Principles of Metal Casting

Principles of Metal Casting

Richard W. Heine

Chairman, Department of Minerals and Metals Engineering
University of Wisconsin, Madison

Carl R. Loper, Jr.

Associate Professor of Metallurgical Engineering
University of Wisconsin, Madison

Philip C. Rosenthal

Dean, College of Applied Science and Engineering
University of Wisconsin, Milwaukee

second edition

McGraw-Hill Book Company

New York St. Louis San Francisco
Toronto London Sydney

Principles of Metal Casting

Library of Congress Catalog Card Number 66-29476

07-027896-2

5 6 7 8 9 0 KPKP 7 9 8 7 6 5 4 3

Preface

The first edition of this book (published in 1955) was written as a textbook for college-level courses in metal casting for metallurgical and mechanical-engineering students. Since that time, there have been many advances in the engineering sciences. Major reorganization of engineering curricula in colleges has completely altered the sequence of presentation of engineering subjects and courses. Metal casting in some schools, for example, may be studied in courses under such headings as transport phenomena, solidification, soils and aggregates, the solid state, and materials science. In other schools, metal-processing or materials-processing courses are offered which include principles of metal casting. Under these circumstances, it is difficult to write a text which will satisfy these different approaches to the teaching of metal casting. In consultation with the Technical Director of the American Foundrymen's Society it was decided that the contents of this edition should be similar to those of the first edition so that it might appeal to persons in the educational field and to those active in metal-casting practice in foundries and be useful as a general reference. This is the objective of the present edition.

This textbook has been sponsored by the American Foundrymen's Society. Thanks are due to its Technical Director, Mr. S. C. Massari, and many other members of the American Foundrymen's Society for their assistance with illustrations and counsel.

We have received excellent assistance from the American Society for Metals, the American Society for Testing Materials, the American Institute of Mining and Metallurgical Engineers, the Gray and Ductile Iron Founders' Society, the Malleable Iron Founders' Society, and the Steel Founders' Society of America. We wish especially to acknowledge Lucille L. Buss, Secretary to the Department of Minerals and Metals Engineering, for her major contribution to our manuscript.

Acknowledgment is also given here to the help obtained from foundries, foundry equipment and supply companies, and the publishing companies which have furnished illustrations for the text.

Richard W. Heine
Carl R. Loper, Jr.
Philip C. Rosenthal

Contents

1
Introduction

A casting may be defined as a "metal object obtained by allowing molten metal to solidify in a mold," the shape of the object being determined by the shape of the mold cavity. Founding, or casting, is the process of forming metal objects by melting metal and pouring it into molds. A foundry is a commercial establishment for founding, or producing castings. Significant in these definitions is the use of liquid metal to cast the shape of the object directly, producing cast metal. Wrought metal products differ from cast metal products in that the metal has received mechanical working treatment such as forging, rolling, or extruding. Practically all metal is initially cast. Castings obtain their shape principally when molten metal solidifies in the desired form. Wrought objects, however, are cast as ingots and then plastically worked to approximately the desired shape.

METAL CASTING, A PROCESS OF SHAPING

The strength of the foundry industry rests on the fundamental nature of casting as a process for causing metals to take shapes that will serve the needs of man. There are other methods of shaping: machining, forging, welding, stamping, hot working, etc. Each has applications in which it is unexcelled and others for which it is unsuited. Rarely is an engineering product completed which does not use several or all of the fundamental metal-processing methods. The foundry industry is thus built on one of the truly basic methods available for shaping metals to useful ends.

Certain advantages are inherent in the metal-casting process. These may form the basis for choosing casting as a process to be preferred over other shaping processes in a particular case. Some of the reasons for the success of the casting process follow:

1. The most intricate of shapes, both external and internal, may be cast. As a result, many other operations, such as machining, forging, and welding, may be minimized or eliminated.

2. Because of their metallurgical nature, some metals can only be cast to shape since they cannot be hot-worked into bars, rods, plates, or other shapes from ingot form as a preliminary to other processing. The highly useful and low-cost cast irons, which exceed the total of all other metals in tonnage cast, illustrate this fact.
3. Construction may be simplified. Objects may be cast in a single piece which would otherwise require construction in several pieces and subsequent assembly if made by other methods.
4. Metal casting is a process highly adaptable to the requirements of mass production. Large numbers of a given casting may be produced very rapidly. The use of castings in the automotive industry provides ample illustration of this point.
5. Extremely large, heavy metal objects may be cast when they would be difficult or economically impossible to produce otherwise. Large pump housings, valves, and hydroelectric plant parts weighing up to 200 tons illustrate this application.
6. Some engineering properties are obtained more favorably in cast metals. Examples are:
   a. Machinability and vibration damping capacity in cast irons.
   b. More uniform properties from a directional standpoint; i.e., properly cast metals can exhibit the same properties regardless of which direction is selected relative to the original casting for the test piece. This is not generally true for wrought metals.
   c. Strength and lightness in certain light metal alloys which can be produced only as castings.
   d. Good bearing qualities are obtained in cast bearing metals.

   In general, a wide range of alloy composition and properties is produced in cast form.
7. A decided economic advantage may exist as a result of any one or a combination of points 1 to 6. The price and sales factor is a dominant one which continually weighs the advantages and limitations of any process used in a competitive system of enterprise.

The list of advantages accruing to the metal-casting process may be expanded beyond that given above. It is also true that conditions may be stated where the casting process must give way to other methods of shaping. Such conditions are those in the area of the principal advantages to be gained by the other metal-processing methods. For example, machining produces smooth surfaces and dimensional accuracy not obtainable in any other way; forging aids in developing the ultimate of fibered strength and toughness in steel; welding provides a convenient method of joining or fabricating wrought or cast products into more complex structures; and stamping produces lightweight sheet-metal parts. Thus the engineer may select from a number of metal-processing methods that one or combination which is most suited to the needs of his work.

THE FOUNDRY INDUSTRY

The scope of the foundry industry encompasses a major segment of our national economy. It has been described as an 8.5 billion dollar industry, employing directly and indirectly 475,000 people; one which produces about 14 to 18 per cent of all ferrous production annually and feeds castings into 90 per cent of all machine shops, produces about 18 million tons of salable casting annually, and itself sustains the subsidiary businesses of foundry equipment and material supplies. The industry's product, castings, enters into every field in which metals serve man. Castings are used in transportation, communication, construction, agriculture, power generators, in aerospace and atomic energy applications, and in other activities too numerous to describe. Because of their widespread use, castings are produced almost everywhere that manufacturing occurs.

Types of Foundries

Foundries may be classified as ferrous or nonferrous, gray iron, steel, malleable, brass and bronze, or light metal (aluminum, magnesium).

The number of foundries in each field is given in the table below.

Foundries in the United States*

Gray cast iron	1896
Steel	367
Malleable iron	90
Nonferrous and others	3321
Total foundries	5674

*From *Foundry*, April, 1963, compiled by the Penton Publishing Co., Cleveland.

Nonferrous foundries, which usually cast more than one group of alloys, are shown as a separate entry and are not further subdivided in the table. Some foundries cast more than one kind of metal.

Foundries are further classified according to the nature of their work and their organizational framework. A jobbing foundry is one having a physical plant that usually contracts to produce a casting or a small number of castings of a given kind. A production foundry, however, is a highly mechanized shop which requires that large numbers of a given kind of casting be made in order to produce them at a low cost. Semi-production shops are those in which a portion of the work is of a jobbing nature and the balance is production casting. A captive foundry is one which is an integral part of some manufacturing company and whose castings are consumed mainly in the products of the parent organization. An independent foundry, however, is usually a separate company that produces castings for any number of customers. The largest foundries, those employing more than 1000 people, are usually captive; but the greatest number of foundries, the smaller shops employing fewer than 100 people, are usually independent.

BASIC STEPS IN MAKING SAND CASTINGS

Practically all the detailed operations that enter into the making of sand castings may be categorized as belonging to one of five fundamental steps of the process:

1. Patternmaking (including core boxes)
2. Coremaking
3. Molding
4. Melting and pouring
5. Cleaning

The details and technical processes involved in each of the above operations are the source of the foundryman's principal problems, other than personnel and marketing. The integration of the various steps to produce a casting is briefly summarized for the benefit of those unfamiliar with the foundry. The processes, and the equipment, are illustrated in part in Fig. 1.1.

Patternmaking

Patterns are required to make molds. The mold is made by packing some readily formed plastic material, such as molding sand, around the pattern, as illustrated in Fig. 1.1. When the pattern is withdrawn, its imprint provides the mold cavity, which is ultimately filled with metal to become the casting. Thus molding requires, first, that patterns be made. A pattern, as shown in Fig. 1.1, may be simply visualized as an approximate replica of the exterior of a casting. If the casting is to be hollow, as in the case of a pipe fitting, additional patterns, referred to as core boxes, are used to form the sand that is used to create these cavities.

Coremaking

Cores are forms, usually made of sand, which are placed into a mold cavity to form the interior surfaces of castings. Thus the void space

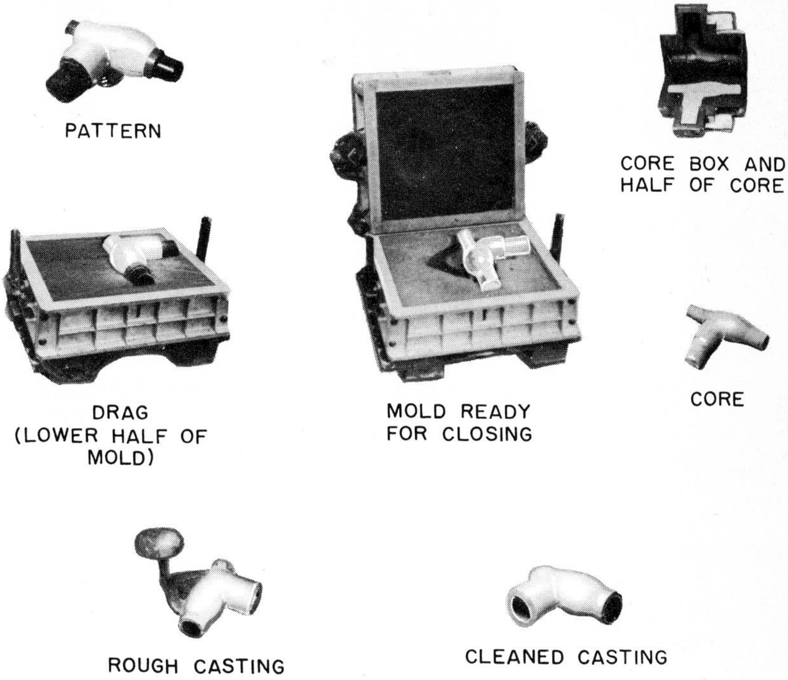

***Fig.* 1.1** **Elements in making a casting. Top half of mold, cope; bottom half, drag.**

between the core and mold-cavity surface is what eventually becomes the casting. A core and core box for a mixing valve are shown in Fig. 1.1. Cores are ordinarily made separately from molds in a designated area of the foundry referred to as a core room. They are then transported to the molding department to be placed in the molds. Core boxes are required to produce cores, so that this operation is again dependent on the pattern department.

Molding

Molding consists of all operations necessary to prepare a mold for receiving molten metal. Molding usually involves placing a molding aggregate around a pattern held within a supporting frame, withdrawing the pattern to leave the mold cavity, setting the cores in the mold cavity, and finishing and closing the mold. The mold is then ready for pouring. A finished mold ready for closing is illustrated in Fig. 1.1.

Melting and Pouring

The preparation of molten metal for casting is referred to simply as *melting.* Melting is usually done in a specifically designated area of the foundry, and the molten metal is transferred to the molding area where the molds are poured.

Cleaning

Cleaning refers to all operations necessary to the removal of sand, scale, and excess metal from the casting. The casting is separated from the molding sand and transported to the cleaning department. Burned-on sand and scale are removed to improve the surface appearance of the casting. Excess metal, in the form of fins, wires, parting-line fins, and gates, is cut off. Defective castings may be salvaged by welding or other repair. Inspection of the casting for defects and general quality follows. The casting is then ready for shipment or further processing, for example, heat-treatment, surface treatment, or machining. A rough mixing-valve casting and a cleaned casting are shown in Fig. 1.1.

The preceding paragraphs have briefly summarized the basic steps in the foundry process. There are, of course, other steps, not discussed, which are exceedingly important in some foundries. For example, with certain alloys, every casting must be given a heat-treatment. The more specialized steps peculiar to certain kinds of foundries and alloys will be considered separately in later chapters.

THE ENGINEER AND THE FOUNDRY INDUSTRY

Because of the scope of the industry and the widespread use of castings, engineers often find themselves in a position where a knowledge of foundry processes and casting problems becomes a vital part of their work. Design of castings, specifications, intelligent use of the properties of cast metals, purchasing of castings, and processing of castings, all require the application of engineering principles unique to castings and the foundry process. The engineer who designs a casting must have accurate information about the properties of the cast metal he would use. Further, he may achieve considerable economies by selecting a design that facilitates molding, coring, and other foundry problems. When specifications are more limiting than necessary, foundry problems and costs rise. Designs which make it difficult to obtain sound castings result in low mechanical properties in the cast metal, so that handbook data are not reliable. Many engineers face these problems in their work even though they themselves are not directly engaged in foundry work. Engineers are also finding increasing opportunity for professional work in the foundry field itself. To provide a foundation for work in this field, indirectly or directly, course work in the principles of metal casting finds a place in the educational preparation of student engineers. In addition, certain principles of materials science and engineering are best studied in the foundry processes.

2
Patterns

Patterns are the foundryman's mold-forming tool. The mold cavity, and therefore ultimately the casting, is made from the pattern. Even if only one casting is desired, it is necessary to have a pattern, but a great many castings may be made from a single pattern. Obtaining suitable pattern equipment is thus the first step in making castings.

PATTERNMAKING

Patternmaking is divided between that which is done within foundries and that which is done by separate businesses called *pattern shops.* Foundries often have pattern departments. For example, 50 per cent, approximately, of the 5674 foundries in the United States have pattern departments. Some foundries have both wood- and metal-pattern facilities. However, most pattern departments in foundries are more concerned with modifying existing pattern equipment and preparing it for molding (work known as rigging) than with producing new patterns. The vast majority of patterns are made by pattern shops which are independent of the foundry and operate as separate businesses.

Patternmaking, the art of making patterns which will produce the desired casting dimensions, is not within the scope of this book. Certain principles which are applied to patterns, however, should be common knowledge to all who may be concerned with castings.

TYPES OF PATTERNS

Several types of patterns are used in foundries. Depending on the casting requirements, the pattern may conform to one of the following types:

1. Single or loose patterns
2. Gated patterns (loose)
3. Match-plate patterns

4. Cope and drag patterns
5. Special patterns and devices

Each of the pattern types has characteristic uses.

Loose Patterns

Loose patterns are single copies of the casting but incorporating the allowances and core prints necessary for producing the casting. They

Fig. 2.1 A loose pattern of a rocker arm. (*Courtesy of the Malleable Founders' Society, Cleveland.*)

generally are of wood construction but may be made of metal, plaster, plastics, wax, or any other suitable material. Relatively few castings are made from any one loose pattern since hand molding is practiced and the process is slow and costly. The parting surface may be hand-formed. Gating systems are hand-cut in the sand. Drawing the pattern from the sand, after rapping it to loosen it from the sand, is also done by hand. Consequently, casting dimensions vary. A loose pattern is shown in Fig. 2.1. Such a pattern might be used for producing prototype castings.

Gated Patterns

Gated patterns such as those shown in Fig. 2.2 are an improvement on ungated loose patterns. The gating system is actually a part of the pattern and eliminates hand-cutting the gates. More rapid molding of small quantities of castings results with this type of pattern.

***Fig.* 2.2** A gated pattern of the rocker arm shown in Fig. 2.1. (*Courtesy of the Malleable Founders' Society.*)

Match-plate Patterns

Large-quantity production of small castings requires match-plate patterns or more specialized types of pattern equipment. The cope and drag portions of the pattern are mounted on opposite sides of a wood or metal plate conforming to the parting line. Match plates are also integrally cast in which cast pattern and plate are cast as one piece in sand or plaster molds. Figure 2.3 shows metal match-plate patterns. Gating systems are almost always attached to the plate. Match plates are generally used with some type of molding machine, as illustrated in Chap. 3, in order to obtain maximum speed of molding. The improved production rate possible with these patterns serves to compensate for their increased cost. Plates also increase the dimensional accuracy of the casting. A limitation of the match-plate pattern arises in the weight of mold and flask which can be handled by the molder. Heavier work is ordinarily put onto larger molding equipment, employing other pattern equipment.

Cope and Drag Pattern Plates

Cope and drag pattern plates are shown in Fig. 2.4. Cope and drag plates consist of the cope and drag parts of the pattern mounted on separate plates. The cope and drag halves of the mold may thus be made separately by workers on different molding machines. The molding of medium and large castings on molding machines is greatly facilitated by this type of pattern equipment. Separate cope and drag plates are more costly, but this type of pattern equipment is usually necessary in

***Fig.* 2.3** A match-plate pattern of the rocker arm shown in Fig. 2.2. (*Courtesy of the Malleable Founders' Society.*)

Fig. 2.4 **Separate cope and drag pattern plates of the rocker arm shown in Figs. 2.1 to 2.3. (*Courtesy of the Malleable Founders' Society.*)**

high-speed mechanized or automated molding. Separate pattern plates require accurate alignment of the two mold halves by means of guide and locating pins and bushings in flasks in order that the upper and lower parts of the casting may match.

Special Patterns and Devices

Specialized pattern equipment is employed when the types discussed above are not suitable. For extremely large castings, skeleton patterns of the kind shown in Fig. 2.5 may be employed. Such equipment is for quite unusual castings where the mold is largely manually constructed. Large work of symmetrical shape sometimes involves the use of sweeps for forming a mold surface. Figure 2.6 illustrates a sweep and shows the type of mold made by this method.

Follow Board

Loose patterns having an irregular parting line are difficult to mold without a follow board, or *match.* The pattern match serves to support the loose pattern during molding of the drag half of the mold and also

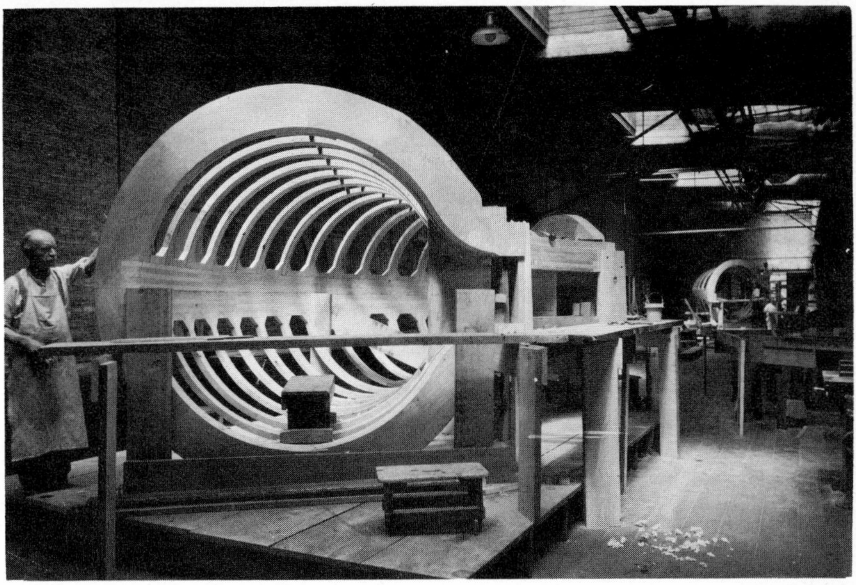

***Fig.* 2.5** **Skeleton pattern of large casting: no. 6 section of spiral casting pattern (no. 5 section in background) for the four 115,000-hp best-efficiency 525-ft-head 150-rpm Francis runners, vertical-shaft hydraulic turbines in cast-steel spiral castings for the U.S. Bureau of Reclamation Boulder Canyon Project. (*Courtesy of Allis-Chalmers Mfg. Co.*)**

establishes the parting surface when the match is removed. Figure 2.7 illustrates a hard-sand match used for molding a ball. The term *hard-sand match* originates in the material used to construct the match. The frame and bottom are of wood, but the match is sometimes made with a mixture of 25 parts dry molding sand, 1 part litharge, and sufficient linseed oil or core oil to make the sand workable as a molding sand. Plaster is also used to make a match.

Master Pattern

A master pattern, often made of wood, as that in Fig. 2.1, is used as an original for casting metal patterns. Several patterns may be cast from the master and mounted on a pattern plate after they have been finished to the proper dimensions. The master pattern in this case may be the first step in obtaining match plates. A master pattern incorporates certain dimensional allowances, discussed in the following section.

PATTERN ALLOWANCES

Although the pattern is used to produce a casting of the desired dimensions, it is not dimensionally identical with the casting. For metallurgi-

***Fig.* 2.6** Top, using a sweep in place of a fully constructed pattern to form a mold surface. Bottom, completed mold ready for closing. The mold is for a flywheel sheave casting weighing 8380 lb. (*Courtesy of Allis-Chalmers Mfg. Co.*)

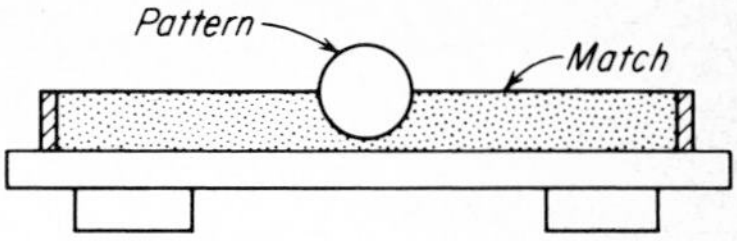

Fig. 2.7 **Hard-sand match used to establish the parting surface when molding a ball-shaped loose pattern by hand.**

cal and mechanical reasons, a number of allowances must be made on the pattern if the casting is to be dimensionally correct.

Shrinkage Allowance

Shrinkage allowance on patterns is a correction for solidification shrinkage of the metal and its contraction during cooling to room temperature. The total contraction is volumetric, but the correction for it is usually expressed linearly. Pattern shrinkage allowance is the amount the pattern must be made larger than the casting to provide for total contraction. It may vary from a negligible amount to ⅝ in. per ft, depending on the metal and the nature of the casting. Typical shrinkage allowances are given in Table 2.1. The linear allowances in Table 2.1 are representative for castings in sand molds. However, special conditions prevail with some metals. White iron, for example, shrinks about ¼ in. per ft when cast, but during annealing it grows about ⅛ in. per ft, resulting in a net shrinkage of ⅛ in. per ft. Spheroidal carbon cast iron may solidify with a contraction of ¼ to ⅛ in. per ft, depending on the degree of graphitization which it undergoes during freezing (i.e., the more graphitization, the less shrinkage).

The patternmaker's *shrink rule* is a special scale which makes unnecessary the computation of the amount of shrinkage allowance which must be provided on a given dimension. For example, on a ⅛-in. shrink rule, each foot is ⅛ in. longer and each graduation is proportionately longer than its conventional length. Shrink rules are available with the standard allowances of Table 2.1. Sometimes double allowances are made if a pattern is first made in wood and then in some other metal, as in making master patterns. For example, an aluminum pattern made from a wood master pattern may require a total allowance of ¼ in. per ft on the wood pattern if a gray-iron casting is to be made. The total allowance on the original wood pattern will then provide for shrinkage of the aluminum pattern casting and of gray-iron castings made from the aluminum pattern.

Machine Finish Allowance

Machine finish allowance is the amount the dimensions on a casting are made oversize to provide stock for machining. Typical finish allowances are presented in Table 2.2. It can be seen that these allowances are influenced by the metal, the casting design, and the method of casting

Table 2.1 Pattern-shrinkage allowances* *Before specifying, consult the patternmaker and foundryman*

Casting alloys	Pattern dimension	Type of construction	Section thickness, in.	Contraction, in./ft
Gray cast iron	Up to 24 in.	Open construction	......	1/8
	From 25 to 48 in.	Open construction	......	1/10
	Over 48 in.	Open construction	......	1/12
	Up to 24 in.	Cored construction	......	1/8
	From 25 to 36 in.	Cored construction	......	1/10
	Over 36 in.	Cored construction	......	1/12
Cast steel	Up to 24 in.	Open construction	......	1/4
	From 25 to 72 in.	Open construction	......	3/16
	Over 72 in.	Open construction	......	5/32
	Up to 18 in.	Cored construction	......	1/4
	From 19 to 48 in.	Cored construction	......	3/16
	From 49 to 66 in.	Cored construction	......	5/32
	Over 66 in.	Cored construction	......	1/8
Malleable cast iron	....	....	1/16	11/64
			1/8	5/32
			3/16	19/128
			1/4	9/64
			3/8	1/8
			1/2	7/64
			5/8	3/32
			3/4	5/64
			7/8	3/64
			1	1/32
Aluminum	Up to 48 in.	Open construction	......	5/32
	49 to 72 in.	Open construction	......	9/64
	Over 72 in.	Open construction	......	1/8
	Up to 24 in.	Cored construction	......	5/32
	Over 48 in.	Cored construction	......	9/64–1/8
	From 25 to 48 in.	Cored construction	......	1/8 –1/16
Magnesium	Up to 48 in.	Open construction	......	11/16
	Over 48 in.	Open construction	......	5/32
	Up to 24 in.	Cored construction	......	5/32
	Over 24 in.	Cored construction	......	5/32–1/8
Brass	....	....	......	3/16
Bronze	....	....	......	1/8–1/4

*From American Foundrymen's Society.[1]

and cleaning. The values in Table 2.2 are for castings made in conventional molding sand. Other casting processes permit different finish allowances to be used, as is pointed out in a subsequent chapter. In general, machine finish allowance may be a minimum if the surfaces to be machined are entirely in the drag half of the mold since dimensional variation and other defects are usually least prevalent there.

Table 2.2 Guide to pattern machine-finish allowances* *Unless otherwise specified*

Casting alloys	Pattern size	Bore, in.	Finish
Cast iron	Up to 12 in.	1/8	3/32
	13 to 24 in.	3/16	1/8
	25 to 42 in.	1/4	3/16
	43 to 60 in.	5/16	1/4
	61 to 80 in.	3/8	5/16
	81 to 120 in.	7/16	3/8
	Over 120 in.	Special instructions	Special instructions
Cast steel	Up to 12 in.	3/16	1/8
	13 to 24 in.	1/4	3/16
	25 to 42 in.	5/16	5/16
	43 to 60 in.	3/8	3/8
	61 to 80 in.	1/2	7/16
	81 to 120 in.	5/8	1/2
	Over 120 in.	Special instructions	Special instructions
Malleable iron	Up to 6 in.	1/16	1/16
	6 to 9 in.	3/32	1/16
	9 to 12 in.	3/32	3/32
	12 to 24 in.	5/32	1/8
	24 to 35 in.	3/16	3/16
	Over 36 in.	Special instructions	Special instructions
Brass, bronze, and aluminum-alloy castings	Up to 12 in.	3/32	1/16
	13 to 24 in.	3/16	1/8
	25 to 36 in.	3/16	5/32
	Over 36 in.	Special instructions	Special instructions

*From American Foundrymen's Society.[1]

Pattern Draft

Draft is the taper allowed on vertical faces of a pattern to permit its removal from the sand or other molding medium without tearing the mold-cavity surfaces. A taper of 1/16 in. per ft is common for vertical walls on patterns drawn by hand. Machine-drawn patterns require about one degree taper. In some cases, even vertical walls 6 to 9 in. deep may be drawn by machine if the pattern is very smooth and clean and the drawing equipment is properly aligned. In the case of pockets or deep cavities in the pattern, considerably more draft is necessary to avoid tearing the mold during withdrawal of the pattern.

Size Tolerance

The variation which may be permitted on a given casting dimension is called its tolerance, and is equal to the difference between the minimum and the maximum limits for any specified dimension. Typical values for heavy castings which require maximum tolerance are given in Table 2.3.

Table* 2.3 *Typical tolerance for casting weighing 1000 lb or more*

Metal	Tolerance, in.
Gray cast iron	1/16
Malleable iron	3/32
Cast steel	5/32
Aluminum alloys	5/64
Magnesium alloys	11/64
Brass	3/32
Bronze	1/8

*Courtesy of American Foundrymen's Society.

The values in Table 2.3 are approximately maximum values. A common rule states that size tolerance should be at least half the shrinkage allowance. However, where there is considerable experience with a casting, and cooperation between the foundry and the casting purchaser exists, much closer tolerance may be established. Where such conditions prevail, tolerance of only a few thousandths of an inch may be maintained with some casting processes.

Distortion Allowance

Certain objects, such as large flat plates and dome- or U-shaped castings, sometimes distort when reproduced from a straight or perfect pattern. In such cases, the pattern may be intentionally distorted, or "faked." The distorted pattern then produces a casting of the proper shape and size.

Example of Allowances

An example of the application of various pattern allowances to a casting is illustrated in Fig. 2.8. The casting design without allowances is also shown in Fig. 2.8. Core prints must be added to the pattern, and some typical allowances for shrinkage and finishing are indicated in the draw-

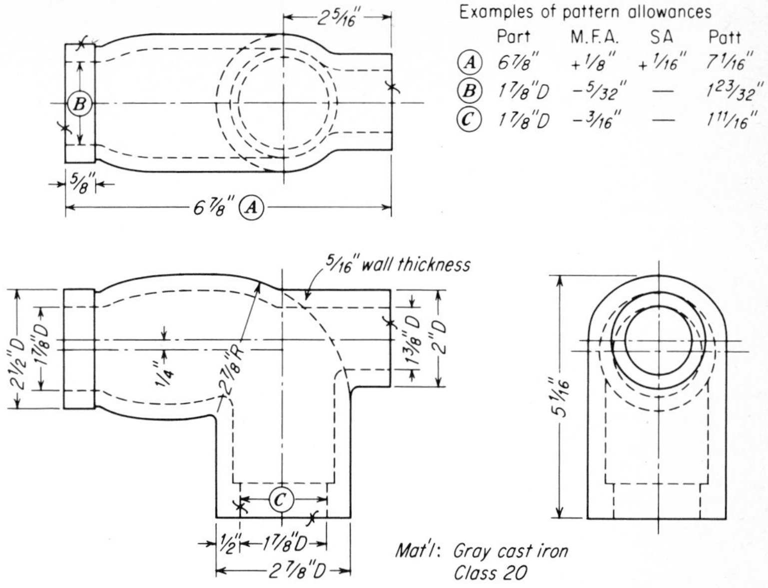

***Fig.* 2.8** **Drawing of mixing-value casting shown in Fig. 1.1. Some typical pattern allowances are listed.**

ing. The actual pattern is shown in Fig. 1.1. The core is located by the walls on the ends of the core print. The actual pattern dimensions are not shown in the drawing, but rather a shrink rule is employed by the patternmaker. However, the machine finish allowance is added to the finished dimension, and so should appear in the drawing. The cored ends must be smaller than the finished diameter. The pattern, made as a loose, split pattern, and the core boxes, core, mold, and casting are shown in Fig. 1.1.

FUNCTIONS OF PATTERNS

The main purpose of a pattern is its use in molding. However, to produce a casting successfully and render it suitable for further processing, the pattern may be required to perform other functions besides producing a mold cavity. These are briefly considered as follows:

Molding the Gating System

Good gating practice for castings generally requires that the system of channels and feeding reservoirs (gates and risers) for introducing metal into the mold cavity be attached to the pattern. The gating system may then obtain the benefits of machine molding.

Establishing the Parting Line

On a flat pattern plate, the parting surface is a simple plane. Many castings, however, require curved parting surfaces (Fig. 2.2) because of their shape, and these are established by the pattern where match plates or cope and drag plates are used (Figs. 2.2 and 2.3). Loose patterns require that the parting surface be cut by hand or that a follow board or match be constructed for establishing the parting surface in successive molds.

Making Core Prints

When a casting requires cores, provision is made on the pattern for core prints. Core prints are portions of the pattern and mold cavity which serve to anchor the core in proper position in the mold. The core print is added to the pattern, but does not appear on the casting because it is blocked off by the core. Core prints are illustrated in Fig. 1.1 and on the pattern in Fig. 2.3.

Establishing Locating Points

The foundry, pattern shop, or machine shop employs locating points or surfaces on the casting to check the casting dimensions. Machining operations may also use the locating points in establishing the position of machined surfaces relative to the balance of the casting.

Minimizing Casting Defects Attributable to the Pattern

Properly constructed, clean, and smooth surfaced patterns are a necessity in making good castings. Patterns with rough, nicked surfaces and undercuts, loosely mounted, and in a generally poor condition contribute substantially to defective castings containing sand inclusions and other imperfections.

Providing for Ram-up Cores

Sometimes a part of a mold cavity is made with cores which are positioned by the pattern before the molding sand is rammed. The ram-up core then is held by the sand which has been packed around it.

Providing Economy in Molding

The pattern should be constructed to achieve all possible savings in cost of the casting. Here such items may be considered as the number of castings in the mold, the proper size of the pattern plate to fit available molding equipment, method of molding, and other factors.

CORE BOXES

Core boxes, although not referred to as patterns, are an essential part of the pattern equipment for a casting requiring cores. Core boxes are constructed of wood or metal. The simplest type of box is the dump box illustrated in Fig. 1.1. The top of the box is flat, and the core is removed by placing a plate over the box and inverting it. A split box is a two-piece box usually having a flat parting surface. A simple gang core box and accompanying pattern are shown in Fig. 2.9. A gang box permits making several cores in the same box simultaneously. More complex multiple-piece core boxes are considered in Chap. 6, which deals with the subject of coremaking. Cores which do not have any flat surfaces impose an additional requirement for the pattern equipment. Support

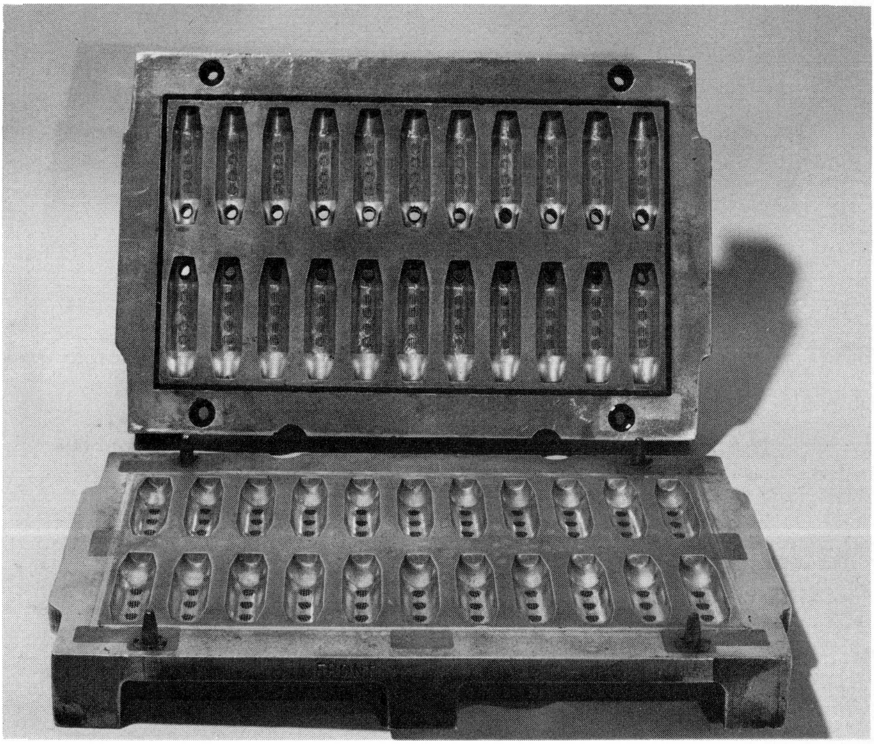

***Fig.* 2.9** Simple gang core box for making rocker arm cores by core blowing. (*Courtesy of the Malleable Founders' Society.*)

must be provided during the baking of cores since the sand is weak until after the baking process. A flat core surface and flat plate (core plate) can provide such support. When the core has only curved surfaces, however, a support conforming to part of the surface must be provided. The supporting device in which the core rests while it is baking is called a *core drier*. Since the drier is used every time a core is baked, the number of driers needed equals the number of cores baked as a batch. Some core boxes require provisions for electrical or gas heating if they are to be used for shell coremaking or hot-box coremaking (Chap. 6).

The importance of good pattern equipment cannot be overemphasized. Patterns which take into account the problems of molding and coremaking, proper gating and risering, ease of cleaning, and further processing promote quality in castings. As was pointed out earlier, the subject is one for detailed treatment, beyond the scope of this text. Further information on construction and principles of patterns may be obtained from some of the references listed in the Bibliography.

BIBLIOGRAPHY

1. American Foundrymen's Society, "Patternmaker's Manual," Des Plaines, Ill., 1953.
2. American Foundrymen's Society, "Cast Metals Handbook," 4th ed., Des Plaines, Ill., 1957.
3. O. Benedict, Jr., "Manual of Foundry and Pattern Shop Practice," McGraw-Hill Book Company, New York, 1947.
4. J. R. Hall and C. L. Webber, "Practical Wood Patternmaking," McGraw-Hill Book Company, New York, 1943.
5. B. R. Hall and H. E. Kiley, "Pattern Design," International Textbook Company, Scranton, Pa., 1941.
6. C. R. Simmons, Liquid Phenolic Casting Resins for Foundry Patterns, *Trans. AFS,* vol. 55, p. 517, 1947.
7. E. Bremer, Pressure Casting Matchplates, *Foundry,* vol. 75, pp. 124–126, April, 1947.
8. W. E. Tharp, Pattern and Allied Equipment, Design, Redesign, and Interchangeability, *Trans. AFS,* vol. 53, p. 368, 1945.
9. W. C. Manwell, Patterns in the Jobbing Foundry, *Trans. AFS,* vol. 53, p. 168.
10. A. J. Howarth, Gating Principles Applied to Gray Iron Castings Production on Match Plates, *Am. Foundryman,* vol. 20, no. 1, p. 28, July, 1951.

3

Molding Processes and Materials

Good castings cannot be made without good molds. Because of the importance of the mold, casting processes and castings are often described by the materials and methods employed in molding. The term *molding process* refers to the method of making the mold and the materials used. The term *casting process* conveys a broader meaning, often including the molding process, the method of introducing the metal into the mold cavity, or all the processes used in making the casting. A brief description of the more common molding and casting processes is given in this chapter. Additional details of each process are given in references listed in the Bibliography.

Molding processes have certain features in common:

1. The use of pattern (or core boxes)
2. Some type of aggregate mixture comprising a granular refractory and binders
3. A means of forming the aggregate mixture around the pattern
4. Hardening of the aggregate or developing its bond while in contact with the pattern
5. Withdrawal of the pattern from the hardened aggregate mold
6. Assembly of mold and core pieces to make a complete mold, metal then being poured into the mold

The various molding processes differ primarily in the method of forming the mold and in the granular refractory and method of bonding it.

Forming the mold is done by:

1. Compaction of the aggregate around the pattern
2. Free flow of dry aggregate around the pattern, illustrated by the shell-molding process
3. Free flow of a slurry or fluid aggregate around the pattern, illustrated by investment and plaster molding
4. Variants of the above mold forming methods

Table 3.1 Some aggregate molding processes

Name of process	Pattern type	Molding aggregate	Molding method	Type and development of aggregate bond	Casting weight	Casting intricacy	Casting dimension and smoothness, general case	Note
Green sand...	Wood, plaster, metal; reusable patterns	75% + sand, 3–15% clay and other binders, water; a moist plastic aggregate; reusable	Compaction of sand around pattern, 20–80% reduction in bulk density	Inorganic, green strength due to plastic clay and compaction; dry strength due to water evaporation during casting	Ounces to 1–2 tons	Limited by pattern drawing, no limit with cores	$\pm 1/64$ – $\pm 1/8$ in., 250–1000 rms μin.	Most common process
Dry sand.....	Same as above	Same as above	Same as above	Dry strength developed by evaporation of moisture	Heavy castings	Same as above	Same as above or better	Baking of mold required, skin drying being a variant of this process
Core sand....	Same as above, or core boxes and driers	90% + sand, 1–3% core oil or resin, 0.25–1.5% cereal, water	Same as above, core blowing	Organic, polymerization of core oil by baking after removal from core box	Ounces to 500 lb	Same as above	Same as above	Baking of mold required
Floor and pit molding	Same as above	Same as green sand, with added binder	Same as above	Inorganic, same as green sand, maximum strength due to baking	No limit	No limit	$\pm 1/4$ in. or less	For very heavy castings

Shell molding	Heated metal pattern	2.5–10.0% thermo-setting resin, balance sand	Free flow of dry sand around pattern or by blowing	Polymerization of resin by heat from the pattern	Usually less than 250 lb	Limited by pattern drawing, no limit with cores	±0.010 in.–±0.025 in., 100–500 rms μin.	Extensively used for making cores
CO_2 process...	Wood or metal patterns or core boxes	2.0–6.0% sodium silicate binder, balance sand	Compaction of sand around pattern, mechanical or by blowing, then CO_2 gassing	Inorganic bond by chemical reaction of CO_2 and silicate	Ounces to several hundred pounds	Same as above	Similar to dry and core sand	
Investment molding	Wax or plastic, expendable	See Table 3.2, slurry with ceramic binder and fine aggregate powder, as ethyl silicate plus silica flour	By dipping pattern in slurry or pouring fluid aggregate around pattern; pattern melted out	Gelling, hydrolysis, or setting of ceramic binder followed by firing	Same as above	Limited to wax patterns that can be ejected from dies and their assemblies	0.002–0.005 in./in., 10–85 rms μin.	Casting weight usually under 10 lb; heat and corrosion-resistant alloys
Ceramic molding	Wood, plastic, or metal; reusable patterns	Same as above	Pouring fluid aggregate around pattern; vibration	Same as above	Same as above	Limited to patterns that can be drawn unless flexible patterns are used	Same as above	Heavier castings
Plaster molding	Metal or plastic patterns	Sand, gypsum binder, and fillers and water	Pouring fluid aggregate around pattern; vibration	Hydration of gypsum followed by drying	Same as above	Same as above	30–50 rms μin., 0.005 in./in. more or less	Aluminum and copper alloy castings mainly

The nature of the molding aggregate largely determines the method of mold forming used. This is pointed out in Table 3.1, which lists some common molding processes, the aggregate, the nature of the bond, the molding method, and the results produced.

Processes of molding with aggregates are classified as follows:

1. Sand molding (or sand casting)
   a. Green-sand molding
   b. Dry-sand molding
   c. Core-sand molding
   d. Shell molding
   e. Miscellaneous sand-molding processes: pit and floor molding, cement-bonded sand, air-set sand, loam molding, CO_2 process, hot box, etc.
2. Investment (or precision) molding
3. Ceramic molding
4. Plaster molding
5. Graphite molding

Casting processes are as follows:

1. Sand casting
2. Permanent-mold casting
3. Die casting
4. Centrifugal casting

Each of the processes listed above has a field of most appropriate application, with certain advantages and limitations.

SAND CASTINGS

Molding processes where a sand aggregate is used to make the mold produce by far the largest quantity of castings. Whatever the metal poured into sand molds, the product may be called a *sand casting*.

Green-sand Molding

Among the sand-casting processes, molding is most often done with green sand. Green molding sand may be defined as a plastic mixture of sand grains, clay, water, and other materials which can be used for molding and casting processes. The sand is called "green" because of the moisture present and is thus distinguished from dry sand.

The basic steps in green-sand molding are as follows:

1. *Preparation of the pattern.* Most green-sand molding is done with match-plate or cope and drag patterns. Loose patterns are used when relatively

few castings of a type are to be made. In simple hand molding the loose pattern is placed on a mold board and surrounded with a suitable-sized flask, as illustrated in Fig. 3.1.

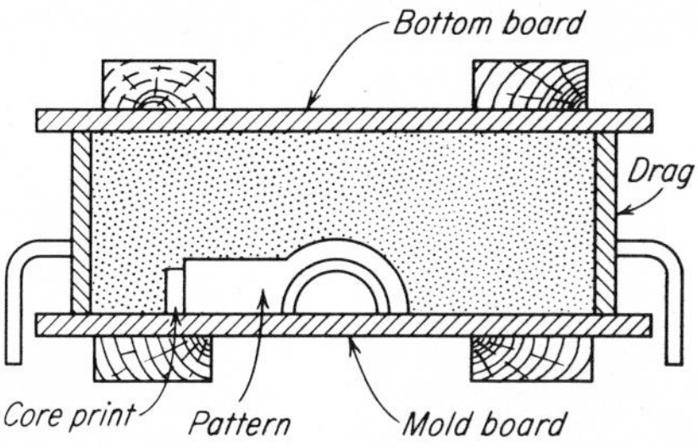

***Fig.* 3.1 Drag half of mold made by hand. Drag is ready to be rolled over in preparation for making the cope.**

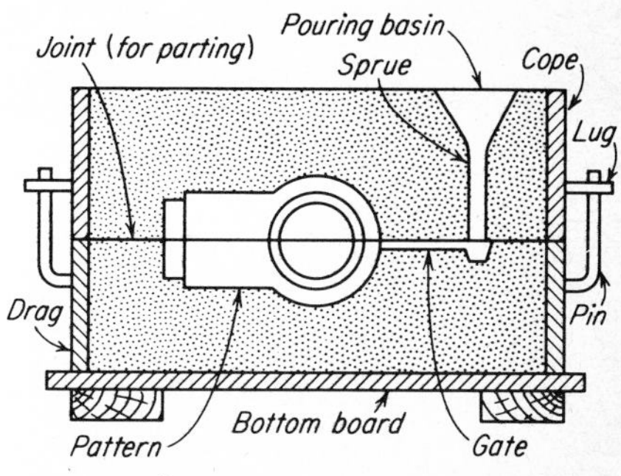

***Fig.* 3.2 Cope mold rammed up. The pattern shown in Figs. 3.1 and 3.2 is shown also in Fig. 1.1.**

2. *Making the mold.* Molding requires the ramming of sand around the pattern. As the sand is packed, it develops strength and becomes rigid within the flask. Ramming may be done by hand, as in the simple setup illustrated in Fig. 3.1. Both cope and drag are molded in the same way, but the cope must provide for the sprue. The gating-system parts of the mold cavity are simply channels for the entry of the molten metal, and can be molded as illustrated in Fig. 3.2. Because of their importance, gating systems are considered in Chap. 9.
3. *Core setting.* With cope and drag halves of the mold made and the pattern withdrawn, cores are set into the mold cavity to form the internal surfaces of the casting. Core setting by hand is illustrated in Fig. 3.3, showing also a mold made by a squeeze-molding machine, a match-plate pattern with attached gating, and an irregular parting surface.
4. *Closing and weighting.* With cores set, the cope and drag are closed. The cope must usually be weighted down or clamped to the drag to prevent it from floating when the metal is poured.

Because of the nature of green-sand molding and molding sands, the process has certain advantages and limitations. Advantages are:

1. Great flexibility as a production process. Mechanical equipment can be utilized for performing molding and its allied operations. Furthermore, green sand can be reused many times by reconditioning it with water, clay, and other materials. The molding process can be rapid and repetitive.
2. Usually, the most direct route from pattern to mold ready for pouring is by green-sand molding.

Fig. 3.3 Setting cores in cavity of mold for making domestic gas-range burner castings. (*Courtesy of Aluminum Co. of America.*)

3. Economy: green-sand molding is ordinarily the least costly method of molding.

Limitations in the use of green-sand molding are:

1. Some casting designs require the use of other casting processes. Thin, long projections of green sand in a mold cavity are washed away by the molten metal or may not even be moldable. Cooling fins on air-cooled-engine cylinder blocks and head, such as those shown in Fig. 3.9, are an example. Greater strength is then required of the mold.
2. Certain metals and some castings develop defects if poured into molds containing moisture.
3. More intricate castings can be made by some other casting processes.
4. The dimensional accuracy and surface finish of green-sand castings may not be adequate. A dimensional variation of $\pm\frac{1}{64}$ in. on small castings and $\pm\frac{1}{16}$ to $\pm\frac{3}{32}$ in. on larger ones may be encountered. However, this

variation on many castings may be much less than that cited if adequate control is exercised.

5. Large castings require greater mold strength and resistance to erosion than are available in green sands.

Dry-sand Molds

Dry-sand molds are actually made with molding sand in the green condition. The sand mixture is modified somewhat to favor good strength and other properties after the mold is dried. Dry-sand molding may be done the same way as green-sand molding on smaller sizes of castings. Usually, the mold-cavity surface is coated or sprayed with a mixture (Chap. 5) which, upon drying, imparts greater hardness or refractoriness to the mold. The entire mold is then dried in an oven at 300 to 650 F or by circulating heated air through the mold. The time-consuming drying operation is one inherent disadvantage of the dry-sand mold.

Skin-dried Molds

The effect of a dry-sand mold may be partially obtained by drying the mold surface to some depth, ¼ to 1 in. Skin drying may be performed by torches, a bank of radiant-heating lamps, or electrical heating elements directed at the mold surface. Skin-dried molds must be poured shortly after drying, so that moisture from the undried sand will not penetrate the dried skin.

Floor and Pit Molding

The production of large intricate castings weighing from 1 to over 100 tons is, of course, one of the special advantages of the casting processes. An example is given in Fig. 3.4. Consider how difficult it would be to make large intricate shapes in some other way. The surface finish and dimensional accuracy of these large castings in ferrous alloys are not as good as in smaller ones, dimensional tolerances of ±¼ in. being acceptable unless special experience permits closer control. The problems of mold construction, handling, coring, gating, pouring, and cleaning of large castings require much engineering effort and control.

When the molds are medium to large in size, considerable heavy equipment, floor space, and time must be allocated to the molding operation. Floor molding is done on the floor of bays of the foundry set aside for these heavy molding jobs. A molding floor is shown in Fig. 3.5. The size of work handled is revealed by comparison with the men in the figure. A completed floor mold, dried, with dry-sand core in place and ready for closing, is shown in Fig. 3.6.

Fig. 3.4 Large intricate casting. Note size relation to railroad flat car. (*Courtesy of Continental Foundry and Machine Co.*)

Fig. 3.5 General view of foundry floor for making large mold by ramming with a motive slinger. (*Courtesy of Beardsley-Piper Division, Pettibone Mulliken Corp.*)

***Fig.* 3.6** Dry-sand floor mold ready for closing. (*Courtesy of Steel Founders' Society of America.*)

When the pattern being molded is too large to be handled in flasks, the molding is done in pits. Molding pits are concrete-lined box-shaped holes in the molding floor. The pattern is lowered into the pit, and molding sand is tucked and rammed under the pattern and up the side walls to the parting surface. The cope of the pit mold is finished off with cores or with sand rammed in a cope flask. An example of a pit mold partially completed is shown in Fig. 3.7. Such large molds are always dried.

When a large mold for a gray-iron casting can be constructed in multiple-piece flasks or by bricking up a large portion of the mold, loam is used as the molding material. Loam is a moist, plastic molding sand containing about 50 per cent sand grains and 50 per cent clay. It is troweled onto a brickwork surface and brought to the pattern dimensions by using skeleton patterns, sweeps, or templates as the molding progresses. A loam mold under construction is shown in Fig. 3.8. Loam molds must be thoroughly dried.

Cement-bonded Sand Molds

Cement-bonded molding sand is a mixture of sand, 8 to 12 per cent high-early-strength hydraulic cement, and 4 to 6 per cent water. This sand develops great hardness and strength by the setting action of portland cement. Molding may be performed by the methods discussed

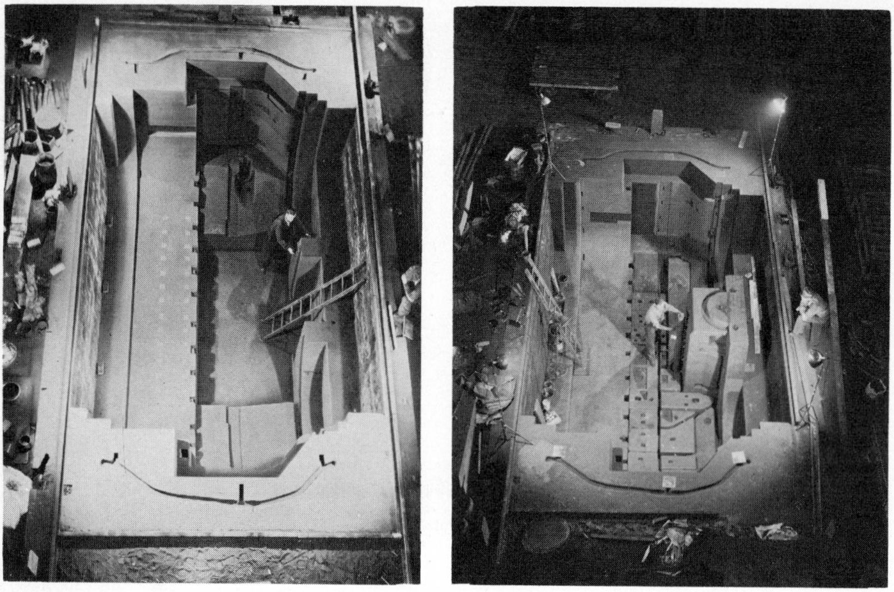

(*a*) (*b*)

Fig. 3.7 **Pit mold for large steam-turbine exhaust end under construction. (*a*) Pit mold with pattern withdrawn. (*b*) Same mold having been dried and in process of being fitted with cores. (*Courtesy of Allis-Chalmers Co.*)**

above and others specially suited to the cement. The sand must be allowed to set or harden before the pattern can be withdrawn. Then the mold is allowed to cure, or continue setting, for up to 72 hr before the mold can be closed or assembled for pouring. When the mold is poured, heat causes the water of crystallization of the cement to be driven off, and thus steam must be allowed to pass off through the sand by means of its porosity and suitably distributed vent holes. Cement-bonded sand molds can be constructed with considerable accuracy, often more than that obtainable in other processes for making large molds. Consequently, more accurate castings may be obtained.[17]

Core Sand or Core Molds

Sometimes molds are made entirely of an assemblage of cores. In place of patterns, core boxes are used for making all parts of the mold. The cores are fitted together to make the mold, being located by alignment bosses and holes. They usually are poured without a flask surrounding the mold.

Core sands usually consist of mixtures of sand grains and organic binders which develop great strength after baking at 250 to 650 F. Their strength after baking makes it possible to cast metal around thin sand

***Fig.* 3.8** Loam mold under construction. (*Courtesy of Allis-Chalmers Manufacturing Company.*)

projections without having them break or erode because of the hot-metal action. The baking operation and the core-sand binders plus difficulties in reusing the sand makes the process more costly. This cost is usually justified, however, in the intricate castings made by this process. Figure 3.9 illustrates intricate castings made in core-sand molds.

Core-sand molds are also sometimes made with dry molding sands or cement-bonded sands, where the great strength and heat resistance of a dry-sand mixture are required, as in large castings.

A process in which the molds do not require baking is known as the air-set process. A mixture of sand, liquid organic binders, and catalysts hardens with time by polymerization of the liquid resins. Molding is mainly done by pouring the free-flowing sand mixture around the pattern. Vibration or ramming is sometimes used to obtain a denser mold. In about 20 min or more, the mixture hardens, and the core box or pattern may be removed. The pieces are then ready for core assembly.

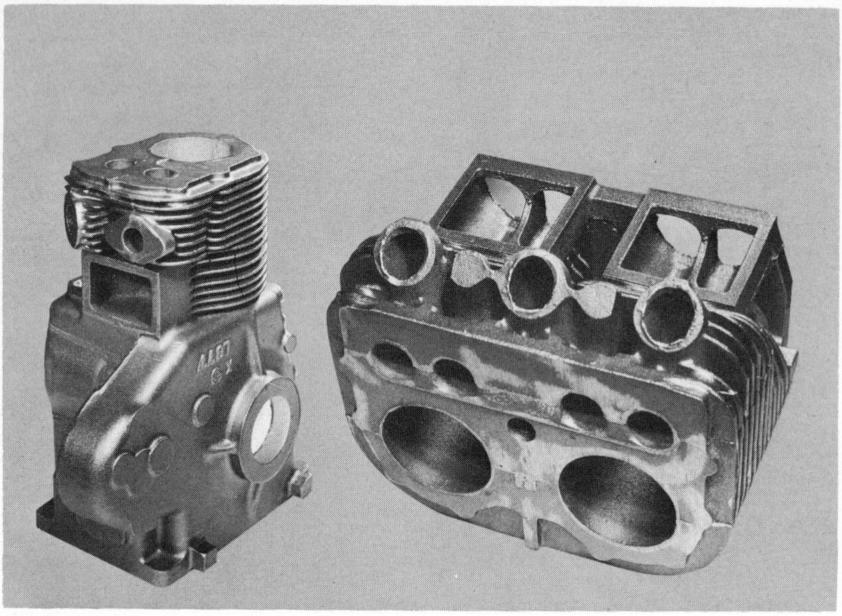

***Fig.* 3.9** Gray-iron air-cooled cylinder-block castings made in core-sand molds. (*Courtesy of Brillion Iron Works, Brillion, Wis.*)

CO_2 *Process*

The CO_2 molding process, also called the sodium silicate process, involves a mixture of sand and 1.5 to 6 per cent liquid silicate. The sand mixture is first packed around the pattern or into the core box. A hardened mold is produced by passing CO_2 gas through the sand mixture. The mold is then assembled from the hardened pieces.[1]

Shell Molding (*Croning Process*)

The sand used for shell molding consists of a mixture of the following ingredients:

1. Dry sand grains, AFS fineness 60 to 140 distributed over 4 to 5 screens.
2. Synthetic resin binder, 3 to 10 per cent by weight. Resins which may be used are the phenolformaldehydes, urea formaldehydes, alkyds, and polyesters. The resin must be a thermosetting plastic, and is used as a powder in dry mixtures. It may also be applied as a liquid and then dried on the sand grains. For molding, the mixture must be dry and free-flowing.

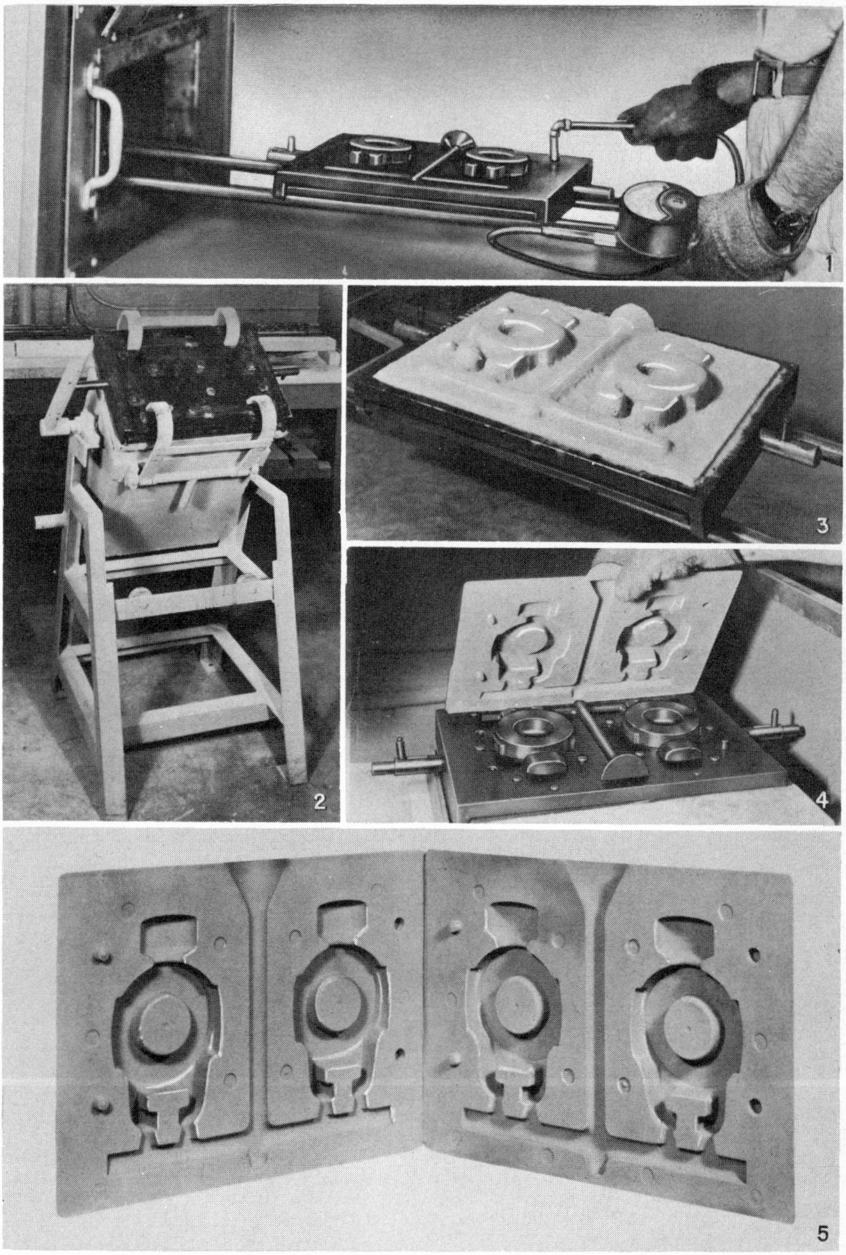

***Fig.* 3.10** Steps in the process of shell molding. (1) Equipment for heating and measuring temperature of shell-molding pattern. (2) Dump box in position for dumping sand on pattern. (3) Shell on pattern. (4) Stripping shell from pattern. (5) Shell-mold halves. (*Courtesy of Monsanto Chemical Company.*)

The steps in shell molding are illustrated in Fig. 3.10. The shell is cured in two stages. When the sand mixture drops onto a pattern heated to about 350 to 700 F, the plastic partially thermosets and builds up a coherent sand shell next to the pattern. The thickness of this shell is about ¼ to ¾ in. and is dependent on the pattern temperature, dwell time on the pattern, and the sand mixture. The shell, still on the pattern, can then be cured by heating it to 450 to 650 F for 3 to 1 min, as, for example, by the method shown in Fig. 3.10. Stripping the shell from the mold presents a problem since the shell is very strong and grips the mold tightly. A mold-release agent, or parting agent, is used to obtain clean stripping when the ejector pins push the shell off the pattern. Silicone parting solutions, sprayed on the pattern, have been found satisfactory. The shell halves may then be assembled and poured.

Shell molding is probably used more for making cores than molds. A variant of the process, known as the hot-box process, employs a heated core box. The molding mixture again contains 1.5 to 4.0 per cent resin of the furane or furfuraldehyde type. Heat from the core box causes the catalysts to start an exothermic polymerization process. As the sand temperature rises, the resin polymerizes and the mass hardens. Molds are made by assembling the hot-box cores.

Advantages claimed for shell molding are exceptionally good surface finish and dimensional accuracy, and hence the possible elimination of some machining operations, decreased casting-weight variation, and less cleaning cost.[1,2,8]

INVESTMENT CASTING

Investment casting is a process also known as the "lost-wax" process, or "precision" casting.[1,3,37] The term *investment* refers to a cloak, or special covering apparel, in this case a refractory mold, surrounding a refractory-covered wax pattern. In this process a wax pattern must be made for every casting and gating system; i.e., the pattern is expendable.

A number of variants of the process exist, but they have the following points in common:

1. Disposable or expendable patterns are used.
2. Molding is done with a fluid aggregate or slurry.
3. The aggregate is hardened in contact with the pattern, providing precise reproduction of the pattern.
4. The aggregate is bonded with an inorganic ceramic binder.
5. The mold is heated to drive off all gases.

6. Pouring is performed with the mold preheated to a controlled temperature in order to pour thin sections which would not otherwise fill out.

The steps in the process, as shown in Fig. 3.11, are as follows:

1. A die for casting the wax patterns is made. The metal die must make allowance for shrinkage of both wax and later the metal casting, about 0.011 to 0.015 in. per in. total.
2. Wax patterns and gating systems are produced from the metal dies by injection. Waxes employed are blends of beeswax, carnauba, ceresin, acrawax, paraffin, and other resins usually obtained as proprietary mixtures. The wax is injected into the mold at 150 to 170 F and at a pressure of 500 to 100 psi. Polystyrene plastics are also used, but require a mold temperature of 300 to 600 F, pressure up to 12,000 psi, and iron or steel dies. Mercury may be used in place of wax patterns but must be frozen to retain the shape desired. Patterns and gating system must be assembled if cast separately. They can be joined by heating the surfaces to be attached in the case of wax or moistening them with a solvent, carbon tetrachloride, in the case of polystyrene patterns.
3. Precoating. The wax assembly is dipped into a slurry of a refractory coating material. A typical slurry consists of 325-mesh silica flour suspended in ethyl silicate solution of suitable viscosity to produce a uniform coating after drying. Some typical coating materials are listed in Table 3.2. After dipping, the assembly is coated by sprinkling it with 40 to 50 AFS silica sand and allowed to dry. Sometimes precoating is not used, and the wax pattern is directly invested in the molding material. In this case, the molding mixture must be vacuumed to remove air bubbles which may lodge next to the pattern.
4. The coated-wax assembly is next invested in the mold. This is done by inverting the wax assembly on a table, surrounding it with a paper-lined steel flask, and pouring the investment-molding mixture around the pattern. The mold material settles by gravity and completely surrounds the pattern as the work table is vibrated. Some typical investment-molding mixtures are given in Table 3.2. The molds are then allowed to air-set.
5. Dewaxing and preheating. Wax is melted out of the hardened mold by heating it in an inverted position at 200 to 300 F. The wax may be reclaimed and reused. Molds with polystyrene patterns in them are preferably dried at 140 to 160 F. For burnout and preheating, the molds are heated at the rate of 100 to 160 F per hr from about 300 F to 1600 to 1900 F for ferrous alloys and 1200 F for aluminum alloys. The finishing temperature of preheating is controlled so that the mold is at a temperature desirable for pouring the particular alloy and casting design. The burnout and preheating cycle must completely eliminate wax and gas-forming material from the mold.
6. Pouring. When the mold is at temperature, the metal is gravity-poured into the sprue. Air pressure may then be applied to the sprue to force-fill the mold cavity. Pouring is also done in a centrifuge to fill out thin sections.
7. Cleaning operations follow cooling of the casting.

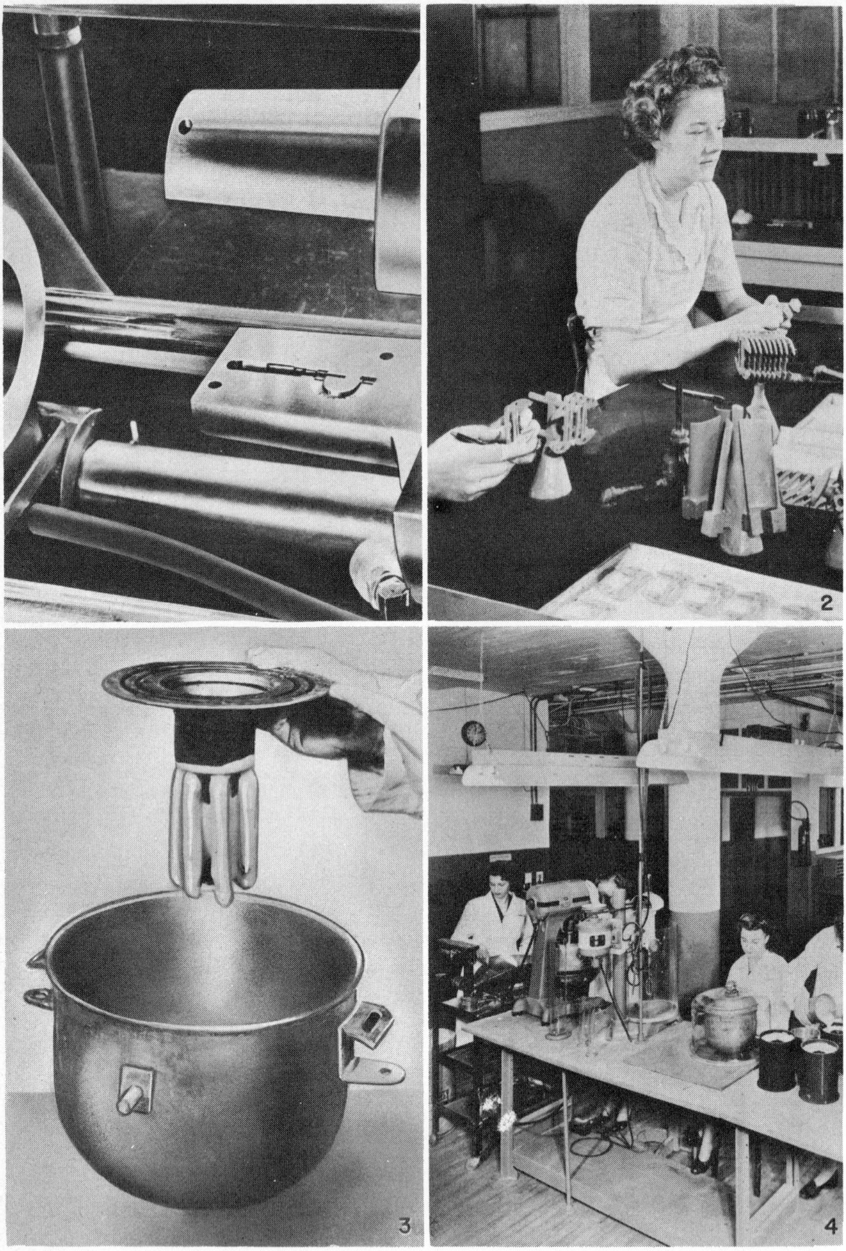

***Fig.* 3.11** Some steps in the process of investment casting. (1) Injection molding die for wax patterns. (2) Assembly of wax patterns. (3) Dipping wax pattern and gating to precoat pattern with in-molding mixture. (*Courtesy of American Foundrymen's Society.*)

Ceramic-shell Molds

A variant of investment molding is ceramic-shell molding. Such molds may be made by alternately dipping the pattern in a coating slurry and coating with silica or other refractory. A shell of ¼ in. or more thickness may be built up in this way. The pattern is then melted out, and the mold processed as described previously.[7,11,12,15,16]

Ceramic Molding

Ceramic molding is an offshoot of the investment-molding process. Reusable patterns are used for this process, as in sand molding. The molding aggregate consists generally of a slurry composed of refractory grains and ceramic binder. In one process, silica grains plus ethyl silicate, water, alcohol, and a gelling agent such as HCl are used. The slurry is poured around the pattern and allowed to gel in about 4 to 7 min. The pattern is then removed. The mold is fired by igniting the alcohol in the aggregate. After the mold has cooled, it is assembled and, if desired, preheated before pouring. In another process of the same type, the refractory grain slurry is bonded by calcium and ammonium phosphates. These processes may be used for making cores as well as molds.[9–14]

Certain advantages characteristic of the investment and ceramic casting processes are:

1. Casting high-pouring-temperature alloys to accurate dimensions. The metallic-mold processes are not suitable for steel and other alloys which must be poured at high temperature. Accuracy of ±0.003 in. per in. is possible in some castings. Machining on castings of many difficult-to-machine alloys is reduced or eliminated. Elimination of machining is one of the great virtues of the process.
2. Castings of great exterior and interior intricacy may be achieved.
3. Thin sections may be cast, even in the high-pouring-temperature alloys, because of the heated molds. Wire forms down to 0.002 in. in diameter and 2 in. long have been cast.

PLASTER MOLDS

Casting in plaster molds, or plaster-bonded molds, has become a useful casting process.[1,41] Copper- and aluminum-base alloys may be cast in plaster molds, but ferrous alloys may not. Plasters used for molding consist of mixtures of gypsum or plaster of paris, $CaSO_4 \cdot \frac{1}{2}H_2O$, and ingredients such as talc, asbestos fiber, silica flour, and others, to control the contraction characteristics of the mold and setting time.

Table 3.2a ***Coating and investment formulas for investment molding****

No.	Material	Amount	Uses
1	Silica	67% Tetraethyl silicate, 8 parts by volume Water, 1 part by volume	Precoating for high-melting alloys
	Liquids	33% Ethyl alcohol, 1–2 parts by volume Hydrochloric acid, a few drops to 1 or 2% of 3% solution	
2	Solids	187 parts 94 parts 325-mesh silica 56 parts 325-mesh alumina 37 parts 40-mesh silica	Same as above
	Liquids	80 parts 4 parts 20 Bé sodium silicate 1 part 2% polyvinyl alcohol	
3	Solids	60% plaster of paris 25% 50-mesh or finer silica 15% talc	Plaster molding for nonferrous alloys
	Liquids	Water to creamy consistency	
4	Solids	90% silica 6% magnesia 3% monobasic ammonium phosphate 1% monobasic sodium phosphate	Precoating for high-melting alloys
	Liquids	Water or 10% hydrochloric or nitric acid	
5	Solids	1464.4 g powder 3 parts china clay 17 parts 140-mesh silica flour	Same as above
	Liquids	800 ml 37.6% No. 40 ethyl silicate 59.8% 190-proof ethyl alcohol 2.6% hydrochloric acid in a 3% water solution	

*In part from K. Geist and R. M. Kerr, Jr.[37]

Table 3.2b Investment-molding mixtures

Ref.	Refractory	Water	Binder	Uses
32	95% sand	27–31%	5% alumina cement	Investment molding
32	Sand	....	3% or more ethyl silicate or sodium silicate	Same as above, suitable for ethyl silicate precoat
32	91.2% sand	33.8%	6.5% primary calcium phosphate 2.30% MgO, 300-mesh	For ceramic or investment molding
32	90.6% sand	51%	7.1% primary calcium phosphate 2.3% MgO, 300-mesh	Same as above
32	93.3% sand	34.1%	5.17% primary ammonium phosphate	Same as above
16	1464.4 g 3 parts china clay 17 parts 140-mesh silica flour	......	800 ml 37.6% No. 40 ethyl silicate 59.8% denatured ethyl alcohol, 190-proof 2.6% hydrochloric acid in a 3% water solution	Same as above

The plaster is added to water and mixed to a consistency of 140 to 180. Consistency is defined as the pounds of water per 100 lb of plaster in the mixture. Dry strength of the plaster depends greatly on the consistency of the mix as revealed in the following table:

Dry compression strength, psi	Consistency, lb water/100 lb mix
11,000	30
6,000	37
4,000	47
2,000	68 (general for plaster of paris)
200	140–180

After mixing, the plaster in a creamy condition is poured over the pattern and retained in a flask. A pattern-parting stearic acid dissolved in petroleum spirits, for example, may be used. Generally, metal patterns are necessary because the water in the plaster raises the grain on wood patterns and makes them almost impossible to draw. After setting 20 to 30 min, the pattern can be rapped and blown off the mold by air. Permeable (porous) casting plaster can be made by beating air bubbles into the plaster slurry with a mechanical mixer. Permeabilities up to 130 in standard permeability tests are possible (see Chap. 5 for meaning of "permeability"). Setting of the plaster involves hydration of the gypsum: $CaSO_4 \cdot \frac{1}{2} + \frac{3}{2}H_2O = CaSO_4 \cdot 2H_2O$ + heat. After setting, the molds are dried at 400 F. The plaster can be partially dehydrated at higher drying temperature, and consequently the mold evolves less steam when the castings are poured. However, mold strength is lost with dehydration. It is obvious that the time required for curing plaster molds is an undesirable part of this process. Because of dimensional accuracy and surface finish, however, many castings such as rubber-tire molds, foam-rubber molds, cast match plates, and the like, are molded in this way.

Antioch Process

Molding in the Antioch process[18] is done with a mixture of sand, gypsum, asbestos, talc, sodium silicate, and water, sand being the bulk ingredient and gypsum the binder. In proportions of 50 parts water to 100 parts dry ingredients, water is added to dry material consisting of 50% silica sand, 40% gypsum cement, 8% talc, and small amounts of sodium silicate, portland cement, and magnesium oxide. This slurry is poured around the pattern in suitable flasks or metal core boxes, and in about 7 min develops a set strength of about 70 psi in compression. After standing about 6 hr, the molds are assembled and autoclaved in steam at about 2 atm pressure. They then are dried in air for about 12 hr, and finally in an oven for 12 to 20 hr at 450 F. The autoclaving and drying process produces permeability, about 25 to 50 AFS permeability. The molds are then ready to be poured.

The advantages of plaster molds are that nonferrous castings can be made with good surface finish and dimensional accuracy. Tolerances of +0.005 in. on small castings and +0.015 in. on large castings such as rubber-tire molds can be obtained. Metallurgical quality in aluminum castings is also claimed for the Antioch process, because metal chills can be embodied in the mold.

GRAPHITE MOLDS

Some reactive metals, such as titanium alloys, for example, can be poured only into inert molds such as those made of graphite. Graphite molds are used either as expendable or as permanent molds. The former are molded with a plastic aggregate consisting 70 per cent of graphite grains of about 85 AFS fineness and 30 per cent of binders composed of pitch, carbonaceous cement, starch, and water.[28–30] The material is molded by squeezing it around the pattern at 60 to 120 psi. It is then dried and fired in a reducing atmosphere at 1800 to 2000 F to form solid mold or core pieces. After assembling the mold, pouring is done under a vacuum to prevent contamination of the metal. References 28 to 30 provide examples of molds and castings made by this process.

Permanent graphite molds are made by machining the mold cavity into solid blocks of graphite. These molds are then used in permanent mold-casting processes. Graphite begins to oxidize above 750 F, and the mold then begins to show wear. A mold coating of ethyl silicate which deposits silica on heating increases the number of castings which may be made before the mold is unsatisfactory. Graphite mold liners are used considerably in centrifugally casting brass and bronze bushings, sleeves, and other shapes.[34] They may also be used for limited runs of permanent mold-type castings. Recently, railroad car wheels have been cast in graphite molds accurately, so that no machining is required.[1]

PERMANENT MOLDS

Molds which can be reused many times are made of metal, usually gray cast iron or steel, though sometimes of bronze. The mold cavity (or die cavity) in a permanent mold is often cast to its rough contour and then is machined to its finished dimensions. Gating-system as well as mold cavities are machined. The machined mold makes it possible to obtain very good finish and dimensional accuracy in the castings. Aluminum, magnesium, zinc, lead, copper-base alloys, and cast irons are the principal alloys so cast. The extremely high temperatures of casting and consequent mold attrition usually make it unsuitable for most steel castings. Pouring temperatures, approximate mold life, and mold operating temperatures are somewhat as follows:

Metal	Pouring temperature range, °F	Approximate mold life, no. of castings	Mold operating temperature, °F
Gray cast iron.....	2300–2700	5–20,000	600–800
Aluminum base....	1300–1400	Up to 100,000	650–800
Copper base......	1900–2100	5–20,000	250–500
Magnesium base...	1200–1300	20,000–100,000	300–600
Zinc base.........	730–800	100,000+	400–500

The process is limited to volume production, and usually requires a continuous cycle of mold preparation, pouring, and casting ejection. This is necessary so that all steps can be timed and the mold thus kept within a fixed operating temperature range at the start of the pour. Operating temperature of the mold is one of the most important factors in successful permanent-mold casting.[22] Automatic machines have been developed to obtain a continuous cycle. The cycle of permanent-mold casting is shown in Fig. 3.12.

Mold life is extended and casting ejection made easier by coating the mold cavity.[21,35] Carbon soot, deposited from an acetylene torch, is used for iron castings. Refractories suspended in liquids may be sprayed on the cavity. The coating can be used for controlling the rate of heat extraction from the casting by varying its thickness. Metal or sand cores may be set in the mold before it is closed, as illustrated in Fig. 3.12. The metal is usually fed into the mold only by gravity (gravity casting), but in some cases air pressure, 3 to 10 psi, is used on the sprue after the casting is poured.

Semipermanent-mold Materials

Aluminum is used to a limited extent as a permanent-mold material. The mold can be cast to shape sufficiently accurately so that only a small amount of machine work is necessary to finish the mold cavity.[31] By anodizing the mold cavity, it is given added heat resistance. The ability of aluminum to extract heat rapidly has made it possible to pour even

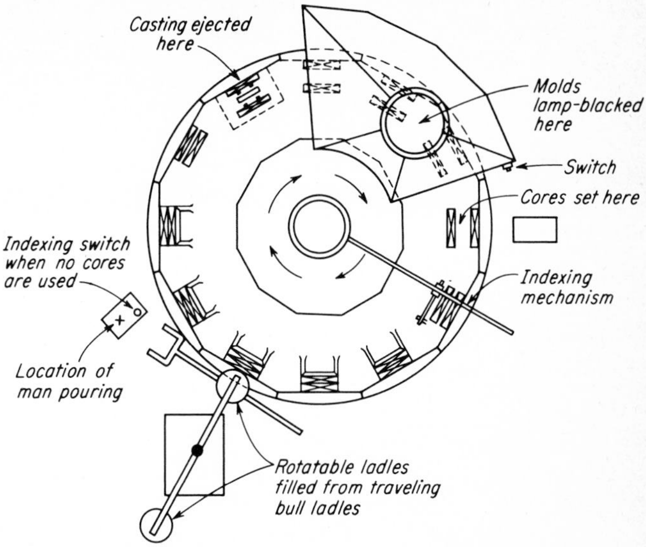

***Fig.* 3.12** **Stations for performing the operations of permanent-mold casting with the Eaton machine. (*Courtesy of Eaton Manufacturing Company.*)**

ferrous castings in these molds.[1] Their main use, however, appears to be for casting low-melting alloys in permanent molds.

Silicon carbide is the mold material in a process used for making permanent molds without the need for machining each mold.[31] Granular silicon carbide is mixed with bentonite (clay) and water containing sodium carbonate. This mixture is plastic, and may be molded like a green molding sand. After the mold is made, it is fired at about 1500 F and is thus converted into a stable, hard mold. This mold has chilling power much greater than that of sand, though not as great as metal.

The use of graphite as a permanent-mold material has been described earlier.

By means of permanent-mold casting, dimensional tolerances of ± 0.010 in. on a dimension for many castings, together with good surface finish, can be obtained. The chilling action of the mold produces better metal properties in many alloys. Holes can be cored and inserts cast into place more accurately than is possible in sand molds. The casting design, though, must be simple enough and with sufficient draft so that ejection from the mold is feasible. Because of mold cost, the process is limited to applications where the advantages named result in an economic or engineering gain over sand castings. Castings in this category include carburetor bodies, refrigeration castings, hydraulic-brake cylinders, connecting rods, washing-machine gears and gear covers, oil-pump bodies, typewriter segments, vacuum-pump cylinders, small crankshafts, flat-iron bases, valve bodies, and many other castings.[21,23,24]

DIE CASTING

Die casting differs from permanent-mold casting in that the molten metal is forced into the mold cavity under high pressures, 1000 to 100,000 psi. Two principal types of die-casting machines are used, the hot-chamber and cold-chamber machines. The submerged-hot-chamber type of machine is illustrated in Fig. 3.13. Molten metal flows into the hot chamber,

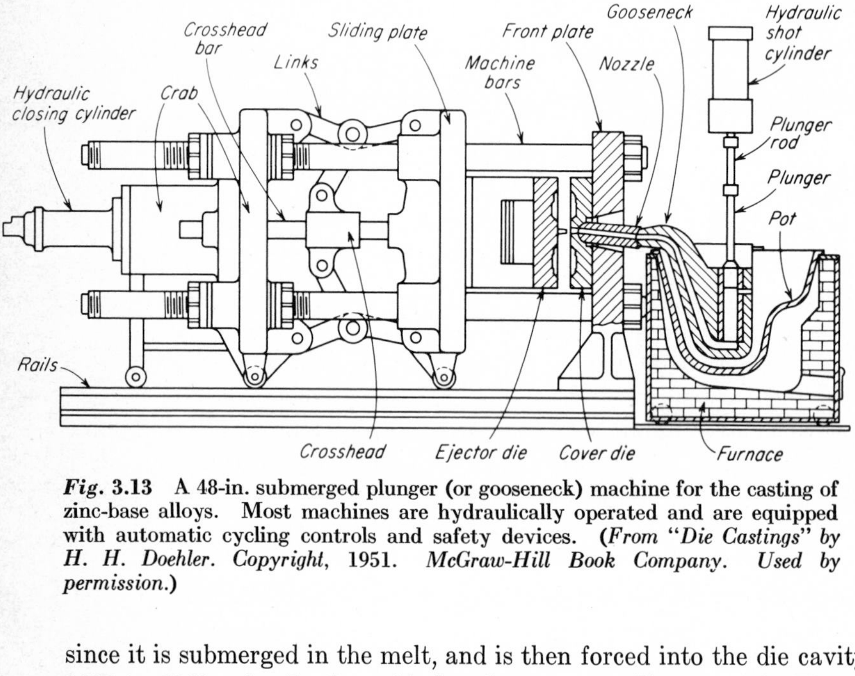

***Fig.* 3.13** **A 48-in. submerged plunger (or gooseneck) machine for the casting of zinc-base alloys. Most machines are hydraulically operated and are equipped with automatic cycling controls and safety devices. (*From "Die Castings" by H. H. Doehler. Copyright*, 1951. *McGraw-Hill Book Company. Used by permission.*)**

since it is submerged in the melt, and is then forced into the die cavity at 1000 to 2000 psi. In the cold-chamber process, illustrated in Fig. 3.14, metal is ladled into the shot chamber. The sequence of operations in cold-chamber die casting is illustrated in Fig. 3.15. Pressures in the cold-chamber machine may go over 30,000 psi. The hot-chamber machine is used for casting zinc, tin, lead, and other low-melting alloys. The cold-chamber machine is used for die-casting aluminum, magnesium, copper-base, and other high-melting alloys. Specific die-casting alloys are discussed later. The ferrous alloys are not as yet commercially die-cast because of their high pouring temperatures. Die-casting temperatures are similar to those used for permanent-mold castings given in the previous section.

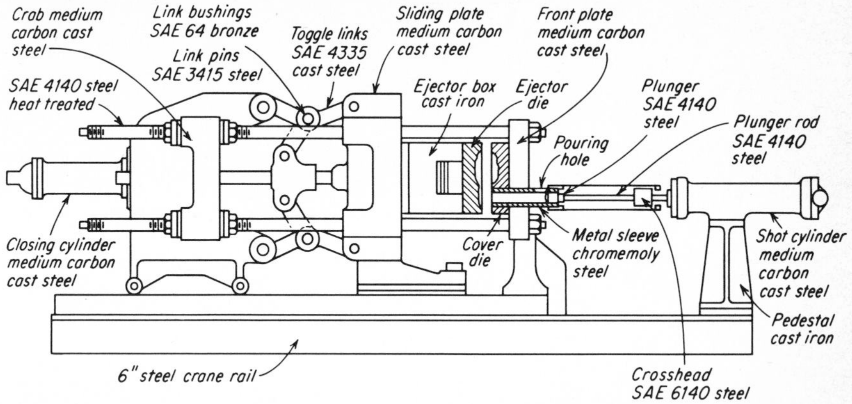

***Fig.* 3.14** A 21-in. cold-chamber machine which has largely replaced the gooseneck machine in production. (*From "Die Castings" by H. H. Doehler. Copyright, 1951. McGraw-Hill Book Company. Used by permission.*)

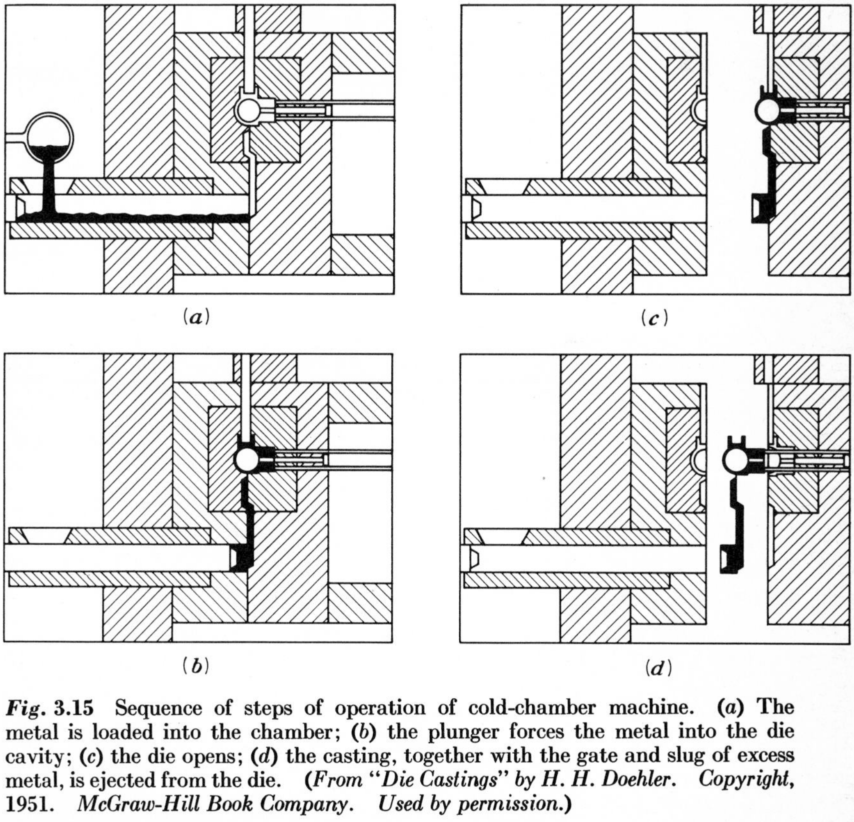

***Fig.* 3.15** Sequence of steps of operation of cold-chamber machine. (*a*) The metal is loaded into the chamber; (*b*) the plunger forces the metal into the die cavity; (*c*) the die opens; (*d*) the casting, together with the gate and slug of excess metal, is ejected from the die. (*From "Die Castings" by H. H. Doehler. Copyright, 1951. McGraw-Hill Book Company. Used by permission.*)

Die casting as a production casting process has certain advantages, some of which are:

1. The production rate is 150 to 250 die-cast cycles per hr, with up to 500 shots per hr possible.
2. Commercial dimensional tolerances of +0.001 to +0.003 in. can be obtained in some castings.
3. Thin sections, down to 0.015 in. in small castings, can be cast because of the pressures involved.
4. Accurate coring and casting of inserts are possible, as illustrated in Fig. 3.16.

***Fig.* 3.16** **Rotors for small electric motors. Aluminum is die-cast around the laminated-steel rotor-and-shaft assembly. (*Courtesy of Aluminum Company of America.*)**

5. Surface finish of many castings is such that they can be buffed directly.
6. Rapid cooling rate produces high strength and quality in many alloys; zinc-base die-casting alloys, for example, would not be used in many of their present applications if they could be sand-cast.

On the other hand, the casting design must be such that the mold cavity and cores allow the casting to be ejected. This is a fundamental difference or limitation of metal molds, however cast, which does not apply to sand-casting processes. Other aspects of the process are described in Refs. 1, 23, 25, and 26.

CENTRIFUGAL CASTING

Centrifugal casting refers more specifically to the forces used to distribute the metal in the mold rather than a specific molding process. However, since molds for centrifugal casting are usually specially designed, it is considered as a process. Centrifugal casting falls into three categories:

1. True centrifugal casting
2. Semicentrifugal casting
3. Centrifuging

Production of pipe castings using equipment of the kind shown schematically in Fig. 3.17 is probably the most familiar example of this pro-

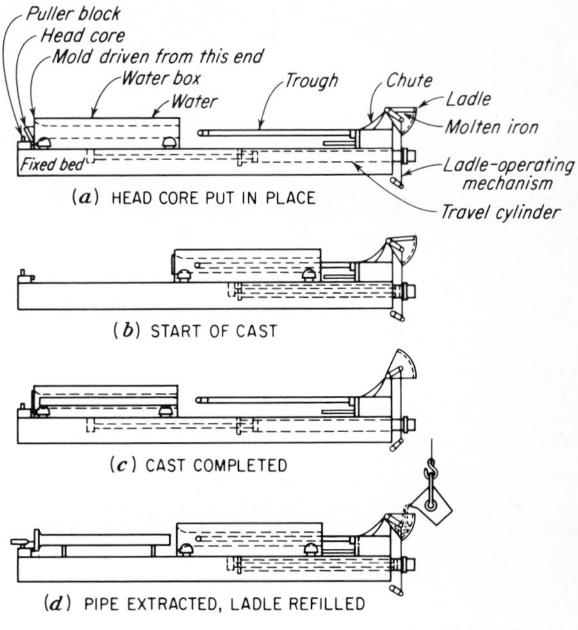

***Fig.* 3.17** Schematic diagram of DeLevaud pipe-casting machine and casting operations. (*Courtesy of American Foundrymen's Society.*)

cess. Either permanent molds or sand-lined tubular flasks are used. Sometimes core-sand molds are centrifugally cast. Shorter castings may be cast with the spinning axis vertical.[34] Castings made by the semi-centrifugal casting process are illustrated in Fig. 3.18. Centrifuging differs from the previous two processes in that the entire mold cavity is spun off the axis of rotation. Metal is fed from a central sprue through a gate into the mold cavity, as illustrated in Fig. 3.19. Extensive discussion of the various aspects of the centrifugal casting process is available in Refs. 1, 33, 34, 36, and 39. Pipe, cylinder liners, bushings, and a variety of centrifugal castings are made by this process.

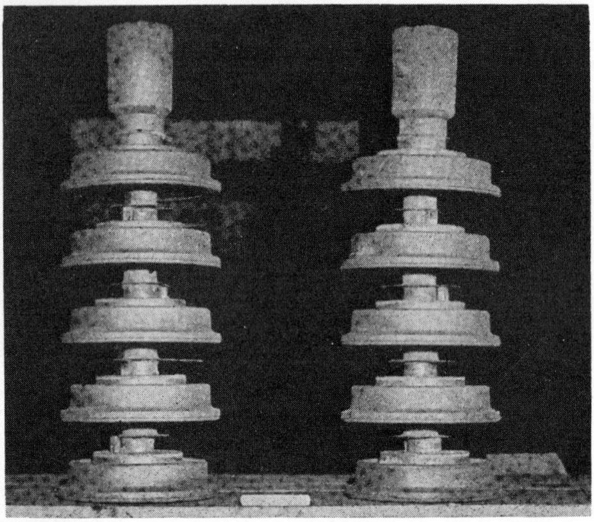

***Fig.* 3.18** Stack of tank track rollers cast by the semi-centrifugal method. (*Courtesy of American Foundrymen's Society.*)

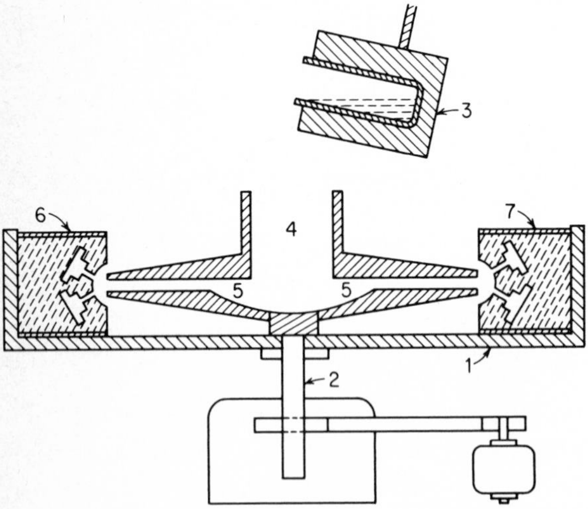

***Fig.* 3.19** Schematic diagram of equipment for centrifuging castings. (*Courtesy of American Foundrymen's Society.*)

BIBLIOGRAPHY

1. American Foundrymen's Society, "Molding Methods and Materials," Des Plaines, Ill., 1963.
2. R. S. L. Andrews, "Shell Process Foundry Practice," American Foundrymen's Society, Des Plaines, Ill., 1963.
3. U.S. Naval Avionics Facility, Fundamentals of Investment Casting, *Indianapolis, Ind., Tech. Publ.* 61, 1958.
4. Steel Founders' Society of America, "Steel Castings Handbook," Cleveland, 3d ed., 1960.
5. Gray Iron Founders' Society, "The Gray Iron Castings Handbook," Cleveland, 1958.
6. Malleable Founders' Society, "Malleable Iron Castings," Cleveland, 1960.
7. T. Operhall, Ceramic Shell, *Foundry,* vol. 86, p. 68, October, 1958.
8. W. C. Truckenmuller, Evaluation of Shell Molding Process Capability, *Trans. AFS,* vol. 66, p. 81, 1958.
9. T. A. Dickinson, New Plant Produces Mercury Investment Castings, *Foundry,* vol. 84, p. 133, November, 1956.
10. R. Greenwood, Ceramic Mold Process, *Foundry,* June, 1959, p. 84.
11. E. Bremer, New Processes Used at New Investment Casting Foundry, *Foundry,* October, 1957, p. 94.
12. A. Dunlop, Precision Castings in a Bigger Way, *Modern Castings,* November, 1956, p. 50.
13. F. C. Quigley and B. Bovarnick, Sintered Alumina Molds for Investment Casting of Steels, *Trans. AFS,* vol. 66, p. 247, 1958.
14. I. Lubalin and R. J. Christensen, Shaw Process Principles and Production, *Trans. AFS,* vol. 68, p. 539, 1960.
15. R. Herrmann, Investment Shell Process, *Foundry,* December, 1959, p. 84.
16. D. J. Kenny and P. A. Rutt, Thickness of Precoat for Investment Castings, *Foundry,* February, 1959, p. 82.
17. K. L. Mountain, Cement Molding at Chambersburg, *Foundry,* vol. 84, p. 102, November, 1956.
18. K. L. Mountain, The Antioch Process for Making Intricate Plaster Mold Castings, *Foundry,* vol. 83, p. 101, November, 1955.
19. C. W. Yaw, Casting Iron Patterns in Zircon Sand, *Foundry,* vol. 86, p. 74, October, 1958.
20. R. Herrmann, Ductile Iron Tire Molds Cast by Complex Process, *Foundry,* August, 1960, p. 60.
21. J. Miske, Permanent Mold Castings, *Foundry,* January, 1960, p. 66.
22. C. L. Goodwin and H. Y. Hunsicker, Cyclic Permanent Mold Operation: Some Thermal Aspects, *Trans. AFS,* vol. 67, p. 431, 1959.
23. E. C. Lewis, Low Pressure Die Casting, *Trans. AFS,* vol. 68, p. 268, 1960.
24. C. B. Curtes, Permanent Mold Casting of Aluminum, *Foundry,* vol. 86, p. 98, January, 1958.
25. M. R. Tenenbaum, Selection and Melting of Die Casting Alloys, *Foundry,* vol. 84, p. 92, February, 1956.
26. D. Morgenstern, Progress in Vacuum Die Casting, *Trans. AFS,* vol. 66, p. 199, 1958.
27. R. H. Herrmann, Aluminum Die Casting Plant, *Foundry,* July, 1959, p. 72.
28. A. L. Feild, Jr., Expendable Molds for Titanium Castings, *Metal Progr.,* vol. 70, no. 4, pp. 92–96, October, 1956.

29. A. L. Feild, Jr., and R. E. Edelman, The Use of Expendable Graphite Molds in Production of Sound Ductile Titanium Castings, *Trans. AFS,* vol. 65, p. 517, 1957.
30. H. W. Antes, J. T. Norton, and R. E. Edelman, Foundry Characteristics of a Rammed Graphitic Mold Material for Casting Titanium, *Trans. AFS,* vol. 66, p. 135, 1958.
31. J. B. McIntyre, Refractory Permanent Molds, *Foundry,* vol. 80, p. 102, August, 1952.
32. W. F. Davenport and A. Strott, Investments for the Precision Casting Process, *Foundry,* vol. 80, July, 1952.
33. M. L. Samuels and A. E. Schuh, Some Recent Developments in Centrifugal Castings, *Foundry,* vol. 79, July, 1951.
34. J. Putchinski, Casting Centrifugally in Graphite Molds, *Foundry,* vol. 78, February, 1950.
35. J. L. Erickson, Die Coating for Permanent Mold Castings, *Foundry,* vol. 77, February, 1949.
36. R. Nieman, Centrifugal Casting, *Trans. AFS,* vol. 52, p. 349, 1944.
37. K. Geist and R. M. Kerr, Jr., Principles of Precision Investment Castings, *Trans. AFS,* vol. 55, p. 17, 1947.
38. Dietert Process for Precision Molds, *Am. Foundryman,* vol. 25, p. 50, July, 1953.
39. American Foundrymen's Society, "Symposium on Centrifugal Casting," publ. 44-37.
40. H. Rosenthal and S. Lipson, Investment Casting of Aluminum, *Trans. AFS,* vol. 60, 1952.
41. R. F. Dalton, Some Practical Applications of Permeable Metal Casting Plaster, *Trans. AFS,* vol. 60, p. 351, 1952.
42. J. B. McIntyre, Casting in Cement Bonded Sand, *Foundry,* vol. 80, p. 90, December, 1952.
43. American Foundrymen's Society, "Cast Metals Handbook," 4th ed., 1957.
44. W. G. Lawrence, Precision Casting Mold Materials, *Trans. AFS,* vol. 68, p. 455, 1960.

4

Molding Processes Equipment and Mechanization

Molding requires specialized equipment for mold making by each of the processes described in Chap. 3. Forming the mold is done in one of several ways:

1. By compaction of the aggregate around the pattern.
2. By free flow of dry aggregate around the pattern. This is well illustrated by shell molding.
3. By free flow of a slurry or liquid aggregate around the pattern. Plaster and investment molding illustrate this method.

Variants of the above are also used. The nature of the molding materials determines the mold-forming method and the equipment needed.

Green-sand molding is done by compacting the aggregate around a pattern by ramming, squeezing, jolting, vibration, slinging, blowing, or by combinations of methods. This work is carried out as bench molding, machine molding, and floor and pit molding. Bench molding is hand work and limited to the production of only a few molds. Today it remains the simplest way to make one or a few small castings of a kind. Floor and pit molding, discussed briefly in Chap. 3, are suited for the larger casting sizes. By far the largest tonnage of castings is produced by machine molding using green sand as the molding material.

MOLDING MACHINES

Machines for the compaction of molding sand may be classified as follows:

1. Squeezers
2. Jolt machines

3. Jolt-squeeze machines
4. Slingers
5. Blowers
6. Combinations of numbers 1 to 5 above

Compaction

For typical limits of compaction, see the bulk-density data in Table 4.1. Minimum bulk density of freshly mixed sand may be as low as 50 lb per cu ft, whereas the maximum after molding may be as high as 115 lb per cu ft, or more.

Even when compacted, the molding-sand mass is composed of approximately 60 to 65 per cent solids and the balance voids (Table 4.1). Regardless of the type of bonding clay in the sand, there is a progressive increase in sand bulk density as the amount of work done in compacting the sand increases. The limiting bulk density is achieved when compaction has occurred to the point of sand-grain to sand-grain contact throughout the mass. This will occur at a density of about 100 to 115 lb per cu ft for typical foundry sands. Application of higher forces will not cause more compaction once the maximum bulk density has been reached.

As compaction of the sand occurs, the mechanical properties of the sand change in the manner shown in Fig. 4.1. As the sand density increases, its green compressive strength, green shear strength, tensile strength, and mold hardness increase.[3] This means that to raise the bulk density from one level to a higher level, more work must be done to over-

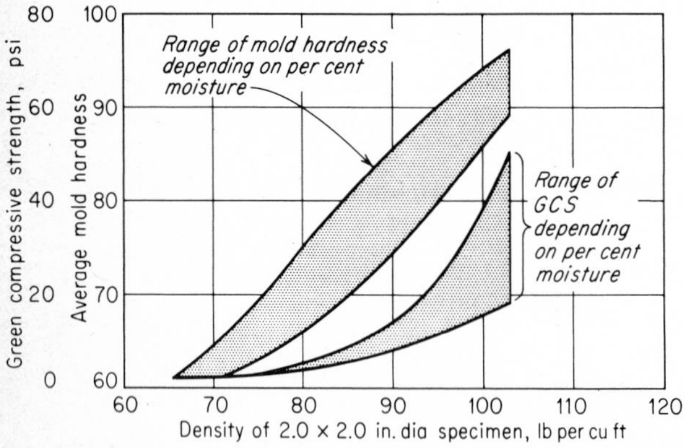

Fig. 4.1 **How mechanical properties change as compaction of sand occurs for a sand mixture of 6% western bentonite, 2% sea coal, 1% cellulose, and the remainder 85 AFS sand.**

come the strength of the sand and cause the increased density. Thus, in green-sand molding, there are interacting processes at work as follows:

1. Gross movement of the sand which must occur as sand flows above and adjacent to the pattern and is compacted
2. Fitting together or packing of sand grains and expression of the gross voids as the maximum bulk density is approached by compaction
3. Increase of mechanical strength of the sand aggregate as gross movement and packing of the sand grains occur

The changes cited are the result of work done on the sand by molding machines. The objective of the molding machine is to compact the molding sand to a uniform bulk density of over 90 per cent of maximum, exceeding about 85 mold hardness, and produce the sand mechanical properties related thereto.[2]

Table* 4.1 *Densities of some typical molding sands

Material	Bulk density, lb/cu ft	Per cent solids*	Per cent voids†
Silica sand (clay-free)	100–115	60.4–69.5	39.6–30.5
Dry sands plus southern or western bentonite and carbonaceous additives having 9–11% AFS clay, 4–8% total combustible, 60–75 AFS fineness	90–105	54.4–63.5	45.6–36.5
Molding sand in No. 2 tempered with water to molding consistency:			
Riddled	50– 65	30.2–39.2	69.8–60.8
Compacted to 70–85 mold hardness	65– 85	39.2–51.3	60.8–48.7
Compacted to 90–95 mold hardness	90–105	54.4–63.5	45.6–36.5
Fire-clay-bonded molding sand; 12–15% AFS clay, 4–8% total combustible, 60–75 fineness; tempered with water:			
Riddled	60– 75	36.2–45.3	63.8–54.7
Compacted to 60–85 mold hardness	75– 95	45.3–57.3	54.7–42.7
Compacted to 90–95 mold hardness	105–115	63.5–69.5	36.5–30.5

*True density of solid silica = 165.4 lb/cu ft

$$\text{Per cent solids} = \frac{\text{bulk density}}{\text{true density}} \times 100$$

Example: $\frac{100}{165.4} \times 100 = 60.4$

†Per cent voids = 100% − % solids

Squeezing

Squeeze molding machines utilize pressure as a means of compacting the sand. The pressure may be applied through a squeeze head or plate as illustrated in Fig. 4.2 by a molding machine such as that shown in Fig. 4.3 (also in Fig. 3.3). The maximum squeezing force of a pneumatically operated squeeze-type machine is defined by

$$\mathrm{MF} = P \times \frac{\pi d_c^2}{4} - W \tag{1}$$

where MF = molding force, 16, a machine limit
P = air pressure in squeeze cylinder, often assumed to be air-line pressure, psi
d_c = piston diameter of squeeze cylinder, in.
W = weight of pattern, flask, sand, and other accessories on work table of machine

Hence the molding force of a squeeze machine is limited by its piston diameter and the air pressure available, usually 90 to 110 psi.

The molding force of the squeeze head is, however, distributed over the entire squeezing area at the top of the flask. Although MF is relatively constant for a particular machine (and air pressure), the flask

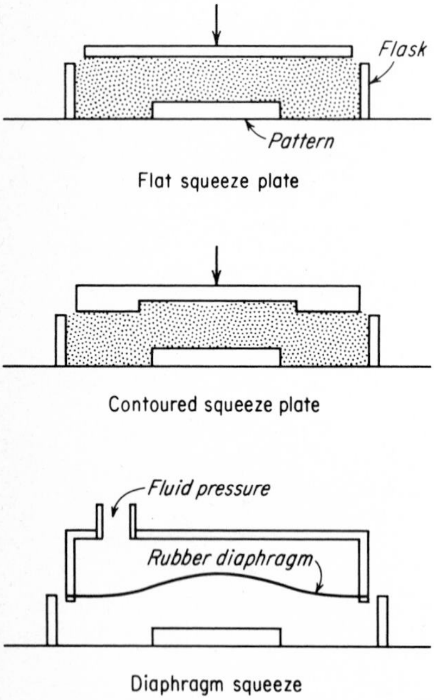

Fig. 4.2 Three methods of squeezing sand to compact it.

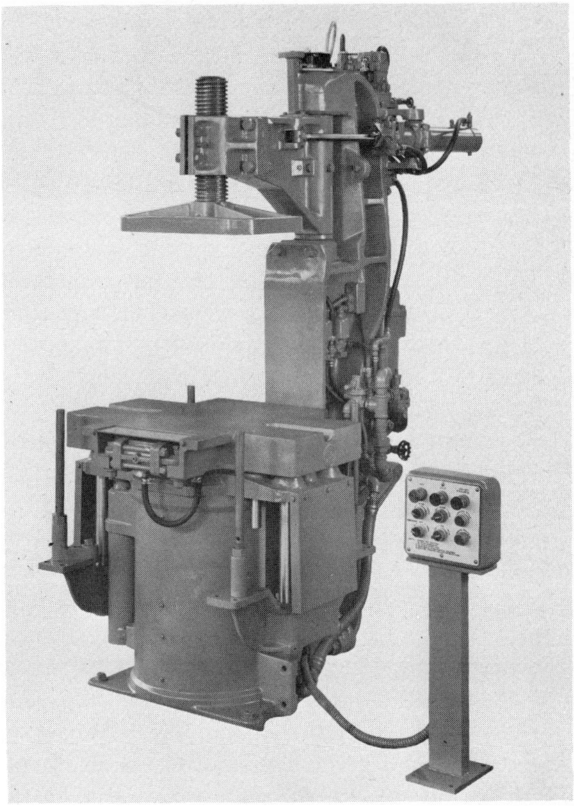

***Fig.* 4.3** Post-type jolt-squeeze pin-lift pattern-drawing molding machine. (*Courtesy of SPO, Inc.*)

size is not. To determine actual molding pressure applied at the flask, the following equation is used:

$$MP = \frac{MF}{A_f} \tag{2}$$

where MP = molding pressure, psi, at flask surface
MF = molding force, lb, applied by squeeze cylinder
A_f = surface area of flask under force MF, sq in.

Molding pressures of 20 to 50 psi are in common use. Pressures of 100 to 150 psi are used to produce densities approaching the maximum. In rare cases pressures up to 1500 psi may be used, although little benefit arises above 150 psi.

Formulas (1) and (2) define the packing forces and pressures applied to the squeezed surface. If molding sand were a perfect fluid, these pressures would be transmitted to the pattern surface and uniformly distributed. However, since molding sand behaves as a plastic aggregate of solid particles, much of the molding force is inefficiently used. Figures 4.4*a* and *b* show how the sand moves nonuniformly from flat squeezing. A column of fully compacted sand builds up over the pattern to support most of the applied squeezing force. Additional force is diverted against the flask walls as revealed by the sand movement shown in Fig. 4.4*b*. This behavior is predictable from principles of soil mechanics as revealed in Refs. 20 and 21. As a consequence, squeezing with a flat plate produces nonuniform density and mold softness at the parting and on vertical walls. Further information on sand movement during molding is reported in Refs. 2, 20, and 23.

Contour squeezing, as illustrated in Fig. 4.2, is a means of distributing squeeze molding forces more uniformly to try to obtain a more uniform mold density.[22] Diaphragm squeezing is another means of contour squeezing.[19] Separately actuated feet squeezing small areas also perform contour squeezing. Whatever type of squeezing is used, the objective is to produce a mold usually in excess of 85 mold hardness and 95 lb per cu ft density.

Bridging and keying of the sand grains against the flask and each other keeps the total applied molding force from reaching the pattern surface. Thus it can be seen that molding by squeezing alone will become less effective for a given pressure as the depth of the mold half increases. Furthermore, there will be a differential in the degree of packing from the squeeze head to the pattern. Sand density is at a minimum adjacent to the pattern, and the hardness of the mold, therefore, is less than that next to the squeeze head. Because of nonuniform pressure distribution, the sand adjacent to the pattern may be nonuniformly rammed. There is, therefore, a limit to flask depth that may be properly molded by squeezing which is dependent on the squeeze-machine capacity, pattern contour, molding sand, etc.[19] To obtain more uniform packing next to the pattern, the squeeze method of molding is used in combination with the jolt method.

Jolting

Jolting is incorporated in the machine shown in Figs. 4.3 and 3.3. The work table with pattern, flask, and sand is raised by a pneumatically operated piston and allowed to fall against the base of the machine under the influence of gravity. Packing of the molding sand is caused by work done by the kinetic energy of the falling sand. The power of jolting

(*a*)

(*b*)

***Fig.* 4.4** (*a*) Mold, flask, and pattern section used to study sand movement. Scale of grid units is 1 in. wide by 2.0 in. high. (*From R. W. Heine, T. J. Bosworth, and J. J. Parker.*[2]) (*b*) Deformation of sand grid caused by squeezing with a flat squeezing plate.

results from the conversion of the momentum of the falling sand to work in foot-pounds per second when the sand is instantaneously halted by the jolt table:

$$\frac{MV}{A} = \text{power of jolting}$$

where M = sand weight, lb
V = velocity at instant of jolt $= \sqrt{2gd}$, fps
A = jolted area, sq ft
d = jolt stroke, ft

For a sand weighing 80 lb per cu ft and 3.0-in. jolt stroke d,

$$\text{Jolting power} = \frac{80 \times \sqrt{2 \times 32.2 \times 3/12}}{1}$$
$$= 320.9 \text{ ft-lb/sec/sq ft}$$

An important characteristic of jolting is evident in the formula. Power for molding is independent of flask area, and determined mainly by the jolt stroke, a machine characteristic. Of course, the number of times that jolting is done will have a great effect on the degree of sand packing. After about 20 jolts, further jolting causes an asymptotic approach to maximum hardness and density, so that 20 or less is a commonly used number.[22]

In this type of sand packing, the maximum molding force is applied at the pattern surface. The mold thus is hardest at the pattern surface and parting. Again, if sand were a perfect fluid, it would flow uniformly against the pattern surface under jolting action. Because of bridging and keying, however, nonuniform flow occurs, especially as the vertical depth of the casting increases, and in deep pockets. Reference 2 shows the sand movement. Because the sand away from the pattern surface packs less than at the pattern surface, it is necessary to finish off the top or back of the mold by squeezing or ramming with a pneumatic rammer. Only the first 1 to 2½ in. of sand above the pattern plate is well rammed.[2,19,23]

Jolt machines, sometimes called bumpers, are useful in handling many sizes of flasks, especially when larger molds are rammed up on a molding floor. The machine shown in Fig. 4.3 has a squeeze head as well as a jolt table. Loose patterns or separate copes and drags may be molded. Heavy flasks are drawn from the pattern by overhead crane. Large core boxes may also be used on jolt machines. It may be noted that the limiting capacity of a jolt machine is that total weight which it is able to lift and let fall, defined as follows:

$$W_j = \frac{\pi d_j^2}{4} \times P$$

where W_j = total weight which can be lifted by jolt cylinder, lb
= flask weight + pattern weight + jolt-table weight + sand weight
d_j = diameter of jolt cylinder, in.
P = air-line pressure

Jolt capacities of 500 lb to several tons are available in commercial machines.

Pattern Stripping

The elimination of the operation of stripping the pattern from the mold by hand speeds molding and removes one of the sources of damaged molds and dimensional variation of the mold cavity. Mechanical pattern stripping is performed by pushing or lifting the flask away from the pattern table, using lifting pins as shown on the machine of Fig. 4.3. The pattern or its mounting table is vibrated before and during the stripping operation. A slow withdrawal of the pattern during the moments when it leaves the sand is desirable. These steps are incorporated in pin lifts, or lifting-bar strippers, which push on the flask, separating the pattern from the mold. Generally, on molding machines, the pattern is lowered away from the mold while the pins or bars hold the flask up. The jolting, squeezing, and pattern-drawing mechanisms on a typical machine are shown in Fig. 4.5.

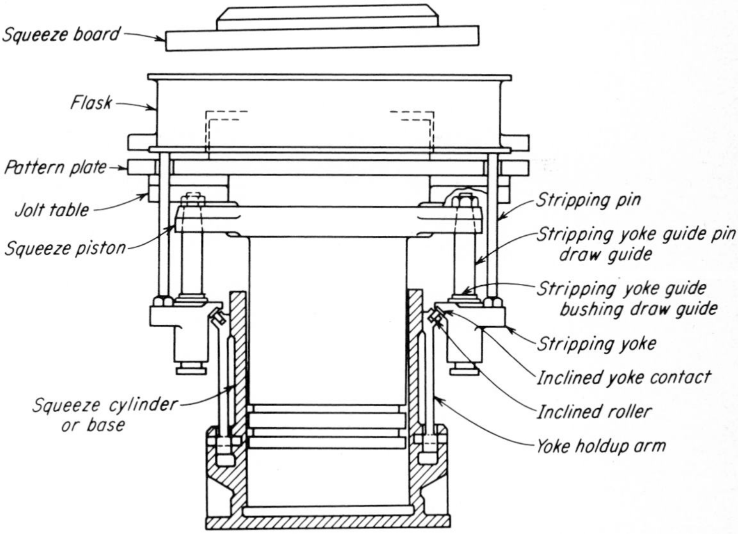

***Fig.* 4.5** Schematic diagram of jolt-squeeze pin-lift pattern-drawing mechanism. (*Courtesy of SPO, Inc.*)

Jolt-squeeze Machines

Jolt-squeeze machines utilize a combination of jolting and squeezing to pack the molding sand. A combination of the beneficial compaction effects of squeezing and jolting on sand density is then obtained. Post-type and cantilever squeeze heads are available, and the machines may be portable or stationary. A portable post-type squeeze-head machine is shown in Fig. 4.3. These machines, without pattern-drawing features, are used mainly for match-plate molding. For this purpose a jolt capacity of 500 lb is adequate, since the molds are generally small enough so that one man can handle them. With the matchplate between cope and drag, the drag half is molded first, using the jolt action. The bottom board, fitting inside the flask, can be jolted against the sand to seat it. Then the assembly is rolled over and the cope molded. On most match-plate work this is done by squeezing with a squeeze plate that fits inside the flask. Thus cope and drag are squeezed simultaneously. The pouring basin can be molded by a pattern attached to the squeeze board, and the sprue may be cut by hand or attached to the pattern. Match-plate molding using jolt-squeeze machines is perhaps the simplest method of speeding up the molding. If a pair of jolt-squeeze machines are used, one machine may be used for making copes and one for drags, to speed up molding. A third man can function as core setter and helper. Some typical machine-capacity characteristics of certain jolt-squeeze pin-lift machines are given in Table 4.2. The limiting size of mold which can be produced depends on table size, maximum jolt load, squeeze capacity, height of pattern draw, stripping-pin center-line distance, and distance from table center to squeeze plate and back support.

Table Size

Table size limits the effective area for attaching patterns or bolster plates. The underside of the work table is provided with recesses and places to bolt the pattern equipment solidly to the table.

Maximum Jolt Load

As defined earlier, the maximum jolt lifting force must be greater than the weight of all patterns, flask, sand, and table pushing down on the jolt piston. These capacities are given in Table 4.2 for the machines being considered.

Squeeze Capacity

The maximum molding force of some typical small-size jolt-squeeze machines is given in Table 4.2. Many machines are equipped with air-pressure relief valves which permit any desired value of air pressure below that of line pressure to be applied. For example, if line pressure

Table 4.2 ***Typical specifications for jolt-squeeze stripper machines, post type with swing-arm squeeze head****

General specifications	Portable or stationary		Stationary	
Table size, in.	20 by 27	21 by 30	23 by 31	25 by 34
Recommended max jolt load, lb, at 80 lb air pressure	600	800	1000	1500
Squeeze-cylinder diam, in.	11	13	14	16
Squeeze capacity, lb, at 80 lb air pressure	7200	10,000	12,000	16,000
Pattern draw, in.	4 or 6	6 or 8	6 or 8	6 or 8 or 10½
Stripping-pin center line, front to back, in.	12 min, 22 max	12 min, 25 max	13½ min, 26 max	14½ min, 31 max
Stripping-pin center line, left to right	14½ min, 21½ max	14½ min, 23½ max	16 min, 25 max	19 min, 29 max
Distance, in., table to squeeze plate	12 min, 20 max	18 min, 24 max	18 min, 24 max	18 min, 24 max 20 min, 26 max
Distance, in., floor to table	27	28	28 or 30	28½ or 32
Distance, center of table to back support, in.	10¾	13	14	17½
Shipping weight, lb, approx.	1500	1900	2200	3650 or 3850

*Courtesy of SPO, Inc.

is 80 psi, the relief valve may be set to bypass anything over 50 psi in the squeeze cylinder. Then the actual molding force is some value less than the maximum, and can be calculated by Eq. (1). Thus, by adjusting the air-pressure relief valve, the molding force can be adapted to the flask size to result in a squeeze pressure [actual molding pressure, Eq. (2)] suitable to the casting requirements. Currently recommended squeeze pressures vary from 25 to 150 psi, depending on the casting size and metal cast.[24]

Height of Pattern Draw

This dimension limits the pattern depth which can be drawn free and clear of the mold. If additional lifting straight up can be done with hoists, much deeper patterns can be drawn.

Stripping-pin Center-line Distance

The stripping pins are adjustable through a swing of 360° and in several positions. The pin center-line distances determine the mimimum and maximum size flask for which the machine is intended. This is indicated in Table 4.2 for some typical machines. Bars, frames, or yokes may be used[1] in place of stripping pins.

Car-type Jolt-squeeze Strippers

Large-size jolt-squeeze stripping machines are often used in high-production work for medium-size castings. A car-type jolt-squeeze stripper, having a 21-in.-diameter squeeze piston, is shown in Fig. 4.6. The jolt-squeeze action is similar to that of the machines already considered. The squeeze plate consists of a car mounted on wheels and a track. In the squeeze position, the car is rolled over the mold before squeezing and functions as the squeeze plate. Stripping is accomplished by lowering the pattern away from the mold while the strip frame or stripping rails hold up the flask. The flask is removed from the machine when the squeeze-platen car is rolled out of the squeeze position. Lifting hooks on the car engage the flask, carry it out, and deposit it on a roll-out conveyor. The machine is used for making copes and drags, although drags must be rolled over outside the machine. It is especially suited to production work when only one size of flask is used, so that the roll-out conveyor and stripping frame are standardized.

Jolt-rockover Pattern Draw

The jolt-rockover pattern draw is a machine used for separate cope and drag work, molding the drag only. The drag is jolted and then finished off by pneumatic ramming and bedding in of a bottom board. The drag

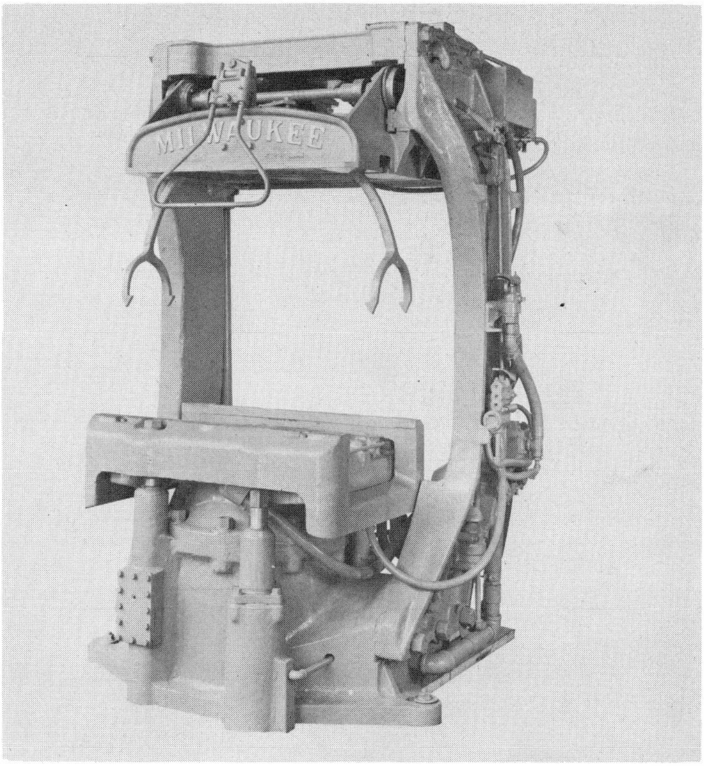

Fig. 4.6 Car-type jolt-squeeze pattern stripper with total squeezing capacity of 27,000 to 56,000 lb and jolting capacity of 3000 lb. (*Courtesy of W. Gerlinger, Inc.*)

is clamped and rocked over onto the leveling bars (equalizers), and the pattern is lifted away from the molds. This drawing action simplifies drawing patterns that have deep pockets on them. A long sand projection will often drop out of a mold when the pattern is stripped by drawing it downward, away from the mold cavity. In the rocked-over position, sand projections in the mold are not hanging in tension; so drops do not occur. Slow drawing of the mold as it first leaves the pattern assists in a clean draw. Many rockover machines are equipped with automatic slow drawing during the first inch of the draw and a more rapid draw for the balance of the pattern-draw travel. The drawing position of the machine is illustrated in Fig. 4.7. Machines of this type can be used on heavy drags which can be rocked over to conveyors or can be transferred by crane to conveyors for closing and pouring.

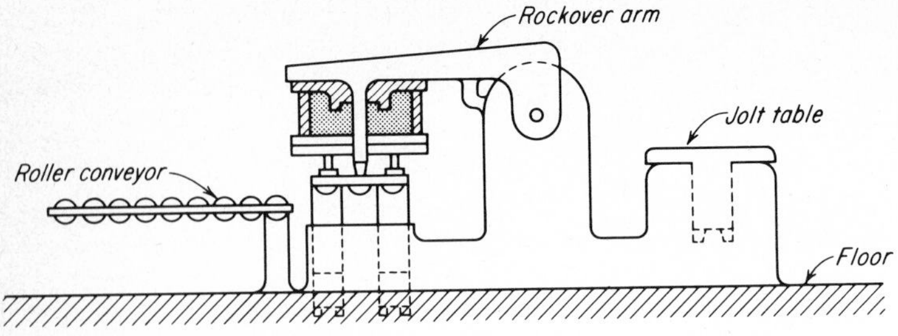

Fig. 4.7 Diagram showing rockover machine in pattern-drawing position.

Jolt-squeeze-rollover Pattern Draw

Jolt-squeeze-rollover pattern-draw machines are used for the drag in cope and drag molding. The rollover mechanism permits pattern drawing by lowering the mold away from the pattern. A machine of this type is shown in Fig. 4.8. The pattern plate is mounted on the rollover table.

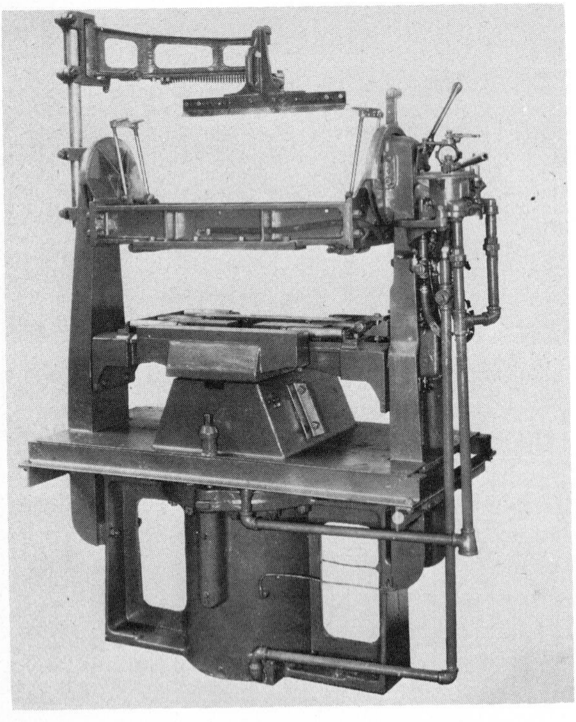

Fig. 4.8 Jolt-squeeze-rollover pattern-draw machine. (*Courtesy Osborne Manufacturing Co.*)

The jolt-table, squeeze-head, and pattern-draw mechanisms are below the rollover table. The jolt table is raised to engage the rollover table for jolting after the flask has been filled with sand. After jolting the rollover table, the flask is struck off by a strike-off bar pivoted on the main frame, leaving a fixed height of sand above the flask bottom. Then a bottom board, which in the case of this machine is also the squeeze board, is held against the sand by the quick-acting clamps that are part of the rollover table. The table and mold are then rotated 180° about their approximate center of gravity (axis of rotation). The squeeze piston in the combination jolt-squeeze–pattern-draw mechanism then squeezes the mold against the rollover table, which is above the mold. The pattern is drawn on the return stroke of the piston by allowing the mold to travel down with the piston. The squeeze action in this case is limited to movement of the bottom board against the flask frame, as can be seen in Fig. 4.9. The effect of squeezing under these conditions depends on the amount of extra sand in the flask, i.e., height of sand above the flask bottom after

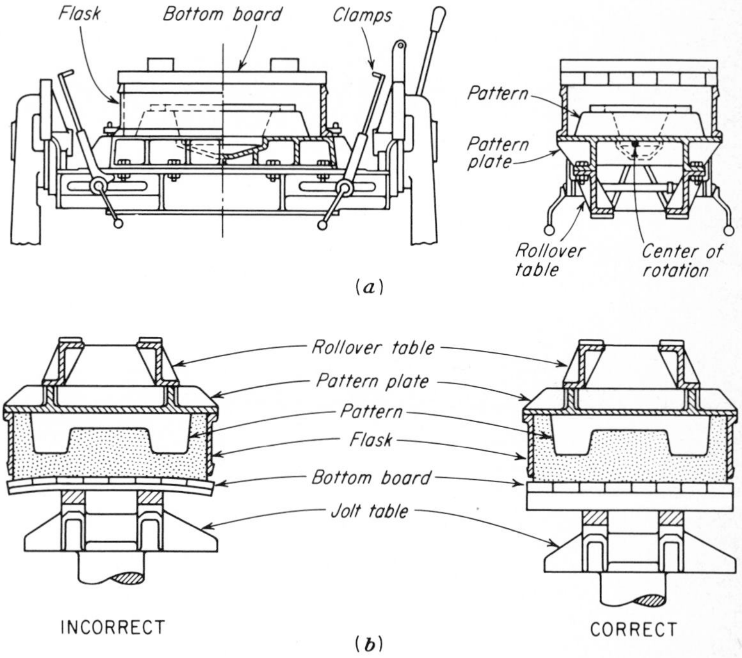

***Fig.* 4.9** Schematic of machine in Fig. 4.8. (*a*) Typical pattern mounting. The ease with which heavy molds are rolled over may be readily understood by noting the manner in which the load is distributed about the center of rotation. (*b*) Squeezing and bottom-board conditions for jolt-squeeze-rollover pattern-draw machine. (*Courtesy of Osborne Manufacturing Co.*)

being struck off. The molding pressure, MP from Eq. (2), does not apply to this type of squeezing, the actual pressure being less than the maximum exerted by the squeeze head, with the balance taken up by the flask frame. The greater the amount of extra sand in the flask before the squeezing, the closer the actual molding pressure approaches the maximum available from the squeeze head.

A variety of special molding machines based on variations of the jolt-squeeze pattern-stripping principles are in use. For instance, a *vibrating-squeeze pattern-draw* machine has been devised. As the mold is squeezed, rapid jolts are applied to the pattern table on the horizontal direction. This assists in sand flow under the squeeze pressure, and is supposed to produce a more uniform mold by squeezing. Simultaneous jolting and squeezing is used in some molding machines.

Special Squeezing Machines

Diaphragm squeezing is illustrated in Fig. 4.2. This method of squeezing is aimed at more efficient use of molding force. Higher average density is obtained by squeezing to develop a contour over mold portions which would be low if a flat squeeze were used. The effect of diaphragm squeezing over a pattern is illustrated in the mold sections in Ref. 23.

Segmented squeeze plates actuated by individual hydraulic cylinders provide another means of developing contours by squeezing.

Sand Slingers

Sand slingers are molding machines which compact the sand moving at high velocity by impact on the pattern. Sand is conveyed by belt into the slinger head, a housing 19 or 22 in. in diameter. The slinger head contains a rotor equipped with 4- or 5-in. blades that pick up the sand as it falls into the head and throw it against the mold. The rotor and blades, traveling at 1800 rpm, are capable of imparting a velocity of about 10,000 fpm to the sand. A slow speed, 1200 rpm, is used to avoid pattern damage in placing the first sand on the pattern, whereas the faster speed is used for the backup sand. The machine operator, by bouncing or rolling the first sand into the mold off the flask edge and sides, can minimize pattern wear caused by the blasting effect of the sand.

Slingers of several different models are used, including:

Stationary Slinger

A model of this type is illustrated in Fig. 4.10. The operator rides a seat next to the slinger head and controls its movements by a joystick which hydraulically operates the translational movements of the head for

***Fig.* 4.10** Stationary speed slinger. (*Courtesy of Beardsley-Piper Division, Pettibone Mulliken Corp.*)

filling the flask. The slinger is fixed in its location and is used for ramming up molds that pass under its head on a conveyor or conveyors. Other stationary models may be operated from remote-control positions.

Tractor Sand Slinger

A tractor slinger can do its own sand conditioning by picking up sand from windrows, reconditioning it, and feeding it back to the slinger head which travels behind. The tractor slinger can ram up molds which are within reach of the slinger head.

Motive Slingers

These are fed with conditioned molding sand in tanks. The unit travels on rails and can ram up molds anywhere within reach of the arc of slinger-head rotation (Fig. 3.5). Motive slingers are generally used in producing medium and larger sizes of castings, for floor and pit work located along the track traveled by the unit. Especially in large work, they have the advantage of filling the flask rapidly and ramming the sand at the same time.

Mold Blowers

Mold blowing is a pneumatic form of slinging. A diagram of a blower is shown in Fig. 6.5 for the making of cores. Blowers are more commonly used for making cores than molds because core sands are more readily blown than molding sands. As the green shear strength of a sand exceeds 1 psi, it becomes more difficult to blow. However, increasing use of mold blowing is occurring. The minimum air pressure required to transport sand is about 3 to 5 psi in the magazine, but sustained blowing and compacting requires 35 to 60 psi in the magazine and about 100 psi available in large volume. Bulk density of molding sand as blown rarely exceeds 85 lb per cu ft, so that additional compaction must be done to obtain a sufficiently dense mold. This is usually done by squeezing the mold against the blower head. Blow-squeeze molding is one of the fastest methods of making shallow flask molds, 2 to 4 in. high.

Dry-aggregate Molding

Mixtures of dry materials can be packed to high density by simply allowing the aggregate to fall or be poured around the pattern. Such aggregates have low unconfined shear strength and will therefore pack with little effort. Vibration is usually sufficient to achieve densities of about 100 to 115 lb per cu ft, or 58 to 65 per cent solids. Mixtures containing 1.0 to 3.0 per cent of a liquid and fine particles become sticky and develop some green shear strength, sometimes up to 1.0 psi or more. These aggregates do not flow freely, and bulk density may drop to 70 to 90 lb per cu ft, or 45 to 55 per cent solids. Core sands and silicate-bonded sands are examples. Squeeze, jolting, or blowing may then be required to gain additional compaction to the full density of vibrated dry aggregates. Obviously, the bond in such mixtures must be developed in contact with the pattern or no mold could be formed.

Shell Molding

Shell molding is an example of dry-aggregate molding. A dry mixture of sand and 3 to 6 per cent resin is usually molded by free fall of the aggregate against the heated pattern, as illustrated in Chap. 3. Shell sand is also made of sand grains that are first coated with liquid resin and then have the resin hardened on the sand grain by heat or catalysts. This sand then behaves as a dry aggregate. Because the sand is heated once it strikes the pattern, the resin melts and becomes sticky before it polymerizes to develop its bond. If the aggregate becomes sticky before the sand packs well, some low-density molds may develop. The shell sand may be blown against the pattern or into a core box rather than be placed by free fall. Reference 25 provides details of various aspects of the process.

Fluid Aggregates

Thin slurries used in plaster molding and ceramic molding flow readily around patterns. Bubbles sometimes become entrapped at pattern surfaces. Vacuuming decreases this problem. Viscosity of the slurry mainly determines the pattern-covering ability.

MOLDING EOUIPMENT

In addition to molding machines, much allied equipment is required for green-sand molding. Some of these items are briefly considered.

Flasks

The flask consists of the frames necessary for molding and handling the cope and drag. Molding flasks may be classified as follows:

1. Removable flasks
   a. Snap
   b. Pop-off
   c. Slip
2. Tight or permanent flasks

Removable flasks are used for match-plate molding and cope and drag molding of small to moderate size. They are convenient since only one flask is required per machine setup. After the mold is made, the flask is removed and replaced with a jacket so that the mold may be weighted and poured. A *slip flask* has sides tapered 4° for removal of the mold. A cam-actuated retractable shelf, called a sand strip, is attached to the cope, so that the cope may be lifted off for pattern removal. In *pop-off-type flasks*, the sand mold is held in place by corrugations on the tapered sides, as in Fig. 4.11. Pop-off flasks have expansible sides, and can therefore be removed after the mold is completed. The double guide pins shown in Fig. 4.11 favor accuracy in pattern drawing and mold assembly.

Snap flasks are hinged on one end so that they can be opened. They have a fixed sand strip at the parting surface for holding up the cope.

Removable flasks are subject to warpage if dropped or mishandled and do not provide the most rigid support of the mold. Flask sizes are usually described by their width and length at the parting surface (thus a 16-32 flask is 16 in. wide and 32 in. long at the parting line) and by their depth. The three dimensions are usually marked on the side of the flask. A minimum of 1½ to 2 in. of sand is desirable at the sides and bottom. The cope height determines the height of the sprue, and thus

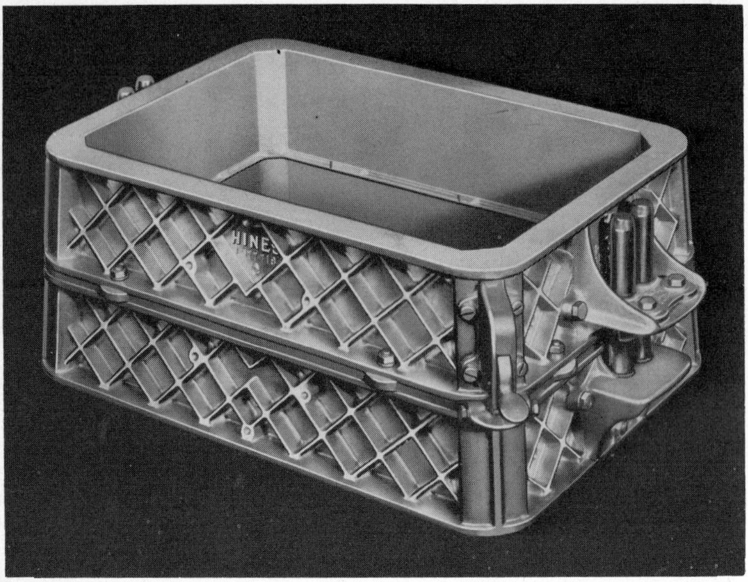

***Fig.* 4.11** Pop-off flasks with double guide pins for squeezer molding with match-plate patterns. (*Courtesy of Hines Flask Co.*)

the metallostatic pressure applied to the molten metal. High copes, i.e., high pressure, favor elimination of gases and promote feeding, but also may cause mold-cavity enlargement. Removable flasks allow the mold to be vented easily.

Tight or *rigid* or *permanent* flasks remain around the mold until after the casting is poured and shaken out. Hence a number of tight flasks are required for any one molding setup, one for each mold being processed. However, jackets are not required, since the flask is used for both molding and pouring. Tight flasks are generally made of steel and have the advantage that they can be barred (reinforced), as illustrated in Fig. 4.12, to make the mold more rigid and less liable to twist. They are more resistant to warpage and assure a positive alignment of cope and drag through pins and bushings. The cope may be clamped to the drag as illustrated, instead of being weighted. However, these flasks are heavy, usually require mechanical handling, and involve greater initial cost.

Upsets

Upsets may be used on any flask to increase the depth of cope or drag. They are frames, usually metal, bolted to the top of the cope or bottom of the drag.

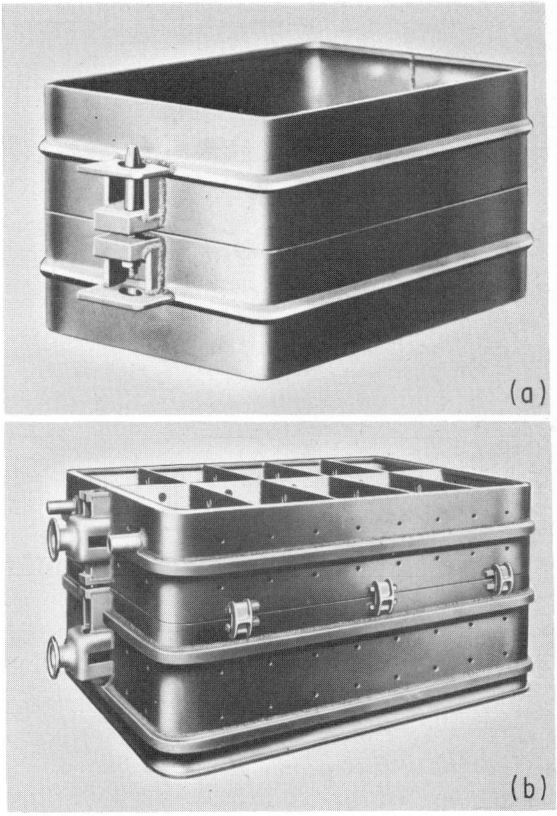

***Fig.* 4.12** Tight or permanent flask. Flask in upper picture shows common type. Flask in lower picture is heavily reinforced for rigidity. (*Courtesy of Sterling Wheelbarrow Company.*)

Jackets

Jackets are used in connection with removable flasks. The unsupported mold is enclosed in a metal, wood, or asbestos board frame, i.e., jacket. The jacket side walls have taper corresponding to that of the removable flasks, about 4° on the vertical. Jackets must fit well—must not be warped or twisted—in order to prevent runouts or mold cracking when the metal is poured. Generally, a jacket is required to have its upper edge below the cope surface so that mold weights may rest on the cope surface of the mold. Jackets may be shifted from mold to mold as pouring progresses, after the casting has solidified.

Bottom Boards, Squeeze Boards

For jolt-squeeze molding, a bottom board is required to fit inside the flask frame with about ¼ in. clearance all around its periphery. Different sizes of flasks therefore require different sizes of bottom boards. If the flask is reinforced, no bottom board is required. In some squeeze work, a bottom board is used which just engages the bottom edge of the flask, as, for example, the rollover molding operation discussed earlier (Fig. 4.9). Bottom boards are made of wood, asbestos board, or aluminum.

Squeeze boards also are usually required to fit inside the flask frame. However, since the squeeze board is used for the cope, only one is needed per molding setup. It may be attached to the squeeze head of the molding machine, where the pattern and flask are in a fixed position as in cope and drag molding or jolt-squeeze machines. A contoured squeeze board may be used to obtain a more uniform squeezing action around the pattern.[19,22] The pattern for the sprue cup or pouring basin can be mounted on the squeeze board.

Weights

The cope mold half must be held down to keep it from floating when the metal is poured. Metallostatic pressure exerts a buoyant effect on the cope, which an be calculated from the following relationship:

$$F_c = P_c \times A_c$$

where F_c = force pushing upon cope
P_c = metallostatic pressure at cope parting surface
A_c = projected mold-cavity area at cope parting surface

P_c is calculated as follows:

$$P_c = w \times h$$

where w = weight per cubic inch of metal
h = effective height of metal head above cope

If the casting is all in the drag, the sprue height is the effective height of metal head above the cope. With some casting in the cope, the effective head is less than the sprue above the parting line. However, the latter may be used as a safe figure. Simplifying, it can be seen that, for ferrous castings, assuming 0.26 lb per cu in. for w, the force pushing up on the cope is 0.26 per square inch of projected cope area per inch of sprue height, or

$$F_c = 0.26 \times A_c \times h_s$$

where h_s is the sprue height in the cope. If the weight of the cope itself is subtracted from F_c, the additional weight required to resist static pressure is obtained.

A safety factor of 1.5 to 2.0 then can be used on the calculated value to overcome dynamic-pressure effect. A mold weight based on the total flask area at the parting line can be a safe weight.

Weights, then, are required to hold down the cope and must be available in different sizes to suit the flasks. Of course, weights may be shifted from mold to mold as pouring progresses. Tight flasks may be clamped together rather than weighted.

FOUNDRY MECHANIZATION

Two developments were required so that foundries could be mechanized. First, machines had to be designed and built which could perform foundry operations such as molding, coremaking, sand mixing, etc. Second, these machines had to be integrated with materials-handling equipment so that continuous processing could be accomplished in the foundry. Since it is estimated that from 50 to 200 tons of material is handled or rehandled to produce a ton of castings, the importance of good materials handling cannot be overemphasized. This basic idea is recognized in mechanization as it is applied in foundries.

Since there are certain basic steps in the metal-casting process, these may be used as units of mechanization. Processing steps which lend themselves to mechanization are the following:

1. Sand preparation for molding and coremaking
2. Coremaking
3. Molding, pouring, and shakeout
4. Melting
5. Cleaning

Since materials and equipment converge at the molding operation and diverge after pouring, this is an important point in the complete cycle. For molding to progress, molding sand must be delivered to the molding machines as rapidly as required.

Sand Preparation and Handling

About 4 or 5 tons of sand is prepared and handled per ton of metal poured in a typical ferrous foundry. Because of this and the fact that the sand so greatly influences the quality of the castings, much attention has been devoted to this part of mechanization. A flowsheet of sand circulation in a mechanized foundry is given in Fig. 4.13.

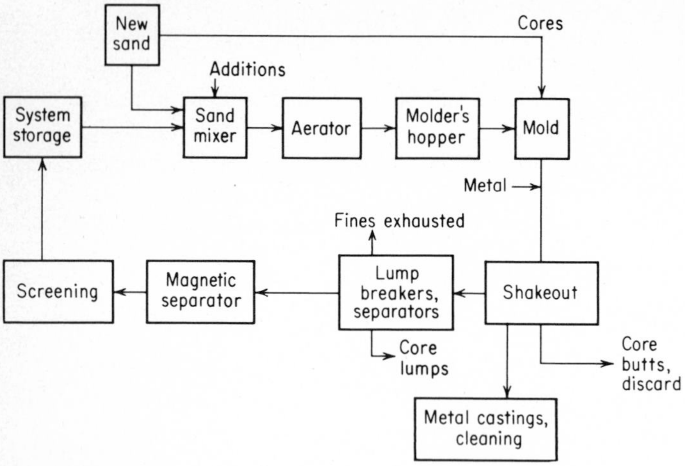

***Fig.* 4.13** Flowsheet of sand circulation in a mechanized foundry.

Although this flowsheet can be built up into a very extensive mechanized sand-handling system, many of its elements exist to some degree in even the simplest system. Mixing of the sand with water and clay is required in all systems. Aeration, separating the coarse-sand agglomerates, may be accomplished by having the molder manually riddle or screen sand onto the pattern. Magnetic separation of tramp iron can be ignored if special facing is used next to the pattern, as can lump breaking and screening after shakeout. However, the best and most thorough sand preparation is necessary in high-production foundries.

Positive sand-mixing action can be obtained through the use of mullers, or intensive mixers. The interior of a typical vertical wheel muller is illustrated in Fig. 4.14. A centrifugal type of muller is illustrated in Fig. 4.15. These mullers can be incorporated into a system of conveyors, hoppers, and storage bins according to the flowsheet above. This machine can be loaded by scoop truck and unloaded into buckets for rapid transfer to molding stations. A typical assemblage of equipment for handling the various stages of sand preparation as a unit is shown in Fig. 4.16. In this case the sand is delivered from the muller discharge to the molding-station hoppers by scoop truck and returned from the shakeout in the same way.

Whatever the sand-conditioning system and equipment, it has a pronounced effect on the quality of the sand for molding. Some of these effects are discussed in Chap. 5 from the standpoint of molding-sand quality rather than handling.

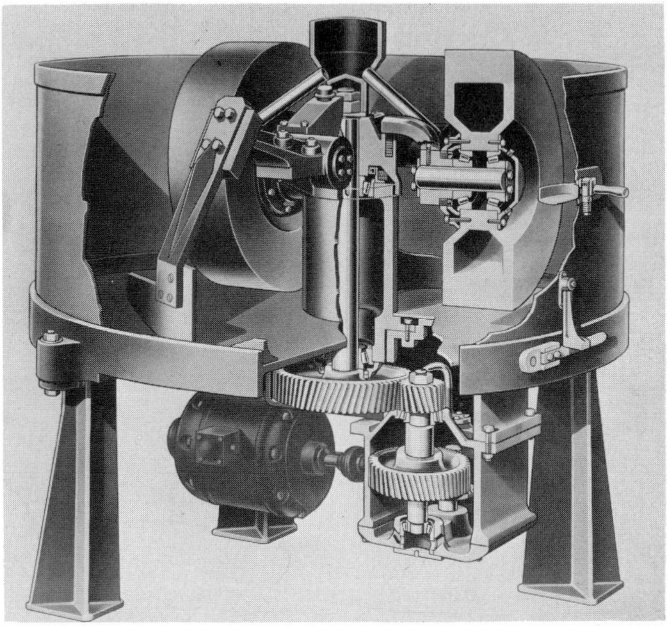

***Fig.* 4.14** Phantom view of sand muller for mixing molding sand. (*Courtesy of Natural Engineering Company.*)

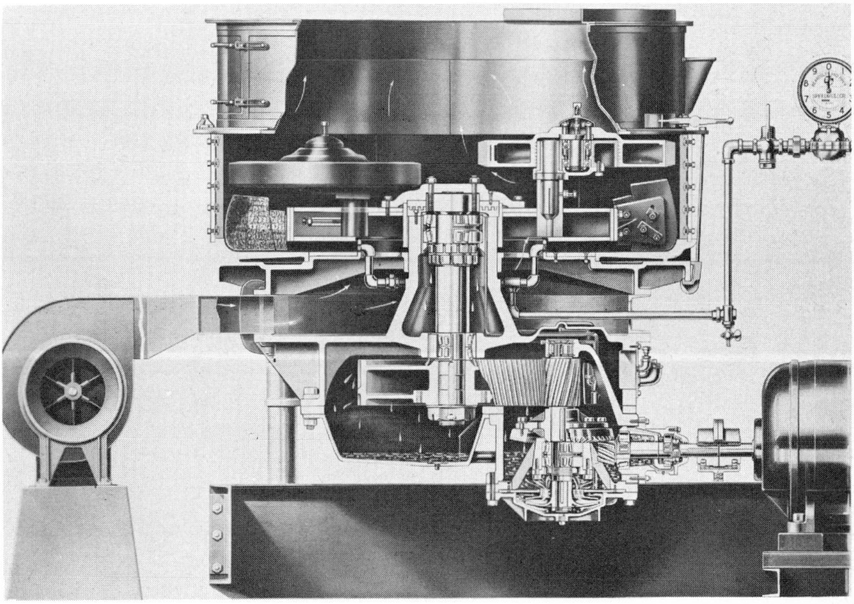

***Fig.* 4.15** Phantom view of a speed muller mixer incorporating a means of cooling hot molding sand. (*Courtesy of Beardsley-Piper Division, Pettibone Mulliken Corp.*)

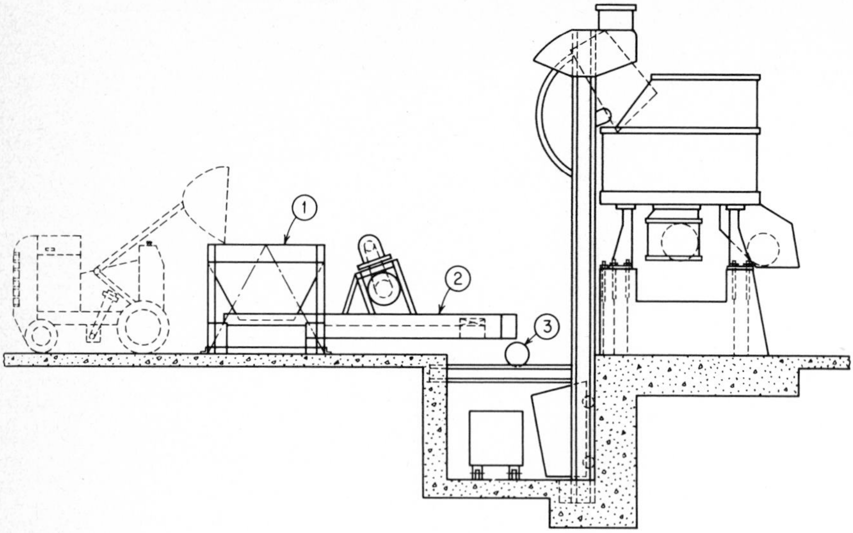

Fig. 4.16 Schematic diagram of a mechanical sand-conditioning system.

Molding-line Mechanization

By combining molding machines with conveyors, a pouring station, cooling, and shakeout, the operations from molding to shakeout may be mechanized. Sand is delivered to the molding stations from the conditioning system, usually into hoppers above the machines. Molding then can be performed using any one or combination of the types of machines discussed earlier. Probably the simplest molding-line mechanization consists of a row of molding machines, usually jolt-squeeze machines doing match-plate, light cope and drag molding, or stack molding located at the end of a roller or rail-type conveyors, as illustrated in Figs. 4.17 and 4.18. Sand is delivered from a preparation system to overhead hoppers at the molding stations. The molding end of the conveyor provides a space for coresetting and mold closing and a buffer zone for the accumulation of unpoured molds. A section of the conveyor is served by monorail or other means of handling ladles for pouring. The balance of the conveyor is for cooling and a buffer zone for mold storage for shakeout. Shakeout may be accomplished by transferring the molds to a separate shakeout or dumping them off the mold conveyor into an oscillating conveyor which delivers them to a shakeout unit. The mold conveyors may be either gravity-acting or powered. The conveyor shown in Fig. 4.17 is a simple rail-type conveyor, unpowered, requiring a minimum of mechanical equipment and upkeep.

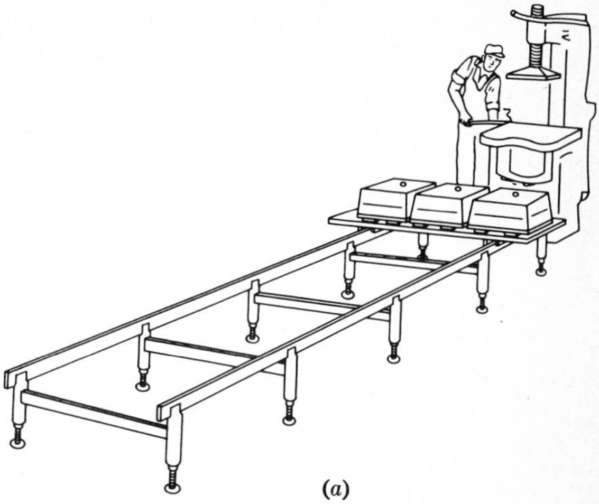

(*a*)

(*b*)

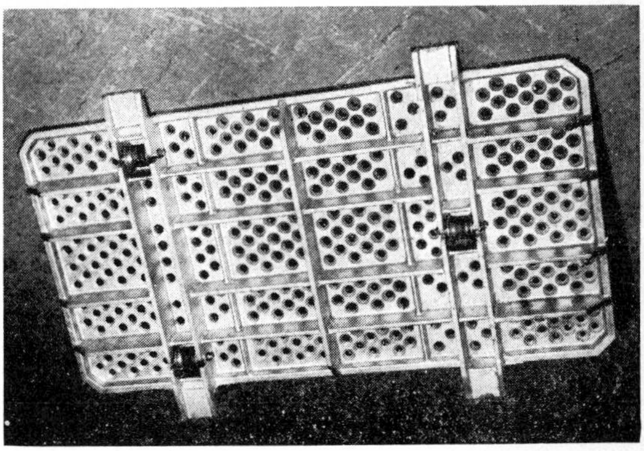

(*c*)

***Fig.* 4.17** Track conveyor with roller-equipped pallets or bottom boards. (*a*) Schematic drawing of arrangement of single-track conveyor and molding machine; (*b*) track conveyor adapted to stack-molding mechanization; (*c*) track-conveyor pallet or bottom board. (*Courtesy of Westover Engineers.*)

***Fig.* 4.18** Roller-conveyor handling of stack molds. Unit incorporates overhead sand hoppers at molding stations fed from a belt conveyor. Sand-conditioning unit is located at far left of the line of molding machines. (*From J. Kropka.*[3])

Some more complex degrees of mechanization are illustrated in Refs. 4, 5, 8, 11, and 15 to 17. The foundry layout illustrated in Ref. 11 provides for complete mechanization of molding-sand preparation, molding and mold handling, charging, melting and pouring of metal, shakeout and cleaning of castings, and handling during annealing and inspection. Almost complete mechanization and automation of the molding operation have been accomplished in some units.

As in the case of molding, the processes of coremaking, melting, and cleaning may be mechanized in various degrees. These subjects, however, will be considered later, when they will require more specific discussion. It should be stated here that there is no intent in this text to consider all the phases of foundry equipment and mechanization, since this is a constantly changing field and one which is best learned by engineers in training or through experience. The subjects of materials handling and detailed mechanization are not considered within the scope of this textbook.

Stack Molding

Stack molding is a type of mechanized molding designed to increase greatly the number of castings made per mold. The mold consists of a number of permanent flask sections stacked up as illustrated in Fig. 4.18. Each flask section has a drag cavity molded in its upper surface and a cope section molded in its lower surface. Both cavities are molded simultaneously by having the cope pattern mounted on the jolt table and the drag pattern mounted on the squeeze platen of a jolt-squeeze pin-lift machine (Fig. 4.19). The amount of sand in the flask is con-

***Fig.* 4.19** Molding machine rigged for stack molding. The cope pattern plate is mounted on the squeeze table, and the drag pattern on the squeeze platen. (*From J. Kropka.*[3])

trolled by means of a strike-off frame, so that after squeezing, the mold hardness is correct and there is sufficient sand for a good seal at the parting. The mold is stacked up with a number of flask sections as they are molded. After pouring and shakeout, the castings may appear as in Fig. 4.20.

Fig. 4.20 Stack-molded castings with the gating system still attached. (*From J. Kropka.*[3])

Stack molding is extensively used for light castings such as piston rings, chain links, levers, etc., where the weight of the stacked castings amounts to from 50 to several hundred pounds. The flask sections require that the castings be relatively shallow. This type of molding requires that the balance of the operations be mechanized for the best production results. Sand conditioning, pouring, shakeout, and cleaning must be suited to handle the volume of castings stack-molded.

BIBLIOGRAPHY

1. American Foundrymen's Society, Molding Methods and Materials, Des Plaines, Ill., 1963.
2. R. W. Heine, T. J. Bosworth, J. J. Parker, E. H. King, and J. S. Schumacher, Sand Movement and Compaction in Green Sand Molding, *Trans. AFS*, vol. 67, p. 47, 1959.

3. J. Kropka, Multiple Molding in a Malleable Shop, *Am. Foundryman,* vol. 24, p. 44, March, 1953.
4. H. W. Zimnawoda, Mechanical Equipment for Medium Sized Gray Iron Foundry, *Trans. AFS,* vol. 59, p. 56, 1951.
5. L. B. Knight, Modernization of the Small Foundry, *Trans. AFS,* vol. 56, p. 297, 1948.
6. E. A. Clake, Molding Machines, *Am. Foundryman,* vol. 55, September, 1947.
7. W. K. Gude, Modern Facilities Incorporated in New Alabama Pipe-foundry, *Foundry,* vol. 60, October, 1952.
8. E. A. Swenson, Limited Mechanization in the Jobbing Foundry, *Foundry,* vol. 80, March, 1952.
9. G. E. Miller, Trends in Molding Machines and Core Blowers, *Foundry,* vol. 80, March, 1952.
10. C. A. Gehrman, How to Select and Maintain Flasks, *Foundry,* vol. 80, February, 1952.
11. L. B. Knight, Modernization with Mechanization, *Foundry,* vol. 80, February, 1952.
12. W. G. Gude, New Process Casts Soil Pipe, *Foundry,* vol. 78, May, 1950.
13. R. Shire, Care of Molding Machines, *Foundry,* vol. 77, September, 1949.
14. R. H. Herrmann, Handling Materials in Metal Charging, *Foundry,* vol. 76, December, 1948.
15. C. O. Bartlett, Mechanized Foundry Design and Operating Phases, *Trans. AFS,* vol. 55, p. 546, 1947.
16. H. W. Zimnawoda, Sand and Mold Handling Equipment, *Foundry,* vol. 80, p. 88, April, 1952.
17. H. W. Zimnawoda, Six Ways to Mechanize a Foundry, *Am. Foundryman,* vol. 15, April, 1949.
18. R. H. Herrmann, How to Specify Conveyor Belting for Foundry Applications, *Foundry,* vol. 81, p. 86, August, 1953.
19. R. W. Heine, Mixing and Molding Green Sand, *Foundry,* October, 1961, p. 68.
20. D. C. Williams, Granular Movement during Squeezing, *Trans. AFS,* vol. 69, p. 8, 1961.
21. K. Terzaghi, "Theoretical Soil Mechanics," John Wiley & Sons, Inc., New York, 1943.
22. R. W. Heine, Molding Sands, Molding Methods and Casting Dimensions, *Trans. AFS,* 1956.
23. R. W. Heine, J. S. Schumacher, and E. H. King, The Jolt Test, *Modern Castings,* April, 1956, p. 59.
24. R. W. Heine, J. S. Schumacher, and E. H. King, Springback in Green Sand Molding, *Trans.* AFS, vol. 71, 1963.
25. R. S. L. Andrews, "Shell Process Foundry Practice," American Foundrymen's Society, 1963.

5
Molding Sands

The major production of castings is in sand molds. Molds for making a ton of castings may require 4 to 5 tons of molding sand. The sand-metal ratio may vary from 10:1 to 0.25:1, depending on the type and size of castings and molding method employed. In any case, the tonnage of sand which must be handled in a sand-casting foundry is large, and its quality must be controlled to make good castings.

Several different types of sand are used for molding. Sand-casting processes involving molds made of green sand, dry sand, core sand, cement-bonded sand, shell-molding sand, and others have been described in an earlier chapter.

GENERAL PROPERTIES OF MOLDING SANDS

From a general viewpoint, the molding sand must be readily moldable and produce defect-free castings if it is to qualify as a good one. Certain specific properties have been identified, and testing procedures adapted for their quantitative description. The AFS "Foundry Sand Handbook"[1] sets forth the standard conditions of testing the sand properties. Those properties of most obvious importance include:

1. Green strength. The green sand, after water has been mixed into it, must have adequate strength and plasticity for making and handling of the mold.
2. Dry strength. As a casting is poured, sand adjacent to the hot metal quickly loses its water as steam. The dry sand must have strength to resist erosion, and also the metallostatic pressure of the molten metal, or else the mold may enlarge.
3. Hot strength. After the moisture has evaporated, the sand may be required to possess strength at some elevated temperature, above 212 F. Metallostatic pressure of the liquid-metal bearing against the mold walls may cause mold enlargement, or if the metal is still flowing, erosion, cracks, or breakage may occur unless the sand possesses adequate hot strength.
4. Permeability. Heat from the casting causes a green-sand mold to evolve a great deal of steam and other gases. The mold must be permeable, i.e.,

porous, to permit the gases to pass off, or the casting will contain gas holes.

5. Thermal stability. Heat from the casting causes rapid expansion of the sand surface at the mold-metal interface. The mold surface may then crack, buckle, or flake off (scab) unless the molding sand is relatively stable dimensionally under rapid heating.
6. Refractoriness. Higher pouring temperatures, such as those for ferrous alloys at 2400 to 3200 F, require greater refractoriness of the sand. Low-pouring-temperature metals, for example, aluminum, poured at 1300 F, do not require a high degree of refractoriness from the sand.
7. Flowability. The sand should respond to molding processes.
8. Produces good casting finish.
9. Collapsibility. Heated sand which becomes hard and rocklike is difficult to remove from the casting and may cause the contracting metal to tear or crack.
10. Is reusable.
11. Offers ease of sand preparation and control.
12. Removes heat from the cooling casting.

This list by no means includes all the properties which might be desirable. Obviously, the most important characteristic of a molding sand is that it facilitate the economic production of good castings.

INGREDIENTS OF MOLDING SANDS

Molding sands are mixtures of three or more ingredients. A green sand contains clay and water, as well as the principal sand constituent, SiO_2. These three components provide the bulk and plasticity required of the molding sand. Other materials may be added to the sand mixture to enhance certain of the properties.

Sand

Granular particles of sand, that is, SiO_2 principally, comprise 50 to 95 per cent of the total material in a molding sand. In different molding sands, these sand particles may differ in the following ways:

1. Average grain size, grain size distribution, and grain shape
2. Chemical composition
3. Refractoriness and thermal stability

The chemical composition of the sand-grain portion of typical molding sand is given in Table 5.1. Generally, the purest silica sand, 99.8+

Table 5.1 Chemical composition of typical sands

Constituents	Washed silica sand*	Washed and dried silica†	Typical bank sand‡	Western bentonite bonded silica sand§		Typical lake sand
				New	Used	
Loss on ignition, %	.....	....	1.02	0.28	0.12	0.80
C, %	.....	....	.....	0.13	0.59	
Free iron, %	.....	....	.....	.....	0.97	
Ferrous iron, %	.....	....	.....	0.44	0.68	
Ferric iron, %	.....	....	.....	0.00	0.12	
Total iron, %	0.10	....	.....	0.44	1.77	
Al_2O_3, %	0.39	....	.....	1.32	0.63	
SiO_2, %	99.08	99.80+	92.09	95.79	95.54	95.0+
TiO_2, %	0.43					
Total $Al_2O_3 + Fe_2O_3$, %	.....	....	6.09	.....	.....	2.0
CaO, %	.....	....	0.58	.....	.....	0.60
Alkali, %	.....	....	.....	.....	.....	0.20
MgO, %	.....	....	0.22	.....	.....	0.40

*New Jersey Silica Sand Co.

†Ottawa silica sand.

‡Great Lakes Sand Co., Juniata.

§A molding sand, from F. L. Orell, Jr., "The Constitution of Discarded Molding Sand," Steel Founders Society of America Report 23, 1950.

per cent SiO_2, is considered the most refractory and thermally stable. The presence of excessive amounts of iron oxide, alkali oxides, and lime can cause objectionable lowering of the fusion point in sands. Average fineness of the sand grains establishes the fineness of the molding sand as a whole, and the grain size distribution affects many of the sand properties, as pointed out later. The shape of sand grains may be rounded, angular, or subangular, depending on their geologic history. Typical sand-grain shapes are illustrated in Fig. 5.1. Compounded grains are agglomerated particles of angular or subangular sands. In molding sands as they are used in foundries, the sand grains are of mixed origin. Some came initially from new molding sand, others as additions of new silica sand, still others as sand from disintegrated cores, and in some cases as used sand which has been reclaimed. Agglomerated grains of sand and clay may also be due to the action of heat and moisture in the mold.

Clay

Molding sands may contain about 2 to 50 per cent of clay. With a suitable water content, it is the principal source of the strength and

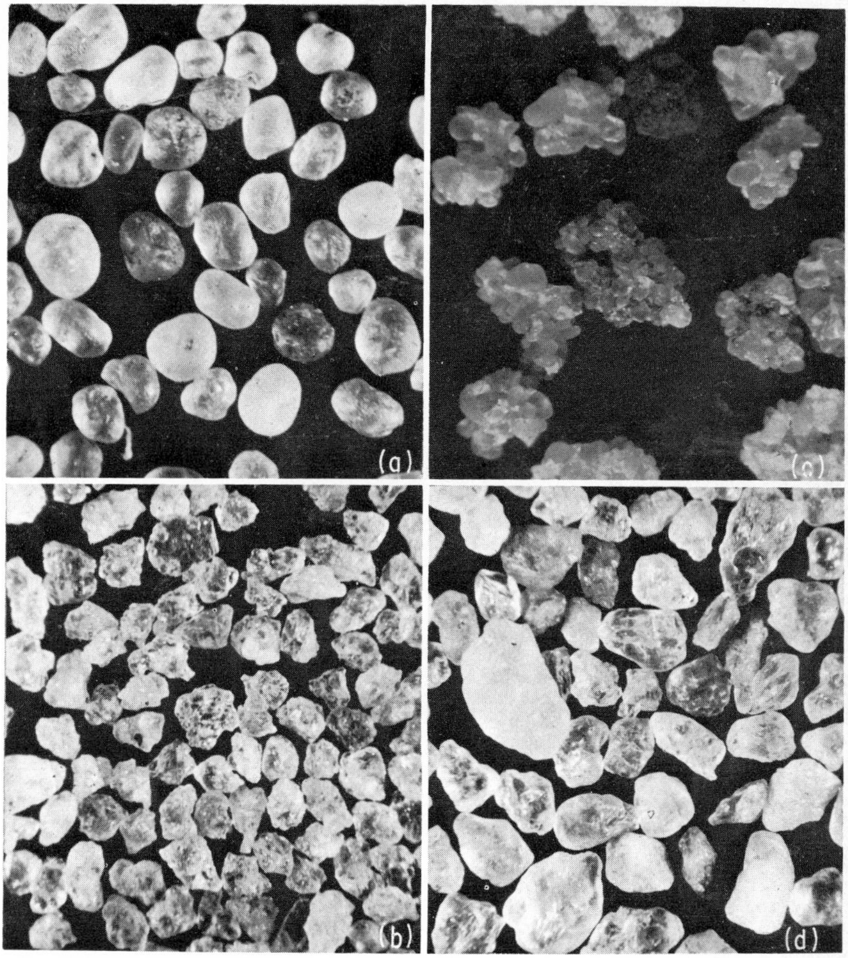

***Fig.* 5.1** Sand grain shapes. (*a*) Rounded sand grains, (*b*) angular sand grains, (*c*) compounded sand grains, (*d*) subangular sand grains. (*From AFS.*[1])

plasticity of the molding sand. Clay is thus the *bond,* or *binder,* of molding sands. In some mineral deposits, clay and sand occur mixed in proper proportions, so that the sand can be mined and used directly for molding. It is then referred to as a "natural molding sand." In other sands, clay bond must be added to develop the proper strength and plasticity. Several types of clay are used for this purpose. In general, these clays are defined as "essentially aggregates of extremely minute crystalline, usually flake-shaped particles that can be classified on the basis of their structure and composition into a few groups which are known as clay minerals. Some clays are composed of particles of a single clay mineral, whereas others are mixtures of clay minerals. Some clays are composed entirely of clay minerals, whereas others contain admixtures of quartz, pyrite, organic matter, etc."[2]

Clay minerals used as bonding additions to sands include the following types:

1. Western and southern bentonites (montmorillonites)
2. Fire clays (kaolinites)
3. Special clays (halloysite, illite, attapulgite)

The first two types are the most commonly used. Table 5.2 lists some of their differences in chemical composition, atomic structure, base exchange characteristics, swelling and shrinkage tendencies, and refractoriness. A clay coating of the sand grains contributes many of the clay properties to the molding-sand aggregate.

Water

Water, present in amounts of about 1.5 to 8 per cent, activates the clay in the sand, causing the aggregate to develop plasticity and strength. Water in molding sands is often referred to as *tempering* water. The water is adsorbed by the clay up to a limiting amount. Only that water rigidly held (adsorbed) by the clay appears to be effective in developing strength.[2] The rigid clay coatings of the grains may be forced together, causing a wedging action and thus developing strength.[2] Additional water, however, can act as a lubricant, and makes the sand more plastic and more moldable, though the strength may be lowered. Thus control of the water percentage in the aggregate is very important. Water may engage in ion exchanges with the clay if dissolved minerals are present.

Special Additives

Besides the three basic ingredients, other materials may be present in molding sands. They are often referred to as *additives* and are used to develop some specific property. These materials will be briefly defined here.

Cereals

Cereal binder, as used in the foundry, is finely ground corn flour or gelatinized and ground starch from corn. Cereals may be used in molding sands for increased green or dry strength or collapsibility in amounts up to 2.0 per cent.

Table* 5.2 *Clay minerals used for bonding molding sands*

Clay mineral type	Composition type	Base exchange	Refractoriness (softening point)	Swelling due to water	Shrinkage due to loss of water	Particle size and shape
Montmorillonite Class IA, western bentonite Source: Wyoming, South Dakota, Utah	$(OH)_4Al_4Si_8O_{20} \cdot nH_2O$ Ex: 90% montmorillonite, 10% quartz, feldspar, mica, etc.	High. Na is adsorbed ion, pH = 8–10	2100–2450 F	Very high, gel-forming	Very high	Flake size of less than 0.00001 in.
Montmorillonite Class IB, southern bentonite Source: Mississippi	$(OH)_4Al_4Si_8O_{20} \cdot nH_2O$ Ex: 85% montmorillonite 15% quartz, limonite, etc.	High. Ca is adsorbed ion, pH = 4–6.50	1800 F+	Slight, little tendency to gel	Very high	Flake size of less than 0.00001 in.
Kaolinite Class IV, fire clay Source: Illinois, Ohio	$(OH)_4Al_4Si_4O_{10}$ Ex: 60% kaolinite, 30% illite, 10% quartz, etc.	Very low	3000–3100 F	Very low, non-gel-forming	Low	Fire clays are often ground and therefore may be relatively coarse or may be ground to a flour
Illite Class III, grundite Source: Grundy, Ill.	$(OH)_4K_y(Al_4Fe_4Mg_4Mg_6)\ (Si_{8-y} \cdot Al_y)O_{20}$	Moderate	2500 F±	Low, non-gel-forming	Moderate	

* Adapted from R. E. Grim and F. L. Cuthbert.[2]

Ground Pitch

Pitch is a by-product of cokemaking, being distilled from soft coals at about 600 F and above. Pitch is used in amounts up to 3.0 per cent to improve hot strength or casting finish on ferrous castings.

Asphalt

Asphalt is a by-product of the distillation of petroleum. It is used for the same purposes as pitch.

Sea Coal

Sea coal is a finely ground soft coal used in molding sands for cast irons, principally for the purpose of improving the surface finish and ease of cleaning the castings. Sea coal may be specified by proximate and ultimate analyses conventionally used for coal. A typical example is given in Table 5.3. The sea coal is usually ground to a fineness similar to that of the molding sand in which it is used. Percentages employed in sands are about 2 to 8 per cent.

Graphite

Synthetic or natural graphite may be used in percentages of 0.2 to 2.0 per cent for the purpose of improving the moldability of the sand and the surface finish of the castings.

Gilsonite

This material is a solid asphaltic mineral, mined in Utah and Colorado, sufficiently volatile so that it functions much as sea coal does in causing improved casting finish.

Fuel Oil

Fuel oil is sometimes used in very small percentages, of 0.01 to 0.10 per cent, and seems to confer improved moldability to the sand.

Wood Flour

Ground wood flour or other cellulose materials such as cob flour, cereal hulls, and carbonized cellulose may be added in amounts of 0.5 to 2.0 per cent to molding sands. They may function to control the expansion of the sand by burning out at elevated temperature. They also can improve collapsibility and flowability of the sand.

Silica Flour

Pulverized silica, finer than 200 mesh, is called silica flour. It may be used in amounts up to 35 per cent for the purpose of increasing hot strength of the sand. It also increases the density of the sand for resisting metal penetration.

Table* 5.3 *Example of sea-coal specification

Proximate Analysis (Moisture-free), %	
Volatile matter (VCM)	36–40.0
Fixed carbon (FC)	55–60
Ash	3–5
Ultimate Analysis	
H	5.6%
C	80–85%
N	1–3%
O	6–8%
S	0.8% max
Ash	3–5%
Ash fusion point	2780 F

Iron Oxide

Fine iron oxide is used in small percentages in some sands to obtain added hot strength.

Perlite

Perlite is an expanded aluminum silicate mineral, useful in small percentages, 0.5 to 1.50 per cent, to obtain better thermal stability of the sand. It may also be used as a riser insulator.[4]

Molasses, Dextrin

Cane or blackstrap molasses, unrefined and containing 60 to 70 per cent sugar solids, may be used for increased dry strength of the sand and edge hardness of molds. Dextrins may be used for the same purpose.

The foregoing list of sand additives is by no means complete, and a number of others may be used.

Rebonding

When molding sands are in continual reuse, materials are added during each sand-preparation cycle to compensate for the material burned or otherwise decrepitated by heat from the castings. Hence the ingredients of the sand as it is used in foundries may consist of burned or partially burned materials, some particles of metal and slag, and other possible foreign matter, as well as new materials of the type described in the foregoing section.

TESTING OF MOLDING SANDS

The nature of a molding sand can be described by means of the results of standard sand tests which have been adopted by the industry. Complete details of the tests, testing procedure, and equipment are set forth in the AFS "Foundry Sand Handbook."[1] The tests will be only briefly reviewed here.

Sample Preparation

All sand tests should be performed on samples which will give results that are representative of the sand. Recommended procedures for sampling and conditioning of the sand should be used.[1] Molding sand may be tempered with water and mixed manually or mechanically, preferably by a method similar to that used in the foundry where the sand tests are being performed. Adequate mixing in a laboratory muller requires about 6 to 10 min, depending on batch size and muller. After mixing, the sand should be kept in a closed container.

Moisture

Since the moisture content of the sand affects so many properties, this is one of the most frequently performed tests. A 50-g sample is weighed, dried 2 hr at 220 F or to a constant weight, and then reweighed. The loss in weight multiplied by 2 gives the per cent moisture in the sand. The moisture teller illustrated in Fig. 5.2 is a device for rapidly drying the 50-g sample. A small fan drives air over a heating element and then through the sand sample, which is retained on a fine screen. The hot air will dry the sand in a time interval in minutes, roughly equivalent to the percentage of moisture in the sand.

Strength

Various types of tests of the strength of molding sands are performed with a universal-type mechanical testing machine as illustrated in Fig. 5.3. Strength in compression, shear, tension, and transverse loading may be performed on green sands, dry sands, and core sands with this machine and its accessories. Most commonly used for molding-sand testing are the compression and shear tests involving a cylindrical sample 2 in. high and 2 in. in diameter.

***Fig.* 5.2** Moisture teller. (*From AFS.*[1])

***Fig.* 5.3** Universal sand-strength testing machine with deformation accessory attached. (*Courtesy of H. W. Dietert Co.*)

AFS Standard Cylindrical Specimen

Since the strength of a molding sand depends greatly on its degree of ramming, the conditions of molding the standard sample must be carefully controlled. Reproducible ramming conditions can be obtained with the standard sand rammer and specimen-tube accessories (Fig. 5.4). The ramming device must be securely mounted.[1] The sand is placed

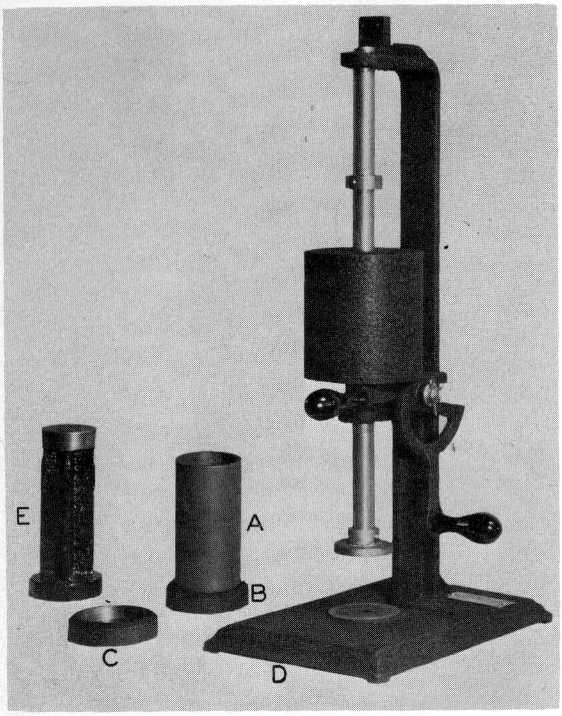

***Fig.* 5.4** Sand rammer, specimen tube, base, and stripping post. (*From AFS.*[1])

in the specimen tube and rammed by impact with three blows of a 14-16 weight. By the manually operated ramming device the weight is dropped from a height of 2.00 in. ± 0.005. Three rams should produce a specimen 2.0 in. ± $\frac{1}{32}$ in height provided the proper weight of sand is put into the specimen tube. Gauge marks are shown at the top of the rammer rod to measure the specimen height. The specimen is removed from the tube by means of a stripping post.

The proper height of specimen is most simply achieved by weighing the sand to be put into the specimen tube. If oversize, the weight can be reduced in increments until a proper weight to produce a 2.0-in. sample height is obtained. The sample weight necessary to produce a 2.0-in. sample height after three rams, usually 145 to 175 g, is actually a valuable piece of information. Specimen weight in grams, multiplied by 0.603, gives the bulk density of the sand in pounds per cubic foot. The bulk density of the specimen may be increased or decreased by changing the number of rams and weight of sand in the 2.0-in.-diameter × 2.0-in.-high specimen. The standard procedure, however, is to use three rams.[1]

Green Compression Test

The green compression test consists in determining the compressive stress in pounds per square inch necessary to cause rupture of the standard cylindrical specimen, using a universal strength tester of the type shown in Fig. 5.3. Green compressive strength is usually simply referred to as the *green strength* of the sand. It is important in this and other green-strength tests that the test be performed immediately after the specimen is stripped from the tube. The strength of green sands increases when the sand specimen begins to air-dry. Green molding sands run from about 5.0 to 22.0 psi green compressive strength, depending on their type.

Green Shear Test

Green shear strength can be determined with the standard specimen and universal testing machine. This is accomplished by changing the loading surfaces on the testing machine from compression plates to shear plates. The specimen then ruptures in shear along its longitudinal axis when sufficiently loaded. Green molding sands usually have about 1.5 to 7.0 psi green shear strength.

Dry Compression and Shear Tests

If standard specimens are dried at 220 to 230 F for 2 hr before they are tested, the dry compression or dry shear strength of the sand may be obtained. Since dry compression strength is usually much greater than green strength, higher loads are required on the universal strength machine. Typical dry-compression values on green sands are 20 to 250 psi, depending on their type.

Deformation (Strain)

Green molding sand has the ability to deform under load. If the sand deforms too readily under low loads, the mold cavity may not remain true to shape. If the sand has too little ability to deform under load, it then is brittle or lacks toughness. Drawing of patterns then may become difficult. This property may be measured by means of a deformation accessory for the universal strength machine (Fig. 5.3). This device measures in inches the amount that the specimen is compressed before it ruptures under compression loading. Deformation of 0.010 to 0.030 in. per in. is observed in many molding sands. The deformation test is, however, considered a nonstandard test.[1] Sometimes the deformation value is used, together with the green compression strength, to describe toughness of the sand, according to the following formula:

$$\text{STN} = D \times \text{GS} \times 1000$$

where STN = sand toughness number
D = deformation, 0.001 in.
GS = green strength

Green Tensile Strength

The tensile strength of a green molding sand using a modified specimen tube for ramming may be determined with the universal sand-strength tester. Green tensile strengths of green molding sands vary from about 1.0 to 6.0 psi, depending on the type of sand.

Hot Strength

Hot-strength tests are performed on a special cylindrical specimen 1⅛ in. in diameter by 2 in. long, which is double-end-rammed with three blows of a 7-lb weight falling 2 in. A hollow specimen may be used for certain tests.[8] Hot-strength tests are performed by means of a special combination furnace and testing device called a dilatometer. The equipment is illustrated in Ref. 1. The specimen is heated to the testing temperature and compression-tested at that elevated temperature. Common testing temperatures are 500, 1000, 1500, 2000, and 2500 F, although others are used.

Hot strength and expansion. With suitable accessories, the dilatometer may also be used to determine the course of thermal expansion of the specimen as it is heated to an elevated temperature.[1] The expansion data are reported as total inches expansion per inch up to the testing temperature. Free-expansion and confined-expansion tests are performed. Free-expansion measurements are performed on the standard hot-strength specimen, and confined-expansion tests employ the same size sample rammed in a silica tube. Usually, an expansion of about 0.016 to 0.020 in. per in. to 2000 F is common.

Permeability

The rate in milliliters per minute at which air will pass through the sand under a standard condition of pressure is used as an index of the permeability of the sand. Standard permeability is determined by measuring the time necessary for 2000 cu cm of air to pass through the standard specimen while it is confined in the specimen tube and under a pressure of 10 g per sq cm. If the time has been determined, the permeability number, defined as the rate in milliliters per minute which will pass through a sand volume one square centimeter in cross section and one centimeter high under a pressure of 10 g per sq cm, can be calculated from the formula

$$P = \frac{V \times H}{p \times A \times T}$$

where V = volume air = 2000 cu cm
H = height of sand specimen = 2.0 in. × 2.54 cm/in. = 5.08 cm
P = pressure = 10 g/sq cm
A = cross-sectional-area sand specimen = 1 sq in. × 2.54 sq cm/1 sq in. = 20.268 sq cm
T = time, sec, for 2000 cu cm air to pass through specimen

The formula reduces to $P = 3007.2/T$ sec.

(a)

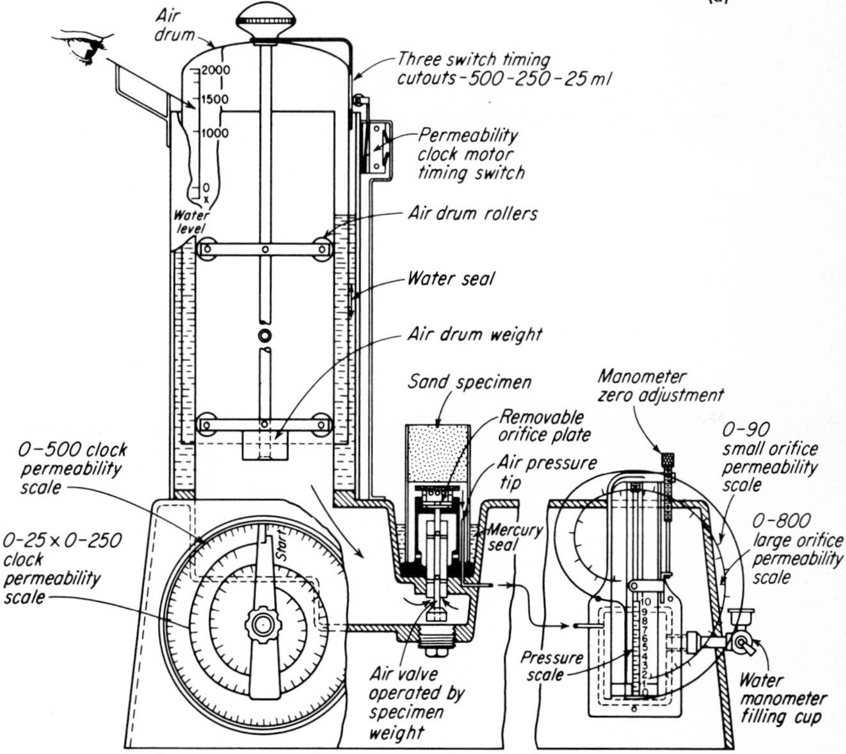

(b)

Fig. **5.5** (*a*) View of one type of permeability apparatus, (*b*) schematic diagram of another design of permeability apparatus.

Table 5.4 Permeability test pressures and corresponding values, as obtained with orifice plates*

Pressure, g/sq cm	Permeability		Pressure, g/sq cm	Permeability	
	Small orifice, 0.5 mm	Large orifice, 1.5 mm		Small orifice, 0.5 mm	Large orifice, 1.5 mm
0.1			3.6	23.4	219
0.2			3.7	22.7	212
0.3			3.8	21.8	205
0.4	....	2450	3.9	21.0	198
0.5	....	2000	4.0	20.0	193
0.6	....	1620	4.1	19.5	185
0.7	....	1350	4.2	19.0	178
0.8	....	1200	4.3	18.4	173
0.9	....	1060	4.4	17.8	167
1.0	....	950	4.5	17.3	163
1.1	....	850	4.6	16.7	156
1.2	....	780	4.7	16.2	151
1.3	....	710	4.8	15.7	146
1.4	....	650	4.9	15.2	142
1.5	....	610	5.0	14.7	138
1.6	....	550	5.1	14.3	134
1.7	....	525	5.2	13.8	128
1.8	....	492	5.3	13.4	126
1.9	....	467	5.4	13.0	122
2.0	49	440	5.5	12.6	119
2.1	47	417	5.6	12.2	115
2.2	44	398	5.7	11.8	112
2.3	42	376	5.8	11.4	108
2.4	40	358	5.9	11.0	105
2.5	38	341	6.0	10.7	102
2.6	36	326	6.1	10.3	99
2.7	34	313	6.2	10.0	96
2.8	33	300	6.3	9.7	93
2.9	31	287	6.4	9.4	90
3.0	30	275	6.5	9.0	88
3.1	29	264	6.6	8.8	85
3.2	28	253	6.7	8.5	82
3.3	27	243	6.8	8.2	80
3.4	25.8	235	6.9	7.9	77
3.5	24.2	226	7.0	7.7	75

* From American Foundrymen's Society.[1]

Table 5.4 Permeability test pressures and corresponding values, as obtained with orifice plates* (continued)

Pressure, g/sq cm	Permeability		Pressure, g/sq cm	Permeability	
	Small orifice, 0.5 mm	Large orifice, 1.5 mm		Small orifice, 0.5 mm	Large orifice, 1.5 mm
7.1	7.5	73	8.6	4.0	40
7.2	7.2	70	8.7	3.7	38
7.3	7.0	67	8.8	3.5	36
7.4	6.7	65	8.9	3.3	
7.5	6.5	63	9.0	3.1	
7.6	6.3	61	9.1	2.9	
7.7	6.0	58	9.2	2.6	
7.8	5.8	56	9.3	2.4	
7.9	5.6	54	9.4	2.2	
8.0	5.3	52	9.5	1.9	
8.1	5.1	50	9.6	1.7	
8.2	4.9	48	9.7	1.4	
8.3	4.7	46	9.8	1.1	
8.4	4.4	44	10.0		
8.5	4.2	42			

A quick permeability test can be performed with a permeability meter of the type shown in Fig. 5.5. In this apparatus, air under constant pressure, 10 cm of water, is caused to flow through an orifice into the open end of the specimen tube and out through the sand specimen. Air delivered by the orifice thus must pass through the sand to escape. If the sand were completely impermeable, the pressure in the specimen-tube (orifice discharge pressure) chamber adjacent to the orifice would rise to a maximum, i.e., that applied by the machine, 10 cm of water. If the sand were completely open, the orifice discharge pressure would be atmospheric or zero on the manometer. Hence the orifice discharge pressure may be calibrated in terms of permeability of the sand specimen. The test then can be made by measuring the pressure in the specimen tube by means of the manometer on the permeability meter (Fig. 5.5). The relationship between orifice discharge pressure and standard permeability is given in Table 5.4. Two different orifices are used, 0.5 and 1.5 mm in diameter. The smaller is used for permeabilities up to 49 ml per min, and the larger is used for permeabilities over 39 ml per min. The meter is provided with a calibrated sector scale which can be rotated until it intersects the meniscus of the manometer water column, and permeability can then be read directly.

Mold Hardness

The hardness achieved by ramming the sand can be measured by a mold-hardness tester of the type shown in Fig. 5.6. This is an indentation-type test. A spring-loaded steel ball is pressed into the sand. If no

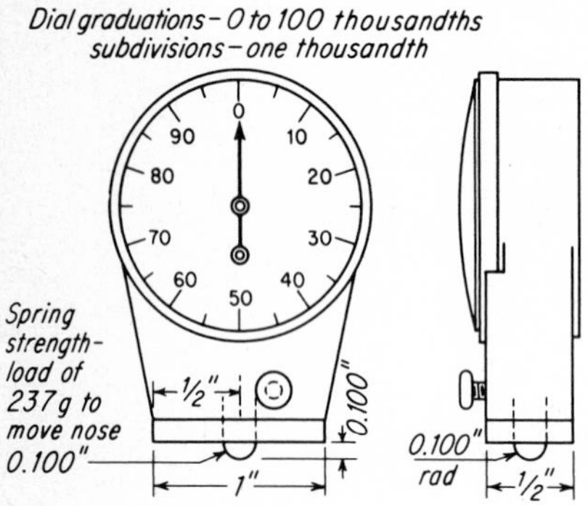

Fig. 5.6 **Mold-hardness tester. (*From AFS.*[1])**

penetration occurs, the hardness arbitrarily is 100. If the ball sinks completely into the sand up to the limiting surface of the tester, the reading is zero; i.e., the sand is very soft. Each scale unit represents 0.001 in. Common mold hardnesses are 80 to 95 for machine molding. Hardness readings are taken on the standard sand specimen as an additional test on that specimen.

AFS Clay Content

For testing purposes, the AFS clay in a molding sand is defined as "particles which fail to settle one inch per minute when suspended in water. These are usually less than 20 microns, or 0.0008 in., in diameter." The latter definition includes all very fine material, fine silica or silt, as well as the clay mineral present, and the total percentage of these particles is called the AFS clay content of the sand.

The clay determination begins with a 50-g sample of dried sand. The 50-g sample is put into a wash bottle and washed according to the following procedures:

1. Add 475 ml distilled water and 25 ml caustic soda solution (25 g per liter).
2. Agitate 5 min with mechanical stirrer or shaker, dilute with water to a height of 6 in. (marker of bottle), and let settle 10 min.
3. Siphon off 5 in. water, dilute again to 6 in. height, and let settle for 10 min.

4. Siphon off 5 in. water, dilute again to 6 in. height, and let settle for 5 min.
5. Repeat step 4 enough times so that, after standing 5 min, the water is clear.
6. Remove the remaining sand grains from the bottle, dry, and weigh. The loss in weight of the original 50 g sample multiplied by 2 gives the AFS clay percentage in the sand. The clay must be removed from all sands containing more than 1 per cent clay if it is intended to perform the AFS sieve analysis test on the sand.

Analysis of the clay content of molding sands is also performed by the hydrometer method and a chemical method given in Refs. 1 and 5.

AFS Sieve Analysis

The size and distribution of sand grains in a sand is determined with the AFS sieve analysis test. A dried 50-g sample or the sand-grain residue from the clay-content determination is used. The latter may be less than 50 g. The sample is placed on top of a series of sieves and shaken for 15 min. The sieve numbers and size of openings are given in Table 5.5. After the shaking period, the sand retained on each sieve and the bottom pan is weighed, and its percentage of the total sample determined. Two uses are made of these data. First, a distribution curve showing the total per cent retained on each sieve may be plotted as in Fig. 5.7, or the cumulative percentage curve showing the total per cent obtained

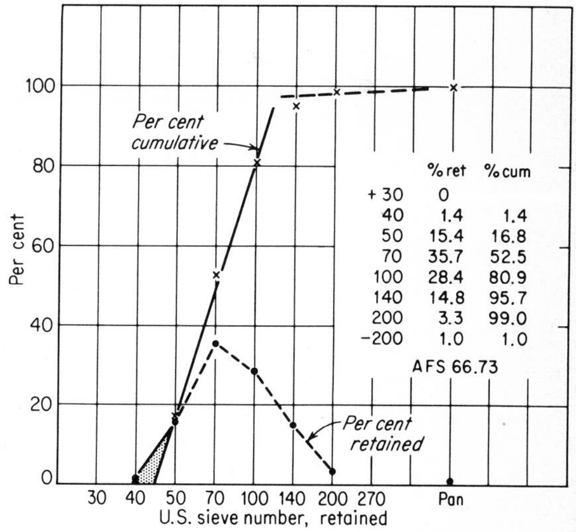

Fig. 5.7 Graph of per cent retained on each sieve vs. sieve number. Data taken from Table 5.6. This sand has a high average fineness number, 173, and might be used for nonferrous castings. Usually, the distribution curve looks more like a probability curve for most ferrous molding sands.

Table 5.5 *Screen scale sieves**

U.S. Series equivalent No.	Tyler screen scale sieves, meshes per lin in.	Openings, mm	Openings, in., ratio $\sqrt{2}$, or 1.414	Permissible variations in avg opening % ±	Diam wire, decimal of an in.	Mesh openings, microns
4	4	4.699	0.187	3	0.065	4760
6	6	3.327	0.132	3	0.036	3327
8	8	2.362	0.0937	3	0.035	2362
12	10	1.651	0.0661	3	0.032	1651
16	14	1.167	0.0469	3	0.025	1167
20	20	0.833	0.0331	5	0.0172	833
30	28	0.589	0.0232	5	0.0125	589
40	35	0.414	0.0165	5	0.0122	414
50	48	0.295	0.0117	5	0.0092	295
70	65	0.208	0.0083	5	0.0072	208
100	100	0.147	0.0059	6	0.0042	147
140	150	0.104	0.0041	6	0.0026	104
200	200	0.074	0.0029	7	0.0021	74
270	270	0.053	0.0021	7	0.0016	53

*From American Foundrymen's Society.[1]

The word "mesh" in terms of measuring "wire cloth" means "the number of openings per lineal inch." The term "mesh" in a technical usage is meaningless unless the diameter of the wire is given, so that the opening can be determined. The size of opening is the measure of the product, and the mesh and diameter of wire are used only as a means of determining the size of opening. The term mesh is secondary, and its use should be discontinued as much as possible.

There is a fixed ratio between the different sizes of the screen scale. This fixed ratio has been taken as 1.414, or the square root of 2 ($\sqrt{2}$). For example, using the U.S. Series equivalent No. 200 as the starting sieve, the width of each successive opening is exactly 1.414 times the opening in the previous sieve. The area, or the surface, of each successive opening in the scale is double that of the next-finer sieve, or one-half that of the next-coarser sieve.

which is coarser than any particular screen may be plotted. Second, the average grain fineness may be computed. An example of the computation is shown in Table 5.6. The percentage retained on each sieve is multiplied by a factor which is the size of the preceding sieve; i.e., the actual size of sand grains retained on one sieve is that permitted to pass through the preceding sieve. The products of sieve numbers multiplied by factors are summed. Then the average grain fineness number is equal to the sum of the sieve number and factor product divided by the total percentage of sand grains retained in the sieve set and pan. By definition, the AFS grain fineness number is the average grain size, and it corresponds to the sieve number whose openings would

Table* 5.6 *Typical calculation of AFS grain fineness number

U.S. Series equivalent No. sieve	Amounts of 50-g sample retained on sieve		Multiplier	Product
	Grams	Per cent		
6	......	.....	3	
12	......	.....	5	
20	......	.....	10	
30	......	.....	20	
40	0.7	1.4	30	42.0
50	7.7	15.4	40	616.0
70	17.85	35.7	50	1785.0
100	14.2	28.4	70	1988.0
140	7.4	14.8	100	1480.0
200	1.65	3.3	145	462.0
270	.....	.....	200	
Pan	0.5	1.0	300	300.0
Total	50.0	100.0	...	6673.0

$$\text{AFS No.} = \frac{\text{total product}}{\text{total per cent retained}} = \frac{6673}{100} = 66.73$$

just pass all the sand grains if all were of the same size. This number is a convenient means of describing the relative fineness of sands, most foundry sands being from about 40 to 220 in average fineness. Most sand properties, however, depend on the size distribution as well as average size. The fineness test makes possible the evaluation of both factors. Other methods of describing the average size and distribution of particles are given in Refs. 12 and 13.

AFS Standard Sand

Sometimes a standard sand is described for comparison tests; for example, the effectiveness of different binders or mixing procedures might be studied. The AFS sand standard is defined as a washed and dried silica sand, AFS fineness number of 50 ± 1, with 100 per cent through a 40-mesh sieve, 95 per cent through a 50-mesh and remaining on a 70-mesh sieve, and the balance retained on a 100-mesh sieve. Another finer sand is sometimes used as a secondary standard.[1]

Other Sand Tests

In addition to the sand tests discussed in the preceding sections, a variety of other tests are used. Among them are:

1. Expansion behavior, and relation to expansion defects.[1,5–10]
2. Sinter point.[1]

3. Durability. The amount of clay required for rebonding the sand to a constant green strength during repeated cycles of use for pouring castings can be used to study the life or durability of clays.[1,5]
4. Mold-gas evolution. The tendency of molding sands to give off gases can be studied by special procedures.[1,5,10]
5. Metal penetration. Metal penetration has occurred when the molten metal seeps into the sand as though it were porous to the liquid. This results in a fused mass of metal and sand which adheres tightly to the casting. A test used to study this tendency has been proposed.[1,5]
6. Loss on ignition. Combustible material in the sand is determined by the per cent loss on ignition of the dry sand.

Many other sand tests have been devised to study molding-sand properties.

PROPERTIES OF GREEN SANDS

The properties of green molding sands and their behavior in the mold are dependent on several factors of major importance. They include:

1. The sand ingredients
2. The methods of preparing the sand for molding
3. The methods of molding employed
4. Variables related to the casting, such as weight, shape, kind of casting alloy, gating design, etc.

A synthetic green molding sand should be viewed as an aggregate composed of silica particles, clay, water, and special additives. The bulk of the aggregate is supplied by the silica particles. The silica comes from the *base sand,* to which the other ingredients are added.

Base Sand

The base sand may be a clay-free, washed, white silica sand or a less pure, tan-colored sand containing some small percentage of clay. Aside from considerations of purity and clay content, the average fineness number and particle size distribution are properties of the base sand of major importance. To illustrate, consider the sieve analysis of a typical silica sand as reported in Fig. 5.7 according to the standard methods of sieve analysis of the AFS.[1] The average fineness number is calculated from the sieve analysis, in this case 66.6. The sieve analysis is graphically presented either as the percentage retained on each sieve or as cumulative percentage retained on successive sieves as shown in Fig. 5.7. In either case there are three major fractions of the sieve analysis to be

Table* 5.7 *Sieve analysis of typical lake and bank sands*

No.	Lake sand	Bank sand	Per cent retained: 60% lake, 40% bank
U.S. Sieve:			
20	0.13	0	0.08
30	0.67	0.03	0.41
40	2.35	0.06	1.43
50	16.02	1.48	10.20
70	45.82	13.30	32.81
100	33.28	43.27	37.28
140	1.23	27.66	11.80
200	0.10	10.90	4.42
270	0.01	1.89	0.76
Pan	0.39	1.42	0.80
AFS No.	56	88.1	68.7

*These are sands which are mined mainly in the Great Lakes region of the United States.

considered, the bulk, the coarse, and the fine fractions. The bulk fraction is that percentage of sand grains represented by the middle portion of the curves (Fig. 5.7). The sand may be defined by the number of screens over which the bulk fraction is spread as a 2-, 3-, 4-, 5-, etc., screen sand.* A screen fraction is arbitrarily defined as one with more than 10 per cent retained on that screen; i.e., a 4-screen sand is one where the bulk of the sand is retained on four adjacent screens, each having more than 10 per cent retained on it. The sieve analysis in Fig. 5.7 is an example of a 4-screen sand. Obviously, the bulk fraction of the sieve analysis of the base sand provides the bulk of the molding sand and normally constitutes more than 80 per cent of the aggregate by weight. A major feature of the bulk fraction which may vary in different sands is the number of screens over which it is spread. Current experience favors the 4-screen type of distribution for synthetic molding sands.[13] Such a sieve analysis may be achieved by mining and blending sands from the same pit to the desired distribution or by blending sands from different pits. For example, Table 5.7 lists two sands, one a 56 AFS number 3-screen lake sand and the other an 88.1 AFS number 4-screen bank sand, which are blended in the ratio of 60:40 to achieve a 68.7 AFS number 4-screen distribution. Four-screen sands may also be obtained as mined. Although 3-, 5-, and 6-screen bulk-fraction sands can be used, the 4-screen type seems to be most versatile over a wide range of conditions.

The coarse fraction of the sieve analysis is composed of the total percentage of sand grains retained on the screens coarser than those of

*Or a 2-, 3-, 4-, 5-, etc., sieve sand.

the bulk fraction, and in amounts of less than 10 per cent. The total coarse fraction must be limited in amount, usually to less than 4 per cent for a sand of the 4-screen distribution type. This limitation is necessary since an excess of coarse particles contributes to a poor casting surface finish. In addition, coarse particles are easily dislodged from the mold-cavity surface and become dirt in the casting. In the case of a typical 60 to 70 AFS sand of the 4-screen type, the coarse fraction occurs on the No. 40 or coarser sieve and must be limited to less than 4 per cent. In a sand of higher AFS fineness number, the coarse fraction might be that on the No. 50 or 70 screens.

The fine fraction of the sieve analysis is composed of the total percentage of sand grains retained on screens finer than those of the bulk fraction and in amounts of less than 10 per cent. The total fine fraction must be limited in amount, usually to less than about 5 per cent for a sand of the 4-screen type. This limitation is necessary since an excess of fine particles causes balling to occur during mulling. When water is added, the fines and clay agglomerate to form balls during mulling and thus prevent the clay from being thoroughly disseminated throughout the mass. Although the percentage of fines must be limited to a maximum percentage as stated above, there is also a minimum percentage desired. In the absence of the fines, clay balling can occur. Mulling causes the clay and water to form balls if there are no fines present and again agglomerates of uniformly dispersed ingredients are not formed from mulling. The ability properly to mull the sand and disseminate the ingredients requires this balance of coarse, bulk, and fine sand particles in the base sand.

Sand Grains and Permeability

Coarser sands with greater void space have greater permeability than finer sands. A base permeability for silica sand (no clay) of one mesh size has been reported in Ref. 18, and is recorded graphically in Fig. 5.8. The finer sand grain sizes show a very low permeability. In addition to average grain size, the grain size distribution has a pronounced effect on permeability. A sand with many fines and a wide range of particle sizes will have low permeability when compared with one of the same average fineness but having only one size of grains present.[18]

Sand Grains and Refractoriness

Refractoriness, i.e., highest fusion point, seems to be obtained in those sand grains of maximum purity and size. Washed and dried white silica sands of AFS number 30 to 45 are regarded as having highest refractoriness, with fusion point above 3000 F. Impurities such as iron oxide, feldspar, and limestone, which discolor, lower its fusion point. Finer grains appear to be more easily fused than coarser ones. Where

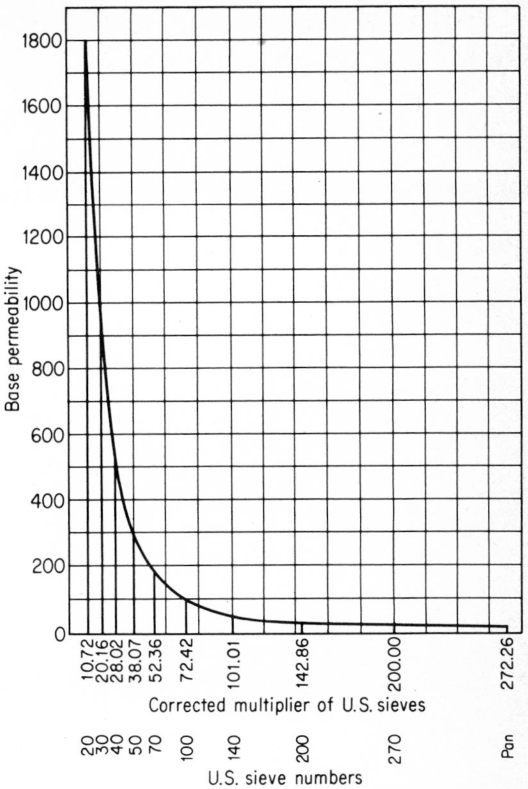

Fig. 5.8 Base permeability of silica sands. (*From AFS.*[18])

maximum refractoriness is required, as in steel molding sands, the coarser, high-purity silica sands are used to advantage.

Sand Grains and Expansion

All sand-expansion characteristics are fundamentally related to the unusual thermal expansion of silica as illustrated in Fig. 5.9. This graph

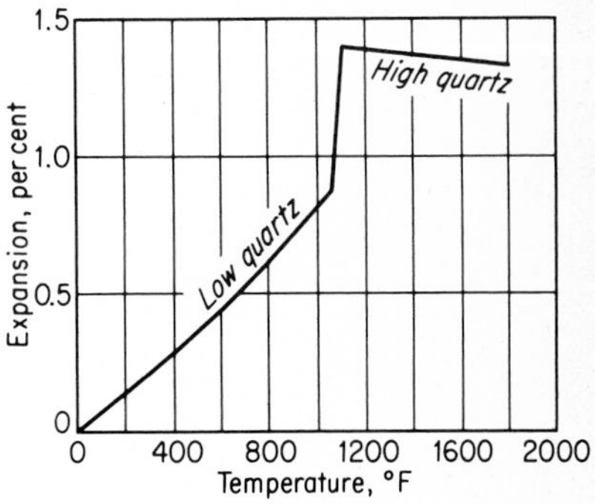

Fig. 5.9 Thermal expansion of silica. (*From AFS.*[18])

shows that major expansion occurs in the temperature range of 1000 to 1200 F because of the allotropic transformation of silica.[28]

Clay and Water

The influence of clay content and percentage of tempering water on the green compression strength of a molding sand is illustrated for western bentonite in Fig. 5.10. The effect of clay and water content on dry compressive stength is shown in Fig. 5.11. Similar curves exist for the

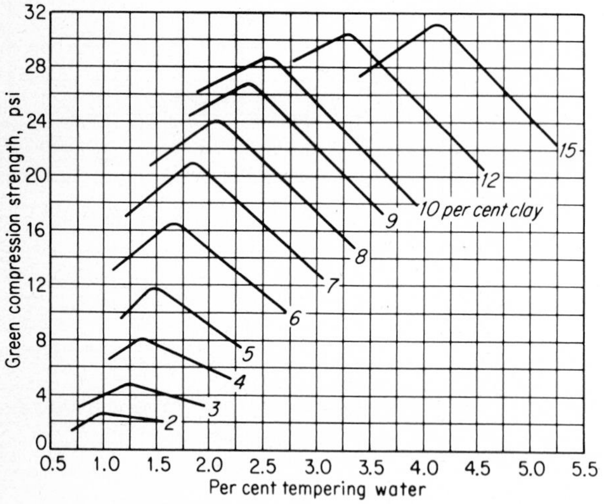

Fig. 5.10 Relationship of green strength, clay, and percentage of tempering water for the AFS standard sand bonded with western bentonite. (*From R. E. Grim and F. L. Cuthbert.*[2])

other clays. For a given clay type and content, there is an optimum water content with reference to Figs. 5.10 and 5.11. Too much water causes excessive plasticity and dry strength. Too little water fails to develop adequate strength and plasticity. Control of moisture in the molding sand so that the best properties are developed is a necessary basis of sand control.

Clay

Green sands may be considered as clay-saturated or unsaturated aggregates according to the clay percentage present. A clay-saturated green sand is defined as one containing a high enough percentage of clay so that any further increase in clay content will not cause an increase in maximum green compressive strength of the aggregate. This defini-

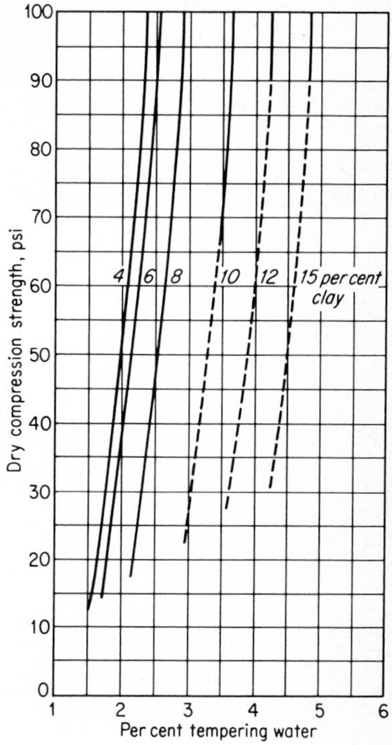

***Fig.* 5.11** Effect of water content on dry strength of standard AFS sand bonded with different percentages of western bentonite. (*From R. E. Grim and F. L. Cuthbert.*[3])

tion is depicted graphically in the schematic diagram of Fig. 5.12.[22,23] The abscissa in Fig. 5.12 refers to the percentage of clay in the clay-sand mixture on the dry basis. The ordinate refers to the *maximum* green compressive strength developed when increasing percentages of water are added to the dry mixture. The moisture percentage which develops maximum green compressive strength can be calculated by a method described in Ref. 23.

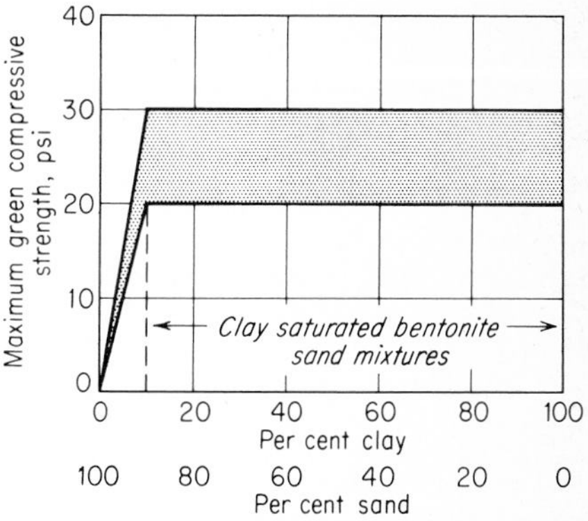

***Fig.* 5.12** Schematic diagram showing the approximate effect of bentonite clays on the maximum green compressive strength of clay-sand-water mixtures.

Figure 5.12 points out that a clay-saturated sand has about the same compressive strength as the clay by itself. The mixture is thus fully bonded. The shaded area on Fig. 5.12 represents variation in maximum strength of the clay-sand mixture due to clay purity and source, sieve analysis of the base-sand mixing efficiency, and other factors. Higher strengths than indicated in Fig. 5.12 can be achieved by more severe mixing.

The specific percentage of clay required for saturation depends on purity and type of clay, base sand, and additives. In most cases, however, about 8 to 12 per cent of bentonites (either sodium or calcium bentonites) or about 20 to 25 per cent fire clay is sufficient to produce a clay-saturated mixture with the sand fineness of 60 to 100 AFS number.

The nature of the bonding action between the clay and sand particles is discussed in Refs. 40 and 41. This subject is not considered here.

With reference to clay content there are three major types of synthetic-sand practices. First, the clay-saturated sands may be considered. These are mixtures containing a percentage of bentonite type of clay corresponding to the saturation point, that is, 8 to 12 per cent.* By AFS clay analysis, the percentage of AFS clay is commonly from 9 to 14 per cent, or true-clay particles of about 8 to 12 per cent (see Ref. 7 for true-clay analysis). The clay-saturated type of sand is currently widely used in iron foundries and in foundries producing the heavier nonferrous alloys. Clay-saturated sands are probably the most versatile green-sand mixtures for a wide range of casting weight and alloy types. Casting defects due to sand expansion, erosion, and cuts and washes are either eliminated or reduced to a negligible percentage attributable to the molding sand itself. Since such sands are normally of high strength (14.0 to 20.0 psi green compressive strength), they require adequate ramming to develop their properties (preferably over 85 mold hardness).

A second type of sand practice involves the use of clay in amounts which are slightly but definitely less than the saturation percentage. The amounts actually carried in sand systems are about 6 to 9.0 per cent AFS clay in bentonite-bonded sand, or about the equivalent amount of 10 to 15 per cent fire clay. Such sands are used more for lighter castings where expansion defects, erosion of cuts, and washes are lesser problems.

A third practice is a low-clay-content practice involving about 4 per cent western (sodium) bentonite and used primarily by steel

*Synthetic molding sands saturated with fire clay are not commonly used. The 20 to 25 per cent fire clay required for saturation produces a sand of low-permeability and high-moisture requirements.

foundries. Expansion problems are at a maximum with this type of sand. However, because of its low green strength, 6 to 9 psi, and high moisture content, it can be readily molded to high density. Cereal is used to offset the expansion problem.

Clay Type

Western bentonites are used in sands requiring a higher level of dry compressive strength, in excess of 80 psi, for example. Southern bentonites are used in sands where a lower dry compressive strength is acceptable, 40 to 80 psi, for example. Fire clay produces moderate dry strength in the sands in which it is used. Maximum dry compressive strengths over 200 psi can be obtained with mixtures of fire clay and western bentonite.[25]

Water

The moisture required to produce the desired properties in a green sand can be calculated. The method is based on first computing the total percentage of water absorbed by all the ingredients of the sand. The maximum adsorbed moisture content is associated with the development of maximum, or peak, green strength, as pointed out in Fig. 5.10. Additional water, called *free water,* is required to develop dry compressive strength and plasticity, or deformation. The method of computation is given in Ref. 23, and examples of its use are described in Ref. 22. The final selection of moisture content to be used in the molding sand is usually a compromise based on many practical factors operating in a given sand foundry. These are not usually accountable in any calculation method.

Additives

The additives used in molding sands were defined earlier. Reference 23 may be studied for more information on this subject.

Effect of Molding on Sand Properties

The foregoing discussion has dealt with the principles of proportioning the ingredients of synthetic molding sands. Although the ultimate properties of the sand are fixed by its ingredients, the properties displayed in a mold are in a large measure determined by the molding operations. As the sand is molded, it is compacted. Compaction, measured as increased bulk density, is accompanied by an increase in the mold hardness, green compressive, shear, and tensile strengths, and dry and hot strengths. Examples of the range of bulk densities existing in sands from minimum to maximum were provided in Table 4.1. When the molding process is finished, the sand is at some level of bulk density between the minimum and the maximum listed in Table 4.1. The bulk density at which molding stops then largely determines the properties which the molded sand aggregate displays. It is extremely important to be able to express the properties of sand over a range of bulk densities and molding or ramming effort. Further, some means of relating the properties measured with laboratory specimens to properties in the mold is necessary.

Mold Hardness

The mold-hardness test provides a convenient measurement for relating properties in the AFS 2.0- by 2.0-in.-diameter specimen to properties in the mold. Fortunately, the mold-hardness test is an indirect measurement of bulk density of a particular sand. In addition, green properties are related to mold hardness in a way similar to that of bulk density. Hence it can be recognized that mold hardness starting at about 60 and increasing to 95+ means that the bulk density of the sand is increasing from the lower to the higher values in Table 4.1, and strength properties are also increasing. Comparison between laboratory specimens and mold then requires that specimens be prepared over a wide hardness range so that any mold hardness measured in a mold can be compared with equivalent hardness in the specimen.[14] Figure 5.13, for example, shows how mold hardness and green compressive strength are related over the hardness range of 60 to 95 MH for new sand mixtures containing 3, 6, 8, and 12 per cent western bentonite. The graph shows a progressive increase of green compressive strength with mold hardness. The graph also demonstrates that green compressive strength at a given mold hardness depends on clay content in unsaturated sands.[30] In clay-saturated sands, green compressive strength reaches a maximum value at any given mold hardness, and is not further increased by increasing clay content. The upper curve in Fig. 5.13 therefore represents the maximum MH-GCS relationship for all clay-saturated sands, regardless of clay type. Further, this relationship is not affected by moisture percentage in the sand within the normal moisture percentages of molding sands.

To correlate specimen properties with the mold, the hardness of the mold is measured. Since most molds are nonuniform in hardness, readings must be taken on the parting surface and on vertical surfaces at varying distance from the parting to gain a picture of the degree of mold-hardness variation within the mold. As in the case of the specimen, when the mold is rammed to high density, it will be uniformly hard. The object of good molding technique is to achieve a uniform and high

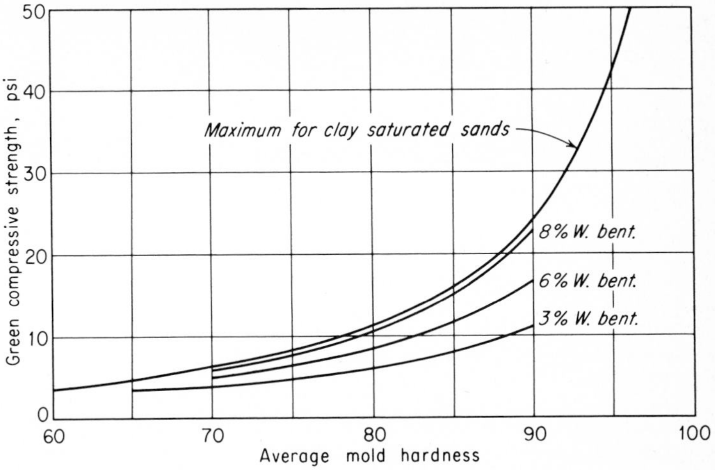

***Fig.* 5.13** Typical effect of clay content on relationship between mold hardness and green compressive strength. Average mold hardness is obtained from three readings on the top and three readings on the bottom of the specimen. The curve marked "maximum" applies equally well to clay-saturated southern and western bentonite and fire-clay-bonded sands.

mold hardness throughout the mold. The practical molding problem involved in obtaining uniformly high mold hardness will not be considered here. It must be recognized, however, that uniform properties and behavior cannot be expected from a well-formulated synthetic molding sand, or any other sand, if it is not molded to a reasonably high and uniform density and mold hardness.

Other properties of the sand, such as green compressive and dry compressive strength[31] and green tensile,[30] are also related to the bulk density and mold hardness achieved by ramming. Figure 5.14 shows such relationships for mold hardness and green and dry compressive strengths and moisture content of a particular sand.[23] Thus the tremendous importance of the combined effects of ramming, clay content, and moisture content of the sand is illustrated. By controlling moisture in the ranges discussed earlier, a suitable combination of green and dry strength is obtained. Obviously, factors such as clay content and type, additives, base sand, molding, etc., have effects on all the properties developed in a sand. Once a sand formulation is selected, however, the major effects are those of moisture and the properties developed by ramming, as discussed above.

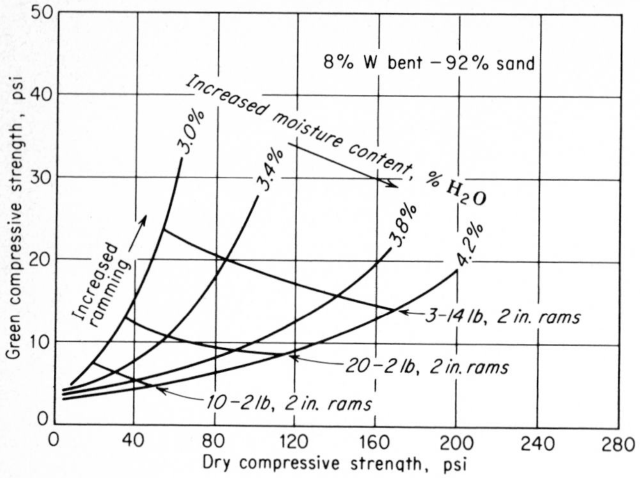

***Fig.* 5.14** **Typical relationship of green compressive strength, dry compressive strength, moisture content, and ramming in an 8% western bentonite–92% sand of 85 AFS fineness number.**

Effect of Sand Conditioning

Effective molding-sand preparation usually consists of certain steps including:

1. Removal of foreign material, principally fines, metal, and hard lumps, as the sand is prepared for reuse.
2. Adequate mixing and tempering. Mulling or other mixing of the sand to distribute the clay, water, and additives should be continued until optimum sand properties are developed. Certain mixers are much more potent than others. Undermixed sand may have a very nonuniform distribution of ingredients.
3. Aerating, consisting in separating sand grains and in fluffing up of the sand by riddling, screening, or beating the sand, is practiced to promote better molding results.
4. Control of sand temperature. Cooling of sand is desirable since hot sand over 100 F causes molding difficulties, e.g., sticking and drops.

These steps are performed with more or less mechanical equipment of the type described in Chap. 4. Conditioning is complicated by the fact that the sand is continually being contaminated with core lumps, metal drippings, scale, and wires, as well as being decrepitated by the action of heat. Metal and lump contamination can be reduced by magnetic separation and screens. Accumulation of fine material can in part be controlled by its removal through exhaust systems under the dusty conditions of the shakeout. However, burnt clay and dilution by core sand can be corrected only by additions of clay and other additives to keep the sand properties at the desired level. Green strength and other properties and the combustible material in the sand are lost as the sand is reused unless such additions are made to recover the losses. The clay and other materials added for each cycle of mixing is about 0.15 to 1.00 per cent of the weight of the sand or about 2 to 20 lb of clay per 2000-lb batch, depending on the size of castings being made. The returned sand is of unknown moisture content, and additions for tempering at the proper water percentage must be made.

Adequate mixing requires the proper use of mixers. A mulling time of 4.5 to 6.0 min is required for mullers of the type shown in Fig. 4.14 to develop the bond for the clay. The centrifugal-type muller (Fig. 4.15) requires about 1.0 to 2.0 min. Overmulling can result in excessive heating of the sand, but more often the sand is hot, and mulling will cool it by water evaporation, especially if the muller is equipped with cooling blowers. Other types of mixers have optimum mixing periods. Any of the equipment must be properly adjusted. After mulling, some sand systems contain storage facilities to take advantage of the fact that some sands seem to improve with time. The mulling effect is considered in Ref. 42.

Before use in molding, aeration is a helpful practice. Aeration may be accomplished by riddling on ¼-in. mesh screens, mechanically, by vibrating screens, or by other devices. Aeration improves the molding qualities of the sand and the casting finish.

MOLDING-SAND TYPES

Sands are classified as natural or synthetic molding sands on the basis of their clay bonding material. A natural sand is one containing sufficient AFS clay as mined from the sand pit so that it can be used directly, needing only to be tempered and conditioned. A synthetic sand, however, is one artificially compounded by mixing sand grains and clay of the selected types considered. Natural sands came first in the chronological development of the foundry industry. Their present advantages consist in the simplicity of their preparation, handling, and use. Synthetic sands have the advantages of lower cost in large volume, widespread availability, and the possibilities of sand reclamation and reuse. Some typical specifications for natural sands are given in Table 5.8.

Listed in Table 5.9 are some properties and mixtures of synthetic sands. A more complete description of one ferrous molding sand is provided in Table 5.10 in which many properties are given quantitative values supposed to be favorable for producing good lightweight gray-

Table 5.8 Sand specifications on some natural sands

Property \ Sand use	Iron	Iron	Heavy brass or iron	No. 00 Albany, small and medium brass	No. 1 Albany, brass and small iron
AFS fineness.	70–80	70–80	23–27	180–200	110–130
Fineness class.	4	4	8	2	3
Clay content, %. . .	15–18	22–30	17–19	11–13	12–15
Clay content class.	F	G	F	E	E
Grain shape.	Subangular	Subangular	Subangular	Subangular	Subangular
Grain distribution.	5:4:3	3:4:3	1:4:7	7:4:0	2:4:2
Moisture, %.	6	7	7	6	6
Permeability, min.	75	40	250	10	15
Compressive strength, psi, min.	7.0	12	10	5	8
Sintering point, °C, min.	1200	1200	1250	1050	1075

iron castings. The latter table is a very complete picture of a particular sand.

Sand Definitions

Certain terms are used in connection with molding sands that should be understood. Definitions are given below. Some of them are standard, taken from AFS references, whereas others are modified according to the authors' experience.

Silica Sand

White washed and dried silica sand grains of high purity, 99.8+% SiO_2.

Bank Sand

Sand from glacial or sedimentary deposits occurring in banks or pits, usually containing less than 5 per cent clay and used in synthetic sands and core sands. In the Great Lakes area these sands usually contain less than 2.0 per cent clay and consist of rounded silica grains in size ranges of 60 to 70, 70 to 80, 80 to 90, and 90 to 100 AFS and over. The sand grains are usually not white because of impurities.

Lake Sand (or Dune Sand)

A subangular sand, from the Great Lakes area, and especially dune and bottom deposits, substantially free of AFS clay and of 45 to 50,

Table 5.9 Typical synthetic-sand practices for small- and medium-weight castings

Clay	Clay-sand type			
	Saturated bentonite	Subsaturated bentonite	Unsaturated	
			W. bentonite	Fire clay
Base sand	60–70 AFS, 4-screen	60–70 AFS, 4-screen	50–70 AFS, 3- to 4-screen	55–65 AFS, 4-screen
AFS clay, %	9–14	7–10	3–6	11–16
True clay, %	8–12	6–8	3–5	10–14
% H_2O, free	+20	+30–50	+50–100	+50–100
Green compressive strength, psi	14–20.0	10–14.0	5–9.0	7–11.0
Green shear strength, psi	4–6.0	3.0–4.0	1.5–2.5	2.0–3.0
Avg mold hardness	84–90	82–88	74–86	76–86
Dry compressive strength, psi:				
W.-bentonite-bonded	Usually >100	>100	>80	
S.-bentonite-bonded	40–80	40–80		
Fire-clay-bonded	....	....	....	60–80
Bulk density, lb/cu ft:				
Freshly riddled	50–65	45–60	40–55	50–65
Fully rammed	100–110	100–110	100–110	110–120
Deformation, in.	0.010–0.020	0.020–0.030	0.025–0.040	0.020–0.035
Total combination, %:				
Fe	5–10	5–10	....	6–12
Cu-base	2–6.0	2–6.0		
Al-base	1.5–2.5	1.5–2.5		
Special additive	Sea-coal cellulose	Sea-coal cellulose	Cellulose	Cereal or dextrin

50 to 60, 60 to 70 AFS fineness. Lake sand is usually not white because of impurities.

System Sand

Any sand employed in a mechanical sand preparation and handling system.

Heap Sand

Sand thought of as being heaped on the floor when it is prepared for use.

Table* 5.10 *An example of a sand for cast iron

	Green Properties		
Moisture, %	4.9	Green compression, psi	18.5
Mold hardness:		Green deformation, in./in.	0.016
Top	88.0	Sand toughness	296.0
Bottom	90.0	Density, lb/cu ft	92.5
Permeability, cu cm	48.0	Flowability, %	68.5
	Dry Properties		
Dry compression, psi	85.0	Combustible material, %	10.94
Air-set strength, psi	28.0		

U.S. sieve No.	*Percentage retained*
6	
12	
20	0.3
30	0.5
40	1.9
50	9.8
70	24.2
100	27.7
140	13.8
200	6.1
270	2.1
Pan	1.8

Clay content, %	14.8	AFS grain fineness No	77.4

Hot Properties

A sintering point, F	2350
Hot strength, psi:	
500 F	99.0
1000 F	76.0
1500 F	193.0
2000 F	38.0
2500 F	3.0
Spalling at 2500 F:	
1 min	No cracks
2 min	Few hair cracks
12 min	Many medium surface cracks
Hollow confined expansion at 1500 F, in./in.	0.021
Pin penetration at 2600 F for 12 min	Very little penetration; diam of pin larger at bottom than at top
Maximum hot gas pressure at 2000 F, in. water	20.0
Sand used to produce lightweight watertight iron castings	

*From H. W. Dietert.[17]

Facing Sand

A specially prepared sand used next to the pattern and backed up with heap or system sand.

Backing Sand

Molding sand used to back up facing sand and not used next to the pattern.

Bonding Sand

Sand high in clay content used to add clay to a molding sand.

Sharp Sand

A sand substantially free of bond. The term has no reference to grain shape. Lake sands are sometimes referred to as sharp sands.

Sand Additive

Any material added to molding sands for a special effect.

Loam

A mixture of sand, silt, and clayey particles in such proportions as to exhibit about 50 per cent sand grains and 50 per cent silt and clay. A material used for loam molding of large gray-iron castings.

Dry Sands

Preceding sections were limited in discussion to the nature of green molding sands. Dry-sand molds have certain desirable features, namely, greater strength and rigidity, thermal stability, and the elimination of defects attributable to water in the sands. Large and heavy castings, because of metallostatic pressure on the mold and the long period during which they may remain molten, require exceptional thermal stability of the mold. Certain metal defects, such as pinholing, can be eliminated in troublesome castings if the mold is dried.

Since the sand is green for molding, its properties are similar to those discussed for green sands. Usually, the sand is tempered on the wet side because this brings out additional dry strength, as was illustrated in Fig. 5.11. Certain ingredients may be added for special effects. Silica flour is extensively used for added hot strength and resistance to erosion. Pitch is often used for greater strength and improved surface finish of iron castings. Some of these variations are indicated in Table 5.11, where some dry-sand molding mixtures are listed. These sands are greatly dependent for their dry strength on their clay and water content and the hardness to which they are rammed.

Mold Coatings

For some castings, the sand surface of a mold is altered after the pattern is drawn by applying a mold surfacing material. This material is called a mold wash, mold coating, spray, blacking, or similar name. The benefits claimed for their use include better surface finish, greater ease of cleaning the casting, and fewer casting-surface defects. Application to the mold surface is usually done by spraying, swabbing, or painting

Table* 5.11 *Examples of dry-sand mixtures

Sand type	Sand green base	Clay binder	Other additives	Comments
Steel, general facing.	Silica sand, 40–60 AFS fineness	7 % western bentonite	14 % silica flour, molasses water	Temper heavy with water and use sufficient dextrin or molasses; bake at 600 F until dry
Steel, heavy.........	50 % new silica sand, 40–60 AFS fineness, 50 % reclaimed system sand	7–8 % fire clay, 1–2 % western bentonite	2–3 % silica flour	Temper heavy with water; bake at 650 F until dry
Gray iron, general...	40 % new silica, 50–60 AFS, 60 % old sand of same source	3–6 % western bentonite	1.0–2.0 % pitch, 1.0–1.5 % cereal	Temper to good workable moisture. Typical sand properties: 8.0–10 psi green strength, 90–120 permeability, 4–5 % moisture. Bake at 350–450 F
Steel, air-dry........	New or reclaimed silica sand, fineness 40–60 AFS	3.5 % western bentonite	5 % silica flour, 1.25 % cereal	3.5–4.5 % moisture, air-dry open mold

of wet materials and sometimes by dusting dry materials. Mold coatings which have been found useful are listed in Table 5.12. Generally, it is simpler for foundrymen to purchase proprietary mixtures than to mix their own washes. The coatings listed in Table 5.12 are suspended in water. However, many mold washes are made which use liquids such as kerosene, some core oils, or other organic media of suspension.

Other Molding Aggregates

This chapter has largely been concerned with green molding sands. Some other aggregates such as core, shell, air-set, and silicate-bonded

Table* 5.12 *Water-base mold coatings

Description	Western bentonite	Silica flour	Graphite	Dextrin	Cereal	Water	Remarks
General purpose......	1.5 %	59.4 %	....	1.5 %	....	37.5 %	+0.1 % sodium benzoate
Cast iron............	0.8 %	....	31.1 %	1.30 %	....	66.7 %	+0.1 % sodium benzoate
Cast iron and brass....	4 parts	....	100 parts	......	4 parts	100 parts	+0.1 % sodium benzoate
Steel................	4 parts	100 parts	....	3 parts	....	100 parts	+0.1 % sodium benzoate
Gray iron............	......	....	x	......	....	x	Slurry testing, 35–40 Bé

sands will be considered under the general topic of core materials, although they may be used for molding as well.

BIBLIOGRAPHY

1. American Foundrymen's Society, "Foundry Sand Handbook," 7th ed., 1963.
2. R. E. Grim and F. L. Cuthbert, The Bonding Action of Clays, Part 1, Clays in Green Molding Sands, *Univ. Illinois Eng. Expt. Sta. Bull.* 357, 1945.
3. R. E. Grim and F. L. Cuthbert, The Bonding Action of Clays, Part 2, Clays in Dry Molding Sands, *Univ. Illinois Eng. Expt. Sta. Bull.* 362, 1946.
4. E. D. Boyle and H. R. Wolfer, Mineral Perlite and Its Use in the Foundry, *Trans. AFS,* vol. 60, 1952.
5. B. C. Yearley, Effect of Heat and Additives on Green Sand, *Foundry,* vol. 91, no. 8, p. 50.
6. H. W. Dietert Co., Tools for Control, catalogue 118, an industrial bulletin.
7. H. G. Lievelink and H. van den Berg, Green Sand Scabbing Tendency Testing by Shock Heating, *Trans. AFS,* vol. 70, p. 152, 1962.
8. R. W. Heine, J. S. Schumacher, W. F. Shaw, and E. H. King, Ramming and Clay Content Effect on Hot Compression Strength of Molding Sand, *Trans. AFS,* 1960.
9. R. W. Heine, J. S. Schumacher, and E. H. King, A New Approach to Molding and Core Sand High Temperature Strength Testing, *Trans. AFS,* 1961.
10. R. W. Heine, J. S. Schumacher, and E. H. King, Thermal Expansion, Hot Deformation, and Associated Defects in Casting, *Trans. AFS,* 1962.
11. H. W. Dietert, Surface Gas Pressure of Molding Sands and Cores, *Trans. AFS,* 1948.
12. M. Granlund, Micrometrics as Applied to Foundry Sands, *Trans. AFS,* vol. 70, p. 37, 1962.
13. C. H. Bowen, Application of Phi Scale to the Description of Industrial Granular Materials, *Mining Eng.,* April, 1956, p. 420.
14. J. Schumacher, Fool Proof Sand Works for Wide Range of Castings, *Am. Foundryman,* June, 1952, p. 54.
15. C. A. Sanders and A. G. Clem, How the One-to-ten Ram Test Measures Sand and Mold Properties, *Am. Foundryman,* vol. 22, October, 1952.
16. H. W. Dietert and A. L. Graham, Ramming of Molding Sands, *Trans. AFS,* vol. 61, 1953.
17. H. W. Dietert, Surface Gas Pressure of Molding Sands and Cores, *Trans. AFS,* vol. 56, 1948.
18. H. W. Dietert, "Foundry Core Practice," American Foundrymen's Society, 1950.
19. J. Schumacher, Fool Proof Sand Works for Wide Range of Castings, *Am. Foundryman,* vol. 21, p. 54, June, 1952.
20. N. J. Dunbeck, Synthetic Sand in Nonferrous Foundries, *Am. Foundryman,* vol. 8, July, 1945.
21. W. F. Bradley, The Green Compression Strength of Natural Bentonites, in "Clay and Clay Minerals," p. 41, National Academy of Sciences and National Research Council, Washington, D.C., publ. 456, 1956.
22. A. H. Zrimsek and R. W. Heine, Clay, Fines and Water Relationships for Green Strength in Molding Sands, *Trans. AFS,* 1955, p. 575.
23. R. W. Heine, J. S. Schumacher, and E. H. King, Green Sand Principles Controlling Casting Quality, *Modern Castings,* April–July, 1960.

24. R. W. Heine, E. H. King, and J. S. Schumacher, How to Determine Moisture Requirements of Molding Sands, *Trans. AFS*, vol. 65, p. 118, 1957.
25. N. J. Dunbeck, American Synthetic Sand Practice, *Trans. AFS*, vol. 49, 1941.
26. G. J. Vingas and A. H. Zrimsek, Systematic Approach to Sand Design and Control, Report Number 6, *Trans. AFS*, vol. 70, p. 321, 1962.
27. B. C. Yearley, A New Look at Green Sand Molding, *Foundry*, vol. 91, no. 8, July, 1963.
28. R. D. Cadle, "Particle Size Determination," Interscience Publishers, Inc., New York, 1955.
29. H. H. Fairfield, Expansion of Silica Sand, *Foundry*, vol. 76, p. 128, May, 1948.
30. R. W. Heine, E. H. King, and J. S. Schumacher, Mold Hardness: What It Means, *Trans. AFS*, vol. 65, p. 123, 1957.
31. R. W. Heine, E. H. King, and J. S. Schumacher, Green Tensile and Shear Strengths of Molding Sands, American Foundrymen's Society, preprint 59-55, 1959.
32. R. W. Heine, E. H. King, and J. S. Schumacher, Correlation of Green Strength, Dry Strength and Mold Hardness of Molding Sands, *Trans. AFS*, vol. 66, p. 59, 1958.
33. J. S. Schumacher, Clay Test for Used Sands, *Am. Foundryman*, vol. 27, no. 3, p. 41, March, 1955.
34. R. W. Heine, E. H. King, and J. S. Schumacher, Sand Movement and Compaction in Green Sand Molding, American Foundrymen's Society, preprint 59-32, 1959.
35. R. W. Heine, Molding Sands, Molding Methods and Casting Dimensions, *Trans. AFS*, vol. 64, p. 398, 1956.
36. R. W. Heine, E. H. King, and J. S. Schumacher, The Problem of Hot Molding Sands, *Trans. AFS*, vol. 66, 1958.
37. R. E. Morey and C. G. Ackerlind, This Mold Wash Works with All Common Alloys, *Am. Foundryman*, January, 1952.
38. R. E. Morey, C. G. Ackerlind, and W. S. Pellini, Effects of Binders and Additives on the High Temperature Properties of Molding Sand, *Trans. AFS*, 1952.
39. J. S. Schumacher, Clay Test for Used Sands, *Am. Foundryman*, vol. 27, no. 3, p. 41, March, 1955.
40. H. F. Taylor and L. M. Diran, The Nature of Bonding in Clays and Sand Clay Mixtures, *Trans. AFS*, vol. 60, p. 356, 1952.
41. R. A. Flinn, "Fundamentals of Metal Casting," Addison-Wesley Publishing Company, Inc., Reading, Mass., 1963.
42. G. J. Vingas and A. J. Zrimsek, The Mulling Effect, *Trans. AFS*, vol. 69, p. 101, 1961.

6

Cores

Most simply defined, cores are sand shapes which form the contour of a casting that is not molded with a pattern. Drawing the pattern from the mold limits the casting exterior to a contour that can be freed from the sand vertically as it is done with molding equipment. Forming internal cavities thus depends mainly on cores which can be inserted into a mold of the casting exterior. Through their use in forming complex internal cavities, cores provide the casting process its ability to make the most intricate of shapes, eliminate much machining, and in fact produce shapes which would be impossible to machine. For instance, the water-cooling chamber in internal-combustion engines and the exterior and interior of air-cooled engines require intricate coring, as revealed in Fig. 6.1.

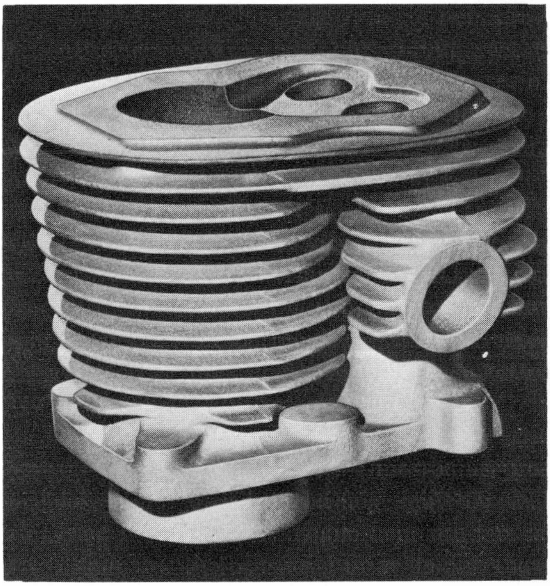

***Fig.* 6.1** Core-sand casting for air-cooled cylinder block. (*Courtesy of Motor Castings Co.*)

Table 6.1 ***Example of some pertinent information on a commercial core blower****

Core-box size (approx max), in.†	36 by 13 by 11
Weight of core (approx max), lb	50
Distance top of table to underside of carriage, in.‡	$25\frac{1}{2}$ to $33\frac{1}{2}$
Distance from floor line to top of table, in	25 to 33
Size intake line required, in	3
Cu ft of free air per cycle of operation at 120 lb line pressure (approx)	11.4

* Courtesy of Osborne Manufacturing Co.

† These dimensions may be increased under certain conditions, using special sizes of sand reservoirs and different clamping arrangements.

‡ This is total space available for sand reservoir, adapter, blow plate, core box, and wearing plate.

Cores may be made of metal, plaster, and investment and ceramic materials, as well as core sand. To achieve the utmost of intricacy in castings, cores must be collapsible after the metal is poured. Metal cores, used in permanent-mold, or die, casting, do not have collapsibility and therefore have shape limitations. However, sand cores and some other materials do not have this handicap and can therefore produce almost any desired degree of casting intricacy. Sand cores, along with sand molding, are the most frequently used.

In addition to their use for forming internal cavities in castings, cores serve a number of other purposes. Among them are:

1. Complete molds may be assembled of core-sand forms. This is a useful molding practice when the intricacy of the casting is such as to make green-sand molding impractical. The motor block of Fig. 6.1 is a good example.
2. Cores may be used to form a part of a green-sand mold. Pattern contours with back draft or projections which cannot be molded can be formed by placing a core in the mold after the pattern is drawn.
3. Cores strengthen or improve a mold surface.
4. Cores may be used as a part of the gating system. Strainer cores, pouring basins or cups (Chap. 9), and slab cores for building the gating system in large molds are examples of this use.
5. Ram-up cores are used for several purposes. These cores are located on the pattern and rammed up along with the molding sand, the core then forming a part of the mold face. They may be used as a means of locating other cores, as supports for chaplets, to hold chills, or to strengthen the mold.

Some of the uses of cores mentioned above will be considered again later in the chapter.

COREMAKING

Most cores are made of a core sand mixture consisting of sand grains and organic binders which provide green strength, cured strength, and collapsibility. Green strength is required so that the core sand may be molded to shape, i.e., for coremaking. The core obtains its real strength and hardness when it is cured to develop the bonded strength.

Coremaking is done manually and with machines. Small cores are made by hand-filling core boxes with the sand, usually done at core benches and described as benchwork. In benchwork, only a core box and core plate are required as equipment. The core box is filled with core sand, rammed, and struck off. Then the core is transferred to a core plate for baking. This is done by placing the plate over the core box, inverting both, and drawing the core box away from the core. A core is shown on a core plate in Fig. 6.2. In this case, inversion of

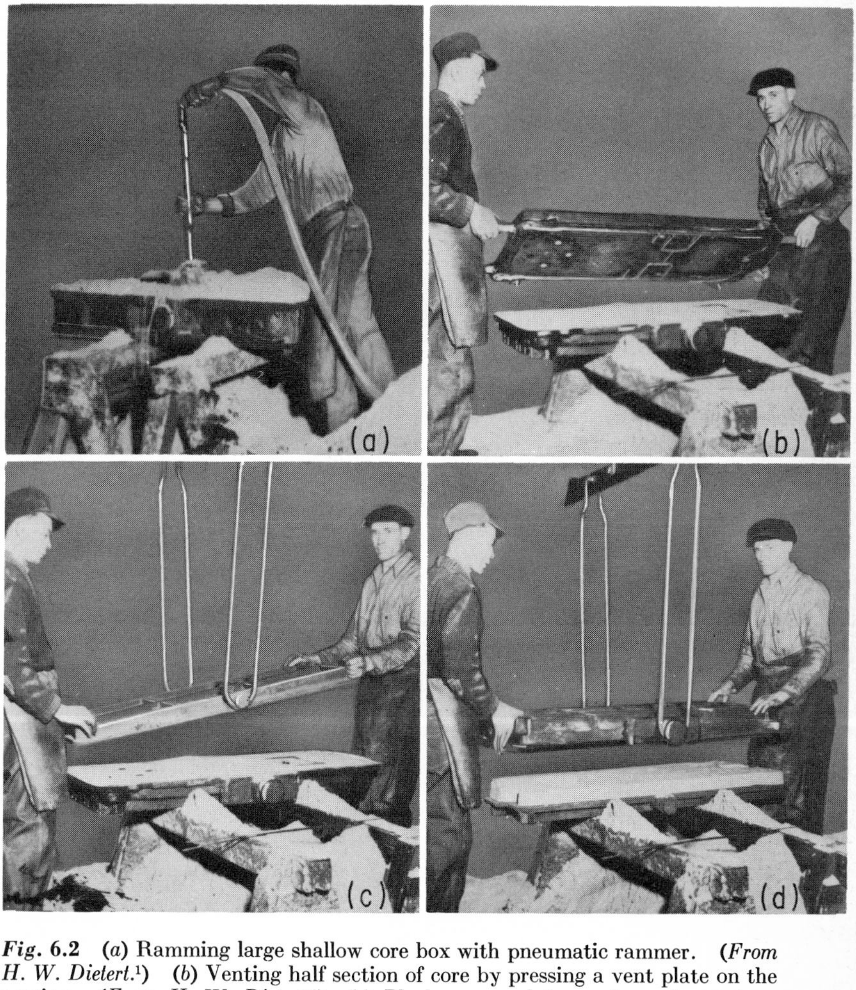

***Fig.* 6.2** (*a*) Ramming large shallow core box with pneumatic rammer. (*From H. W. Dietert.*[1]) (*b*) Venting half section of core by pressing a vent plate on the parting. (*From H. W. Dietert.*[1]) (*c*) Placing core plate on face of core box. (*From H. W. Dietert.*[1]) (*d*) Stripping core box from core with aid of a crane. (*From H. W. Dietert.*[1])

the box and drawing was performed mechanically, employing the rock-over machine. The core which is to be baked on a core plate, shown in Fig. 6.2, must have a flat surface to rest on. Cores with no flat surfaces must be supported on a core drier until they are baked. Bench coremaking is limited in production and in size of work to core boxes which can be handled by one man. Larger work, however, may be handled by two or more men with cranes and may shift from the bench to the floor. The making of a medium-sized shallow core is illustrated in Fig. 6.2*a* to *d*. Figure 6.2*d* shows the same sequence of operations on larger work as was described for benchwork.

COREMAKING MACHINES

The operation of coremaking is performed by machines similar to those used for making molds.

Jolt Machine

A simple jolt table is useful in ramming many core boxes. These machines are very versatile in the size and shape of a dump-type core box which can be jolt-rammed. After jolting, the back may be hand- or pneumatic-rammed, and is then struck off.

Shell-core Machines

The principle of shell molding as presented in Chap. 3 is also used for making cores. A shell-coremaking machine is shown in Fig. 6.3. In this process the core box must be heated. Gas burners or electrical heaters are used for this purpose. The core box is heated at the back so that the cavity surface is heated by conduction through the box. Sand is fed into the box either by gravity or by blowing the sand into the box. After a dwell period which establishes the thickness of the shell, the unheated interior sand may be drained from the shell. The sand drained from the shell may be reused in subsequent cycles of the operation. The shell built up adjacent to the hot box is generally ¼ to ½ in. in thickness and produces a core that faithfully duplicates the dimensions of the cavity. The core may be readily stripped from the box and can be handled directly as illustrated in Fig. 6.3. No further baking may be required, although sometimes additional curing is performed in an oven. Shell cores may be placed directly into molds for the casting operation.

***Fig.* 6.3** Machine for producing shell cores with heated core boxes. *(Courtesy of Beardsley-Piper Division, Pettibone Mulliken Corp.)*

Sand Thrower, or Slinger

The principle of the sand slinger may be used for ramming up core boxes. These machines are suitable for larger sizes of core boxes, since so much sand is delivered in a short time. Separate facilities for drawing the core must be provided.

Core Blower

The core blower has become established as the principal means of rapid production of small and medium-sized cores. In a core-blowing machine, the core box is simultaneously filled with sand and rammed by a sand-carrying air stream. Typical core-blower construction is illustrated in Fig. 6.4. An important part of the machine is the movable sand reservoir from which the sand is blown into the core box. It has an opening at the top which admits sand when the reservoir is in the fill position under a sand hopper. The reservoir has a plate covering its bottom, but with holes in the plate for blowing the sand out of the reservoir. The full reservoir slides into its blow position over the core box, with the sand-fill opening connected to the air blow valve. When air pressure is applied to the sand reservoir through a hand-actuated valve, the sand

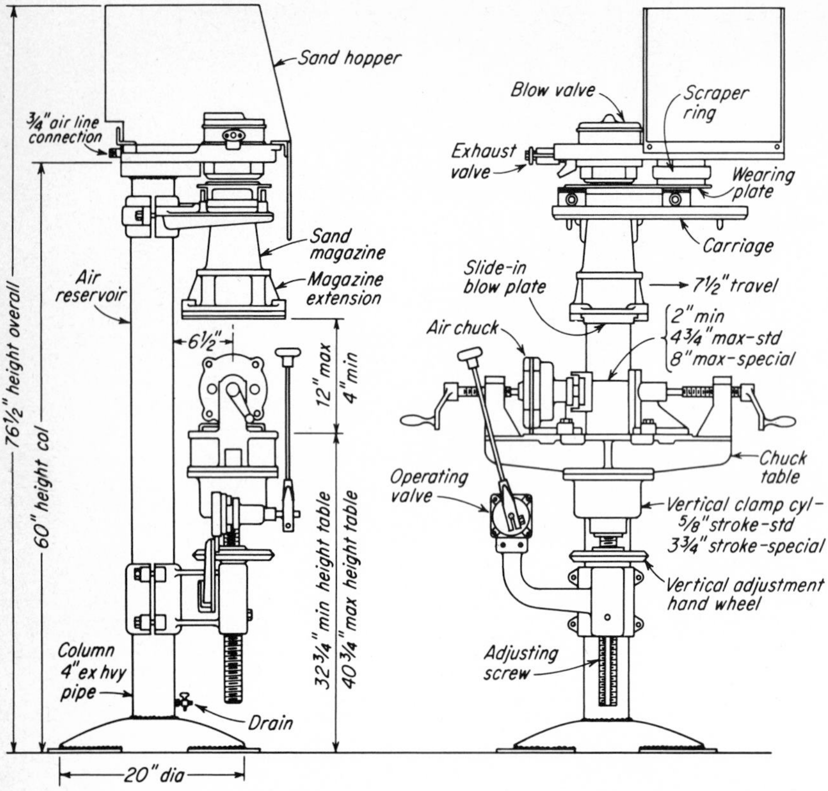

Fig. 6.4 Core-blower construction. (*From H. W. Dietert.*[1])

is blown from the sand reservoir through the blow-plate holes (blowholes) and into the core box. Before blowing begins, the core box and table are raised tightly against the sand reservoir, and it in turn is raised against a sealing gasket in the blow valve so that the full line air pressure may be built up in the sand reservoir. This action, pneumatically powered, is all initiated by the hand-operated valve. The vertical clamping mechanism may be observed in Fig. 6.4. There is also a horizontal clamping mechanism (air chuck) shown in Fig. 6.4 which is used on vertically split core boxes so that air pressure in the box will not blow it open. During the blow cycle, air pressure at the top of the reservoir causes air and sand to flow through the blowholes and into the core box. The air is vented through vent holes located at suitable places in the box. The blowing action is very rapid, and less than 1 or 2 sec is required to fill and ram the sand, even in large core boxes.

Blowers are manufactured in various sizes, producing cores ranging in weight from only a few ounces to more than 300 lb. A bench-type blower is shown in Fig. 6.5. In this machine small cores in gang boxes may be rapidly produced on the bench, usually being hand-drawn. A larger machine is shown in Fig. 6.6. Descriptive data on a typical commercial core blower such as the machine shown in Fig. 6.6 are given in Table 6.1. The limiting core-box size is governed by the reservoir blow-plate opening and the maximum clamping capacity, as well as the maximum weight of sand which can be contained in the reservoir. Core sand weighs approximately 100 lb per cu ft.

Air Requirements

Core blowers require high-pressure air delivered at 90 to 110 psi. If a core is to be blown to maximum density, the air pressure must be kept high, above 90 psi, during the blow cycle. Considerable air may

Fig. 6.5 Bench-type blower. (*Courtesy of Beardsley-Piper Division, Pettibone Mulliken Corp.*)

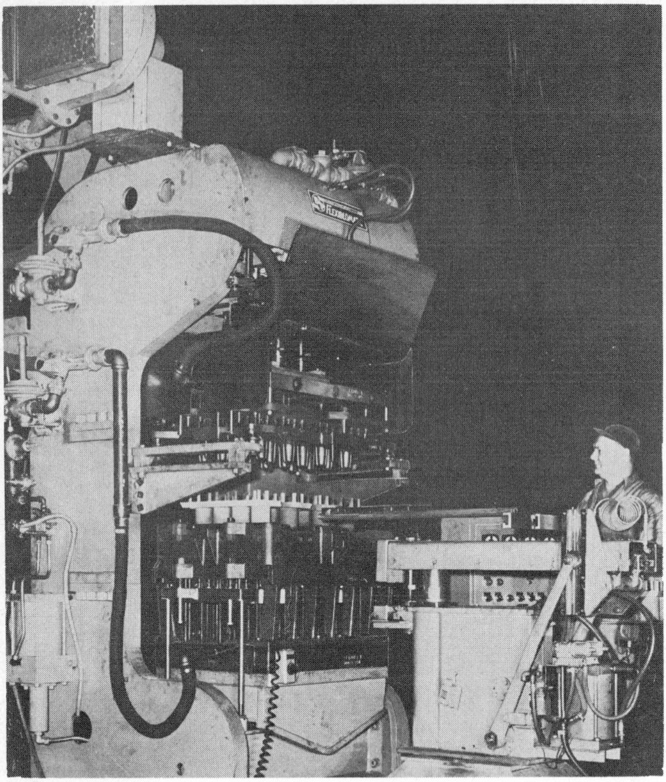

Fig. **6.6** Core blower for making automotive engine cylinder cores by the hot-box process. (*Courtesy of Beardsley-Piper Division, Pettibone Mulliken Corp.*)

be required for a blow, as much as 11.4 cu ft free air for the machine described in Table 6.1. The flow of this much air can cause a serious pressure drop in the air line if it does not supply the necessary volume at a high enough rate. A narrow-diameter pipe would not permit rapid enough flow. In the machine considered in Table 6.1, a 3-in. pipeline for the air is required. Many core blowers have pressure-tank air reservoirs to supply the air required and maintain a high pressure during the period of maximum air flow. If a number of blowers are to be serviced from a central pipe, the main line must have sufficient capacity to carry the air to the machines without serious pressure drop. Air lines should also be provided with drains and filters to prevent water and oils from entering the sand reservoir.

The movement of sand from a blowhole occurs when sand immediately above the hole moves first as the air pressure reaches about 5.0 psi.

Higher pressures of 35 to 50 psi inside the sand reservoir will keep the sand moving into the core box. A channel is formed, and the adjacent sand column collapses into the air stream. Aspiration resulting from the pressure drop also drives the sand into the air stream as long as the strength of the core sand is not too high, up to about 1.50 psi in compression. Stronger sands pile up adjacent to the hole unless some type of agitator is used inside the sand reservoir.

Core-box Equipment

Core boxes for blowing are almost always constructed of metal, usually aluminum. Since the boxes are clamped in the blower, the sides, top and bottom, should be flat and machined parallel. Since they are air-clamped, they must be ribbed and braced to prevent distortion. A most important provision incorporated in the box is adequate blowholes and venting.

Blowholes. A slide-in blow plate fits the bottom of the sand reservoir, as in Fig. 6.4. The blow plate has holes in it to allow the sand to be blown from the reservoir into the core box. These holes are about $\frac{3}{16}$ to $\frac{1}{2}$ in. in diameter, and are located in strategic places to fill the box completely. The center line of the box should be lined up with the center line of the blow plate. Blowholes may be located over large cavities and hard-to-fill places. If the box is flat and open at the top, the blowholes in the blow plate lead directly into the core cavity. If the core box is parted horizontally, however, the upper half must have blowholes drilled in it to connect the blow-plate holes to the core cavity. The two conditions are illustrated in Fig. 6.7. The number of blow-

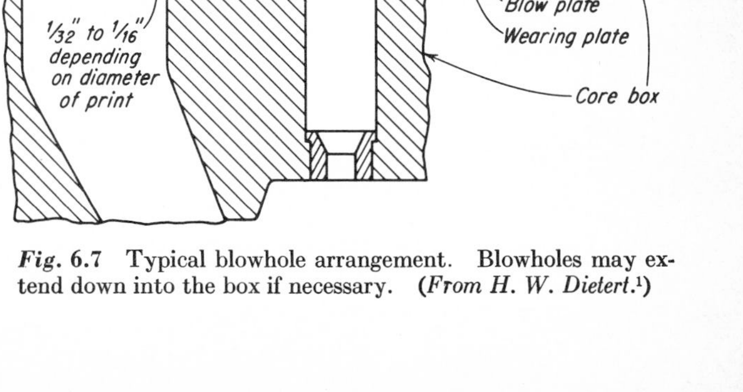

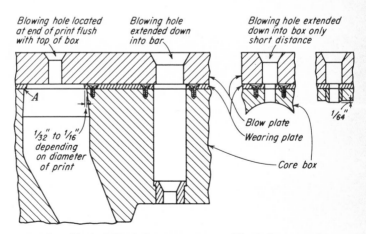

Fig. 6.7 Typical blowhole arrangement. Blowholes may extend down into the box if necessary. (*From H. W. Dietert.*[1])

holes required by a core box is a matter for experimentation. In general, too many holes are not desirable because the box fills before the sand has a chance to flow into all recesses in the box. Too few holes will prevent the box from filling because of channeling in the sand reservoir. The air bores a hole through the sand in the reservoir to the blowholes and then will carry no more sand with it. To control the wear problem, blowholes are often fitted with bushings. Since blowholes for various cores are located differently, each box must have its own blow plate or a means of adapting to it. Universal blow plates contain a large number of blowholes and vent holes which may be opened or blocked off in any position required.[5]

Core-box venting. Along with blowholes, proper venting is necessary to obtain an evenly rammed core by blowing. Vent holes, or other venting means, allow the air to be exhausted from the core box, leaving the sand behind. As the air-sand stream passes through the blowholes into the core-box cavity, it expands, there is a drop in velocity, and the sand is deposited as the air continues on its way out of the box. If there were no vents, sand would not be conveyed into the core box. The venting must be balanced with the blowhole area to get good ramming; over-all core softness indicates insufficient venting area if sufficient blowholes are present. Vent holes may be used to direct air flow (and sand) to a given section of a core box. An illustration of blowholes and venting in a two-piece core box is given in Fig. 6.8. The blowholes in this case are located over core prints so that they will not cause casting-surface imperfections. Also shown in Fig. 6.8 are vent grooves connected to holes which exhaust air at the parting surface. Some small boxes may be blown with vent grooves 0.005 to 0.008 in. deep as the only venting means. Vent plugs, slotted or screened, are used for venting on the core-box cavity. Slotted vent plugs are illustrated in Fig. 6.8. They may be driven into drilled holes and contoured to suit the core box. Screens lie flat, and hence leave spots on the core which may be objectionable. With screens, the venting area should be about two times the blowhole area, but with vent plugs a greater area is required.

Considerable core-box wear can occur because of sand abrasion in blowing. Areas under the blowholes and near vents may wear rapidly and cause the core to be oversize. This can be rectified by putting in inserts at wearing areas as they develop, as illustrated in Fig. 6.9. The core-box surface or parting also wears rapidly and usually is faced off with replaceable $\frac{1}{8}$- to $\frac{1}{4}$-in. steel or brass plate. The wear plate or wear strips may be replaced when wear has occurred. Wearing strips are illustrated in Fig. 6.10.

Core venting. Core boxes are often required to provide a means of venting the core itself. Cores are often largely surrounded by hot metal

***Fig.* 6.8** Blowholes, vents, and vent grooves in a two-piece core box for a valve-body core. (*Courtesy of W. Demmier and Bros.*)

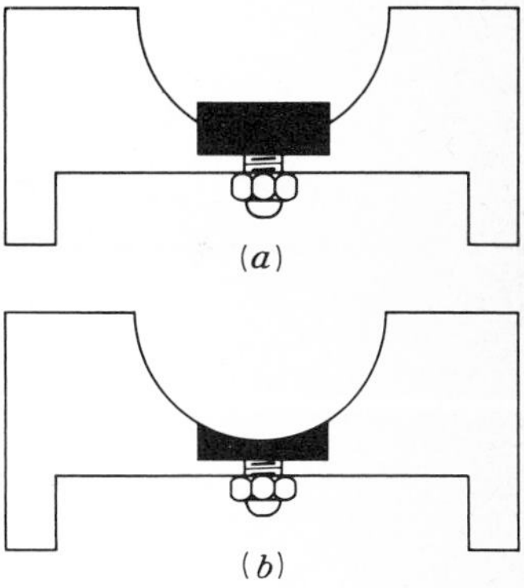

***Fig.* 6.9** Core-box insert used to compensate for wear under blowholes. (*a*) New insert bolted into hole in core box at location of wear; (*b*) insert after contouring to shape of box.

***Fig.* 6.10** Automotive core box and drier. Vent rods and reinforcing wires are shown in place. The vent rod is removed, and the core is drawn onto a plate after placing the drier under the barrel end of the core. (*From H. W. Dietert.*[1])

after the casting is poured. They are thus required to be sufficiently permeable to allow core gases to pass through the core and into the mold or atmosphere. Vent holes through the core assist in gas escape. The vent holes are usually made with wires or rods which are present when the box is blown but withdrawn before the core is stripped, leaving a vent hole. This type of core-box fitting is shown in Fig. 6.10. The core vent hole is formed by withdrawal of the rod protruding from the end of the core box in Fig. 6.10.

Reinforcing wires, arbors. Some cores require internal reinforcing to prevent breakage or shifting when the casting is poured. Wires or arbors within the sand serve this purpose. Figure 6.10 shows wires being used to support the barrel of the cylinder core. Wires should be surrounded with sand to keep them from fusing to the casting and making their removal difficult.

Core driers. If a core requires a drier for support (Figs. 2.9 and 6.12), the drier may sometimes be used as a part of the core box. The lower half of a horizontally split box may be used as the drier. Each time a core is blown, another core-box half is required. This practice eliminates the operation of removing the lower half of the core box and replacing it with a drier each time the core is stripped. A further refinement of this practice consists in attaching the upper core box to the sand reservoir and positioning the lower half below it. The operator then may only need to slide in the drier and remove the blown core and drier after the blow cycle. This practice requires shallow cores or clamping mechanisms with sufficient travel to clear the core and drier.

Stock-core Machines

Cores may be made by extrusion through a die with a stock-core machine operating on the meat-grinder principle. Small cylinders and hexagonal and rectangular cross-sectioned cores may be extruded. Stock cores are made in standard sizes and stored for future use. They may be cut to length and tapered if desired.

CORE BAKING

Cores are baked at temperatures up to about 650 F to develop the strength obtainable from the organic binders in the core sand. During baking, moisture is driven off first, holding the core temperature to 212 F. Then the core oil or other binder changes chemically and molecularly from a liquid to a solid by oxygen absorption and polymerization as the temperature rises to 400 to 500 F or more. The importance of temperature and time of baking is illustrated by its influence on core tensile strength as revealed in Fig. 6.11. Baking cycles of 2 to 6 hr at 400 to 460 F are quite commonly used. Proper baking is essential if a core is to perform satisfactorily when the metal is poured. Underbaked cores give off much gas and can cause a variety of defects. Overbaked cores may collapse too soon and break or erode before the casting is solidified. When baked, a core-oil-bonded core assumes a nut-brown color, darkness indicating overbaking and lightness underbaking. Proper baking depends upon good baking equipment if the core sand mixture is correct.

Core-baking Equipment

Equipment for baking cores may be classified as follows:

- I. Core ovens
  - *A*. Batch-type
  - *B*. Continuous
    - 1. Horizontal
    - 2. Vertical
- II. Dielectric bakers
- III. Radiant bakers

The various types of baking equipment are used to advantage in different ways.

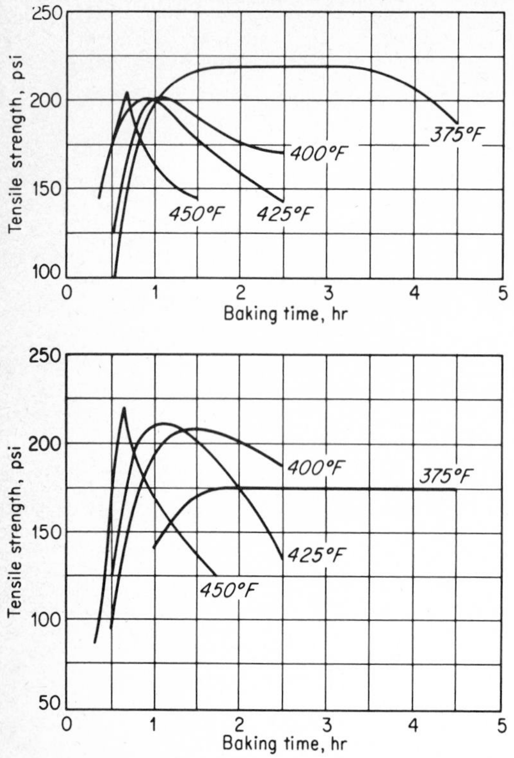

***Fig.* 6.11** Influence of temperature and time of baking on tensile strength developed by two different core-sand mixtures. (*From H. W. Dietert.*[1])

Core Ovens

Batch-type core ovens are useful for handling a wide variety of work in small- and medium-sized castings. The drawer-type oven shown in Fig. 6.12 is useful for baking batches of small cores. The drawers make it possible to bake cores of varying size and thickness for different lengths of time suitable to the core size. Ovens of this type are usually gas- or oil-fired. Larger batch ovens, such as that shown in Fig. 6.13, are loaded by placing cores on racks. The size of core is not limited in this case. The large batch ovens are fired with gas, oil, or coal. They may have separate firing chambers for heating the air, and should have circulating fans to obtain a uniform temperature throughout the baking chamber. For baking of most cores to proceed properly, an adequate supply of fresh air is required since oxygen is needed for many core oils to harden.

Continuous core ovens are conveyorized so that core racks may continually enter and leave the oven. A vertical oven is schematically illustrated in Fig. 6.14. The cores are loaded on racks on one side of the oven tower and unloaded on the opposite side. Horizontal ovens, usually located overhead, are also conveyorized. These are loaded at

***Fig.* 6.12** Drawer-type batch oven for baking cores. (*From H. W. Dietert.*[1])

one end as illustrated in Fig. 6.15, provide a certain temperature and time of travel in the oven, and then are unloaded at the opposite end. Continuous ovens require that all sizes of cores receive the same cycle of baking. Small cores thus may be overbaked when the large cores are properly baked. By adjusting the core sand mixture and the placement in loading, however, this problem can be largely overcome. Continuous ovens lend themselves readily to production layouts since they will handle a steady stream of cores and deliver them baked for further work. A coremaking and baking flow diagram is shown in Fig. 6.15.

Dielectric Baking

A relatively recent development is the dielectric baking of cores. Dielectric baking depends upon the principle that heating of nonconducting materials on a molecular scale can be caused in a rapidly fluctuating electrostatic field. The heating system may comprise a pair of flat-plate electrodes to which is applied a rapidly oscillating alternating-current voltage. Plate voltage of 1000 to 5000 volts and frequencies up to 20 million cycles are employed. The cores are passed between the electrodes long enough for heating to complete the baking process. Dielectric bakers

***Fig.* 6.13** Batch-type core oven loaded with core racks. (*From H. W. Dietert.*[1])

are conveyorized, with the cores traveling at such a rate that the time under the electrodes is sufficient for baking. The conveying belt passing through the baking tunnel is made of steel links and is used as the bottom electrode as well as a means of moving the core plates. The top electrode is an aluminum plate. The belt may be driven at 0 to 10 fpm, depending on the core size, with actual baking time varying from 20 to 30 sec to 2 or 3 min. Baking dielectrically requires the use of special binders, namely, thermosetting resins such as urea or phenolformaldehyde, melamines, resorcinols, or blends of these. The thermosetting resins develop strength immediately when they are heated to 200 to 300 F. An extended holding period at temperatures such as that required for core oils is not needed. Core sand mixtures for dielectric baking are considered in Chap. 7, but it should be recognized here that the mixture is an important part of the successful use of dielectric bakers. Since time at temperature is not required, baking time under the electrodes is governed mainly by the period required to heat the core sufficiently to drive off its water. Water is the ingredient of the sand which is most easily dielectrically heated. Hence, when the water has been driven off (steam at 212 F), there is relatively little further heating and the binder has thermoset and de-

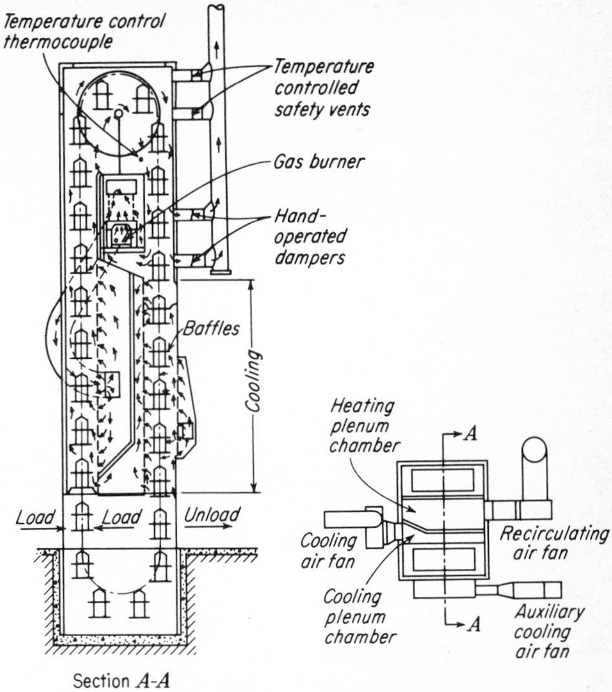

Fig. 6.14 **Schematic diagram of vertical core oven. (*From H. W. Dietert.*[1])**

veloped its strength. The water percentage in the core mix and the size of the core are thus the principal factors governing baking time. Since little temperature rise occurs after the water is driven off, there is virtually no danger of overbaking the cores.

Core driers for dielectric baking. Metal driers or core plates are not used to support cores which are dielectrically baked. Voltage failure, arcing, or flashing can occur if any conductor narrows the gap between the electrodes. Metal core plates also interfere with potential distribution in the electrostatic field and disturb the heating cycle. As a substitute, Transite (a cement-bonded asbestos) is suitable for core plates. Plywood is also used. Driers can be made of plastics. Since baking is done rapidly, fewer driers are required in dielectric baking as compared with core ovens. Other metal objects such as core wires, arbors, or chills can also cause flashover trouble, especially if they are in a vertical position, where flashover of voltage from the electrodes may occur. In the horizontal position they are unlikely to have this effect. However, many cores containing reinforcing wire can be baked without trouble.

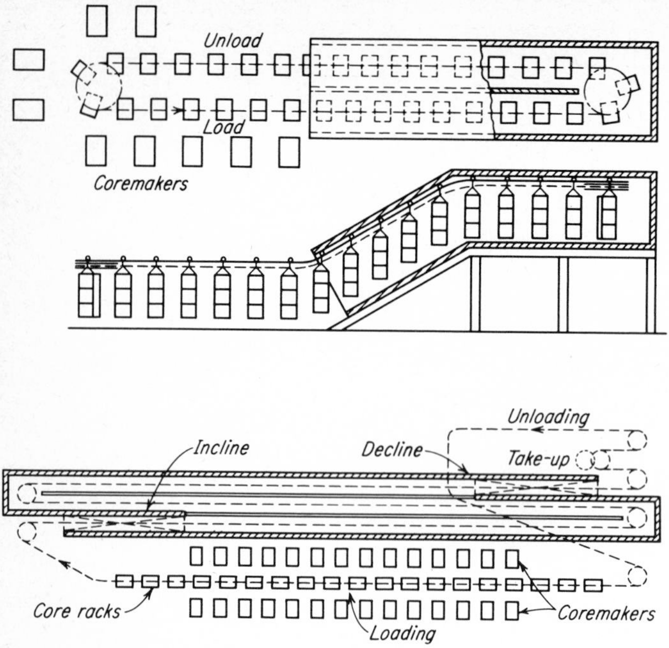

Fig. 6.15 Layouts for continuous production of cores. (*From H. W. Dietert.*[1])

Hot-core-box Processes

Baking of cores can be eliminated in the hot-core-box processes. Shell molding and furan resin coremaking accomplish this in heated core boxes. Sand is transferred into the box by gravity free fall in simple boxes and by blowing into complex boxes. Metal boxes, commonly gray cast iron, are heated to 400 F or higher. As described earlier in Chap. 3, the thermosetting resin-sand mixture forms a hard shell in contact with the hot box. The unheated sand interior may be drained out to make hollow shell cores. When furan resins are used, exothermic polymerization causes baking throughout after the hardened core is withdrawn from the hot box.[1,2,7,8] Wires and arbors can often be eliminated by these processes because the core is hardened in the box and has sufficient strength immediately for handling and use in the mold.

FINISHING OF CORES

After the cores are baked, a certain number of operations are performed on them before they can be set in the mold. These operations are termed *core finishing.* Finishing work may be classified as follows:

1. Cleaning
2. Sizing (making it dimensionally accurate)
3. Core assembly
4. Inspection

Cleaning Operations

Cleaning operations include all work done on the core except sizing or assembly of cores. Work included in this category is trimming, brushing, venting, coating, and mudding. Trimming consists in removing fins, bumps, or other sand projections by rubbing them or filing with an emery stone, core file, or other abrasive tool. Fins arise from loose joints or loose pieces in the core box. Blowholes and vent plugs often leave marks on the core which must be smoothed off. Brushing cores with a brush of moderate stiffness is performed to remove loose sand. Brushing is required on cores which, before baking, have been bedded in sand rather than on a core drier.

Cores may be coated with refractory or protective materials which improve their resistance to molten metal or produce a better casting. These coatings may be applied by spraying, dipping, or swabbing. The subject of core coating will be considered in Chap. 7. Mudding is a localized coating used to make the core completely smooth. Graphite or red talc moistened with water to a putty consistency may be used to fill up any cavities, rough spots, soft rammed areas, or the joint lines of assembled cores. Another mud consists of 94% silica flour, 3% western bentonite, and 3% dextrin moistened to a putty with water. The mud is applied by hand, rubbed into the cavities, and smoothed off. Cores which have been coated or rubbed may cause trouble with defects in the casting because of steam evolution when the metal is poured. Drying in a core oven for 20 min to 1 hr can eliminate this problem. With some core coatings, air drying is often adequate.

Venting of cores is sometimes included as a cleaning operation. Baked cores which are to be assembled may be vented into the core prints by scratching grooves on the surfaces to be joined. More often grooves or vent holes are put into the core before it is baked, as, for example, in Figs. 6.2*b* and 6.8. Then it may be desirable to inspect the vents to see that they are open. Small holes may be reamed open with a wire or rod. Wax vent holes are made by ramming up a string of wax in the core. The wax melts out when the core is baked and leaves a vent hole. It is frequently necessary during cleaning to open this hole to complete the vent.

Sizing Operations

Sizing is done to make cores dimensionally accurate. Sizing usually involves gauging the core to see if its size is correct and then removing material. Sizing is thus in part dimensional inspection. Gauges may be used to check critical dimensions. Templates, pieces of sheet metal cut out to the contour required of the core, may be used to determine whether the core has sagged or slumped during baking. The cores may be inserted in a gauging fixture which will check a number of dimensions at once. In some cores with large flat surfaces exact height is necessary so that casting-wall thickness and location are accurate. Such cores may be made slightly oversize and ground to correct height. This may be done by hand filing with a scraper or on a core-grinding machine. In either case the core is put into a fixture which positions the core and the excess material is removed. Hand-sizing operations may be performed on cores which are slightly out of shape. Crooked core plates or driers, vibration during baking, and weak sands or ramming may cause cores to be off dimension and are good reason for gauging and sizing.

Core Assembly

Some cores are of one piece and may be set directly into the mold after cleaning and sizing. Other cores are assembled of two or more pieces before they can be used. Core assemblies may be held together by pasting, bolting, or leading.

Pasting is most commonly used on small work. A core paste, usually a proprietary mixture of talc, dextrin, flour, molasses, water, or other ingredients, is applied to the surfaces to be joined. The paste may be put on with a paste bulb, brush, the finger, or by means of dipping with a pasting fixture. A pasting fixture consists of a metal rack which is lowered into a tank of paste and then raised against the prepositioned core, depositing paste at the desired points. Care must be exercised to avoid sealing off vent holes and grooves when cores are pasted. The pasted surfaces are pressed together and allowed to dry so that a strong assembly results. Often it is desirable to mud the joint lines to prevent metal penetration and give a smoother casting surface. Pasted and mudded cores are best if dried to avoid the danger of blow defects in the castings.

Cores may be bolted together if pasting does not produce a sufficiently strong assembly. Bolting is useful in larger core work. Recessed holes are left in the cores so that they may be bolted together. The bolt and nut heads are covered over with a core plug or mud.

Joining cores by leading is occasionally used where a strong joint is desired in small cores. Cavities are left in the core parts to be joined.

These are filled with molten lead. When the lead freezes, it holds the core together, just as a bolt would.

Inspection

As a final finishing operation, the cores may be inspected before they are sent to the molding floor or core storage. Sometimes gauging is done at this point to check the final dimensional accuracy. The cores should be smooth, free of loose sand or projections, mudded if necessary, and dry, to be ready for the core-setting operation.

CORE SETTING

Core setting is the operation of placing cores in molds. Cores must be of correct size and positioned properly with respect to the mold cavity so that cored-out cavities are in their required location in the casting. Cores are positioned in the mold by core prints. When the metal is poured, cores are buoyed up and may rise unless they are securely anchored. Good core setting then involves advance planning so that the cores will be correctly positioned and firmly held when the metal is poured.

Small cores are placed in the mold by hand, as in Fig. 3.3. Larger cores may require hoist or crane service as in Fig. 6.16*b*. Sometimes a number of cores are assembled and set in at one time. This usually requires an assembly fixture such as that shown in Fig. 6.16*a* for automotive-motor-block cores. The core assembly may be bolted together or held together by the fixture, as in Fig. 6.16*b*, when it is transferred to the mold. When a number of cores are assembled, dimensional errors are additive and some kind of fixture or gauge, as in Fig. 6.16*a*, is necessary.

Location of Cores

Cores may require positive location in three directions, one vertically and two horizontally. Horizontal location can be based on locating surfaces in the mold cavity or on the flask pins. In Fig. 6.16*b*, the cores are positioned by the assembly fixture relative to the flask pins. Locating cores in that way requires that the mold cavity also bear a fixed position relative to the flask pins and so must the pattern. Thus the flask pins and bushing are reference points for locating both mold cavity and cores. This usually requires rigid or tight flasks and constant attention to flask pins and bushings. Loose pins and bushings will allow shifts of the cope and core-setting fixture and consequently cause dimensional inaccuracy of

***Fig.* 6.16** (*a*) Locating fixture for assembling motor-block cores. (*b*) Locating fixture used as transfer fixture to set cores in mold. (*From H. W. Dietert.*[1])

the casting. A more common practice of locating is to use surfaces in the mold cavity to position the cores. The ends of the core may butt up against the mold core prints, or a locating bead may be placed around the prints. The tapered arrangement is not nearly so positive as the bead. If three or more core prints extend into the mold, these alone may be sufficient to position the core. In any event, worn or inaccurate core prints on the core, the core box, or pattern or in the mold cause sloppy fits and may permit the core to shift or rise when the metal is poured. Horizontal location often, though not always, also establishes the vertical location of cores, especially when a print fits into both the cope and drag mold-cavity surfaces. However, vertical location may be easily upset when the metal is poured, because of buoyancy of the core.

Chaplets

Chaplets are metal forms placed between mold and core surfaces. Various types of chaplets are illustrated in Fig. 6.17. They are often used to overcome vertical movement of the core due to buoyancy. Long thin

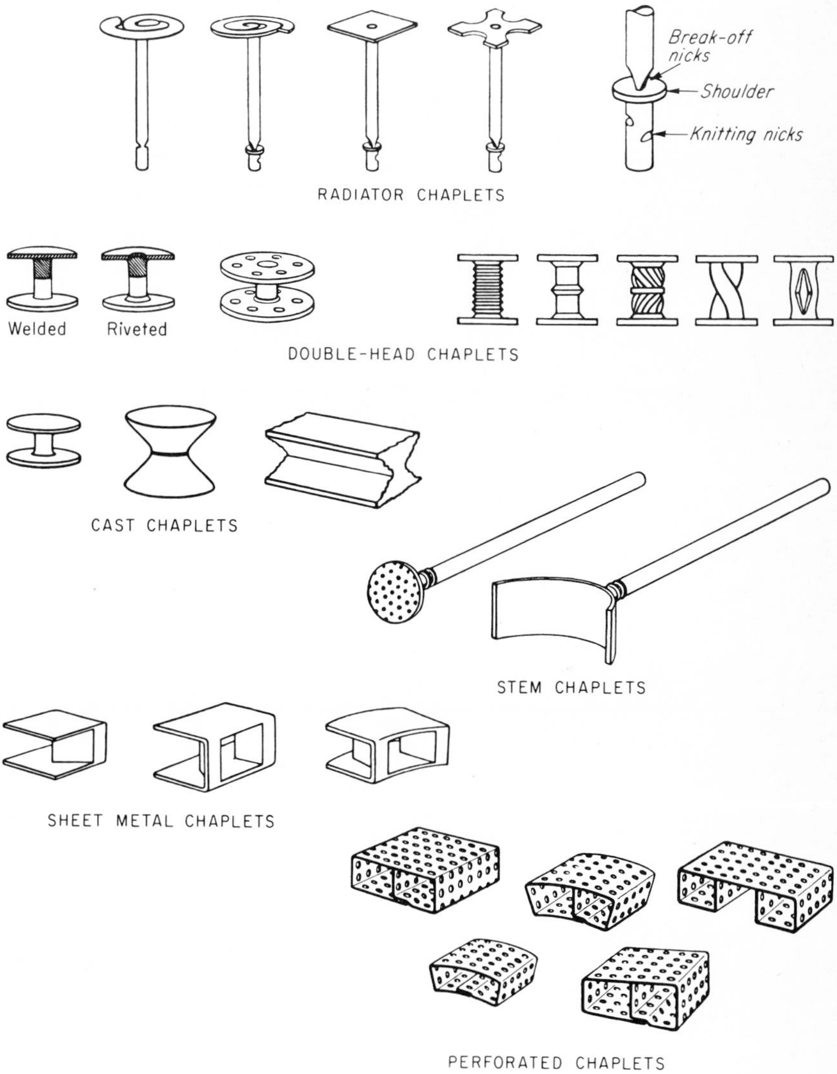

Fig. 6.17 Chaplets. (*From H. W. Dietert.*[1])

cores tend to float more easily than short chunky cores. If the metal is molten for a long time, the core has greater opportunity to float, shift, or crack. Buoyancy is due to the weight of liquid metal displaced by the core, an application of the familiar Archimedes' principle. The buoyant force on a core is equal to the weight of the liquid displaced minus the weight of the core. Cores weigh approximately 100 lb per cu ft. If molten iron is used as the liquid and its weight taken as 450 lb per cu ft, the buoyant force on a cubic foot of core sand surrounded by iron is 450 — 100, or 350 lb. Since this is true regardless of the submerged depth of the core, a ratio between the weight of the core and the buoyant force exists, and is 350 ÷ 100, or 3.5. Ratios of buoyant force

Table 6.2 Ratio of buoyant force to weight of core*

Material	Ratio
Aluminum	0.66
Brass	4.25
Copper	4.50
Gray iron	3.50
Steel	3.90

*From H. W. Dietert.[1]

to core weight are given in Table 6.2 for different metals. Thus, by weighing a core and multiplying by the proper ratio, the buoyant force, if it is wholly submerged, may be quickly determined. Cores not completely surrounded by metal necessitate an estimation of the submerged weight to determine the lifting force. Cores in aluminum castings will not float.

To cause the core to float, the lifting force on the core must exceed the hold-down force of the core prints. Molding sand in a core print will support loading to about 5 psi, according to one expert.[1] Thus the force relationships can be expressed as follows:[1]

$$\text{Core buoyancy, lb} - \text{core-print support, lb} = \text{unsupported load, lb} \quad (1)$$

$$\text{Core-print support, lb} = \text{core-print area, sq in.} \times 5 \text{ psi} \quad (2)$$

If the unsupported load has a negative value, the core has no tendency to float. If the unsupported load has a positive value, the force on the core will cause it to crush the sand in the core prints and move upward. This can be prevented by placing chaplets in the mold cavity between the cope and the core, i.e., by increasing the supporting area. Since the chaplet usually rests on molding sand, the chaplet head will sink into the sand if it is overloaded. The required chaplet area for supporting the core can then be calculated as follows:

$$\text{Unsupported load} \times 0.20 = \text{chaplet area required, sq in.} \tag{3}$$

since each pound on the chaplets requires 0.20 sq in. of chaplet area.

The foregoing formulas are based on a molding-sand strength of 5 psi, chaplets which will not weaken before the metal freezes, and cores which will not crush under the chaplet load. Small cores may be rammed up in the cope to seat chaplets and take up the load from the chaplet head, or the conditions may be modified in other ways. Placement of the chaplets to distribute the lifting load properly is also very important.

Chaplets for ferrous alloys are generally made of low-carbon steel and are tin-coated or otherwise protected from rusting. When the casting is poured, the chaplets become hot and bond to the casting by diffusion processes. Since chaplets span the section thickness, they may result in leaks unless bonding is good. Rusty or wet chaplets may cause this difficulty.

Closing the Mold

When the cores have been set, the mold can be closed. Since some sand falls into the mold during core setting, it may be blown out with air. Strainer cores or other gate cores may be required, as well as those for cored casting cavities. When cores extend into the cope, they may loosen sand and drop it into the drag unless positioning is accurate and flask pins and bushings fit well. When the cope is closed, mold inspection is completed.

CORE APPLICATIONS

It was pointed out earlier that cores are used in many ways besides their principal one of coring out internal casting cavities. Strainer, gate, pouring cup, and riser cores are described in Chaps. 9, 16, and 20. Core-sand molds are discussed in Chap. 3. In centrifugal castings, the strength of core molds may be necessary to resist the centrifugal force of the metal as the mold is spun. Stack molds can be made by piling up core slabs. These can be either centrifugally or statically cast. Sometimes cores are used for increasing production from match-plate molding. A slab core positioned between the cope and drag as shown in Fig. 6.18 makes it possible to double the castings output from one mold. In certain castings metal forms may be combined with cores to produce holes above or below the parting line which could not otherwise be readily molded. Figure 6.19 illustrates the use of hinge tubes and metal forms which are molded

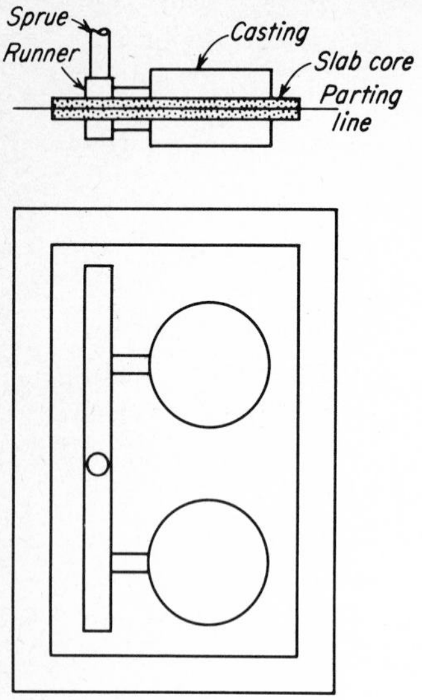

***Fig.* 6.18** Slab core used at parting line to double the number of castings made per mold.

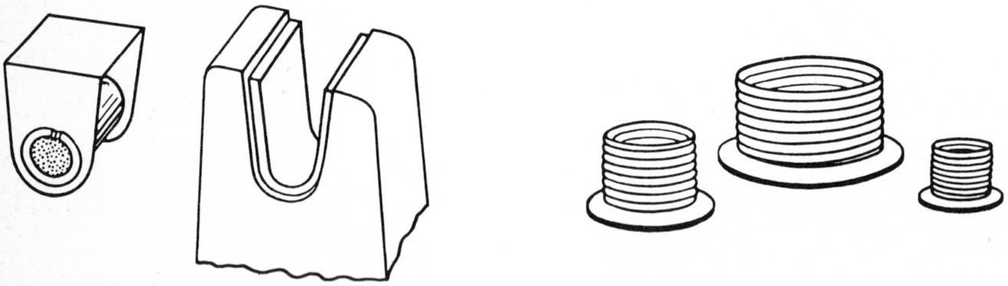

***Fig.* 6.19** Metal chaplets, or forms for casting hinge holes, threads, and lifting bars. (*From H. W. Dietert.*[1])

into place to make cored holes or other forms. Threaded holes can also be made in this way. Cores and core forms greatly increase the versatility of molding and casting operations.

CORE-SAND DISPOSAL

When molds are poured and shaken out, a certain percentage of the core sand enters the molding sand. The amount depends on the size of the cores, the mass of the castings, the degree to which the core binder burns out and frees the sand, and the severity of shakeout. Excessive contamination of molding sand by core sand is considered undesirable. The burned-out sand has an adhering coating of partially decomposed organic binder, which does not bond well with clay in the molding sand. The molding sand thus deteriorates. Therefore efforts are made to separate much of the core sand from the molding sand in the shakeout operations. Large cores which hold together may be removed completely by remaining with the casting. These cores are removed separately by a core-knockout operation, and this sand does not enter the molding sand. Core pieces which become mixed with the molding sand are screened out in the molding-sand system (Chap. 5). In spite of these precautions, some core sand becomes mixed with the molding sand. Its harmful effects on the sand can be partly mitigated if the core-sand grain size and distribution are the same as or close to those of the molding sand. Hence, in many synthetic-sand systems, the same base silica sand grains are used for the molding sands and the cores. This is not always possible, however. Core-sand admixture to the molding sand is particularly harmful if it occurs in large slugs at one time, since it contains no clay or other ingredients, as does the molding sand.

Core Knockout

The most rapid removal of cores can occur when the core binders burn out completely and allow the sand to run freely out of the casting cavities. The cores may then be vibrated or hammered, and the sand will flow out. Hollow cores such as shell and furan cores usually collapse readily. Many simple cores are removed in handling or in cleaning. Pneumatic hammers may be used in hand-knockout work. In large castings, the very hard strong cores are difficult to remove, and special equipment may be required. Hydroblasting is one means: A stream of water under a pressure of 1500 to 7000 psi is directed at the casting in a special blasting room. The core is washed out of the casting gradually. Many adaptations of this method of core removal have been made. Both the exterior and interior of the casting may be cleaned in this way. Wires and arbors greatly hinder the knockout of cores by any method, and so should be used only when necessary.

The core sand coming from the knockout must be disposed of in some way. Wet methods of knockout require that the sand be dewatered. It may then be hauled away to dumps or reclaimed for reuse. Burned-out sand and lumps from dry-core removal may also be hauled away to dumps. Because of haulage costs, many foundries have become interested in reclaiming the sand for reuse. A discussion of sand reclamation is outside the scope of this textbook, however. See Ref. 16 for an extensive treatment of sand reclamation.

BIBLIOGRAPHY

1. H. W. Dietert, "Foundry Core Practice," American Foundrymen's Society, 1950.

2. R. L. S. Andrews, "Shell Process Foundry Practices," American Foundrymen's Society, 1964.
3. W. E. Mason, Metal Core Box Equipment, *Trans. AFS,* vol. 65, p. 443, 1957.
4. A. M. Clark, Principles of Core Blowing, *Trans. AFS,* vol. 64, p. 577, 1956.
5. Z. Madacey, Pattern and Core Box Equipment for Blowing Foundry Sands, *Trans. AFS,* vol. 68, p. 193, 1960.
6. W. E. Sicha, Aluminum Pattern Castings, *Trans. AFS,* vol. 69, p. 479, 1961.
7. E. E. Harkess, Hot Core Box Design and Engineering, *Trans. AFS,* vol. 69, p. 123, 1961.
8. P. Jasson, Core Production in Hot Core Boxes, *Trans. AFS,* vol. 69, p. 287, 1961.
9. C. A. Barnett, Modern Foundry Core and Mold Ovens, *Trans. AFS,* vol. 57, 1949.
10. E. Blake, Design of Core Boxes and Driers for Core Blowers, *Foundry,* vol. 79, June, 1951.
11. Z. Madacey, Core Blowing as a Factor in a Semiproduction Foundry, *Foundry,* vol. 71, June–July, 1943.
12. J. W. Cable, Recent Advances in Dielectric Core Baking, *Trans. AFS,* vol. 59, p. 159, 1951.
13. R. F. Lincoln, Arrangements of Cores, Blowholes, and Vents for Blowing Purposes, *Trans. AFS,* vol. 51, June, 1943.
14. H. M. Gade, Core Blowing, *Foundry,* vol. 78, May, 1950.
15. E. J. Jory, Core Practice as Related to Malleable Foundry Losses, *Trans. AFS,* vol. 59, p. 300, 1951.
16. American Foundrymen's Society, Symposium on Sand Reclamation, *Trans. AFS,* vol. 61, 1953.
17. American Foundrymen's Society, "Molding Methods and Materials," 1963.

7

Core Materials

In molds, the cores must withstand the severest abuse. In spite of being submerged in hot metal, the core must resist erosion, breakage, thermal shock, and metal penetration, as well as retain its dimensional location and produce no casting defects. Yet cores should not be so permanent that their removal from the casting becomes too difficult. These requirements demand that cores be made of suitable materials. Core sands are established as the most versatile of materials for cores. However, cores may be made of metal, ceramics, and green molding sand.

CORE SANDS

Core sands may be simply defined as sand mixtures suitable for cores. To satisfy this definition, the sand mixture is expected to have certain properties, among them:

1. Green strength adequate for the operations of coremaking
2. Response to core baking so that strength, hardness, and other properties are brought out by the baking operation
3. After baking, adequate strength for handling, core setting, and retention of dimensional accuracy
4. Resistance to the action of the molten metal, i.e., erosion, fusion, thermal shock, and venting ability to pass off gases
5. Ease of removal from the solidified casting
6. Retention of desirable properties during periods when baked cores are stored

The above properties pertain particularly to conventional core sands, which are still the most commonly used. Other core-sand mixtures such as shell, furan resin, air-set, and silicate sands need not require baking response since they may not be baked.

CORE-SAND INGREDIENTS

Core-sand mixtures consist of sand grains, binders for green and cured strength, and other additives used for special purposes.

Base Sands

Silica is the basis of most sands used for cores, and zircon, olivine, and others are also used. The word "sand" in foundry terminology may refer to any granular material of 0.05 to 1.0 mm average particle size. Some properties of the common sands used in core mixtures are compared in Table 7.1. Of importance are refractory behavior, including fusion point and dimensional and chemical stability with temperature change, heat-transfer capability, and sieve analysis.

The higher fusion point, higher bulk density, and thermal capacity of zircon and olivine are revealed in Tables 7.1*a* and *b*. These may be reasons for their use in cores where silica does not perform satisfactorily. Chemical stability refers to inertness, or absence of chemical reactions.

Silica may be reduced by some metals such as magnesium or may react with others such as iron to form silicates. However, silica is the most widely used base sand.

Sieve Analysis

Sieve analysis has been discussed in conjunction with molding sands (Chap. 5). Some typical core-sand sieve analyses are given in Table 7.2*b*. The table shows that coarser sands, and those with a narrow size distribution, have much higher base permeability. Core sands are commonly 3-sieve sands for this reason. Coarse white silica sands of high refractoriness are much used for steel foundry cores. The finer bank and lake sands are more frequently used for cast irons and nonferrous work. Blending of sands, one coarser and one finer, as was shown in Table 5.7, may be used to increase the size distribution and obtain greater strength, with some sacrifice of permeability. The increased grain surface area in contact when wider grain size distribution prevails, 4- or 5-sieve sand for example, permits the binders to develop more strength. For example, from Table 7.2 a mixture of 60 to 65 per cent Michigan No. 3 lake sand and 35 to 40 per cent Michigan No. 4 bank sand may be used for some core work in gray iron and malleable foundries. The same blend bonded with clay can be used as a molding sand, as shown in Table 5.7.

Density

Heat-transfer capability, resistance to metal penetration, surface finish, bonded strength, and other properties of cores are much influenced by the bulk density of the aggregate. The bulk density of a silica sand depends on sieve analysis and particle packing. Possible modes of packing and the densities achieved expressed as per cent of solids are illustrated in Fig. 7.1. Measurements of bulk density reveal that typical

Table 7.1a Properties of common granular refractories used in core-sand mixtures

Property	Silica	Zircon	Olivine	Carbon	Chamotte
Vibrated bulk density, lb/cu ft....	110 (95–125)	188	128	68	90–110
Specific gravity...	2.65	4.6–4.7	3.25–3.40	....	2.5–2.7
Melting point, °F..	3119	3452–4622	3200–3450	6400	3100–3200
Mean specific heat	0.275	0.131	0.22–0.33	....	0.25
Temperature, °F..	0–2400	0–2400	0–2800	....	1800
Mean thermal conductivity, Btu/hr/sq ft/°F/in. .	0.3–0.6	0.9–1.0	0.6–0.70	....	0.6–0.70
Temperature, °F..	0–2800	2000	2000	....	2000
Chemical formula	SiO_2	$ZrSiO_4$	$2MgO \cdot SiO_2$ 84%, $2FeO \cdot SiO_2$ 9%, balance enstatite serpentines, chromite	C	Granular, calcined, aluminous fire clay
Thermal expansion, in./in. to 2000 F	0.020	0.005	0.015	0.008	0.007

Table 7.1b Typical sieve analysis

	Portage 420		Wedron 5030		No. 70 olivine, ret	Zircon, ret
	Ret*	Cum†	Ret	Cum		
U.S. No. sieve						
20						
30..................	2.2	2.2				
40..................	18.1	20.3	1.2	1.2		
50..................	30.7	51.0	30.4	31.6	26.2	
70..................	25.2	76.2	48.2	79.8	31.0	0.60
100..................	15.7	91.9	17.8	97.6	23.7	11.66
140..................	6.0	97.9	2.0	99.6	9.5	48.02
200..................	1.7	99.6	0.40	....	5.8	39.57
270..................	.....	......	......	....	2.2	
Pan..................	0.4	1000	......	....	1.6	0.15
% AFS clay...........	0.50	......	0.50			
AFS No...............	51.3	......	51.6	....	69.0	112.3

*Ret—retained on the sieve.

†Cum—cumulative; total on the sieve.

*Table 7.2 Sand grains of typical core sands**

Characteristics	Source										
	New Jersey		Michigan				Wisconsin				Illinois
			Bank		Lake or dune		Berlin				
	1	6	1	4†	3	7	1	3	Doyles-town	Portage screened	Ottawa coarse
Sieve analysis:											
6											
12											
20	1.7	...	0.10	...	...	0.20	...	...	...	0.60	
30	15.4	...	0.30	0.20	0.1	5.80	0.2	...	...	4.0	11
40	30.1	...	1.10	0.8	1.5	41.6	0.6	1.2	1.0	13.40	74
50	33.5	...	8.7	5.0	17.5	48.2	5.2	12.5	7.0	24.40	14
70	18.8	0.3	27.2	14.0	54.3	4.0	24.5	43.6	32.0	34.40	1
100	1.5	15.3	31.2	29.0	24.9	...	28.9	24.5	36.0	41.60	
140	...	41.6	21.6	36.0	1.10	...	27.6	12.5	18.3	5.20	
200	...	31.6	5.10	10.0	0.10	...	9.40	3.3	4.20	0.40	
270	...	7.8	2.30	4.30	0.10	...	1.6	0.9	0.60	1.80	
Pan	...	3.4	0.30	0.30	0.20	...	0.7	0.8	0.40	0.20	
AFS Fineness, No.	36.4	124	75	90	54	45	83	68	72	54	30.5
AFS clay, %	...	...	2.10	0.7	0.3	0.20	1.3	0.7	0.50	1.0	
Base permeability	300	58	70	45	150	260	80	145	120	200	650
Grain shape	Rounded	Subangular	Subangular	Subangular	Subangular	Subangular	...	...	...	...	Rounded
Type	Silica	Silica	Bank	Bank	Lake	Lake	Bank	Bank	Silica	Silica	Silica
Typical use	Steel, large	Ferrous, brass, light	Blending, nonferrous, light, medium		Gray, malleable, nonferrous	Gray, malleable	Gray, malleable, nonferrous	Gray, malleable, nonferrous	Gray, malleable	Ferrous, steel	Steel

* Adapted from H. W. Dietert.[5]

† Chemical analysis in Table 5.1.

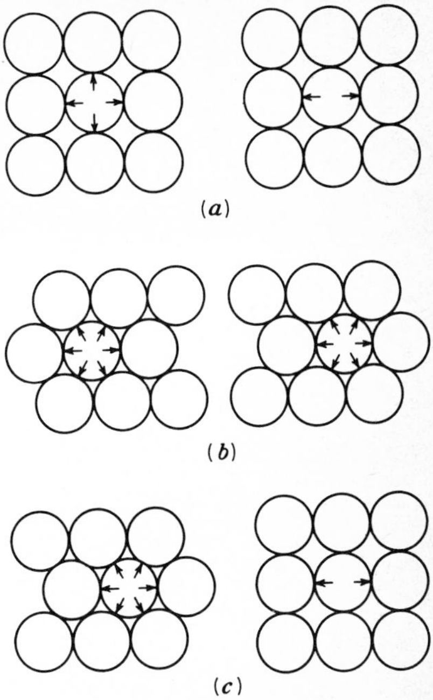

***Fig.* 7.1** **Sand-grain packing configurations.**

foundry sands pack to about 55 to 75 per cent solids, commonly about 62 per cent.[1,2] Sieve analysis, particularly size distribution, affects bulk density by raising it as the number of screens over which the sand spread increases from 1 to 10, as shown by Fig. 7.2.

To use Fig. 7.2, a curve relating AFS number and average particle size is needed as in Fig. 7.3. To predict bulk density, the AFS number is calculated from the sieve analysis. The number of screens exceeding 10 per cent retained is determined from the sieve analysis, one additional screen being added for each 10 per cent total on the screens having less than 10 per cent.

The average particle size for the AFS number of the sand is determined from Fig. 7.3. The bulk density is then determined from Fig. 7.2. For example, the P420 sand in Table 7.1*b* has an AFS number of 51.3. Average particle size from Fig. 7.3 is 0.308 mm. From the sieve analysis it is seen to be a 4½-screen sand. On Fig. 7.2, at 0.308 mm and 4- to 5-screen, spread bulk density is 112 to 114.5 cu ft.

Blending of sands is sometimes practiced to increase bulk density. In blending, the sands used must spread out the sieve analysis if the density is to be increased appreciably. This points to the effectiveness of silica flour (325-mesh) for raising bulk density, as shown in Fig. 7.4. References 1 to 3 and their bibliographies describe further principles in connection with particle packing.

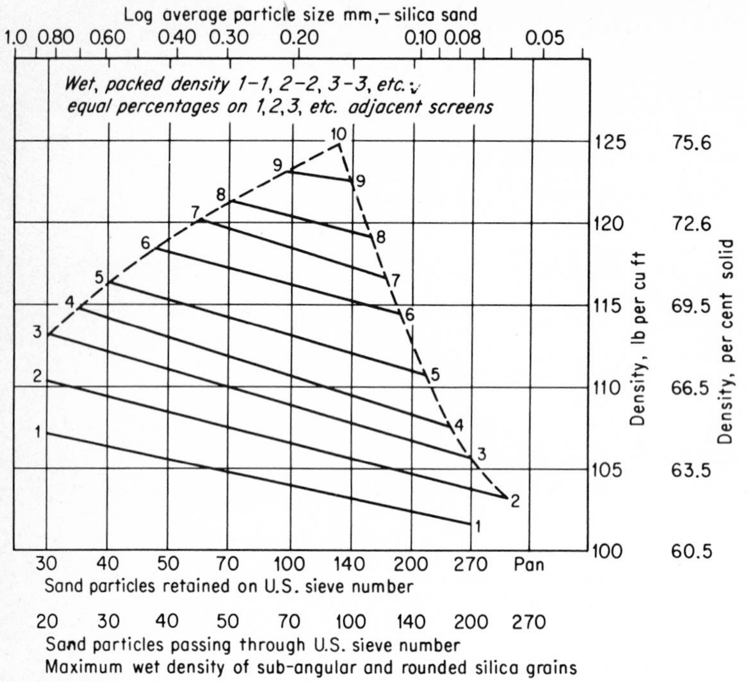

***Fig.* 7.2** Empirical relationship of vibrated bulk density of sand to AFS number and average particle size when the sand grains are equally distributed on the number of sieves indicated for each line on the graph.

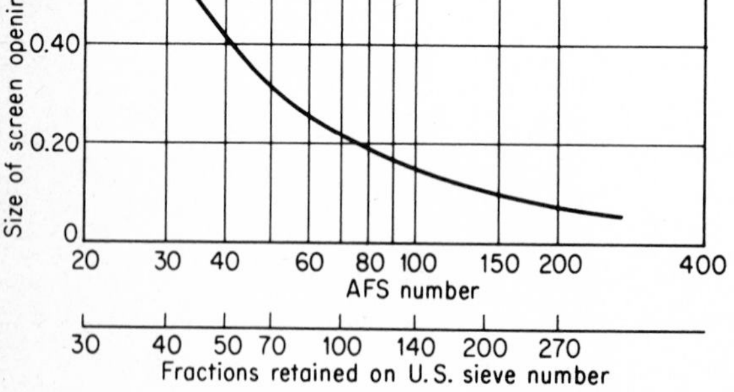

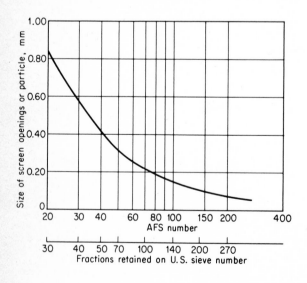

***Fig.* 7.3** Relationship of AFS number and average particle size.

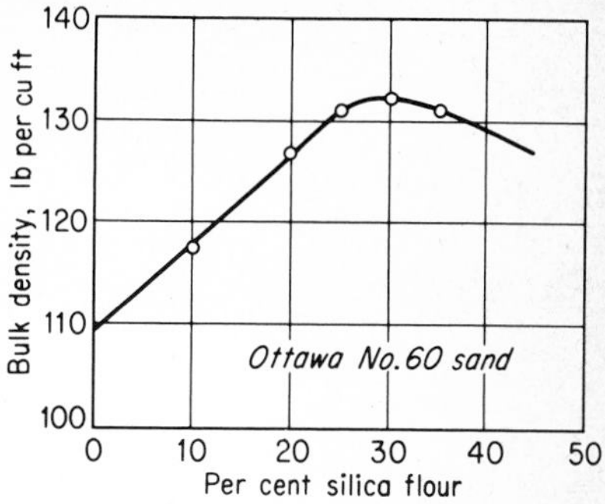

Fig. 7.4 **Effect of silica flour on increasing bulk density of 60 AFS silica sand.**

Binders

Core binders serve to hold the sand grains together and impart strength, resistance to erosion and to breakage, and degree of collapsibility. They may be classed as organic, inorganic, and metallo-organic binders. Organic binders are combustible, and are destroyed by heat. Hence they contribute a degree of collapsibility to the core-sand mixture. Inorganic binders are not combustible and may have considerable strength at high temperatures, may have resistance to erosion, and may be relatively noncollapsible, depending on their nature.

Organic Binders

Core oil, cereal, resins, plastics, pitch, dextrin, molasses, rosin, rosin oil, lignin, casein, gelatin, and other materials are used as organic binders. Tables 7.3*a* and *b* present data on common organic binders.

Core oil. Core oils in amounts of 0.5 to 3.0 per cent by weight are used in many core-sand mixtures. Core oils contribute little to the green strength of core sands, but are the most commonly used binder for baked strength. Core oils are manufactured by blending various ingredients, such as linseed, soy, fish, and petroleum oils, and coal tar and extenders polymerizable by heat or oxidation to convert them from a liquid to a solid. Baking converts the liquid film on the sand grains to a solid. The percentage of oil required depends on the fineness of the sand and the strength and hardness required of the core. The amount of oil needed is increased if clay is present in the sand since clay soaks up core oil as well as the liquids. Air-set oil-type binders contain catalysts which accelerate polymerization and may cause it at ambient temperatures.

Driers. Driers are added to core sands to hasten the curing process. They function as catalysts to the polymerization process or provide additional oxygen and heat for the reaction. Ammonium nitrate is used in amounts of 0.10 per cent or more in core-oil-bonded sands.

Table 7.3a Data on core binders*

Binder	Hardness of cores, comparative	Moisture for machine tempering, % by volume	Mixing time, min	Bond ratio by volume	Removal from castings, comparative
Linseed oil	Hard	8	5–7	1:40–120	Good
Core oil	Hard	8	5–7	1:40–100	Good
Wheat flour	Medium	10	7–10	1:12 20	Good
Corn flour†	Medium	10	6–10	1:25-50	Good
Dextrin†	Medium	8	7–10	1:10–20	Good
Clay†	Frail	8	7–10	....	Fair
Molasses†	Frail	7	5–8	....	Good
Hydrol†	Frail	7	5–8	....	Good
Sulfite solution	Hard shell	3–5	7–10	1:50–100	Good
Dry sulfite	Medium	8	7–10	1:50–100	Good
Pitch	Hard	7	5–7	1:15–25	Hard
Oil-less binder	Hard	7	5–7	1:35–40	Fair
Rosin	Soft	7	5–10	1:15–20	Good

Table 7.3b Data on core ingredients

Binder	Specific gravity, approx	Weight per gal, lb	Baking temp, F	Binder destroyed, F	Baking speed, comparative
Linseed oil	0.93	7.8	450–500	600–700	Slow
Core oil	0.90	7.5	450–500	600–700	Slow
Wheat flour	0.60	4.5–5.5	325	500–600	Fast
Corn flour†	0.45	2.5–4.5	325	500–600	Fast
Dextrin†	0.47–0.65	3.9–5.5	350	500–600	Fast
Clay†	1.0–2.0	8.5–17	300	2000–3000	Fast
Molasses†	1.3	10.5–11.5	250	400–500	Fast
Hydrol†	1.4	11.7	250	400–500	Fast
Sulfite solution	1.25	10.5	350	600–700	Fast
Dry sulfite	0.6	5	350	600–700	Fast
Pitch	0 46–0.59	3.9–5.0	350–400	500–600	Fast
Oil-less binder	0.47	4	350	500–600	Fast
Rosin	1.07	4–9	325	600–700	Fast
Silica flour	1.3	10.0	...	3000	Slow
Fire clay	1.2	9.6	...	2700	Medium
Wood flour	0.23	2.0			
Iron oxide	1.3	10.8	...	2500	Slow
Bentonite	0.5	7.2	...	2700	Medium
Silica sand	1.3	10–13			

*From H. W. Dietert.[5]

†These binders are seldom used alone.

Sodium perborate, manganese dioxide, manganese oleate, and other metallo-organic compounds are used with liquid oils and resins for this purpose. Baking time may be reduced by 20 to 80 per cent by driers.

Cereal and water-soluble binders. Cereal is the binder commonly used for green strength. An amount of 0.5 to 2.0 per cent by weight is used to provide 1.0 to 2.5 psi green compressive strength. The percentage used generally must be less than three times the percentage of core oil in the mixture or there will be a reduction in hardness and strength after baking. Starches, dextrin, and to a limited extent other dry binders such as casein provide some green strength. One virtue of a water-soluble binder is its ability to air-dry or air-harden rapidly to resist sagging during handling. In all cases, the proper water addition is required to develop the green-strength and baked-strength potential of the binder. For cereal this amounts to about two to five times the percentage cereal in the sand. At the lower water percentages, less baked tensile strength and scratch hardness are developed. Completely water-soluble binders such as sugar, molasses, and dextrin require water to about one to three times their percentage in the sand. Again, higher moisture percentages develop higher baked scratch and edge hardness and tensile strength.

Sulfite binder. Sulfite, or lignin, binders are water-soluble compounds of wood sugars produced as a by-product of papermaking. They are used as a liquid containing 60 to 70 per cent solids or dried as a brown powder. They provide strength on evaporation of water and produce very high surface hardness during baking. Lignin binders are useful in green-sand or dry-sand core mixtures because they are readily compatible with clays and water. Up to 1.50 per cent may be used. They unfortunately readsorb water readily, and therefore the cores soften on standing. Sulfite binders are used as an ingredient of pitch compounds for large dry sand cores.

Pitch. Pitch is a solid-coal-tar by-product of the making of coke. It is used as a ground powder in percentages up to 3 per cent or sometimes more. Pitch core compounds contain pitch and other ingredients such as clay and sulfite lignin. The pitch portion fuses and partially distills at temperatures of 300 to 600 F during baking, leaving a solid film which binds the sand grains together. Upon casting the metal around the core, the pitch cokes and develops hot strength to resist the metal.

Wood flour. Ground hardwood cellulose is used in core sands in percentages of usually less than 1.0 per cent, rarely up to 3.0 per cent. Wood flour is useful in decreasing hot strength of any core or molding sand. A mix of 2 per cent wood flour in a 4 per cent western bentonite–silica sand lowers hot strength and dry strength to 30 to 40 per cent of that of the wood flour-free mixtures over the entire temperature range.

For practical purposes, 1 per cent or less is sometimes useful in decreasing veining and increasing collapsibility of cores.

Release agents. These are organic fluids such as hydrocarbons used in amounts of less than 0.10 per cent to reduce sticking of sand in core boxes and for improving drawing. Silicones and various waxes dissolved in solvents are used for the purpose.

Thermosetting plastics. Phenolformaldehyde is a polymerization product of the organic compounds phenol and formaldehyde. Urea formaldehyde is similarly a polymerization product of urea and formaldehyde. These plastics are thermosetting, and may be obtained as partially polymerized liquids or powders having properties like those listed in Table 7.4. When heated, they polymerize to a strong solid

Table 7.4 Properties of typical synthetic resins used as core binder*

Property	Urea resins		Phenol resins	
	Liquid	Dry†	Liquid	Dry†
Solids content, %	50	97	70	97
Color	White	White	Red brown	Red brown
Clarity	Milky	Milky	Clear	Turbid
Viscosity, centipoises, at 70 F	85	94	250	650
pH	7.8	6.0	7.9	10.3
Specific gravity—60/60 F	1.202	1.180	1.207	1.189
Dilutability with water	1:1	1:1	1:10	1:2
Combustibility	Complete		Complete	

*From H. W. Dietert.[5]

†Values in the dry columns are for 50 per cent solutions.

and bake in a short time. Manufacturers of these plastics control their processing and partial polymerization so that in core mixtures the thermosetting action will occur properly during the baking cycle. In dielectric or other baking, these binders thermoset almost as soon as they are heated to 200 to 400 F. Their baking thus is limited almost entirely by the time necessary to evaporate the water in the core mixture, the latter being the material which is heated in dielectric baking.

The two thermoset binders mentioned have a tendency to cause core sand to stick to core boxes. About 0.25 per cent kerosene or light fuel oil or a proprietary "release" agent may be added to the sand to reduce this trouble.

Inorganic Binders

Fire clay, bentonites, silica flour, and iron oxide are inorganic binders used in core mixes. They may be used to obtain green strength, baked strength, hot strength, or a smooth finish. Since they are all finely pulverized materials, they greatly increase the amount of oil which is necessary in oil-sand mixes. Fire clay is used sparingly, in the smallest amounts which will give the strength desired, under 2.0 per cent. If a fine sand is added to a coarser sand, added strength can be obtained, and this may be due in part to the fine material and clay present in it. Bentonite, 0.5 to 2.0 per cent, may be used to gain green strength, but a substantial increase in core oil is required when this is done. Bentonite retards collapsibility. However, about 0.30 per cent southern bentonite is reported to reduce sagging of cores during baking.[15] Iron oxide is used to obtain added hot strength or prevent veining (cracking). Silica flour in amounts up to 30 per cent in core sands is used to obtain hot strength in cores of large castings which remain molten for a long time or in small thin cores which must resist erosion. Cores which have high hot strength and do not collapse sufficiently can cause tears in a casting as it shrinks around the core.

Water

Water is not usually thought of as a binder. Other binders and additives, however, do not seem to function properly unless an optimum percentage of water exists in the mixture, usually somewhere between 2.5 and 7.0 per cent. Failure to use enough water results in not developing green strength from cereals and poor scratch hardness, edge hardness, and low baked tensile strength after baking. Excessive water causes stratification of binders by seepage, stickiness, and surface crusting and also causes coremaking and drawing problems and prolongs baking time.

CORE-SAND MIXTURES

The simplest core-sand mixture commonly used comprises sand, 1% core oil, 1% cereal, and 2.5 to 6.0 per cent water. Other mixtures for coring purposes are listed in Table 7.5. The ingredients are varied to suit the needs of the cores as determined by the alloy being cast and its temperature, the size and shape of the casting, the method of making the core, and any special requirements of the core. The weights of typical core-sand ingredients are given in Table 7.6.

CORE-SAND MIXING

Sand for cores requires adequate storage and proper mixing if the best cores are to be obtained. Storage out of the weather is desired to keep moisture and dirt out of the sand. Bins, tanks, and silos are used. If

Table 7.5 Some typical core-sand mixtures*

Application	Sand base	Binders	Other ingredients	Remarks
Light gray iron	Silica, 56 AFS, 113 parts	2 parts core oil	None	Waterless oil-bonded sand, collapsibility, cleans well
	Lake sand, 280 qt	5 parts core oil, 4 qt cereal	None	Add water to develop green strength, 2.5–3.5 %
Large gray iron	200 lb new silica; 720 lb burned core, AFS 45	3 lb w. bentonite, 5 lb pitch core component	None	Temper with water to 4.5–5.5 %
Malleable, light to medium	20 parts lake sand, 75 parts bank sand, 99 AFS	1 part core oil, 2.5 parts cereal	None	4.20 % H_2O, 44 green permeability, 1.2 psi green compression, 80 baked tensile strength
Light	New Jersey silica, 88 AFS, 280 qt	5 lb urea, 10 lb cereal	Kerosene 2 qt, deodorant 8 oz, liquid parting 3 oz	16 qt water, core blowing, baked at 400 F
Aluminum	50 parts silica, 50 parts bank, 85–90 AFS	1 part core oil, 1 part dextrin base, dry		Water to temper, small casting
	480 lb lake sand, AFS 55; 240 lb bank sand, AFS 80	6 lb cereal, 4 qt urea resin, liquid	1 qt kerosene	Baked at 350 F
Steel, general	1300 lb silica, 45 AFS	5 qt core oil, 16 qt cereal	16 lb iron oxide	
	325 lb silica	1 qt w. bentonite, 30 lb core oil, 3 qt cereal	5 lb iron oxide	Mix for blowing
Centrifugal casting, light	2000 lb	20 lb w bentonite, 30 lb pitch, 40 lb resin	120 lb silica flour	High hot strength required

*Adapted from H. W. Dietert.[5]

the sand is dried at the mine, shipped in box cars, and stored inside, it may be used directly for mixing. Some foundries dry the sand and screen out refuse just prior to its use, thus ensuring dry, clean sand of known moisture content. Dried sand still retains about 0.8 to 1.0 per cent adsorbed moisture, which would require considerably more heating to remove. Drying is performed in rotary kilns. With a dried sand, the moisture content of the sand may be more positively controlled.

Mixing Equipment

Sand mixing is performed in paddle mixers, mullers, or kneading-type mixers. A muller set up for core mixing is shown in Fig. 7.5. Sand is delivered from storage to the overhead weigh hoppers. Weighed amounts are transferred to the muller, and then the additions are made. Volume measurement of material by gallons, quarts, shovels, or wheel-

Table 7.6 Weights of common core materials

Material	Approximate pounds per quart	Pounds per cubic foot	Volume per cent per wt per cent*	Per cent fixed carbon in binder after carbonizing
Cereals range	0.6–1.40	18–42	5.33–2.35	6–12
Mogul	1.30	38.9	2.53	
Wheat flour	1.15	34.4		
Dextrin	1.40	41.9	2.33	
Core oils	1.85–2.0	55.5–60	1.67–1.8	Variable
Wood flour	0.58	17.3	5.50	5–12
Glutin	2.75	82.3		
Pitch	1.25	37.4	2.63	6–20
Sea coal	1.47	44	2.24	55–65
Air-set	2.2	66	1.50	
Carbonized cellulose	1.4	41.9	2.33	15–30
W. bentonite	1.8	53		
S. bentonite	1.74	53		
Fire clay	2.4	72		
Iron oxide	2.7	81		
Silica, general	3.34–3.67	100–110		
Silica flour	2.5	90		
Olivine	4.2	126		
Zircon	6.0	180		

*Volume per cent equaling one weight per cent in core sand at 100 lb per cu ft.

barrows is also used, but is not as accurate as weighing. Kneader types of mixers are also used.[5] The mixers may be equipped with meters or weighing devices to measure water, oil, cereal, etc. Conveying of sand to and away from the mixers to the coremaking stations is also incorporated in mechanized core rooms.

Mixing Cycle

Mixing begins with the addition of sand first and then dry binders to the mixers. The dry ingredients are mixed for a short time, and then the liquids are added. There seems to be some controversy as to whether oil or water should be added last. One author[9] states that core properties are more consistent if the oil is added first, mixed, and followed by the water. Another states that for a 3-min mixing cycle, water should be first, then oil. The latter practice is probably more common.

The total mixing time may require 3 to 6 min in the usual muller

Fig. 7.5 View of mechanical equipment incorporating muller for mixing core sand, crane, and hoppers for handling and distribution of sand. (*Courtesy of Beardsley-Piper Division, Pettibone Mulliken Corp.*)

or 60 to 90 sec in a centifugal muller. The objective, of course, is to bring out the best properties of the binders added to the sand. To retain their properties, mixed sands should be protected from drying out.

TESTING OF CORE SANDS

The nature of core sands is best described in terms of the sand mixture and its properties based on sand tests. Sand mixtures are tested for control purposes by determining their moisture content, green strength, permeability, and baked strength. A number of other tests are used when special information is desired. Many of the tests are identical with those used on molding sands in Chap. 5, and these will not be discussed again.[6]

Sample Preparation

For control purposes, mixed core sand taken from hoppers is used for testing. When the standard AFS sands are used to test binders, a dried-sand sample of 2500 g is used. The dry sand is mixed with the desired amount of cereal binder or oil for 2 min. Water is then added, and mixing continued for 2 min more. The sand specimen can then be prepared for testing. The standard AFS 2-in.-diameter specimen is used for many tests, but tensile strength after baking requires a special specimen.

Green Strength

Green compression, shear, or tensile strength and permeability tests may be performed on core sands in the same way and with the equipment similar to that described in Chap. 5 for molding sands. Some typical values for core sands are given in Table 7.7. Core mixtures are quite

Table 7.7 Common room-temperature properties of core sands

Sand type	Green tests			Baked tests			
	Comp. str., psi	Shear str., psi	Permeability, ml/min	Comp. str., psi	Tensile str., psi	Scratch hardness	Permeability, ml/min
Oil-sand	<1.0	<0.60	Depends on base perm. of sand, 70–300	500–1000	150–400	>92 80–90 70–80	80–300
COMMENTS: Baked hardness and strength increase with per cent oil, 92 and above for strong edges and abrasion resistance, 80 to 90 for general use, 70 to 80 for weak collapsible cores; poor handling when green							
Oil-cereal-water-sand	<3.0	<1.2	60–250	500–1000	150–400	>92 80–90 70–80	80–300
COMMENTS: Same as for oil-sand plus improved green strength for coremaking; air drying rapid to reduce sagging							
Oil–cereal–w. bentonite–water–sand	<4.0	<1.5	60–300	300–800	100–400	>92 80–90 70–80	
COMMENTS: Same as for oil-sand plus improved hot strength							
Oil–cereal–w. bentonite–silica flour–water–sand	<5.0	<2.0	20–100	300–800	100–400	>92	
COMMENTS: Same as for oil-sand plus improved hot strength and resistance to metal penetration; bulk density and reduced permeability							

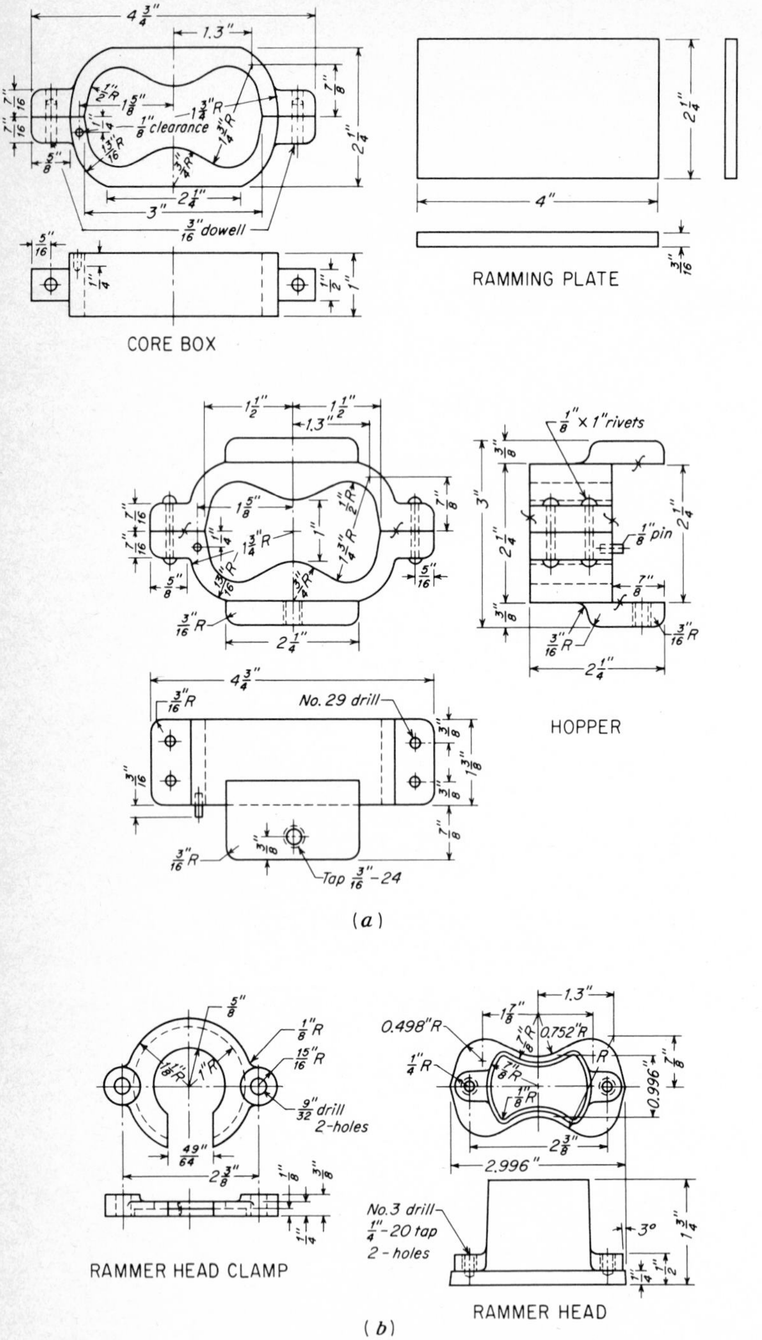

Fig. 7.6 **(a)** Core box, ramming plate, and hopper used in making briquets for testing tensile strength of core-sand mixtures; **(b)** rammer-head attachment for ramming tensile briquets. **(*From AFS.*)**

weak compared with molding sands. Values of 0.5 to 1.5 psi green compression strength are quite common in most cases, 5.0 psi being very unusual. Because of its low green strength, it is difficult to use the universal sand-strength machine without special attachments; so a vertically acting compression tester may be used instead.

Baked Strength

Determination of the baked strength of cores requires a standardized procedure for baking. For control tests, the specimens may be baked along with regular cores. For laboratory tests, an oven conforming to AFS specification,[2] having accurate temperature control, ±5 F, circulating air with five to eight changes of air per hour, and otherwise reproducible in baking conditions is required. The baking cycle is such as to develop optimum properties of the binder. Tensile and transverse tests are most commonly used on baked cores. The standard tensile specimen core box is shown in Fig. 7.6. The specimen is molded by ramming three times with the standard rammer. If the baked strength developed after core blowing rather than impact ramming is desired, a core-box arrangement as shown in Fig. 7.7 may be used. Accessories for the

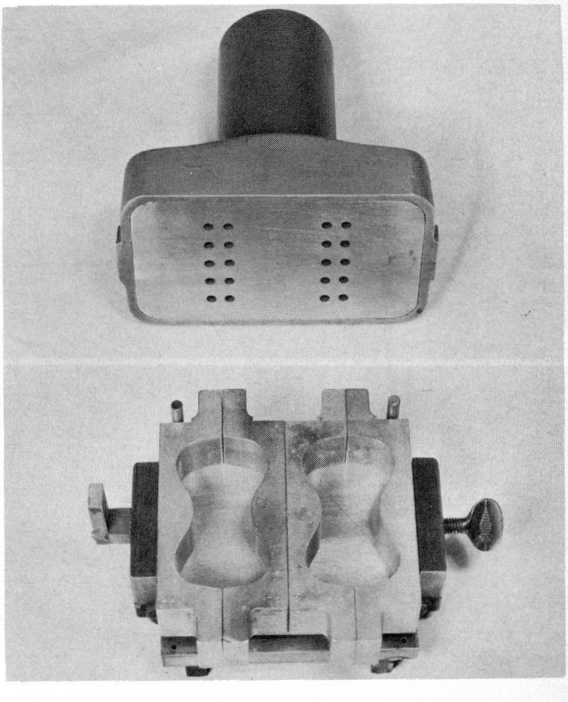

***Fig.* 7.7** Blow head and core box for blowing tensile test samples for core-sand mixtures. (*From H. W. Dietert.*[5])

universal sand-strength machine permit that device to be used for tensile and transverse strength tests on baked cores. The baked tensile strength of strong core mixes is as high as 250 to 300 psi or more. The 1- by 1- by 8-in. transverse bar will take as high as 150 to 200 lb load on a 6-in. span.

Warm Strength

Cores do not develop maximum strength until they have cooled to room temperature. At 150 to 300 F, cores may be substantially weaker than at room temperature. If specimens are tested immediately on removal from the oven, the warm-strength data are obtained. This, however, is not a standard test. Warm strength does not appear to be directly related to room-temperature strength.

Hot Strength

Tests on the high-temperature properties of core sands may be run in the manner discussed in Chap. 5. The specimen must be baked before it is tested. Expansion measurements are also made, using dilatometer equipment.

The change in properties with time of exposure to high temperature may be tested by methods described in Ref. 13. This method of testing simulates exposure of the sand to the heat of the metal poured around the core. Figure 7.8 shows an example of results obtained by the method.

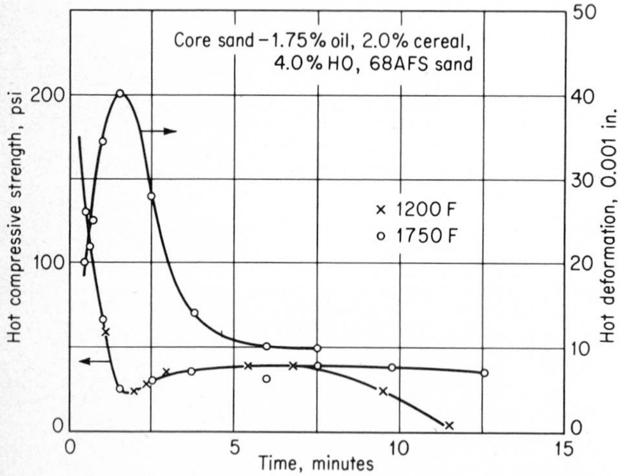

Fig. 7.8 **Effect of time of exposure to a dilatometer furnace temperature of 1750 F on hot strength and deformation of hollow core-sand specimens. Baked strength at ambient temperature was 1000 psi.**

Retained Strength

Retained strength is determined on the 1.125-in.-diameter by 2-in. specimen with the dilatometer discussed in Chap. 5, by heating the baked specimen to temperatures above 1000 F, holding it for 12 min, and allowing it to cool down to room temperature. It is then tested in compression. A core-sand mixture of silica sand and core oil will exhibit no retained strength after heating to 1000 F. It will thus be easy to shake out of a casting. Sands exhibiting over 10 psi retained compression strength can be difficult to shake out.

Permeability

Permeability may be determined on green and on baked core sand. Ordinarily green permeability is considered adequate for control testing. The baked permeability is often 110 to 130 per cent of the green permeability; so the latter is used as a guide. Baked-permeability testing requires that the standard specimen be baked, cooled, and then inserted in a special tube for the test. The permeability of core sands is ordinarily much higher than that of molding sands. Values of 150 to 300 ml per min permeability are quite common.

Core Hardness

Testing the hardness of baked and green cores requires a hardness-testing device. Green hardness may be determined with a tester similar to that used on molds, except that a larger indenter and lighter load are used in the tester. A scratch type of baked-core hardness tester is shown in Fig. 7.9. The plow indenter is spring-loaded with 1100 g and

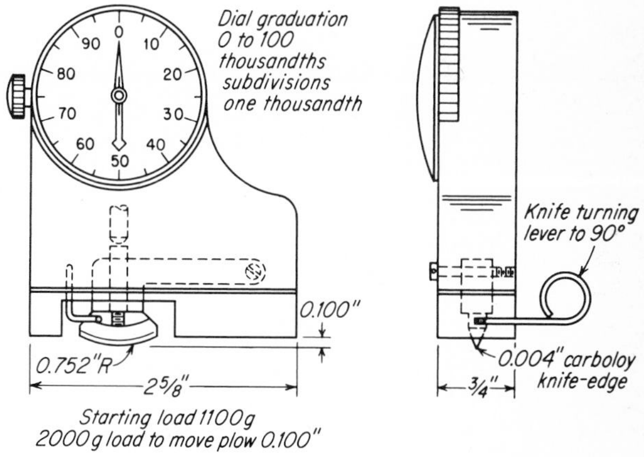

Fig. 7.9 Scratch-hardness tester for baked cores. (*From H. W. Dietert.*[5])

protrudes 0.100 in. from the flat comparison surface (bottom). The tester is slowly drawn over a flat core surface, and hardness is read directly from the dial. Each unit represents 0.001 in. A reading of 90 indicates that the indicator protrudes 0.100 to 0.090, or 0.010 in. from the bottom. The range from soft to hard cores is about 30 to 95 with this tester.

Moisture Content

Moisture determination of core-sand mixtures encounters the problem that some ingredients of core oils are volatile at 220 to 230 F, the temperature of drying. Hence moisture tests with the carbide bomb tester are made according to the procedure described in Ref. 6.

Other Tests

AFS clay content and sieve analyses are performed on the sands used in the core mixtures before any binders are added. Other tests such as sintering point, core-gas evolution, metal penetration, binder evaluation, core toughness, and organic chemical properties of binders and many others may be used to study the properties of core mixtures. Special testing methods for the newer core-sand materials have been devised. For example, the testing and equipment for shell-core sands are described in Refs. 14 and 15.

CORE-SAND PROPERTIES

The properties of the sand in a core depend on a number of variables. The ingredients of the mix, the operations of mixing, coremaking, and baking, all have effects. Mixing is supposed to be performed so that binders are uniformly distributed in order to obtain uniformity of coremaking and baking.

Core Baking

Core baking develops the properties of the organic binders. The importance of temperature and time of baking in its effect on baked tensile strength has been illustrated in Fig. 6.11. Certain temperature-time combinations develop the maximum strength and hardness which can

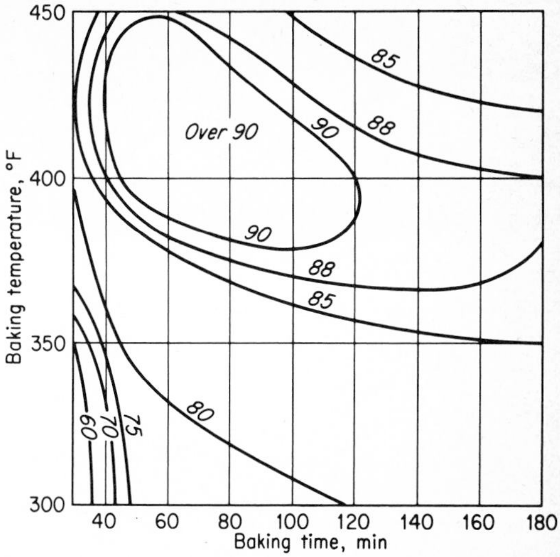

***Fig.* 7.10** **Relationship between core hardness of standard AFS samples and baking time and temperature. (*From H. W. Dietert.*[5])**

be obtained from a particular mix. Figure 7.10 shows how the same variables affect core hardness as judged by the scratch-hardness test. It must be recognized, however, that Fig. 7.10 applies only to a certain size core, the AFS test core, as well as one particular mix. Larger cores would require substantially longer baking time to reach the full baked hardness. The baking cycle must allow time for the evaporation of water, the first step in baking; heating to the baking temperature; and thorough baking of the various-sized cores. An optimum baking cycle is a best compromise between core properties and practical difficulties of baking. Mixtures bonded with core oil or urea or phenolformaldehyde display similar response of properties to baking.

Properties and Ingredients

Obviously, the sand mixture has a great influence on the properties of the core. Baked hardness and strength may be greatly increased by increasing the amount of binder. This fact is illustrated in Fig. 7.11. For each type of core sand, however, depending on its fineness, clay content, and distribution, there is an optimum sand-oil ratio. The proper amount of water must also be used. Softer cores can always be made by using less oil.

Binders other than oil will give different baked strength; for instance, sands bonded with the thermosetting plastics described earlier may exhibit baked tensile strength of 300 to 1000 psi.

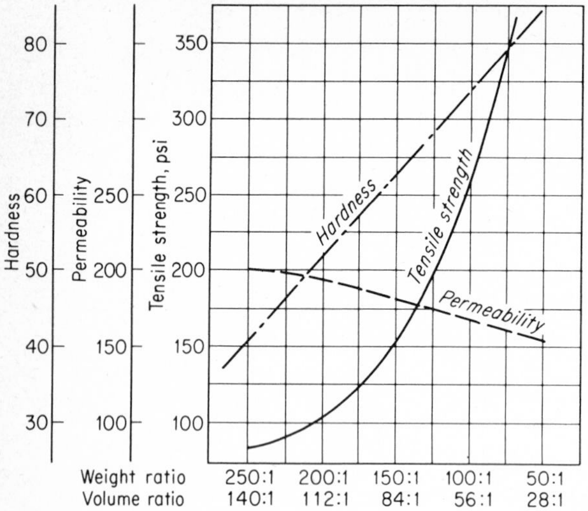

***Fig.* 7.11 Effect of sand-oil ratio on baked properties of an oil-bonded sand mixture made in standard AFS test samples baked 1.5 hr at 350 F. (*From H. W. Dietert.*[5])**

Core mixtures with insufficient green strength cause difficulties in core-making and baking. The cores may slump or sag, and thus be off size.

Hot Strength

When oil-cereal-bonded core sand is heated, the organic matter softens as temperature increases above about 200 F. At 400 to 900 F, the binders partially liquefy, distill, and char, or carbonize. Liquefaction and distillation cause a large increase in hot deformation, as shown in Fig. 7.8. This increased hot deformation reaches a maximum at the minimum strength of the mixture. This shows the need for adequate core prints, chaplets, and arbors to support cores until they are surrounded by solidified metal.

The bulk of the unheated core mass permits the core to retain its shape during the low-strength–high-deformation period. As carbonization proceeds, a coke bond is established. This provides the hot strength of the core surface until other binders may function. The coke bond develops over the range of 600 to 1200 F and up to 1850 F, as in the coking of coal. It is in this temperature range and above that supplementary inorganic binders are useful in core-sand mixtures. Silica flour in amounts up to 30 per cent, as much as 5.0 per cent iron oxide, and several per cent of bentonite or fire clay may be used individually or in combinations to obtain the higher hot-strength properties. A core with hot strength may show from 10 to 300 psi compressive strength at 2500 F in the standard hot-strength test. Collapsible cores would show 0 psi hot strength under the same conditions.

Collapsibility

Rapid loss of core strength after the metal is poured is promoted by the use of organic binders and nonuse of inorganic binders. Of course, low binder concentrations are helpful. Cellulose and starches are effective in promoting burnout. Cereals may reduce burnout time and hot strength by 50 per cent or more when used in amounts up to 2.0 per cent. Rosin and urea formaldehyde also promote collapsibility. Collapsibility is really a combination of two factors, the absence of hot strength and the rate of loss of strength with heating. Lack of collapsibility may cause hot-tear defects, warpage, and difficulty in shaking out. Retained strength is present in unheated parts of a core or in cores which contact very little hot metal. Retained strength from organic binders which are not thermally decomposed leaves the core at close to its baked strength, and therefore not collapsible.

Core Density

Core-sand density is an important factor related to collapsibility and hot strength. A core rammed to high density resists collapse and displays more hot strength. The density of the base sand, as discussed earlier, approximates the limiting density which a core can have.

Refractoriness

The starting point for refractoriness in cores is the sand-grain base of the core moisture. Washed and dried, white, high-purity silica sand in coarser sizes seems to have a maximum fusion point of about 3100 F. The less pure, discolored bank and lake sands in finer sizes have fusion points of 2900 to 3000 F. In addition to the sand base, however, certain things may be done to improve the heat resistance of cores. Core coatings which change the properties of surface layers of the core may be used. These may put additional refractories on the surface or may reinforce the surface by applying more binders to the surface. Resistance of the core surface to the heat of the metal determines the coating surface quality.

CORE COATINGS

Core coatings are more commonly known as core washes, core dips, blacking, or facing. Core coatings may be applied as liquids by spraying, dipping, or brushing and as solids by dusting. Core coatings are usually proprietary materials formulated by the manufacturer for use on certain types of castings. Some mixtures which may be used for coatings are given in Table 7.8. They usually consist of a liquid carrier, a refractory material, and binders. The powder is mixed with water, core oil, or other liquid to a suitable consistency for dipping or spraying. Water-base coatings, containing organic binders, are likely to ferment, although 0.15 per cent sodium benzoate may be added to the solution as a preservative.

Core coatings for steel casting work are largely based on silica flour, magnesite, or chrome ore as the refractory material, as indicated in Table 7.8. Core coatings for cast irons make use of the refractoriness of graphite and its effectiveness in reducing the amount of sand fused onto the casting. Graphite-bearing washes may also be used for copper-base alloy castings. Since coatings are most commonly applied as liquids, the problem of drying the core arises. Coating before baking may be practiced, or the coating may be applied after the core is baked. Coated baked cores should be oven-dried unless there is adequate time for air drying. Cores for iron castings may be coated for a metallurgical effect. Tellurium-bearing core coatings are able to cause a gray iron to freeze as a white iron for a considerable depth from the coated surface.[9] Conveyor wheels, cams, and similar wearing surfaces may be cast with a white (hard) iron surface by this means.

Table* 7.8 *Typical core-coating materials

Casting type	Liquid	Refractory	Other materials
Steel..........	25 gal water	150 lb silica flour	12 lb western bentonite
Steel..........	Water as required	100 parts magnesite	20 parts western bentonite, 20 parts cereal, 0.15% sodium benzoate
Steel..........	3–4 gal water	8 qt silica flour	1 qt western bentonite, 0.5 gal water-soluble resin
Brass, bronze..	15 parts water	11 parts plumbago	1 part western bentonite

CORES AND CASTING DEFECTS

Cores can be the source of casting defects. Poor or defective cores should not be delivered to the molding operations. Cores should therefore be inspected before they are sent to the molders. Some core defects which may be caught by inspection in the core room include:

1. *Off gauge or off size.* Cores which are not of correct size will not produce the desired casting dimensions. The cores may be gauged for size in the finishing operations (Chap. 6), and the off-size cores rejected.

2. *Core sticker.* Some core-sand mixtures give trouble by sticking to the core box. The sand sticking to the box gives the core a rough, pitted surface which will be transferred to the casting. Such cores can be rejected.
3. *Inaccurate core assemblies.* Core assemblies may be shifted or not well fitted together, causing dimensional errors.
4. *Fins.* All fins and projections on the core will definitely show up as cavities in the casting unless they have been cleaned off in core-finishing operations.
5. *Cracked cores.* Some cores will show cracks on their surface after they are baked. Metal may run into these cracks and produce fins on the casting.

In spite of delivering good, clean, dimensionally accurate cores to the molder, cores may still be the source of casting defects other than those considered above. The core-sand mixture and the method of locating and securing cores in the mold can cause trouble. When the metal is poured, thermal effects cause the core to burn out, and buoyancy or the momentum of the metal can cause it to shift from where it was set into the mold. Some of the defects which can be encountered from these sources include:

1. *Blow.* Since cores give off gases, they may cause blows or gas cavities in the casting. One of the chief reasons for core blows is underbaked cores. Cores which are underbaked and have green centers may give off substantial amounts of gas.
2. *Dirt.* Loose or easily eroded sand may result in dirt defects in castings.
3. *Core raise.* This defect occurs when the core floats and moves up close to the cope. It may even touch the cope surface and seal off the section. A weak core or one which is not properly supported with chaplets may be the cause of this defect. An undersize core not held tightly by the core prints may also raise.
4. *Core shift.* A core may shift horizontally if it is not securely held by chaplets or prints or if it was not centered when set. The characteristic evidence of a core shift is that one casting wall is thinner and the opposite one thicker than required.
5. *Cracked core, fins.* A core may crack because of buoyancy effects. A stronger core or better support with prints or chaplets is indicated. Cracks or fins can seal off internal passages.
6. *Metal penetration.* This defect is especially troublesome in large castings where cores become heated up to the melting point of the metal before it freezes. Metal then seeps into the core, developing an adhering mass of sand and metal. This defect is a very troublesome one to remove from the casting. Soft ramming and sand with a low sintering point seem to aggravate this defect.
7. *Core wash, cut* (see Chap. 5, wash defect in molding sand). A core will wash (erode) when the surface collapses too fast. Washes may be prevented by using a refractory coating on the core or strengthening it by the use of more binder. Sand additions which increase hot strength, silica flour or clay, for example, develop more resistance to washing.

8. *Hot tears.* This defect is amply illustrated in Chaps. 9 and 23. A hard core which does not allow the casting to contract may rupture or tear the metal. Too high a hot strength of the sand mixture, obtained usually through inorganic binders, may cause this defect. The defect is most common in malleable, steel, and nonferrous castings.
9. *Veins.* Veins on castings are fin-shaped protuberances in cored areas. It appears that a crack-shaped opening develops in the core as it becomes heated by the metal. The crack is then filled with molten metal, and a vein appears on the casting when it is cleaned. Certain materials added to core sands, such as iron oxide, that flux the sand and make it tough at high temperature seem to overcome this defect. However, it is known to be caused by several sand conditions, described in Ref. 6. The defect is most often encountered in ferrous castings where a small or thin core is surrounded by a substantial mass of metal.
10. *Scabs and buckle.* Sand-expansion defects of the type considered for molding sand in Chap. 5 are also encountered on cored casting surfaces.
11. *Crush.* A crush is most commonly a defect in the mold which is caused during the core setting or closing of the mold. In a crush, sand on the mold cavity is displaced by the cores. If a core is oversize, when the mold is closed, the core prints will be enlarged by the core, and this can flake sand off the mold walls. The defect shows up on the casting as a depression where the mold wall is crushed in toward the mold cavity. Careless closing of the mold or poor flask guide pins may also cause the trouble.
12. *Fissures.* Fissures appear as rough, grainy-looking masses attached directly to cored surfaces of the castings. They appear to be locations where the core sand has collapsed and has been pushed aside by the still molten metal.

It is evident that the defects which may be related to cores are in part mechanical problems and in part problems associated with the properties of core-sand mixtures. A careful control of the core-sand properties can reduce defects from that source.

OTHER CORE PROCESSES

A number of special coremaking processes have come into general use. These usually involve a combination of core-sand mixture and coremaking equipment that offers some special advantage either in making the core or in the casting.

Shell cores require a heated core box and a sand mixed with about 2 to 5 per cent thermosetting resin, commonly the phenolic type. Sands precoated with the resin are most frequently used. The sand is either blown into the box or fed in by gravity. After a dwell period, to produce a hardened shell, the unhardened sand is drained out, producing a hollow core. Curing of the shell is continued for a short time longer.

The shell core is then extracted from the box. The process produces hardened cores that require no further baking. Thus driers are not needed. The shell-core process is fully described in Ref. 15.

The hot-box process produces solid cores from a mixture of 2 to 4 per cent furan resins, a catalyst, and sand. The cores are blown using cores boxes heated to 400 to 600 F. Heat from the box initiates exothermic polymerization of the resin. After less than a minute, the core may be removed from the box, and it is cured outside the box by continuation of the exothermic reaction. Baking is again not required. The silicate process, referred to in Chap. 3 for making molds, may also be used for hardening a core sand within the core box.

The processes above have the common feature of hardening the core within the core box. This step produces an accurate reproduction of the core-box cavity, and consequently leads to accurately cored castings.

BIBLIOGRAPHY

1. J. Caine and C. MacQuiston, Theoretical Concepts of Packing Small Particles, *Trans. AFS,* vol. 66, p. 36, 1958, and accompanying bibliography.
2. J. Grott, Particle Packing: Principles and Limitations, *Trans. AFS,* vol. 66, p. 553, 1958.
3. R. W. Heine and T. W. Seaton, Density of Sand Grain Fractions of the AFS Sieve Analysis, *Trans. AFS,* vol. 66, p. 40, 1958.
4. C. W. Briggs (ed.), "Fundamentals of Core Sands and Binders," Steel Founders' Society of America, Cleveland, 1961.
5. H. W. Dietert, "Foundry Core Practice," American Foundrymen's Society, 1950.
6. American Foundrymen's Society, "Foundry Sand Handbook," 1963.
7. H. K. Salzberg, Plastic Binders for Foundry Sand Practice, *Trans. AFS,* vol. 60, 1952.
8. J. E. McMillan and J. A. Wickett, Phenolic Resin Core Binders, *Trans. AFS,* vol. 58, 1950.
9. O. J. Myers, Which Comes First, Oil or Water? *Foundry,* vol. 77, September, 1949.
10. C. R. Austen, Using Tellurium in Promoting Chills on Gray Iron, *Foundry,* vol. 77, July, 1949.
11. R. E. Morey, G. G. Ackerlind, and W. S. Pellini, Effects of Binders and Additives on the High Temperature Properties of Foundry Sands, *Trans. AFS,* vol. 60, 1952.
12. A. E. Murton, H. H. Fairfield, and B. Richardson, Core Oil Evaluation Method, *Trans. AFS,* vol. 59, p. 276, 1951.
13. R. W. Heine, E. H. King, and J. S. Schumacher, A New Approach in Testing the High Temperature Strength of Molding and Core Sand, *Trans. AFS,* vol. 69, p. 410, 1961.
14. H. W. Dietert Co., Tools for Control, *Bulls.* 118, 364, and 365; *Foundrymen's News Letter,* vol. 2, Detroit, 1962.
15. R. S. L. Andrews, "Shell Process Foundry Practice," American Foundrymen's Society, 1964.
16. J. Pelleg, Core Binder Properties, *Trans. AFS,* vol. 70, p. 57, 1962.

8

Solidification of Metals

INTRODUCTION

It is the purpose of this chapter to consider the major fundamental problems in connection with the solidification of foundry alloys. Before doing so, however, it will be helpful to review briefly some of the more important factors involved.

If attention is confined for the time being to binary alloy systems,* it is apparent immediately that solidification proceeds:

1. At constant temperature (pure metals and eutectic alloys)
2. Over a temperature range (solid solutions)
3. By a combination of solidification over a temperature range followed by constant-temperature freezing (proeutectic-plus eutectic-type freezing)

Solidification occurs by the nucleation of minute grains or crystals, which then grow under the influence of the crystallographic and thermal conditions that prevail. The size and character of these grains are controlled by the composition of the alloy and by the cooling rate. Growth ceases when all the available liquid metal has solidified.

Other changes are also taking place during the freezing process. Heat is being extracted from the molten metal as soon as the metal enters the mold. This heat is often referred to as *superheat,* since it represents that which must be removed before solidification can begin. The latent *heat of fusion* is also evolved. This must be transferred to the surrounding mold before complete solidification can be achieved. Finally, the solid metal transfers heat to the mold, and then to the atmosphere as it cools to room temperature.

During the three stages of cooling, i.e., liquid, liquid-solid, and solid, shrinkage is also occurring. Thus the metal contracts as it loses super-

*It is assumed that the student has been introduced to the physical metallurgy of binary alloys. If not, it will be well at this point to review the subject. Sources of this information are numerous, and include, among others, Clark and Varney, "Physical Metallurgy for Engineers," D. Van Nostrand Company, Inc., Princeton, N.J., 1962; Albert G. Guy, "Elements of Physical Metallurgy," Addison-Wesley Publishing Company, Cambridge, Mass., 1959; Committee on Metallurgy, "Engineering Metallurgy," Pitman Publishing Corporation, New York, 1957.

heat, as it transforms to the solid, and as the solid cools to room temperature.

There are, therefore, three major points for consideration when a casting solidifies:

1. Growth of the solid grains
2. Heat evolution and transfer
3. Dimensional changes

Additional variables are present which add to the complexity of the process. These include the effect of the mold material and its thickness, the mold geometry, the metal thickness, and such metal properties as its thermal conductivity and solidification temperature range, heat transfer from the mold to the atmosphere, control of grain size by the use of inoculants or vibration, and others. Since these variables operate through their effect on the solidification process, major attention is given to the process itself. The effect of the variables is considered secondarily, or can be deduced from the discussion. The relationship of other properties, such as fluidity, hot-tearing tendencies, and gas evolution, to the solidification process is also covered in this chapter.

FREEZING OF A PURE METAL

Skin Effects; Solidification in a Mold

The freezing (or melting) temperatures of pure metals have been established very accurately, so accurately, in fact, that these points serve as a means for standardizing thermocouples. When a pure metal is allowed to freeze in a mold, that portion of the liquid which first reaches the freezing temperature begins to solidify. This usually occurs next to the mold wall, where heat extraction is greatest. The chilling action of the mold wall results in the formation of a thin "skin," or shell, of solid metal surrounding the liquid. With sufficient extraction of heat through this thin wall of metal, the liquid begins to freeze onto it and the wall increases in thickness, growing progressively inward to the center, as determined by the existing temperature gradient. The interface between the liquid and solid is relatively smooth because the metal is freezing at constant temperature. Actually, there is a mild change in the character of the interface as the front advances, as described later. The interface, in effect, represents an isothermal surface which moves away from the mold wall. Figure 8.1 illustrates how the solid metal wall increases in thickness during the course of freezing a 2- by 12- by 12-in. plate of 99.8 per cent aluminum cast into a baked sand mold. These samples were produced by pouring out the remaining liquid after the time intervals indicated.

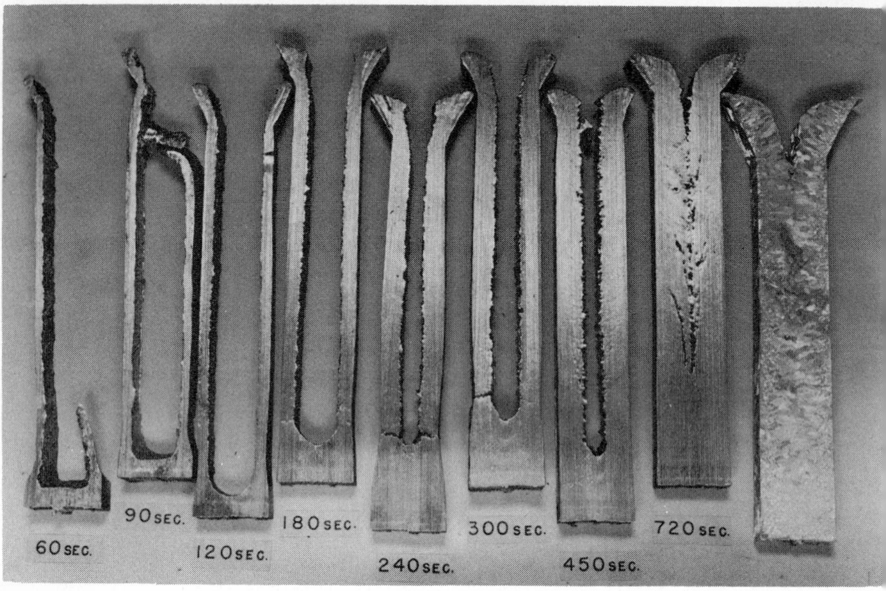

Fig. 8.1 Cross sections through the center of 2- by 12- by 12-in. plates of 99.8 per cent aluminum cast in baked-sand molds and poured after the time intervals indicated. Section at right was macroetched. (*From H. Y. Hunsicker.*[1])

It has been found that the thickness of the skin frozen in any given time can be expressed by the function

$$D = k\sqrt{t} - c$$

where k, c = constants
t = time
D = thickness

The magnitude of the constant k is determined by the size of the casting and how fast heat can be extracted by the mold. The constant c is determined largely by the degree of superheat. During the growth of this skin, the liquid which remains is close to the freezing temperature, and, depending on the rate at which heat is removed through the walls, it may finally be nucleated in a random manner, with final solidification occurring by uniform growth of scattered nuclei in the liquid.

At the instant of freezing, the general drop in temperature accompanying the solidification process is interrupted as the first solid metal releases its latent heat of fusion. This release of energy by the freezing metal has the effect of equalizing the temperature of the remaining liquid near its freezing point and of increasing the over-all time required for the liquid in the interior of the casting to freeze, since the liquid is actually absorbing heat from the solid metal which surrounds it. Only after all the heat of fusion has been absorbed can normal cooling again be expected to occur. The effects described above may be seen in an idealized manner by the sketch in Fig. 8.2.

Nucleation and Growth

That part of the casting which is near the mold wall is, in effect, supercooled, and solidifies as fine equi-axed grains. Nucleation of the supercooled grain is governed by two factors: The first factor is the free energy *available* from the solidification process. This is dependent upon the volume of the particle formed. The second factor is the energy *required* to form a liquid-solid interface. This is dependent upon the surface area of the particle. It can be shown that the net effect of these two factors is that the total energy of the particle reaches a maximum at a given particle size for a given supercooling temperature.[2] This is the critical particle size which must be created before the nucleus is stable for that particular supercooling temperature. As the degree of supercooling increases, the free energy available from the liquid-solid transformation also increases, and consequently, the critical particle size required for stability decreases, but simultaneously the thermal fluctuations which tend to create stable nuclei also decrease. As a consequence, the rate of nucleation builds up to a maximum with increasing supercooling and then drops off.[3]

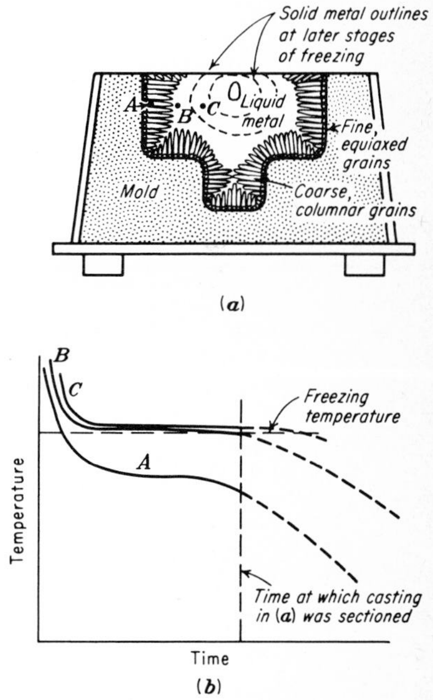

***Fig.* 8.2** (*a*) Cross section through a freezing casting of pure metal poured in an "open-face" mold; (*b*) schematic representations of cooling curves at indicated points in pure-metal casting shown in (*a*).

The preceding explanation represents so-called *homogeneous nucleation,* or self-nucleation. Usually foreign particles are present which alter the liquid-solid interface energy enough to assist in nucleation, thereby reducing the amount of supercooling required to effect nucleation. This *heterogeneous* nucleation usually prevails in castings at least to a certain extent. The thermodynamic principles governing nucleation are discussed in Refs. 2 and 4.

Once a stable nucleus is formed, it grows by acquiring atoms from the liquid. The rate of growth is governed by the amount of undercooling below the melting point, growth rate increasing with the degree of undercooling until it reaches a maximum and then drops off.[3,5] It is apparent, therefore, that the rate of nucleation and the rate of growth follow the same general trend with increasing amount of supercooling. The relative rates differ, however, to the extent that nucleation is predominant in the early stages of freezing, and as a consequence the first layer of solid metal at the metal-mold interface consists of the fine equi-axed grains mentioned previously.

During the time the first skin of solid metal is being produced, the latent heat of fusion is being released, and the remaining liquid rapidly loses most of its undercooling. The effect of this change is to stop further nucleation. Growth continues, however, on some of the grains already formed. This growth is controlled by the rate of heat transfer from the casting, and since this establishes a temperature gradient toward the casting surface, the growth occurs in a direction opposite to the heat flow. In

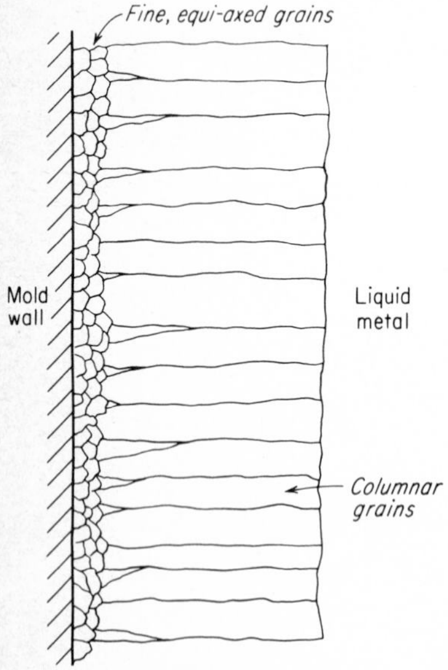

***Fig.* 8.3** Development of columnar grains from the initial fine-grained surface layer during the freezing of a pure metal. (*After B. Chalmers.*[6])

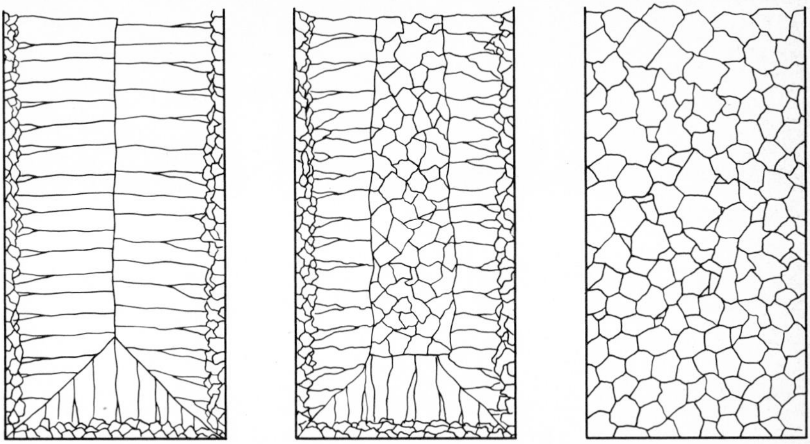

(*a*) (*b*) (*c*)

***Fig.* 8.4** Possible casting structures. (*a*) Wholly columnar, except for chilled zone of fine equi-axed grains, typical of pure metals; (*b*) partially columnar and partially equi-axed, typical of solid-solution alloys; (*c*) wholly equi-axed grains, indicative of the absence of thermal gradients or the use of a nucleation catalyst to induce heterogeneous nucleation. (*From G. W. Form and J. F. Wallace,*[2] *J. L. Walker,*[4] *and A. Cibula.*[7])

addition, because growth is also dependent on crystallographic direction as well as the direction of heat flow, only those grains which happen to be favorably oriented will grow toward the center of the castings and other less favorably oriented grains will be pinched off. The net effect will be to create a zone of columnar grains next to the outer layer of fine grains as depicted in Figs. 8.2 and 8.3. In pure metals these columnar grains extend to the center of the casting,[6] but in alloys the columnar grain growth may be interrupted by an equi-axed grain growth. These possibilities are shown schematically in Fig. 8.4.

If the liquid metal is supercooled, grain growth can occur dendritically, that is, in a treelike fashion. This type of growth represents only about 10 per cent of the total freezing process of pure metals,[6] whereas it is commonplace for the freezing of alloys. Dendritic growth of grains will therefore be discussed in the section dealing with solid solutions.

Shrinkage

While the changes that have been described are occurring, shrinkage of the metal also occurs. The effects of shrinkage may perhaps best be illustrated by using a hypothetical case.

Suppose that the mold illustrated in Fig. 8.5 is filled to level *A* with metal at a temperature of, say, 100°, above its freezing temperature. If

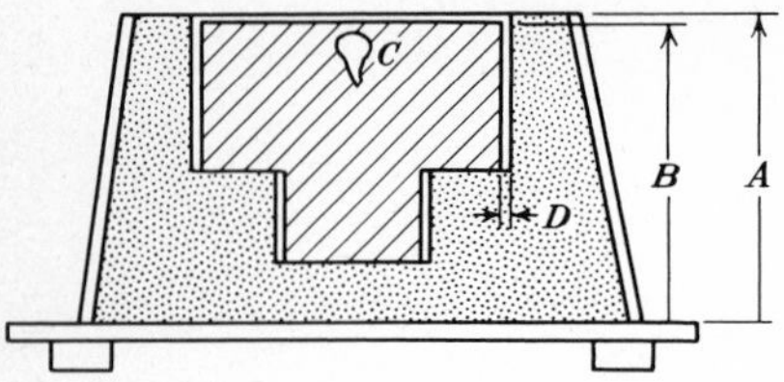

Fig. **8.5** If superheated metal is filled to the top of the mold (level *A*), it will shrink somewhat on cooling to the freezing temperature (level *B*). During liquid-solid contraction, further reductions in volume take place, usually localized near the top of the casting, in the region which freezes last (area *C*). Finally, the solid metal pulls away from the mold wall as it contracts (distance *D*).

no additional metal is allowed to enter the mold, the liquid metal will begin to contract on cooling because of the normal contraction that occurs in the liquid. Thus, just at the freezing point, the metal may have contracted sufficiently to lower it to the level *B* depicted in Fig. 8.5. When the freezing temperature is reached, the metal begins to freeze next to the mold surface, because this is where most of the heat has been extracted, and freezing progresses inward as already described. Since solid metal is denser than liquid metal (unlike water), a further contraction takes

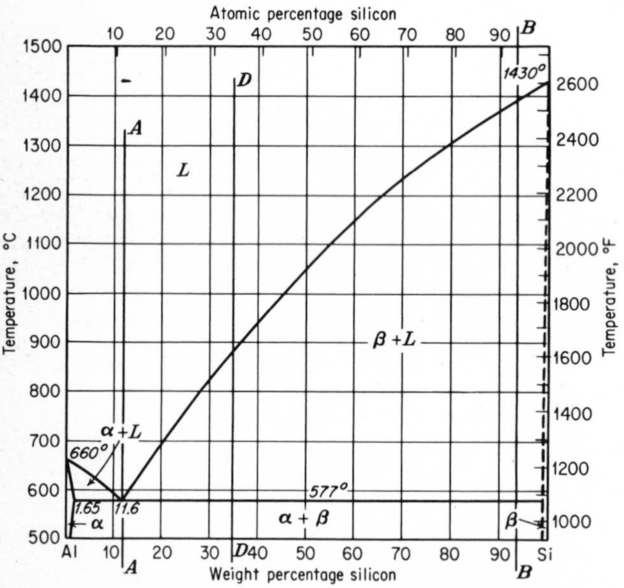

Fig. **8.6** Examples of alloys exhibiting (*a*) eutectic-type freezing (alloy *A*), (*b*) precipitation of an essentially pure component (alloy *B*), (*c*) solid-solution freezing (alloy *C*), (*d*) precipitation of an essentially pure component followed by eutectic freezing (alloy *D*), (*e*) solid-solution freezing followed by eutectic freezing (alloy *E*). (*Courtesy of American Society for Metals.*)

place during freezing. Finally, the solid metal contracts as it cools to room temperature. This latter effect is demonstrated by the metal pulling away from the mold wall a slight distance (*D* in Fig. 8.5). The liquid-solid contraction results in having insufficient metal to feed all the initial volume in the mold, with the result that a so-called "pipe," or shrinkage region, develops in the interior at point *C*.

The fact that there is increasingly less liquid metal available for feeding the casting as solidification progresses, together with the coarser grain size in the interior, is probably responsible for the decreased density that has been noted in the center of castings as compared with the outer portions.[1]

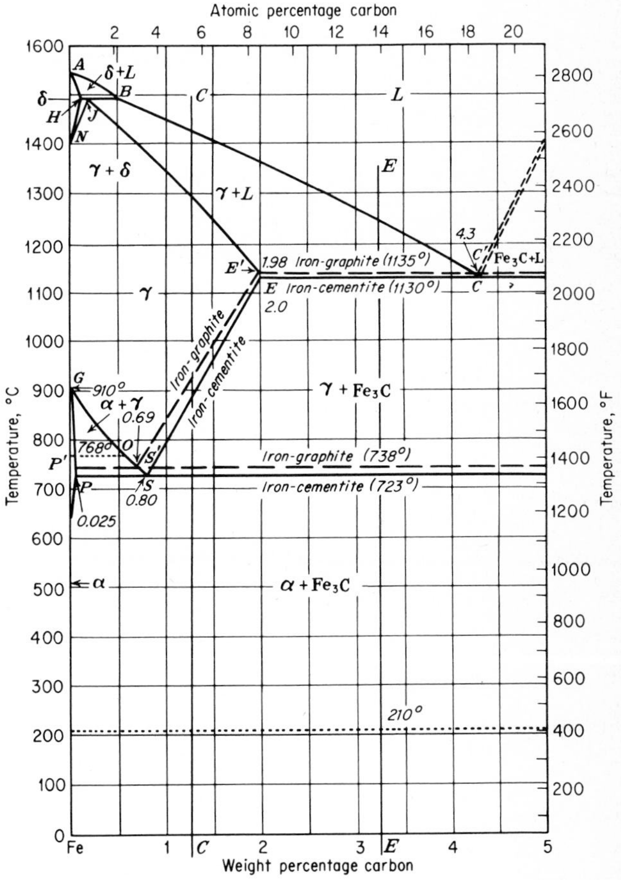

Fig. **8.6** (*Continued*)

FREEZING OF ALLOYS

Classification

Alloys can be divided into those which:

1. Start and complete their freezing by precipitating an essentially pure component, but over a temperature range (alloy B, Fig. 8.6).*
2. Start and complete their freezing as solutions (alloy C, Fig. 8.6).
3. Freeze at constant temperature by precipitating simultaneously two phases (binary systems) or three phases (ternary systems). These alloys are known as *eutectics* (alloy A, Fig. 8.6).
4. Start their freezing by precipitating an essentially pure component and complete it with eutectic-type freezing (alloy D, Fig. 8.6).
5. Start their freezing as solutions and complete it as eutectic type (alloy E, Fig. 8.6).

*Note that a *small* amount of eutectic precipitation completes the freezing process.

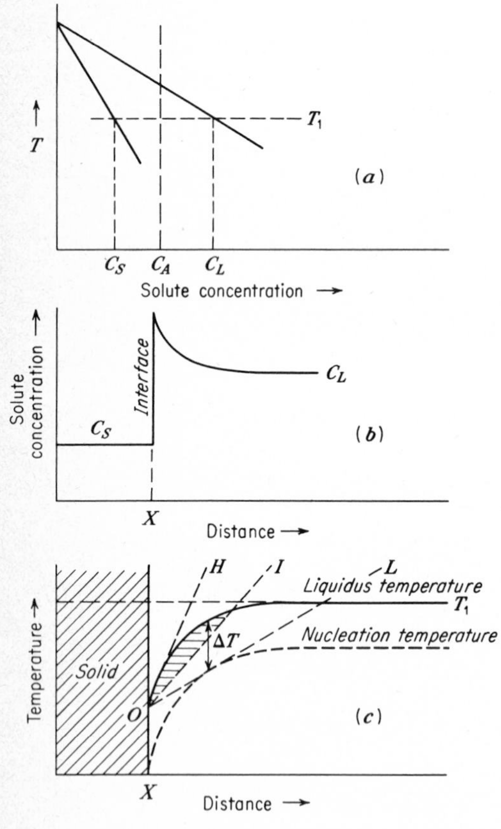

Fig. 8.7 Schematic illustration of (*a*) the solute concentration in solid, C_S, and in liquid, C_L, at temperature T_1; (*b*) the composition gradient existing in the liquid at the solid-liquid interface; (*c*) the effect of this gradient on the liquidus temperature in the vicinity of the interface. (*After G. W. Form and J. F. Wallace*[2] *and J. L. Walker.*[4])

Alloy Freezing Where No Eutectic Occurs (Cases 1 and 2)

Freezing occurs over a temperature range the extent of which is determined by the alloy system and by the composition of the alloy. Thus, in the iron-carbon system, the freezing range for which is shown in Fig. 8.6, the freezing range is small at low carbon contents, reaches a maximum at about 2.0 per cent carbon, and decreases again thereafter.

In this type of freezing, the precipitating solid differs in composition from the liquid. This sets up concentration gradients in the liquid which have a profound effect on the freezing process. A schematic illustration of what can happen is given in Fig. 8.7. Because the solid is lower in solute concentration than the liquid at T_1, a concentration gradient develops immediately ahead of the interface as shown in Fig. 8.7*b*. This concentration gradient will affect the liquidus temperature as shown in Fig. 8.7*c*. If this concentration gradient is not as steep as the temperature gradient (line *OH* in Fig. 8.7*c*), the interface will advance uniformly. If the temperature gradient is in some intermediate position such as shown by line *OI* in Fig. 8.7*c*, there will be a small amount of supercooling ahead of the advancing front represented by the shaded area. This results in what is referred to as *constitutional supercooling*. The instability created by this condition promotes the growth of spikes which extend into the liquid. Continued growth of these spikes into the liquid in a direction opposite the heat flow, and in a lateral direction as well, results in a typical treelike, or dendritic, structure, represented by Fig. 8.8.

If the cooling rate eventually results in a temperature gradient indicated by line *OL* in Fig. 8.7*c*, the supercooling temperature differential ΔT may then be low enough to promote random nucleation and equi-axed grains. As these new nuclei grow, constitutional supercooling develops in advance of the growing interface, and these grains also grow in a dendritic manner, until constitutional supercooling has ceased because of thermal and com-

***Fig.* 8.8** Aluminum-alloy dendritic structure developed during solidification. (*From J. F. Wallace, E. E. Stonebrook, W. L. Rudin, R. A. Clark, and B. C. Yearly.*[8])

***Fig.* 8.9** Grain structure of stainless-steel ingots, the one to the right being poured from metal treated with a nucleation catalyst. (*From J. L. Walker.*[4])

positional adjustments.[4,6] Commercial alloys poured into castings and cooled in the normal manner will exhibit the columnar dendritic grains near the surface and the equi-axed dendritic grains near the center of the casting. The ratio of equi-axed to columnar grains is:

1. Inversely proportional to the effective superheat*
2. Inversely proportional to the critical degree of supercooling necessary for nucleation to occur at a fairly high rate
3. Proportional to the freezing range
4. Inversely proportional to the thermal conductivity[2]
5. Inversely proportional to the slopes of the solidus and liquidus lines

By proper control of alloying elements to promote constitutional supercooling and the additional use of inoculating agents to promote heterogeneous nucleation, relatively fine grained structures are possible. This is illustrated in Fig. 8.9. The use of inoculating agents reduces the amount of supercooling required for nucleation, but very fine equi-axed grains are obtained only when elements are present which produce concentration gradients to restrict the growth rate of each grain, thereby producing nucleation of additional grains.[6,7]

*It has been shown that the percentage of columnar grain structure and the size of the interior equi-axed grains both increase with pouring temperature. This has been attributed to the effect of pouring temperature on the survival of nuclei produced initially at the metal-mold interface. A low pouring temperature creates more nuclei, which survive in the liquid and which drift away from the interface by convection. These serve as nuclei for equi-axed grains. The number of these grains is inversely proportional to the pouring temperature; consequently, the lower the pouring temperature, the greater the number of equi-axed grains, the finer their grain size, and the more restricted the growth of columnar grains.[49]

The fact that alloys of this type freeze over a range of temperature means that, when a casting is poured and cools to the freezing temperature, there is no fine line of demarcation between the liquid and solid as in the case of pure metals. The first metal to freeze is at the mold surface as before, and freezing progresses inward as before, but here the similarity ends. It would be better, in fact, to say that the *start of freezing* progresses inward as before, because even though the metal dendrites extend themselves into the metal, they leave behind islands of liquid which do not freeze until further heat is extracted. Eventually, however, these islands also freeze and their solidification also progresses inward. The result is that, when these alloys solidify, the start of freezing proceeds in a wavelike manner toward the center of the casting, with the *end of freezing* lagging behind, but also moving toward the center of the casting.[9] At any one particular time, therefore, a region can be found in the casting which is composed of both liquid and solid metal. This has a mushy consistency when hammered, squeezed, or deformed in any way, leading to the expression *mushy stage* of freezing.* The time separation between the start and end of a freezing wave is controlled by external variables as well as by the characteristics of the particular alloy, and such extremes as a completely mushy condition throughout or only a slight separation of the start and end wave can occur. The latter condition can occur when heat is extracted rapidly. This is not the only controlling variable, however, and others will be discussed in the next section. Figure 8.10 illus-

*The mushy, or pasty, stage of freezing is a term sometimes reserved for the case where dendrites are suspended in liquid metal rather than attached to the side walls. This condition can occur during the freezing of the interior equi-axed zone.[6]

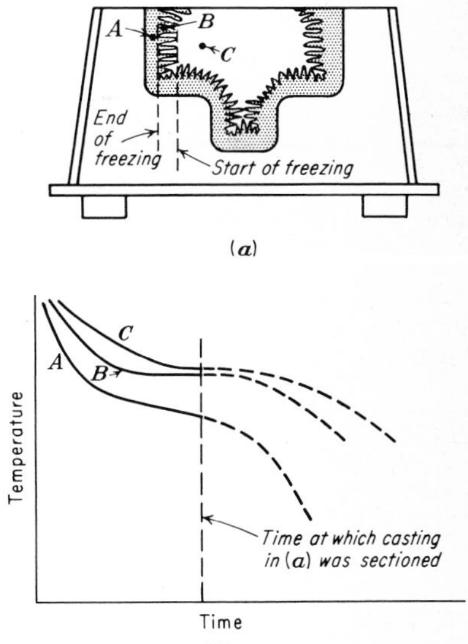

***Fig.* 8.10** (*a*) Cross section through a casting which freezes over a temperature range; (*b*) schematic representation of cooling curves at indicated points in the casting.

trates schematically the relationship between the conditions existing during the freezing of this type of alloy and the cooling curves at various points in the casting. This figure shows that there is no single temperature of solidification, as was the case for pure metals. However, the effect of the latent heat of fusion is such that the remaining liquid is held virtually at constant temperature after freezing begins. Only the metal near the surface (point A) is cooled rapidly enough to avoid the extreme thermal lag evident in the interior. The general similarity in the curves for points B and C in Figs. 8.2 and 8.10 illustrates the inadequacy of using cooling-curve data alone to study solidification characteristics. Metallographic examination of castings interrupted in their freezing process is also essential to reveal the exact nature of the process. This is demonstrated in the discussion of eutectic alloys in a later section.

Variables Affecting the Start and End of Freezing for Cases 1 and 2

The foregoing information has established the fact that alloys freeze differently from pure metals in that they develop a band where both solid and liquid metal coexist. The width of this band is affected by a large number of variables, including:

1. The solidification range of the alloy
2. Thermal characteristics of the mold
3. Conductivity of the solidifying metal
4. Temperature level of solidification

The Solidification Range of the Alloy

If cooling data taken at various points in a casting are rearranged to give a plot of distance from the mold-casting interface against time in minutes, the effect of these variables can be readily revealed. Such so-called *TTT* curves* (time-temperature-transformation) are illustrated in Fig. 8.11 for steel of several carbon contents cast in chill and green-sand molds. These curves show that solidification proceeds by the simultaneous travel of *start-of-freeze* and *end-of-freeze waves*. Since an increase in carbon content increases the solidification range, the effect of this variable is made apparent by comparing the three sets of curves and the graphic representations below. For a given mold material, the effect of increasing the solidification range is to increase the separation between start and end of freezing.

*It should be pointed out that the *TTT* curves herein described are not the same as the *TTT* curves from the heat-treating process.

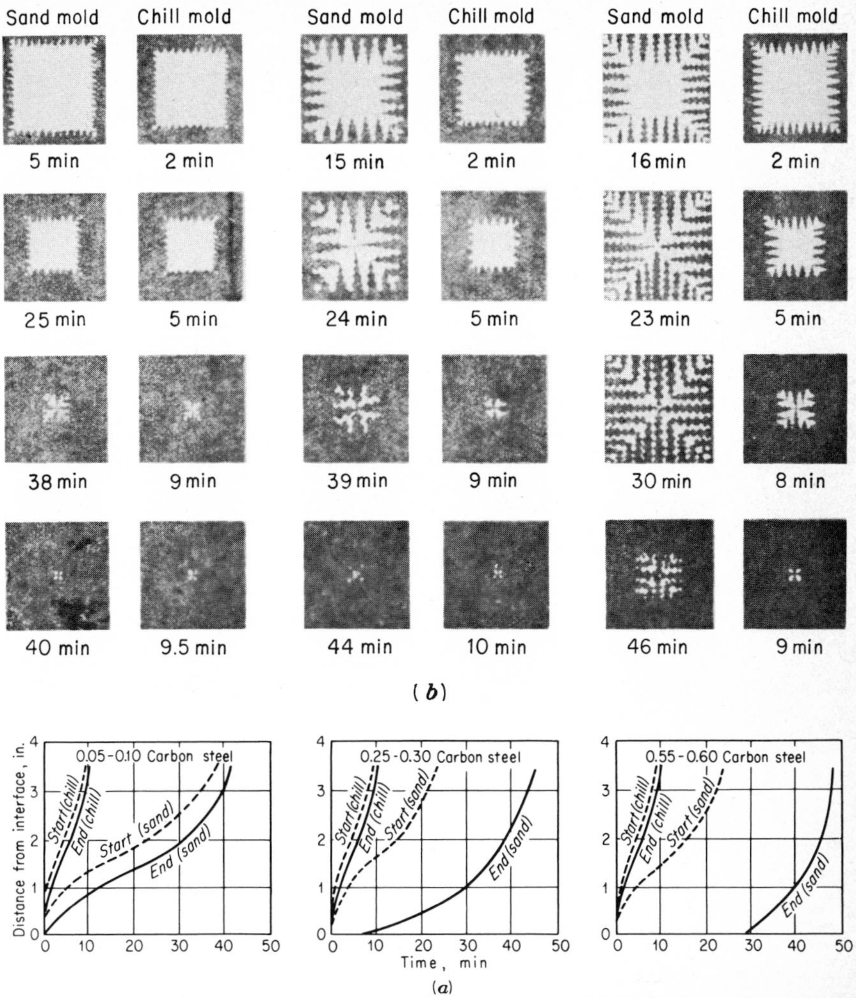

***Fig.* 8.11** Effect of carbon content on the solidification of steel in sand and chill molds expressed (*a*) as *TTT* solidification curves and (*b*) as graphic representations. (*From H. F. Bishop and W. S. Pellini.*[9])

Thermal Characteristics of the Mold

These curves also show that, for steel cast into chill molds, the space separation of the two waves is relatively narrow; hence the solidification process consists basically of the movement of the solidification band from the mold wall into isothermal liquid which is holding constant at essentially the liquidus temperature. Solidification of steel from sand walls, on the other hand, although still progressive, is such that the solidification band is much wider or never develops. Solidification in sand molds, therefore, is more general throughout the casting.[10]

Thickness of the mold walls will affect the position of the curves shown in Fig. 8.11. Up to a certain point, increasing the thickness of a chill-mold wall will increase solidification rates. Beyond that point, little additional effect is realized. In the case of sand molds, heat-removal rates are increased by a *decrease* in mold thickness below a certain critical thickness. Above this thickness little effect from mold-thickness variation is experienced. Increasing the superheat of the metal has the tendency of moving the start and end curves somewhat to the right in both chill and sand molds.[10]

Thermal Conductivity of the Solidifying Metal

The effect of a high thermal conductivity of the metal is to decrease thermal gradients in the casting, thus favoring a wide separation between the start and end of freezing, even in alloys that have a short solidification range.

For example, a 99 per cent aluminum alloy was found to have approximately a 40-min spread between the start and end of freezing when cast in a sand mold even though the solidification range was only 10 F.[9]

Temperature Level of Solidification

A low temperature level of solidification which reduces temperature gradients between the mold and casting will decrease the temperature gradient within the casting. The effect of this last variable can also be revealed by comparing the sand casting of the aluminum alloy referred to above with that of the low-carbon steel (Fig. 8.11). Here both alloys have a low solidification range, but the steel shows much better progressive solidification than the aluminum alloy.

The effect of the four variables mentioned previously is shown schematically in Fig. 8.12.

Dendritic Growth and Segregation

Dendrites grow by extending their main spines into the liquid and sending out lateral branches, as previously explained. The metal which freezes on these spines is of different composition from the liquid from which it originated. This can be demonstrated by passing an isotherm through a binary diagram in the liquid-solid region and noting that the solid metal is always richer in the component of higher melting point as compared with the liquid with which it is in equilibrium. The result of this difference in composition between liquid and solid is segregation of elements in the final casting. This segregation of elements is really of two types. First, there is a general, or *ingot,* type of segregation, which results in a slightly different composition on the outer portions of the cast-

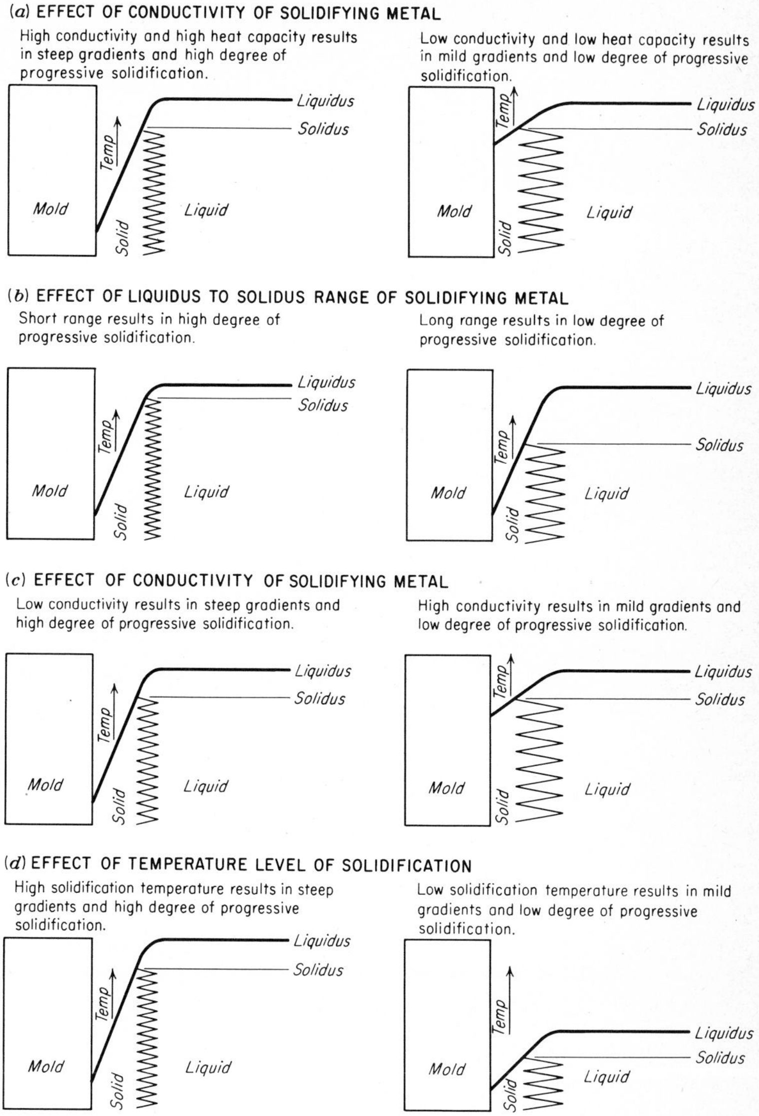
(a) EFFECT OF CONDUCTIVITY OF SOLIDIFYING METAL
High conductivity and high heat capacity results in steep gradients and high degree of progressive solidification.
Liquidus
Solidus
Temp
Mold
Solid
Liquid
Low conductivity and low heat capacity results in mild gradients and low degree of progressive solidification.
Liquidus
Solidus
Temp
Mold
Solid
Liquid
(b) EFFECT OF LIQUIDUS TO SOLIDUS RANGE OF SOLIDIFYING METAL
Short range results in high degree of progressive solidification.
Liquidus
Solidus
Temp
Mold
Solid
Liquid
Long range results in low degree of progressive solidification.
Liquidus
Solidus
Temp
Mold
Solid
Liquid
(c) EFFECT OF CONDUCTIVITY OF SOLIDIFYING METAL
Low conductivity results in steep gradients and high degree of progressive solidification.
Liquidus
Solidus
Temp
Mold
Solid
Liquid
High conductivity results in mild gradients and low degree of progressive solidification.
Liquidus
Solidus
Temp
Mold
Solid
Liquid
(d) EFFECT OF TEMPERATURE LEVEL OF SOLIDIFICATION
High solidification temperature results in steep gradients and high degree of progressive solidification.
Liquidus
Solidus
Temp
Mold
Solid
Liquid
Low solidification temperature results in mild gradients and low degree of progressive solidification.
Liquidus
Solidus
Temp
Mold
Solid
Liquid

Fig.* 8.12** **Schematic illustration of the effect of mold and metal variables on progressive solidification.** ***(From W. S. Pellini, Trans. AFS, vol. 61, p. 603, 1953.)

ing as compared with the interior. Because the first solid to freeze is richer in one component, it is natural that the remaining liquid in the interior should change composition slightly from its initial composition.

The other type of segregation is on a microscopic scale and involves the liquid metal which is entrapped by the various branches of the dendrites. Since this liquid is being constantly depleted of one component and there is generally insufficient time to establish equilibrium, the last metal to freeze around and between the dendrite spines is often considerably different in chemical composition from that which froze first. Thus each dendrite exhibits a segregation pattern, and as a result, a single grain (the dendrite) will differ widely in chemical composition from point to point. When this structure is etched, segregation accounts for a difference in etching rate from point to point, and structures such as exhibited by Fig. 8.13 result.

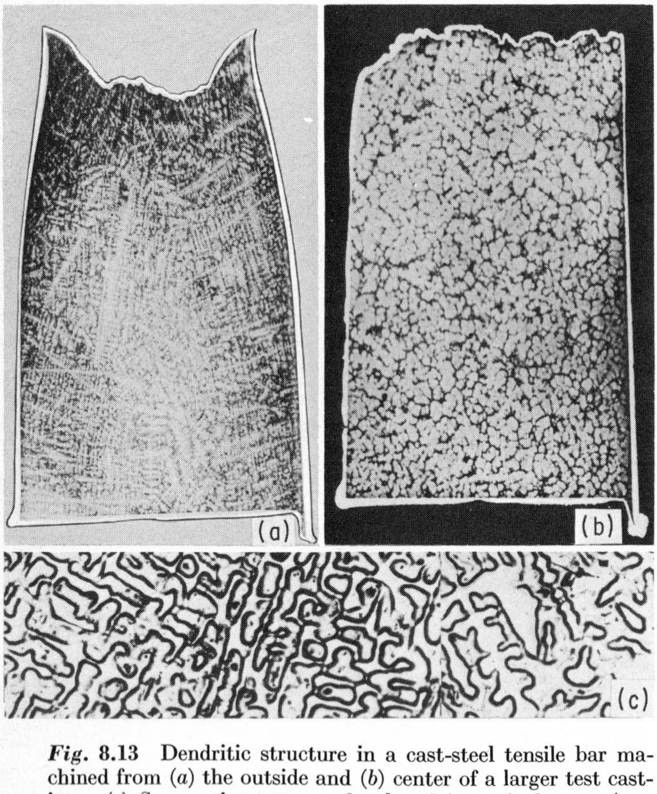

***Fig.* 8.13** Dendritic structure in a cast-steel tensile bar machined from (*a*) the outside and (*b*) center of a larger test casting. (*c*) Segregation pattern developed in a tin bronze (gun metal), commonly referred to as a "cored" structure. [(*a*) *and* (*b*) *from A. Cibula;*[7] (*c*) *from Ames and Kahn, Trans. AFS, vol.* 58, *p.* 229, 1950.]

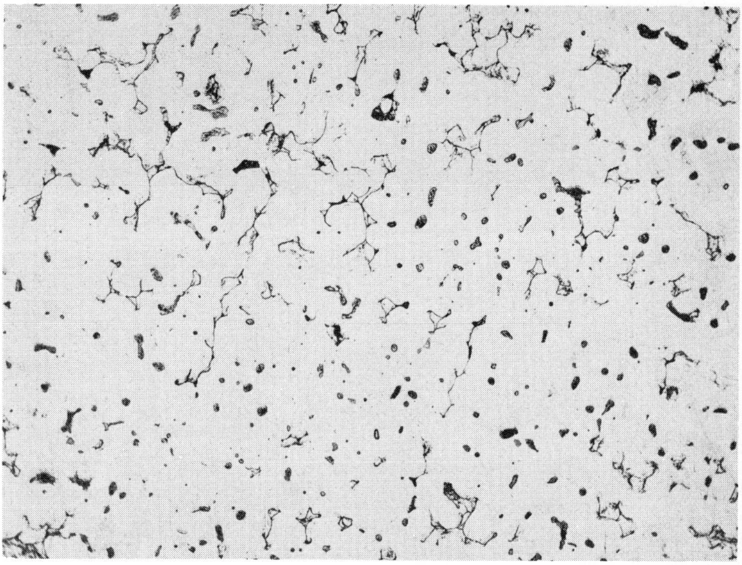

***Fig.* 8.14** Interdendritic fissure-type microporosity in brass, ×100. (*From J. F. Ewing, C. Upthegrove, and F. B. Rote.*[12])

Shrinkage

The shrinkage effects in these alloys are also complicated by the interlacing dendrite system that develops during freezing. Not only can we expect the localized shrinkage found where the last liquid froze, but the liquid entrapped between dendrites also shrinks, developing widely distributed voids referred to as *microporosity* (Fig. 8.14.) Thus the dendritic growth illustrated in Fig. 8.15*a* would develop substantial microporosity, whereas that represented by Fig. 8.15*b* would not. Tin bronzes exhibit the type of dendritic growth shown in Fig. 8.15*a*.

If gases such as hydrogen and nitrogen are dissolved in liquid metal, they also tend to segregate in the same manner as alloying elements, with the result that, as freezing progresses, the gases accumulate in the same interdendritic areas in which microporosity is most likely to occur. The result is that these gases aggravate the porosity condition developed by the dendritic freezing process by precipitating in these voids. Although porosity induced by gas precipitation will assume the form of spherically shaped holes if enough liquid metal is still present, once ample solidification has occurred, it is difficult or impossible to distinguish the effects of gas segregation from that caused solely by localized shrinkage because of the irregularly shaped voids that are formed in both cases. Frequently, microporosity can be attributed to the combined effect of gas precipitation and inadequate feeding. The need for proper melting procedures and for proper mold design to reduce the range between the start and end of freezing is indicated.

Commercial Alloys

Steel and copper- or nickel-base alloys are the best examples of commercial metals freezing as solid-solution alloys. The aluminum casting alloys usually end up with some eutectic freezing.

Eutectic Alloys

Only a narrow range of composition, or more strictly speaking, only one composition, in a particular alloy system exhibiting the eutectic-type freezing will freeze at constant temperature. Furthermore, when additional elements are added to a system of two metals, chances for isothermal freezing become even less.

The solidification of a casting poured from a eutectic composition (alloy *A*, Fig. 8.6) might be presumed to occur in much the same manner as that of a pure metal. It is true that under equilibrium conditions solidification takes place at constant temperatures as for pure metals, but some

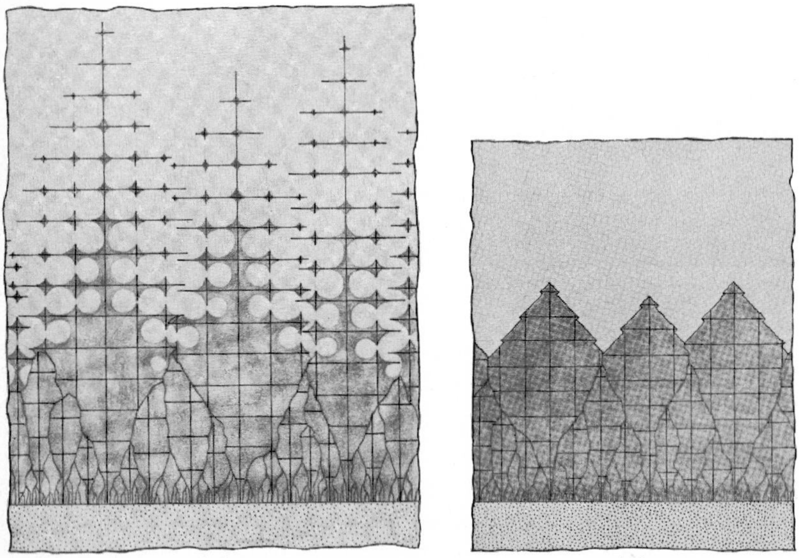

(*a*) (*b*)

Fig. 8.15 (*a*) Characteristic freezing habit of tin bronzes which leads to microporosity and little apparent shrinkage, (*b*) freezing of dendrites in alloys where microshrinkage is no problem and more localized shrinkage occurs in the last metal to freeze (piping). (*After C. L. Frear.*[25])

differences should be noted. The grain size of the two precipitating phases, for example, is much finer than that of a pure metal, and freezing starts at a lower temperature than that of either component in the alloy.

The shape of the precipitating particles can be quite varied, and includes such morphologies as:

1. Lamellar structure
2. Rodlike precipitation of one phase in the other
3. Globular precipitation of a phase
4. Precipitation of polyhedrally shaped particles of one phase in the other[15,16]

It has been shown that the morphology of the eutectic structure in Al-Si alloys is dependent upon the temperature at which the silicon phase nucleates,[16] the order in terms of decreasing nucleation temperature being polyhedrally shaped silicon grains, coarse silicon plates, fine silicon plates, and globular silicon particles. The globular structure is produced most readily by an addition of a modifying agent such as sodium. The resultant alloy is referred to as a *modified* alloy. A type of globular eutectic can also be produced by chill casting.

From a casting standpoint, the eutectic alloys are known to freeze either *exogenously,* that is, from the surface to the center of the casting, or *endogenously,* represented by a more or less random nucleation of eutectic cells or colonies consisting of individual clusters of the two phases growing in the liquid as essentially spherical solid masses. The result of exogenous freezing is to provide a wall-like solidification from the surface to the center of the casting. Endogenous solidification leads to a mushy, or pasty, condition during the solidification process due to the liquid surrounding each eutectic cell. Modified Al-Si alloys are found to freeze exogenously whereas the normal Al-Si alloys freeze endogenously, as demonstrated in Fig. 8.16.[17]

Normal eutectic alloys will freeze in the endogenous cellularlike fashion which tends to produce the mushy condition; nevertheless, the greater nucleation of cells near the surface of the casting does cause the solidification to progress in a wavelike fashion, with the start of eutectic freezing advancing toward the interior some distance in advance of the completion of freezing.

Near the surface of a casting more and finer cells are found than in the interior. If the cell growth is uniform throughout, the finer and more numerous cells must complete their freezing before the larger, less numerous cells in the interior; in the latter, the cells would have to grow for a longer time before they would meet other growing cells. This mechanism of freezing would explain the fact that freezing does not occur along a sharp interface between solid and liquid, and would also explain the almost complete lack of temperature gradients during eutectic solidification

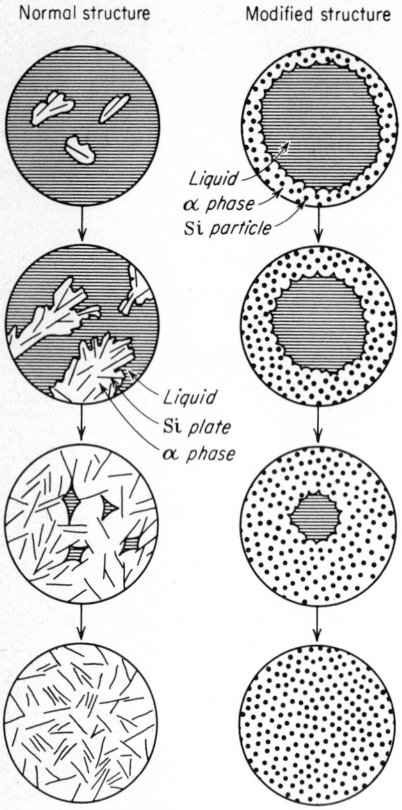

***Fig.* 8.16** Mode of solidification in normal and modified aluminum-silicon alloys. (*After C. B. Kim.*[17])

that has been noted.[19] It would appear, therefore, that it is only the modified, or exogenously freezing, eutectic alloys which behave similarly to pure metals in their freezing process.

Alloy Freezing in Two Stages

This type of freezing involves cases 3 and 4 listed on page 186. In these cases, it is convenient to think of freezing as taking place in two stages: the dendritic growth of the primary phase, followed by the final solidification of the liquid as a eutectic mixture. A good example of a commercial alloy exhibiting this type of freezing is cast iron.

In alloys of this type the first stage of freezing proceeds essentially as already described; namely, dendritic growth starts and moves inward, followed by the "end" wave after the "start" wave has completed its travel, thus creating a semisolid condition throughout the casting. Near the surface the eutectic freezing seems to start coincidental with the completion of the dendritic end wave, although the thermal methods used to detect these cycles may not be able to identify their timing exactly.

The rate at which the eutectic structure extends into the interior appears to slow down drastically as soon as the eutectic begins to develop, because the beginning of eutectic freezing near the center of the casting is delayed until well after the dendrites have completed their growth. This no doubt results from the combined effect of the heat of fusion and poor heat transfer out of the casting. The difference in time between the start and end of eutectic freezing at any one point in a casting would not be expected to be very great since the eutectic solidification range in a ternary system such as cast iron is not very great.

These effects are illustrated in Fig. 8.17, which shows, in addition, that, compared with steel, cast iron has a much more extensive "mushy stage." Note, for instance, that at certain time periods, after the dendrite formation has started, the end is still not complete anywhere in the casting; on the other hand, for the eutectic portion of the freezing, the end wave follows closely on the heels of the start wave.

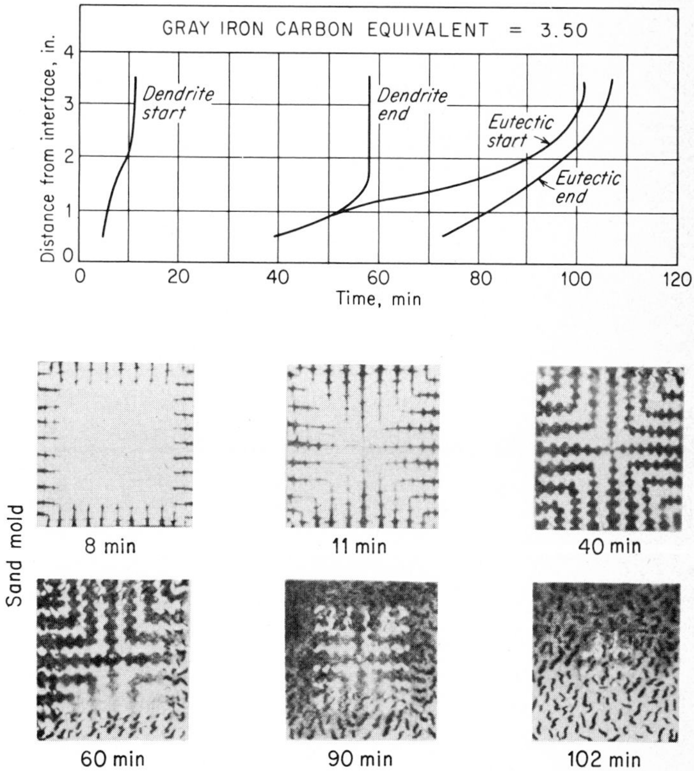

***Fig.* 8.17** Solidification mode of gray cast iron. (*From H. F. Bishop and W. S. Pellini.*[9])

As has already been discussed, the initial freezing results in the formation of an interlacing network of crystals that grows in a treelike manner. The eutectic, however, although it apparently begins forming first near the surface of the casting, is not so prone to be influenced in its nucleation by the mold wall. Nucleation apparently appears throughout the liquid, and the eutectic cells grow outwardly in all directions. This is probably because the liquid is very close to being isothermal. There appear to be more nuclei near the mold wall and fewer as the center of the casting is approached. As discussed for eutectic alloys, this may result in freezing of the eutectic liquid taking longer in the center than on the outside.

Effects of Variables

The effect of composition is demonstrated by Fig. 8.18, which shows that, in cast iron, as the carbon or silicon contents or both increase (equivalent to an increase in "carbon equivalent" value; see Chap. 21), the time required for completion of dendritic freezing is shortened whereas the time required for completing the eutectic freezing is increased. Superheat tends to delay the start and end of freezing, whereas an addition of sea coal to the molding sand speeds up the solidification process.

Segregation and Shrinkage

As in the preceding cases that have been discussed, segregation and shrinkage accompany the solidification process. The extent and severity of these effects are controlled by variables such as superheat and cooling rate, which have already been discussed, as well as by the type of alloy being formed. Thus it would be expected that a cast iron of a composition close to that of the eutectic would show a minimum of segregation and microporosity, whereas one having an extended temperature range of solidification would be more likely to exhibit these effects.

In the case of gray cast iron, graphitization of the iron occurs during the freezing process. Graphitization results in an expansion of the iron which can, in part at least, nullify the shrinkage that normally would be expected. The graphitization mechanism is considered in greater detail in Chap. 21.

OTHER PROPERTIES RELATED TO THE FREEZING MECHANISM

Fluidity

The term *fluidity*, as used by the foundryman, does not mean the reciprocal of viscosity. What is meant by fluidity in the foundry sense is the ability to fill a mold. It is measured by pouring a standard mold that will provide a good indication of metal flow. Usually a thin, long casting is poured in the form of a spiral, the length of the spiral serving as a measure of fluidity. One such spiral casting, illustrated in Fig. 21.7, was used to obtain the data given in Fig. 8.20.

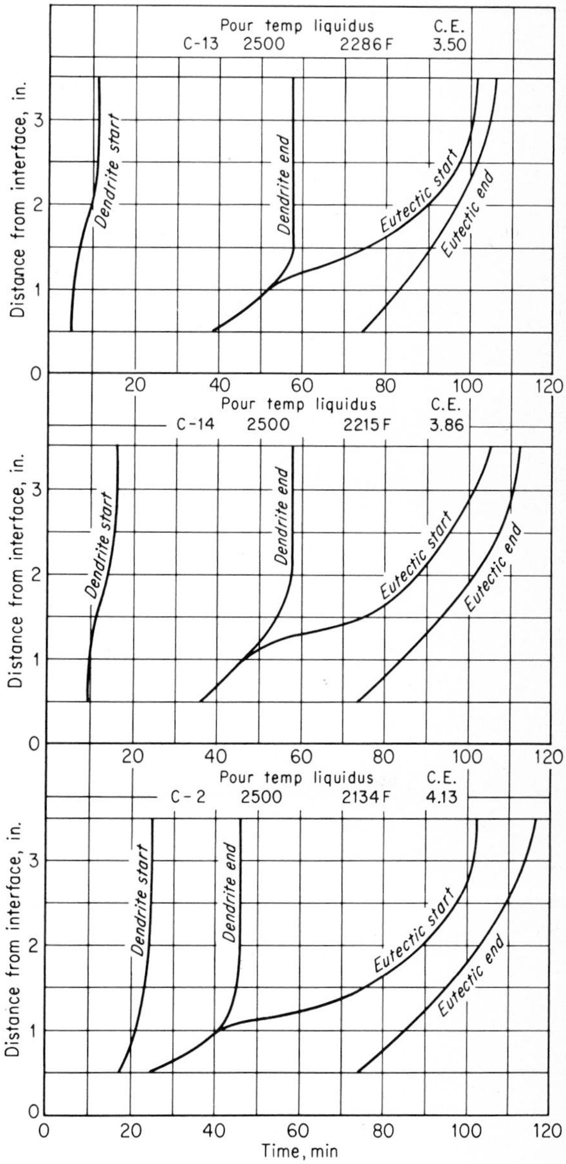

***Fig.* 8.18** Progression of solidification for gray-iron castings of three different compositions poured at 2500 F. (*From R. P. Dunphy and W. S. Pellini.*[32])

Both metal and mold characteristics are involved in determining fluidity. As far as metal characteristics are concerned, the following metallurgical factors can be listed as those which have a greater or lesser effect on fluidity:

1. Metal composition, with particular emphasis on its relation to the freezing process
2. Superheat
3. Metal viscosity
4. Surface tension
5. Surface oxide films
6. Adsorbed gas films
7. Suspended inclusions
8. Inclusions precipitating during freezing

Of these factors, the first two are most important. With regard to superheat, it stands to reason that metal that is heated to a higher temperature will have a longer period in the mold in which it is liquid, and hence it will flow farther than metal not so highly heated.

It has been amply demonstrated that changes in metal composition, insofar as these changes are reflected by changes in the solidification process, can markedly affect fluidity. Consider, for example, Fig. 8.19, which shows a plot of fluidity superimposed over the constitution diagram for the lead-antimony and antimony-cadmium systems. Note that best fluidity is attained for pure components, eutectics, or phases that freeze congruently (at constant temperature), whereas poorest fluidity is had when the solidification range is the greatest. Since a long solidification range is indicative of a condition where the metal is in a mushy condition, consisting of interlacing dendrites surrounded by liquid at practically its freezing temperature, it would seem only natural that this condition would restrict fluidity. On the other hand, if pure metal freezes, it does so by a gradual inward growth of solid metal which does not restrict the flow of the still liquid interior metal. Likewise, freezing of a modified eutectic can be considered in somewhat the same light (Fig. 8.16).

In a study of the fluidity of a group of aluminum alloys as compared with their solidification characteristics, it was found that there was a direct correlation between the fluidity of the alloys and their freezing range.[34] Those alloys having the longer freezing range were lower in fluidity than those with a short freezing range. In fact, it was possible to calculate with reasonable accuracy the fluidity of various alloys simply from information regarding their freezing range.

Another example showing the close correlation between fluidity and solidification temperature, as well as with superheat temperature, is given by Fig. 8.20, which shows data obtained for gray and malleable cast iron.

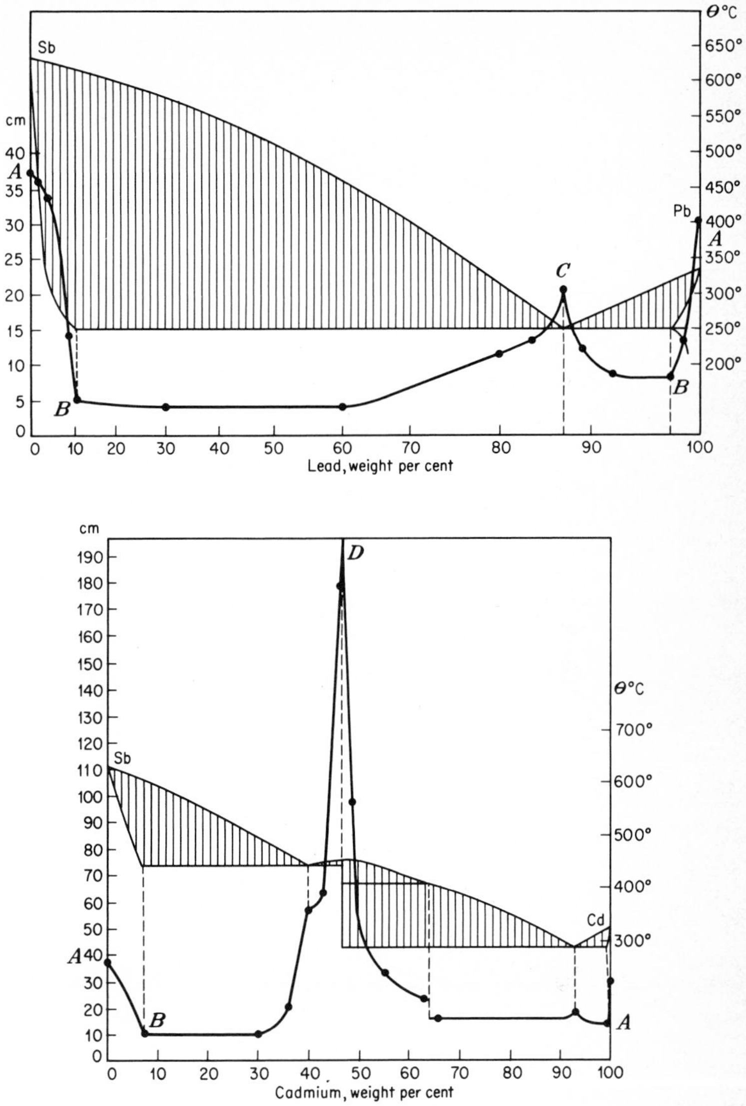

***Fig.* 8.19** Fluidity curves superimposed on the binary diagrams indicate the close relationship between the fluidity of the metal and the solidification process. (*After A. Portevin and P. Bastien.*[33])

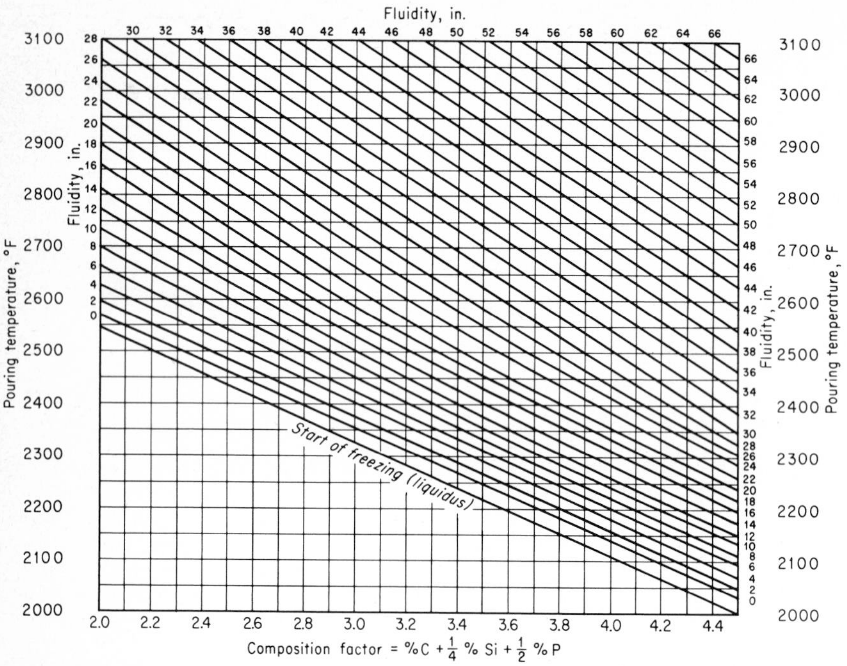

Fig. 8.20 **Fluidity related to pouring temperature and composition of gray and malleable cast iron.** (*From L. F. Porter and P. C. Rosenthal.*[35])

Hot Tearing or Hot Cracking

As castings cool, they contract; and if they are restrained from contracting in certain areas because of their geometry or because of mold conditions, parts of the castings may then be placed in tension. If these tensile stresses arise when the metal is weak, it cannot resist these stresses and cracks. There is considerable controversy in the literature as to the time when cracking occurs, some authors arguing that it occurs after solidification, others that it occurs before. The fact that cracking is associated with the solidification process has, however, been firmly established. It has been suggested that the cracking occurs during a later stage in freezing, when solidification is complete except for a thin film of liquid surrounding the dendrites. The condition is aggravated by the presence of low-melting segregates and coarse grain size.[40–42] The mechanism is depicted graphically in Fig. 8.21.

A somewhat similar explanation has been advanced for hot cracking of aluminum-base alloys.[38] It is stated that, during solidification, the aluminum-base alloys become coherent after a certain portion has solidified. If there is a relatively large reduction in temperature during subsequent solidification, thermal contraction may cause cracking. The cracking tendency seems to be aggravated if only a small quantity of eutectic is present, and is progressively reduced if large amounts of eutectic are formed. The small quantities of eutectic are believed to form interdendritic films which constitute zones of weakness. An empirical correlation between the solidification range and alloy behavior has been used to rate the resistance of various aluminum alloys toward hot cracking. These results are given in Table 8.1 in terms of a coherence temperature range, the lower values corresponding to superior resistance.

In studies of the hot tearing of white cast iron for malleableizing, it was also concluded that hot tearing occurs in the latter stages of freezing, but here results are complicated by the graphitization ("mottling")

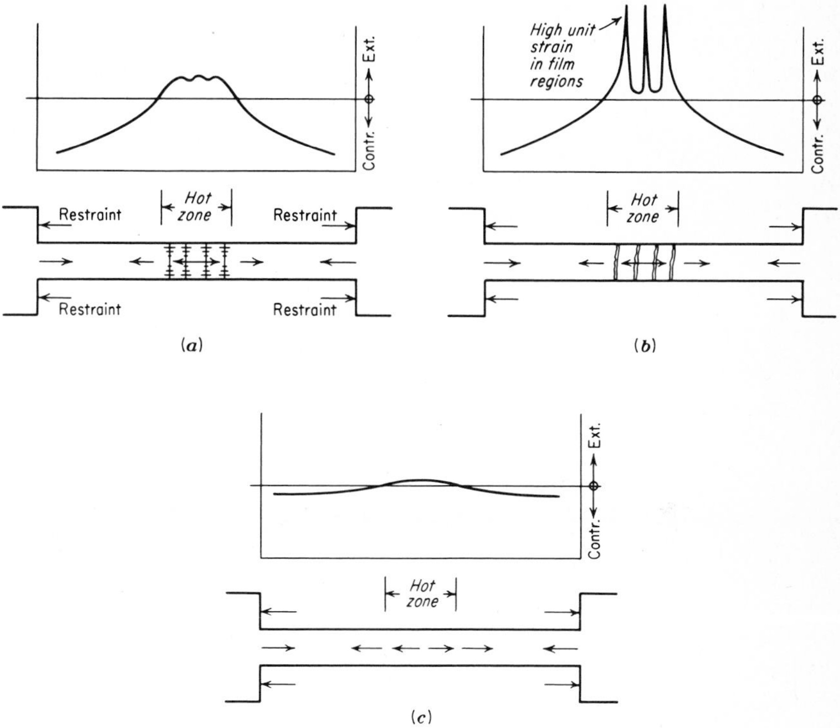

***Fig.* 8.21** Schematic illustration of a proposed basic mechanism of hot tearing. (*a*) Hot zone in mushy stage. Extension of hot zone is essentially uniform, resulting in low unit strains which are insufficient to cause a separation. (*b*) Hot zone in liquid-film stage. Extension of hot zone is highly concentrated in film regions, resulting in high unit strains which may be sufficient to cause separation. (*c*) Hot zone in solid stage. Extension of hot zone occurs by uniform creep flow of highly ductile solid metal. (*From H. F. Bishop, C. G. Ackerlind, and W. S. Pellini.*[36])

tendency of the iron.[37] If some graphite is formed during freezing, the normal contraction is partly alleviated and cracking is less likely to occur.

Although it appears that cracking is most likely to occur when the casting is almost frozen, it is not possible to generalize too much in relating the hot-cracking tendencies to the solidification characteristics, since quite a number of other factors, both metallurgical and mechanical, are involved.

Evolution of Dissolved Gases

Information already presented has revealed how the normal shrinkage which occurs when metals freeze may result in either such local effects as cavities, or a spongy mass of interconnecting voids, or a more widespread distribution of voids referred to as microporosity. Whether local or widespread porosity occurs depends on composition and the way the casting is fed (Chap. 9).

Table 8.1 Relative resistance to hot cracking of commercial aluminum casting alloys *Ratings obtained from solidification curve analysis based on coherence ranges**

Alloy No.	Coherence range, F	Alloy No.	Coherence range, F
43	15	B195	54
B214	18	113	61
A132	27	319	66
C113	27	108	67
356	29	214	88
355	33	122	91
D132	34	212	92
333	36	112	99
A108	46	195	146
F214	49	220	176

* From E. E. Stonebrook and W. E. Sicha.[34] Lower coherence-range values indicate higher resistance to hot cracking.

Associated with cavities resulting from shrinkage effects is porosity, which may come from dissolved gases that are evolved during solidification as already discussed. Occasionally, as in the case of copper castings, a reaction between dissolved oxygen and hydrogen to form water vapor may be instrumental in creating porosity. The effect of the evolved gas (generally hydrogen) may be manifested in a number of ways. If the alloy is inclined to exhibit local shrinkage, the gas may eliminate or reduce it by preventing liquid metal from feeding the casting in the normal manner, thereby leading to widespread microporosity rather than the local shrinkage usually occurring. If the alloy is inclined toward microporosity, gas evolution will accentuate this form of defect by creating a back pressure, making it more difficult to feed through the mushy range.[43] The problem of dissolved gases and their evolution during freezing is discussed in greater detail in connection with specific alloys considered in subsequent chapters.

Effect of Inoculation

Another problem connected with the solidification characteristics of alloys is the modification of the structure and properties by the addition of a small amount of another metal to the alloy before pouring. Examples of this are the addition of sodium to aluminum–12 per cent silicon alloys, of titanium to aluminum, and of magnesium to cast iron. In the latter case, a nodular-type graphite structure develops (Chap. 22).

In all cases, the additions act to delay and alter precipitation of the solid from the liquid, as previously discussed for modified Al-Si alloys. Various explanations have been advanced for these effects, but none has been universally accepted. The effects may be related to the question of homogeneous vs. heterogeneous nucleation. The modification of the aluminum–12 per cent silicon alloy by sodium and of the cast irons by magnesium has been attributed to the addition effecting a change in the interfacial tensions between the two solid phases (aluminum and silicon in the first case and austenite and carbon in the second).[15] Grain refinement by vibration is also possible.[29]

BIBLIOGRAPHY

1. H. Y. Hunsicker, Solidification Rates of Aluminum in Dry Sand Molds, *Trans. AFS,* vol. 55, p. 68, 1947.
2. G. W. Form and J. F. Wallace, Solidification of Metal, *Trans. AFS,* vol. 68, p. 145, 1960.
3. R. F. Mehl, The Growth of Metal Crystals, p. 24 in "The Solidification of Metals and Alloys," American Institute of Mechanical Engineers, 1951.
4. J. L. Walker, Structure of Ingots and Castings, p. 319 in "Liquid Metals and Solidification," American Society for Metals, 1958.
5. W. K. Bock, Solidification of Metals, *Trans. AFS,* vol. 68, p. 691, 1960.
6. B. Chalmers, Melting and Freezing, *J. Metals,* vol. 200, p. 519, May, 1954.
7. A. Cibula, The Mechanism of Grain Refinement of Sand Castings in Aluminum Alloys, Part 4, *J. Inst. Metals,* vol. 76, p. 321, 1949.
8. J. F. Wallace, E. E. Stonebrook, W. L. Rudin, R. A. Clark, and B. C. Yearly, Solidification and Heat Treatment, *Foundry,* vol. 87, p. 84, September, 1959.

9. H. F. Bishop and W. S. Pellini, Solidification of Metals, *Foundry*, vol. 80, p. 87, February, 1952.
10. H. F. Bishop, F. A. Brandt, and W. S. Pellini, Solidification of Steel against Sand and Chill Walls, *Trans. AFS*, vol. 59, p. 435, 1951.
11. J. F. Wallace, J. H. Savage, and H. F. Taylor, Mechanical Properties of Cast Steel, *Trans. AFS*, vol. 59, p. 223, 1951.
12. J. F. Ewing, C. Upthegrove, and F. B. Rote, Melt Quality and Fracture Characteristics of 85-5-5-5 Brass, *Trans. AFS*, vol. 57, p. 433, 1949.
13. W. A. Tiller, Grain Size Control during Ingot Solidification, *J. Metals*, vol. 11, p. 512, August, 1959.
14. W. A. Tiller, Grain Size Control during Ingot Solidification, Part 2, Columnar-equiaxed Transition, *Trans. Met. Soc. AIME*, vol. 224, p. 448, June, 1962.
15. W. A. Tiller, Polyphase Solidification, p. 276 in "Liquid Metals and Solidification," American Society for Metals, 1958.
16. H. Weart, The Eutectic Reaction in Certain Binary Metallic Systems, Ph.D. thesis, University of Wisconsin, Madison, Wis., 1962.
17. C. B. Kim, A Study of the Solidification and Eutectic Modification of Al-Si Alloys, Ph.D. thesis, University of Wisconsin, Madison, Wis., 1962.
18. A. Boyles, "The Structure of Cast Iron," American Society for Metals, 1947.
19. R. W. Ruddle, A Preliminary Study of the Solidification of Castings, *J. Inst. Metals*, vol. 77, p. 1, 1950.
20. D. Jaffee and M. B. Bever, Solidification of Al-Zn Alloys, *Trans. AIME*, vol. 85, p. 972, 1956.
21. R. W. Ruddle, The Solidification of Castings, *Inst. Metals Monogr. Rept. Ser.* 7, 1957.
22. M. C. Flemings, S. Z. Uram, and H. F. Taylor, Solidification of Aluminum Castings, *AFS Trans.*, vol. 68, p. 670, 1960.
23. A. Cibula, The Grain Refinement of Aluminum Alloy Castings by Addition of Titanium and Boron, *J. Inst. Metals*, vol. 80, p. 1, 1951.
24. J. P. Dennison and E. V. Tull, The Refinement of Cast Grain Size in Cu-Al Alloys Containing 7–9% Aluminum, *J. Inst. Metals*, vol. 85, no. 1712, 1956.
25. C. L. Frear, Shrinkage in Tin Bronze Castings, *Foundry*, vol. 85, p. 81, December, 1957.
26. W. A. Tiller and J. W. Ritter, Effect of Growth Conditions upon the Solidification of a Binary Alloy, *Can. J. Phys.*, vol. 34, p. 96, January, 1956.
27. K. A. Jackson and B. Chalmers, Kinetics of Solidification, *Can. J. Phys.*, vol. 34, p. 473, May, 1956.
28. J. A. Reynolds and C. R. Tottle, Nucleation of Cast Metals at the Mold Face, *J. Inst. Metals*, vol. 80, p. 93, 1951.
29. W. C. Winegard and B. Chalmers, Supercooling and Dendritic Freezing in Alloys, *Trans. ASM*, vol. 46, p. 1214, 1954.
30. D. Walton, W. A. Tiller, J. W. Rutter, and W. C. Winegard, Instability of a Smooth Solid-Liquid Interface during Solidification, *Trans. AIME*, vol. 203, p. 1023, 1955.
31. W. S. Pellini, Solidification of Various Metals in Ingot and Sand Molds, Electric Furnace Steel Conference, *AIME preprint*, Dec. 5–7, 1956.
32. R. P. Dunphy and W. S. Pellini, Solidification of Gray Iron in Sand Molds, *Trans. AFS*, vol. 59, p. 425, 1951.
33. A. Portevin and P. Bastien, Fluidity of Ternary Alloys, *J. Inst. Metals*, vol. 61, 1934.
34. E. E. Stonebrook and W. E. Sicha, Correlation of Cooling Curve Data with

Casting Characteristics of Aluminum Alloys, *Trans. AFS,* vol. 57, p. 489, 1949.
35. L. F. Porter and P. C. Rosenthal, Factors Affecting Fluidity of Gray Cast Iron, *Trans. AFS,* vol. 60, p. 725, 1952.
36. H. F. Bishop, C. G. Ackerlind, and W. S. Pellini, Metallurgy and Mechanics of Hot Tearing, *Trans. AFS,* vol. 60, p. 818, 1952.
37. E. A. Lange and R. W. Heine, A Test for Hot Tearing Tendency, *Trans. AFS,* vol. 60, p. 182, 1952.
38. D. C. G. Lees, Factors Controlling the Hot Tearing of Aluminum Casting Alloys, *Foundry Trade J.*, vol. 87, p. 211, Aug. 8, 1949.
39. C. W. Briggs, Solidification of Steel Castings, *Trans. AFS,* vol. 68, p. 158, 1960.
40. C. F. Christopher, Hot Tearing Characteristics of Acid and Basic Steel Castings Determined by High Temperature Testing, *Trans. AFS,* vol. 64, p. 293, 1956.
41. H. F. Bishop, C. G. Ackerlind, and W. S. Pellini, Investigation of Metallurgical and Mechanical Effects in the Development of Hot Tearing, *Trans. AFS,* vol. 65, p. 247, 1957.
42. R. A. Dodd, W. A. Pollard, and J. W. Meier, Hot Tearing of Magnesium Alloys, *Trans. AFS,* vol. 65, p. 100, 1957.
43. L. W. Eastwood, "Gas in Light Alloys," John Wiley & Sons, Inc., New York, 1946.
44. I. C. H. Hughes, K. E. L. Nicholas, A. G. Fuller, and T. J. Szajda, Factors Influencing Soundness of Gray Iron Castings, *Modern Castings,* vol. 35, p. 73, March, 1959.
45. P. Bastien, J. C. Armbruster, and P. Azou, Flowability and Viscosity, *Modern Castings,* vol. 41, p. 72, June, 1962.
46. A. H. Freedman and J. F. Wallace, The Influence of Vibration on Solidifying Metals, *Trans. AFS,* vol. 65, p. 578, 1957.
47. R. G. Garlick and J. F. Wallace, Grain Refinement of Solidifying Metals by Vibration, *Trans. AFS,* vol. 67, p. 366, 1959.
48. R. S. Richards and W. Rostoker, The Influence of Vibration on the Solidification of an Aluminum Alloy, *ASM Trans.*, vol. 48, p. 884, 1956.
49. B. Chalmers, The Structure of Ingots, *J. Australian Inst. Metals,* vol. 8, p. 255, August, 1963.

9

Pouring and Feeding Castings

INTRODUCTION

The soundness of a casting depends upon how the metal enters a mold and solidifies. At first glance, it would appear to be a relatively simple procedure to pour a casting; actually, many factors must be controlled if a good casting is to be obtained. A sound knowledge of the behavior of the various alloys in the molten state, of the flow of liquids, and of solidification characteristics is necessary. The importance of these physical properties is considered in the following discussions.

If metals were perfectly inert chemically, if they absorbed no gases, if they exhibited no shrinkage on cooling, and if they were not erosive to the mold and of various specific gravities, it would be much simpler to make a casting. Unfortunately, the reverse is true, and those factors, plus others, must all be accounted for when designing for castings.

POURING LADLES

It is usually easier to transport metal from the melting furnace to the mold than vice versa. Therefore some means of handling the molten metal must be available. Often, the molten metal is temporarily stored in large *holding* ladles, from which it is tapped off as needed. These holding ladles are constructed of steel plate lined with a suitable refractory such as firebrick. They are usually designed to receive metal from the melting furnace simultaneously with the pouring off of metal from them into smaller ladles.

Other ladles that are used include *bull,* or *crane, ladles* that are handled by crane or monorail, *two-man ladles* handled by either hand, crane, or monorail, and *hand ladles,* usually carried by hand (Fig. 9.1).

Ladles also differ as to the facilities available for preventing impurities such as slag or dross from entering the mold. In ordinary *lip-pouring ladles,* metal at the pouring lip is skimmed clean before pouring by means of metal skimming bars. Some ladles are equipped with a refractory

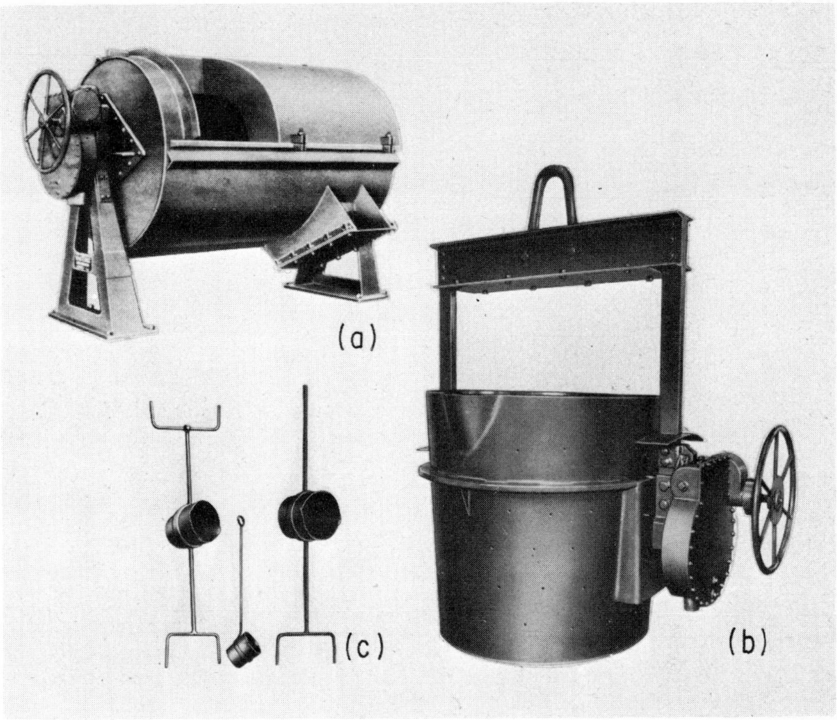

***Fig.* 9.1** Various sizes of foundry ladles. (*a*) Large reservoir, or holding, ladle; (*b*) bull, or crane, ladle; (*c*) two-man and hand ladles. (*Courtesy of Whiting Corporation.*)

dam in front of the lip that aids in holding back impurities. *Teapot-pour ladles* have a refractory spout which extends down beneath the surface of the metal so that only clean metal can pass through the spout. *Bottom-pour ladles* have a taphole at the bottom suitably stoppered by a refractory-covered *stopper rod* manipulated from the outside. A number of these ladles are illustrated in Fig. 9.2.

GATING SYSTEM

Chapter 8 described the solidification characteristics of metals and alloys and how these were influenced by composition and external variables. All these factors must be accounted for in designing a gating system for a casting. More specifically, the shrinkage behavior, as presented schematically in Fig. 8.5, and the crystal-growth morphology must be recognized if the gating design is to be effective. In considering the freezing characteristics in Chap. 8, the usual growth from the out-

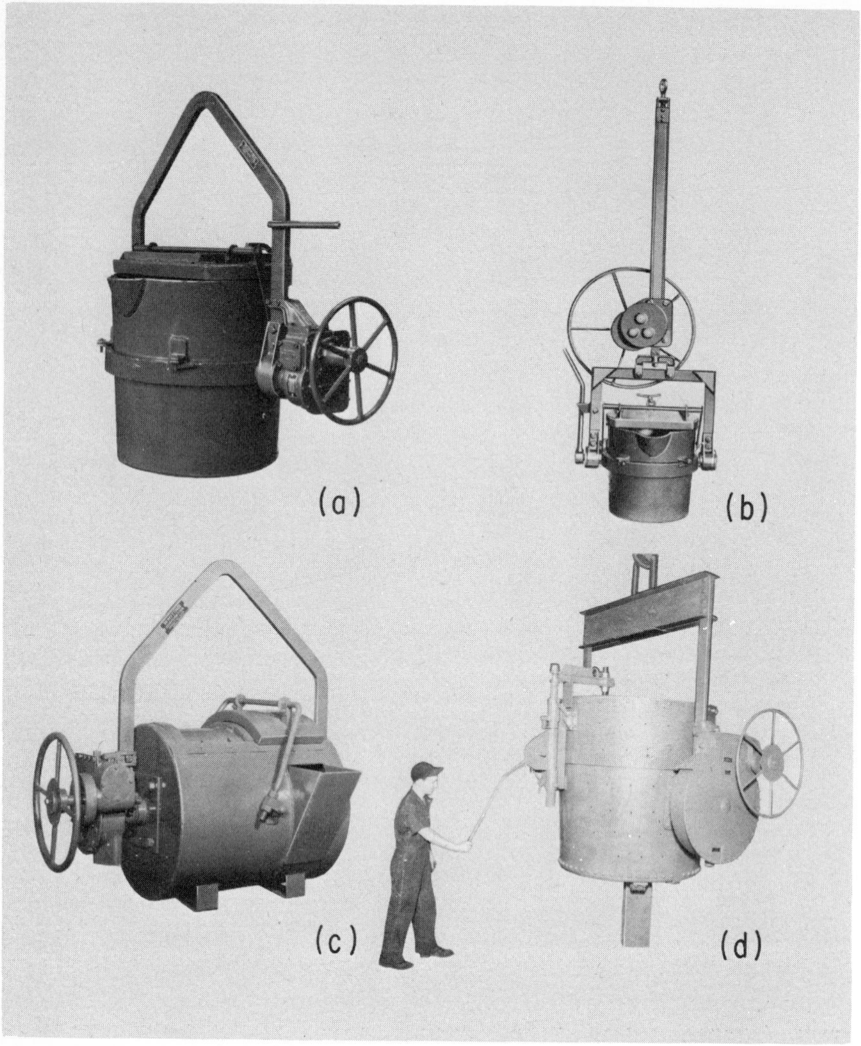

Fig. 9.2 Ladle types. (*a*) Covered lip-pour ladle with geared handwheel, (*b*) covered lip-pour monorail or crane ladles with ladle handles, (*c*) teapot-spout ladle, (*d*) bottom-pour ladles. (*Courtesy of Whiting Corporation.*)

side to the interior of the casting was revealed. This condition of having a partially solid, partially liquid zone growing from the outside inward is what is referred to as *progressive solidification.* Gating design must control this progressive solidification in such a way that no part of the casting is isolated from active feed channels during the entire freezing cycle. This is referred to as *directional solidification.*

Progressive solidification is a product of freezing mechanism and cannot be avoided. The degree of progressive solidification can, however, be controlled. Thus a rapidly cooled casting which results in a short distance between the start and end of freezing is said to have a high degree of progressive solidification, whereas one which is slowly cooled would possess a low degree of progressive solidification.* Directional solidification is a product of casting design, location of gates and risers, and the use of chills and other means for controlling the freezing process. It therefore is subject to the controls available to the foundryman. In principle, it means that if a casting is so proportioned and disposed with respect to the feeding system that the sections most distant from the available liquid metal will solidify first, there will be a successive feeding of the contracting metal by still liquid metal until the heaviest and last-to-freeze section is reached. This, in turn, can be fed by extra reservoirs of metal provided for that purpose and referred to as *risers,* or *heads.* These risers, or heads, are attached to the casting at the right locations and so that they can continually supply hot liquid metal to the shrinking casting until it is completely solidified. Imagine, for example, what would happen had the casting in Fig. 8.2 been poured in the reverse position, with the small section on top. Freezing would have occurred first in the small section, as before, but then there would be no liquid metal available to feed the heavier section by gravity, and it would have developed a general porosity that could not be eliminated. On the other hand, additional metal provided by an extra head, or riser, on top of the heavy section in Fig. 8.5 would eliminate completely the localized shrinkage shown. An example of the application of this directional solidification is given in Fig. 9.3. The system devised to feed the casting cavity serves the dual function of delivering the metal to this cavity, as well as of serving as a reservoir for the additional metal required as shrinkage takes place. In a very general way, delivery of the metal is accomplished by the *gating system,* whereas reserve metal is supplied by risers, or heads. Both functions,

*As discussed in Chap. 8, inoculation can also increase the tendency toward progressive solidification.

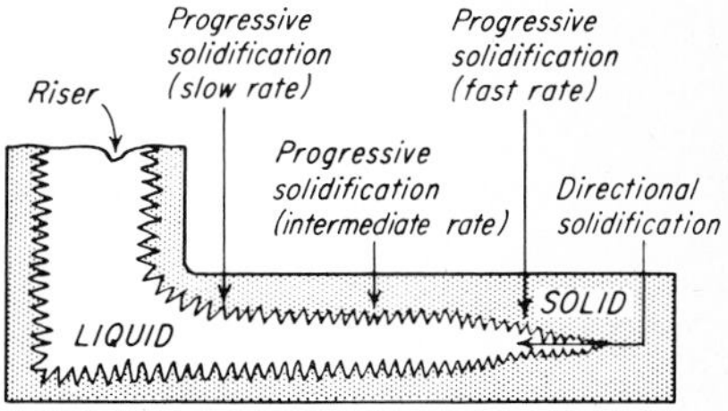

***Fig.* 9.3** An example of progressive solidification, directional solidification, and feeding of a casting with a riser. (*From E. T. Myskowski, H. F. Bishop, and W. S. Pellini.*[1])

however, may be served by either one of these parts of the mold; hence no clear-cut distinction can be made.

Gating System Defined

The Gating and Risering Committee of the American Foundrymen's Society has done much toward standardizing the nomenclature in connection with the feeding of castings. Therefore the definitions evolved by these groups serve as a useful reference for this purpose. Accordingly, the information given below is used practically verbatim as supplied by the Gating and Risering Committee, Gray Iron Division.

The elements of a basic and very common *gating system* are the *downsprue,* through which metal enters the *runner,* and from which it in turn passes through the ingates into the *mold cavity* [Fig. 9.4]. That part of the gating system which most restricts or regulates the rate of pouring is the *primary choke,* more often called simply the *choke.* At the top of the downsprue may be a *pouring cup* or *pouring basin* to minimize splash and turbulence and promote the entry of clean metal only into the downsprue. To further prevent the entry of dirt or slag into the downsprue, the pouring basin may contain a *skim core,* a *strainer, a delay screen,* or *a sprue plug.* To prevent erosion of the gating system when a large amount of metal is to be poured, a *splash core* may be placed in the bottom of the pouring basin, at the bottom of the downsprue, or wherever the flowing metal impinges with more than normal force.

Castings of heavy section or of high shrinkage alloys commonly require a *riser* or reservoir where metal stays liquid while the casting is freezing. The riser thus provides the *feed metal* which flows from the riser to the casting to make up for the *shrink* which takes place in the casting metal as it changes from liquid to solid. Depending on the location, the riser is described as a *top riser* or *side riser* and may be either an *open riser* or a *blind riser.* Since risers are designed to stay liquid while the casting solidifies, *riser height* and *riser neck* are important dimensions as are those of the body of the riser itself. *Riser distance* and the shape of the *riser base* are additional important details that pertain only to side risers.

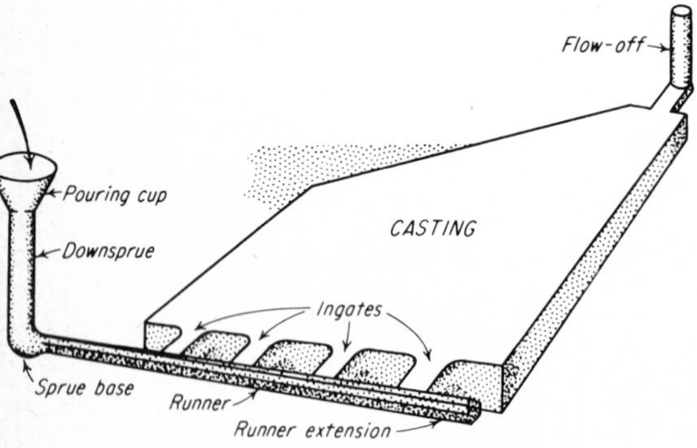

***Fig.* 9.4** Finger-gated casting with flow-off. (*Courtesy of AFS Gating and Risering Committee.*)

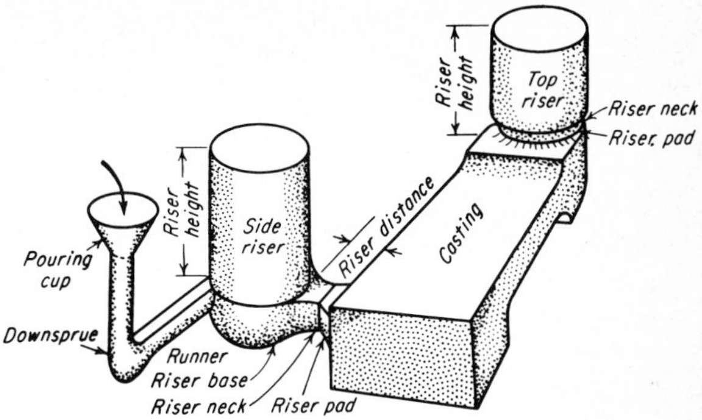

***Fig.* 9.5** Riser-gated casting with side riser and top riser. (*Courtesy of AFS Gating and Risering Committee.*)

Gates and risers are often designed to take advantage of the principle of *controlled directional solidification* which requires that freezing start farthest from the riser and proceed toward the riser. To accomplish this, castings are *riser-gated* with metal entering the riser through a downsprue and runner, heating both the riser base and riser neck while flowing into the mold cavity [Fig. 9.5].

Additional definitions are found in publications of the AFS Gating and Risering Committee.

Types of Gates

Metal can be directed into a mold cavity in various ways. The design of each gating system depends upon its primary objectives. Thus a gate may be designed for ease of molding, to avoid turbulent flow, or to prevent washing of sand from the mold walls. Again, a principal objective might be to avoid inclusion of dross or slag with the metal entering the mold. Naturally, other factors are not disregarded when a gate is designed with a particular purpose in mind. Various designs of gates are shown in Fig. 9.6, and the following discussions pertain to the gates illustrated.

Parting Gate

These gates enter the mold cavity along the parting line separating the cope and drag portions of the mold. They may contain devices such as *skim bobs* or *relief sprues* to collect dross or slag (*a*, *b*, and *c*) or relieve pouring pressure. Design *d* illustrates the use of a pouring basin to serve this function; design *e* contains a *shrink bob* serving the dual function of slag or dross collector and metal reservoir to feed the casting as it shrinks. Designs *f* and *g* illustrate the use of core inserts to filter the metal or prevent erosion of the mold.

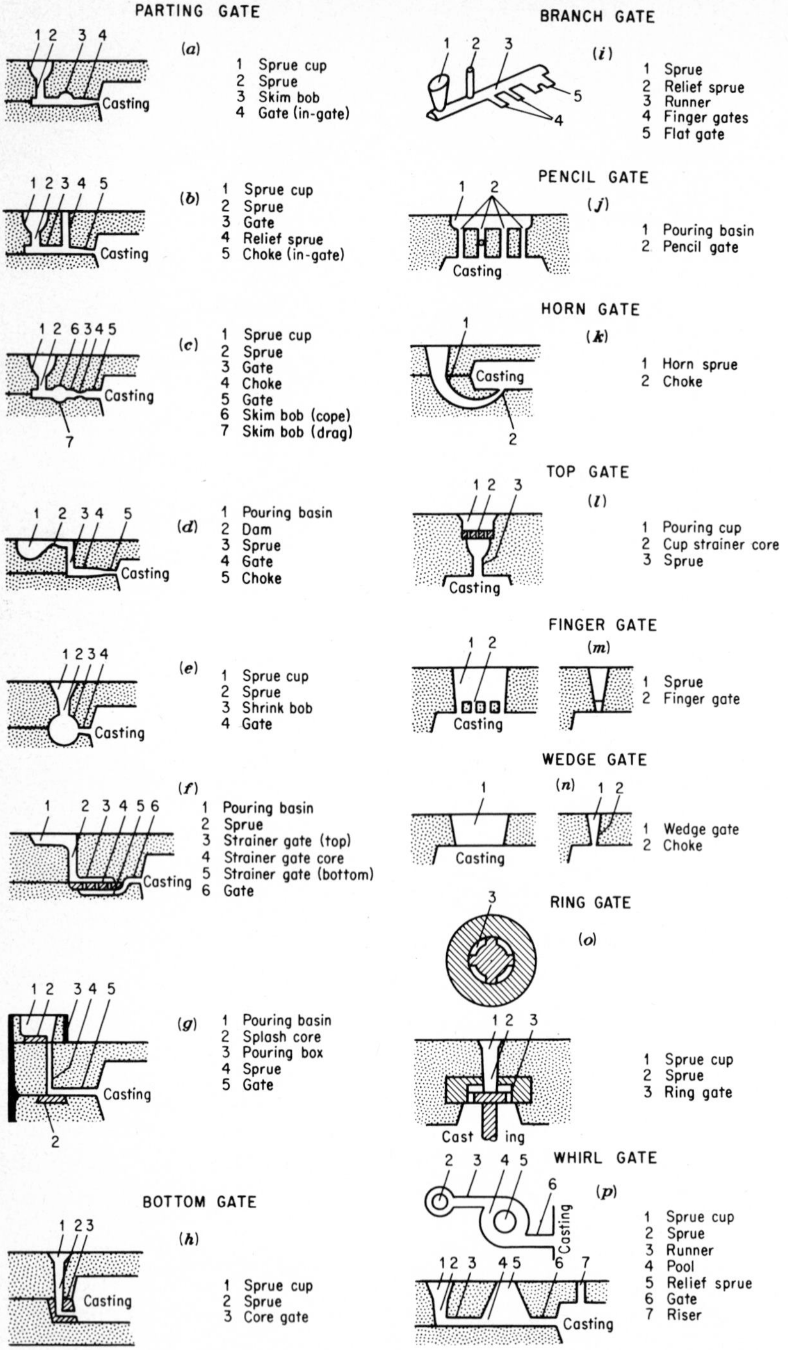

***Fig.* 9.6** Examples of gating systems. (*Courtesy of AFS Gating and Risering Committee.*)

Bottom Gate

The bottom gate enters the casting cavity at the bottom of the drag half of the mold. It is illustrated by design *h* in Fig. 9.6, although other variations are also used. For example, a well at the base of the sprue or a change in the direction of flow of the metal may be incorporated to reduce flow rates in the systems. A bottom gate is advocated for steel castings in particular to reduce erosion and gas entrapment and to prevent splashing, which can result in cold shots.

Branch Gate

A branch gate is designed either to feed a single casting at several points or a number of individual castings (*i*, Fig. 9.6).

Horn Gate

This is a variety of bottom gate (*k*, Fig. 9.6). One objection to its use is a tendency for producing a fountain effect in the casting. However, it is a means of bottom gating without the necessity of a core for the gate.

Others

With the exception of the *whirl gate,* the remaining gate types illustrated in Fig. 9.6 are essentially variations of a top-gating system since the metal enters the mold from above. The designs are intended to break up the metal stream so that it enters the mold with a minimum of turbulence and erosive action. The *whirl gate* accomplishes somewhat the same purpose as the parting gates illustrated in *a*, *b*, and *c*. The *step gate* is intended to have hot metal enter successively the various gates from bottom to top of the casting. If this objective were accomplished, the situation would promote directional solidification. Unless the step gates are properly designed, however, this gating system does not function as desired. Each gate must be slanted upward and properly proportioned relative to the other gates to attain the desired goal.

DESIGN OF GATING SYSTEM

Mold Materials

Wherever possible, the gating system is made of the same molding material as that used for the mold cavity. There are occasions, however, where, from the standpoint of convenience or for other reasons, some other material is used for a part of the gating system. Thus the pouring basin or pouring cups are frequently made as baked-sand cores. Skim gates or strainer cores and splash cores are also made of baked sand since they must withstand a considerable amount of erosive action and pressure from the metal which could not be sustained by similar constructions made of green sand. Strainers, downsprues, and gate cores may also be obtained in ceramic materials called tile. Occasionally, a certain portion of the gating system may be constructed of a high-density sand such as zircon sand to prevent washing or metal penetration.

Fluid Flow

Such problems as gas contamination, inclusion of dross or slag, and aspiration of gas are factors that must be recognized when designing a gating system. A little reflection will show that these problems are connected with the major problem of having the metal enter the mold in quiet and uniform manner. In other words, these are problems concerned with fluid flow, and the laws governing fluids can be studied profitably to improve any design.

First of all, it should be recognized that liquids flow either in a streamlined *laminar* fashion or in a *turbulent* manner. Whether smooth or turbulent flow results depends upon the velocity of the liquid, the cross section of the flow channel, and the viscosity of the liquid. The relationship is expressed as the Reynolds number

$$R_n = \frac{\text{mean velocity of flow} \times \text{diameter of tube} \times \text{density of liquid}}{\text{kinematic viscosity of liquid}}$$

When the Reynolds number reaches a certain critical value, turbulent flow prevails. Apparently, most metals reach turbulent-flow conditions quite readily. Investigations show that steel always flows under turbulent conditions ($R_n > 3500$).[2] Turbulent flow creates such problems as inclusion of dross or slag, aspiration of air into the metal, erosion of the mold wall, and roughening of the casting surface.

The flow of a liquid in a mold is also governed by a number of other variables, best summed up in terms of Bernoulli's theorem, which states that the sum of the potential energy, the velocity energy, the pressure energy, and the frictional energy of a flowing liquid is equal to a constant.[3] This theorem can be expressed in the following equation:

$$wZ + wPv + \frac{wV^2}{2g} + wF = K$$

where w = total weight of fluid flowing, lb
Z = height of liquid, ft
P = static pressure in the liquid, lb/sq ft
v = specific volume of the liquid, cu ft/lb

g = acceleration due to gravity, 32 ft/sec^2
V = velocity, ft/sec
F = frictional losses, ft
K = a constant

If this equation is divided by w, all the terms have the dimensions of length and may be considered, respectively, to represent:

1. Potential head (Z)
2. Pressure head (Pv)
3. Velocity head ($V^2/2g$)
4. Frictional loss of head (F)

Bernoulli's theorem, which is based on the first law of thermodynamics, can be usefully applied to a proper understanding of the flow of metal in a mold. The potential energy of the metal can be considered a maximum as the metal enters the pouring cup or basin. This form of energy is then rapidly changed to kinetic or velocity energy and pressure energy as the metal passes through the mold system. Once flow is established and the potential and frictional heads are virtually constant, the velocity is high when the pressure is low, and vice versa. While metal is flowing, there is a constant loss of energy in the form of fluid friction between the metal and mold wall. (There is also a heat loss which is not represented in Bernoulli's theorem, but which eventually leads to solidification of the metal.)

It would be impossible to consider all the implications of this theorem and its application to the design of gating systems, but a number of examples have been given in the literature.[3–5] Figure 9.7 gives a schematic illustration of the application of this principle to a typical gating system.

Factors Involved in Gating Design

The physical aspects of gating systems have already been considered. How these gates are to be used to produce a sound casting is a question of gating design. Improper design of a gating system can cause one or more of the following defects in the casting:

1. Sand, slag, dross, or other impurities
2. Rough surface
3. Entrapped gases
4. Excessively oxidized metal
5. Localized shrinkage (pipe shrinkage, or macroshrinkage)
6. Dispersed porosity, or microporosity
7. Incomplete fusion of liquid metal where two streams meet (*cold shuts*)

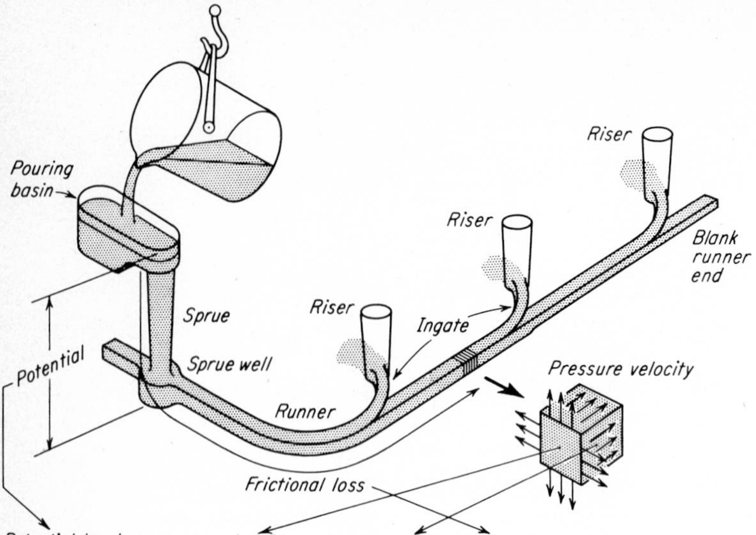

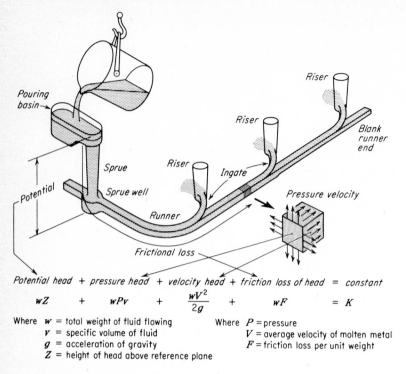

Potential head + pressure head + velocity head + friction loss of head = constant

$$wZ + wPv + \frac{wV^2}{2g} + wF = K$$

Where w = total weight of fluid flowing
v = specific volume of fluid
g = acceleration of gravity
Z = height of head above reference plane

Where P = pressure
V = average velocity of molten metal
F = friction loss per unit weight

Fig. 9.7 Application of Bernoulli's theorem to a gating system. (*After J. F. Wallace and E. B. Evans.*[5])

8. Entrapped globules of presolidified metal (*cold shots*)
9. Unfilled molds (misruns)
10. Metal penetration into sand mold and/or core

The gating system must therefore be designed to accomplish the following objectives as quoted from Wallace and Evans:[6]

1. Fill the mold rapidly, without laps or requiring excessively high pouring temperatures.
2. Reduce or prevent agitation or turbulence and the formation of dross in the mold.
3. Prevent slag, scum, dross, and eroded sand from entering the casting by way of the gating system.
4. Prevent aspiration of air or mold gases into the metal stream.
5. Avoid erosion of molds and cores.
6. Aid in obtaining suitable thermal gradients to attain directional solidification and minimize distortion in the casting.
7. Obtain a maximum casting yield and minimum grinding costs.
8. Provide for ease of pouring, utilizing available ladle and crane equipment.

It is evident that not all these requirements are compatible, and compromises may have to be made to get as close as possible to the desired goal.

Pouring Time

A slight trickle of metal or metal poured too cold is undesirable because the metal would freeze too fast to fill out the mold or would develop cold shuts. Very rapid filling of the mold also would present such problems as having an adequate gating system to handle a large volume of metal in a short time, erosion of the mold wall, rough surface, excessive shrinkage, and other possible defects. There is, therefore, an optimum pouring rate, or pouring-rate range, for most castings that must be established by experience. In die castings or special casting techniques where metal is forced into a mold under pressure, this upper limit is probably set by the fluidity of the metal itself.

In conventional sand casting, establishing the optimum pouring rate is the first step in the design of the gating system. Once this is done, the next step is the proper proportioning and distribution of the various parts of the gating system in order to achieve this rate. The characteristics of the various foundry alloys have a strong influence on the importance of this first step. Geometry of the casting is, of course, also a factor.

Some metals like cast iron are not so sensitive to pouring rate as others. Yet even for cast iron an optimum pouring rate, which is a function of the casting size and shape,[7] is advocated. A metal like steel must of necessity be poured fast to avoid premature freezing because it has a high freezing range compared with most other casting alloys. Metals like aluminum or magnesium alloys can be poured more slowly, and here the problem is one of avoiding turbulence, drossing, and gas pickup.

Effective pouring rates for all commercial casting alloys have not been published. These would be expected to reflect to some extent the practices in a given foundry or the limitations of the available equipment, as well as the casting geometry. Some data are available for cast iron, steel, brass, and bronze:[6,8,9]

1. Gray-iron castings <1000 lb:

$$\text{Pouring time } t, \text{ sec} = K\left(0.95 + \frac{T}{0.853}\right)\sqrt{W}$$

where K is a fluidity factor determined by dividing the fluidity of the specific iron obtained from Fig. 8.20 by 40 (the fluidity value for iron of CE = 4.3 at a temperature of 2600 F). As seen from Fig. 8.20, this factor is affected by iron composition and pouring temperature. T is the average thickness in inches, and W is the weight in pounds.

2. Gray-iron castings > 1000 lb:

$$\text{Pouring time } t\text{, sec} = K\left(0.95 + \frac{T}{0.853}\right)\sqrt[3]{W}$$

3. Shell-molded ductile iron (vertical pouring):

$$\text{Pouring time } t\text{, sec} = K_1\sqrt{W}$$

where $K_1 = 1.8$ sections from $\frac{3}{8}$ to 1 in., 1.4 for thinner sections, and 2.0 for heavier sections.

4. Steel castings:

$$\text{Pouring time } t\text{, sec} = k\sqrt{W}$$

where K varies from about 1.2 for 100-lb castings to about 0.4 for 100,000-lb castings, when casting weight is plotted on a log scale.

Comparing these statistics for a 400-lb casting of 1 in. average wall thickness, the following pouring-time values would be obtained:

1. Gray cast iron of 4.0 carbon equivalent poured at 2700 F:

$$t = 1\left(0.95 + \frac{1}{0.853}\right)\sqrt{400} = 42 \text{ sec}$$

2. Shell-molded ductile iron:

$$t = 1.8\sqrt{400} = 36 \text{ sec}$$

3. Steel:

$$t = 1.0\sqrt{400} = 20 \text{ sec}$$

For comparison, a pouring time of 15 to 45 sec is recommended for brass or bronze castings of less than 300 lb.[10]

With the optimum pouring time established by whatever means are available, the next step is to proportion the gating system properly to achieve the desired rate while complying as closely as possible with the other desired characteristics of the gating system previously enumerated.

Pouring Basin

The ideal situation is to establish the proper flow system as rapidly as possible. This means that, when a metal enters the sprue, it should be flowing under conditions that are as nearly as possible those which are present when full flow has been established. Good results can be accomplished by:

1. Streamlining the pouring basin and providing a dam so that essentially constant conditions are established when the metal enters the sprue
2. Use of a strainer core in the pouring basin
3. Use of a delay screen or sprue plug

It is not always necessary that the utmost precaution be exercised to get the metal to flow properly in the mold, and in this case the pouring-basin or pouring-cup design may be dictated largely by the ease with which it can be filled or made. The diameters of the cups should be large enough to make it possible to keep the sprue full of metal and to avoid splashing.

Choke Area

The smallest area in the feeding channels controls the flow rate into the mold cavity and consequently controls the pouring time. Usually, this choke area occurs at the bottom of the sprue to establish the metal velocity as soon as possible, but this is not always the case.[11] If the choke area occurs at the base of the sprue, the proper area can be calculated by applying a formula based on the application of Bernoulli's theorem. For example, the choke area can be determined by using the following formula:[12]

$$A = \frac{W}{dtC\sqrt{2gH}}$$

where A = choke area, sq in.
W = casting weight
d = density of molten metal
H = effective height of metal head
C = efficiency factor or nozzle coefficient which is a function of the gating system used
g = acceleration of gravity, 386.4 in./sec^2
t = pouring time, sec

Sprue Design

As the metal gains velocity in passing through the sprue, it loses its pressure energy, or head. This is demonstrated by the constriction in cross section that appears in a metal stream at points some distance from the pouring spout. The loss of pressure head in a sprue may result in a tendency to form a vortex on the metal in the sprue or a negative pressure effect in the metal column so that gas from the mold is sucked into the metal stream. The remedy is to taper the sprue opening. This also reduces mold erosion and metal turbulence.

As mentioned in the preceding section, sprue size is often selected so that it controls the pouring rate; i.e., the major restriction to flow in the gating system occurs in the sprue. This has the advantage of early establishment of the proper flow characteristics and of reducing the rate of flow of metal entering the mold cavity from the gates.

In alloys such as aluminum that are subject to drossing, the use of a restricted sprue area to reduce the velocity of the metal may lead to drossing of the metal as it enters the runners. A suggested ideal sprue and gating design to overcome these effects is shown in Fig. 9.8.

Some metals such as cast iron and steel are not so prone to dross, and therefore these precautions are not so necessary. Furthermore, since steel is poured at a high temperature and chills very rapidly, the factor that may determine the sprue design is not drossing and quiet entry of metal into the mold, but the need to get the metal into the mold fast enough to avoid excessive chilling. If this is the predominant consideration, sprue-runner ratios may differ radically from those advocated for the light-metal alloys.

Sprue-runner-gate Ratios

If the primary choke of the feeding system occurs in the sprue, the balance of the feeding areas is commonly expressed as ratios of the sprue-choke area. Thus, in some of the succeeding references to aluminum alloys, a ratio of 1:2:4 is used. The deviations that can be encountered in pouring practices for other metals are indicated by the ratios given in Table 9.1.

Table* 9.1 *Selected sprue-runner-gate area ratios

Metal	Ratio	Ref.
Steel	1:2:1.5	19
	1:3:3	19
	1:1:07	19
	1:2:2	20
Fin-gated	1:1:1	16
Gray cast iron	1:4:4	6
Pressurized system	1:1.3:1.1	22
Ductile iron, dry-sand molds	10:9:8	11
Shell-molded, vertical pouring	1:2:2	8
Pressure system	4:8:3	18
Reverse choke	1.2:1:2*	18
Aluminum	1:2:4	15
Pressurized system	1:2:1	17
Unpressurized system	1:3:3	17, 20
Brass	1:1:1–1:1:3	21

*With enlargements in runner varying from 3 to 6.

Thus it is seen that the gating system can vary widely from one leading to a nonpressurized, or "reverse choke," system, such as 1:2:4 or 1:3:3, to one where the choke and pressure are at a maximum at the

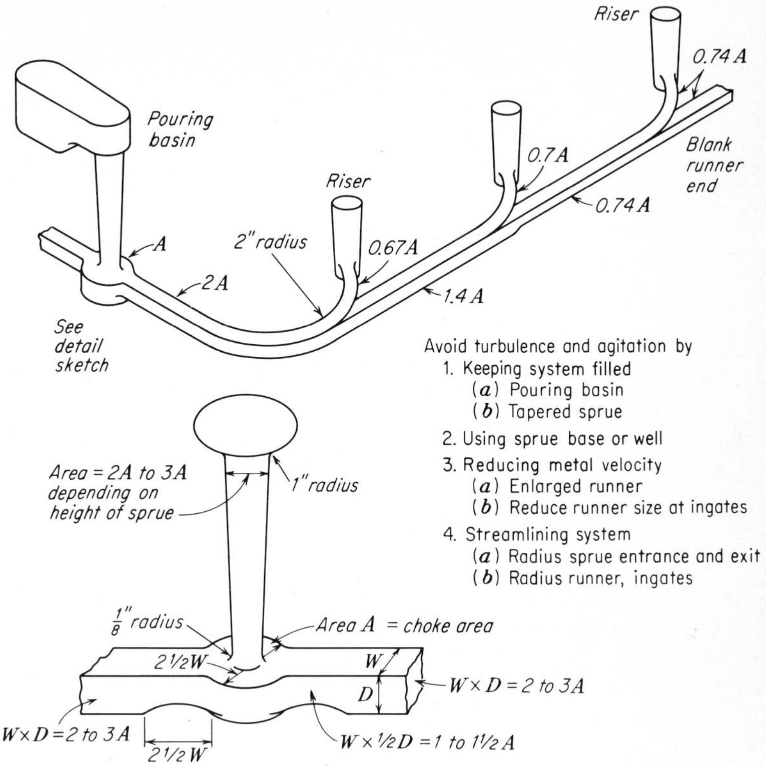

***Fig.* 9.8** **Gating system and sprue design developed for light-metal systems using horizontal gates. (*After J. F. Wallace and E. B. Evans,*[5] *L. W. Eastwood,*[13] *and J. G. Kura.*[14])**

ingate, such as 4:8:3 or 1:2:1. If more than one ingate is used, the ratios pertain to the total area of all the ingates. In other words, in changing from one ingate to two while maintaining the same ingate ratio, the areas of the two ingates should equal that of the single ingate system.

Runners and Gates

Runners and gates should be designed to obtain the following characteristics:

1. Absence of sharp corners or changes of section that may lead to turbulence or gas entrapment
2. Proper relation between cross-sectional areas of the several gates, between gates and runners, and between the runners and the sprue
3. Proper location of the gates to ensure adequate feeding of low-velocity metal into the mold cavity

Studies of the gating systems now employed show that in some instances the systems do not function as anticipated. For example, whirl, riser, and horn gates were found to be ineffective in preventing turbulence in the molds when pouring steel.[23] In multiple-finger gating systems, it has been found that often most of the feeding is accomplished by the fingers farthest from the sprue. This is the result of improper proportioning of the cross section of the gate and runners. Because of frictional losses and the abrupt change in cross section at these points, the liquid metal has a relatively low velocity and a fairly high pressure. Hence it will readily flow into the farthest gate. The gates nearer the sprue will have less metal flowing through them because of higher velocities and lower pressures. This effect is demonstrated by Fig. 9.9*a*, which shows the proportion of liquid which flows through gates supplying a block casting.[15] In this instance, the total sprue area to total runner area to total gate area was 1:2:4. Some correction was obtained by cutting down the ingate area to a 1:2:2 ratio because this tended to maintain a more uniform distribution of the metal in the feeding system and hence more constant velocity and pressure conditions (Fig. 9.9*b*). To be completely satisfactory, however, the runner beyond each gate should also be reduced in cross section to balance the flow in all parts of the system and thereby to equalize further the velocity and pressure. Such a design is illustrated in Fig. 9.8. In this case the runner is proportioned so that reasonably constant velocity and pressure are maintained. Furthermore, the design is streamlined to avoid sudden changes in direction that might create turbulence.

Thus, to satisfy the demands imposed by Bernoulli's theorem, it is necessary that those gates farthest from the sprue be of smallest cross section so that the volume of metal through these gates is the same as that through those closer to the sprue. If such proportioning is not done, there is a tendency for the pressure to be a maximum at the farthest gate and, therefore, for the flow to be greatest at that point. In some instances, there may even be a negative pressure existing at some of the first gates leading toward an actual flow of metal out of the mold back into the runner.

Other measures in addition to proper proportioning of ingate are:

1. To develop enlargements in the gating system to dissipate momentum effects
2. To bend the runner away from the casting
3. To use a tapered runner[24]

To summarize, streamlining of a gating system reduces turbulence to a minimum, and proper proportioning of the various parts of the gating

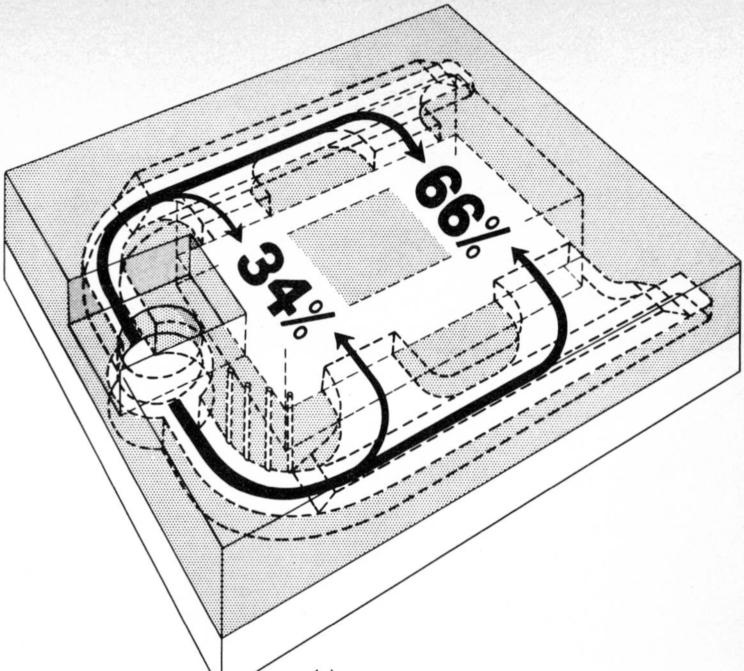

(a)

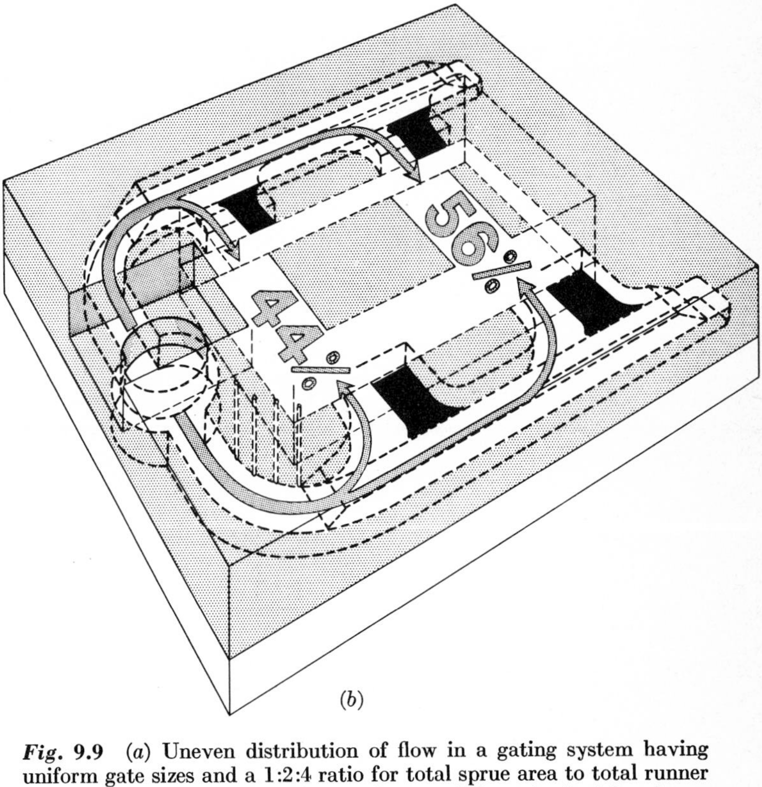

(b)

Fig. 9.9 (*a*) Uneven distribution of flow in a gating system having uniform gate sizes and a 1:2:4 ratio for total sprue area to total runner area to total gate area, (*b*) improved flow conditions obtained by changing sprue-runner-gate ratio to 1:2:2. (*From K. Grube and L. W. Eastwood.*[15])

system so adjusts the pressure and velocity head of the metal that it flows as desired.

Vertical Gating Systems

In permanent molds, shell molds, and sand molds for castings that are best cast on edge, vertical gating systems are required. Examples

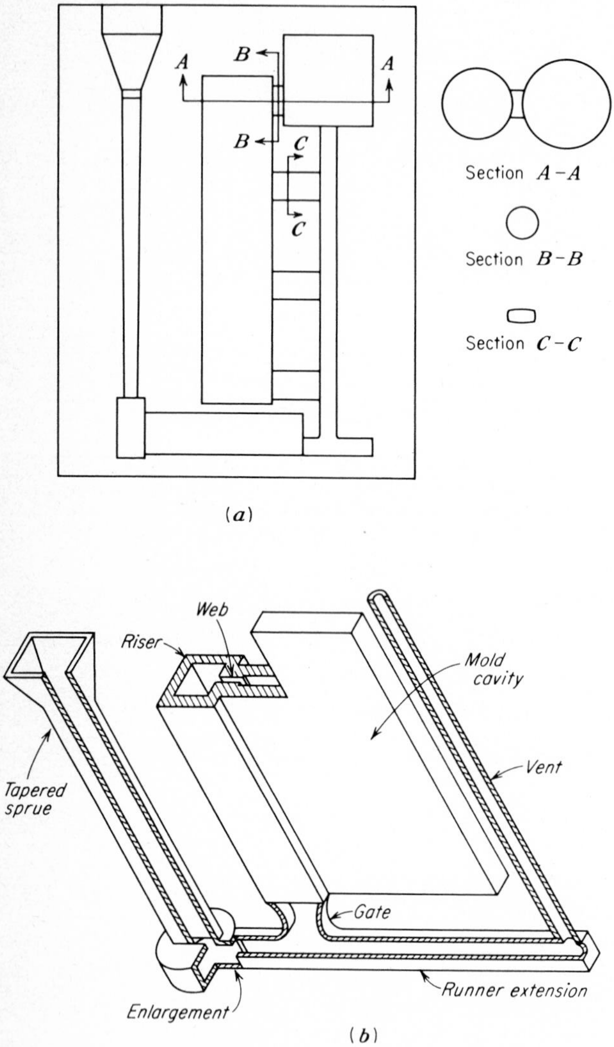

***Fig.* 9.10** Examples of vertical gating systems. (*a*) Ductile iron in shell molds. (*From H. O. Meriwether.*[8]) (*b*) Light-metal alloy. (*From K. R. Grube, R. M. Lang, and J. G. Kura.*[26])

of this type are given in Fig. 9.10*a* for ductile iron cast in shell molds and in Fig. 9.10*b* for an Al-7 Mg alloy.[8,25,26]

In some instances, the riser has been omitted[27] and the sprue connected to the casting by a continuous slot. The purpose of this arrangement is to obtain directional solidification. The sprue is fitted with an annular screen of tinned steel, and coarse steel wool is placed inside the screen to aid in securing proper flow as well as to screen out oxides from the metal.

Vertical gating is claimed to be superior for certain copper-base alloys in shell molds.[28]

Top gating of castings (Fig. 9.11) and mold-reversal manipulation as demonstrated in Fig. 9.12 are additional methods used to favor directional solidification. The shrink bob illustrated in Fig. 9.6*e*, which is really a form of riser, is another method that is used frequently in malleable-iron work to provide proper feeding of a casting.

Elimination of Slag and Dross

Use of pouring basins, strainer cores, and suitable dams in a gating system helps to filter out slag and dross from the metal stream before it enters the mold cavity. Some examples of such methods have already been given. In the case of light-metal alloys, the difficulties are somewhat greater than for copper or ferrous alloys since there is so little difference in specific gravity between the impurities and the metal. Enlargements in the feeding system to reduce the velocity of flow, or special devices such as the whirl gate, which whirls the dross and slag

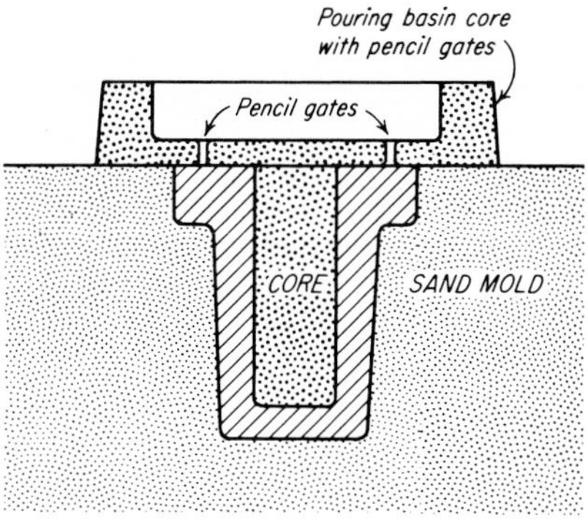

***Fig.* 9.11** Top gating through pencil gates.

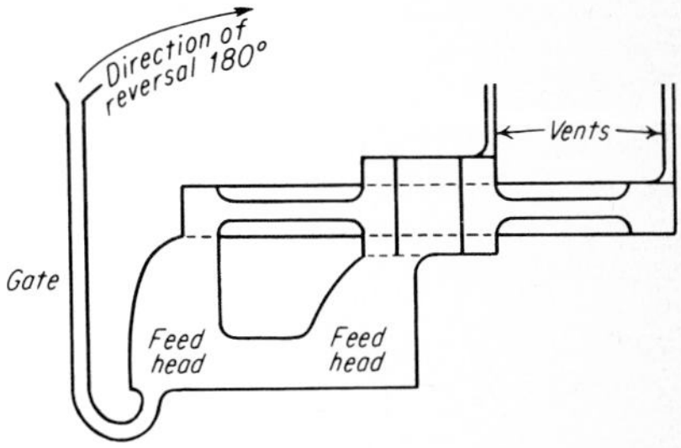

***Fig.* 9.12** Mold-reversal method for securing proper feeding. (*Batty, Trans. AFS, vol.* 42, *p.* 237, 1934.)

into the center of the riser, are other means of cleansing the metal. For aluminum castings it has been recommended that the runners be placed in the drag with the ingate in the cope of the mold to reduce the inclusion of dross in the mold cavity. For ferrous metals, on the other hand, the reverse situation has been suggested, with the runner in the cope and the ingate in the drag.

Economy and Ease of Removal of Gates and Sprues

In addition to the factors already discussed, it is quite obvious that changes in design of the gating system to reduce costs without affecting the quality of the casting are something for which one should strive. Quite frequently it is found that some modifications in practice, such as, for example, the inclusion of a chill in a strategic location, may greatly reduce the amount of metal required to feed a casting. In other instances, it may be found that gating in a particular location will result in much greater ease of removal of the gate than if located in another part of the casting. The immediate connection between the ingate and the mold is sometimes reduced to permit the gate to be removed readily from the casting; or a neck-down, or Washburn, core may be used for this purpose. There are so many factors in connection with each metal and each particular casting that it is still necessary that each particular job be studied individually with the viewpoint of improving the gating system to achieve a quality casting at a minimum cost.

RISERS

Primary Function of a Riser

The primary function of a riser is to feed metal to the casting as it solidifies. In some instances, it may also be considered as a part of the gating system. The riser requirements depend considerably on the type of metal being poured. Gray cast iron needs less feeding than some alloys because a period of graphitization occurs during the final stages of solidification which causes an expansion that tends to counteract metal shrinkage. Steel or white cast iron, and many of the nonferrous alloys which have an extended solidification range, require excessive and sometimes elaborate feeding systems to obtain sound castings. The variation that can be expected in the volumetric shrinkage of some metals is shown in Table 9.2.

The values given in Table 9.2 represent minimal requirements that must be satisfied by the riser. Any bulging or extension of a casting beyond its normal limits because of a soft mold or excessive metal pressures in the mold will require additional feed metal that must be provided by the riser.

Table* 9.2 *Approximate solidification shrinkage of some foundry alloys

Material	Volumetric shrinkage, %
Medium carbon steel	2.5–3.0
1% carbon steel	4.0
Pure aluminum	6.60
Pure copper	4.92
Gray cast iron	1.90 to negative depending on graphitization, composition, etc.
White cast iron	4.0–5.50

Although shrinkage and mold-wall movement are important factors in determining riser size, they are not the only factors. The susceptibility of various alloys to shrinkage defects, and hence the need for risering, is also related to the freezing mechanism. This is demonstrated in a quantitative way in Table 9.3, which expresses alloy behavior in two ways:

1. Thickness of casting completely solid when freezing begins at the center of a 7-in.-thick casting
2. A so-called "center-line resistance factor" which is the ratio of center-line freezing time (at a depth of 3.5 in.) to casting freezing time × 100

Data for sand and chill molds are included. Alloys with a high center-line resistance factor would be expected to be more difficult to feed than those with a low value.

These data also illustrate the importance of heat-transfer rates as a factor in the feeding of castings. Note from Table 9.3 that the greater heat-transfer rate obtained from the chill mold improves the possibility of getting a sound casting.

Theoretical Considerations

The riser and the casting it feeds should be considered an integral system because a casting cannot be made sound without adequate feed metal, no matter how much attention may be paid to other details. Since Table 9.2 indicates that only a relatively small amount of feed metal is necessary, one might conclude that risering is fairly simple and that only small reservoirs are necessary to compensate for shrinkage. But the metal in risers is subject to the same laws of solidification as the metal in the castings, and a little reflection will show that, to be effective, a riser must stay fluid at least as long as the casting and must be able to feed the casting during this time. Consequently, the problem of providing this feed metal during the entire solidification period of the

Table 9.3 Quantitative evaluation of solidification behavior*

Material	Thickness of casting completely solid when freezing begins at center (3.5 in. from surface)		Center-line resistance factor: center-line freezing time × 100 (casting freezing time)	
	Sand mold	Chill mold	Sand mold	Chill mold
Copper (99.8)	3.2	3.2	<1	3.2
Lead (99)	2.5	....	17	
60-40 brass	2.2	3.2	26	2.5
12% Cr steel	0.5	3.0	38	9.3
18-8 (0.2%)	0.5	2.7	35	9.4
0.6 C cast steel	0 + 10% liquid at surface	2.5	54	25.0
Monel	0 + 50% liquid at surface	2.2	64	19.0
Al-4 Cu	0 + 90% liquid at surface	0 + 25% liquid at surface	96	46.0†
88-10-2 bronze	0 + 90% liquid at surface	0.6	95	63.0
Al-8 Mg	0 + 90% liquid at surface	0 + 50% liquid at surface	19	65.0

*From R. A. Flinn.[29]
†Shows anomalous freezing.

casting involves quite a few variables, of which the important ones are listed below and discussed in succeeding paragraphs:

1. Riser shape
2. Riser size as a function of casting shape
3. Location of risers
4. Grouping of castings
5. Riser connections to the casting
6. Use of chills
7. Use of insulators and exothermic compounds
8. Special conditions arising from joining sections

Riser Shape

A casting loses its thermal energy by transferring it to its surroundings by radiation, conduction, and convection. Without establishing the relative importance of these three modes of heat transfer, it is apparent that the surface area of the casting relative to its volume is important in determining the rate of this heat transfer. This concept was expressed mathematically by Chvorinov[30] as follows:

$$\text{Solidification time } t \approx \frac{\text{square of volume}}{\text{square of area}} \approx \frac{V^2}{A^2}$$

Although this equation is somewhat oversimplified, it does indicate that, for a riser to have a solidification time equal to or greater than that of the casting, the minimum riser size would be obtained from a sphere.

Spheres are usually difficult to mold, however, and would present feeding problems as well, since the last metal to freeze would be near the center of the sphere, where it could not be used to feed a casting. Practicalities dictate the use of cylinders for most risers, and the discussion hereafter will refer to such shapes unless noted otherwise. The base of a side riser may be hemispherical in shape (Fig. 9.5), and a blind riser, i.e., one which is enclosed by sand, may have a hemispherical top in order to provide the smallest possible surface-area–volume ratio.

Riser Size as a Function of Casting Shape

Two simple examples can be used to indicate the relation between riser size and casting shape. If a cylindrical casting poured on end is to be fed by a riser, it is obvious that this riser must have a diameter at least as large as that of the cylinder. On the other hand, if the same volume of metal used in the cylindrical casting is distributed over a greater area in the form of a plate, having a thickness less than the diameter of the cylinder, the riser needed to feed this plate will not be as large as the one for the cylinder, since it will not have to remain molten as long as the riser on the cylinder. Obviously, then, the surface-area–volume ratio of the riser can be related to the surface-area–volume ratio of the casting.

Thus Caine[31] developed an equation for steel which expresses the relative freezing time of riser and casting in terms of the relative volume of the riser and casting:

$$X = \frac{0.10}{Y - 0.03} + 1.0^*$$

where X = freezing ratio or relative freezing time

$$= \frac{\text{casting area/casting volume}}{\text{riser area/riser volume}}$$

Y = riser volume/casting volume

This is one of the curves plotted in Fig. 9.13.[32] This curve provides the theoretical locus of points which separate sound (right) and unsound (left) castings.

*In the original equation, the constants were slightly different.

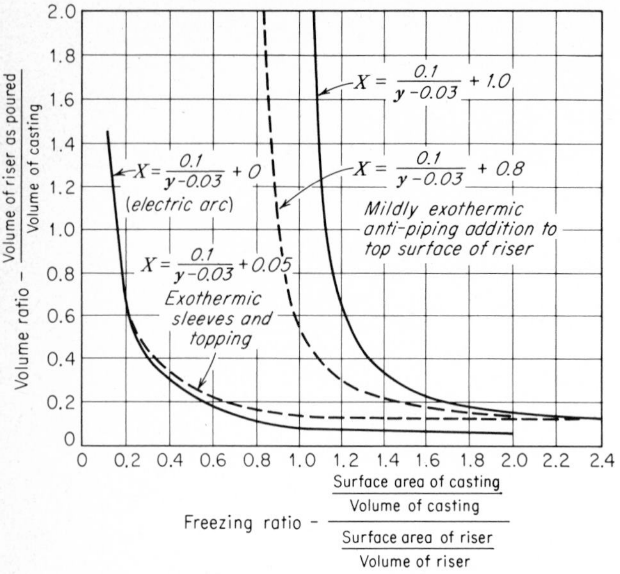

***Fig.* 9.13** Plot of riser-volume to casting-volume ratio vs. freezing ratio $\left(\frac{\text{casting area/casting volume}}{\text{riser area/riser volume}}\right)$ for various conditions existing in the riser. (*From J. F. Wallace.*[32])

This relation, together with the additional information provided by the other curves in Fig. 9.13, has contributed much to the basic understanding of risering principles, but it requires trial-and-error calculation to arrive at the desired riser size.

Another factor is the shape of the cavity, or pipe, formed in the riser. If this pipe should extend into the casting, it may be necessary to enlarge the riser sufficiently to avoid the situation, even though the casting may otherwise be sound. Consequently, the nature of shape of the shrinkage cavity generated in the riser must be observed.

Various alternative procedures are available to calculate riser size.[33–37] One of these takes into account the shape factor of the casting, which is expressed as the sum of the length and width of the casting divided by the thickness $(L + W)/T$. Research on this approach has shown that the riser-volume–casting-volume ratio is related to the shape factor as presented in Fig. 9.14*a*.[36] Ready conversion to riser diameter is made with the help of Fig. 9.14*b*. Others have developed riser-size data based on casting geometry and shrinkage factors.[34]

One method which has proved successful with malleable-iron castings is outlined below.[38] The method is based on the actual measurement of

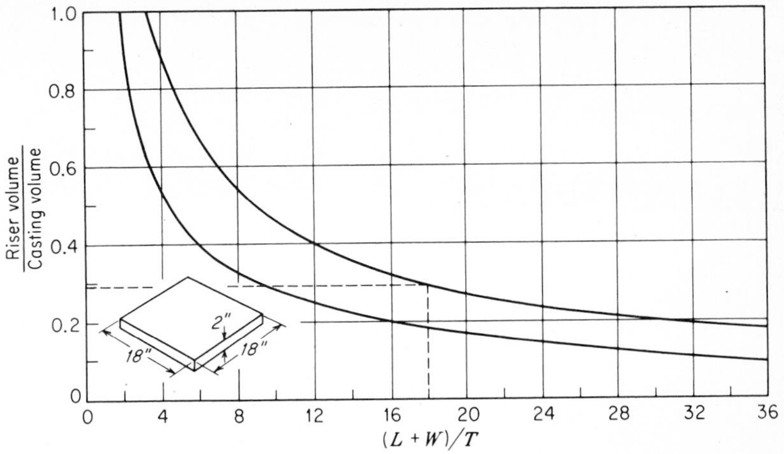

(a)

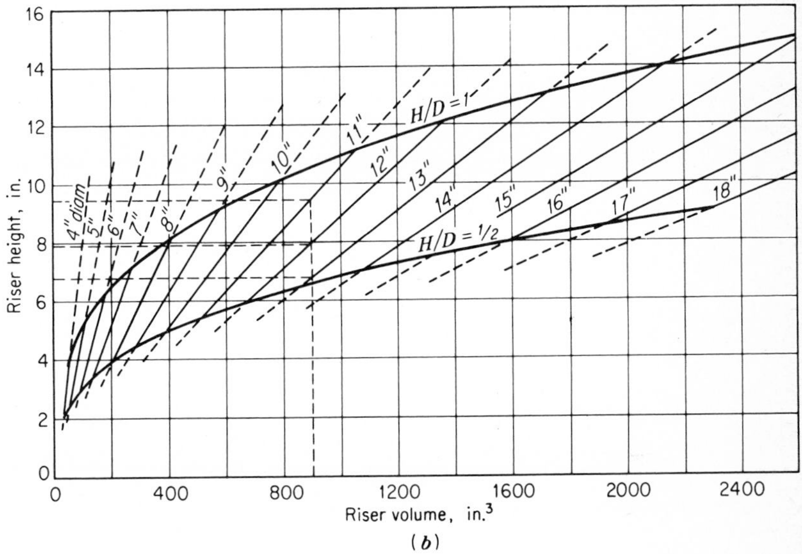

(b)

Fig. **9.14** (*a*) Riser-volume to casting-volume ratio as a function of the shape factor, (*b*) chart for determining riser diameter. (*From E. T. Myskowski, H. F. Bishop, and W. S. Pellini.*[35])

the pipe in a casting and riser system that is known to produce a sound casting. This measurement can be made by filling the pipe with water and measuring the volume or by comparing the weight of the riser with the expected weight calculated from the external dimensions. If this measurement is not feasible, a shrinkage percentage can be estimated based on prior knowledge of the casting characteristics of the alloy. The procedure then follows, using Fig. 9.15 for reference:

1. Obtain the weight of the casting.
2. Calculate the volume of feed metal required by the castings:

$$\frac{\text{Casting weight} \times \text{feed-metal percentage}}{\text{Weight per cubic inch}} = V_F$$

where V_F is the feed-metal volume required. (For white iron the feed-metal percentage is about 6 per cent and the weight per cubic inch would be about 0.27.)

3. Calculate D_P and H_P, the diameter and height of the pipe:

$$V_F = \pi \left(\frac{D_P}{2}\right)^2 \times H_P$$

Obviously, a number of combinations of D_P and H_P could supply the required V_F. Measurement of D_P and H_P of piping risers on a number of castings, however, shows that H_P usually is about 1.5 to 3.0 times D_P. Most commonly, the ratio H_P:D_P is about 2.5:1. These values could be substituted in V_F above, and the equation solved. It is easier to set up the relationship graphically for all the possible combinations as in Fig. 9.16. For 6 cu in. of feed metal with H_P:D_P at 2.5:1, the feed metal will be provided with $H_P = 3.6$ in., and $D_P = 1.45$ in., if only one riser is used. These dimensions are obtained from Fig. 9.16 by entering the graph on the dashed line at H_P:$D_P = 2.5$:1 and advancing to the intercept with the line marked 6 cu in. (this is V_F). Then H_P is read on the ordinate at the left, and D_P on the abscissa at the top of the graph. If two or more risers were used, the volume required from each would establish the necessary H_P and D_P in the same way.

4. Determine D_R. This is the diameter of the riser as shown in Fig. 9.15, $D_R = 2W + D_P$, where W is the representative section thickness of the casting. It is possible to verify W after the casting is made, since it can be

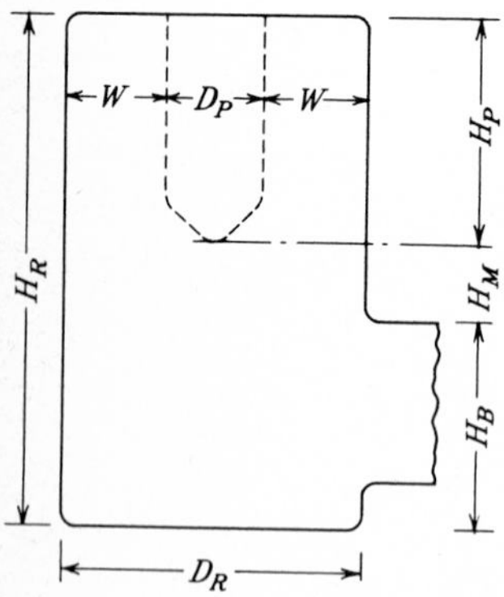

***Fig.* 9.15** Cross section of piping type of side riser. (*From R. W. Heine.*[38])

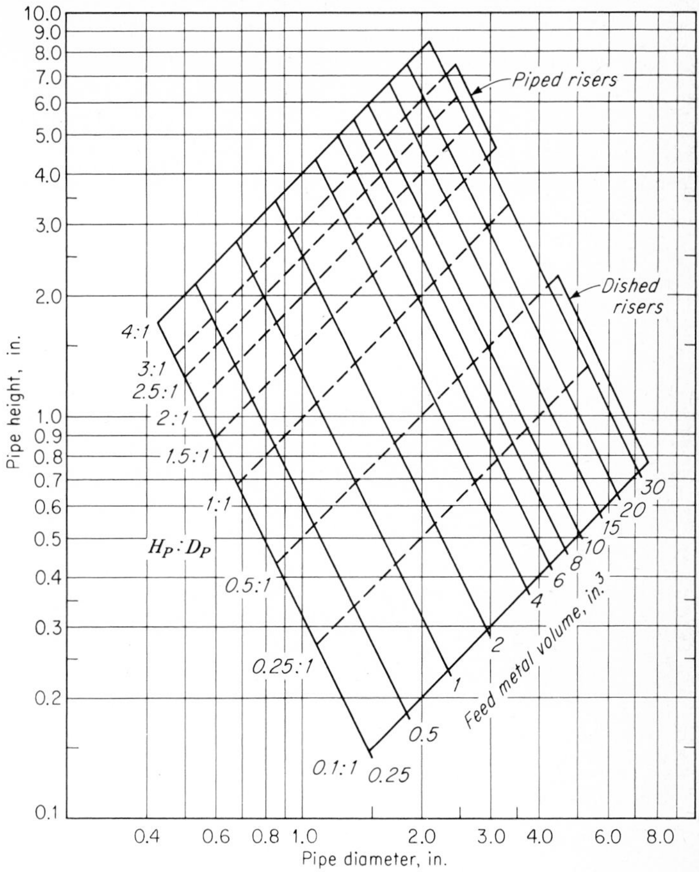

***Fig.* 9.16** Graph relating D_p, H_p, and volume of feed metal. (*From R. W. Heine.*[38])

measured on piped risers. W is the effective plate thickness, or one-half the bar diameter when bars are to be fed, or $0.35E$ on cubes, where E is the edge length of the cube.

Example: Assume a 27-lb hub casting with a 0.75-in. uniform section thickness. D_P and H_P were determined in steps 2 and 3 above. Then

$$D_R = 2 \times 0.75 + 1.45$$
$$= 2.95 \text{ in.}$$

when one riser is used. If two risers are used and 3 cu in. is fed from each,

$$D_P = 1.125$$

$$H_P = 2.8 \text{ in.}$$

$$D_R = 2 \times 0.75 + 1.125 = 2.625 \text{ in.} \qquad \text{for each riser}$$

5. Design the pressure section. Keeping pressure on liquid metal in the casting during the final stage of feeding is the function of the pressure section of the riser, H_M. The diameter of the pressure section is the same as that of the feeding section, D_R. The height of the pressure section, H_M, depends on the location of the highest point to be fed in the casting. For hypoeutectic alloys like white iron, H_M should usually be a minimum of 1 in. above the highest point of the casting to maintain positive pressure in the final stages of feeding. When the highest point to be fed is above the parting line, H_M can be decreased by putting part or all of the riser connection in the cope. If the highest point of the casting is below the side riser gate, $H_R = H_P + H_B + 1.0$.
6. Design the bottom section. The bottom section of the riser is that portion of the height below the top of the riser connection. It functions as a channel for the feed metal to reach the casting. The diameter of this section is D_R. The height H_B is a minimum of $2W$, and need not be more than $2W + D_P$ or D_R. A safe height is $H_B = 3W$.
7. The riser connection should be $2.5W$ to $0.8D_R$ in width and W in height for rectangular connections. For cylindrical connections it should be $2W \times 2W$. Distance from riser to casting is 0.5 to $1.5W$.
8. Determine the riser height. The total height of the piping riser equals $H_P + H_M + H_B$. As a minimum the height $H_R = H_P + 1.0 + 3W$ in inches, where W is section thickness. The height is greater than the minimum when H_M is required to be more than 1.0 in.

If the riser dishes at the top rather than forming a pipe, somewhat different dimensions of the riser are involved, as indicated by the plot in Fig. 9.16. Reference 38 supplies the procedures that should be followed to calculate the size of a dished riser. Piping risers provide more positive feeding pressure and require less flask area, whereas dishing risers do not require as much cope height. A dishing riser develops because the heat-transfer system is such that no clear-cut flow channel for liquid metal is produced in the center of the riser.

In arriving at the final riser dimensions, one should make certain that the bottom of the pipe lies above the level of the highest point of the casting. Also, to allow for variations in casting volume or pipe height, an additional inch or two should be added to the riser height. In general, the riser height must exceed 1.5 times the diameter to get piping. For complicated castings where several risers may be necessary to assure soundness, the volume calculations for step 1 should be for that part of the casting fed by a given riser. If one riser is to be used to feed several castings, the feed-metal volume will be that for a single casting multiplied by the number of castings. Such an arrangement when feasible leads to maximum casting yield.

The advantage of this method of riser design is that it provides an approach which determines the amount of feed metal required regardless of the shape of the casting. Once the feed-metal requirements are established, the optimum riser dimensions can then be formulated in a simple manner.

One factor that must not be overlooked is the effect of pouring temperature on the feeding of castings. Changing the pouring temperature not only affects the thermal gradients in the casting; it affects the extent of nucleation as well. For every surface-area–volume ratio formed in castings, there is an optimum pouring temperature. Pouring a casting of a given surface-area–volume ratio at too low a temperature will cause skulling over of the riser and ineffective feeding. Pouring at too high a temperature tends to cause the riser to dish rather than to pipe, which will reduce feeding action unless the riser is specifically designed to account for this. The dishing results from extensive dendritic growth during the freezing process.

Location of Risers

When a long bar or plate is cast without a riser, it is found that a certain length from each end of the bar or plate is sound. This results from the directional solidification that develops at the ends because of the greater heat extraction from those points compared with others. This effect occurs despite the absence of a riser. Similarly, if a long bar or plate is cast horizontally with one adequate riser at the center, it will be found that, for a certain distance from the riser, the casting will be sound because of the feeding action of the riser, whereas beyond this point, some form of shrinkage will be evident. These two effects can be referred to as the *end effect* and *riser effect,* respectively. Figure 9.17

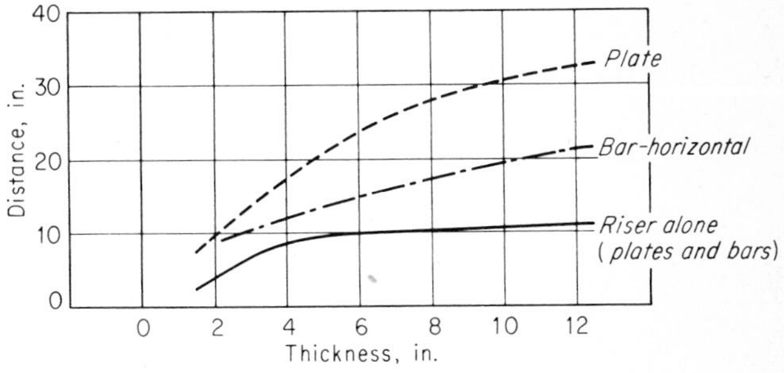

***Fig.* 9.17** Maximum feeding distance of risers only and of total riser plus end effect on steel plates and bars. (*From J. F. Wallace.*[32])

illustrates the consequence of these effects in feeding steel plates and bars.[32]

If castings having a variety of section thicknesses are produced, the adjacent sections will have an effect on the soundness of the casting in a specific section. Thus, if a light section is attached to a heavy section, the extent of the sound region in the heavy section will not be as great as in the absence of the light section. Conversely, the presence of the heavy section next to the light section would tend to increase the length of sound metal in the light section as compared with the case where the heavy section is absent.

Another similar situation is the case where both a light and a heavy section are attached to a section of intermediate distance. Table 15.2 gives formulas to calculate finding distances for a number of these possibilities for steel castings, but similar equations could be developed for other metals as well. One of the results of these studies is to demonstrate that it is easier to produce a sound tapered section than a section of uniform thickness.

With the effect from risers and ends established, it is possible to use these data to determine the location of risers to effect complete soundness in a bar or plate. Only a simple case will be used as an example. More specific examples can be found in Ref. 32.

Problem. What is the theoretical length of a 4-in.-thick bar of steel that can be cast sound with the two top risers? In this case the riser size is assumed to be adequate to feed the casting if spacing is correct.

Solution. It will be noted that each riser will feed to one end on one side of the riser and toward the center of the bar on the other. Therefore, from Table 15.2, the end effect would be $6\sqrt{T} = 6\sqrt{4} = 12$ in. On the other side of the riser the feeding distance would be $D = 3.6\sqrt{T} = 3.6 \times 7.2$ in. Therefore each riser would feed a total distance of 19.2 in., and the total length of bar that could be cast sound would be 38.4 in.

Problems of this type may be more complex, depending on casting geometry. In some instances, graphical solutions using a compass to prescribe the circle of influence of a given riser are easier to handle. In the case of side risers, the radius of the riser must be added to the feeding distance to locate the circle of influence from the center of the riser. A schematic example of the development of an adequate riser and padding system is provided in Fig. 9.18.

Blind Risers

The conventional riser is open to the atmosphere. The so-called *blind riser* is enclosed by the sand mold and is usually designed for a minimum

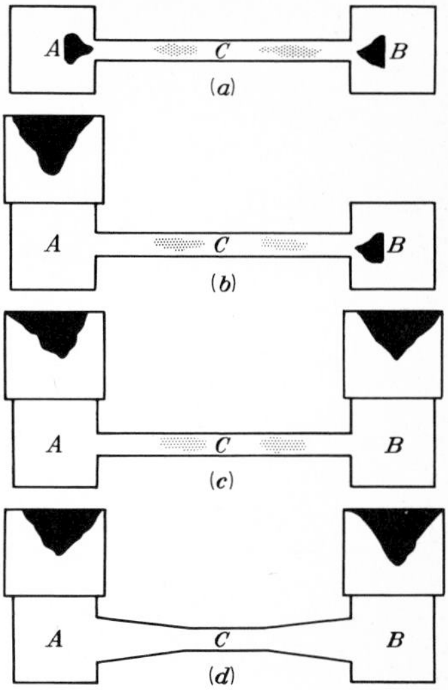

***Fig.* 9.18** The development (*a* to *d*) of a riser and padding system to ensure casting soundness. Shaded areas represent microporosity. (*From J. B. Caine.*[31])

surface area per unit volume (Fig. 9.19). In the case of steel, which forms a solid outer skin of metal during solidification, the sprue solidifies early, and the casting and blind riser thereby constitute a closed shell of metal, which develops a partial vacuum by virtue of the shrinkage that occurs during solidification. As shrinkage takes place in the casting, metal is drawn in from the riser to compensate for it. This can occur even though the riser is no higher than the casting, but the temperature gradient must be such that the casting freezes first. Of course, if the riser is of greater height than the casting, additional benefit is gained. If, in addition, the skin of the casting is strong enough and the skin of the blind riser is pierced to allow atmospheric pressure to exert an influence, the riser can then feed a casting of greater height than itself, the atmospheric pressure forcing liquid metal into the shrinkage areas as

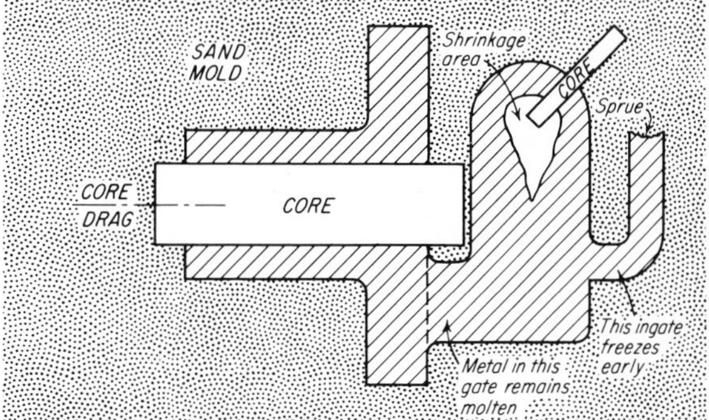

***Fig.* 9.19** Cross-sectional diagram of a casting fed by a blind riser with atmospheric vent produced by a pencil core.

they develop. The skin of the riser can be kept open by using sand or graphite core inserts as illustrated in Fig. 9.19 (the use of cores is patented). When a blind riser is used in this manner, it is referred to as an *atmospheric,* or *pressure,* riser. There is no advantage in providing atmospheric pressure feeding for metals which do not readily form a solid skin during solidification, because the partial vacuum necessary for the success of this method is not created.

The blind riser has a number of advantages, among which are:

1. The hottest metal is in the riser, and the coldest is in the casting. This promotes directional solidification.
2. Considerable latitude is allowed in positioning the blind riser.
3. A blind riser can be smaller than a comparable open riser.
4. Blind risers can be removed more easily from a casting.

A disadvantage, particularly if it is to feed a section of the casting at a greater height, is that a break in the skin of the casting itself will tend to equalize the pressure and reduce the effectiveness of the riser.

Internal Risers

Risers surrounded in whole or in part by the casting to be fed are referred to as *internal risers.* Risers of this type can be employed inside circular or cylindrically shaped castings. Since the risers are partially surrounded by the casting, their cooling rate is lower than that of risers which are located above or to one side of a casting. This means that they can be made smaller than in the conventional case, thereby contributing to casting yield. Two examples of the internal riser are given in Fig. 9.20.

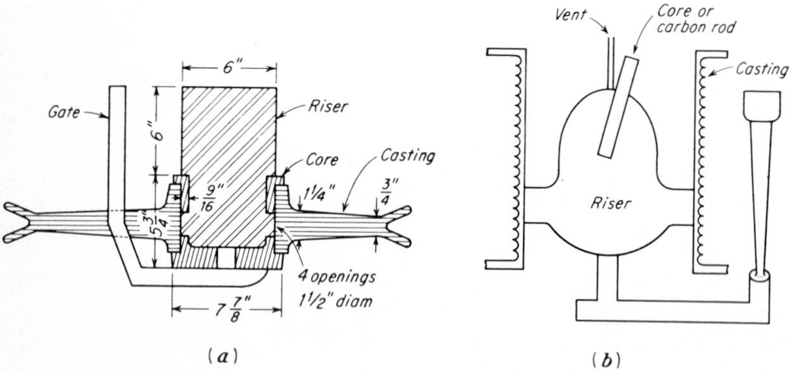

Fig. **9.20** Examples of (*a*) an open-top internal riser and (*b*) a blind internal riser. (*From J. F. Wallace.*[32])

Grouping of Castings

Closely related to the use of internal risers is the improved efficiency obtained when several castings can be grouped about a single riser. Not only does one riser do the work of several, but the grouping of castings near the riser lowers its cooling rate so that a smaller riser can be used. This principle is illustrated in Fig. 9.21.

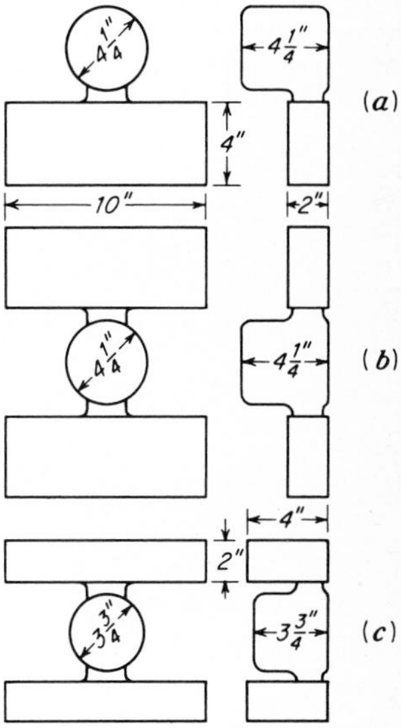

***Fig.* 9.21** Improving casting yield by grouping castings about a single riser. Note the smaller riser diameter required for case *c*, where the proximity of the castings has lowered the riser cooling rate. (*From J. F. Wallace.*[32])

Riser Connections to the Casting

How the riser is attached to the casting is important because it determines, first, how well the riser can feed the casting, and second, how readily the riser can be removed from the casting. It may also control to some extent the depth of the shrinkage cavity by solidifying just before the riser freezes, thereby preventing the cavity from extending into the casting. Riser-neck dimensions for three types of risers are given in Table 9.4, which is to be used with reference to Fig. 9.22. These dimensions are for cases where the material surrounding the neck has the same thermal properties as the molding material used elsewhere. If insulating necks or necks made from core sand are used, the dimensions may be smaller.

Use of Chills

The foregoing discussion of risers deals largely with methods for securing directional solidification by delaying the freezing process in some part

Table 9.4 Riser-neck dimensions*

Type riser	Length L_N	Cross section L_N
General side.	Short as feasible, not over $D/2$	Round, $D = 1.2\ L_N + 0.1D$
Plate side.	Short as feasible, not over $D/3$	Rectangular, $H_N = 0.6$ to $0.8D$ as neck length increases, $W_N = 2.5L_N + 0.18D$
Top.	Short as feasible, not over $D/2$	Round, $D_N = L_N + 0.2D$

*From J. F. Wallace.[32]

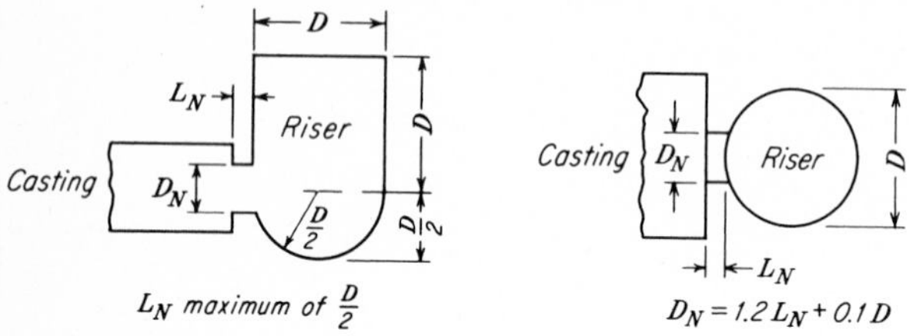

(*a*) General type of side riser

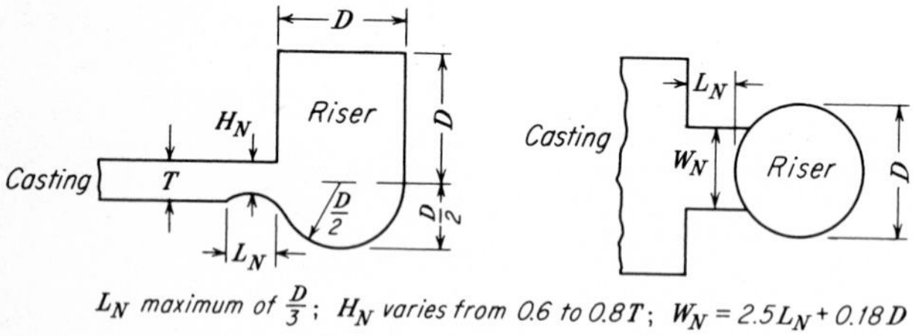

(*b*) Side riser for plate casting

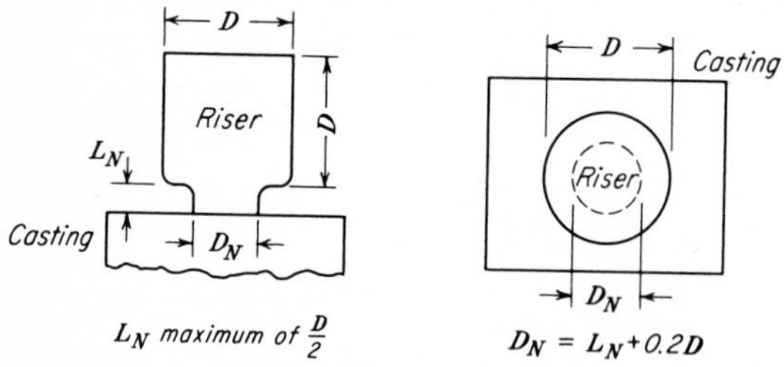

(*c*) Top round riser

Fig. 9.22 **Location of dimensions used in Table 9.4 for three types of risers.** (*From J. F. Wallace.*[32])

of the mold system. It is entirely possible, however, that the same objective of directional solidification can be accomplished by the reverse procedure of chilling the metal in those portions of the casting that are more remote from the liquid-metal source. Both *external* and *internal chills* can be used for this purpose. External chills are placed in the mold walls at the mold-metal interfaces, whereas internal chills are placed in the mold cavity.

External Chills

External chills are metal inserts of steel, cast iron, or copper that are placed at appropriate locations in the mold to increase the freezing rate of the metal at those points. They may be standard shapes or, in special cases, may be shaped to conform to the required mold-cavity dimensions; their size is determined by the cooling requirements. They are used effectively at junctions or other portions of a casting that are difficult to feed by risers. A number of examples of the use of external chills are given in Fig. 9.23. The effect of chills in altering the freezing cycle of steel castings was demonstrated in Fig. 8.11. This figure showed that the gap between the start and end of freezing was drastically reduced by the use of external chills. This effect causes a notable improvement in the chance for getting a sound casting since:[32]

1. It sets up steep temperature gradients.
2. It promotes good directional and progressive solidification.
3. It reduces the incidence of macro- and microporosity.

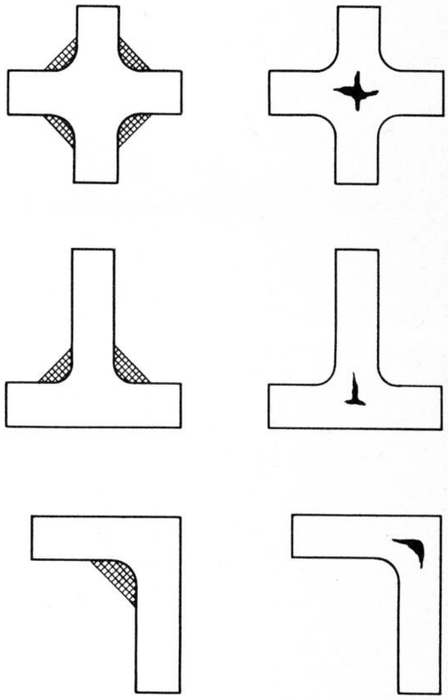

Fig. 9.23 External chills of appropriate size can be used to eliminate porosity at casting junctions.

Chills must be dry to avoid forming blowholes in the metal. They are frequently given a protective wash of silica flour or other refractory material. This wash should be thoroughly dried before the chill is inserted in the mold. When chills are placed in green sand, moisture from the mold may condense on them if they are allowed to stand too long in the mold. This can be prevented by preheating the chill before its insertion or pouring the mold shortly after it is made. Condensation of moisture on the chill should be avoided because it leads to gassing of the metal.

Although not strictly in the category of an external chill, the same effects can be accomplished by a variety of molding materials that will change the cooling characteristics of the mold. An example of this is shown in Fig. 9.24. Here, the use of a chill plus crushed magnesite and bonded silicon carbide in the manner shown results in the proper directional solidification. In some instances, similar effects can be obtained by varying the thickness of the molding material.

Internal Chills

Internal chills are placed in the mold at locations that cannot be reached effectively with external chills. They are also used in spots that are subsequently machined out, such as in bosses and lugs that are to be drilled or bored. Examples of internal chills are shown in Fig. 9.25.

The use of internal chills is somewhat more critical than external ones for the following reasons:

1. The chill may not fuse with the casting, thereby establishing points of weakness.
2. Cleanliness of the chill is more important since it will be completely surrounded by metal, and any gas that is created cannot readily escape.
3. The chill may alter the mechanical properties of the casting where it is used.
4. The composition of the chill must be compatible with the metal being

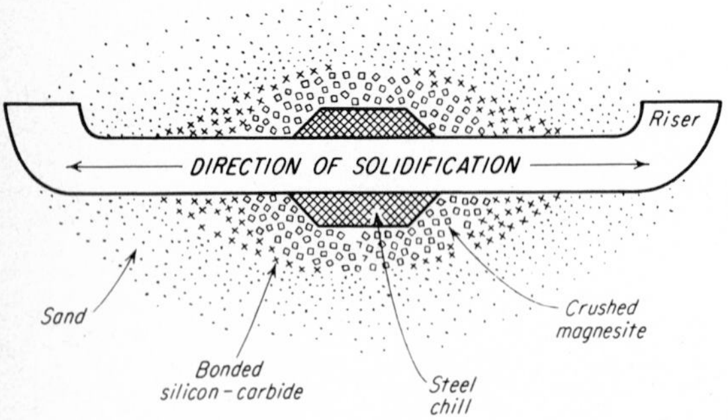

Fig. 9.24 Directional solidification can be secured by the use of a variety of mold materials that change the cooling characteristics of the mold. (*From C. W. Briggs.*[2])

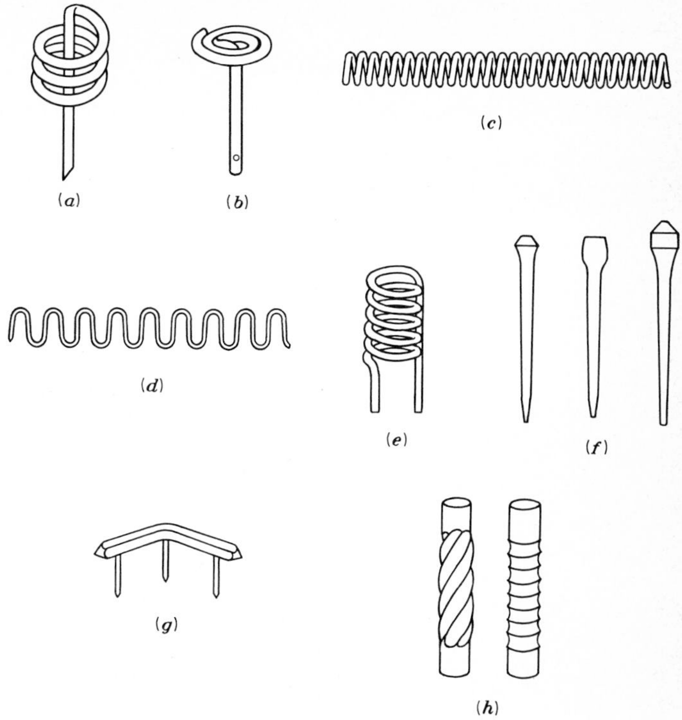

***Fig.* 9.25** Examples of internal chills. (*a*) Chill coil nail, (*b*) flathead chill coil nails, (*c*) chill coil, (*d*) grid chill, (*e*) hub chill, (*f*) chill nails, (*g*) spider chill, (*h*) chill rods. (*Courtesy of Fanner Manufacturing Co.*)

poured. Thus a cast-iron internal chill would not be used for a steel or a nonferrous casting. Usually, the chill should have approximately the composition of the metal in which it is to be used.

Use of Insulators and Exothermic Compounds

A riser can be made more efficient by employing some artificial means to keep the top of the riser from freezing over so that the molten metal beneath can be exposed to atmospheric pressure. This can be done by use of certain additions made to the surface of the molten metal in the riser, preferably as soon as possible after the metal enters the riser.

These additions serve as *antipiping compounds* through an insulating effect or from heat given off by an exothermic reaction in the compound. Insulating effects are obtained by such additions as powdered graphite or charcoal, rice or oat hulls, and refractory powders. The carbonaceous compounds, as well as other mixes specifically designed for that purpose, also provide additional heat from exothermic reactions. In the case of the carbonaceous materials, this effect may merely result from oxidation of carbon. With other mixes, the oxidation may be more rigorous, resulting from reactions of the type

$$2Al + Fe_2O_3 = 2Fe + Al_2O_3$$

which is strongly exothermic. Other oxidants and oxidizers, together with other additions, may also be employed.[55] Figure 9.26 indicates the improvement in riser efficiency obtained from the use of insulating- and exothermic-type compounds. Figure 9.13 illustrates the effect of these compounds and the use of an electric arc on the riser-to-casting freezing ratio.

Oxidation of the metal in the riser with a stream of oxygen and heating with an electric arc are other means that have been used to keep the riser open in very large castings.

Besides supplying insulation on the top of the riser, it is also possible to use *insulating* sleeves to form the sides of the riser, thereby making it possible to secure a lower solidification rate in the riser and hence better feeding of the casting. For nonferrous work such sleeves can be made from plaster of paris, but this material is not satisfactory for ferrous metal because it reacts with the metal.

Insulating pads can also be employed in various parts of the mold to decrease the cooling rate in thin sections where such an effect is desired to promote directional solidification. An illustration of the use of an insulating sleeve and pad is given in Fig. 9.27. Moldable exothermic compounds could be used in place of the insulating pads.[57, 58]

The net effect on the risers in using chills on the casting or insulators or exothermic compounds is to reduce the size of the riser relative to the

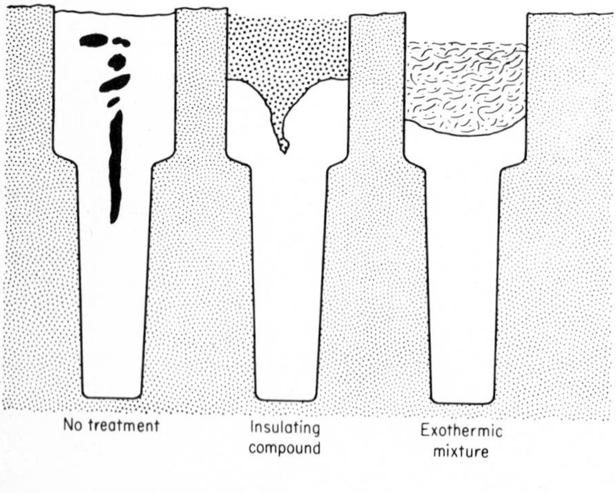

Fig. 9.26 Use of an insulating compound or exothermic mixture in the riser reduces the piping tendency and decreases the amount of metal required in the riser.

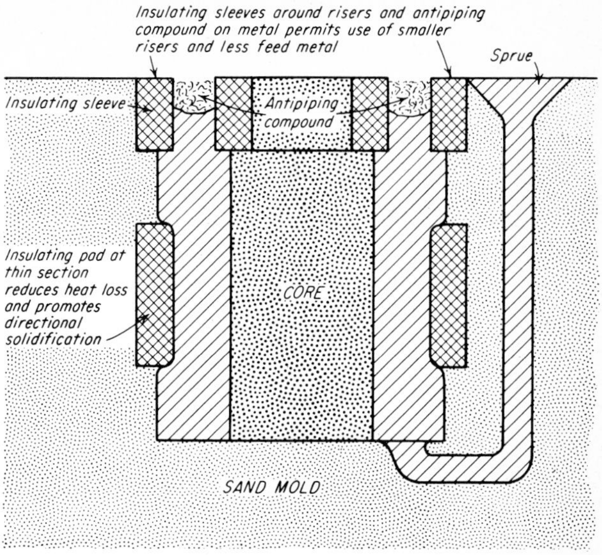
Insulating sleeves around risers and antipiping compound on metal permits use of smaller risers and less feed metal
Sprue
Insulating sleeve
Antipiping compound
Insulating pad at thin section reduces heat loss and promotes directional solidification
CORE
SAND MOLD

***Fig.* 9.27 The combination of insulating sleeves around risers and insulating pads at thin sections of a casting increases metal yield and promotes directional solidification.**

size of the casting. It is obvious that this means a higher casting yield.* The use of chills or the addition of insulating materials or exothermic compounds to the molds means added costs, not only because of the use of these materials, but also with respect to any additional conditioning the system sand may require to remove these materials. Therefore there are economic considerations as well as technical ones that will dictate whether or not these means of increasing casting yield are sound. There are, of course, certain instances where these practices are the only feasible ones to use, and in such instances the question of cost is not involved.

Special Conditions Arising from Joining Sections

Figure 9.23 gives examples of the shrinkage that can develop at section junctions and the use of chills to prevent it. Section junctions present special feeding problems that can be handled by using chills or by redesign of the casting. Figure 9.28 gives an example of a redesign to accomplish the same objective of eliminating shrinkage at a junction.

Applications

In designing the feeding system for a casting, the first step is to determine the location of risers and chills to assure that directional solidification

*Weight of casting relative to total weight of casting plus risers and gates.

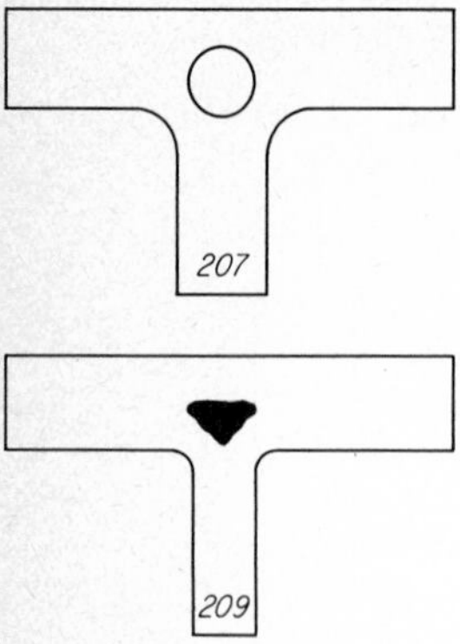

Fig. 9.28 **Effect of casting design on soundness at a junction.** (*From J. F. Wallace.*[32])

is achieved. This can be done with the use of published information on feeding distances such as given in Table 15.2 and elsewhere or on the basis of previous experience. The use of exothermic compounds, insulators, or other special techniques must be studied from both the technical and economic aspects. Once the riser locations are established, the riser sizes can be calculated, using the procedure outlined in this chapter or one of the other methods given in chapters dealing with specific casting alloys.

With the risering system established, the gating system can be planned, using the principles presented in the first part of this chapter. These steps are not necessarily performed in the order given here, but the point to be made is that design of castings can be established on the basis of sound engineering principles and need not be hit-or-miss.

In a very general way, a riser or gating system designed for steel ought also to be applicable to other metals. However, there are certain restrictions to this generalization.

Certain alloys, such as gray cast iron and some aluminum- and copper-base alloys, have an extended freezing range which precludes the possibility of developing a gastight skin such as is found in cast steel and some copper-base alloys. This eliminates the possibility of using atmospheric or pressure risers. In addition, gray cast iron undergoes some expansion during solidification as a result of graphitization occurring during the freezing period. As a consequence, gray cast iron requires less risering than other metals.

Experience has indicated which alloys require extensive feeding systems and which are less critical, and this has largely governed the selection of the risering and gating system used for a specific alloy. It is undoubtedly true that, as more basic information is accumulated, economies in the design of these systems can be effected through a more judicious proportioning and positioning of the feeding system.

BIBLIOGRAPHY

1. E. T. Myskowski, H. F. Bishop, and W. S. Pellini, Application of Chills to Increasing the Feeding Range of Risers, *Trans. AFS*, vol. 60, p. 389, 1952.
2. C. W. Briggs, "The Metallurgy of Steel Castings," McGraw-Hill Book Company, New York, 1946.
3. M. J. Berger and C. Locke, A Theoretical Basis for the Design of Gates, *Foundry*, vol. 79, p. 112, February, 1951.
4. M. J. Berger and C. Locke, "Fluid Flow Mechanics of Molten Steel," Armour Research Foundation, Chicago, Apr. 12, 1951.
5. J. F. Wallace and E. B. Evans, Principles of Gating, *Foundry*, vol. 87, p. 74, October, 1959.
6. J. F. Wallace and E. B. Evans, Gating of Gray Iron Castings, *Trans. AFS*, vol. 65, p. 267, 1957.
7. H. W. Dietert, How Fast Should a Mold Be Poured? *Foundry*, vol. 81, p. 205, August, 1955.
8. H. O. Meriwether, Shell Molded Ductile Iron Castings Gating and Risering for Vertical Pouring, *Trans. AFS*, vol. 68, p. 516, 1960.
9. E. A. Lange and A. T. Bukowski, Pouring Times for Steel Castings, U.S. Naval Research Laboratory Report, Washington, D.C., 1958.
10. C. V. Knobeloch, Choke That Gate, *Modern Castings*, vol. 84, p. 48, December, 1956.
11. D. M. March, Gating and Risering Ductile Iron Castings Poured in Dry Sand Molds, *Trans. AFS*, vol. 68, p. 512, 1960.
12. Report of IBF Subcommittee TS24, Ingots, *Foundry Trade J.*, vol. 99, p. 691, Dec. 15, 1955.
13. L. W. Eastwood, Tentative Design of Horizontal Gating System for Light Alloys, in "Symposium on the Principles of Gating," p. 25, American Foundrymen's Society, 1951.
14. J. G. Kura, Calculation of Horizontal Gating Systems, *Am. Foundryman*, vol. 27, p. 123, May, 1955.
15. K. Grube and L. W. Eastwood, A Study of the Principles of Gating, *Trans. AFS*, vol. 58, p. 76, 1950.
16. T. Finlay, Fin Gating: New Cost-cutting Steel Techniques, *Modern Castings*, vol. 40, p. 53, September, 1961.
17. M. C. Flemings and H. F. Taylor, Gating Aluminum Castings, *Foundry*, vol. 88, p. 72, April, 1960.
18. R. W. White, Gating of Ductile Iron Castings, *Foundry*, vol. 88, p. 101, February, 1960.
19. C. W. Briggs, Gating Steel Castings, *Foundry*, vol. 88, p. 124, June, 1960.
20. R. F. Polich, A. Saunders, Jr., and M. C. Flemings, Gating Premium Quality Castings, *Trans. AFS*, vol. 71, p. 418, 1963.
21. C. W. Ward, Jr., and T. C. Jacobs, Kiss Gating Brass Castings, *Trans. AFS*, vol. 70, p. 865, 1962.
22. E. Bjorklund, Calculating Ingate Dimensions for Gray Iron Castings, *Trans. AFS*, vol. 70, p. 193, 1962.
23. J. G. Mezoff and H. E. Elliott, A Study of Factors Affecting the Pouring Rates of Castings, *Trans. AFS*, vol. 56, p. 279, 1948.
24. W. H. Johnson, W. O. Baker, and W. S. Pellini, Principles of Gating Design: Factors Influencing Molten Steel Flow from Finger Gating System, *Trans. AFS*, vol. 58, p. 661, 1950.
25. K. R. Grube and J. G. Kura, Principles Applicable to Vertical Gating, *Trans. AFS*, vol. 63, p. 35, 1955.

26. K. R. Grube, R. M. Lang, and J. G. Kura, Modifications in Vertical Gating Principles, *Trans. AFS,* vol. 64, p. 54, 1956.
27. H. E. Elliott and J. G. Mezoff, Effect of Gating Design on Metal Flow Conditions in the Casting of Magnesium Alloys, *Trans. AFS,* vol. 56, p. 223, 1948.
28. F. E. Murphy, G. J. Jackson, and R. A. Rosenberg, Bronze Valve Vertical Gating in Shell Molds, *Modern Castings,* vol. 40, p. 51, July, 1961.
29. R. A. Flinn, Quantitative Evaluation of the Susceptibility of Various Alloys to Shrinkage Defects, *Trans. AFS,* vol. 64, p. 665, 1956.
30. N. Chvorinov, Theory of the Solidification of Castings, *Geisserei,* vol. 27, pp. 177–225, 1940.
31. J. B. Caine, Risering Castings, *Trans. AFS,* vol. 57, p. 66, 1949.
32. J. F. Wallace (ed.), "Fundamentals of Risering Steel Castings," Steel Founders' Society, 1960.
33. J. T. Berry and T. Watmough, Factors Affecting Soundness in Alloys with Long and Short Freezing Range, *Trans. AFS,* vol. 69, p. 11, 1959.
34. H. D. Merchant, Dimensioning of Sand Casting Risers, *Modern Castings,* vol. 35, p. 73, February, 1959.
35. E. T. Myskowski, H. F. Bishop, and W. S. Pellini, A Simplified Method for Determining Riser Dimensions, *Trans. AFS,* vol. 63, p. 271, 1955.
36. J. F. Wallace, Risering of Castings, *Foundry,* vol. 87, p. 74, November, 1959.
37. C. W. Briggs, Risering of Commercial Steel Castings, *Trans. AFS,* vol. 63, p. 287, 1955.
38. R. W. Heine, Piping Risers for White Iron Castings, *Malleable Founders' Soc. Tech. Bull.* 63-3, 1963.
39. H. F. Bishop, Risering Steel Castings, *Foundry,* vol. 88, p. 75, August, 1960; p. 116, September, 1960; p. 114, October, 1960.
40. R. W. White, Risering of Ductile Iron Castings, *Foundry,* vol. 88, p. 96, March, 1960.
41. J. F. Bishop and W. H. Johnson, Risering of Steel, *Foundry,* vol. 84, p. 70, February, 1956; p. 136, March, 1956.
42. H. F. Taylor, M. C. Flemings, and T. S. Piwonka, Risering Aluminum Castings, *Foundry,* vol. 88, p. 216, May, 1960.
43. D. Miller, Feeding Systems for Permanent Mold Castings, *Foundry,* vol. 86, p. 70, December, 1958.
44. R. W. Ruddle, Risering of Copper Alloy Castings, *Foundry,* vol. 88, p. 78, January, 1960.
45. J. Varga, Jr., A New Method for Studying Riser Requirements for Castings, *Foundry,* vol. 85, p. 106, July, 1957.
46. H. F. Bishop and C. G. Ackerlind, Dimensioning of Risers for Nodular Iron Castings, *Foundry,* vol. 84, p. 115, December, 1956.
47. Gating and Feeding for Light Metal Castings, American Foundrymen's Society, 1962.
48. H. Chappie, Gating Affects Quality in Production of Steel Castings, *Foundry,* vol. 84, p. 90, April, 1956.
49. R. Namur, Calculation of Riser-necks for Sand Castings, *Giesserei,* vol. 44, p. 665, Oct. 24, 1957.
50. C. W. Briggs, Necked-down Risers for Production Steel Castings, *SFSA Res. Rept.* 11, March, 1947.
51. C. W. Briggs, R. A. Gezelius, and G. R. Donaldson, Steel Casting Design for the Engineer and Foundryman, *Trans. AFS,* vol. 46, p. 605, 1938.
52. V. Pulsifer, Gray Iron Chilling Practice, *Foundry,* vol. 86, September, 1958.

53. V. Paschkis, Range of Effectiveness of Chills, *Trans. AFS,* vol. 63, p. 13, 1955.
54. C. Locke, Application of Indirect Chills, *Trans. AFS,* vol. 63, p. 291, 1955.
55. S. L. Gertsman, A Study of Insulating and Mildly Exothermic Antipiping Compounds Used for Steel Castings, *Trans. AFS,* vol. 57, p. 332, 1949.
56. J. Gotheridge and D. H. Snelson, How to Use Moldable Exothermic Compounds, *Foundry,* vol. 84, p. 150, May, 1956.
57. H. F. Bishop, H. F. Taylor, and R. G. Powell, Risering of Steel Castings with Exothermic Sleeves, *Foundry,* vol. 86, p. 54, June, 1958.
58. T. C. Bunch and G. E. Dalbey, Feeding of Castings, *Trans. AFS,* vol. 63, p. 503, 1955.
59. W. A. Mader, Application of Insulated Risers to Production of Aluminum Alloy Sand Castings, *Trans. AFS,* vol. 63, p. 553, 1955.
60. D. L. Gertsman and R. K. Buhr, Use of Rice and Oat Hulls as Riser Insulation, *Foundry,* vol. 83, p. 92, February, 1955.
61. A. J. Stone, H. B. Kinnear, and A. R. Fraser, Better Castings with Less Metal, *Foundry,* vol. 83, p. 118, July, 1955.
62. W. A. Mader, Make Small Risers Do the Work of Large, *Modern Castings,* vol. 83, p. 32, September, 1955.
63. H. Present and H. Rosenthal, Feeding Disturbance of Bars in Investment Molds, *Trans. AFS,* vol. 69, p. 138, 1961.
64. M. C. Flemings, R. W. Strachan, E. J. Poirier, and H. F. Taylor, Performance of Chills on High Strength Magnesium Alloy Sand Castings of Various Section Thicknesses, *Modern Castings,* vol. 34, p. 336, July, 1958.

10

Metals Cast in the Foundry

The preceding nine chapters have dealt largely with general principles applicable to all types of casting alloys. For an understanding of how these principles can be applied, it is now necessary that attention be given to specific alloys and the specific problems associated with these alloys. Just as our industrial complexity requires certain combinations of properties to meet certain requirements, so it is that selection can be made from a wide variety of available alloys to obtain the necessary combination of properties to meet specified conditions. Each of these alloys or groups of alloys possesses certain foundry characteristics that necessitate giving them special consideration beyond that possible in a discussion of general principles.

Accordingly, the succeeding chapters deal with the various commercially important casting alloys. To prepare the student for this section of the book, a classification of these alloys is given here, together with a tabulation of some of the more important properties of these alloys.

CLASSIFICATION OF FOUNDRY ALLOYS

Castings are frequently classified as *ferrous* (iron-base) and *nonferrous*. Subdivisions of these major groupings are given in the following outline.

I. Ferrous
  A. Steel
    1. Plain carbon steel
    2. Low-alloy steel
    3. High-alloy steel
  B. Cast iron
    1. Gray cast iron
    2. Ductile or nodular cast iron
    3. White cast iron
    4. Malleable iron; pearlitic malleable iron

II. Nonferrous
- *A*. Aluminum-base
- *B*. Copper-base
- *C*. Lead-base
- *D*. Magnesium-base
- *E*. Nickel-base
- *F*. Tin-base
- *G*. Zinc-base
- *H*. Miscellaneous

The nonferrous alloy castings can be divided into *heavy-metal castings* (copper-, zinc-, lead-, and nickel-base) and *light-metal castings* (aluminum- and magnesium-base alloys).

It would be impossible to present a complete list of all the cast alloys that can be produced and that do not fall into any of the other classifications given in preceding paragraphs. However, a few are worthy of mention:

1. *High-temperature alloys.* Although these parts can be fabricated by other processes, one of the commercially useful methods of producing the complex high-temperature alloys is by applying precision-casting methods (Chap. 3). A discussion of the various alloy types is outside the limitations of this book, but elements such as cobalt, chromium, columbium (niobium), tantalum, tungsten, nickel, and titanium are used in a wide variety of different combinations.
2. *Castings for atomic-energy work.* Various special alloys that are peculiarly suited to atomic-energy applications have been produced.
3. *Dental alloys.* These are cast by the precision-casting process. They rank with the high-temperature alloys in cost, base elements used, and complexity of composition.
4. *Precious-metal castings.* Parts of silver, gold, or platinum can be fabricated by casting where the need for the high corrosion and oxidation resistance or aesthetic qualities of these metals is indicated.

Each group of alloys in the preceding lists can be further subdivided into a number of alloy variations. In some cases these variations are quite extensive. This seeming complexity in the number of alloys cast in the foundry and available to the designer results from a large number of factors, any one or more of which may be responsible for the final selection of an alloy for a given application. Factors that determine the selection of a casting alloy include:

1. Cost
2. Corrosion resistance
3. Strength
4. Toughness

5. Weight
6. Tradition
7. Appearance
8. Casting properties
9. High- or low-temperature properties
10. Electrical properties
11. Susceptibility to heat-treatment
12. Personal preferences
13. Special property requirements, such as wear resistance and machinability
14. Sales effort for certain alloys

PROPERTIES OF METALS AND ALLOYS

In connection with the foregoing, certain physical properties of the base elements used for casting purposes are tabulated in Table 10.1. Comparison of the values listed in this table will show the rather large differences in properties that exist between some metals and that account for their use or elimination for a particular application. Thus aluminum and copper are found to be superior to iron in electrical conductivity (reciprocal of the resistivity). The electrical resistivity listed for aluminum is somewhat higher than that for copper. This comparison is on a volume basis; if it were to be made on a weight basis, aluminum would be found to have an electrical conductivity superior to that of copper.

Differences in melting point are of significance in determining the foundry practice for a particular metal and may be of significance in the use of the metal at elevated temperatures. Table 10.1 shows that there is a wide difference in melting points for some of the elements listed.

The modulus of elasticity is another property that is significant in determining the usefulness of a particular metal. The data show, for example, that iron is about 2½ times as stiff as aluminum. Thus it would take 2½ times the load to deflect an iron bar as compared with an aluminum bar of similar size. Again, however, if the weight factor is considered and bars of equal weight per unit length are considered (but differing in cross-sectional area), the difference would not be so marked, particularly if the added volume given the aluminum bar were properly distributed to stiffen the bar relative to the applied load.

These are just a few of the factors that need to be considered when selecting a metal for a particular application. Other examples will be found in other chapters. In addition to the basic physical data for pure metals, other data on alloys are useful, and some of these have been collected in Table 10.2.

Table 10.1 ***Some physical properties of the elements****

Element	Aluminum	Carbon (graphite)	Copper	Iron	Magnesium	Manganese	Nickel	Tin	Zinc	Lead
Symbol	Al	C	Cu	Fe	Mg	Mn	Ni	Sn	Zn	Pb
Atomic no.	13	6	29	26	12	25	28	50	30	82
Atomic weight (1947)	26.98	12.011	63.54	55.85	24.32	54.93	58.71	118.70	65.38	207.21
Density at 20 C (68 F), g/cu cm	2.699	2.25	8.96	7.87	1.74	7.43	8.902	7.298	7.138[a]	11.36
Density at 68 F (20 C), lb/cu in.	0.09751	0.081	0.324	0.284	0.0628	0.270	0.322	0.2637	0.258[a]	0.4097
Atomic volume, cu cm/g atom	9.996	5.33	7.09	7.10	14.0	7.39	6.59	16.26	9.17	18.27
Melting point, °C	660	3727	1083.0 ± 0.1	1536.5	650 ± 2	1245	1453	231.9 ± 0.1	419.46	327.4
°F	1220	6740	1981.4 ± 0.2	2797.7 ± 2	1202 ± 4	2273	2647	449.4 ± 0.2	787.11	621.4
Boiling point, °C	2450	4830	2595	3000 ± 150	1110	2150	2730	2270	906	1725
°F	4442	8730	4703	5430 ± 270	2025 ± 20	3900	4950	4120	1663	3137
Specific heat at 20 C, cal/g/°C	0.215	0.165	0.092	0.11	0.245	0.115	0.105	0.054	0.0915	0.031
Heat of fusion, cal/g	94.5	....	50.6	65.5	89 ± 2	63.7	73.8	14.5	24.09	6.26
Btu/lb	170	....	91.1	117.9	160	114.7	132.8	26.1	43.36	11.27
Coefficient of linear thermal expansion:										
Near 20 C, μin./°C	23.6	0.6–4.3	16.5	11.76	27.1	22	13.3	23	39.7[b]	29.3
Near 68 F, μin./°F	13.1	0.3–2.4	9.2	6.53	15.05	12.22	7.39	13	22.0	16.3
Thermal conductivity near 20 C, cal/(sq cm/cm)/°C/sec	0.53	0.057	0.94	0.18	0.367	....	0.22	0.15	0.27	0.083
Electrical resistivity, μohm-cm	2.655 (20 C)	1375 (0 C)	1.673 (20 C)	9.71 (20 C)	4.45 (20 C)	185 (20 C)	6.84 (20 C)	11.0 (20 C)	5.916 (20 C)[c]	20.65 (20 C)
Modulus of elasticity in tension, 10^6 psi	9	0.7	16	28.5 ± 0.5	6.35	23	30	6–6.5	[d]	2.0
Crystal structure	Face-centered cubic	Hexagonal[e]	Face-centered cubic	Body-centered cubic	Close-packed hexagonal	Cubic (complex)[e]	Face-centered cubic	Body-centered tetragonal	Close-packed hexagonal	Face-centered cubic

* Adapted from the ASM "Metals Handbook," 8th ed., vol. 1, 1961.
[a] At 40 C (104 F).
[b] For polycrystalline zinc; in single crystals, varies from 61.5 (parallel to hexagonal axis) to 15 (perpendicular to hexagonal axis).
[c] For polycrystalline zinc; in single crystals, varies from 6.16 (parallel to hexagonal axis) to 5.89 (perpendicular to hexagonal axis).
[d] Pure zinc has no clearly defined modulus of elasticity.
[e] Ordinary form; other modifications known or probable.

Table* 10.2 *Casting properties of foundry products*

Metal or alloy	Nominal composition, %	Solidification range, F	Shrinkage, in./ft	Specific gravity	Wt., lb/cu in.
Steels:					
Carbon cast steel	Less than 0.20 C; 0.50–1.00 Mn; 0.20–0.75 Si; 0.05 P max; 0.06 S max	2730–2615	1/8–1/4	7.86	0.284
	0.20–0.40 C; 0.50–1.00 Mn; 0.20–0.75 Si; 0.05 P max; 0.06 S max	2695–2590	1/8–1/4	7.86	0.284
	More than 0.40 C; 0.50–100 Mn; 0.20–0.75 Si; 0.05 P max; 0.06 S max	2670–2160	1/8–1/4	7.80–7.86	0.282–0.284
Alloy cast steel	......	2730–2280	Up to 5/8	7.50–8.10	0.271–0.293
Cast irons:					
Gray iron	......	2400–2000	1/8	7.00–7.50	0.252–0.271
White iron	......	2550–2065	3/16–1/4	7.70	0.277
Malleable iron	......	2550–2065	3/16	7.20–7.45	0.259–0.268
Aluminum alloys:					
Aluminum	99+ Al	1215 M.P.	5/32+	2.70	0.098
Aluminum-copper alloy	92 Al; 8 Cu	1165–975	5/32	2.83	0.102
Aluminum-copper-silicon alloy	4 Cu; Si; 93 Al	1170–970	5/32	2.75	0.099
Aluminum-magnesium alloy	4.0 Mg; 96.0 Al	1185–1075	5/32	2.63	0.095
Aluminum-manganese alloy	2.0 Mn; 98.0 Al	1255–1215	5/32	2.73	0.099
Aluminum-silicon alloy	12.0 Si; 88.0 Al	1150–1070	5/32	2.65	0.096
Aluminum-zinc alloy	2.5 Cu; 1.3 Fe; 11.0 Zn; 85.2 Al	1165–980	5/32	2.94	0.106
Copper alloys:					
Copper	99+ Cu	1980 M.P.	3/16	8.80	0.317
Copper-nickel alloy	45 Ni; 55 Cu	2325–2235	1/4	8.60	0.310
Cupronickel	30 Ni; 70 Cu	2250–2140	3/16	8.80	0.317
Bell metal	20 Sn; 80 Cu	1600–1450	3/16	8.70	0.313
Nickel brass (nickel silver)	20 Ni; 15 Zn; 65 Cu	2060 approx	3/16	8.50	0.316
Red brass	5 Zn; 5 Pb; 5 Sn; 85 Cu	1775 approx	3/16	8.75	0.314
Medium red brass	77 Cu; 10 Zn; 10 Pb; 3 Sn	1775 approx	3/16	8.68	0.312
Gun metal	8 Sn; 4 Zn; 88 Cu	1825–1775	1/8	8.30–8.60	0.300–0.310
Aluminum bronze	10 Al; 90 Cu	1920 approx	7/32	7.50	0.271
Manganese bronze	55–60 Cu; 38–42 Zn; 3.5 max Mn	1675 approx	7/32	8.40	0.303
Leaded bearing bronze	80 Cu; 10 Pb; 10 Sn	1725 approx	3/16	8.90	0.324
Silicon bronze	94 Cu; 5 Si; 1 Mn	1830 approx	3/16	8.20	0.297
Lead alloys:					
Lead-base bearing alloy	75 Pb; 15 Sb; 10 Sn; 0.50 max Cu; 0.20 As	515–465	......	9.73	0.350
Lead-antimony alloys	90 Pb; 10 Sb	500–475	......	10.67	0.386
Lead-tin-antimony alloys	80 Pb; 5 Sn; 15 Sb	500–460	......	10.04	0.363
Magnesium-base alloy	3.5–10 Al; 3.5 max. Zn; remainder Mg	1150 approx	5/32–1/8	1.83 max	0.066
Nickel alloys:					
High nickel-copper alloy	70 Ni; 30 Cu	2500–2400	1/4	8.80	0.317
High nickel-copper-silicon alloy	65 Ni; 30 Cu; 3–5 Si	2400–2300	1/4	8.65	0.312
Tin alloy, babbitt	90 Sn; 5 Cu; 5 Sb	690–430	......	7.34	0.265
Zinc-base alloy (die casting)	0.10 max Cu; 3.5–4.3 Al; remainder Zn	720 approx	5/32	6.60–6.70	0.238–0.242

* Adapted from *Metals and Alloys*, April, 1949.

11

Aluminum and Magnesium Foundry Practice

Historically, the development of casting practices for aluminum and its alloys is a relatively recent accomplishment. Aluminum alloys were not available in any substantial quantity for casting purposes until long after the discovery in 1886 of the electrolytic process of reduction of aluminum oxide by Charles Martin Hall in the United States and Paul Heroult in France. Although Hall's invention provided aluminum at a greatly reduced cost, the full value of aluminum as a casting material was not established until alloys suitable for foundry processes were developed. Since about 1915, a combination of circumstances—gradually decreasing cost, the expansion of air transportation, development of specific casting alloys, improved properties, and the impetus provided by two world wars—has resulted in an ever-increasing use of aluminum castings. Production figures for the light-metal casting alloys for the past few years are given in Table 11.1. Aluminum- and magnesium-alloy castings, the light metals, are making rapid strides toward more extensive engineering use.

Table* 11.1 *Production of aluminum and magnesium castings*

Year	Aluminum				Magnesium, total
	Total	Sand	Permanent mold	Die	
1962	926,698	146,731	295,567	481,034	29,325
1961	761,821	124,623	261,866	375,896	23,373
1960	774,548	129,804	258,042	385,617	23,530
1959	786,399	141,987	274,855	368,101	27,253
1958	641,700	125,487	224,092	290,275	28,776
1957	751,656	144,151	232,326	369,086	30,322
1956	801,036	171,733	245,451	376,116	36,168
1955	827,162	165,482	298,349	355,203	27,854
1954	624,973	158,473	214,408	245,291	25,777
1953	658,022	214,553	200,025	239,330	34,517

*Thousands of pounds. Adapted from *Foundry*, Penton Publishing Co., Cleveland.

ALUMINUM CASTINGS

Advantages of Aluminum Castings

Certain engineering advantages are inherent in the use of aluminum alloys for castings. Light weight (per unit volume) is the one most commonly cited. Some of the numerous other desirable properties include:

1. *A wide range of mechanical properties.* Strength, hardness, and other properties may be greatly altered by alloying and/or heat-treatment. Properties of the strongest alloys can be favorably compared with those of the cast irons and lower-strength steels, especially if the weight factor is considered. Suitable strength for many engineering uses is thus available.
2. *Architectural and decorative value.*
3. *Corrosion resistance.* This property is, of course, relative, but resistance to atmospheric- and water-corrosion conditions makes possible the use of aluminum for building construction, outboard-motor parts, food-handling-equipment castings, etc.
4. *Nontoxicity.* The use of aluminum castings for cooking utensils and other food-handling equipment requires that no chemical-reaction products toxic to humans be formed by action of the food on the aluminum alloy.
5. *Electrical conductivity.* Rotor bars in induction motors are cast of aluminum because of its desirable electrical conductivity. See Fig. 3.16, which illustrates this point.
6. *Ease of machining.*
7. *Casting properties.* Since aluminum has a relatively low melting point, about 1200 F, the problems of melting and pouring are greatly simplified when compared with steels and cast irons. Permanent metal molds may be used, and die casting is extensively practiced. Problems with furnace refractories and molding sands are reduced because of the lower pouring temperatures.
8. *Lower casting shipping costs per piece.*

A number of other factors relating to the characteristics of aluminum as a castings material will be considered in the following chapter, along with more specific information about the casting alloys.

Limitations

Since the cost of aluminum alloys in cents per pound is greater than that of cast irons and many steels, this fact is often considered a disadvantage. However, the cost in cents per pound is misleading unless it is recognized that the volume per pound of aluminum is about 2.90 times that of a pound of the ferrous alloys.

Engineering limitations include the following:

1. Lack of resistance to abrasion and wear.

2. Absence of aluminum alloys which can develop the combination of high tensile strength, toughness, and hardness obtainable in ferrous alloys.
3. Lack of resistance to severe corrosion to the degree offered by numerous copper- and nickel-base alloys and stainless steels.

Obviously, the selection of aluminum as a castings material demands that its advantages outweigh its limitations in any particular application. As in the production of other castings, the basic processes of molding, coring, melting, and cleaning are necessary. These processes, however, must be modified in aluminum founding to suit the metallurgical properties characteristic of the alloy.

MELTING OF ALUMINUM

One of the most easily controlled processes, although frequently overlooked in importance, is melting. Certain casting problems are directly related to failure to exercise adequate control during the melting process. These problems will be discussed in terms specifically related to the melting of aluminum, but the reader should recognize that there is a more extensive application of the principles to other metals.

Melting Furnaces

The types of melting furnaces[2] employed in aluminum foundries include the following:

1. Crucible furnaces, lift-out type
2. Pot furnaces
   a. Stationary, fuel-fired
   b. Tilting, fuel-fired
3. Reverberatory furnaces, fuel-fired, stationary, and tilting types
4. Barrel-type furnaces, fuel-fired
5. Induction furnaces, electrically operated
   a. Low frequency
   b. High frequency

Each of these furnaces has certain advantages. Fuel-fired furnaces are of two types: the indirect-flame type, in which the products of combustion do not come into direct contact with the metal, and the direct-flame type, in which there is direct contact of the combustion products and metal charge. Pot furnaces are usually indirect-flame or electrical-resistance furnaces whereas reverberatory furnaces are direct-flame furnaces. However, some constructions of pot and crucible furnaces approach the direct-flame conditions.

***Fig.* 11.1** Lift-out-type crucible furnace. The crucible is lifted out of the furnace and used as a pouring ladle. (*Courtesy of Hevi-Duty Electric Company.*)

Crucible Furnaces

A typical crucible furnace of the lift-out type is illustrated in Fig. 11.1. A cross section of another type of crucible furnace is shown in Fig. 11.2. The capacity of such furnaces is limited by the crucible size. Crucibles are made of a clay-graphite mixture or of silicon carbide. Table 11.2 provides data of the standard sizes of crucibles. Lift-out crucibles are especially useful for flexibility in small operations and in number of alloys melted. After the melt has been prepared, the crucible is lifted out of the furnace with tongs, placed in a ring shank ladle, its temperature measured, and then it is poured directly from the ladle. Unless a crucible cover is used, crucible melting approaches open-flame conditions.

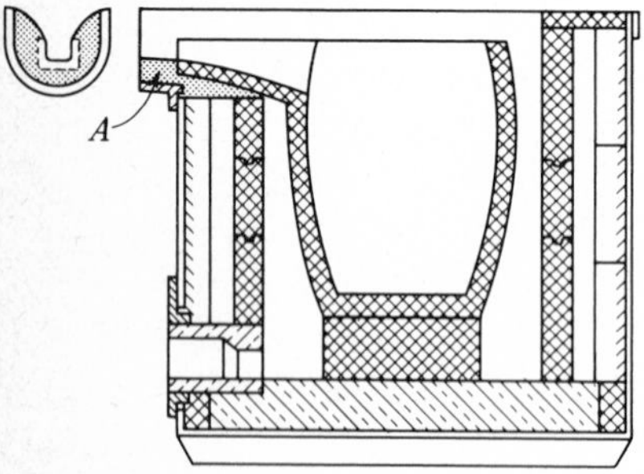

***Fig.* 11.2** Cross section of a crucible furnace in which the pouring spout is an integral part of the crucible. See Fig. 11.5 for a view of the exterior of this type of furnace. (*From L. W. Eastwood.*[2])

Table* 11.2 *Standard sizes of graphite crucibles

No.	Height outside, in.	Diameter top out, in.	Diameter bilge out, in.	Diameter bottom out, in.	Approx capacity, lb, water full*	Approx working capacity, lb, red brass
0000	2 15/16	2 3/8	2 3/8	1 3/4	0.25	1.19
1	3 5/8	3 1/4	3 1/8	2 1/4	0.50	2.96
2	4 1/2	3 3/4	3 11/16	2 7/8	0.75	4.74
3	5 3/8	4 1/4	4 1/8	3	1.0	8.5
4	5 3/4	4 5/8	4 9/16	3 1/8	1.50	10.07
6	6 1/2	5 1/4	5 1/4	3 7/8	2.25	15.41
8	7 1/8	5 7/8	5 7/8	4 1/4	3.0	20.74
10	8 1/16	6 1/16	6 9/16	4 15/16	4.81	36.0
12	8 1/2	6 3/8	6 7/8	5 1/16	5.0	42.0
14	8 7/8	6 11/16	7 3/16	5 1/4	5.75	48.0
16	9 1/4	6 15/16	7 1/2	5 1/2	7.18	53.0
18	9 13/16	7 5/16	7 15/16	5 13/16	8.6	64.0
20	10 5/16	7 11/16	8 3/8	6 1/8	10.0	74.0
25	10 15/16	8 3/16	8 7/8	6 1/2	12.0	89.0
30	11 1/2	8 5/8	9 5/16	6 13/16	14.0	104.0
35	12	9	9 3/4	7 1/8	16.0	119.0
40	12 1/2	9 3/8	10 1/8	7 7/16	18.0	134.0
45	13 3/16	9 7/8	10 11/16	7 13/16	21.0	157.0
50	13 3/4	10 1/4	11 1/8	8 1/8	24.0	179.0
60	14 7/16	10 13/16	11 11/16	8 9/16	28.0	209.0
70	15 1/16	11 1/4	12 3/16	8 15/16	32.0	239.0
80	15 5/8	11 11/16	12 11/16	9 1/4	36.0	269.0
90	16 3/16	12 1/8	13 1/8	9 9/16	40.0	298.0
100	16 11/16	12 1/2	13 1/2	9 7/8	44.0	328.0
125	17 3/8	13	14 1/16	10 5/16	50.0	373.0
150	18 3/8	13 3/4	14 7/8	10 7/8	60.0	468.0
175	19 1/4	14 3/8	15 9/16	11 3/8	70.0	523.0
200	20	15	16 1/4	11 7/8	80.0	597.0
225	20 3/4	15 1/2	16 13/16	12 5/16	90.0	672.0
250	21 3/8	16	17 5/16	12 11/16	100.0	747.0
275	22	16 7/16	17 13/16	13	110.0	822.0
300	22 1/2	16 7/8	18 1/4	13 3/8	120.0	896.0
400	24 5/16	18 3/16	19 11/16	14 7/16	160.0	1195.0

* Multiply water capacity by specific gravity of metal to find capacity in other alloys.

Crucible heats are also made by induction heating using the lift-coil-type furnace illustrated in Fig. 11.3.

Pot Furnaces

A stationary-pot furnace is illustrated in Fig. 11.4. Capacities of these indirect-flame furnaces are limited by the cast-iron- or steel-pot size to a

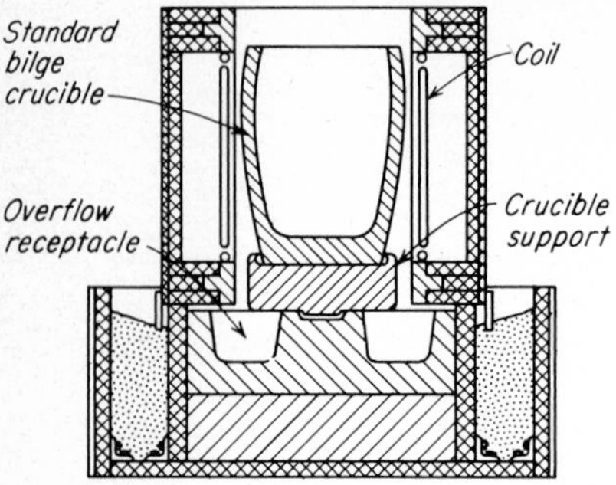

Fig. 11.3 Lift-coil induction-heated crucible. The coil is lifted off, and the crucible is used directly as a pouring ladle. (*From L. W. Eastwood.*[2])

relatively few hundreds of pounds. Metal is ladled from the pot for pouring. Larger melts, up to 3000 lb, may be handled in tilting-pot furnaces of the type shown in Fig. 11.5. The melt is poured from the tilting furnace into ladles for distribution to the molds.

Reverberatory Furnaces

These furnaces are used mainly for production of large quantities, up to 100,000 lb per charge, primarily by producers of foundry ingot and the largest of aluminum foundries. However, the tilting reverberatory furnace shown in Fig. 11.6 is a unit melting smaller amounts at a high rate. For example, heats of 500 lb may be melted in about 30 min in the tilting reverberatory furnace whereas 30 to 45 min may be required for 100 lb in

Fig. 11.4 Stationary crucible melting and holding furnace. (*Courtesy of Hevi-Duty Electric Company.*)

***Fig.* 11.5** A hydraulically tilted melting crucible furnace. (*Courtesy of Hevi-Duty Electric Company.*)

a pot furnace. The barrel-type reverberatory furnace is also a rapid-melting unit more commonly used for melting of copper-base alloys rather than aluminum. Reverberatory furnaces are, of course, direct-flame furnaces, and the melt may therefore be subject to the extremes of drossing and gas absorption which can occur.

Induction Furnaces

In recent years more extensive use is being made of the induction furnace for melting of many nonferrous alloys. High-frequency furnaces of the lift-coil type (Fig. 11.3) are limited by crucible size to about 90-lb heats of aluminum. A schematic diagram of the furnace coil and melting pot of the high-frequency-type furnace is illustrated in Fig. 11.7. Motor-generator sets of 5 to 1000 kw providing frequencies up to 10,000 cycles may be used. Low-frequency furnaces in sizes ranging from 60 to 500 kw at frequencies below 1000 cycles and having pouring capacities of 200 to 5000 lb of aluminum are available and are capable of melting 5 to 7 lb per hour per kw rating of the furnace.[19] Low-frequency furnaces have the characteristic that they must be started with a heel of molten metal, and so are emptied only when cleaning is necessary. A low-frequency unit is illustrated in Fig. 11.8, which also illustrates the transformer core and passages for the initial charge of molten metal.

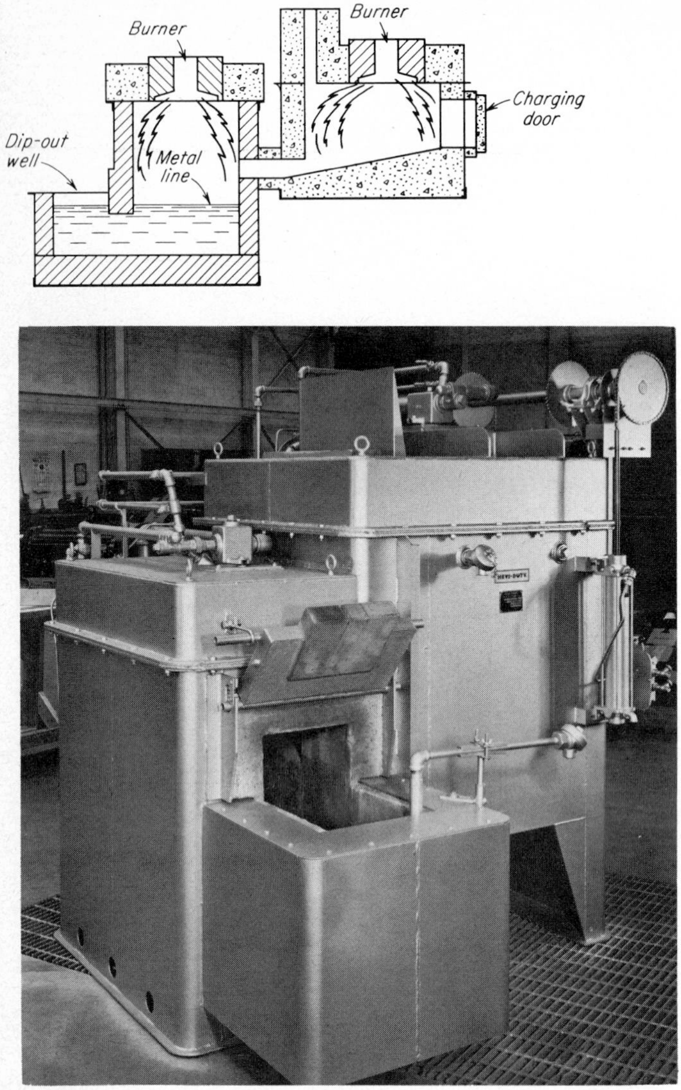

Fig. **11.6** Dip-out, double-chamber, dry-hearth melting and holding furnace, used for aluminum alloys. (*Courtesy of Hevi-Duty Electric Company.*)

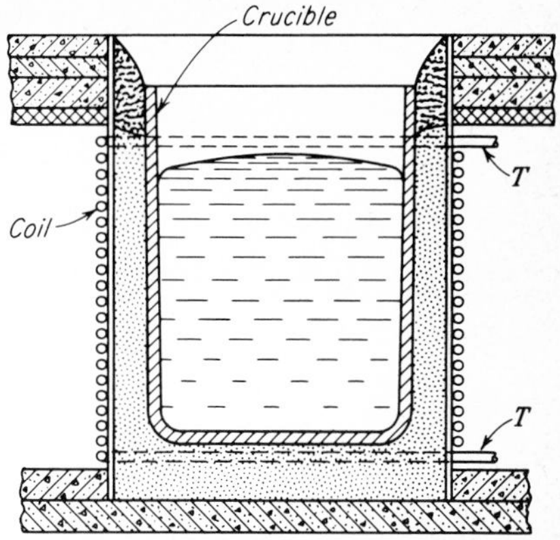

***Fig.* 11.7** Schematic diagram of cross section of a high-frequency induction furnace. The high-frequency current is carried by the water-cooled copper coil *T*. (*From L. W. Eastwood.*[2])

Automatic stirring and mixing of the melt due to the induced currents and their motor effect is another characteristic of low- and high-frequency furnaces. Since melting is rapid and no combustion products are present, oxidation losses are at a minimum.

Melting Procedure

The normal metal charge consists of *clean* foundry scrap (remelt) and prealloyed aluminum pig. Aluminum-casting-alloy pigs of specified anal-

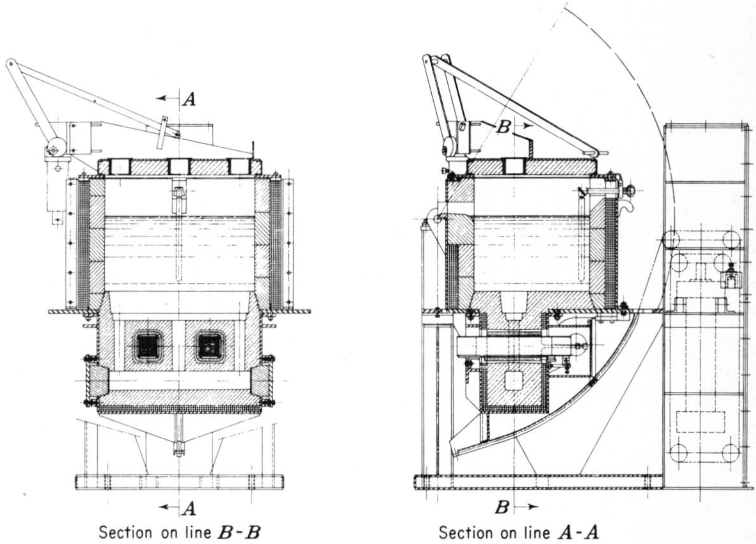

***Fig.* 11.8** Two sections of a low-frequency, twin-coil, 125-kw, lip-axis tilting furnace, for the melting of nonferous alloys. (*From L. W. Eastwood.*[2])

ysis are purchasable from primary and secondary smelters and refiners. Most commonly, analysis control is obtained by using a charge of known analysis, i.e., carefully segregated remelt and new pig. Alloying of virgin aluminum is not generally practiced, except in the largest of aluminum foundries under rigid analysis control. When it is necessary to add alloying elements to aluminum, low-melting-point metals such as zinc and magnesium may be added in elemental form. However, higher-melting-point metals such as copper, nickel, manganese, silicon, titanium, and chromium are best added as rich alloys or *hardeners*. The composition of some alloy-rich aluminum pigs is listed in Table 11.3.

Table* 11.3 *Nominal composition of rich alloy ingot*
Composition in per cent—maximum unless shown as a range

Alloy	Cu	Fe	Si	Mn	Zn	Ni	Cr	Ti
2107	38.0–42.0	0.7	0.6	0.30				
2108	18.0–22.0	0.50	0.35					
2301	....	0.25	0.35–0.50					
2309	....	0.7	13.0–16.0					
2311	....	0.6–1.0	10.0–12.0					
2312	....	0.65	11.0–13.0					
A2312	....	0.40–1.0	11.0–13.0					
2314	....	0.40	4.5–6.0					
2351	1.0–1.5	0.14–0.25	4.5–5.5	....	.....	....	....	0.08–0.20
A2351	1.0–1.5	0.13	4.5–5.5	....	.....	....	....	0.08–0.20
2370	....	0.12–0.25	6.5–7.5	....	.....	....	....	0.08–0.20
A2370	....	0.11	6.5–7.5					
2400	....	0.7	0.45	4.0–6.0				
2402	....	0.7	0.45	6.0–8.0				
2509	0.6	0.6	0.50	....	.....	9.0–11.0		
2801	0.6	16.0–20.0	1.0	0.30	0.30			
2803	0.6	28.0–32.0	1.0	0.30	0.30			
2919	....	0.55	0.30	....	.....	....	2.0–3.5	

*Aluminum Co. of America.

Scrap of heterogeneous origin should not be mixed with pig and remelt if analysis standards are to be maintained. Turnings, borings, and other cuttings loaded with cutting oils and water can cause serious difficulties.

Good melting practice requires that the furnace, as well as the metal charge, be clean. Crucibles and pots should be cleaned after each heat, by scraping them clean of adhering dross and entrapped metal. Broken pieces of crucible or dross lumps may become entrained in subsequent melts if not removed. Objectionable contamination of the melt with iron from metal pots will occur unless the pot is coated in some way. A wash of powdered whiting, talc, or mica containing some sodium silicate can be applied when the pot is hot, over 212 F, to act as pot coating. A wash which is being used consists of 7 lb whiting, $CaCO_3$, per gal water plus 4 oz sodium silicate. Coated pots should dry at a red heat before melting is begun. Extremely low iron contents can be maintained only with the use of silicon carbide or clay-graphite pots.

Drossing

Melting occurs most rapidly if a heel of molten aluminum is present when the charge is added. Melting down with minimum dross formation occurs when the charge is protected from combustion products and melting is rapid. Drossing is the formation of aluminum oxide and other oxides which accumulate on the melt surface. Complete separation of dross and metal would be favored by large differences in their specific gravities. Unfortunately, the specific gravities of the oxides and the molten metal are of similar magnitude, as revealed in Table 11.4. Some oxides float on the melt surface (i.e., dross) whereas others sink and form a sludge.

Table* 11.4 *Specific gravity of some materials in drosses

Compound	Specific gravity (20 C)
Al_2O_3	3.99
$Al_2O_3 \cdot 3H_2O$	2.42
Al	2.70
MgO	3.65
Mg	1.74
Si	2.40
SiO_2	2.20–2.60
CuO	6.40
Cu_2O	6.0

Practices aimed at providing clean metal containing a minimum of dross will be discussed under fluxing and flushing.

Gas Absorption

If given the opportunity, aluminum alloys will absorb or dissolve harmful quantities of hydrogen gas. Temperature exerts a profound effect on the maximum solubility of hydrogen in aluminum, as illustrated in Fig. 11.9. At the melting point an abrupt increase in solubility occurs, as shown in Fig. 11.9. If the solubility limit is reached at pouring temperatures, subsequent cooling and solidification will result in gas evolution and, probably, gas or pinholes and microscopic gas porosity. This type of metal defect is illustrated in Fig. 11.10.

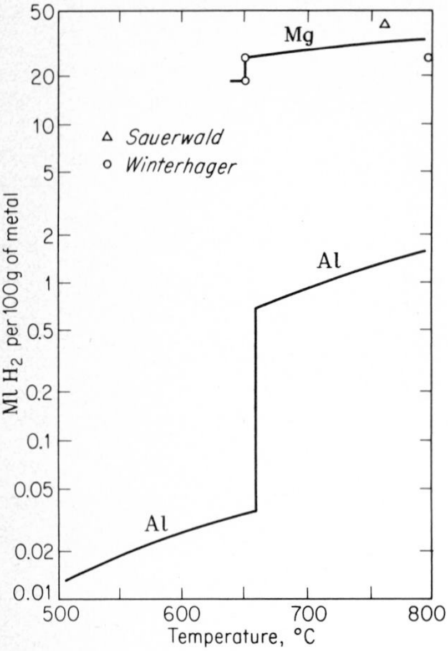

***Fig.* 11.9** Solubility of hydrogen at atmospheric pressure in aluminum and magnesium. (Data on aluminum from Ransley and Neufeld; data on magnesium from Sauerwald and from Winterhager.) (*From D. P. Smith, L. W. Eastwood, D. J. Carney, and C. E. Sims.*[3])

Water vapor is particularly harmful in causing gassing of aluminum alloys because of the following reaction:

$$2Al + 3H_2O \rightarrow Al_2O_3 + 6H \text{ (dissolved in Al)} \qquad (1)$$

Combustion gases containing H_2O then may cause both oxidation and hydrogen absorption. Increased solubility of hydrogen with increased partial pressure of hydrogen above the melt [formula (1)] has been reported[4] and indicates that the water content of combustion gases and the atmosphere is capable of seriously increasing the harmful defects caused by hydrogen. Fortunately, hydrogen can be removed to a substantial extent by flushing or purging of the melt and its harmful effects are thus reduced.

Fluxing and Flushing

Fluxing and flushing of aluminum melts is practiced mainly for two reasons:

1. To provide more effective separation of molten metal and dross
2. To remove dissolved hydrogen and entrapped dross

Gaseous fluxes used to flush or purge the melt include nitrogen, helium, argon, and chlorine. The gases are bubbled slowly through the melt for hydrogen removal. Hydrogen dissolved in the aluminum diffuses into the gas bubbles and is carried away. Dross separation is probably a mechanical action of the inert gas bubbles carrying oxides to the surface. However, chlorine reacts chemically to form chlorides which change the wetting characteristics of the metal and result in separation of dross and melt. Flushing is carried out by skimming off surface dross and then bubbling the dry gas through the melt for 10 to 20 min at the rate of about 0.5 to 0.75 cu ft gas per minute for a 300- to 400-lb melt. Flushing is practiced at the lowest possible temperature, about 1250 F, to obtain maximum hydrogen removal. After flushing, the temperature of the melt is quickly raised to that required for pouring; the melt surface is skimmed, and pouring begins. The beneficial effects of flushing the melt are demonstrated in Fig. 11.10.

Fluxing with solid fluxes is a simpler procedure, more widely practiced although not so effective as purging. Flux to the extent of about 0.10

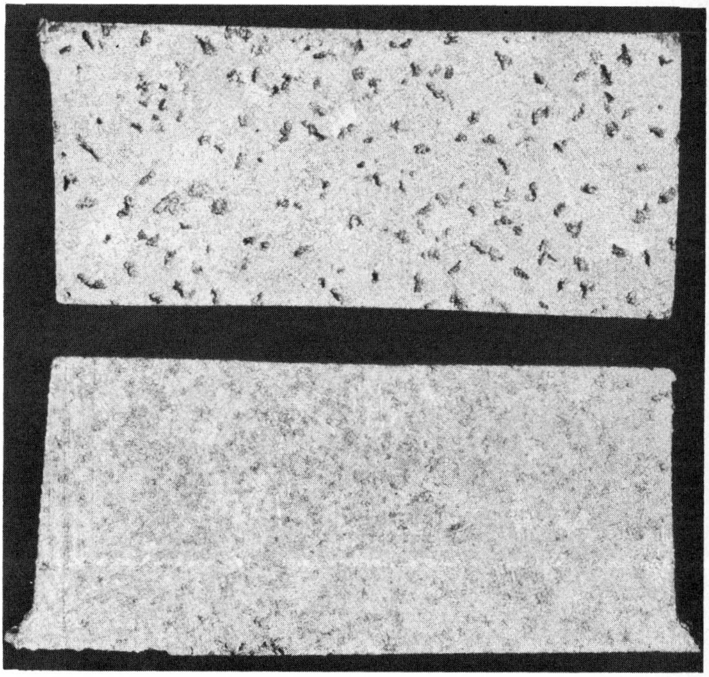

***Fig.* 11.10** Pinholes and microporosity caused by hydrogen. Top, section of a casting of aluminum alloy CS43 gassed with water vapor at a metal temperature of 1500 F and poured in a sand mold. Bottom, section of a casting made of the same metal as shown in upper view after purging the melt 15 min with dry nitrogen while cooling it from 1500 to 1300 F before pouring. Both samples etched with dilute NaOH, ×2.

lb per 100 lb of metal is added to the melt by forcing it to the bottom of the bath in a perforated container. Aluminum and zinc chlorides, as well as a number of proprietary compositions containing these compounds, are used as solid fluxes. Solid fluxes serve to facilitate separation of the metal and oxides through their chemical action.

Grain Refining

Several procedures have been discovered which will cause a minimum grain size to be developed during freezing of the casting. These methods include:

1. Chill casting, as in metal molds
2. Temperature adjustment
3. Late additions to the melt[5]

Rapid solidification, of course, causes a smaller grain size in all casting alloys. Boron, titanium, chromium, columbium, and sodium may be used as grain-refining additions to the melt shortly before pouring. It has been pointed out that pouring at the lowest possible pouring temperature aids in obtaining a fine-grained casting.

Pouring Temperature

When the melt has been properly prepared, a final checking of temperature for pouring is essential. Immersion thermocouples consisting of No. 8 gauge asbestos-covered chromel-alumel wire are suitable for this measurement. The bare couple is satisfactory for rapid temperature measurement. A pouring temperature of 1250 to 1400 F may be employed, depending on casting size, alloy composition, and a number of other factors. Selection of the proper temperature is essential to producing the most desirable castings.

Melting Procedures—Summary

Aluminum melting practices aimed at producing the most favorable results may include the following measures:

1. Start with clean materials of known analysis.
2. Use clean melting practice.
3. Keep temperature of melt low until pouring is imminent.
4. Use a minimum holding time in the molten condition.
5. Avoid water vapor or hydrogen-bearing gases whenever possible.
6. Do not agitate or stir melt more than is absolutely necessary.
7. Use adequate flushing or fluxing practices.
8. Skim only when ready to pour.

9. Avoid turbulence when pouring the molten aluminum to minimize drossing and hydrogen pickup.
10. Use a proper pouring temperature and pouring practice.

The nature of aluminum is such that excessive turbulence and sloppy and erratic pouring can ruin an otherwise properly prepared melt.

MOLDING FOR ALUMINUM CASTING

Aluminum alloys can be cast by any of the commonly used processes: sand casting, plaster molding, permanent mold, and die casting. Because of the low pouring temperature and specific gravity of aluminum alloys, molds are less affected by heat than in the case of iron and steel. Consequently, excellent surface finish and dimensional accuracy may be obtained even in large sand castings. The minimum section thickness for aluminum castings produced by the commonly used processes is illustrated in Table 11.5. Sand castings weighing several tons have been made. Permanent-mold castings weighing 650 lb and die castings up to 70 lb are in use.

An important effect of the casting process used for aluminum alloys is its influence on the properties of the metal. One author[6] gives the figures in Table 11.6 to illustrate the effect of casting method on the mechanical properties of Al-Cu-Si and Al-Si alloys.

Undoubtedly, the rapid chilling of the metal mold, and in the case of die casting, the effect of casting under pressure, produces the improved properties. Data for the effect of casting process on the mechanical properties of specific alloys will be considered in the next chapter. At this point, however, it should be recognized that mere chemical specification of a certain alloy is no guarantee of mechanical properties. Casting process, casting design, melting practice, and the complete history of foundry processing must be considered. In spite of the improved mechanical properties obtained with metal molds, sand casting remains as a major process because of its inherent advantages. A comparison of annual production by the three processes can be obtained from Table 11.1.

Sand Casting

Casting in molds made by any of the usual sand-molding processes is practiced with aluminum alloys. Green-sand molding with conventional molding equipment is used to the greatest extent, although dry-sand molds are preferred where large or intricate work is involved. Low squeeze pressures, 20 to 30 psi, are used in machine molding, since a high mold hardness is not required as a rule.

Table **11.5** ***Minimum section thickness for aluminum castings produced by different processes****

Section thickness, in.	For length of:
SAND CASTINGS	
1/8	Under 3 in.
5/32	3 to 6 in.
3/16	Over 6 in.
PERMANENT-MOLD CASTINGS	
0.100	Under 3 in.
0.125	3 to 6 in.
0.160	Over 6 in.
DIE CASTINGS	
0.050	Small parts
0.080	Large parts
PLASTER-MOLD CASTINGS	
1/16	2 in. or less
3/32	3 to 6 in.
1/8	Over 6 in.
SHELL-MOLD CASTINGS	
1/16	Under 1/2 in.
3/32	1/2 to 3 in.
1/8	3 to 6 in.
5/32	Over 6 in.
PRECISION SAND CASTINGS	
0.080	Under 3 in.
0.100	3 to 6 in.
0.100	Over 6 in.
INVESTMENT CASTINGS	
0.035	1/4 in.
0.060	2 in. or less
0.090	2 to 4 in.
0.125	4 to 8 in.
0.150	Over 8 in.
CENTRIFUGAL PERMANENT-MOLD CASTINGS	
0.070 in. for up to 4 sq in. per casting; 0.080 for 5 to 10 sq in.; 0.090 for 11 to 20; 0.100 for 21 to 30; 0.110 for 31 to 70; 0.120 for 71 to 100; and 0.156 in. for over 100 sq in. per casting.	

*From American Society for Metals.[16]

Table 11.6*

	Al-Cu-Si		Al-Si	
	Tensile strength, 1000 psi	Elongation, % in 2 in.	Tensile strength, 1000 psi	Elongation, % in 2 in.
Sand cast	20–25	1–3	17–25	3–8
Permanent mold	25–35	1–5	20–28	3–10
Die cast	30–35	1–3	25–32	1–5

*From L. F. Mondolfo.[6]

Molding Sands

Both natural and synthetic sands of the types listed in Table 5.11 are employed in green-sand molding for aluminum castings.

Whether a natural or synthetic sand is used, good sand conditioning is required. Excessive moisture, lumps, clay balls, or other matter may cause serious casting defects. Collapsed blows from excessive moisture are illustrated in Fig. 11.11. Reaction of the molten metal with excess

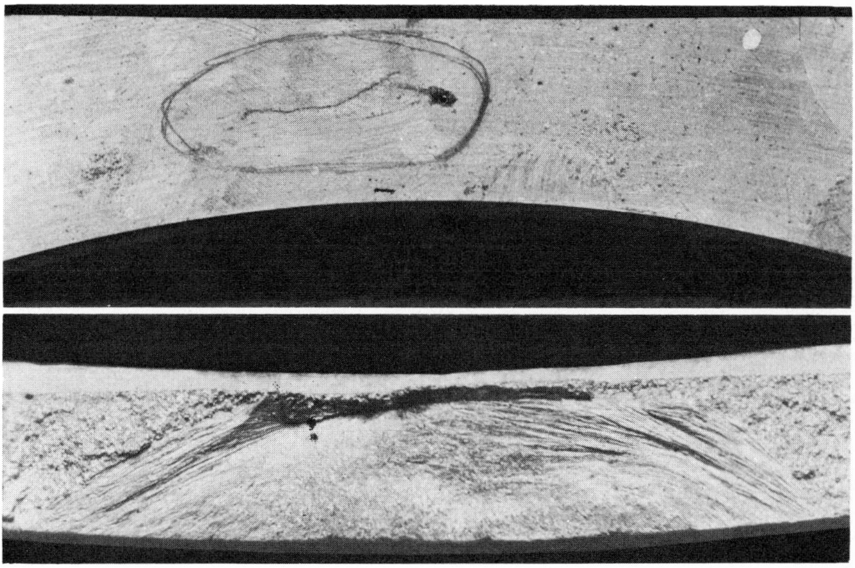

Fig. **11.11** Above, a collapsed blow shown on a machined surface and, below, as opened by fracturing. The more characteristic appearance of an uncollapsed blow is simply a balloon-shaped smooth-surfaced cavity. (*From D. A. LaVelle.*[9])

***Fig.* 11.12** Casting pits caused by steam from clay balls in the molding sand. These defects are actually small localized blows. (*From D. A. LaVelle.*[9])

moisture in the sand may result in reaction porosity, a concentration of small spherical voids usually just under the casting skin. Clay balls in the sand may explode when covered by molten metal and cause pits or small blows. The latter defects are illustrated in Fig. 11.12. Severe generation of steam within the mold, together with turbulent metal flow, may result in extreme gas porosity like that illustrated in Fig. 11.10. Most of these problems can be avoided by the proper use of molding sands and molding practices.

Core Sands

Cores and core-sand mixtures for aluminum castings were listed in Chap. 7. Core collapsibility is especially desired because of the tendency of aluminum alloys to hot tear if they are not allowed to contract freely. Hence the mixtures used are weaker and more collapsible than those used for heavier, high-temperature metals.

Inserts

Cast-iron or steel inserts are often cast into aluminum castings. Shafts, bushings, sleeves, cylinder liners, and other surfaces requiring wear resistance may be obtained in this way. An example of an insert is shown in Fig. 11.13, the flatiron casting having a cast-in heating element. Inserts are knurled or otherwise provided with a mechanical bond to the casting. Metal inserts are molded into the molding or core sand or located in die or permanent molds, and must be absolutely dry and clean to prevent blows.

GATING AND RISERING OF ALUMINUM

Proper gating and risering of aluminum (and magnesium) castings has long been recognized as a major factor in producing good castings. To function satisfactorily, good gating and feeding systems must take into account certain well-known characteristics of aluminum-casting alloys, namely:

1. Drossing tendency
2. Gas entrainment
3. Gas absorption
4. Solidification shrinkage (feeding requirements)
5. Difficulty of eliminating microshrinkage
6. High thermal conductivity

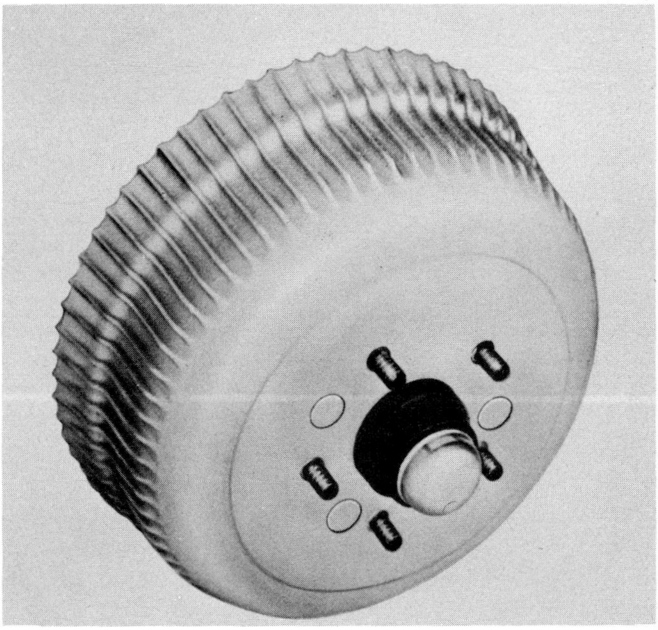

***Fig.* 11.13** Aluminum-alloy permanent-mold cast brake drum. (*Courtesy of Reynolds Metals Co.*)

Oxidation of the molten aluminum and also hydrogen absorption can occur readily in the mold and during pouring. Oxygen and water vapor from the atmosphere and mold gases are abundantly present. The turbulence of pouring and the flow of metal in the gates promote mixing and reaction of gases and melt. Hence dross may form and hydrogen may dissolve in the liquid metal as the mold is poured. In addition, gas bubbles may become mechanically entrained in the flowing metal, as illustrated in Fig. 11.14.

Metal adversely affected by gating or pouring may be referred to as "damaged" metal. Gating and pouring problems are so important in making aluminum castings that much research has been aimed at their understanding. Some of these principles have been discussed in Chap. 9, and are now considered in relation to aluminum castings.[12,13,15]

Gating Design

Pouring basin, sprue, runners, and ingates all enter into a successful gating system. Since the point of entry into the mold is the sprue cup or pouring basin, this item may be considered first.

Pouring Basin

If metal is poured directly into the sprue, a high velocity, turbulence, formation of a vortex, and mechanical washing of dross into the mold cavity are all favored. Hence a pouring basin of the type shown in Fig. 11.15 or those illustrated in Chap. 9 may be used to prevent these difficulties. The basin of this type is made of core sand or may be formed in the mold. Streamlining of the basin and all other parts of the gating system is a method of minimizing turbulence. The streamline dam in the pouring basin minimizes cascading (turbulence) of the

***Fig.* 11.14** Air bubbles adjacent to a gate. They may be due to the entrainment of gases in the metal by a poor gating system. (*From D. A. LaVelle.*[1])

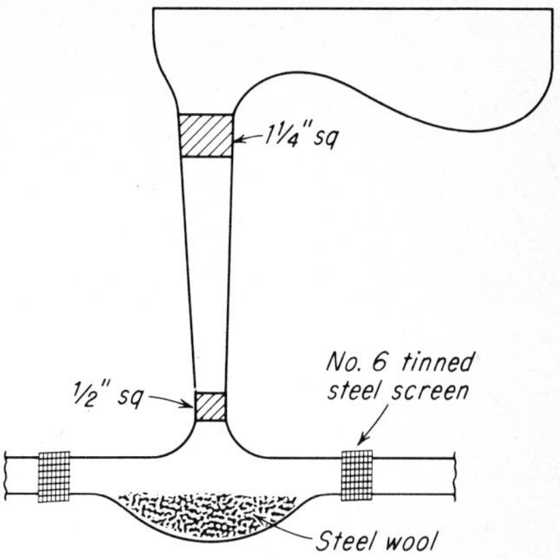

***Fig.* 11.15** Sprue system designed to minimize gas entrainment and drossing during pouring and while the metal is in the gating system. Screens permit gas bubbles to rise out of the metal in the runners, and the steel wool traps dross and reduces turbulence. Round sprues are often considered preferable to the square sprue shown here. (*From T. E. Kramer.*[35])

first metal into the sprue and permits the operator to reach an optimum pouring speed before any metal enters the sprue.

Sprue

In the gating designs recommended for aluminum[12,15] the sprue is employed as the metering portion of the gating system. Gating ratios of 1:2:2, 1:4:4, and 1:6:6 (ratio of sprue area to the runner area to ingate area) are used in unpressurized systems. The sprue then is the choke or restrictive area metering the flow of metal. Pressurized systems of 1:2:1 are not as common in aluminum since they encourage turbulence at the ingate.

Tapered, straight, and reverse-tapered sprues are used in molding. For the light metals, however, it has been proved[12,13] that tapered sprues will eliminate aspiration of air from the sprue walls into the metal stream. Aspiration, of course, may cause gas entrapment and damaged metal. A side-wall taper of about ¼ in. per ft of sprue height has been used satisfactorily. From a gating standpoint, it is desirable that the sprue be molded hard and clean rather than be cut with sprue cutter. Rectangular-cross-section sprues are considered less likely to develop a vortex than round ones, though this may not be true if the sprue size and balance of the gating are right.

Sprue Base

Since the base of the sprue represents a sharp change in direction and also in area (with 1:4:4 ratio), it can also be a source of turbulence, aspiration, and damaged metal. Streamlining like that of a venturi or a well or enlargement at the sprue base has been proposed as different means of treating this point.

Runners

In general, runners for aluminum castings should encircle a large part of the casting periphery. This is done to provide ingates at a number of points on the casting. Multiple ingating is necessary to avoid introducing too much metal through one gate. Cross-sectional area of the runner may be about four times the sprue area. Current practice is to locate the runner in the drag, although this is a controversial point. The runner should be streamlined to avoid aspiration and turbulence. In order to obtain flow of approximately equal metal volumes through each ingate, the size of the runner is reduced in area after each ingate by an equal amount in the ingate area. This is an application of Bernoulli's theorem, as discussed in Chap. 9. Proportioning of the runner for a simple plate casting is illustrated in Fig. 11.16. A runoff (*B*, Fig. 11.16) is provided at the runner's end to carry off the first metal into the runner and its accompanying dross.

Ingates

Multiple ingating of aluminum castings is usually advised for two reasons. First, misruns are avoided. Second, excessive metal flow through one gate often results in shrinks adjacent to the gate because of local heating of the sand and consequent delay in freezing (Fig. 11.17).

With gating using the ratio of 1:4:4, the total area of all the ingates approximately equals the sprue area multiplied by 4. The ingates should be streamlined as indicated in Fig. 11.16 to avoid aspiration or turbulence. Ingates may be located in cope or drag, depending on which gives the best results in a given casting.

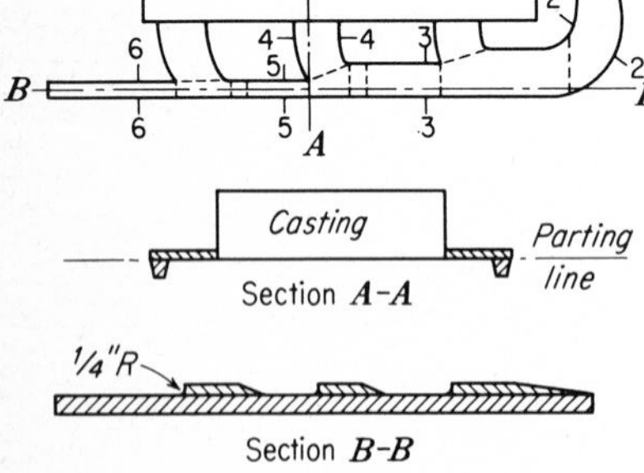

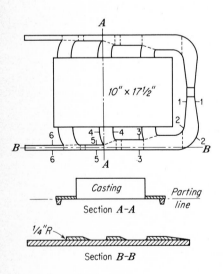

Fig. 11.16 Suggested runner and gate design to avoid abrupt changes in cross-sectional area and flow direction. Note 4:1 reduction in flow velocity before first gate is reached and constant flow velocity thereafter. (*From R. E. Swift, J. H. Jackson, and L. W. Eastwood.*[12])

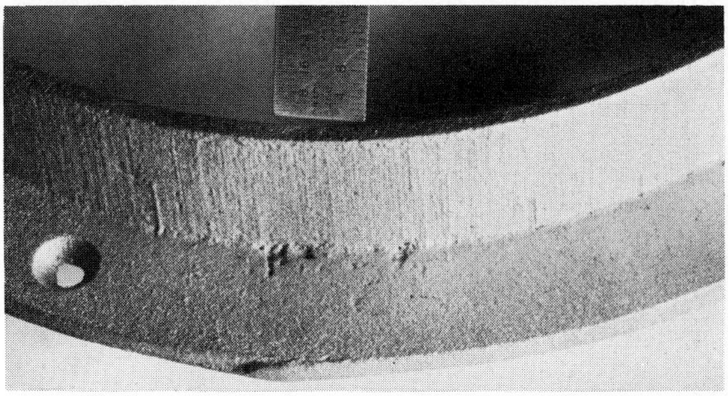

***Fig.* 11.17** Shrinkage due to excessive metal flow through one ingate. (*From D. A. LaVelle.*[9])

In order to obtain equal metal flow through each ingate, the simplest design appears to be one using equal areas in all ingates and a reduction in runner size by the amount of the ingate area immediately after each ingate. Adjustment of ingate and runner area at each ingate location can, however, be used to cause more metal to flow through a certain ingate.

Screens

In order to prevent foreign material in the flowing stream from reaching the casting, it is possible to resort to various steps to clean the metal in the runner system. One technique has been described in Fig. 11.16, where a runoff at the end of the runner is provided. Another technique is to make the runners wide and shallow to allow air or dross to separate and adhere to the cope surface. Screens may also be inserted at various points in the gating systems to clean the metal.

Ratio-gating Principles

Since ratio gating involves sprue, runners, and ingates as one unit, it is well to examine their interrelationships. The sprue, being the minimum area, markedly controls the rate of flow. The delivery rate of a sprue has been described approximately by formula:[14]

$$W = KA\sqrt{H} \tag{2}$$

where W = flow rate, lb/sec
K = an orifice coefficient
A = minimum sprue area
H = sprue height

In a given mold (H is constant), the delivery rate depends mainly on the area of the sprue and its orifice coefficient, area being the most important factor. The actual delivery rate of the sprue depends also on the influence of the runner and ingates on flow in the system. Different runner and ingate areas could exert drastic effects on flow, especially if their cross-sectional area approached or became smaller than the sprue area or their length was great. Experiments indicate that the orifice coefficient K is related to the ratio of the sprue area to the total ingate area, or

$$K \approx \frac{A_s}{A_g}$$

where A_s = sprue area
A_g = ingate area

The relation of K to A_s/A_g is shown graphically in Fig. 11.18. This graph applies to round tapered sprues up to 0.75 in. in diameter, a full sprue during pouring, runner area four times sprue area, T or streamlined ingates, 4- to 6-in. sprue height, and plate castings limited to about 15 lb weight. However, certain principles are illustrated in the graph. For a fixed sprue size, the orifice coefficient increases rapidly as the ratio changes from 1:4:1 to 1:4:4, a change which shows that the sprue becomes the limiting orifice as the ingates are enlarged. Hence the flow rate is largely determined by the sprue size at gating ratios of 1:4:4. With a gating ratio of 1:4:4, the dimensions of the gating systems based on Fig. 11.18 are listed in Table 11.7. The flow rate does not seem profoundly affected by sprue-height changes in the ranges investigated in the case of Table 11.7, but probably would be with substantially higher sprues.

If gating ratios are used in which the ingate or runner acts as the metering orifice, then obviously these dimensions become the most important in influencing the over-all orifice coefficient. Small changes in their dimensions will then affect the flow rate drastically. In aluminum, it is undesirable to have the ingates function as the choke, since they will cause a jet effect resulting in substantial drossing and gas entrainment. Note from Table 11.7 that increasing the sprue diameter

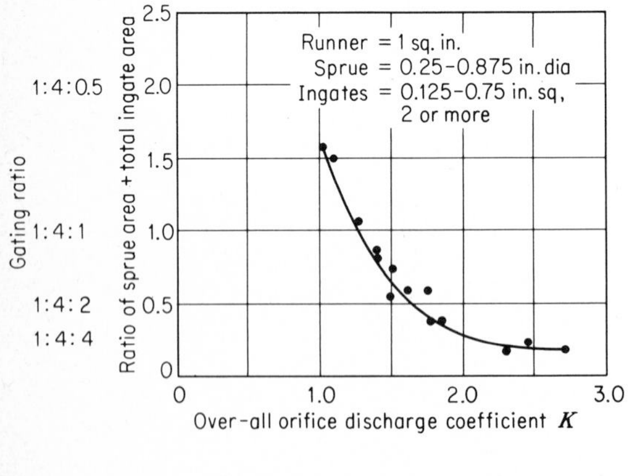

***Fig.* 11.18 Relationship of over-all orifice discharge coefficient K to ratio of sprue to total ingate area (runner area equivalent to form twice the sprue area). The curve applies to a single runner, one to four ingates, with gating in the drag, and a 4- to 8-in. cope height.**

Table* 11.7 *Flow rate and gating areas for 1:4:4 ratio*

Diam sprue, in.	Sprue area, sq in.	Runner area, sq in.	Total ingate area, sq in.†	K	Approx flow rate $W = KA_s\sqrt{H}$, lb/sec
0.50	0.196	0.785	0.785	2.25–2.5	1.07–1.19
0.625	0.307	1.228	1.228	2.25–2.5	1.68–1.86
0.75	0.442	1.765	1.765	2.25–2.5	2.41–2 68

* Based on data used for Fig. 11.18, $H = 5.875$ in,
† Two or more.

permits a rapid increase in the flow rate when the sprue is the metering orifice as it is in 1:4:4 gating systems.

Since ratio-gating designs for aluminum are aimed at minimum turbulence and smooth metal flow, the time necessary for pouring the casting must be sufficiently prolonged so that excessive metal-flow rates are avoided. Information of the type shown in Fig. 11.18 and Table 11.7 and formula (2) can be used to design a gating system so that it will pour a casting in a specified time. The time obviously must be short enough to avoid misruns, long enough to minimize gas entrainment. It should be recognized that there is no attempt here to offer data which provide a final method for such designs. The information provided in Fig. 11.18 and Table 11.7 was experimentally derived on specific mold design, and is given only as illustrative of significant factors in ratio-gating design to control flow rate. With pouring basin, sprue, runners, and ingate and flow rate designed to avoid damaged metal, the best results in casting soundness and freedom from defects are obtained.

Risering

The proper feeding of solidifying aluminum castings involves the solution to two problems:

1. Prevention of macroshrinkage, large, visually detectable shrinkage cavities, usually concentrated at hot spots.
2. Prevention of microshrinkage, shrinkage which can usually be observed only by microscopic examination or X-ray or radiographic inspection and which usually is quite widely dispersed. Dissolved gases are particularly harmful if the elimination of microshrinkage is desired.

The principles of risering in general have been discussed in Chap. 9. This discussion pertains more specifically to aluminum alloys.

Riser Size

In addition to the rather high percentage of volume contraction, 6.6 per cent, for the element aluminum (Table 9.3), the solidification mechanism of aluminum alloys results in the following general principles for designing risers:[17]

1. The mushy nature of the solidification of most aluminum alloys requires the use of fairly large risers and a large number of risers. Based on weight poured, casting yield percentages of 25 to 45 per cent are quite common.
2. Very steep thermal gradients are required to eliminate completely all traces of microporosity.
3. Surface defects due to inadequate risering may occur since a solid skin does not form on most aluminum-alloy castings until late in the solidification process.
4. Overheating of the sand in one location may result in surface shrinkage because of weak skin formation. Overheating may result from excessive metal flow in one area or placing a riser too close to the casting.

The size of risers necessary to feed aluminum castings is at present still largely a matter of experience. Naturally, the riser must remain molten longer than the section it is to feed, and the principles of directional solidification must be obeyed. The principles of risering discussed in Chap. 9 may be used, although the necessary graphs and data for aluminum castings have not appeared in the literature.

Simple riser and casting combinations having volume and freezing-ratio values to the right of the curve in Fig. 9.14 can be sound with respect to macroshrinkage. Microshrinkage, however, can be eliminated only with the most favorable of temperature gradients within the casting and from casting to riser. The application of Caine's method to risering of aluminum is limited in its use since no information is available which reveals the distance over which a riser will effectively feed and prevent microshrinkage. Feeding distances of most aluminum alloys, however, appear to be quite large compared with steel.[17] Since dissolved hydrogen may be evolved during solidification, this gas can be particularly harmful in aggravating the microshrinkage problem. Nevertheless, the method of Caine is useful as a starting point.

Riser Location

Extensive use of top risers is made on aluminum castings. Maximum benefit of metallostatic pressure in risers is obtained with top risers. This point is important in light metals because of their low specific gravity. Side risers, however, must often be used. Whenever possible these are "hot" risers; i.e., metal flows from the gates into the riser and then into the castings. Difficulties with microshrinkage can be minimized by close spacing of risers, development of severe temperature gradients, and use of directional solidification to the fullest extent. Radiographic, or X-ray, study of the effect of changes in the gating and risering system is probably the most positive method of arriving at a suitable gating and feeding system.

ALUMINUM PERMANENT-MOLD CASTINGS

Permanent metal molds are made of steel or cast iron. Coring may be done with metal cores in permanent molds, but these must be removable after the metal has solidified. More intricate coring may be done by using sand cores in the permanent mold. The mold surface is coated by spraying the hot mold with a suspension of a fine-particle-size refractory in water. The mold coating can be used to promote directional solidification. Sections required to freeze more slowly can be given a thicker coating of refractory. Mold coatings serve to prevent sticking of the casting to the mold, provide a smooth surface, and assist in controlling solidification so that sound castings are obtained. The castings shown in Fig. 11.13 are typical permanent-mold castings produced for their surface finish and dimensional accuracy. Production of quality permanent-mold castings requires a careful control of pouring temperature, mold temperature (600 to 800 F), mold coating, gating, pouring, mold manipulation, and continuity of operation. Only certain alloys are favorably cast in permanent or die-casting molds, because of hot tearing and other problems, which are discussed in Chap. 12.

MAGNESIUM CASTINGS

Magnesium-base casting alloys have undergone their greatest development through the growth of air transportation. The use of magnesium-alloy castings in this field is of course based on the very low specific gravity of these alloys, about 1.74 to 1.82 in different alloys, the lowest of commercial casting alloys. In fact, the cast form represents the major consumption of magnesium alloys.

Foundry Practices

Green- and dry-sand molding, permanent molds, and die-casting methods are all suitable for magnesium-castings production. Castings weighing over 1000 lb have been produced. In addition to aircraft castings, parts for portable hand tools, typewriters, appliances, X-ray machines, and other places where lightness is desired have been made by these three casting processes. The casting properties of magnesium require that special precautions be observed in molding, melting, and processing.[26,28,29]

Molding

Sand molding requires provision for the reactiveness of molten magnesium with the moisture in the sand and the need for correct gating practices. Synthetic sands are preferred. They consist of silica sand or bank sand bonded with 3 to 4 per cent western bentonite. Sands of AFS fineness of 60 to 90 and permeability of 80 to 150 ml per min are bonded to a green strength of 7 to 10 psi with a minimum moisture content for molding. A protective agent is added to the sand to inhibit the following reaction between water in the sand and the molten magnesium:

$$\text{Mg (molten)} + \text{H}_2\text{O (vapor)} \rightarrow \text{MgO (dross)} + 2\text{H (dissolved in melt)}$$

Two harmful effects accompany this reaction: oxide inclusions may be entrapped in the casting, and hydrogen-gas defects, pinholes, may develop. The inhibitors minimize these effects. Sulfur and boric acid, about 1 per cent or more of each, may be used. Ammonium fluoride compounds, ammonium fluoborate, for example, also are employed. Sometimes 1 per cent of diethylene glycol (a sirupy liquid) is employed, the latter decreasing the amount of water needed and also the drying-out tendency of the sands. A total of 3 to 6 per cent of the foregoing protective agents is used in the sand. Since the melting point of magnesium is 1202 F, thermal requirements of the sand are similar to those of aluminum alloys.

Core sands are required to be relatively collapsible because magnesium alloys are susceptible to hot tearing during solidification. Some typical sand mixtures and their properties are given in Table 11.8. Protective agents (inhibitors) are also added to core sands to prevent oxidation. The urea-formaldehyde-resin-bonded sand (Table 11.8) is useful in providing collapsibility and also, because of its low baking temperature, prevents the inhibitors from being lost during baking.

It is very important that adequate venting be provided in all molds and cores and that opportunity for contamination of the mold with moisture be minimized. Venting is exceedingly important because the very low metallostatic pressures developed by molten magnesium are not sufficient to overcome much back pressure from mold or core gases. Cores, because of their cereal content, may pick up water if not stored under dry and warm conditions, 85 to 100 F.

Table* 11.8*a* *Molding sands for magnesium castings*

Type	Ingredients	Properties
1	Silica, AFS fineness, 60 Western bentonite, 3–4.0% Inhibitors, 3–6% Diethylene glycol, 1%	Permeability, 150 Moisture, 3.0% Green strength, 7–10.0 psi
2	Silica, AFS fineness, 85 Western bentonite, 3–4.0% Inhibitors, 3–6% Diethylene glycol, 1%	Permeability, 80 Moisture, 3.–4.0% Green strength, 7.0–10.0 psi

Table* 11.8*b* *Core sands for magnesium castings*

Type	Ingredients						Properties				
	Sand, lb	Sulfur, lb	Boric acid, lb	Corn flour, lb	Urea form-aldehyde, dry, lb	Water, lb	Green permeability	Green compression	Baked tensile strength	Baked hardness	Baked permeability
1	1000	10	5	5	8	40	80	1.1	275	90	100
2	1000	10	5	10	8	20	90	1.8	230	90	110
3	1000	5	3	4	9	16	90	1.1	275	90	110

* From American Foundrymen's Society.[26]

Gating

Proper gating has been found to be one of the most important factors in producing quality magnesium casting. "Damaged" metal, drossy and gassed, is more easily produced by faulty gating and pouring practice in magnesium alloys than in any other alloy group. Bottom gating is desired for this reason. Less turbulent flow and less cascading occur when metal is introduced at or near the bottom of the mold and can rise uniformly throughout the mold cavity. A number of ingates are required to introduce the metal rapidly if the casting is of the spread-out type. Magnesium has a low heat content per unit volume of metal and therefore loses temperature rapidly as heat is extracted. For this reason it is not possible to run metal over long distances in thin castings, and it must be introduced at a number of points.

Because magnesium oxidizes so readily various devices are employed to restrain dross from entering the casting. First of all, every effort must be made to minimize dross formation during pouring. Gating principles and practices discussed in Chap. 9 and for aluminum should be observed. Slot sprues ¼ to ½ in. thick by 1½ to 2 in. wide are often used because it is claimed that vortexing occurs less frequently in the former than in round sprues. The use of slot sprues is illustrated in Fig. 11.19. A coarse-steel-wool pad (strainer pad, or screen) may be used at the base of the slot sprue to restrain oxides from entering the casting. Whether the slot sprue is more efficient than the round sprue in preventing vortexing is debatable since the proportioning of the balance of the gating system has such a profound effect. In either case, a full sprue during pouring is necessary to prevent aspiration and drossing. Rather extensive use is made of screens, coarse steel wool, and other gating arrangements for preventing damaged metal from reaching the casting. A combination of the aforementioned practices is shown in Fig. 11.19, where a slot sprue, screen in the runner, and bottom gating through a slot gate are employed. This figure also shows a top-riser ring which would normally be needed above the aircraft wheel hub.

Feeding solidification shrinkage of magnesium is largely accomplished with top risers, although it is sometimes necessary to use side risers. Top risers are needed to obtain pressure feeding because of the low metallostatic pressure of the metal. The riser must of course be proportioned to remain molten longer than the section to be fed. Because of heavy riser requirements, yield is low, 20 to 35 per cent.

Melting

Melting equipment is of the pot or crucible type described previously for aluminum. Large heats of 1200 to 2000 lb are melted in steel pots. The pots are often aluminized to prevent iron contamination. The melt is transferred from large pots to smaller steel crucibles for treatment before pouring. Smaller heats may be melted directly in steel

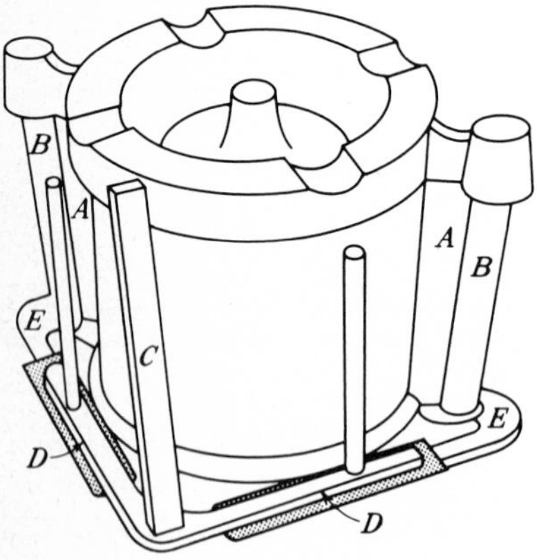

***Fig.* 11.19** Gating system showing the use of a slot sprue screen in the runner, and bottom gating through a slot in the side runner. (*A*) Side gate, (*B*) side runner and feeder, (*C*) sprue, (*D*) bottom runner and screen, (*E*) bottom runner. (*From H. E. Elliott and J. G. Mezoff.*[28])

crucibles. Oil- or gas-fired furnaces with a slightly reducing atmosphere are commonly used. About 1 part of new ingot to 4 parts of remelt is charged to the large pot, and melting is carried on under a flux cover. The flux, such as numbers 230 and 232 in Table 11.9, forms a fluid slag covering which prevents burning of the metal. Some typical fluxes are listed in Table 11.9.

Table* 11.9** ***Fluxes for magnesium-alloy melting*

Flux No.†	KCl	$MgCl_2$	MgO	CaF_2	$BaCl_2$	$MnCl_2$	Use
230	55.0	34.0	....	2.0	9.0	....	Remelting pots, fluid slag
232	37.5	42.0	7.5	8.5	4.5	....	Remelting pots, fluid slag
250	23.0	....	....	2.5	2.5	72.0	Higher melting temp
310	20.0	50.0	15.0	15.0	...	....	One pot, crucible melting, dries during use
320	....	....	11.0	13.0	...	76.0	Higher-temperature melting

* From American Society for Metals.[27]

† Proprietary numbers, Dow Chemical Co., Midland, Mich.

The principal purpose of the flux is to prevent burning. Numbers 230 and 232 are more fluid and provide good protection of large open pots. However, their fluidity makes them too easily entrained in the melt and carried into the casting during pouring. The other fluxes are less fluid and dry on standing over the melt, so they can be held back during pouring. The latter are used for crucible melting where no metal transfer before pouring is involved.

Metal in the crucibles may be purged with dry nitrogen (oil-pumped) for 15 to 20 min to remove hydrogen. Several other refining treatments may be employed to improve melt quality. Fluxing and gentle stirring assist in separating sludge- or dross-forming oxides from the melt. Chlorination, or bubbling chlorine gas or carbon tetrachloride vapor or both, through the melts assists in fluxing and grain refinement. Grain refinement can be accomplished in several ways. Carbon-powder additions to the melt seem to promote fine grain size. It has been found that superheating to 1650 to 1700 F followed by rapid cooling in air to the pouring temperature also promotes grain refinement.

Another grain-refining treatment involves the use of hexachlorobenzine (C_6Cl_6). The melt is treated with 20 to 25 g of hexachlorobenzine per 100 lb metal at 1450 to 1500 F. This grain-refining treatment is employed after normal fluxing and purging and just prior to adjusting the temperature to the pouring temperature. Pouring temperatures are measured at the mold with portable pyrometers, and are usually in the range of 1350 to 1500 F. Because of its combustibility, molten magnesium must be protected from air during pouring. This is accomplished with SO_2, generated by sprinkling a mixture of sulfur and boric acid powder on the metal in the crucible during pouring. Gentle pouring, with pouring lip close to pouring cup, to avoid turbulence, and ladle skimming, to avoid drossy-slag entrapment, are desirable.

Cleaning

The castings are allowed to cool in the mold until there is no danger of developing cracks during shakeout. This may require an hour or more for larger castings. After shakeout, the castings are sand-blasted with a sand of about 35 AFS fineness to reveal surface defects. Gates and risers are removed by band sawing (Chap. 24). Grinding and rotary filing are employed to remove fins and excess metal. In all metal-cutting operations, the fire and explosion hazard of magnesium chips or powder must be recognized. For example, at grinder stations dust washers, in which exhaust air is wet down with water, remove the magnesium as a fire hazard. After cleaning, a final sand or grit blasting is used to provide a uniform appearance. Impregnation, or sealing, may be used on a casting which must be leakproof. The castings are given a chrome-pickle treatment before shipment. This is primarily for protection against corrosion during shipment and storage before machining. The pickling treatment consists in dipping for a short time in an aqueous solution of 1.5 lb per gal of sodium dichromate and 1.5 pt per gal of concentrated nitric acid. The dip is followed by rinsing in hot water. The castings are given a bronze color by this treatment. Coatings suitable for more permanent corrosion protection may be applied after the part is finished, the latter treatments being described in Ref. 27.

BIBLIOGRAPHY

1. F. A. Lewis, Aluminum Alloy Castings, *Foundry,* vols. 75 and 76, December, 1947–November, 1948.
2. L. W. Eastwood, Melting Aluminum and Magnesium-base Alloys, *Trans. AFS,* vol. 59, 1951.
3. D. P. Smith, L. W. Eastwood, D. J. Carney, and C. E. Sims, "Gases in Metals," American Society for Metals, 1953.
4. W. R. Opie and N. J. Grant, Hydrogen Solubility in Aluminum and Some Aluminum Alloys, *J. Inst. Metals,* vol. 188, p. 1237, October, 1950.
5. W. Bonsack and O. Tichy, Grain Refining of Al and Its Effects on Properties, *Trans. AFS,* vol. 57, 1949.
6. L. F. Mondolfo, "Metallography of Aluminum Alloys," p. 22, John Wiley & Sons, Inc., New York, 1943.
7. Aluminum Co. of America, "Casting Alcoa Alloys," 1952.
8. American Foundrymen's Society, "Recommended Practices for Sand Casting Nonferrous Alloys," 1948.

9. D. A. LaVelle, Aluminum Sand Casting Defects: Their Identification, Causes, and Corrections, *Trans. AFS,* vol. 60, 1952.
10. H. W. Dietert, "Foundry Core Practice," American Foundrymen's Society, 1950.
11. American Society for Metals, "The Physical Metallurgy of Aluminum Alloys," 1949.
12. R. E. Swift, J. H. Jackson, and L. W. Eastwood, A Study of the Principles of Gating, *Trans. AFS,* vol. 57, 1949; continued in subsequent transactions.
13. H. E. Elliott and J. G. Mezoff, Effect of Gating Design on Metal Flow Conditions in the Casting of Magnesium Alloys, *Trans. AFS,* vol. 56, 1948.
14. C. Benkoe, Determination of Sprue Size in Aluminum Castings, *Foundry,* vol. 72, p. 88, November, 1944.
15. American Foundrymen's Society, "Symposium on Principles of Gating," 1951.
16. American Society for Metals, "Metals Handbook," 8th ed., vol. 1, 1961.
17. H. F. Taylor, M. C. Flemings, and T. S. Piwonka, Risering Aluminum Casting, *Foundry,* vol. 88, p. 216, May, 1960.
18. M. C. Flemings and H. F. Taylor, Gating Aluminum Castings, *Foundry,* vol. 88, p. 72, April, 1960.
19. W. N. Brammer, Melting Practice for Aluminum Casting Alloys, *Trans. AFS,* vol. 66, p. 497, 1958.
20. J. P. Moehling, Aluminum Melting Practice in the Die Casting and Permanent Mold Fields, *Trans. AFS,* vol. 66, p. 533, 1958.
21. V. C. Reid, Induction Melting in a Nonferrous Jobbing Foundry, *Foundry,* April, 1953.
22. H. K. and L. C. Barton, Low-frequency Induction Heating in the Die Casting Shop, *Machinery,* Sept. 24–Oct. 29, 1954.
23. E. W. Rearwin, Gating of Aluminum Die Castings, *Foundry,* vol. 88, p. 106, November, 1960.
24. R. K. Owens, H. W. Antes, and R. E. Edelman, Effect of Nitrogen and Vacuum Degassing on Properties of a Cast Al-Si-Mg Alloy (Type 356), *Trans. AFS,* vol. 65, p. 424, 1957.
25. A. F. Taylor et al., Effect of Pressure during Solidification on Microporosity in Aluminum Alloys, *Trans. AFS,* vol. 66, p. 129, 1958.
26. American Foundrymen's Society, "Recommended Practice for Sand Casting Aluminum and Magnesium Base Alloys," 1948.
27. American Society for Metals, "Metals Handbook," 1948.
28. H. E. Elliott and J. G. Mezoff, A New Gating Technique for Magnesium Alloy Castings, *Trans. AFS,* vol. 55, 1947.
29. H. H. Fairfield and A. E. Murton, Some Causes of Pinholes in Magnesium Alloy Castings, *Trans. AFS,* vol. 55, 1947.
30. AFS Light Metals Division, Magnesium Alloy Characteristics, *Am. Foundryman,* vol. 23, p. 156, April, 1953.
31. R. M. Brick, R. B. Gordon, and A. Phillips, "Structure and Properties of Alloys," 3d ed., McGraw-Hill Book Company, New York, 1965.
32. K. E. Nelson and F. P. Strieter, Casting of Magnesium–Rare Earth–Zirconium Alloys in Sand Molds, *Trans. AFS,* vol. 58, p. 400, 1950.
33. P. F. George, Metallography of Cast Magnesium Alloys, *Trans. AFS,* vol. 57, p. 133, 1949.
34. C. E. Nelson, Grain Size Behavior in Magnesium Casting Alloys, *Trans. AFS,* vol. 56, p. 1, 1948.
35. T. E. Kramer, Gating Aluminum Castings in "Symposium on Principles of Gating," American Foundrymen's Society, 1951.

12

Aluminum and Magnesium Casting Alloys

Pure aluminum and magnesium being relatively poor casting materials, aluminum and magnesium castings are actually produced from alloys. The casting alloys used are those having properties peculiarly suited to casting purposes. Since a large number of aluminum- and magnesium-base casting alloys are available, it is evident that quite widely different properties may be obtained from the various alloys. For all these alloys two types of properties should be considered: the casting properties, those characteristics of the alloy which determine the ease or difficulty of producing acceptable castings, and the engineering properties, those properties which are of interest to the designer or user of the castings. These two sets of properties can be used as a basis for studying the similarities and differences of the large number of aluminum and magnesium casting alloys.

ALUMINUM ALLOYING PRINCIPLES

The aluminum-base alloys may in general be characterized as eutectic systems, containing intermetallic compounds or elements as the excess phases. Because of the relatively low solubilities of most of the alloying elements in aluminum and the complexity of the alloys that are produced, any one aluminum-base alloy may contain several metallic phases, which sometimes are quite complex in composition. These phases usually are appreciably more soluble near the eutectic temperatures than at room temperature, making it possible to heat-treat some of the alloys by solution and aging heat-treatments. Specific instances of the application of these heat-treatments are given in subsequent paragraphs.

All the properties of interest are, of course, influenced by the effects of the various elements with which aluminum is alloyed. The principal alloying elements in aluminum-base casting alloys are copper, silicon, magnesium, zinc, chromium, manganese, tin, and titanium. Iron is an element normally present and usually considered as an impurity. Some of the simpler effects of alloying can be considered.

Copper

The structural effects of copper in Cu-Al-base alloys are presented in the equilibrium diagram in Fig. 12.1. The diagram shows solubility of copper in aluminum increasing in the solid state from less than 0.50 per cent at room temperature to 5.65 per cent at 1018 F. Copper above the solubility limit at any temperature appears microstructurally as the θ phase. The latter phase has a composition approximating the formula $CuAl_2$ (46.5% Al–053.5% Cu) and is a hard brittle constituent. By comparison the solid-solution phase is relatively soft and ductile. The two phases are illustrated in Fig. 12.2. Structurally, then, increasing copper content in Cu-Al-base alloys results in an increasing percentage of the hard θ phase. The mechanical properties of hardness and strength can then be expected to increase as copper content increases while the ductility decreases. These property trends are illustrated in Fig. 12.3. A limited percentage of copper thus has a beneficial effect of strengthening and hardening in Cu-Al-base alloys. However, Fig. 12.3 also shows that an excessive copper percentage will cause tensile properties to fall below the maximum values obtained. Furthermore, ductility is reduced to a very low level and brittleness results in alloys of high copper content. Therefore copper percentages do not exceed 12 per cent in most aluminum casting alloys. Actually, the copper percentages in aluminum casting alloys are adjusted so that the lower contents, 2 to 5 per cent, are used in alloys required to have optimum ductility (or toughness), whereas the higher percentages are used when greater hardness and strength are desired.

Heat-treatment of Cu-Al *Alloys*

The mechanical-property curves of Cu-Al alloys in Fig. 12.3 are shown to be markedly shifted by solution heat-treatment and age hardening. In fact, the degree of strengthening obtainable by heat-treatment is greater than that gained by alloying alone. A few elements, namely, Cu, Mg, Zn, and combinations of Mg and Si confer heat-treating potentialities to Al-base alloys in which they are present. These are referred to as "heat-treatable" grades of aluminum alloys, and they greatly extend the range of properties available in aluminum castings.

Detailed study of the metallurgical principles of solution heat-treatment and aging phenomena is outside the scope of this book. However,

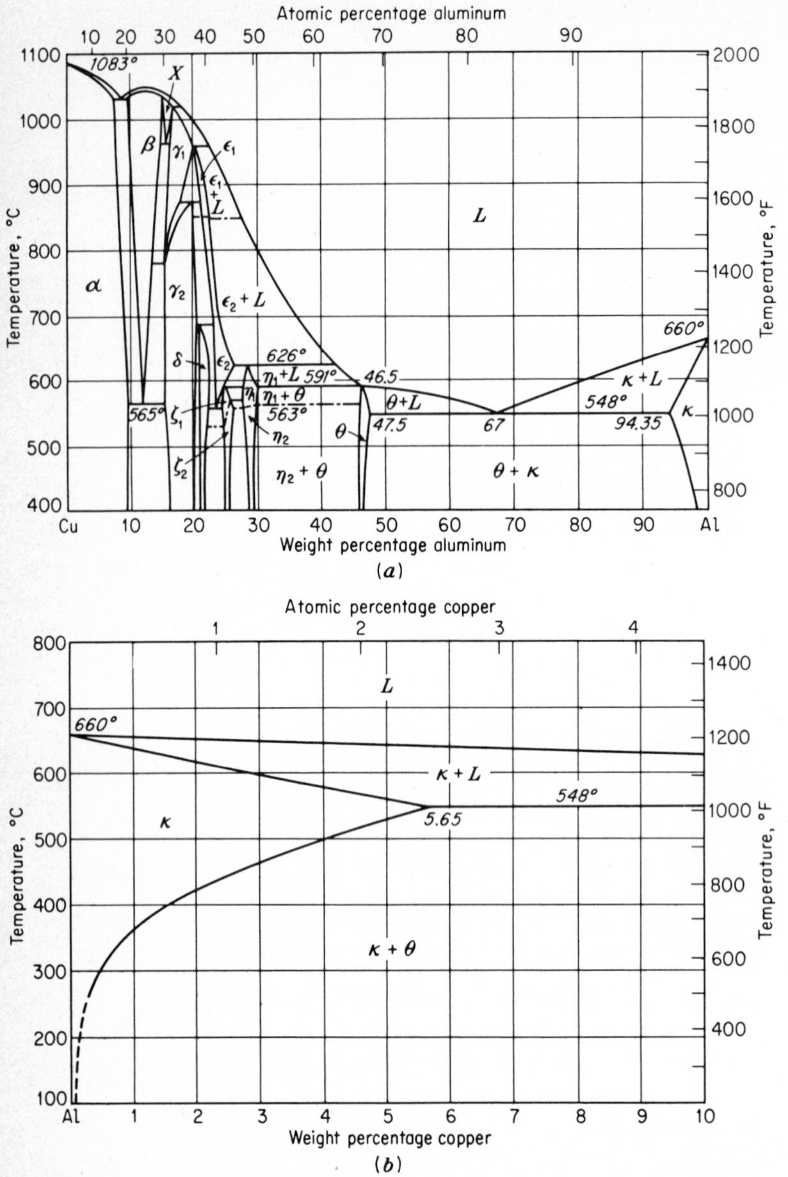

Fig. **12.1** The Al-Cu equilibrium system. (*a*) Entire diagram, (*b*) the Al-rich end of the Al-Cu system. (*From American Society for Metals.*[1])

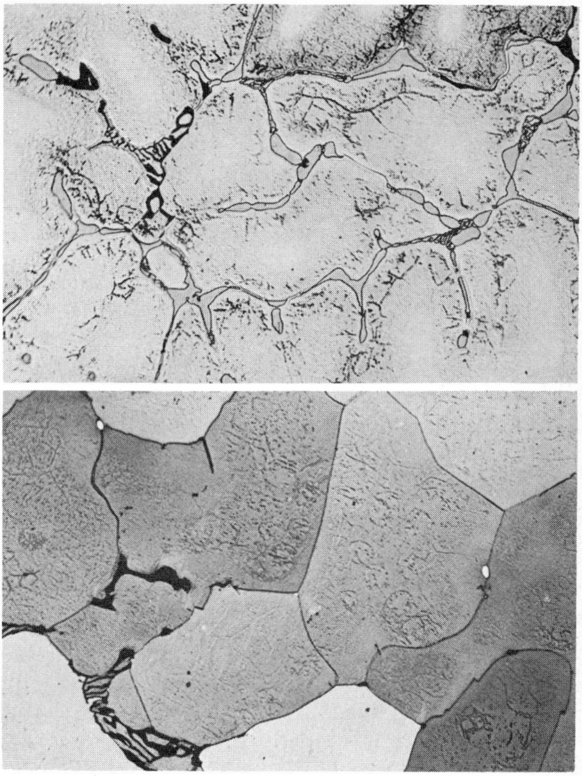

***Fig.* 12.2** Microstructure of commercial aluminum casting alloy with about 4% Cu as the principal alloying element. Top, sand-cast alloy 195-F. Almost continuous interdendritic network of θ Al-Cu and α Al-Fe-Si surrounding cored-aluminum solid-solution dendrites. Coring is indicated by the precipitated θ Al-Cu in the shaded areas. Keller's etch, ×250. Bottom, the same alloy as solution heat-treated, 195-T6. Heat-treatment has dissolved practically all θ Al-Cu and eliminated coring. Notice that the "Chinese script" α Al-Fe-Si is unchanged. Keller's etch, ×250. (*Courtesy of the Aluminum Company of America.*)

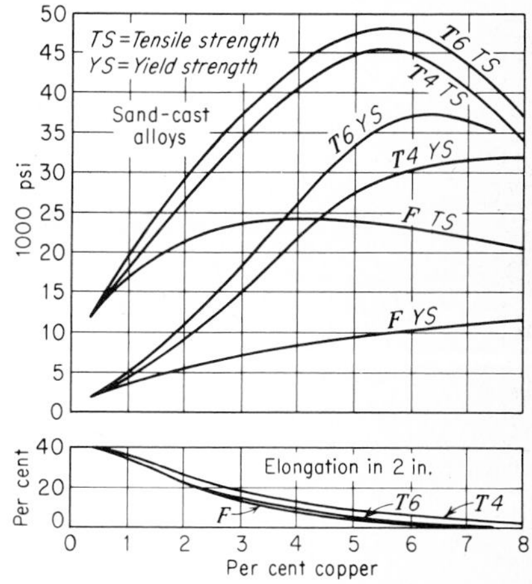

***Fig.* 12.3** Tensile properties of sand-cast aluminum-copper alloys of high purity. Tensile specimens cast to size, ½ in. in diameter at reduced sections. F, as cast; T4, quenched in water after solution treatment at high temperature; T6, precipitation-hardened after solution treatment. (*From American Society for Metals.*[1])

the mechanical operations and a few of the more general aspects of these heat-treatments are discussed so that the aluminum casting alloys may be better understood.

Solution heat-treatment. Solution heat-treatment of aluminum casting alloys consists of a thermal cycle of heating, a suitable period of holding the metal at some elevated temperature, and then rapid cooling of the castings, usually by quenching in water. The temperature and time of holding are exceedingly important factors in the treatment. The temperature must be high enough to cause a substantially large amount of the alloying elements (usually present as intermetallic compound phases) to dissolve in the aluminum-rich solid-solution phase.

As a simplified example of the principles, a 4% Cu–96% Al alloy may be considered with due attention to the equilibrum diagram in Fig. 12.1. After sand casting and slow cooling to room temperature, this alloy consists microstructurally of the aluminum-rich phase κ and the hard θ phase, copper being concentrated mainly in the latter phase. A typical microstructure would be like that shown in Fig. 12.2. Reheating the alloy to a temperature of about 900 to 950 F causes the θ phase to disappear from the microstructure, since, according to Fig. 12.1, the higher temperature permits all the copper in the alloy to be dissolved by the aluminum; hence the name "solution" heat-treating. Of course, adequate time for dissolving of the θ phase into the κ phase (Fig. 12.1) must be allowed. Thus emphasis is placed on the "time at temperature" of the solution heat-treatment. A sufficient holding period at the solution heat-treating temperature is one which results in the aluminum-rich phase having reached a uniformly high percentage of dissolved alloying elements. When this condition exists, rapid cooling from the elevated temperature will retain the enriched solid-solution phase, 4% Cu–96% Al in the present case, down to room temperature. The end microstructure after solution heat-treating then is a supersaturated Al-rich solid-solution phase. A typical microstructure after solution heat-treatment would appear as shown in Fig. 12.2, lower view. In this case, the κ phase contains 4 per cent dissolved copper rather than the normal amount of less than 0.50 per cent for the slow or equilibrium-cooled condition. Since solution heat-treating results in a more uniform distribution of soluble alloying elements, it also assists in minimizing the harmful effects of segregation developed during solidification.

Accompanying the microstructural effects of solution heat-treatment are improvements in mechanical properties. A marked increase in tensile and yield strengths and an improvement in ductility are revealed in Fig. 12.3 as a consequence of this treatment. *Most important is the fact that solution heat-treatment is the necessary step in preparing the alloys for age or precipitation hardening* from which further benefits may be obtained.

Solution heat-treatment by chill casting. Rapid cooling from any elevated temperature, particularly above 700 to 800 F, will cause retention of a supersaturated Al-rich phase down to room temperature. Hence casting processes such as permanent-mold or die casting which are inherently rapid in their cooling effect have this possibility. Sand casting, by contrast, is a slow cooling process. Therefore, if a given alloy, Cu-Al, for example, is cast in a metal mold, it will usually show higher hardness, strength, and ductility than if the same alloy is cast in a sand mold. This point will be considered again later.

Age hardening or precipitation hardening. Natural age hardening is a gradual increase in hardness (and strength) which occurs with the lapse of time at atmospheric temperatures. The increased hardness may reach a maximum value in a few days but may require several years in some alloys. More rapid aging can be caused to occur at elevated temperatures, 300 to 400 F. Heat-treating to cause aging is called artificial age hardening, or "precipitation" hardening. Aging effects by either method are obtained only from alloys which have been previously solution heat-treated. Or the alloy can be aged, if it has been processed so that effects similar to solution heat-treatment are retained, as, for example, by chill casting. The metallurgical changes associated with aging are exceedingly complex, so that only the more simple details are considered here.

Aging or precipitation-hardening temperatures are such as to promote precipitation from the supersaturated solid solution remaining from solution heat-treatment. In the case of the 4% Cu–96% Al alloy considered earlier, the direction of microstructural changes during aging is toward reprecipitation of the θ phase from the supersaturated κ phase developed by solution heat-treatment. However, the most beneficial aging effects are obtained before microstructural evidence of precipitation is revealed. In fact, when the precipitating phase is metallographically visible, overaging has occurred. Overaging results in a substantial decrease in hardness, strength, and other properties.

Temperature and time of aging are exceedingly important factors, determining the end effect of aging. Change of hardness with aging temperature and time is illustrated in Fig. 12.4 for a typical cast alloy used as an example. High temperatures are seen in Fig. 12.4 to cause rapid aging or overaging at extended times. Low temperatures can prevent aging. Thus it is evident that a proper temperature and time interval will produce the most desirable properties. Aging treatments for specific alloys will be considered later.

Solution heat-treatment and aging processes are dependent on alloying elements having effects such as those of copper. The effect of copper concentration in binary Al-Cu alloys was illustrated in Fig. 12.3. Excessive copper contents are undesirable even in the heat-treated condition,

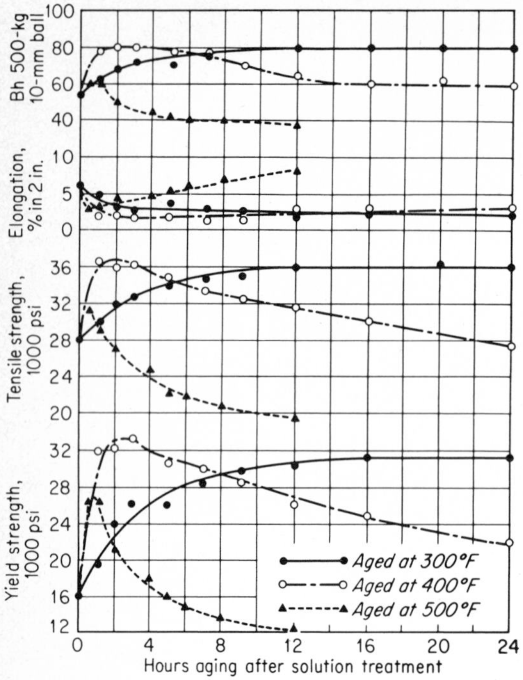

Fig. 12.4 The effect of artificial aging temperature and time on the mechanical properties of sand-cast solution heat-treated aluminum alloy ASTM SG1. See Table 12.1 for composition. *(Courtesy of Aluminum Company of America.)*

since they cause loss of ductility and strength. Hence commercial alloy compositions are aimed at developing optimum combinations of hardness, strength, and toughness after suitable heat-treatment. Other elements used in heat-treatable alloys are Mg, Zn, and certain combinations of Mg and Si.

Silicon

Silicon is present in all commercial aluminum casting alloys. As an alloying element it is used in amounts up to about 14 per cent Si. The binary Al-Si system is shown in Fig. 12.5. The solubility of Si in aluminum, the α phase, is limited to 1.65 per cent at 1072 F and less than 0.05 per cent at room temperature. Undissolved silicon is present as β, silicon particles containing an extremely small percentage of aluminum. The silicon phase in an aluminum alloy, containing 14.0 per cent Si, is illustrated in Fig. 12.6. The size of the silicon-rich β particles may be varied greatly. A rather coarse particle size occurs with normal melting and sand-casting practice; for an example, see the illustration in Fig. 12.6, bottom. Structural refinement by special melting practices is discussed in Chap. 11. The casting process may also cause microstructural refinement. The permanent-mold and die-casting processes can produce refinement of the type illustrated in Fig. 12.6. This is an effect over and above their ability to produce solution heat-treating effects.

The effect of silicon on the properties of Al-Si alloys is largely one of alloying since no significant benefits are obtained by attempts at solution heat-treating and aging. The percentage of silicon in the alloy is first in importance, closely followed by the microstructural effects of modification by permanent-mold or die casting or special melting practices. These factors are summarized in Fig. 12.7. The general effect of increasing silicon contents is shown in Fig. 12.7 to be that of increasing the strength until the eutectic silicon percentage is reached. Ductility, however, is lowered. The beneficial effects of modification with elements such as sodium and by chill casting are also evident in Fig. 12.7. From these observations it follows that aluminum-silicon alloys will be at their best when modified by suitable additions, or better, when cast in metal molds. Furthermore, since additional improvement cannot be obtained by heat-treatment, these alloys will be used in the as-cast condition. Other elements used in aluminum alloys which, like Si, do not confer response to solution heat-treatment are manganese and nickel.

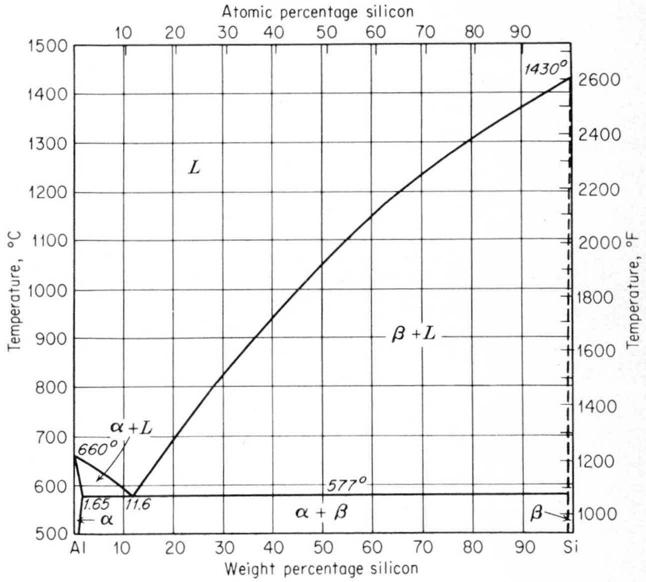

***Fig.* 12.5** The Al-Si equilibrium system. (*From American Society for Metals.*[1])

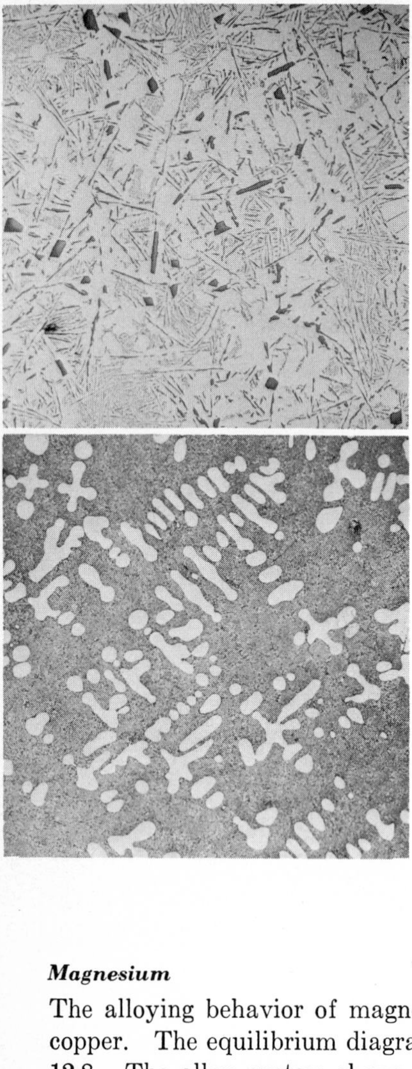

***Fig.* 12.6** Modification of the as-cast structure of an Al–11.8% Si alloy. Top, coarse polyhedral and platelet particles of silicon characteristic of unmodified eutectic solidification. Bottom, fine particles of silicon obtained in modified eutectic caused by addition of sodium to the melt. (*Courtesy of C. B. Kim.*)

Magnesium

The alloying behavior of magnesium in aluminum is similar to that of copper. The equilibrium diagram for the binary system is shown in Fig. 12.8. The alloy system shows a solid-solubility change of the α phase with temperature, 14.9 per cent Mg being soluble at 844 F and less than 2.90 per cent at room temperature. A second, harder β phase exists when the solid-solubility limit is exceeded. The opportunity for solution and aging heat-treatments is present, and the mechanical-property relationships with magnesium percentage are similar to those in the Cu-Al alloys. Several alloys are based on this binary system, and normally contain 4, 8, and 10 per cent Mg. Complex alloys containing other elements, along with a substantial percentage of magnesium, are also listed in Tables 12.1 to 12.3.

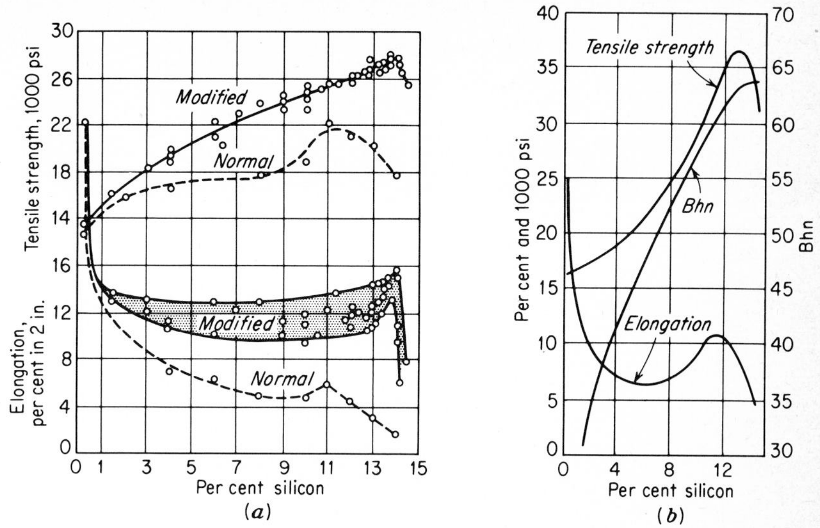

***Fig.* 12.7** Properties of Al-Si casting alloys as a function of silicon in the alloy. (*a*) Applies to normal and modified alloys (sodium-treated) in sand castings; (*b*) applies to chill castings. (*From American Society for Metals.*[1])

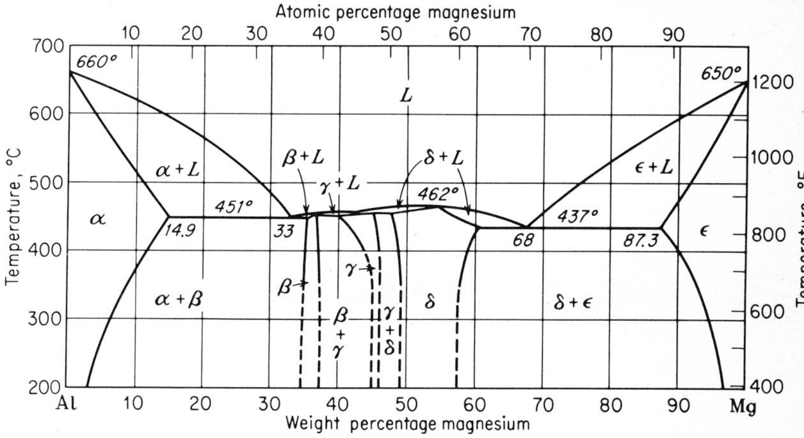

***Fig.* 12.8** The Al-Mg equilibrium system. (*From American Society for Metals.*[1])

Magnesium and Silicon

Certain combinations of magnesium and silicon have been found to exhibit important alloying effects in aluminum. The two elements are able to combine and form the metallic compound Mg_2Si. They then behave as a quasi-binary alloy system, as illustrated in Fig. 12.9. The Al-Mg_2Si system is also of the type permitting solution and aging treatments and their accompanying property changes. Ternary alloys taking advantage of this quasi-binary system and the beneficial effects of silicon contain small percentages of Mg, up to about 0.30 per cent, and larger percentages of Si, 6 to 8.0 per cent. The excess of silicon is present to improve casting properties of these alloys since it is not needed to form Mg_2Si.

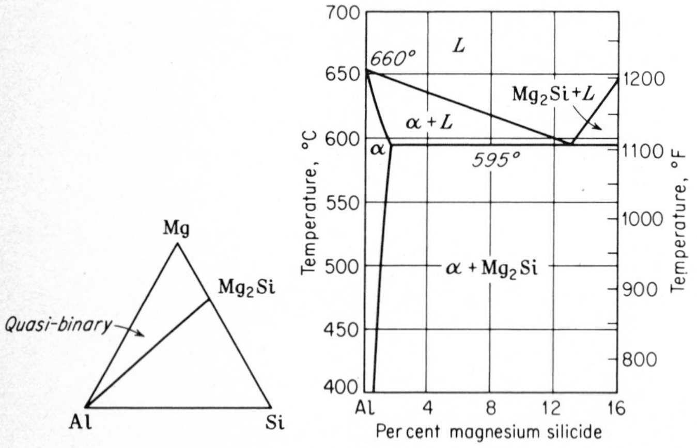

***Fig.* 12.9** The Al-Mg-Si equilibrium system and the quasi-binary system Al-Mg_2Si. (*From American Society for Metals.*[1])

In some alloys, the combined effects of Si and Mg are undesirable, and they may then be limited as impurities.[13] Since all aluminum alloys contain silicon, the addition of magnesium is all that is necessary to obtain the hardening effect of Mg_2Si. The alloys may then become brittle. For this reason impurity limits for magnesium in many alloys (the Cu-Al, Si-Al, and their complex alloys, for example) are set at 0.03 to 0.10 per cent maximum. Thus the combined effects of the Mg and Si in Al alloys provide another case study of elements which are beneficial in some alloys when used as alloying elements or harmful when unintentionally present as impurities in other alloy types.

ASTM Alloy Specification B26-60T	Nominal composition, %								Commercial designation	Similar specifications for comparative purposes			
										Federal QQ-A-601a	U.S. Navy 46A1f	SAE	
	Cu	Si	Mg	Zn	Ni	Mn	Cr	Ti				Handbook (1951)	AMS[b]
C4A	4.5	.....	.....	.....	.....	.....	.....	.....	195	Class 4	Class 4	38	4230 4231A
CG100A	10.0	.....	0.2	.....	.....	.....	.....	.....	122	Class 7	.....	34	
CN42A	4.0	.....	1.5	.....	2.0	.....	.....	.....	142	Class 6	.....	39	4222B
CS43A	4.0	3.0	.....	.....	.....	.....	.....	.....	108	Class 8			
CS72A	7.0	2.0	.....	.....	.....	.....	.....	.....	113	Class 9	.....	33	
G4A	.....	.....	4.0	.....	.....	.....	.....	.....	214	Class 5	Class 5	320	
G10A	.....	.....	10.0	.....	.....	.....	.....	.....	220	Class 16	.....	324	4240A
GM70B[c]	0.1	0.2	7.0	.....	.....	0.2	.....	0.2					
GS42A	.....	1.8	4.0	.....	.....	.....	.....	.....	B214				
S5A[d]	.....	5.0	.....	.....	.....	.....	.....	.....	43	Class 2	Class 2	35	
S5B[e]	.....	5.0	.....	.....	.....	.....	.....	.....	5% Si				
SC51A	1.3	5.0	0.5	.....	.....	.....	.....	.....	355	Class 10	Class 7	322	4210D 4212C 4214B
SC64C[f]	3.7	6.3	.....	.....	.....	.....	.....	.....	319	Class 18	.....	329	
SC64D[g]	4.0	6.3	.....	.....	.....	.....	.....	.....	.....	.....	.....	326	
SC82A	1.5	8.0	0.4	.....	.....	0.4	.....	.....	Red X-8	.....	.....	327	
SG70A	.....	7.0	0.3	.....	.....	.....	.....	.....	356	Class 3	Class 3	323	4217A
ZC81A	0.7	.....	0.4	7.5	.....	.....	.....	.....	Tenzaloy				
ZG32A	.....	.....	1.6	3.0	.....	0.5	0.3	.....	Ternalloy 5				
ZG42A	.....	.....	2.1	4.3	.....	0.5	0.3	.....	Ternalloy 7				
ZG61A	.....	.....	0.55	5.6	.....	.....	0.5	0.2	40E	Class 17	Class 1	310	
ZG61B	0.5	.....	0.7	6.5	.....	.....	.....	.....	A612				

* From American Foundrymen's Society[4] and ASTM Specification B26-63. [a] For specified compositions refer to applicable specifications. [b] Aeronautical Materials Specifications. [c] Iron plus silicon not to exceed 0.40. [d] Copper, 0.1% max. [e] Copper, 0.3% max for cooking utensils. Other uses, 0.6% max. [f] Iron, 1.2% max; magnesium, 0.5% max. [g] Iron, 1.0% max; magnesium, 0.1% max.

Table 12.1b Sand-cast aluminum alloys, properties and characteristics*

1 indicates best of group; 5 indicates poorest of group

Alloy	Pattern shrinkage allowance, in./ft[a]	Approximate melting range, °F[b]	Foundry characteristics: Resistance to hot cracking[c]	Pressuretightness	Fluidity[d]	Solidification shrinkage tendency[e]	Normally heat-treated	Other characteristics: Resistance to corrosion[f]	Machining[g]	Polishing[h]	Electroplating[i]	Anodizing (appearance)[j]	Chemical oxide coating (protection)[k]	Strength at elevated temp[l]	Suitability for welding[m]	Suitable for brazing[n]
C4A	5/32	970–1190	4	4	3	3	Yes	3	2	2	1	2	3	3	3	No
CG100A	5/32	965–1155	3	3	3	3	Yes	4	1	2	1	3	4	1	4	No
CN42A	5/32	990–1175	4	3	3	4	Yes	4	2	2	1	3	4	1	4	No
CS43A	5/32	970–1160	2	2	2	2	No	4	3	3	2	3	3	3	2	No
CS72A	5/32	965–1160	3	3	2	3	No	5	2	2	2	3	4	3	3	No
G4A	5/32	1110–1185	4	5	5	5	No	1	1	1	5	1	1	2	4	No
G10A	1/10	840–1120	2	5	4	5	Yes	1	1	1	4	1	1	[o]	5	No
GM70B	5/32	1020–1165	3	5	5	5	No	1	1	1	5	1	1	3	4	No
GS42A	5/32	1090–1170	3	4	3	4	No	1	2	2	4	2	1	3	4	No
S5A	5/32	1065–1170	1	1	1	1	No	2	5	5	2	5	2	4	1	Ltd
S5B	5/32	1065–1170	1	1	1	1	No	3	5	5	2	5	2	4	1	Ltd
SC51A	5/32	1015–1150	1	1	1	1	Yes	3	3	3	1	4	2	2	2	No
SC64D	5/32	950–1125	2	2	2	2	Yes	3	3	4	2	4	3	3	2	No
SC82A	5/32	960–1135	1	1	1	1	Yes	3	4	5	2	4	2	2	2	No
SG70A	5/32	1035–1135	1	1	1	1	Yes	2	4	5	2	4	2	3	2	No
ZC81A	3/16	1100–1185	5	3	4	4	Aged only	2	1	1	2	2	3	5	4	Yes
ZG32A	3/16	1105–1180	5	3	4	4	Aged only	2	1	1	3	2	2	5	4	Yes
ZG42A	3/16	1085–1165	5	3	4	4	Yes	2	1	1	3	2	2	5	4	Yes
ZG61A	3/16	1110–1185	5	3	4	4	Aged only	2	1	1	2	2	3	5	4	Yes
ZG61B	3/16	1105–1195	5	3	4	4	Aged	2	1	1	2	2	3	5	4	Yes

* From ASTM Specification B26-63.

[a] Allowances for average castings. Shrinkage requirements will vary with intricacy of design and dimensions.

[b] Temperatures of solidus and liquidus are indicated; pouring temperatures will be higher.

[c] Ability of alloy to withstand contraction stresses while cooling through hot-short or brittle temperature range.

[d] Ability of liquid alloy to flow readily in mold and fill thin sections.

[e] Decrease in volume accompanying freezing of alloy and measure of amount of compensating feed metal required in form of risers.

[f] Based on alloy resistance in standard-type salt-spray test.

[g] Composite rating based on ease of cutting, chip characteristics, quality of finish, and tool life. Ratings, in the case of heat-treatable alloys, based on T6-type temper. Other tempers, particularly the annealed temper, may have lower rating.

[h] Composite rating based on ease and speed of polishing and quality of finish provided by typical polishing procedure.

[i] Ability of casting to take and hold an electroplate applied by present standard methods.

[j] Rated on lightness of color, brightness, and uniformity of clear anodized coating applied in sulfuric acid electrolyte.

[k] Rated on combined resistance of coating and base alloy to corrosion.

[l] Rating based on tensile and yield strengths at temperatures up to 500 F, after prolonged heating at testing temperature.

[m] Based on ability of material to be fusion-welded with filler rod of same alloy.

[n] Refers to suitability of alloy to withstand brazing temperatures without excessive distortion or melting.

[o] Not recommended for service at elevated temperatures.

Zinc

Zinc is used as a principal alloying element in some alloys. Its chief beneficial effect seems to be that of making it possible to obtain a maximum of mechanical properties in the as-cast condition.[11]

Impurities

The impurities present in the aluminum casting alloys greatly influence their properties. Two alloy characteristics which may be seriously impaired are ductility (and toughness) and corrosion resistance. Although other properties may also be affected, the latter are the most frequently afflicted by the various elements which are sometimes looked on as alloying elements and at other times as impurities. The case of magnesium and silicon has been considered above.

Silicon

Silicon as an impurity in most aluminum casting alloys can be tolerated up to several per cent. It is only when brittleness is induced, as by combination with magnesium, that it must be limited to 0.2 to 0.3 per cent.

Iron

Iron in amounts of 0.8 to 2 per cent is an omnipresent impurity because of the ability of molten aluminum to dissolve iron from furnace pots, ladles, etc. It forms iron-aluminum and iron aluminum–silicon phases in the microstructure which cause embrittlement and loss of corrosion resistance. Another harmful effect of excessive iron content is a coarsening of the as-cast grain size of the metal.

Zinc

Zinc is used as a beneficial alloying element in a certain group of alloys; types ZC and ZG in Tables 12.1 to 12.3. In other alloy types, however, it may cause loss in corrosion resistance if it exceeds 0.1 to 0.3 per cent in some grades. In the copper-free, silicon-aluminum alloys it is allowable up to 0.50 per cent. In other alloys amounts up to 2.50 per cent are permissible.

Other Elements

A number of other elements are often given limits of 0.05 to 0.10 per cent individually because of impurity effects. These may include lead, tin, antimony, arsenic, cadmium, etc.

ASTM Alloy Specification B108-62T	Cu	Si	Mg	Zn	Ni	Mn	Cr	Ti	Commercial designation	Federal QQ-A-596a	Military Mil-A-958A	SAE Hand-book (1951)	SAE AMS
CG100A	10.0	...	0.25	...	...	...	...	...	122	Class 2	Class 2	34	
CN42A	4.0	...	1.5	...	2.0	...	...	...	142	Class 3	Class 3	39	
CS42A	4.5	2.5	...	...	...	...	...	...	B195	Class 4	Class 4	380	4282B
													4283
CS66A	6.5	5.5	0.4	...	...	...	...	...	152	...	...	300	
CS72A	7.0	2.5	...	...	...	...	...	...	113	Class 1	Class 1	33	
CS104A	10.0	4.0	1.0	...	...	...	...	...	138				
GM70B[b]	0.1	0.2	7.0	...	...	0.2	...	0.2					
GS42A	...	1.8	4.0	...	...	...	...	...	B214				
GZ42A	...	...	4.0	1.8	...	...	...	...	A214				
S5A[c]	...	5.0	...	...	...	...	...	...	43	Class 7	Class 7	35	
S5B[d]	...	5.0	...	...	...	...	...	...	5% Si				
SC51A	1.3	5.0	0.5	...	...	...	...	...	355	Class 6	Class 6	322	4280B
													4281
SC64A	4.5	5.5	...	...	...	...	...	...	A108	Class 5	Class 5	330	
SC64B[e]	3.7	6.3	...	...	...	...	...	...	...	Class 11	...	326	
SC64C[f]	3.7	6.3	...	...	...	...	...	...	319				
SC103A	3.0	9.5	1.0	...	...	...	...	...	...	...	...	332	
SC122A	1.5	12.0	0.7	...	...	0.7	...	...	Red X-13	...	...	328	
SG70A	...	7.0	0.3	...	...	...	...	...	356	Class 8	Class 8	323	4284A
SN122A	1.0	12.0	1.0	...	2.5	...	...	...	A132	Class 9	Class 9	321	
ZC60A	0.5	...	0.35	6.5	...	...	...	...	C612				
ZC81B	0.7	...	0.35	7.5	...	...	...	...	Tenzaloy				
ZG32A	...	...	1.6	3.0	...	0.5	0.3	...	Ternalloy 5				
ZG42A	...	...	2.1	4.3	...	0.5	0.3	...	Ternalloy 7				

* From American Foundrymen's Society[4] and ASTM Specification B108-62T. [a] For specified compositions refer to applicable specifications. [b] Iron plus silicon, 0.40% max. [c] Copper, 0.1% max. [d] Copper, 0.3% max for cooking utensils. Other uses, 0.6% max. [e] Iron, 1.0% max; magnesium, 0.1% max. [f] Iron, 1.2% max; magnesium, 0.5% max.

Table 12.2b Permanent-mold cast aluminum alloys, properties and characteristics*

1 indicates best of group; 5 indicates poorest of group

Alloy	Approximate melting range, °F	Foundry characteristics					Other characteristics								
		Resistance to hot cracking[b]	Pressure-tightness	Fluidity[c]	Solidification shrinkage tendency[d]	Normally heat-treated	Resistance to corrosion[e]	Machining[f]	Polishing[g]	Electroplating[h]	Anodizing (appearance)[i]	Chemical oxide coating (protection)[j]	Strength at elevated temp.[k]	Suitability for welding[l]	Suitable for brazing[m]
CG100A	965–1155	4	4	3	4	Yes	5	1	2	1	3	4	1	4	No
CN42A	990–1175	4	4	3	4	Yes	4	2	2	1	2	3	1	4	No
CS42A	970–1170	4	3	3	3	Yes	4	3	2	1	3	2	2	4	No
CS66A	930–1110	2	3	3	3	Yes	5	3	2	2	4	3	2	4	No
CS72A	965–1160	3	3	2	3	No	5	2	2	2	3	4	3	4	No
CS104A	945–1110	2	3	2	3	No	5	2	2	5	4	5	2	3	No
GM70B	1020–1165	4	5	5	5	No	1	1	1	5	1	1	3	4	No
GS42A	1090–1170	3	4	4	4	No	1	1	1	5	2	1	3	5	No
GZ42A	1075–1180	4	5	5	4	No	1	1	1	4	1	1	3	5	No
S5A	1065–1170	1	1	1	2	No	2	5	4	2	4	2	4	1	Ltd
S5B	1065–1170	1	1	1	2	No	3	5	4	2	4	2	4	1	Ltd
SC51A	1015–1150	1	1	2	2	Yes	3	3	3	2	4	2	2	2	No
SC51B	1015–1150	1	1	2	2	Yes	3	3	3	2	4	2	2	2	No
SC64D	950–1125	2	2	2	3	Yes	3	3	3	2	4	3	3	2	No
SC103A	970–1080	1	2	1	2	Aged only	3	3	4	3	5	3	3	2	No
SC122A	980–1060	1	2	1	3	Yes	3	4	5	3	5	2	2	2	No
SG70A	1035–1135	1	1	2	1	Yes	2	3	3	1	4	2	3	2	No
SG70B	1035–1135	1	1	2	1	Yes	2	3	3	1	4	2	3	2	No
SN122A	1000–1050	1	2	1	3	Yes	3	4	5	4	5	2	2	2	No
ZC60A	1120–1190	5	4	4	5	Aged only	2	1	1	2	1	2	5	4	Yes
ZC81B	1100–1185	5	4	4	5	Aged only	2	1	1	2	1	2	5	4	Yes
ZG32A	1105–1180	5	4	4	5	Aged only	2	1	1	3	1	2	5	4	Yes

* From ASTM Specification B108-62T.

[a] Ability of alloy to withstand stresses from contraction while cooling through hot-short or brittle temperature range.

[b] Temperatures of solidus and liquidus are indicated; pouring temperatures will be higher.

[c] Ability of liquid alloy to flow readily in mold and fill thin sections.

[d] Decrease in volume accompanying freezing of alloy and measure of amount of compensating feed metal required in form of risers.

[e] Based on resistance of alloy in standard-type salt-spray test.

[f] Composite rating based on ease of cutting, chip characteristics, quality of finish, and tool life. Ratings, in the case of heat-treatable alloys, based on T6-type temper. Other tempers, particularly the annealed temper, may have lower rating.

[g] Composite rating based on ease and speed of polishing and quality of finish provided by typical polishing procedure.

[h] Ability of casting to take and hold an electroplate applied by present standard methods.

[i] Rated on lightness of color, brightness, and uniformity of clear anodized coating applied in sulfuric acid electrolyte.

[j] Rated on combined resistance of coating and base alloy to corrosion.

[k] Rating based on tensile and yield strengths at temperatures up to 500 F, after prolonged heating at testing temperature.

[l] Based on ability of material to be fusion-welded with filler rod of same alloy.

[m] Refers to suitability of alloy to withstand brazing temperatures without excessive distortion or melting.

Table 12.3a Die-cast aluminum alloys, compositions and specifications*†

ASTM Alloy Specification B85-60	Nominal composition, %				Commercial designation	Similar specifications for comparative purposes			
	Cu	Si	Mg	Fe max		Federal QQ-A-591a	Military Mil-A-15153 (Ships)	SAE Handbook (1951)	SAE AMS
G8A....	....	.....	8.0	1.8	218	Class 7	Class 7		
S5C....	....	5.3	....	2.0	43	Class 3	Class 3	304	
S12A...	....	12.0	....	1.3	13	Class 1	Class 1	305	4290D
S12B...	....	12.0	....	2.0	A13	Class 2			
SC84A..	3.5	8.5	....	1.3	A380	Class 11	....	308	4291
SC84B..	3.5	8.5	....	2.0	380				
SC114A	3.8	11.3	....	1.3	384				
SG100A	....	9.5	0.5	1.3	A360				
SG100B	....	9.5	0.5	2.0	360	Class 12	....	309	4290D

*From American Foundrymen's Society,[4] American Society for Metals,[33] and ASTM Specification B85-60.

†For specified compositions refer to applicable specifications.

Complex Alloys

The foregoing discussion has described a few of the beneficial and limiting results of alloying in the Al-base metals. Improvements in strength and hardness and response to heat-treatment are obtained with proper percentages of copper, magnesium, zinc, or certain combination of magnesium and silicon in aluminum alloys. Excessive percentages of these elements, however, result in a complete loss of ductility and toughness. Other elements, among them silicon, show improved properties through alloying effects but demonstrate no significant benefit from heat-treatments. The latter alloys are especially susceptible to improvement by modification treatments or chill casting.

Obviously, the details and principles have been greatly simplified by a consideration of only the simple binary-alloy systems. Commercial alloys are complex in composition. Also, only simple mechanical-property effects of alloying have been examined. Changes in conductivity, corrosion resistance, machinability, thermal expansion, endurance limit, etc., have not been examined. However, the simple principles advanced are helpful in understanding the classes of aluminum casting alloys which have been developed. Additional engineering and casting properties are considered later in the chapter.

Table 12.3b ***Die-cast aluminum alloys, properties and characteristics**** *1 indicates best of group; 5 indicates poorest of group*

Alloy	Approximate melting range, °F	Die-casting characteristics: Resistance to hot cracking[a]	Die-casting characteristics: Pressure-tightness	Die-casting characteristics: Die-filling capacity[b]	Other characteristics: Normally heat-treated[c]	Other characteristics: Resistance to corrosion[d]	Other characteristics: Machining[e]	Other characteristics: Polishing[f]	Other characteristics: Electro-plating[g]	Other characteristics: Anodizing appearance[h]	Other characteristics: Chemical oxide coating[i] (protection)	Other characteristics: Strength at elevated temperature[j]	Other characteristics: Suitable for welding	Other characteristics: Suitable for brazing
G8A......	995–1150	5	5	5	....	1	1	1	5	1	1	4	No	No
S5C......	1065–1170	2	3	3	....	2	5	4	2	4	3	5	No	No
S12A.....	1065–1080	1	2	1	....	3	4	5	3	5	3	3	No	No
S12B.....	1065–1080	1	2	1	....	3	4	5	3	5	3	3	No	No
SC84A....	1000–1100	2	2	2	....	5	3	3	1	3	5	2	No	No
SC84B....	1000–1100	2	2	2	....	5	3	3	1	3	5	2	No	No
SC114A...	960–1080	2	2	1	....	5	3	3	2	4	4	2	No	No
SG100A...	1035–1105	1	1	1	....	3	3	3	1	3	3	2	No	No
SG100B...	1035–1105	1	1	1	....	3	3	3	1	3	3	1	No	No

* From ASTM Specification B85-60.

[a] Ability of alloy to withstand stresses from contraction while cooling through hot-short or brittle temperature range.

[b] Ability of liquid alloy to flow readily in die and fill thin sections.

[c] Heat-treatments generally confined to low temperature to provide stress relief or increased ductility. Treatments to improve properties not generally applicable.

[d] Based on resistance of alloy in standard-type salt-spray test.

[e] Composite rating based on ease of cutting, chip characteristics, quality of finish, and tool life.

[f] Composite rating based on ease and speed of polishing and quality of finish provided by typical polishing procedure.

[g] Ability of the die casting to take and hold an electroplate applied by present standard methods.

[h] Rated on lightness of color, brightness, and uniformity of clear anodized coating applied in sulfuric acid electrolyte.

[i] Rated on combined resistance of coating and base alloy to corrosion.

[j] Rating based on tensile and yield strengths at temperatures up to 500 F, after prolonged heating at testing temperature.

ALLOY DESIGNATION

A standard four-part system of alloy designation for aluminum- and magnesium-base alloys was first adopted by the ASTM in 1948 and is used for identifying approximate nominal compositions of casting alloys.[33]

1. The first part of the code indicates the two principal alloying elements. This consists in using two code letters representing the two main alloying elements arranged in order of decreasing percentage (or alphabetically if percentages are equal). The code numbers designated are:

A	aluminum	L	beryllium
B	bismuth	M	manganese
C	copper	N	nickel
D	cadmium	P	lead
E	rare earths	Q	silver
F	iron	R	chromium
G	magnesium	S	silicon
H	thorium	T	tin
K	zirconium	Z	zinc

2. The second part indicates the amounts of the two principal alloying elements and consists of two whole numbers corresponding to rounded-off percentages of the two main alloying elements and arranged in the same order as alloy designations in the first part.
3. The third part distinguishes between different alloys with the same percentages of the two principal alloying elements. Differences in permissible impurities or some other specified variation in analysis such as the addition of 0.25% Cr for use in grain refining may be indicated. Letters of the alphabet, except I and O, are assigned as compositions become standard.
4. Conditions and properties are indicated in the fourth part. A letter followed by a number is used and is separated from the third part by a hyphen. When only the alloy is referred to, and not its properties, this part is generally omitted. Common designations used for aluminum and magnesium casting alloys are:

F	as fabricated
T2	annealed
T4	solution heat-treated
T5	artificially aged only
T6	solution heat-treated and artificially aged

For a complete description of temper designation, see Ref. 33.

Examples of the numbering system used for aluminum-base alloys are as follows:

Alloy CS43A—copper 4%, silicon 3%

Alloy SC64B—silicon 6.3%, copper 3.7%, 1% iron max, 0.1% magnesium max
Alloy ZG61A—zinc 5.6%, magnesium 0.55%

Since the system is standard for both aluminum- and magnesium-base alloys, the designation should be preceded by the name of the base metal unless the base metal is obvious.

ALUMINUM CASTING ALLOYS

Most of the aluminum casting alloys can be classified into one of the following alloy groups:[3]

1. Aluminum-copper, heat-treatable and non-heat-treatable, identified by ASTM code letter C
2. Aluminum-silicon alloys, non-heat-treatable, code letter S
3. Aluminum-copper-silicon, heat-treatable and non-heat-treatable grades, code letter CS or SC
4. Aluminum-silicon-magnesium, heat-treatable, code letter SG
5. Aluminum-magnesium, heat-treatable and non-heat-treatable, code letter G
6. Aluminum-zinc, code letter ZC or ZG
7. Special alloys: copper-nickel-aluminum, copper-tin, high Si-Al, etc.

In these groupings, alloys are classed as non-heat-treatable for one of two principal reasons. First, their properties are not significantly benefited by solution heat-treatment and aging, the Al-Si alloys, for example. Or second, if heat-treated, they become so brittle after aging as to be useless for castings. Impurities have a great influence on the latter effect, so that in general it is necessary to place much lower limits on impurities tolerable in the heat-treatable alloys.

The nominal chemical-composition specifications of a number of commercial casting alloys and their distinctive properties are given in Tables 12.1 to 12.3. ASTM Specifications B26-52T, B108-52T, and B85-53T[3] may be consulted for specific analysis ranges and impurity limits for the alloys listed.

ENGINEERING PROPERTIES OF ALUMINUM CASTING ALLOYS

Probably the first requirement of aluminum casting alloys is adequate mechanical strength for the intended use. Other extremely important factors are machinability; ability to be polished, welded, brazed, or surface-treated; appearance; corrosion resistance; conductivity; leaktightness; and cost. Selection of a particular alloy depends usually on the most favorable compromise of all the factors.

Mechanical Properties

As discussed previously, the mechanical properties of the casting alloys are dependent on alloying, heat-treatment, and casting process. A summary of the typical tensile-property ranges for the three casting processes and different conditions of heat-treatment is presented in Tables 12.4 to 12.6.

In general, the tensile properties vary from 17,000 to 43,000 psi mimimum tensile strength, from 9000 to 43,000 yield strength, and 0 to 12.0 per cent elongation. The higher strengths are obtained by heat-treatment and by casting in metal molds.

Heat-treatment

Heat-treatments may be applied to aluminum castings for one or several of the following reasons:

1. To obtain the most favorable or desired mechanical properties
   a. Strengthening
   b. Toughening
2. To obtain dimensional stability of castings
   a. Minimize or prevent growth
   b. Stress relief
3. To stabilize mechanical properties and uncontrolled change of properties during use (room-temperature aging)

The alloys which usually receive heat-treatments are indicated in Tables 12.1 to 12.3.

Solution and aging heat-treatments. The desired mechanical properties are usually obtained by some combination of solution heat-treatment and age- or precipitation-hardening treatment embodying the principles discussed earlier. The temperatures and time required for these heat-treatments are given in Table 12.7. Additional data of the type found in Table 12.7 may be found in Ref. 1. Conventional heat-treating furnaces of the air-chamber type may be used. Molten salt baths are also possible. Temperature control is essential, and variations within the furnace should be within 5 F of the required temperature. Since the strength of the castings is very low at solution heat-treating temperatures, careful stacking and support of the castings are desirable to prevent warpage. Overshooting of the solution heat-treating temperature can be disastrous, since melting begins at temperatures only a little above those of heat-treatment. Quenching of the castings from the solution heat-treating temperatures is done in hot water or in air. Cold water causes cracking or serious distortion of the castings.

To obtain improved ductility or toughness with increased strength, the castings may be left in the solution heat-treated condition. For

Table* 12.4 *Tensile properties of sand-cast aluminum alloys, tensile requirements*

Alloy	Condition	Yield strength (0.2 per cent offset), min, psi[a]	Tensile strength, min, psi	Elongation in 2 in., min, %
C4A	T4 (solution heat-treated)	13,000	29,000	6.0
	T6 (solution treated and aged)	20,000	32,000	3.0
	T62 (solution treated and aged	28,000	36,000	[b]
	T7 (solution treated and overaged)	16,000	29,000	3.0
CG100A	T2 (annealed)	....	23,000	[b]
	T61 (solution treated and aged)	....	30,000	[b]
CN42A	T21 (annealed)	....	23,000	[b]
	T61 (solution treated and aged)	20,000	32,000	[b]
CS43A	F (as cast)	12,000	19,000	1.5
CS72A	F (as cast)	12,000	19,000	1[c]
G4A	F (as cast)	9,000	22,000	6.0
G10A	T4 (solution heat-treated)	22,000	42,000	12.0
GM70B	....	18,000	35,000	9.0
GS42A	F (as cast)	10,000	17,000	[b]
S5A	F (as cast)	6,000	17,000	3.0
S5B	F (as cast)	7,000	17,000	3.0
SC51A	T6 (solution treated and aged)	20,000	32,000	2.0
	T51 (aged)	18,000	25,000	[b]
	T71 (solution treated and overaged)	22,000	30,000	[b]
SC64D	F	13,000	23,000	1.5
	T6	20,000	32,000	2.5
SC82A	F (as cast)	14,000	25,000	1.0
	T6 (solution treated and aged)	21,000	34,000	1.0
SG70A	F (as cast)	....	19,000	2.0
	T6 (solution treated and aged)	20,000	30,000	3.0
	T7 (solution treated and overaged)	....	31,000	[b]
	T51 (aged)	16,000	23,000	[b]
	T71 (solution treated and overaged)	18,000	25,000	3.0
ZC81A	T5[d]	22,000	30,000	3.0
ZG32A	T5[d]	17,000	30,000	5.0
ZG42A	T5[d]	22,000	33,000	2.0
	T7	30,000	37,000	1.0
ZG61A	T5[d]	25,000	32,000	3.0
ZG61B	T5[e]	20,000	32,000	2.0

*From ASTM Specification B26-63. If agreed upon by the manufacturer and the purchaser, other mechanical properties may be obtained by other heat-treatments such as annealing, aging, or stress relieving.

[a]Yield strength to be determined only when specified in the contract or purchase order.

[b]Not required.

[c]For information only, not required for acceptance.

[d]Aged 21 days at room temperature or artificially aged.

[e]Aged 21 days at room temperature.

Table 12.5 *Tensile properties of permanent-mold cast aluminum alloys, tensile requirements**

Alloy	Condition	Yield strength,[a] (0.2 per cent offset), min, psi	Tensile strength, min, psi	Elongation in 2 in., or 4 × diameter, min, %
CG100A	T551 (aged)	....	30,000	[b]
	T65 (solution treated and aged)	....	40,000	[b]
CN42A	T571 (aged)	....	34,000	[b]
	T61 (solution treated and aged)	....	40,000	[b]
	T4 (solution heat-treated)	15,000	33,000	4.5
CS42A	T6 (solution treated and aged)	22,000	35,000	2.0
	T7 (solution treated and overaged)	16,000	33,000	3.0
CS66A	T5 (aged)	25,000	32,000	[b]
CS72A	F (as cast)	14,000	23,000	[b]
CS104A	F (as cast)	[b]	[b]	[b]
GM70B	As cast	18,000	35,000	8.0
GS42A	F (as cast)	....	19,000	1.5
GZ42A	F (as cast)	12,000	22,000	2.5
S5A	F (as cast)	6,000	21,000	2.5
S5B	F (as cast)	7,000	21,000	2.0
SC51A	T6 (solution treated and aged)	23,000	37,000	1.5
SC51B	T61 (solution treated and aged):			
	Separately cast specimens	30,000	40,000	3.0
	Castings, designated area	30,000	40,000	3.0
	Castings, no location designated[c]	30,000	37,000	1.0
SC64D	F (as cast)	14,000	27,000	2.5
	T61 (solution treated and aged)	24,000	40,000	2.0
SC103A	T5 (aged)	....	31,000	[b]
SC122A	T5 (aged)	26,000	32,000	[b]
	T65 (solution treated and aged)	37,000	42,000	[b]
SG70A	F (as cast)	....	21,000	3.0
	T6 (solution treated and aged)	22,000	33,000	3.0
	T71 (solution treated and overaged)	....	25,000	3.0
SG70B	T61 (solution treated and aged):			
	Separately cast specimens	26,000	38,000	5.0
	Castings, designated area[c]	26,000	38,000	5.0
	Castings, no location designated[c]	26,000	33,000	3.0
SN122A	T551 (aged)	....	31,000	[b]
	T65 (solution treated and aged)	....	40,000	[b]
ZC60A	T5[d]	18,000	28,000	7.0
ZC81B	T5[e]	22,000	32,000	4.0
ZG32A	T5[e]	17,000	37,000	10.0
ZG42A	T5[e]	25,000	42,000	4.0
	T7	35,000	45,000	3.0

* From ASTM Specification B108-62T. If agreed upon by the manufacturer and the purchaser, other mechanical properties may be obtained by other heat-treatments such as annealing, aging, or stress relieving.

[a] Yield strength to be evaluated only when specified in contract or purchase order.

[b] Not required.

[c] These properties apply only to castings having section thicknesses not over 2 in.

[d] Aged 21 days at room temperature.

[e] Aged 21 days at room temperature or artificially aged.

Table* 12.6 *Typical mechanical properties of aluminum-alloy die castings*

Alloy	Tensile strength, psi	Yield strength (0.2 per cent offset), psi	Elongation in 2 in., %	Shear strength, psi	Fatigue strength (R. R. Moore specimen), 500 million cycles, psi
G8A......	45,000	28,000	5	29,000	20,000
S5C......	33,000	14,000	9.0	19,000	17,000
S12A.....	42,000	19,000	3.5	25,000	19,000
S12B.....	43,000	21,000	2.5	25,000	19,000
SC84A....	47,000	23,000	3.5	27,000	20,000
SC84B....	46,000	23,000	2.5	28,000	20,000
SC114A...	48,000	24,000	2.5	29,000	20,000
SG100A...	46,000	24,000	3.5	26,000	18,000
SG100B...	44,000	25,000	2.5	28,000	20,000

* From ASTM Specification B85-60.

Table* 12.7 *Heat-treatments for some aluminum casting alloys*

Alloy No.	Solution heat-treatment			Aging		Typical Bhn	Description
	Temp, F	Time, hr	Quench	Time, hr	Temp, F		
C4A, sand-cast	960	12	Water, 150–212 F	.....	...	60	Solution heat-treated, T4
	960	12	Water, 150–212 F	3–5	310	75	Solution heat-treated
	960	12	Water, 150–212 F	12–16	310	95	and aged, T6 and T62
CN42A, sand-cast	Omitted	..	....	2–4	650	70	Annealed, T21
CG100A, permanent-mold cast	950	12	Water, 150–212 F	5–7	310	100	Solution heat-treated and aged, T52
	950	12	Water, 150–212 F	5–7	340	140	Solution heat-treated and aged, T65
	950	12	Water, 150–212 F	18–22	340	115	Solution heat-treated and aged, T551
	Omitted	..	....	2–4	600	80	Annealed, T2
SG70A, sand-cast	1000	12	Water, 150–212 F	2–5	310	70	Solution heat-treated and aged, T6
permanent mold	1000	12	Water, 150–212 F	3–5	310	90	Solution heat-treated and aged, T6

* Adapted from American Society for Metals.[1]

maximum strength and hardness, aging treatments must be used after solution heat-treatment. Table 12.7 also gives typical aging treatments. The properties and casting dimensions are more stable after aging. In the case of some permanent-mold and die castings, only aging is utilized for stress relief and property improvement.

Annealing. Annealing may be accomplished by heating the castings to about 650 F for 1 to 4 hr and then air or furnace cooling. Maximum ductility and low hardness and strength are then obtained. However, the casting dimensions and properties will be most stable. In the unannealed condition, Al-Si alloys can grow 0.0016 in. per in. because of gradual precipitation of silicon from the aluminum-rich solution promoted by die and permanent-mold castings. Dimensional changes of this order can be objectionable but can be avoided by heating at 400 to 450 F for 10 to 20 hr.

Foundry variables and heat-treatment. As with other properties, the results of heat-treatments are susceptible to the foundry history of the alloy. For example, in Table 12.7 the hardness after heat-treatment of alloy SG70A is shown to be dependent on the casting process. The permanent-mold cast alloy has a Brinell hardness number (Bhn) of 90 as compared with 70 for the same alloy sand-cast even though both receive the same heat-treatment. Hence the heat-treatment used must account for the influence of foundry variables and be adjusted to develop the desired properties.

Other Mechanical Properties

The properties of shear strength, endurance limit, and compressive strength are of importance in some applications. Endurance limits of 6500 to 10,000 psi based on 500 million cycles with the R. R. Moore type of testing equipment are common for many aluminum casting alloys. Shear strengths of 16,000 to 32,000 psi are obtained, being higher in heat-treated alloys and generally increasing with the yield and tensile strengths. Compressive yield strengths of 10,000 to 46,000 psi are developed, the higher values always being obtained in the higher-tensile-strength alloys. Young's modulus of 10,300,000 psi, modulus of rigidity of 3,850,000 psi, and Poisson's ratio of 0.33 apply to most alloys. Specific values for these properties may be obtained for some alloys from Refs. 1 and 5.

Importance of Test Bars

Because the mechanical properties of aluminum alloys are markedly influenced by the casting process, it is necessary that mechanical-property tests be made on test bars representative of the casting process. A typical sand-cast tensile test bar is illustrated in Fig. 12.10. A setup for casting permanent-mold test bars is illustrated in Fig. 12.11. A number of other factors such as pouring rate, mold temperature, metal temperature, and time in the mold, all affecting cooling rate, have been found to alter the properties.[6] Hence it is evident that any evaluation of the mechanical properties of an aluminum alloy used for casting purposes requires careful attention to the details of obtaining a representative test bar (Fig. 12.12).

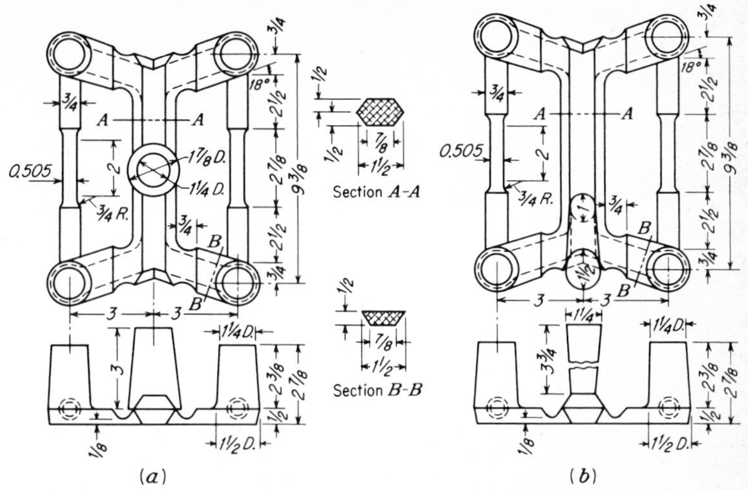

Fig. **12.10** Drawings of two test-bar castings with different gating systems. (*Courtesy of the Aluminum Company of America.*)

Fig. **12.11** Equipment setup and mold for casting permanent-mold test bars. (*From L. J. Ebert, R. E. Spear, and G. Sachs.*[6])

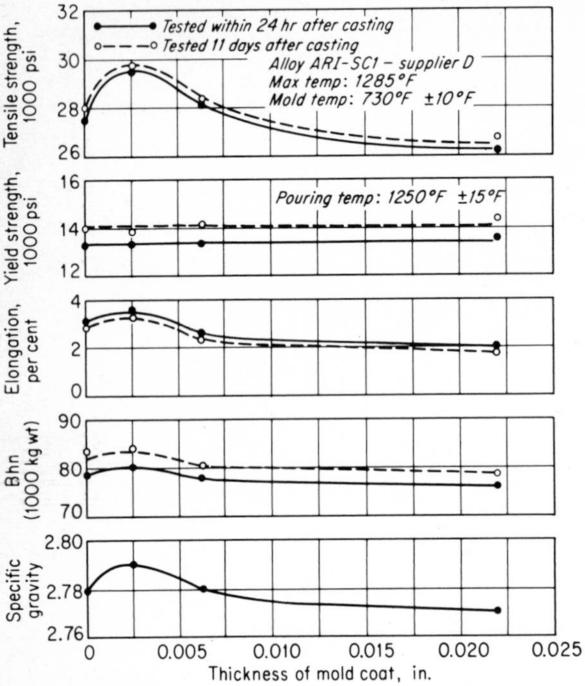

***Fig.* 12.12** Effect of the thickness of permanent-mold coating on the properties of an aluminum alloy. (*From L. J. Ebert, R. E. Spear, and G. Sachs.*[6])

Corrosion Resistance

Resistance to many types of corrosion is an important virtue of aluminum alloys in many applications. Cooking utensils, food containers, food-processing equipment, and outboard motors operate in a variety of corrosive media. Important differences exist in corrosion resistance of the various alloys, and they are rather simply rated in Tables 12.1 to 12.3. The magnesium-aluminum alloys, types G4A, G10A, and GS42A, have been found most favorable in this respect. Next-best types are ZG and ZC, zinc-magnesium-aluminum and zinc-copper-aluminum alloys. Poorest are the alloys containing substantial percentages of copper. It should be recognized that these ratings are based on salt-spray corrosion tests. Corrosion resistance is an extremely complicated property, and actual field tests are necessary to establish the true behavior of the alloy in specific applications.

Processing Properties

Only certain of the aluminum casting alloys are suitable for welding or brazing, as indicated in Tables 12.1 to 12.3. Fabrication by joining castings or castings and structural shapes is thus limited to those alloys.

Machinability of most of the aluminum alloys is excellent. In general, the high-copper-content alloys have better machinability whereas the high-silicon-content alloys have poorer machinability. Specific machining practices are given in Ref. 7.

Surface Treatments

Several surface treatments may be applied to aluminum castings. Anodizing to obtain a bright silvery luster may be performed. The cleaned casting is immersed for 15 to 45 min in an electrolyte of 15 to 18 per cent H_2SO_4 as the anode at 14 to 30 volts and a current density of 12 to 15 amp per sq ft. A chemical coating may be obtained by dipping the cleaned casting in a solution of 2 per cent sodium carbonate–0.10 per cent potassium dichromate at 160 to 180 F. Either the anodized or chemical coatings may be sealed for added corrosion resistance by dipping in hot 5 per cent potassium dichromate. Maximum protection from corrosion can be obtained if the sealed casting is then painted. Other treatments such as polishing and electroplating are possible, but their consideration is outside the scope of this text. However, Tables 12.1 to 12.3 indicate the relative response of the various alloys to these treatments.

ALUMINUM-ALLOY CASTING PROPERTIES

The production of good castings requires that the casting alloys possess favorable foundry properties. Those considered of importance for aluminum casting alloys are:

1. Minimum solidification shrinkage (and maximum yield)
2. Adequate fluidity
3. Freedom from hot tearing or cracking
4. Minimum difficulty in producing pressuretight castings
5. Minimum problems with gas absorption and drossing

The metallurgical principles relating to these properties have been discussed in Chap. 8. However, some of the more notable effects in aluminum alloys are briefly considered.

Shrinkage

Shrinkage problems are at a minimum in the Si-Al alloys containing 5 or 13 per cent Si according to Tables 12.1 to 12.3. Accordingly, foundry yield is at a maximum, and difficulties with hot tearing and microporosity are minimized. It may be noted in the tables that alloys having low shrinkage tendencies accompanied by a narrow freezing temperature have the better ratings of resistance to tearing, pressuretightness, and fluidity. This follows the general principle related to solidification mechanisms described in Chap. 8. Rated second to the Si-Al alloys are the high-silicon–low-copper-aluminum alloys, the SC types. Because of their favorable casting properties, the silicon-rich aluminum alloys are extensively used for permanent-mold and die castings. Percentages of 5, 7, 9, and 12% Si are used in combination with other elements for castings made by the metal-mold processes. Since most of the same alloys can be heat-treated, it is evident that this class of alloys is good for general-purpose use.

Patternmakers' shrinkage for the various alloys is given in Table 12.1. A low value of patternmakers' shrinkage, however, does not mean that the shrinkage problems of microporosity, pressuretightness, and cracking will be low. The mechanism of freezing rather than the total contraction is a dominant factor in the latter problem. For example, alloy G10A having a long freezing range is troublesome in leaktightness, even though its pattern shrinkage is a minimum.[13]

Fluidity

Few quantitative studies have been reported of the fluidity of aluminum alloys using fluidity spirals of the type described in Chap. 8. A ribbon-type spiral has been used successfully and is reported in Ref. 8. However, the generalized ratings reported in the tables are based primarily on foundry experience in running thin and intricate sections in practical castings. The silicon-rich alloys favor fluidity and resistance to tearing. Table 12.3 shows that most all die-casting alloys are silicon-rich alloys. Figure 12.13 illustrates a variety of die castings which require fluidity and tearing resistance if they are to be successfully cast. Thus it appears that silicon improves many of the casting properties of the aluminum alloys. This appears to be the reason that the general-purpose casting alloys contain substantial amounts of silicon, along with smaller percentages of copper or other elements.

Drossing and Gas Absorption

The drossing problems of the different alloys vary somewhat. The more oxidizable element, magnesium, causes extensive drossing in the high-magnesium-content alloys G4A, G10A, and GS42A. Gas absorption, the dissolving of hydrogen, has been said to be more serious in some of the alloys. However, the few experimental results available seem to indicate

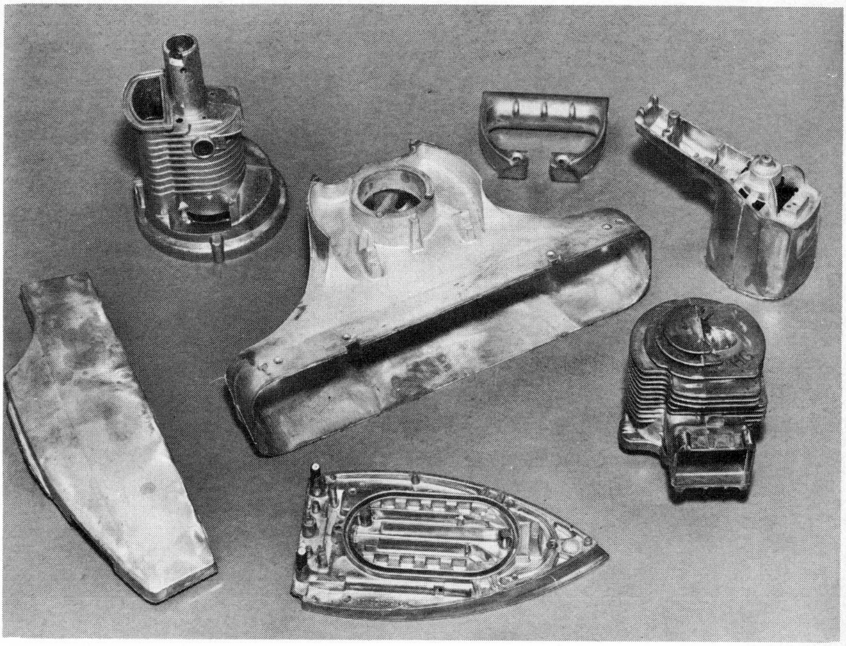

Fig. **12.13** Aluminum-alloy die castings. (*Courtesy of the Aluminum Company of America.*)

that alloying elements decrease the solubility of hydrogen in aluminum.[16] Even the most troublesome alloys can be safely cast if good melting, pouring, and other foundry practices are followed.

Pressuretightness

Absence of leakage of fluids, especially those under pressure, is a requirement of some casting applications. Pump housings, valve bodies, and pipe manifolds are examples. Leakage of fluids through the casting walls may occur as a result of two different defects in the metal, namely:

1. Highly localized cavities extending through the leaking section. Gross unfed solidification shrinkage is the usual reason for this defect. An improvement in gating and risering or other foundry practice can eliminate these leakers.
2. Dispersed cavities which, when interconnected, permit gradual passage of the fluid through the casting walls. This type of leakage is more difficult to cure. Often it is related to the alloy type and the design of the casting. The alloys G4A and G10A (magnesium) are especially troublesome in showing dispersed or fine leakage, whereas the silicon-rich alloys, S, SC, and

SG types, are less difficult to cast leaktight.[14] Dispersed shrinkage is reduced to a minimum in any alloy type by pouring at a minimum temperature (1250 F), making every effort to obtain directional solidification, proper gating and metal flow, and use of the best melting practices.

Leaks may be detected by pressure testing. Air pressure, 40 to 90 psi, is applied to the casting, and it is immersed in warm soapy water or sprayed with a warm soap solution (1.6 oz neutral soap per gallon of water). If leaks are found, measures may be taken to seal them. In spite of the best of foundry practices, *leakers** occur and many may be made usable by sealing. Indeed, sealing is almost a necessity for certain combinations of casting designs and casting alloys to produce leakproof castings even with the best foundry practices.

Sealing

The simplest sealing method for localized leakage is peening. The area may be hammered to close up the leak. Impregnation is necessary where dispersed leakage is found. Impregnation consists in causing a liquid to penetrate the shrinkage holes. After being forced into the cavities, the liquid turns into a solid. Commonly used impregnants are:[14]

1. Sodium silicate
2. Drying oils: tung, linseed oil, etc.
3. Various types of synthetic resins

Castings may be immersed in a sodium silicate solution (30 to 40 Bé, 65 F) at 150 to 200 F for 2 to 4 hr. They are then washed and air-dried or baked at 215 to 300 F. Castings which are to be aged may be baked during the aging treatment. The silicate can be more effctively applied with pressure. In this case, the casting is closed off, except for one opening, the silicate solution is introduced to its interior, and then air pressure, about 30 psi, is applied. Pressure silicating may also be performed on small castings by immersing them in silicate solutions contained in pressure tanks. After pressure silicating, the castings are air-dried or baked.

Various types of synthetic resins may be used as sealers using methods similar to those described above.[14]

It should be recognized that sealing and impregnation are not substitutes for correct aluminum-foundry practice. Rather, they are methods of handling problem castings that are difficult to produce pressuretight by other means.

* Castings which are not pressuretight.

MAGNESIUM CASTING ALLOYS

Certain types of magnesium alloys have been found most suitable for casting purposes. These have been adopted by the ASTM as standard alloys, and are listed in Tables 12.8 to 12.10. The principal alloy systems in these tables include:

1. Magnesium having aluminum and manganese as the principal alloying elements, designated type AM
2. Magnesium having aluminum and zinc as the principal alloying elements, designated type AZ
3. Magnesium having rare earths and zirconium present, including types EK, EZ, and ZE
4. Magnesium having zinc and zirconium as the principal alloying elements, designated type ZK
5. Magnesium having thorium and zirconium as the principal alloying elements, including types HK, HZ, and ZH

Other magnesium alloys are also cast, but the five systems above have attained more widespread use.

Table* 12.8*a* *Sand-cast magnesium alloys, composition and specifications*

ASTM Alloy Specification B80-62	Nominal composition, %						Similar specifications for comparative purposes		
	Al	Zn	RE†	Zr	Th	Mn	Federal	SAE	AMS‡
AM100A....	10.0	....	....	.....	....	0.10 min			
AZ63A......	6.0	3.0	....	.....	....	0.15 min	QQ-M-56	50	4420
AZ81A......	7.5	0.7	....	.....	....	0.13 min			
AZ91C......	8.7	0.7	....	.....	....	0.13 min	QQ-M-56		
AZ92A......	9.0	2.0	....	.....	....	0.10 min	QQ-M-56	500	4434
EZ33A......	.....	2.6	3.3	0.75					
HK31A......	.....	0.3 max	....	0.70	3.3				
HZ32A......	.....	2.1	0.1 max	0.75	3.3				
K1A........	.....	....	....	0.70					
QE22A§	.....	....	2.2¶	0.70					
ZE41A......	.....	4.3	1.3	0.70	....	0.15 max			
ZH62A......	.....	5.7	....	0.75	1.8				
ZK51A......	.....	4.6	....	0.75					
ZK61A......	.....	6.0	....	0.80					

* From AFS Light Metals Division[18] and ASTM Specification B80-62. For specific compositions refer to applicable specifications.

† RE stands for total rare-earth-metal content, usually misch-metal content.

‡ Aeronautical Materials Specifications.

§ Silver content for alloy QE22A shall be 2.0 to 3.0.

¶ Rare-earth elements are in the form of didymium.

The alloying behavior of the various elements in magnesium is similar in principle to that described in the case of the aluminum alloys. Reference 1 may be studied for details, and an excellent consideration of the metallurgical principles is provided in Ref. 20. Only differences important to casting applications of the alloys are considered here.

Table 12.8b Sand-cast magnesium alloys, properties and characteristics*

Alloy	Melting range, approximate, °F			Pattern shrinkage allowance, in./ft[b]	Foundry characteristics[c]				Other characteristics[e]				
	Nonequilibrium solidus[a]	Solidus	Liquidus		Pressure-tightness	Fluidity[d]	Microporosity tendency[e]	Normally heat-treated	Machining[f]	Electroplating[g]	Surface treatment[h]	Suitability to brazing[i]	Suitability to welding[j]
AM100A	810	867	1100	5/32	2	2	2	Yes	1	2	2	No	1
AZ63A	685	850	1130	5/32	3	1	3	Yes	1	1	1	No	3
AZ81A	790	882	1115	5/32	2	1	2	Yes	1	2	2	No	1
AZ91C	785	875	1105	5/32	2	1	2	Yes	1	2	2	No	2
AZ92A	770	830	1100	5/32	2	1	2	Yes	1	2	2	No	2
EZ33A	.....	1010	1189	3/16	1	2	1	Yes	1	2	1	No	1
HK31A	.....	1092	1204	7/32	1	2	1	Yes	1	2	1	[k]	1
HZ32A	.....	1026	1198	3/16	1	2	1	Yes	1	[k]	2	[k]	2
QE22A	.....	1020	1190	5/32	2	2	2	Yes	1	2	1	No	1
ZE41A	.....	......	......	.....	[k]	2	[k]	Yes	1	1	1	No	[k]
ZH62A	.....	......	1169	5/32	2	2	2	Yes	1	1	1	No	[k]
ZK51A	.....	1020	1185	5/32	3	2	2	Yes	1	2	1	No	3
ZK61A	.....	985	1175	5/32	3	2	2	Yes	1	2	1	No	3

* From ASTM Specification B80-62.

[a] As measured on metal solidified under normal casting conditions.

[b] Allowance for average castings. Shrinkage requirements will vary with intricacy of design and dimensions.

[c] Rating of 1 indicates best of group; 3 indicates poorest of group.

[d] Ability of liquid alloy to flow readily in mold and fill thin sections.

[e] Based on radiographic evidence.

[f] Composite rating based on ease of cutting, chip characteristics, quality of finish, and tool life. Ratings, in the case of heat-treatable alloys, based on T6-type temper. Other tempers, particularly the annealed temper, may have lower rating.

[g] Ability of casting to take and hold an electroplate applied by present standard methods.

[h] Ability of castings to be cleaned in standard pickle solutions and to be conditioned for best paint adhesion.

[i] Refers to suitability of alloy to withstand brazing temperature without excessive distortion or melting.

[j] Based on ability of material to be fusion-welded with filler rod of same alloy.

[k] Inexperience with these alloys under wide production conditions makes it undesirable to supply ratings at this time.

The AZ-type alloys were the first extensively used for magnesium castings. They still account for the principal quantity of castings for general-purpose use. The castability of these alloys is good. AZ91 and AZ81 are gradually replacing AZ63, and are widely used where good ductility and moderately high yield strength are required up to 350 F. These alloys have high yield strength, making them suitable for aircraft landing wheels, levers and linkages, housings, etc. The ZK and ZH

Table* 12.8c *Sand-cast magnesium alloys, tensile requirements*

Alloy	Condition	Tensile strength, min, psi	Yield strength (0.2 per cent offset), min, psi	Elongation in 2 in., min, %
AM100A	T6 (solution heat-treated and artificially aged)	35,000	17,000	†
AZ63A	F (as cast)	26,000	11,000	4
	T4 (solution heat-treated)	34,000	11,000	7
	T5 (artificially aged only)	26,000	12,000	2
	T6 (solution heat-treated and artificially aged)	34,000	16,000	3
AZ81A	T4 (solution heat-treated)	34,000	11,000	7
AZ91C	F (as cast)	23,000	11,000	†
	T4 (solution heat-treated)	34,000	11,000	7
	T5 (artificially aged only)	23,000	12,000	2
	T6 (solution heat-treated and artificially aged)	34,000	16,000	3
AZ92A	F (as cast)	23,000	11,000	†
	T4 (solution heat-treated)	34,000	11,000	6
	T5 (artificially aged only)	23,000	12,000	†
	T6 (solution heat-treated and artificially aged)	34,000	18,000	1
EZ33A	T5 (artificially aged only)	20,000	14,000	2
HK31A	T6 (solution heat-treated and artificially aged)	27,000	13,000	4
HZ32A	T5 (artificially aged only)	27,000	13,000	4
K1A	F (as cast)	24,000	6,000	14
QE22A	T6 (solution heat-treated and artificially aged)	35,000	25,000	2
ZE41A	T5 (artificially aged only)	28,000	19,000	2.5
ZH62A	T5 (artificially aged only)	35,000	22,000	5
ZK51A	T5 (artificially aged only)	34,000	20,000	5
ZK61A	T6 (solution heat-treated and artificially aged)	39,000	26,000	5

*From ASTM Specification B80-62.
†Not required.

Table 12.9a Permanent-mold cast magnesium alloys, composition and specifications*

ASTM Alloy Specification B199-62	Nominal composition, %						Similar specifications for comparative purposes		
	Al	Zn	Re	Zr	Th	Mn	Federal	SAE	AMS
AM100A	10.0	....	....	....	....	0.10	QQ-M-55	502	
AZ81A	7.5	0.7	....	....	....	0.13 min			
AZ91C	8.7	0.7	....	....	....	0.13			
AZ92A	9.0	2.0	....	....	....	0.10	QQ-M-55	503	4484
EZ33A	....	2.6	3.3	0.75					
HK31A	....	0.3 max	....	0.70	3.3				
QE22A†	....	....	2.2‡	0.70					

* From AFS Light Metals Division[18] and ASTM Specification B199-62. For specific compositions refer to applicable specifications.

† Silver content of QE22A shall be 2.0 to 3.0.

‡ Rare-earth elements are in the form of didymium.

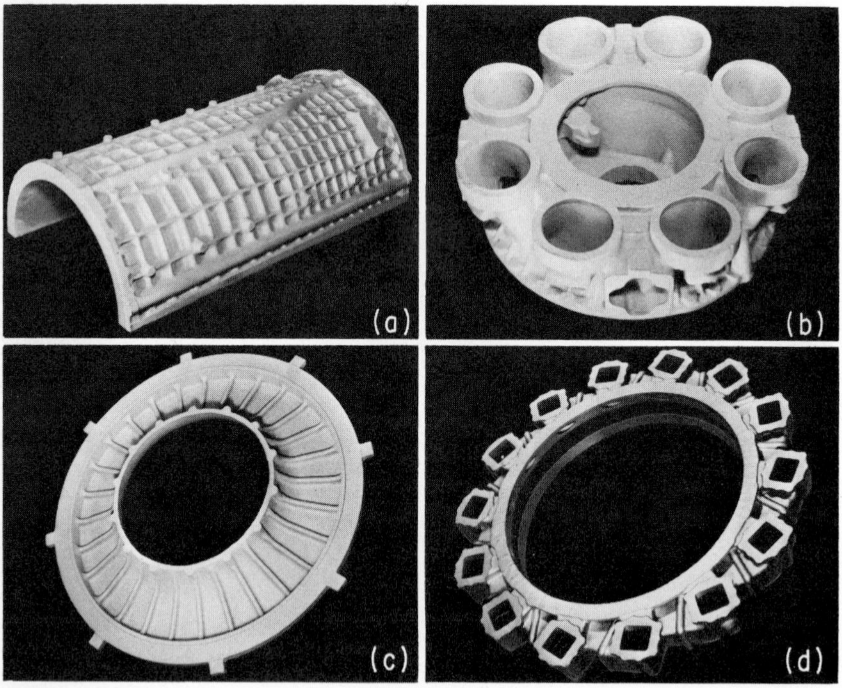

***Fig.* 12.14** Magnesium-alloy, EK30, aircraft-engine castings which operate at elevated temperatures. (*From K. E. Nelson and F. P. Strieter.*[22])

alloys develop the highest yield strength of the casting alloys, and they can be cast into complicated shapes. These grades, however, are more costly than the AZ series. Magnesium–rare earth–zirconium alloys are used at temperatures between 350 and 500 F since they are able to resist deterioration of strength from extended exposure to these elevated temperatures. These alloys may be used for elevated-temperature housings in jet-engine and other aircraft castings. Typical castings are shown in Fig. 12.14. The magnesium-thorium-zirconium alloys are intended for use at temperatures of 400 F and higher. These alloys have been used at temperatures up to 650 and 700 F for a few applications.

Table* 12.9*b* *Permanent-mold cast magnesium alloys, properties and characteristics*

Alloy	Melting range, approximate °F			Foundry characteristics[a]				Other characteristics[a]				
	Nonequilibrium[b] solidus	Solidus	Liquidus	Pressure-tightness	Fluidity[c]	Microporosity tendency[d]	Normally heat-treated	Machining[e]	Electro-plating[f]	Surface treatment[g]	Suitability to brazing[h]	Suitability to welding[i]
AM100A	810	867	1100	2	1	2	Yes	1	1	2	No	1
AZ81A	790	882	1115	2	1	2	Yes	1	2	2	No	1
AZ91C	785	875	1105	2	1	2	Yes	1	1	2	No	2
AZ92A	770	830	1100	3	1	3	Yes	1	1	2	No	2
EZ33A	.....	1010	1189	1	2	1	Yes	1	1	1	No	1
HK31A	.....	1092	1204	1	2	1	Yes	1	2	1	[j]	1
QE22A	.....	1020	1190	2	2	2	Yes	1	2	1	No	1

* From ASTM Specification B199-62.

[a] Rating of 1 indicates best of group; 3 indicates poorest of group.

[b] As measured on metal solidified under normal casting conditions.

[c] Ability of liquid alloy to flow readily in mold and fill thin sections.

[d] Based on radiographic evidence.

[e] Composite rating based on ease of cutting, chip characteristics, quality of finish, and tool life. Ratings, in the case of heat-treatable alloys, based on T6-type temper. Other tempers, particularly the annealed temper, may have lower rating.

[f] Ability of casting to take and hold an electroplate applied by present standard methods.

[g] Ability of castings to be cleaned in standard pickle solutions and to be conditioned for best paint adhesion.

[h] Refers to suitability of alloy to withstand brazing temperature without excessive distortion or melting.

[i] Based on ability of material to be fusion-welded with filler rod of same alloy.

[j] Inexperience with this alloy under wide production conditions makes it undesirable to supply a rating at this time.

Table* 12.9*c* Permanent-mold cast magnesium alloys, tensile requirements

Alloy	Condition	Tensile strength, min, psi	Yield strength (0.2% offset), min, psi	Elongation in 2 in., min, %
AM100A..	F (as cast)	20,000	†	†
	T4 (solution heat-treated)	34,000	.	6
	T61 (solution heat-treated and artificially aged to full hardness)	34,000	17,000	†
	T6 (solution heat-treated and artificially aged to intermediate hardness)	34,000	15,000	2
AZ81A....	T4 (solution heat-treated)	34,000	11,000	7
AZ91C....	F (as cast)	18,000	10,000	†
	T5 (artificially aged only)	20,000	11,000	2
	T4 (solution heat-treated)	34,000	11,000	7
	T6 (solution heat-treated and artificially aged)	34,000	16,000	3
AZ92A....	F (as cast)	20,000	10,000	†
	T5 (artificially aged only)	20,000	11,000	†
	T4 (solution heat-treated)	34,000	11,000	6
	T6 (solution heat-treated and artificially aged)	34,000	18,000	†
EZ33A....	T5 (artificially aged only)	20,000	14,000	2
HK31A...	T6 (solution heat-treated and artificially aged)	27,000	13,000	4
QE22A....	T6 (solution heat-treated and artificially aged)	35,000	25,000	2

* From ASTM Specification B199-62.
† Not required.

Table* 12.10*a* Die-cast magnesium alloys, composition and specifications

ASTM Alloy Specification B94-58	Nominal composition, %				Similar specifications for comparative purposes		
	Al	Zn	Mn	Cu	Federal	SAE	AMS
AZ91A........	9.0	0.7	0.13 min	0.10 max	QQ-M-38	501	4490
AZ91B........	9.0	0.7	0.13 min	0.35 max	....	501A	

* From ASTM Specification B94-58. For specific compositions refer to applicable specifications.

Table* 12.10*b* *Die-cast magnesium alloys, typical properties*

	Alloys AZ91A and AZ91B
Tensile strength, 1000 psi	32–36
Tensile yield strength, 1000 psi	22–24
Compression yield strength, 1000 psi	22–24
Elongation in 2 in., %	2–5
Impact, ft-lb†	2
Shear strength, 1000 psi‡	20
Fatigue strength, 1000 psi§	14
Brinell hardness	63
Rockwell hardness, E scale	75

* From ASTM Specification B94-58.
† Unnotched.
‡ Double-shear tests converted to single-shear value.
§ 5×10^8 cycles.

Casting properties of the alloys are rated in Tables 12.8 and 12.9. Differences in tendency for hot cracking, pressuretightness, microporosity, etc., that the tables show are based on foundry experience with making castings of the various alloys. It might be noted that alloy AZ63A is one with a long freezing temperature and is rated as one of the poorer casting alloys. The alloys with substantially higher solidus temperatures are the ones with better high-temperature properties.

Heat-treatment[21]

All but a few of the alloys in Tables 12.8 to 12.10 can be profitably solution heat-treated and aged. Conditions for heat-treatment are given in Table 12.11. Solution heat-treatment may be started at 300 to 500 F, raising the temperature to the heat-treating temperaure in about 2 to 3 hr. An addition of about 1% SO_2 to the heat-treating-furnace atmosphere is required to prevent burning of the castings, since it appears that the ignition point of magnesium is about 700 F without the SO_2 in the atmosphere. After solution heat-treatment, the castings are quenched by cooling in still air or by an air blast. Stabilizing heat-treatment (Table 12.11) is used to prevent growth or distortion of solution heat-treated castings. Solution heat-treatment may be followed by aging, as indicated in Table 12.11, when it is desired to develop maximum yield and tensile strengths with reduced ductility. Heat-treatment symbols T4, T6, and T7 stand for solution heat-treatment, solution treatment plus aging, and solution heat-treatment plus stabilizing, respectively, as shown in Table 12.11. The same designations are used in Tables 12.8 and 12.9.

Table* 12.11 *Typical heat-treating schedules for magnesium casting alloys*

Alloy	Solution heat-treatment (T4)†		Aging after solution heat-treatment (T6)		Stabilizing after solution heat-treatment (T7)		Stabilizing treatment (T2)	
	Time, hr	Temp, F	Time, hr	Temp, F	Time, hr	Temp, F	Time, hr	Temp, F
A10	18–24	780–800	10–12	325–400	4	500		
AZ92	18–22‡	760–775	5–15	400–425	4	500		
AZ91C	18–20‡	775–790	3–5	400–425	4	500		
AZ63	10–15§	720–740	5–15	400–425	4	500		
ZK61	2	930	48–72	300				
ZK51	.....	....	.....	....	..	...	12	350
EZ33	.....	....	.....	....	..	...	12	350
EK30A	16	1050	16	400				

* From E. G. Gingerich.[19]

† Castings are brought up to holding temperature at uniform rate of temperature rise in approximately 2 hr before treatment at times and temperatures shown.

‡ The step of interrupted-cycle heat-treatment described in the text may be necessary to prevent germination.[21]

§ This treatment is usually preceded by heating to 650 F in 2 hr, holding for 2 hr, and heating to heat-treating temperature in 2 hr to prevent eutectic melting.

OTHER CASTING ALLOYS

Other important applications of casting alloys available to engineers are nickel-base alloys; heat- and corrosion-resistant alloys; zinc-, tin-, and lead-base alloys; titanium-base alloys; and alloy groups listed earlier in the text. The volume of these alloys produced is far smaller than that of the other alloys covered in this book. This does not indicate that they are less important, but rather that their cost and characteristic properties suit them best for certain applications which the more widely used alloys cannot satisfy. The interested reader is referred to the bibliography for this chapter for technical literature dealing with these casting alloys.

BIBLIOGRAPHY

1. American Society for Metals, "Metals Handbook," 1948.
2. American Society for Metals, "Physical Metallurgy of Aluminum Alloys," 1949.
3. ASTM Standards, Metallic Materials, Nonferrous, Specification B26-50T, Aluminum Base Alloys for Sand Castings; B108-50T, Permanent Mold Castings; B86-60T, Die Castings.
4. AFS Aluminum and Magnesium Division, Aluminum Alloy Characteristics, *Am. Foundryman*, vol. 22, p. 56, November, 1952.

5. American Foundrymen's Society, "Cast Metals Handbook," 4th ed., 1944.
6. L. J. Ebert, R. E. Spear, and G. Sachs, The Development of a Permanent Mold for Aluminum Tensile Test Bars, *Trans. AFS,* vol. 56, 1948.
7. Aluminum Co. of America, "Machining Aluminum and Its Alloys," 1952.
8. W. E. Sicha and R. C. Boehm, A Fluidity Test for Aluminum Casting Alloys, *Trans. AFS,* vol. 56, 1948.
9. D. A. La Velle, Aluminum Sand Casting Defects: Their Identification, Causes, and Corrections, *Trans. AFS,* vol. 60, 1952.
10. E. E. Stonebrook and W. E. Sicha, Correlation of Cooling Curve Data with Casting Characteristics of Aluminum Alloys, *Trans. AFS,* vol. 57, 1949.
11. W. Bonsack, High Strength Non-heat-treated Aluminum Casting Alloys, *Trans. AFS,* vol. 60, 1952.
12. R. A. Quadt and E. C. Reichard, Corrosion and Stress Corrosion of a High Strength Al-Zn-Mg-Cu Casting Alloy, *Trans. AFS,* vol. 58, 1950.
13. R. A. Quadt and J. J. Adams, Effect of Mg on Al-Cu-Si Casting Alloys, *Foundry,* vol. 77, July, 1949.
14. E. V. Blackmun, Impregnation of Aluminum and Magnesium Castings, *Trans. AFS,* vol. 55, 1947.
15. R. H. Heyer, "Engineering Physical Metallurgy," D. Van Nostrand Company, Inc., Princeton, N.J., 1939.
16. W. R. Opie and N. J. Grant, Hydrogen Solubility in Aluminum and Some Aluminum Alloys, *J. Metals,* vol. 188, p. 1237, October, 1950.
17. R. H. Dyke, Modification of Al-Si Alloys, *Trans. AFS,* vol. 59, p. 28, 1951.
18. AFS Light Metals Division, Magnesium Alloy Characteristics, *Am. Foundryman,* vol. 23, p. 156, April, 1953.
19. E. G. Gingerich, Heat Treatment of Magnesium Alloy Castings, *Trans. AFS,* vol. 60, p. 641, 1952.
20. R. M. Brick, B. Gordon, and Arthur Phillips, "Structure and Properties of Alloys," 3d ed., McGraw-Hill Book Company, New York, 1965.
21. R. C. Cornell, Die Casting Magnesium Alloys, *Trans. AFS,* vol. 59, p. 398, 1951.
22. K. E. Nelson and F. P. Strieter, Casting of Magnesium–Rare Earth–Zirconium Alloys in Sand Molds, *Trans. AFS,* vol. 58, p. 400, 1950.
23. R. C. Lemon and H. Y. Hunsicker, New Aluminum Permanent Mold Casting Alloys C355 and A356, *Trans. AFS,* vol. 64, p. 255, 1956.
24. R. C. Lemon and C. R. Howle, Premium Strength Aluminum Casting Alloys 354 and 359, *Trans. AFS,* vol. 71, 1963.
25. K. E. Nelson and F. P. Strieter, A Castability and Property Comparison of Several Magnesium–Rare Earth–Sand Casting Alloys, *Trans. AFS,* vol. 59, p. 532, 1951.
26. J. W. Meier and M. W. Martinson, Development of High-strength Magnesium Casting Alloy ZK61, *Trans. AFS,* vol. 58, p. 742, 1950.
27. D. W. Grobecker, An Investigation of Melting and Casting Procedures for High Purity Nickel, *Trans. AFS,* vol. 58, p. 720, 1950.
28. International Nickel Co., "Heat Resistant and Corrosion Resistant Castings in Industry," 1952.
29. The New Jersey Zinc Co., "Die Casting for Engineers," 1946.
30. H. H. Doehler, "Die Casting," McGraw-Hill Book Company, New York, 1951.
31. J. W. Smith and T. A. Hamm, Factors Contributing to the Soundness of Titanium Castings, *Trans. AFS,* vol. 68, p. 337, 1960.
32. G. D. Chandley and D. G. Flack, Uranium Foundry Practice, *Foundry,* February, 1960, p. 76.
33. American Society for Metals, "Metals Handbook," 8th ed., vol. 1, 1961.

13

Copper-alloy Foundry Practice

Historically, copper-alloy castings were among the earliest metallic objects made by man from molten metal. Since copper could be found as native metal, it has been worked into artifacts, far back into antiquity. Its melting point and that of its alloys with gold, tin, and zinc are low enough to be within the range of temperatures which can be reached by wood and charcoal fires. Copper melting and casting by artisans are known to have occurred as early as 3000 B.C. The full value of copper alloys as casting materials, however, had to await the metallurgical developments of the past several hundred years, discoveries which made the metal more abundant, with a greater variety of useful properties. Foundry-production data for copper-alloy castings during the past few years are presented in Table 13.1. It may be noted that sand-casting processes account for the greater percentage of castings produced in these alloys.

Advantages of Copper Alloys

Certain engineering advantages are inherent in the use of copper alloys for castings. Some of these include:

1. Electrical and thermal conductivity
2. Corrosion resistance
3. Appearance
4. Nontoxicity
5. Bearing qualities

Although the above items are all favorable to the use of copper-base casting alloys, it must be recognized that certain limitations prevail. Cost is a factor of great import, being sufficiently high so that copper-base castings are not used unless their special advantages, as listed above, present a real engineering or economic advantage over other metals. Figure 13.1 shows some characteristic uses of copper-base castings.

Table* 13.1 *Production of copper-base castings*

Year	Total	Sand	Permanent mold
1962	768,717	571,951	40,945
1961	730,094	639,031	39,246
1960	759,658	667,875	45,391
1959	871,032	765,246	52,456
1958	740,155	670,873	36,429
1957	875,389	788,319	44,696
1956	966,306	866,545	57,522
1955	1,011,748	907,852	82,201
1954	835,930	753,179	48,848
1953	993,750	892,126	61,211

* Thousands of pounds. Adapted from *Foundry*, Penton Publishing Co., Cleveland.

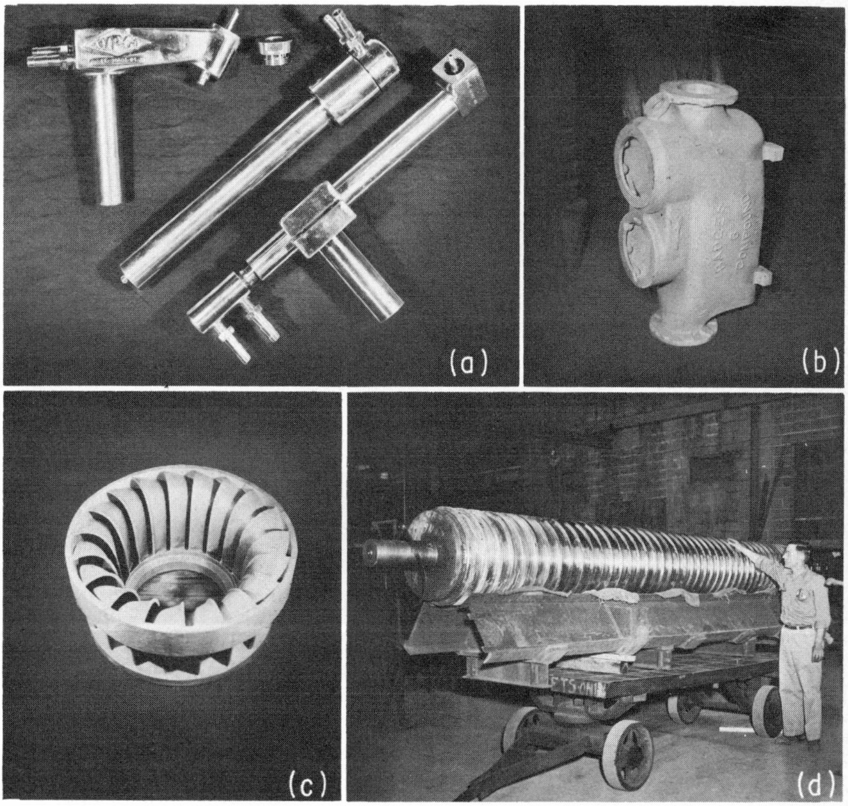

***Fig.* 13.1** Groups of nonferrous copper-base castings. (*a*) High-conductivity Cr-Cu ejector-type resistance-welding tip holders, (*b*) aluminum-bronze turbine runner, (*c*) tin-bronze water-meter housing, (*d*) aluminum-bronze idler roll. (*Courtesy of Ampco Metal, Inc.*)

MOLDING

Copper-base alloys may be cast by any of the processes: sand casting, permanent-mold and die casting, plaster molds, precision casting, etc. Because of the high specific gravity and intermediate pouring-temperature range, molds are affected by heat to a moderate degree, mold attrition being less than that caused by irons and steels but far more than caused by aluminum alloys. In fact, compared with aluminum, copper-alloy die casting can be accomplished only with a relatively few alloys, and is much more limited in casting shape, size, and number of castings which can be produced before the metal mold deteriorates. Cement-bonded sand molds are widely used for large castings such as ship-propeller castings. Propellers weighing up to 35,000 lb have been cast by this method with maximum dimensional variation of $\frac{1}{32}$ in. over the entire casting. Plaster molds are used for making small intricate castings, hardware, fittings, and also ornamental and statuary castings. Nearly all the copper-base alloys may be cast by the centrifugal process, with castings varying in size from a few ounces to over 50,000 lb, the latter being perforated cylinders for the wood-pulp and paper industry.[18] In general, however, green-sand molding accounts for the major quantity of castings of copper-base alloys.

Suggested dimensional tolerances for copper-base alloy castings produced by various molding methods are presented in Table 13.2.

Molding Sands

Molding sands employed for copper-base alloys vary somewhat, depending on the alloy type, weight, and section thickness of the casting. Some values for sand permeability, green strength, and moisture as related to casting weight and section thickness are listed in Table 13.3.

The unusual emphasis on permeability in Table 13.3 is due to the observable connection between that property and casting-surface finish. Many copper-alloy castings require excellent surface finish as cast. For example, plumbing fittings which are chromium-plated or must have accuracy, valves, for example, need good surface finish. Low-permeability sands have been found to give a more desirable finish. Of course, fine sand, AFS 120 to 270, will have a lower permeability than coarse sands when both are bonded with clay. However, fineness is not the only factor. Flowability is required so that a uniformly dense and smooth mold-cavity surface will be developed. Natural sands having a large proportion of fines and AFS clay seem to possess this flowability to a favorable degree. If a fine synthetic sand is overbonded with clay, it usually does not have flowability. Hence, even though it may be very fine, the latter sand does not produce a good finish because it does not pack (flow) well during molding. Its permeability will, of course, be high by comparison because of its lack of flowability.

Higher permeability may be required on the larger sizes of castings. Gas formation is more pronounced when the casting mass is large. Blows, pinholes, and similar gas defects can be more readily avoided in sands when permeability is higher and moisture lower (Table 13.3). Coarser sands may be required to achieve this end, with a consequent reduction in surface-finish quality. Furthermore, certain copper-base alloys require higher permeability. For instance, leaded nickel brasses and bronzes give trouble with pinholes under the casting skin and other gas-hole defects unless poured in molds of higher permeability than that listed in Table 13.3. The molding-sand permeability and other property requirements of the various copper-base casting alloys cast in different section sizes are set forth in Ref. 1 and Tables 13.3 and 13.4.

Facing materials may be used in copper-base sands to improve the surface finish of large castings. In some cases, cereal, flour, plumbago, or very fine sea coal may be added to a specially prepared facing sand. Plumbago, graphite, or flour may be dusted directly on the mold-cavity face to improve surface finish. Major emphasis for surface finish, however, is placed on the permeability and fineness of the sand itself.

Core Sands

Cores for copper-base castings are made by conventional methods, using core sands which are required to allow for the properties of these alloys. Hot tearing can occur if the cores are too hard and resistant to collapse after the metal is poured. Typical mixtures are given in Chap. 7. Core coatings employing graphite, mica, or other washes may be employed for smoother surfaces.

Gating

Gating of copper-base alloys involves many of the principles discussed in Chaps. 9, 11, and 20. In copper-base alloys, however, these principles have been largely applied through experience. Applications of ratio gating have not thus far been reported in the literature. In many small, thin, uniform section castings the runner and gates may also serve to feed the casting. Figure 13.2 shows a simple gating arrangement with the choke (minimum cross-sectional area) in the ingate. The choke controls the rate at which the casting can be filled and also makes removal of the gates during cleaning easier. Since all metal in the casting passes through the ingate, it is rapidly heated to the metal temperature. This fact causes it often to be the last part of the casting to freeze and makes it possible to feed the casting from the runner. An arrangement which

Table 13.2 ***Suggested dimensional tolerances for copper-alloy castings produced by various molding methods****

Sand mold	Shell mold	Permanent mold	Die casting	Plaster mold	Investment casting
TOLERANCE, PLUS OR MINUS, AVERAGE					
3/32 in./ft in general; optimum, 0.005 in./in.; as little as 0.005 in. total on some casting dimensions. Dry sand similar to or better than green sand	0.005 in./in.; as little as 0.003 in. total on some dimensions	0.015 in./in. for first inch. Add 0.001 to 0.002 in. for each additional inch. May be reduced to ±0.010 in. total in some castings	0.003 in./in.; 0.005 in. min	0.005 in./in. or less	0.002 in./in. min; 0.005 in./in. avg on dimensions over 1 in.
TOLERANCE ACROSS PARTING LINE					
Add 0.010 in. to above for green sand	Add 0.005 to 0.015 in. to above	Add 0.010 to 0.020 in. to above	Add 0.003 to 0.010 in. to above	Add 0.010 in. to above or total of 0.010 in./in.	Add 0.001 in./in. to above
TOLERANCE BETWEEN POINTS PRODUCED BY ONE PART OF MOLD, MIN					
3/32 in.	0.003 in.	0.010 in.	0.005 in.	0.005 in.	0.002 in.
TOLERANCE BETWEEN POINTS PRODUCED BY CORE AND MOLD, MIN					
3/32 in.	. . . .	. . . .	0.017 in.		
OUTSIDE DRAFT					
1/2° min.	0° with 2 in. max draw	2° min	1° min	1 1/2° min	

Draft in Recess					
½° min	...	2° min	2° min	2° min	
Draft in Cores					
½° min	...	...	4° min		
Minimum Cored-hole Diameter					
¼ in. optimum in green sand; 3/16 to ¼ in. in dry sand	½ to ¼ in.	3/16 to ¼ in.	3/16 in.	0.500 in.	0.020 to 0.050 in.
Section Thickness, Min					
3/32 in.	3/32 in.	3/32 to ½ in.	0.031 to 0.062 in.	0.040 to 0.060 in., depending on surface area of section	0.025 to 0.050 in., depending on surface area of section
Section Thickness, Max†					
No limit on floor or pit mold	...	2.0 in.	5/16 in. preferable; normally less than 0.125	...	Normally 0.500 in.; may sometimes be more

* From ASM Metals Handbook, 8th ed., vol. 1, 1961.

† Values shown are subject to individual design and alloy composition.

Table* 13.3 *Sand properties vs. section size and weight*

Weight, lb	Section thickness, in.	AFS permeability	Green compressive strength, psi	Moisture, %
Up to 1	½	20	7	6.5
1–10	1	30	7	6.0
10–50	2	40	7	6.0
50–100	3	50	8	5.5
100–200	4	60	10	5.5
200–250	5	80	12	5.5
1000 and up	6	100	15–20	5.0

* From American Foundrymen's Society.[1]

Table* 13.4 *Some brass and bronze molding sands*

Properties	Natural sands		System sand	
	Sand No. 1	Sand No. 2	Synthetic sand	Natural sand
Moisture, %	7.0	7.0	6.8	7.6
Permeability	18.4	49.0	11.4	18.4
Green shear, psi	1.8	2.7	1.7	1.9
Green compression, psi	6.9	11.2	7.6	7.8
Dry shear, psi	3.0	5.1	18.0	21.0
Dry compression, psi	22.0	29.0	85.0	93.5
Retained on mesh, %:				
12	......	......	1.40	
20	......	......	0.80	2.60
30	......	0.60	0.80	0.40
40	0.80	0.60	1.40	1.60
50	0.60	0.80	4.20	4.00
70	1.00	7.80	13.40	12.80
100	6.60	40.20	16.20	20.20
140	28.60	26.20	14.60	13.20
200	40.00	4.40	21.20	12.20
270	3.40	0.60	2.80	4.20
Pan	2.20	0.40	20.00	15.60
Total screen	83.20	82.00	96.80	86.80
Clay	16.80	18.00	3.20	13.20
B sintering point, F	2606	2651		
Deformation, in	0.016	0.014	0.012	0.018
Tensile strength, psi	6.8	9.8	2.7	4.2
AFS avg grain fineness	125	82.0	135	125

* From American Foundrymen's Society.[6]

takes advantage of runner size and pressure effect due to fluid head in order to feed the casting is shown in Fig. 13.3. The runner feeds the casting through the ingates, using to good advantage the temperature and pressure gradients in this arrangement. This practice is, of course, limited to small castings of uniform section weighing less than a few pounds. Larger castings require feeding from risers because of the large solidification shrinkage of copper-base alloys, 4.5 to 9.0 per cent.

Since copper-base alloys contain elements such as zinc, tin, and aluminum, which readily form oxides, they may be subject to drossing similar to that discussed in Chap. 11 for the aluminum alloys. However, since the drosses have much lower specific gravity than the molten metal, they have a greater tendency to separate by floating out than is the case for aluminum alloys. Gating arrangements for catching dross and preventing its entry into the casting are therefore useful. The practice of using metal-flow reversal at ingates as indicated by Fig. 13.3 arises from this objective. Bottom gating, traps, dams, and strainer cores are also used in the gates to prevent dross from entering the casting.

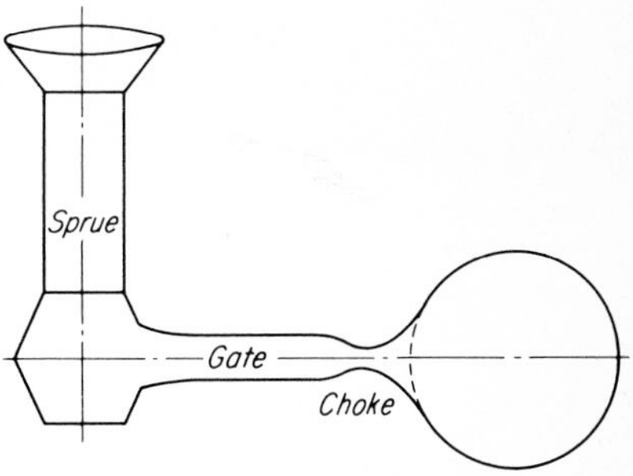

***Fig.* 13.2** **A simple choke gate is recommended for light uniform-section leaded red and semi-red brasses.** (*From American Foundrymen's Society.*[1])

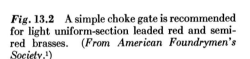

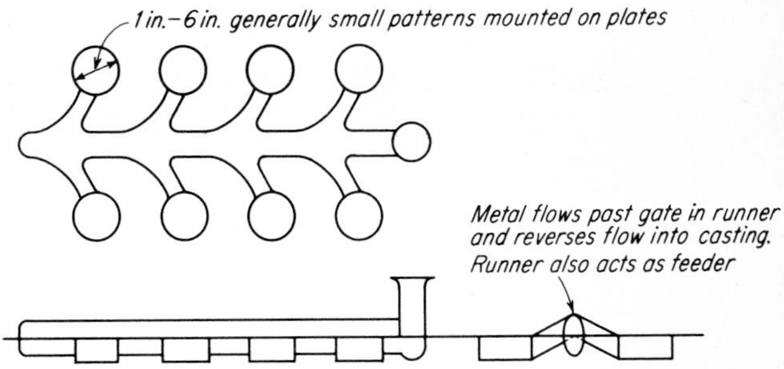

***Fig.* 13.3** **Gating arrangement for match-plate molding, taking advantage of the feeding action of runner in cope and cleaning action of flow reversal.** (*From American Foundrymen's Society.*[1])

Gating Design

Gating of copper-base alloys is like that of gray iron in that the constriction controlling metal-flow rate in the gating system is recommended to be in the ingate or in the runner just ahead of hot risers feeding the casting. This differs from the case of aluminum alloys, where current theory places the minimum gate area or choke in the sprue (Chap. 11). The ratio of cross-sectional areas of sprue to runners to total ingates can then be expressed as

$$S_A : R_A : G_A$$

where S_A = sprue cross-sectional area, greater than G_A but less than R_A usually

R_A = runner cross-sectional area, greater than S_A by 3 to 8 times; the maximum area

G_A = total cross-sectional area of all ingates; the minimum area in the system

To permit dross to float out in the runner, it appears that a gating ratio of about 2:8:1 or 3:9:1 is favorable. To feed from runner to casting, a minimum ratio of R_A:G_A would be about 4:1 to 6:1. However, to feed from a riser to the casting where the metal flows from runner into the riser and then into the casting, as illustrated in Fig. 13.4, the runner may be much smaller, a 1:2 ratio, for example. In the latter case, the runner is not expected to do any feeding, and dross separation can occur in the riser.

The actual ingate area selected for castings of various sizes may be based on experience or on different empirical methods of calculation. One method of ingate-area calculation for gray-iron castings is presented in detail in Chap. 20. Since the specific gravity of copper-base alloys is approximately in the same range as that of irons, 7.6 to 7.8 for the latter compared with 7.5 to 8.85 in various copper alloys, the formulas advanced in Chap. 20 might be used as a basis for calculating ingate areas

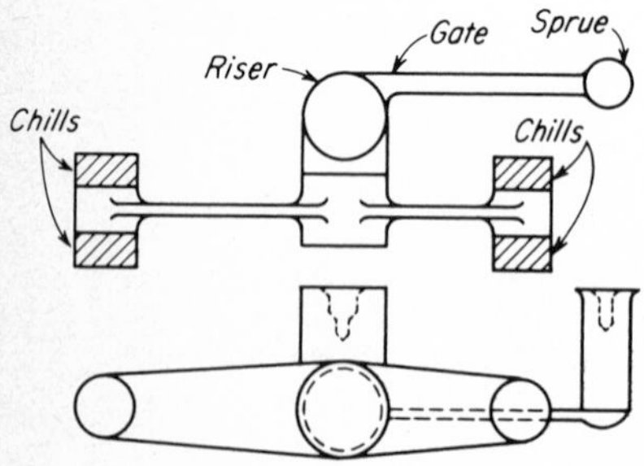

***Fig.* 13.4** Gating arrangement making use of chills and a hot riser to obtain soundness in heavy sections separated by thin sections. In this system the choke is in the gate (runner) between the sprue and riser. (*From American Foundrymen's Society.*[1])

for castings of a wide range of weights. The total ingate area may be divided between any number of ingates that might be needed. The sprue and runner sizes can be determined by using area ratios similar to those cited in the preceding paragraph. The reader is referred to Chap. 20 for examples of this method of selecting sprue, runner, and ingate sizes. To the authors' knowledge, however, this method has not been applied to copper-base alloys.

Risers

The solidification characteristics of copper-base alloys are in general unfavorable to efficient feeding of castings. Solidification contraction is high, 4.5 to 9.0 per cent. Many of the alloys have a long freezing range and freeze with the dendritic mechanism that makes transfer of molten metal from risers to casting difficult. The same freezing mechanism favors dispersed shrinkage and thus increases the difficulty of obtaining sound castings. The principles of freezing mechanisms and casting properties related to them as discussed in Chap. 8 apply directly to these alloys and are further considered in the following chapter. The problems of properly feeding copper-base castings thus are similar to those cited in Chap. 11 for aluminum alloys, namely, prevention of gross shrinkage, or macroshrinkage, and the prevention of microshrinkage. Gross-shrinkage cavities can be eliminated by the use of risers sufficient in amount, size, and placement and utilization of the directional-solidification principles. Figure 13.4 is an example of the use of chills on a lever-arm casting to establish steep temperature gradients from the remote parts of the casting toward risers and thus increase the effective feeding life of risers.

Even though a riser is kept molten for a considerably longer time than the casting, it does not follow that the casting will be successfully fed, particularly with respect to microshrinkage. To achieve a fully fed casting without dispersed shrinkage, it is necessary to have temperature gradients within the casting so that parts freezing first will be completely fed by parts freezing later, the latter finally fed by risers. The distance which liquid metal can feed through partially solidified metal to the advancing solid wave is greatly influenced by the thermal gradient between solidified and unsolidified metal and the freezing mechanism of the alloy. Consider the gating in Fig. 13.5 as an example. Although a hot riser and tilting of the mold to obtain pressure are used in this case, the gating does not produce a casting having no dispersed shrinkage. This is true because the feeding distance is excessive, and over the distance which must be fed from the riser into the casting there is insufficient temperature gradient to permit the first solidified sections to be fed by those close to the riser. The casting then shows microshrinkage some distance

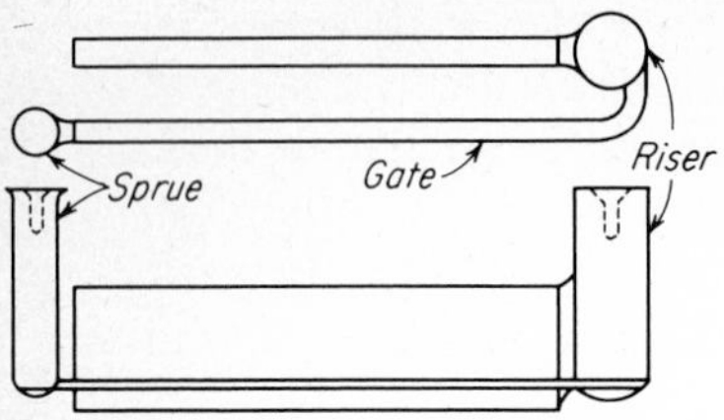

***Fig.* 13.5** Sprue, gate, and hot-riser arrangements for casting flat bars of manganese bronze. Molds are poured with riser end ¾ in. lower than sprue and then tilted back so that the riser will feed. (*From American Foundrymen's Society.*[1])

removed from the riser. Keeping the riser molten longer with an insulator would do no good at all in this case. The use of chills at the far end of the casting in Fig. 13.5 would assist in producing more complete soundness. Figure 13.6 shows a gating system for nickel-brass or bronze disk castings. The use of chills, a hot riser, and the padded gate connecting riser and casting illustrates a method of obtaining steep temperature gradients to promote feeding during solidification of the casting. This gating arrangement favors the elimination of dispersed shrinkage and maximum metal soundness.

The many copper-base casting alloys may differ widely in freezing-temperature range and mechanism, and no actual data are available which inform the foundryman of the feeding distance of risers and the necessary temperature gradients which must exist in different section thicknesses so that soundness can be fully achieved. The experience of the foundryman and experimentation are the present bases of risering to eliminate gross and dispersed shrinkage.

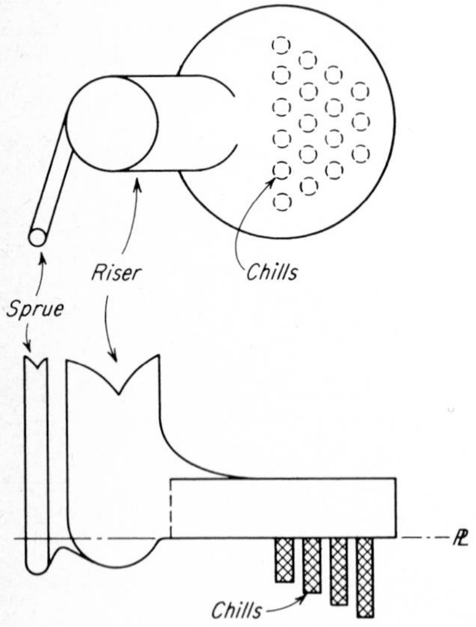

***Fig.* 13.6** Methods of gating and risering nickel-brass or bronze disk castings. Note use of chills, padding, and a hot riser to promote directional solidification. (*From American Foundrymen's Society.*[1])

The importance of absolute soundness in castings should not be over-emphasized. In many castings dispersed shrinkage does no harm whatever. In fact, in bearing applications, dispersed microshrinkage may act as oil-retaining cavities and actually be beneficial. Dispersed shrinkage then is an asset. The heavy risering and directional-solidification devices required to produce an absolutely sound casting can so greatly add to its cost as to prohibit its use. Hence the need for complete soundness should be fully established and the difficulty of achieving it analyzed in a particular casting to arrive at a suitable application of the principles.

The difficulty of removing large risers from copper-base castings provides another incentive for reducing risering to a minimum. The metal is usually tough, and risers must be sawed off if they are of any size at all. However, this problem can be handled in part through the use of knockoff risers described in Ref. 14. Such risers have a necked-down, or reduced, section at the point where the riser attaches to the casting. The reduced section is obtained by using a thin doughnut-shaped core made of core sand or graphite at the junction of riser and casting. The reduced section permits the riser to be knocked off with a hammer. The use of knockoff risers and cleaning of castings having such risers are discussed in Chap. 24.

MELTING

The quality of copper-base alloy castings is greatly influenced by melting and pouring operations. The perfect mold produces a low-quality casting if correct metallurgical practices are not followed. Copper-base alloys involve higher temperatures than melting of aluminum-base alloys considered in Chap. 11. The melting point of copper is about 1981 compared with 1220 F for aluminum. Nevertheless, about 60 per cent more heat in Btu is required to melt a unit weight of aluminum than is needed for copper. This is due to the greater heat capacity, in Btu per pound per degree Fahrenheit, and latent heat of fusion, in Btu per pound, of aluminum as compared with copper (values may be obtained in Ref. 7). Hence heat capacity is a fundamental factor in the melting of all metals and determines the heat input required.

Melting Equipment

The furnaces used for melting copper-base alloys consist of crucible furnaces, reverberatories, and electric-arc and induction furnaces. Since these have been described in Chap. 11, they are not considered again here. Contact of molten metal with furnace gases varies greatly in the aforementioned furnaces, and pertinent information in Chap. 11 should be reviewed because of the very important reactions which may occur. The reverberatories and crucible furnaces permit varying degrees of direct contact of furnace combustion atmosphere and melt. Induction furnaces may be covered, have no combustion products, and have a virtually stagnant atmosphere over the melt. This, then, is a marked difference in the two types of furnaces. The possible effects of melting-furnace atmospheres will be considered.

Melting Procedure

The normal metal charge consists of clean foundry scrap (remelt) and pig or ingot of the desired analysis. The metal is melted down, generally under an oxidizing atmosphere if a fuel-fired furnace is employed. An oxidizing atmosphere implies that free oxygen, about 0.50 per cent, is present in the products of combustion. After meltdown, additions such as alloying elements, zinc, tin, lead, or special hardeners are made as needed to achieve the desired analysis. The metal can then be heated to its pouring temperature plus 50 to 100 F, and is then ready for transfer from the furnace to the pouring operation. Temperature readings must be taken with base-metal thermocouples so that the pouring temperature may be accurately controlled. A minimum time at temperatures in the molten range decreases the danger of damaged metal due to gas absorption or composition changes.

Drossing

Most, though not all, copper alloys contain readily oxidizable elements, such as zinc, tin, aluminum, magnesium, and manganese. The oxides separate more or less completely from the melt and form a dross. In many cases, the oxide has a low specific gravity and would be expected to float out of the melt. However, surface tension and other effects make the separation difficult in some alloys, such as high-zinc brasses and aluminum bronze. The dross may then entrap considerable metal and cause high melting losses. Sometimes fluxes or charcoal covers are employed to minimize drossing. A cover of bottle glass thinned with borax is fluid and helps keep the metal surface clean. Charcoal as a protective cover is often used to minimize oxidation. Proprietary fluxes may be purchased which are claimed to cleanse the metal of oxides and prepare it for pouring. Undoubtedly, a minimum of agitation and melting under favorable combustion conditions decreases drossing.

Oxygen in Copper Melting

Copper as an element is a metal which is readily oxidized in the molten condition. This possibility is illustrated in Fig. 13.7, which shows that the solubility of oxygen in molten copper increases rapidly with tempera-

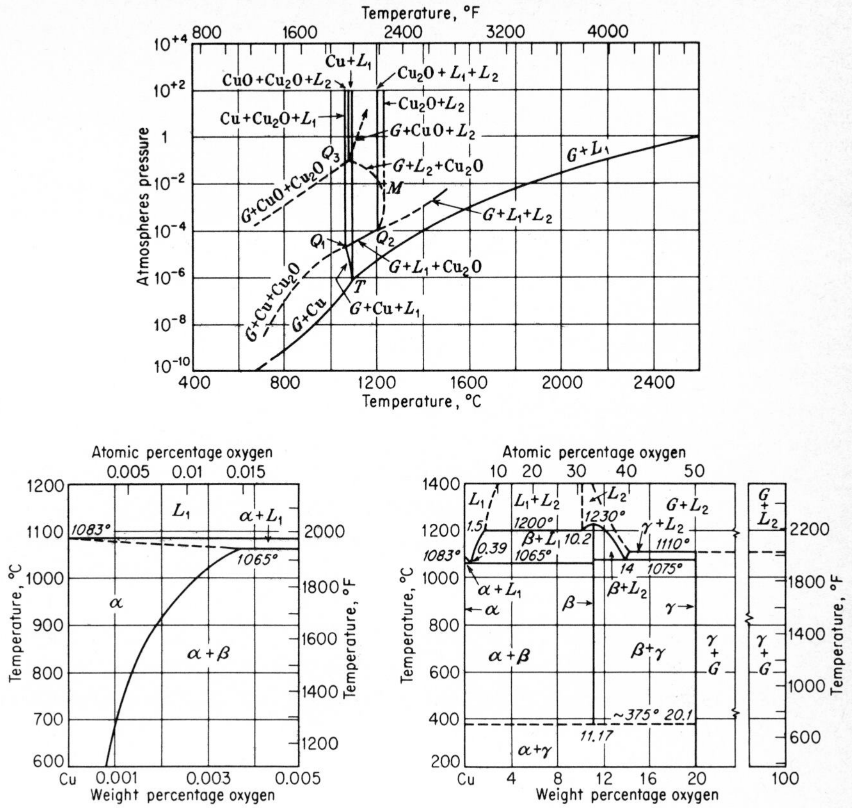

***Fig.* 13.7** **The Cu-O equilibrium system.** (*From American Society for Metals.*[7])

ture above its melting point. In the solid state copper can dissolve up to about 0.0035 per cent of oxygen, any excess occurring as Cu_2O, according to Fig. 13.7. Hence it is evident that melting copper in the presence of free oxygen (or an oxidizing gas such as Co_2) favors oxidation or an increased percentage of oxygen in the molten copper. The actual percentage of dissolved oxygen reaches a value of 0.04 to 0.05 per cent by weight when pure copper is melted under oxidizing atmospheres. Another means of raising the oxygen content of the metal is to cover the melt with an oxidizing flux, for example, a mixture of 20 parts cupric oxide, 34 parts borax, and 54 parts sand. Copper alloys contain substantially less oxygen under the same melting conditions than does pure copper. Many of the elements in the alloys, for example, zinc, tin, or aluminum, are deoxidizers to a degree, in that they may form oxides more strongly than copper and thus prevent the maximum dissolved oxygen content from being reached.

Hydrogen in Copper Melting

As in the case of aluminum alloys, the solubility of hydrogen in copper and copper alloys increases markedly with temperature, as shown in Fig. 13.8. A pronounced solubility increase is noted at the melting point of copper. Figure 13.8 also shows that the solubility of hydrogen is lower in copper-tin alloys (bronzes) than in pure copper. Hydrogen pickup by the molten metal can come from the furnace atmosphere, moisture or oils on the furnace charge, ladles, and molding and core sands. Its effects in the metal are harmful since it can cause gas holes and microporosity. Dissolved hydrogen can add to the difficulties of dispersed shrinkage since the gas will readily diffuse to cavities, precipitate as molecular hydrogen gas bubbles, and prevent the cavities from being fed from riser or adjacent areas of the casting. Gas holes in a copper-base alloy casting are illustrated in Fig. 13.9. Gas evolution during freezing prevents normal solidification shrinkage from showing up in risers. In place of a pipe, the riser top may swell or exude, as shown in Fig. 13.10. Thus gases are a factor which cause part of the difference between apparent shrinkage and true shrinkage of alloys (Chap. 8).

Reaction of Oxygen, Hydrogen, and Impurities

Since both hydrogen and oxygen may be present in molten copper alloys, interactions are possible and steam or water vapor may be formed. In fact, the two gases have a regulating effect on each other's solubility. If a high oxygen content is produced by melting under an oxidizing atmosphere or adding solid CuO to the melt, the hydrogen content of the

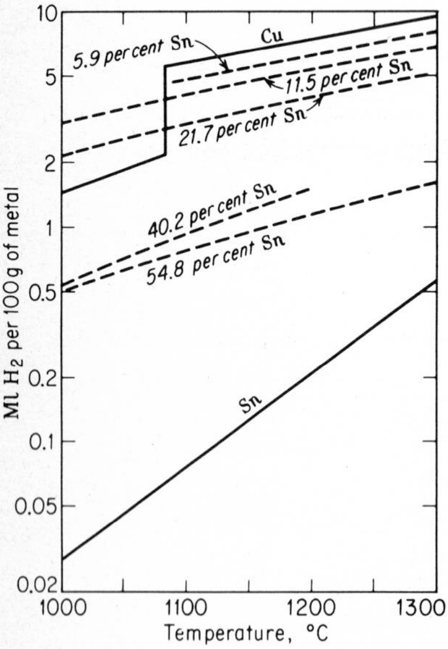

Fig. **13.8** Solubility of hydrogen in copper, tin, and copper-tin alloys as related to temperature at 1 atm pressure. Note that tin and many of the alloys are molten throughout the temperature range of the graph whereas copper is not. (Data from Bever and Floe, and Sieverts. *From American Society for Metals.*[4])

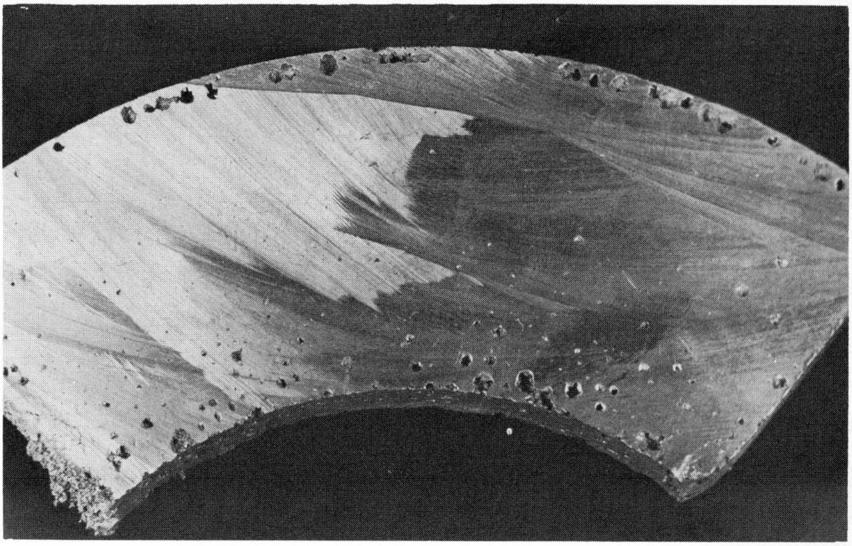

***Fig.* 13.9** Gas holes in section of a copper-base alloy casting. (*From American Foundrymen's Society.*[1])

***Fig.* 13.10** Failure of a riser to show pipe due to gas evolution during solidification. (*From American Foundrymen's Society.*[1])

metal is held low by the water-vapor reaction. For this reason, many foundrymen prefer to melt copper-base alloys under oxidizing atmospheres in order to minimize contamination of the melt with hydrogen. The evidence[8] appears to indicate that reducing atmospheres, containing a high CO percentage, promote porosity and poor properties even though the dissolved gases are not sufficient to cause gas holes such as shown in Fig. 13.9. Another means of reducing the hydrogen content of copper alloys during melting is to employ purging or flushing out of the hydrogen with nitrogen gas in the manner described for aluminum alloys; Refs. 9 and 12 provide examples of this practice.

Zinc flaring is another means of reducing the hydrogen content of yellow brass, manganese bronze, or any high-zinc copper-base alloy. Flaring is due to the vapor pressure–temperature relationships of zinc in these alloys, as indicated in Table 13.5. Zinc vapor distills from the brass more readily as temperature increases to the point where the vapor pressure equals barometric pressure. The zinc vapor reacting with oxygen forms a brilliant white flame, or "flare."

Flaring becomes pronounced when the temperature is raised to the point where boiling is incipient or occurs. Table 13.5 shows that this occurs over a fairly narrow temperature range, so that flaring is often used as a gauge of proper melting temperature for pouring. The formation of zinc vapor flushes out hydrogen and reduces it to a level where it does not present a severe gas-defect hazard. Zinc losses from flaring require the addition of 1 to 1.5 lb zinc per 100 lb melt for composition adjustment.

However, even high-zinc brasses can result in hydrogen-porosity if dirty charges are used, if melting occurs in a severely reducing atmosphere, or if flaring is improperly used to flush out hydrogen.

In addition to hydrogen, carbon and sulfur are gas-forming impurities which can be present in copper alloys. They may react as follows:

$$C\ (\text{dissolved}) + O\ (\text{dissolved}) \rightarrow CO\ (g) \tag{1}$$

$$S\ (\text{dissolved}) + 2O\ (\text{dissolved}) \rightarrow SO_2\ (g) \tag{2}$$

Table* 13.5 *Vapor pressure of zinc in molten brass, mm* Hg

Temp	Composition, Cu-Zn			
	60-40	65-35	70-30	80-20
900 C (1652 F)	160	125	90	30
1000 C (1832 F)	430	330	230	80
1100 C (2012 F)	980	760	540	180
1200 C (2192 F)	2000	1550	1100	370

* From D. R. Hull.[3]

The gaseous reaction products of Eqs. (1) and (2) may cause gas-hole defects, especially since these reactions occur more readily as temperature drops while a casting freezes. The solubility of carbon in copper is very low, under about 0.004 per cent, so that CO does not appear to be a frequent source of gassing, especially since the oxygen needed for reaction (1) can be removed by the addition of deoxidizers. Considerable sulfur can be present in copper alloys, and it is therefore regarded as an impurity which must be held below certain limits, generally under 0.05 to 0.08 per cent in most alloys. The most common means of preventing gassing from reactions (1) and (2) is to reduce the oxygen content by deoxidation below a percentage which will cause them to proceed to the right.

Deoxidation

Elements which combine more effectively with oxygen than copper does can be used to remove or decrease the oxygen content of a molten copper-base alloy melted under oxidizing conditions. Phosphorus, lithium, boron, calcium, magnesium, aluminum, silicon, and beryllium are such elements. Most commonly employed is a low-melting-point alloy of phosphorus and copper, 15% P–balance Cu. About 0.02% P or less is added to the melt for deoxidation purposes. This amounts to about 1 to 2 oz of 15% P–Cu per 100 lb of melt. After the addition is made, pouring should proceed at once. With the phosphorus residual in the alloy, the metal is no longer in an oxidized condition, and it can therefore pick up hydrogen again. The action of the phosphorus residual in reducing the oxygen content of a Cu–10% Sn bronze is illustrated in Fig. 13.11. It is evident from Fig. 13.11 that a residual of 0.020% P is fully as effective as a higher percentage of phosphorus in reducing the oxygen content to as low a value.

Melting for Control of Gases—Summary

The important role of gas reactions in copper-base alloy melting is evident from the foregoing discussions. Gas holes and microporosity are possible

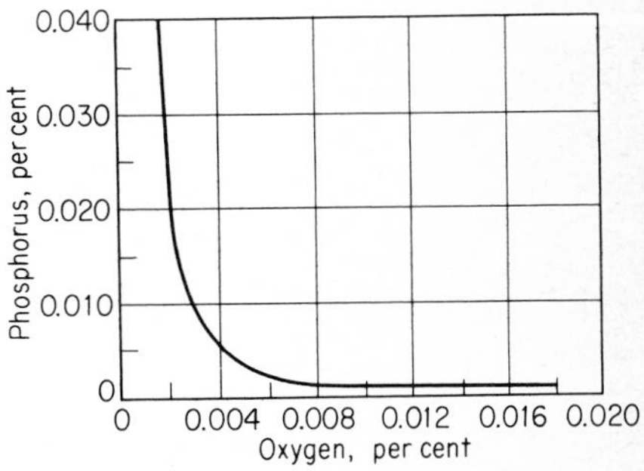

***Fig.* 13.11** **Effect of percentage of phosphorus residual on oxygen content of a 90-10 Sn bronze.** (*From O. W. Ellis.*[2])

defects. Metal quality is lowered by the embrittling effect of excessive copper or other oxides in the solid metal. One procedure of melting to control these gas effects consists of, first, an oxidizing stage during melting and heating to control hydrogen. Second, deoxidation is practiced to control oxygen effects. Flushing and flaring are other practices aimed at hydrogen control. With increasing use of induction melting, the use of an oxidizing melting-furnace atmosphere may decrease and flushing, purging with nitrogen gas, or flaring only may be practiced. Although the aforementioned oxidizing-atmosphere melting practice is more commonly practiced, it should be stated that other practices are used. One author[15] advocates melting under a reducing atmosphere to decrease drossing and slag troubles. Hydrogen removal can be accomplished just before pouring by adding copper oxide to the ladle or by blowing dry air through the melt. The deoxidation practice of adding phosphor copper may then be used.

Melt quality. As a guide to melt quality in any particular melting practice, test bars of various kinds are poured. Round cylinders of various diameters, 1 to 2 in., may be poured before castings are poured to study the shrinkage which may be expected from the metal.

For instance, a round bar displaying a freezing behavior of the kind illustrated in Fig. 13.10 would immediately indicate that the metal is in a gassy condition. A deep pipe in the same test would indicate that the metal is very low in gas content.

Another test involves the use of a fractured test bar to gauge melt quality.[16,17] A test mold employed for the purpose of determining melt quality of 85 Cu–5 Zn–5 Sn–5 Pb red brass is shown in Fig. 13.12. The base of the mold is a cast-iron chill plate. Metal is poured into the mold at temperatures of 2000 to 2200 F, and the block water quenched after it has cooled to about 1500 F. The block is then notched with a hack saw and fractured. High-quality melts display a blue-gray fracture extending more than 1¾ in. from the chilled surface. Low-quality melts show much less of a blue fracture, and may reveal a rough, mottled fracture surface much coarser in appearance than high-quality melts. Melt quality is regarded as high if the metal shows good tensile strength and ductility and freedom from porosity in castings. Fracture testing requires carefully standardized conditions and varies among the different alloys. References 16 and 17 and others at the end of this chapter are recommended reading for more detailed information on this subject.

Temperature control. Melt quality, metal properties, and casting quality are greatly influenced by the temperatures employed in melting and pouring of copper-base alloys. High temperatures encourage the entrance of gases into the metal, especially if the time at temperature is

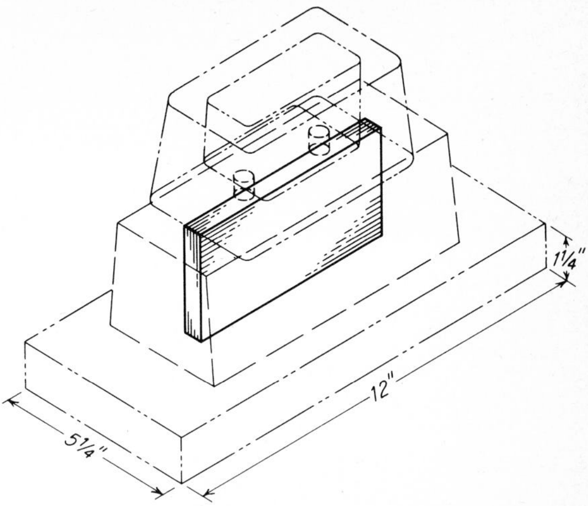

Fig. **13.12** Core-mold and chill-plate assembly for fracture testing of 85-5-5-5 red brasses. The bar is fractured across the middle, and the fracture appearance related to melt quality. (*From R. O. Shilling, C. Upthegrove, and F. B. Rote.*[15])

prolonged. However, the maximum temperatures used in melting must allow for the temperature drops encountered during reladling, 50 to 100 F, and temperature loss during the time required for pouring the castings. Pouring temperature has a considerable influence on casting quality. Table 13.6 lists pouring-temperature ranges for different copper-base alloys. Too high a pouring temperature may be accompanied by:

1. Damaged metal due to gassing during melting
2. Increased possibility of reactions between molding sands and metal
3. Excessive drossing in the gating system
4. Development of porosity because of increased feeding requirements
5. Defects from flaring in the mold

Pouring too cold may of course result in misruns. There is also the danger that porosity and shrinkage may be aggravated, since the risers may not have time to function or adequate temperature gradients to promote feeding may not be developed.

Impurities. Another factor having a great bearing on metal quality is the presence of certain impurities in the alloys. In addition to the gas-forming impurities in the alloy, a number of copper-base alloys develop harmful casting defects when certain unwanted elements are present. Some of these are listed in Table 13.7. Lead sweat is a defect which may be caused by silicon and aluminum in the leaded alloys. This defect is an exudation of lead from the casting during the last stages of solidification. It appears that porosity caused by the aforementioned elements, possibly in combination with evolved gases, forces liquid lead to the casting surface since the latter separates late in freezing. Silicon and

Table* 13.6 *Melting and pouring data for copper-base alloys*

Alloy type	Temp in furnace, F	Pouring temp, F	Flux	Deoxidizer
Leaded red brass, leaded semi-red brass	2050–2300	1950–2250	a,b	1 oz/100 lb 15% P-Cu
Leaded yellow brass	2050–2100	2050 max	a,b	P or Al but not together
High-strength yellow brass, leaded strength yellow brass (manganese bronze)	1850–1950 temp required for flaring	1900 max	a,b,c	If used, 1 oz/100 lb 15% P-Cu
Tin bronze, leaded tin bronze	2050–2350	1950–2250	a,b,d	2 oz/100 lb 15% P-Cu
High-leaded tin bronze	2200–2375	1850–2200	a,b,d,c	1–2 oz/100 lb 15% P-Cu
Leaded nickel brass, bronze	Pouring temp plus 50–100 F	2050–2600 depending on alloy and casting	....	4 oz 50–50 Cu Mn, 1 oz stick Mg, 3 oz 15% P-Cu, per 100-lb melt
Silicon brass, bronze	Pouring temp plus 50–100 F	1900–2150	a,b	Not needed
Aluminum bronze	Pouring temp plus 50–100 F	1950–2250	a	Not needed

* Adapted from American Foundrymen's Society.[1]
[a] Not needed.
[b] Glass and borax.
[c] Charcoal.
[d] Lime and fluorspar.

aluminum form lead silicates in leaded alloys and cause a white scum to appear on the casting surface and also a wormy or wrinkly surface. Some elements may be beneficial or harmful, depending on how they are used. Phosphorus is necessary as a deoxidizer in many of the alloys. It also promotes fluidity. Excessive fluidity, however, may cause the alloy to wet the molding sand and give a rougher casting surface. Iron is another element which may be harmful or beneficial. If the melt is not heated to a high enough temperature to cause the iron to dissolve fully in the melt, amounts over 0.15 to 0.25 per cent can exist as local areas of high iron content, which are hard spots in the metal. Properly alloyed, up to several per cent iron may be used for grain refining, hardening, and strengthening in manganese and aluminum bronzes. Table 13.7 briefly summarizes some of the important impurity effects of a number of the elements which are usually present in copper-base casting alloys.

Test bars. Metal quality is ultimately determined by the properties exhibited by castings. Extensive studies have been made of test-bar designs which should give properties representative of the casting. Several types of test-bar castings have been adopted by the ASTM (Specification B208-58T). An example of a commonly used bar is given in Fig. 13.13. Numerous factors affecting test-bar results such as design, gating, mold materials, and cooling rate have been investigated.[17]

*Table 13.7 Effects of impurities and modifying elements in copper casting alloys**

Alloy type	Aluminum	Antimony	Iron	Phosphorus	Magnesium	Silicon	Sulfur	Others
Leaded red brass, leaded semired brass	<0.001–0.003 %, causes lead sweat, porosity	<0.25 %, not harmful	<0.40 %, causes hard spots	<0.02–0.05 %, deoxidizer, casting roughness if too much	Similar to aluminum and silicon, trace	0.01 %, causes unsoundness, dross, wormy, white appearance		
Leaded yellow brass	0.3–0.50 % max, produces yellow color; none in pressure castings	....	0.6–0.75 % max, grain refiner	Not recommended as deoxidized	....	....	....	Nickel, grain refiner; P and Al should never be used together
Manganese bronze	1.50–7.50 %, strengthener	....	2.0–4.0 %, grain refiner	....	....	....	....	0.20 % Pb max when strength must be max
Tin bronze	Held as low as possible in pressure castings, like silicon in effects	<0.25 % up to 0.75 % may be present	0.15–0.25 %, hard spots	0.05 % max as deoxidizer	....	Held low as possible in pressure castings, causes lead sweat, porosity in leaded alloys	0.08 max, causes gassing	P up to 1.00 % used for hardness and strength in phosphor bronzes
Leaded nickel brass and bronze alloys	....	....	....	Deoxidizer	Sometimes used as deoxidizer	....	Causes embrittlement in Ni alloys	
Aluminum bronze	Alloying element	....	Up to 4 % used as grain refiner	Not ordinarily used as deoxidizer	....	0.05 max, causes embrittlement	....	Sn, 0.5 % max; Pb, should be under 0.07 %; Mn, up to 3.5 %

* Adapted from American Foundrymen's Society.[1]

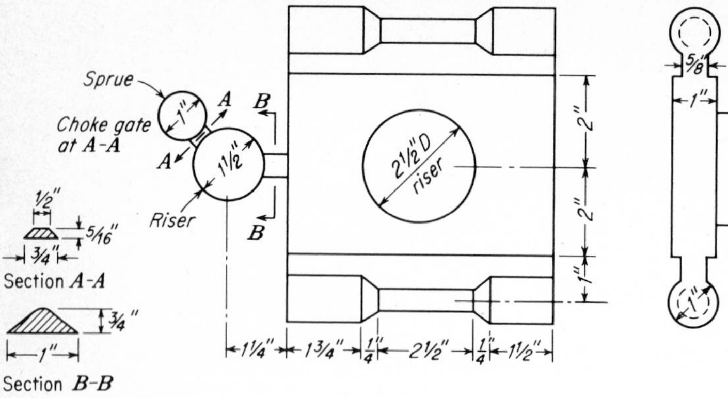

Fig. **13.13** Example of horizontal ⅝ in. web-Webbert-type tensile-test-bar casting.

BIBLIOGRAPHY

1. American Foundrymen's Society, "Copper-base Alloys Foundry Practice," 1952.
2. O. W. Ellis, "Copper and Copper Alloys," American Society for Metals, 1948.
3. D. R. Hull, "Casting of Brass and Bronze," American Society for Metals, 1950.
4. American Society for Metals, "Gases in Metals," 1953.
5. American Smelting and Refining Co., Copper-base Casting Alloys, *Federated Metals Div. Bull.* 102.
6. L. B. Osborn, Molding Sand for Brass and Bronze Foundries, *Trans. AFS,* vol. 54, 1946.
7. American Society for Metals, "Metals Handbook," 1948.
8. J. W. Bolton, discussion of Pearson and Baker's paper, *J. Inst. Metals,* vol. 67, p. 370, 1941; T. F. Pearson and W. A. Baker, Causes of Porosity in Tin-Bronze Castings, *J. Inst. Metals,* vol. 67, p. 231, 1941.
9. R. A. Colton, Melting Practice for Copper-base Alloys, *Foundry,* vol. 78, January, 1950.
10. V. C. Reed, Induction Melting in a Non-ferrous Foundry, *Foundry,* vol. 81, April, 1953.
11. R. A. Colton, Copper-base Alloys Have Wide Range of Properties, *Am. Foundryman,* vol. 17, February, 1950.
12. E. Kurzinski, Degassing Non-ferrous Metals, *Foundry,* vol. 76, December, 1948.
13. H. F. Taylor and W. C. Wick, Insulating Pads and Riser Sleeves for Bronze Castings, *Trans. AFS,* vol. 54, p. 262, 1946.
14. S. W. Brinson and J. A. Duma, Knock-off Risers for Non-ferrous Castings, *Trans. AFS,* vol. 54, 1946.
15. R. O. Shilling, C. Upthegrove, and F. B. Rote, Melt Quality and Fracture Characteristics of 85-5-5-5-red Brass and 88-8-4 Bronze, *Trans. AFS,* vol. 58, p. 7, 1950.

16. M. Glassenberg, L. F. Mondolfo, and A. H. Hesse, Refining of Secondary Copper Alloys, *Trans. AFS,* vol. 59, p. 465, 1951.
17. G. H. Clamer, Testbars for 85-5-5-5 Alloy, Their Design, and Some Factors Affecting Their Design, *Trans. AFS,* vol. 54, 1946.
18. American Society for Metals, "Metals Handbook," 8th ed., vol. 1, 1961.
19. C. L. Frear, Shrinkage Prevention in Bronze Castings, *Foundry,* vol. 86, September–November, 1958.
20. W. H. Johnson, H. F. Bishop, and W. S. Pellini, Methods for Improving Soundness of Gun-metal Bronze Castings, *Foundry,* vol. 83, p. 120, November, 1955.
21. V. R. Fulthorpe and F. M. Bunbury, Producing High-conductivity Copper Castings, *Foundry,* vol. 89, p. 84, March, 1961.
22. F. E. Murphy, G. J. Jackson, and R. A. Rosenberg, Bronze Valve Vertical Gating in Shell Molds, *Trans. AFS,* vol. 69, p. 313, 1961.
23. R. A. Flinn et al., Research Reports, Brass and Bronze Division, AFS T and R Inst., *Trans. AFS,* vols. 66–70, 1958–1962.
24. H. St. John, Gating and Risering in the Brass Foundry, *Foundry,* vol. 84, p. 108, November, 1956.
25. R. W. Ruddle, Risering Copper Alloy Castings, *Foundry,* vol. 87, p. 78, January, 1960.

14

Copper-base Casting Alloys

Copper may be alloyed with many elements, singly and in combinations, with beneficial effects on the properties of the alloy. Hence it is not surprising that the number of alloys which might be used for castings purposes is great. The variety of alloying possibilities is so numerous that their classification necessitates separation of the metals into major groups differing broadly from each other in composition. For this purpose the American Society for Testing Materials has adopted a standard classification of the copper-alloy groups (ASTM Specification B119-45).

ASTM Descriptions

Specifications which cover the casting alloys listed above include:

ASTM B22-61	Bronze Castings for Turntable and Movable Bridges and for Bearings and Expansion Plates of Fixed Bridges
ASTM B61-60	Steam or Valve Bronze Castings
ASTM B62-60	Composition or Ounce Metal Castings
ASTM B66-52	Bronze Castings in the Rough for Locomotive Wearing Parts
ASTM B67-52	Car and Tender Journal Bearings, Lined
ASTM B132-52	Lead High Strength Yellow Brass (Manganese Bronze) Sand Castings
ASTM B143-61	Tin Bronze and Leaded Tin Bronze Castings
ASTM B144-52	High Leaded Tin Bronze Castings
ASTM B145-61	Leaded Red Brass and Leaded Semi-red Brass Sand Castings
ASTM B146-52	High Strength Yellow Brass (Manganese Bronze) and Lead High Strength Yellow Brass (Leaded Manganese Bronze) Sand Castings
ASTM B148-52	Aluminum Bronze Castings
ASTM B149-52	Leaded Nickel Brass (Leaded Nickel Silver) and Leaded Nickel Bronze (Leaded Nickel Silver) Sand Castings
ASTM B198-58	Silicon Bronze and Silicon Brass Sand Castings

The above specifications by no means cover all the copper-base alloys supplied as castings by the foundry industry.

Copper

Conductivity copper castings, defined in the ASTM classification above, are used for a wide variety of electrical- and thermal-conductivity applications. Fittings, cable connectors, cable dead ends, spacers, inductor heads, switch parts, etc., require differing degrees of conductivity of copper. These castings are ordinarily of high copper content because other elements adversely affect the conductivity of copper. This idea is illustrated graphically in Fig. 14.1. Note the drastic effect of phosphorus on conductivity in Fig. 14.1. Deoxidation with P must therefore be carefully controlled to keep the residual percentage low, below 0.01 per cent preferably. Although the best conductivity is obtained with pure copper, the metal is soft, low in strength, and difficult to machine and has less desirable casting properties than many of its alloys. A comparison of electrical conductivity of the conductivity grade of copper alloys with the general-purpose alloys is made in Table 14.1. The table shows that the latter class of alloys has exceedingly low conductivity compared with conductivity copper alloys, although their other properties such as strength and hardness may be better.

The thermal-conductivity property behaves in a manner analogous to

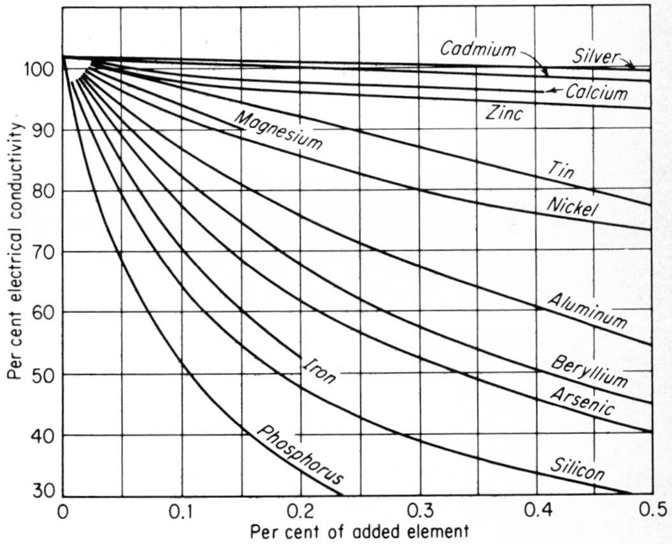

***Fig.* 14.1** Influence of alloying elements (impurities) on electrical conductivity of copper. (*From R. A. Colton.*[4])

Class	Addition elements	Remarks
Copper	Not over 2% total of arsenic, zinc, cadmium, silicon, chromium, silver, or other elements	Conductivity copper castings, pure copper, deoxidized copper and slightly alloyed copper
Brasses:		
Red brass	2 to 8% zinc. Tin less than zinc. Lead less than 0.5%	Alloys in this class without lead seldom used in foundry work
Leaded red	2 to 8% zinc. Tin less than 6%, usually less than zinc. Lead over 0.5%	Commonly used foundry alloys. May be further modified by addition of nickel. See ASTM Specifications B62 and B145
Semired	8 to 17% zinc. Tin less than 6%. Lead less than 0.5%	Alloys in this class without lead seldom used in foundry work
Leaded semired	8 to 17% zinc. Tin less than 6%. Lead over 0.5%	Commonly used foundry alloys. May be further modified by addition of nickel. ASTM Specification B145
Yellow	Over 17% zinc. Tin less than 6%. Under 2% total aluminum, manganese, nickel, iron, or silicon. Lead less than 0.5%	Commonly used foundry alloys
Leaded yellow	Over 17% zinc. Tin less than 6%. Under 2% total aluminum, manganese, nickel, or iron. Lead over 0.5%	Commonly used foundry alloys. See ASTM Specification B146
High-strength yellow	Over 17% zinc. Over 2% total of aluminum, manganese, tin, nickel, and iron. Silicon under 0.5%. Lead under 0.5%. Tin less than 6%	Commonly used foundry alloys under name of "manganese bronze" and various trade names. See ASTM Specification B147
Leaded high-strength yellow	Over 17% zinc. Over 2% total of aluminum, manganese, tin, nickel, and iron. Lead over 0.5%. Tin less than 6%	Commonly used foundry alloys. See ASTM Specifications B132 and B147
Silicon	Over 0.5% silicon. Over 3% zinc	Commonly used foundry alloys. See ASTM Specification B198
Tin	Over 6% tin. Zinc more than tin	Alloys in this class seldom used in foundry work
Nickel (nickel silver)	Over 10% zinc. Nickel in amounts sufficient to give white color. Lead under 0.5%	Commonly used foundry alloys sometimes called "german silver"
Leaded nickel (leaded nickel silver)	Over 10% zinc. Nickel in amounts sufficient to give white color. Lead over 0.5%	Commonly used foundry alloys sometimes called "german silver." See ASTM Specification B149

Class	Addition elements	Remarks
Bronzes:		
Tin	2 to 20% tin. Zinc less than tin. Lead less than 0.5%	Commonly used foundry alloys. May be further modified by addition of some nickel or phosphorus or both. See ASTM Specifications B22 and B142
Leaded tin	Up to 20% tin. Zinc less than tin. Lead over 0.5 and under 6%	Commonly used foundry alloys. May be further modified by addition of some nickel or phosphorus or both. See ASTM Specifications B61 and B144
High-leaded tin	Up to 20% tin. Zinc less than tin. Lead over 6%	Commonly used foundry alloys. May be further modified by addition of some nickel or phosphorus or both. See ASTM Specifications B22, B66, B67, and B144
Lead	Lead over 30%. Zinc less than tin. Tin under 10%	Used for special bearing applications
Nickel	Over 10% nickel. Zinc less than nickel. Under 10% tin. Under 0.5% lead	Commonly used foundry alloys. Sometimes called "german silver" or "nickel silver"
Leaded nickel	Over 10% nickel. Zinc less than nickel. Under 10% tin. Over 0.5% lead	Commonly used foundry alloys. Sometimes called "german silver" or "nickel silver." See ASTM Specification B149
Aluminum	5 to 15% aluminum. Up to 10% iron, with or without manganese or nickel. Less than 0.5% silicon	Commonly used foundry alloys. Some may be heat-treated. May be further modified by addition of some nickel or tin or both. See ASTM Specification B148
Silicon	Over 0.5% silicon. Not over 3% zinc. Not over 95% copper	Commonly used foundry alloys. Some are readily heat-treated. See ASTM Specification B198
Beryllium	Over 2% beryllium or beryllium plus metals other than copper	Most of these alloys are heat-treatable

Table 14.1 Properties of copper-base alloys used in electrical industry*

Alloy	Cu	Sn	Pb	Zn	Al	Be	Others	Tensile strength, psi	Yield strength, psi	Elongation, % in 2 in.	Bhn	Electrical conductivity, min, % Cu
High-strength bronzes:												
Herculoy electrical bronze	89	1	...	5	..	...	5 Si	65,000	30,000	30.0		
Aluminum bronze	81	...	...	...	11	...	4 Fe	90,000	40,000	10		
High strength	....	...	...	...	..	...	4 Ni	112,000†	70,000†	5†		
Aluminum bronze	86	...	...	...	10	...	4 Fe	75,000	30,000	20		
								100,000†	40,000†	12†		
Aluminum bronze	89	...	...	...	10	...	1 Fe	72,000	25,000	25		
								90,000†	40,000†	15†		
General-purpose alloys:												
85-5-5-5	85	5	5	5	..	...	....	35,000	17,000	30	60	15
83-4-6-7	83	4	6	7	..	...	....	33,000	15,000	25	55	16
Regular Herculoy	89	1	...	5	..	...	5 Si	50,000	20,000	50	90	6
Everdur	95	...	...	...	..	...	4 Si, 1 Mn	50,000	15,000	50	75	6
Navy M	88	6	1.5	4.5	..	...	....	38,000	17,000	35	65	14
High-strength–high-conductivity alloys:												
Chromium copper	99.5	...	...	...	..	...	0.5 Cr	50,000	25,000	20	..	85
Beryllium copper	97.5	...	...	...	..	2.0	0.5 Co	160,000	140,000	2†	..	25
Beryllium copper	98.2	...	...	...	..	0.3	1.5 Ni	75,000	45,000	5.0†	..	55
Beryllium copper	95.0	...	...	...	..	1.0	2.0 Co 2.0 Ni	95,000	45,000	10†	..	50
Moderate-strength–moderate-conductivity alloys	97	1	1	1								
	96	1	1	2								
	95	1	2	2	..	...	....	20,000	10,000	25	..	25
	94	2	2	2	..	...	....	33,000	14,000	50	..	40
	94.5	1.5	1	3								
	94.5	...	0.5	4.5	..	...	....	32,000	13,000	45	..	52
	97	...	...	3	..	...	....	23,000	10,000	55	..	65

* From R. A. Colton.[4]

† Properties obtained by suitable heat-treatment of castings.

electrical conductivity. Castings for water-cooled blast-furnace tuyeres, cooling glands, heat-exchanger parts, and similar applications may be made of conductivity copper.

Copper-Zinc Alloys

The alloying behavior of zinc in copper-zinc alloys is presented in the binary equilibrium diagram in Fig. 14.2. The diagram shows solubility of zinc in copper up to 32.5 per cent at the solidus temperature and about 35 per cent at room temperature. The solid-solution phase α is the major microstructure constituent of most brasses except for the high-zinc-content, high-strength type of brass (manganese bronze). The latter alloys contain a substantial amount of the β' constituent. The α phase is a relatively soft, ductile, and low-strength phase, and this is reflected in the hardness of cast alloys of varying zinc content. A really substantial increase in hardness (and strength) does not occur until the percentage of zinc in the alloy is high enough to cause an appreciable amount of the β' constituent to be present. The latter phase is a hard, brittle constit-

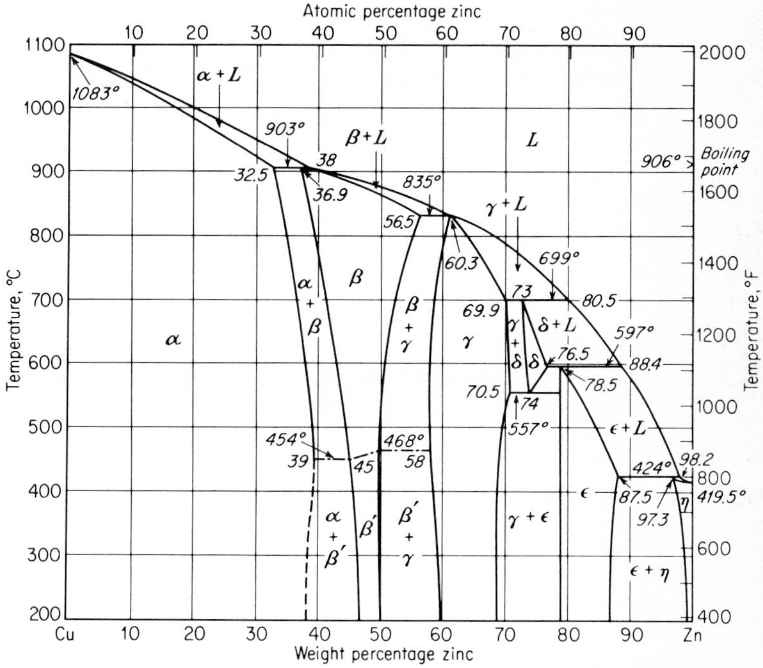

Fig. **14.2** The Cu-Zn equilibrium system. (*From American Society for Metals.*[1])

uent, which, although it increases the strength of $\alpha + \beta'$ mixtures, unfortunately also reduces ductility to the point of destroying the usefulness of the alloys if the zinc content is too high. Hence it is evident that the zinc content of casting alloys is limited to a maximum of that which produces a desirable combination of hardness and strength without a harmful loss of ductility. The maximum zinc content is about 36 per cent.

Characteristics other than microstructure and properties are exceedingly important in certain applications.

Color

The color of copper-zinc alloys is greatly influenced by zinc content of the alloys. Color is related to zinc content approximately as follows:

1. 98% Cu; characteristic copper color
2. 90% Cu–10% Zn; dark bronze yellow or antique gold color
3. 85% Cu–15% Zn, 80% Cu–20% Zn; red brass, copper color
4. 70% Cu–30% Zn, 65% Cu–35% Zn; yellow brass, bright yellow
5. 60% Cu–40% Zn; yellow, tendency toward lighter or whiter yellow brass color

Sometimes color is an important reason for using yellow brasses for castings. A particular casting may be required to blend in color with wrought brass parts, for example. Yellow brasses are primarily used for small castings because the mechanical properties are not especially good and casting difficulties due to shrinkage are aggravated in larger castings.

Flaring

Vaporization of zinc (flaring) increases with zinc content at any particular temperature of melting and pouring. The relationship was pointed out in Table 13.5. Flaring can cause surface-finish difficulties, wrinkles and pinholes, for example, if it is necessary to pour the castings at high temperature.

Electrical and Thermal Conductivity

These properties decrease with increasing zinc content, as pointed out earlier in Fig. 14.1.

Freezing-temperature Range

As can be seen in Fig. 14.2, the liquidus is lowered and temperature range of freezing is increased as the zinc content of the alloys increases. Some liquidus and solidus temperatures for various alloys are listed in Table 14.2. The alloys in Table 14.2 are not simple Cu-Zn brasses and have freezing ranges different from the diagram in Fig. 14.2.

Table 14.2 ***Copper-base alloy casting information****

Alloy name	Nominal composition					Liquidus, solidus, F†	Impurities, max %							Density, lb/cu in.
	Cu	Sn	Pb	Zn	Others		P	Si	Al	Fe	Sb	S	Others	
Leaded red brass	85	5	5	5	...	S1810–1840	0.05	0.003	..	0.30	0.25	0.080	1.0 Ni	0.318
	83	4	6	7	...	S1800	...	...	..	...	...	...	...	0.312
Leaded semi-red brass	81	3	7	9	...	S1750	0.02	0.003	..	0.40	0.20	0.080	1.0 Ni	0.314
	76	3	6	15	...	S1725	...	...	..	...	...	...	...	0.310
Leaded yellow brass	71	1	3	25	...	S1700	0.01	0.05	..	0.60	0.10	0.05	0.75	0.307
	66	1	3	30	...	S1700	...	...	..	...	...	...	...	0.303
	60	1	1	38	...	S1675–1925	...	...	..	...	...	...	...	0.304
High-strength yellow brass No. 8C	62	0.5 max	0.20 max	36	3 Fe, 5.5 Al 3.5 Mn	L1650	...	...	..	...	...	...	9.5 Ni	0.285
No. 8A	58	1.0 max	0.40 max	39.15	1.25 Fe, 1.25 Al, 0.25 Mn	L1660	...	...	..	...	...	...	0.50 Ni	0.269
Leaded high-strength yellow brass, No. 7A	59	0.75	0.75	37	1.25 Fe, 0.75 Al, 0.5 Mn	S1675–1725	...	...	..	...	...	...	0.5 Ni	0.296
Leaded tin bronze	88	6	1.5	4.5	...	S1800–1830	0.05 max	...	..	0.25	0.25	0.05 max	1.0 Ni	0.315
Leaded tin bearing bronze	87	8	1	4	...	L1830–S1570	...	...	..	0.20	0.30	...	1.0 Ni	0.318
High-leaded tin bronze	80	10	10	0.75 max	...	...	0.05	...	..	0.15	0.55	...	0.75 Ni	0.320
Aluminum bronze	88	1 Fe	10 Al											
Aluminum bronze	87.5	3.5	9	...	...	...	...	...	..	...	...	...	...	0.267

* Adapted from American Society for Metals.
† Liquidus L, solidus S.

Density

The density of copper-zinc alloys decreases with increasing zinc content and decreasing copper content but does depend on the presence of other elements such as lead and tin. Table 14.2 lists density in pounds per cubic inch of common copper-base casting alloys.

Coring

A solid-solution-type alloy exhibits the microstructural phenomenon of coring. Coring is due to the dendritic freezing mechanism illustrated in Fig. 8.12, which causes segregation of the alloying elements. The higher-freezing-temperature solid-solution phase, usually lower in alloy content, forms the dendritic structure as freezing begins, and the lower-freezing-temperature solid-solution alloy completes the freezing and filling in of the dendrite. This results in a nonuniform chemical composition within the grains which can be brought out by metallographic means as in Fig. 14.4. A wide freezing-temperature range accentuates coring. Coring in alloys is accompanied by less favorable corrosion resistance and mechanical properties than when it is absent.

Brass Casting Alloys

Actual casting brasses are not simple Cu-Zn alloys, nor do they have simple α or $\alpha + \beta'$ structures referred to earlier. Instead, the composition may be complicated by the presence of tin, lead, antimony, iron, sulfur, nickel, silicon, aluminum, manganese, phosphorus, and other elements. The influence of some of these elements and also of other copper alloys will become more understandable as other alloy systems are considered. The analyses and properties of some typical casting brasses are included in Tables 14.3 and 14.4. In these brasses, the copper is alloyed with tin and copper as well as zinc. The tin provides increased strength, and the lead, improved casting characteristics with respect to soundness, and also better machinability. The latter effects of lead are discussed again later, under the subject of copper-lead alloys. The influence of lead and of the other alloys to be discussed on casting characteristics is demonstrated in Table 14.5. The terms used here should not be confused. Fluidity is the ability of a molten metal to fill a mold cavity completely in every detail, whereas castability is the ease with which an alloy responds to ordinary foundry practice, without undue attention to gating, risering, melting, sand conditions, and any of the other factors involved in making good castings. Fluidity improves many of these aspects of castability.[10]

The leaded red brasses are very commonly used for valves, valve seats, handles, plumbing fixtures, nuts, hardware, lock parts, etc. In this group 85% Cu, 5% Sn, 5% Pb, and 5% Zn alloy is the most commonly

Table* 14.3 *Chemical requirements for sand-cast leaded red and leaded semired brasses*

Classification	Leaded red brass				Leaded semired brass			
Alloy designation	4A		4B		5A		5B	
	Min	Max	Min	Max	Min	Max	Min	Max
Copper, %	84.00	86.00	82.00	83.75	78.00	82.00	75.00	76.75
Tin, %	4.00	6.00	3.25	4.25	2.25	3.50	2.50	3.50
Lead, %	4.00	6.00	5.00	7.00	6.00	8.00	5.25	6.75
Zinc, %	4.00	6.00	5.00	8.00	7.00	10.00	13.00	17.00
Nickel, %†	.....	1.00	.....	1.00	.....	1.00	.....	1.00
Iron, %	.....	0.30	.....	0.30	.....	0.40	.....	0.40
Phosphorus, %	.....	0.05	.....	0.03	.....	0.02	.....	0.02
Total other constituents, %‡	.....	0.50	.....	0.50	.....	0.50	.....	0.50

* From American Foundrymen's Society[6] and ASTM Specification B145-61.

† In this alloy, minimum copper may be computed as copper plus nickel.

‡ Analysis shall regularly be made only for copper, tin, and lead. If the presence of excessive amounts of other elements is suspected, or indicated in the course of routine analysis, further analysis shall be made to determine that the total of these other elements is not in excess of 0.50%.

used copper-base casting alloy and accounts for the bulk of copper-base castings.

Composition and properties of leaded yellow brasses are given in Tables 14.6 and 14.7. These alloys have a pleasing yellow color which may be desirable in some applications. In general, their properties are not better than the leaded red brasses and they have less favorable casting properties. However, their corrosion resistance is better than the former alloys when in contact with fuel oil, gasoline, or other petroleum products.

Table* 14.4 *Minimum tensile requirements for sand-cast leaded red and leaded semired brasses*

Classification	Leaded red brass		Leaded semired brass	
Alloy designation	4A	4B	5A	5B
Tensile strength, min, psi	30,000	29,000	29,000	25,000
Yield strength, min, psi†	14,000	12,000	13,000	12,000
Elongation in 2 in., min, %	20	15	18	15

* From American Foundrymen's Society.[6]

† Yield strength shall be determined as the stress producing an elongation under load of 0.5%; i.e., 0.01 in. in a gauge length of 2 in.

Table 14.5 ***Nominal compositions and relative foundry ratings of principal sand-mold copper casting alloys****

Common name	Composition								Relative rating, sand-mold casting		
	Cu	Sn	Pb	Zn	Ni	Mn	Al	Other	Cost†	Castability‡	Fluidity‡
Leaded red brass	85	5	5	5					100	2	6
Leaded semired brass	81	3	7	9					95	2	6
	76	3	6	15					89	2	6
Yellow brass	63	1	1	35					91	9	3
Yellow brass with Al	63	1	1	35			0.25§		91	4	4
Leaded yellow brass	67	1	3	29			0.25§		85	4	4
Manganese bronze	58			Rem		0.5	1.0	1.0 Fe	103	6	2
	62			Rem		3.5	5.5	2.5 Fe	128	6	2
Nickel silver	64	4	4	8	20				112	5	7
	65	5	1.5	2	25				118	5	7
Tin bronze	88	8		4					153	3	6
	88	6	2	4					120	3	6
	80	19.5		6				0.5 P	182	3	4
Silicon brass	81			15				4.0 Si	138	7	1
Silicon bronze	95					1.0		4.0 Si	118	3	3
Aluminum bronze	89						10.0	1.0 Fe	140	8	5
	81				4.5		10.0	4.5 Fe	140	8	5
High-lead tin bronze	80	10	10						124	1	6
	70	5	25						118	1	6

* From American Society for Metals.[10]
† Relative cost; 85-5-5-5 leaded red brass = 100.
‡ Relative rating; 1 is highest or best possible rating.
§ Maximum.

Table* 14.6 *Chemical requirements for sand-cast leaded yellow brasses*

Classification	Leaded yellow brass					
Alloy designation	6A		6B†		6C	
	Min	Max	Min	Max	Min	Max
Copper, %	70.00	74.000	65.00	70.00	60.00	65.00
Tin, %	0.75	2.00	.....	1.50	0.50	1.50
Lead, %	1.50	3.75	1.50	3.75	0.75	1.50
Zinc, %	Remainder		Remainder		Remainder	
Iron, %	.....	0.60	.....	0.75	.....	0.75
Aluminum, %	.....	......	.....	0.30‡		0.50

* From American Foundrymen's Society[6] and ASTM Specification B146-52.

† The chemical requirements of SAE Specification 41 conform in general to the requirements for alloy 6B.

‡ Maximum aluminum "none" in pressure casting.

High-strength yellow brasses, leaded and not leaded, are employed where high mechanical properties are desired in the as-cast condition. Ship propellers illustrate an application requiring high strength as well as resistance to the corrosive effects of salt water. Chemical and tensile requirements of manganese bronzes are given in Tables 14.8 and 14.9. The presence of aluminum in these alloys improves strength since 1 per cent of it is equivalent to about 6 per cent of zinc in increasing the tendency to form the β' constituent, the hardening and strengthening phase in the microstructure. Iron in these alloys assists in obtaining a finer grain size, as it may in any of the copper casting alloys (see section on aluminum bronze). Tin may be present to enhance corrosion resistance. Since strength in the as-cast condition is a prime virtue of these alloys, the use of manganese bronze should be evident in its applications.

Table* 14.7 *Minimum mechanical properties for sand-cast leaded yellow brasses*

Classification	Leaded yellow brass		
Alloy designation	6A	6B	6C
Tensile strength, min, psi	35,000	30,000	40,000
Yield strength,† min, psi	12,000	11,000	14,000
Elongated, min, % in 2 in.	25	20	15

* From American Foundrymen's Society.[6]

† Yield strength shall be determined as the stress producing an elongation load of 0.5%; i.e., 0.01 in. in a gauge length of 2 in.

Table 14.8 Chemical composition for high-strength yellow brass castings*

Alloy	7A	8A	8B	8C
Copper, %, min	56.00	55.00	60.00	60.00
max	62.00	60.00	68.00	68.00
Zinc, %	Remainder	Remainder	Remainder	Remainder
Manganese, %, min	.....	.....	2.50	2.50
max	1.50	1.50	5.00	5.00
Aluminum, %, min	.....	0.50	3.00	3.00
max	1.50	1.50	7.50	7.50
Iron, %, min	.....	0.40	2.00	2.00
max	2.00	2.00	4.00	4.00
Tin, %, max	1.50	1.00	0.20	0.20
Lead, %, min	0.50			
max	1.50	0.40	0.20	0.20
Nickel, %, max	.....	0.50		
Total other constituents, %, max	0.25	0.25	0.25	

* From American Foundrymen's Society[6] and ASTM Specification B147-52.

Table 14.9 Physical properties for sand-cast high-strength yellow brasses*

Alloy	7A	8A	8B	8C
Ultimate tensile strength,[a] min, psi	60,000	65,000	90,000	110,000
Yield strength in tension,[a] min, psi	20,000	25,000	45,000	60,000
Elongation,[a] min, % in 2 in.	15	20	18	12
Reduction of area,[b] %[e]	18	20	18	10
Modulus of elasticity, psi[e]	12,000,000	12,200,000	13,500,000	14,000,000
Bhn (500-kg load, 10-mm ball)[e]	100	120	180	210
Compression of 0.001 in.,[c] psi[e]	20,000–26,000	20,000–26,000	....	55,000–65,000
Compression of 0.1 in.,[c] psi[e]	85,000–90,000	85,000–90,000	....	90,000–120,000
Specific gravity[e]	8.4	8.4	....	79
Weight, lb/cu in.[e]	0.303	0.303	....	0.284
Patternmakers' shrinkage, in./ft[e]	7/32	7/32	....	5/16–1/4
Izod impact resistance,[d] ft-lb	30–50	20–40	10–20	10–15
Electrical conductivity, % annealed copper at 20 C	22.0	20	13	12
Coefficient of thermal expansion, per F	70–400 F, 0.0000114	70–600 F, 0.00001077; 70–200 F, 0.00001210	....	70–500 F, 0.000011

* From American Foundrymen's Society.[6]

[a] Minimum requirements according to ASTM Specification B147-52. Remainder of properties listed are not to be used for specification purposes.

[b] As determined on tensile specimens machined to provide ½-in. diameter by 2-in. gauge length.

[c] As determined on compression specimens machined to 1.128 in. diameter by 1.0 in. high.

[d] As determined on impact specimens machined to standard Izod cantilever dimensions, 10 by 10 mm with 45° V notch.

[e] Average properties.

For example, large propellers should be strong as-cast since heat-treatment of such large objects is not desirable, or indeed possible.

Copper-Tin Alloys

The alloying behavior of tin in copper is similar to that of zinc. The equilibrium diagram for the binary system is shown in Fig. 14.3. The system shows solubility, the α phase, up to about 13.5 per cent during solidification. At lower temperatures, an $\alpha + \delta$ eutectoid occurs. The α phase is a softer solid-solution phase, but the δ phase is exceedingly hard and brittle. It is evident from Fig. 14.3 that the alloys containing 5 to 15 per cent tin have an unusually long freezing-temperature range over 400 F. The long solidification range makes castings of these alloys very hard to riser adequately and also promotes severe coring. The latter condition is illustrated for a leaded tin bronze in Figs. 14.4 and 14.5.

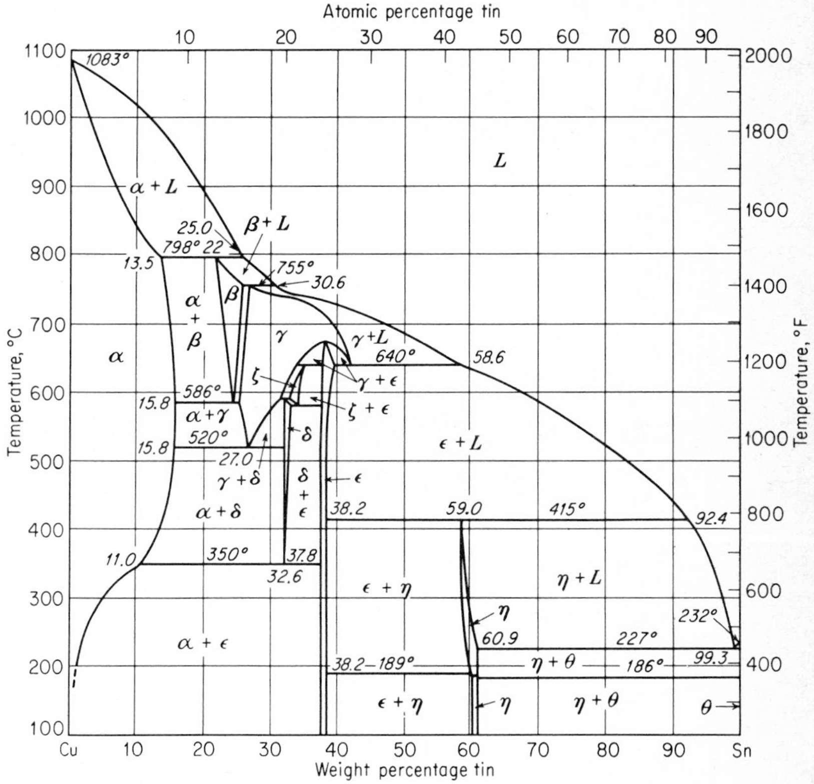

***Fig.* 14.3** The Cu-Sn equilibrium system. (*From American Society for Metals.*[1])

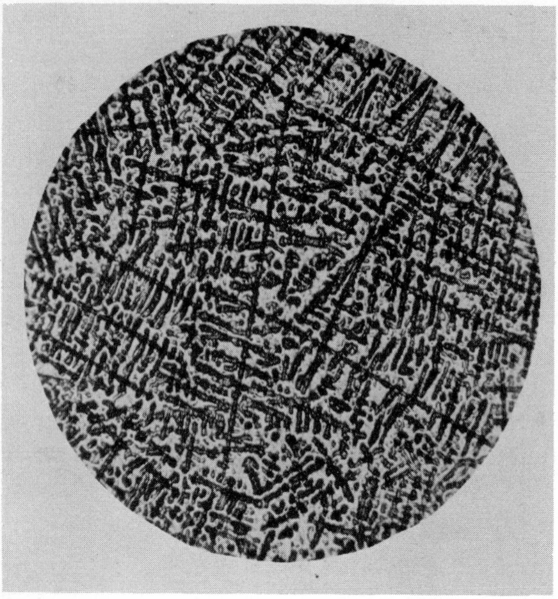

***Fig.* 14.4** Cored dendritic structure in 87% Cu, 10% Sn, 1% Pb, 2% Zn alloy. This photomicrograph is characteristic of a casting section cooled fairly rapidly and has a relatively fine dendritic structure. Etched with ammoniacal copper chloride to show the dendritic pattern, ×250. (*From American Foundrymen's Society.*[6])

Because so much segregation occurs during freezing, alloys as low as 7 per cent tin contain the δ constituent and show the $\alpha + \delta$ eutectoid even though the "equilibrium" diagram does not indicate this fact. In sand castings, the nonequilibrium microstructures containing α or $\alpha + \delta$ eutectoid remain after cooling to room temperature. Only prolonged

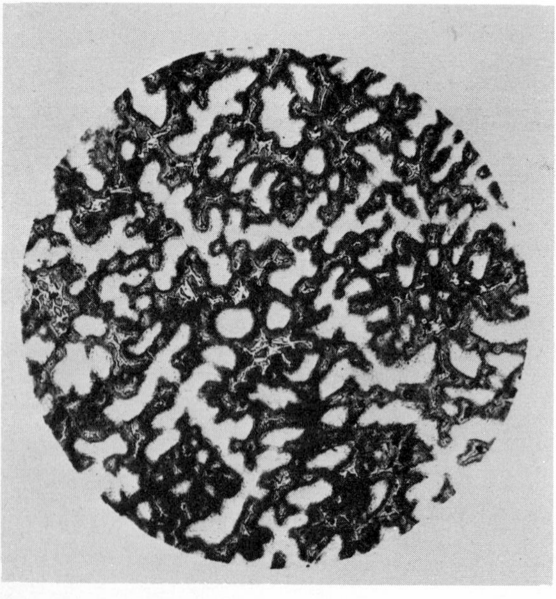

***Fig.* 14.5** Cored structure is 88% Cu, 10% Sn, 0% Pb, 2% Zn alloy etched with ferric chloride to reveal the delta constituent. The delta constituent is pale blue in color and appears in the photomicrograph as white islands within dark areas, ×100. (*From American Foundrymen's Society.*[6])

annealing at elevated temperatures would produce the equilibrium structures. Copper alloys are limited to lower maximum tin content than is the case for zinc since embrittlement occurs with the presence of increasing amounts of the δ constituent at relatively low tin content. Tin is more effective percentagewise in strengthening copper than zinc is. The tin bronzes based on the Cu-Sn system have strength, hardness, and bearing qualities which make them suitable for gears, worms, bearing plates, turntables, sleeves, and liners. Because of corrosion resistance, these applications find frequent use in marine construction, naval vessels, bridges, dams, hydroelectric plants, chemical-processing industries, and the like. The tin bronzes are, of course, complex alloys modified by the presence of elements other than copper and tin. Tables 14.10 and 14.11 present the chemical and tensile requirements of tin-bronze casting alloys. The alloy 88% Cu, 10% Sn, 2% Zn is known as G-bronze, or gun metal. The alloys are possessed of better all-around resistance to sea water than the brasses, so that they are used extensively in that field. Bell bronzes contain 20 to

***Table* 14.10 *Chemical composition for sand-cast tin-bronze alloys**[a]**

Alloy designation	1A[b]	1B[c]	2A[d]	2B[e]	3[f]	4[g]	5[h]
Copper, %, min	86.00	86.00	86.00	85.00	79.00	82.00	88.00
max	89.00	89.00	89.00	89.00	82.00	85.00	90.00
Tin, %, min	9.00	7.50	5.50	7.50	18.00	15.00	10.00
max	11.00	9.00	6.50	9.00	20.00	17.00	12.00
Lead, %, min	....	.....	1.00				
max	0.30	0.30	2.00	1.00	0.25	0.25	0.50
Zinc, %, min	1.00	3.00	3.00	2.50			
max	3.00	5.00	5.00	5.00	0.25	0.25	0.50
Phosphorus, %, min	....	....	....	....	....	....	0.10
max	0.05	0.05	0.05	0.05	1.00	1.00	0.30
Nickel, %, min							
max	1.00	1.00	1.00	1.00			
Iron, %, min							
max	0.15	0.15	0.25	0.25	0.25	0.25	0.15
Total other constituents, %, max	0.25	0.25	0.35	0.35			

* From American Foundrymen's Society[6] and ASTM Specifications B143-61 and B22-61.

[a] Alloy designations 1A, 1B, 2A, and 2B are official ASTM alloy designations. The remainder of the alloy numbers have no significance other than numerical sequence.

[b] ASTM Specification B143-61-1A, ASTM Specification B22-61, Class D; SAE 62-AMS 4845-C.

[c] ASTM Specification B143-61-1B, Fed. QQ-B-691B, Comp. 5, Navy 46M6h.

[d] ASTM Specification B143-61-2A, Fed. QQ-B-691B, Comp. 1, Navy 46B8i.

[e] ASTM Specification B143-61-2B.

[f] ASTM Specification B22-61, Class A.

[g] ASTM Specification B22-61, Class B.

[h] SAE 65.

Table* 14.11 *Physical properties for sand-cast tin-bronze alloys*

Alloy designation†	1A[b]	1B[c]	2A[d]	2B[e]	3[f]	4[g]	5[h]
Tensile strength, psi, min.	40,000	40,000	34,000	36,000	....	....	35,000
Yield strength,‡ psi, min.	18,000	18,000	16,000	16,000			
Elongation, % in 2 in., min.	20.0	20.0	22.0	18.0			10.0
Deformation limit, psi, min.	.....	.....	.....	.....	24,000§	18,000§	
Permanent set in 1 in., under 100,000 psi, in.	.....	.....	.....	.....	0.04–0.12	0.10–0.20	
Bhn (500-kg load)	65	.....	57				
Patternmakers' shrinkage, in./ft	3/16	.....	3/16				
Specific gravity (approx)	8.75	.....	8.70				

* From American Foundrymen's Society[6] and ASTM Specifications B143-61 and B22-61.

† For meaning of superior letters, see footnotes under Table 14.10.

‡ Stress producing an elongation under load of 0.5% (0.01 in.) in gauge length of 2 in.

‡ Compression load which produces a permanent set of 0.001 in. in a cylindrical specimen 1 sq in. in cross-sectional area and 1 in. in height.

23 per cent tin, are relatively hard and brittle, and have the ability to produce musical tones when struck, which makes for their use in bell castings. Lead is added to tin bronzes for machinability or to obtain antifrictional properties. High-leaded tin bronzes are useful for sleeves, bushings, and bearings for railroad, rolling mill, and papermaking applications where good bearing qualities against steel or iron surfaces are needed.

Copper-Lead Alloys

The copper-lead equilibrium system is illustrated in Fig. 14.6. The solid solubility of lead in copper is about 0.002 to 0.005 per cent at room temperature. The presence of other elements may increase this limit slightly. However, it is known that leaded copper alloys have most of their lead present as islands of the element distributed throughout the microstructure. The lead islands dispersed throughout the microstructure of 85% Cu, 5% Sn, 5% Pb, 5% Zn are illustrated in Fig. 14.7. Since the lead is precipitated late during freezing of the metal, it segregates in areas which freeze last. At the end of freezing it may fill in areas which might otherwise become shrinkage porosity. Lead in copper alloys thus often makes it easier to produce leakproof castings for valves and fittings. Another beneficial effect of lead is its use for improving machinability of copper alloys. The weak lead islands

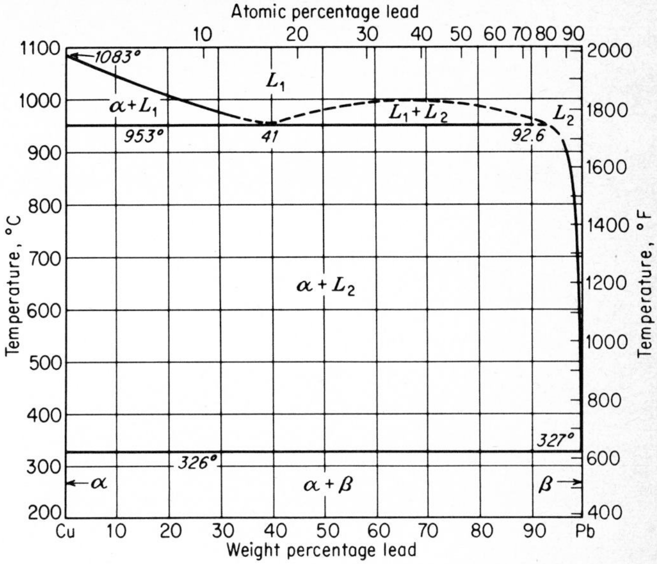

***Fig.* 14.6** The Cu-Pb equilibrium system. (*From American Society for Metals.*[1])

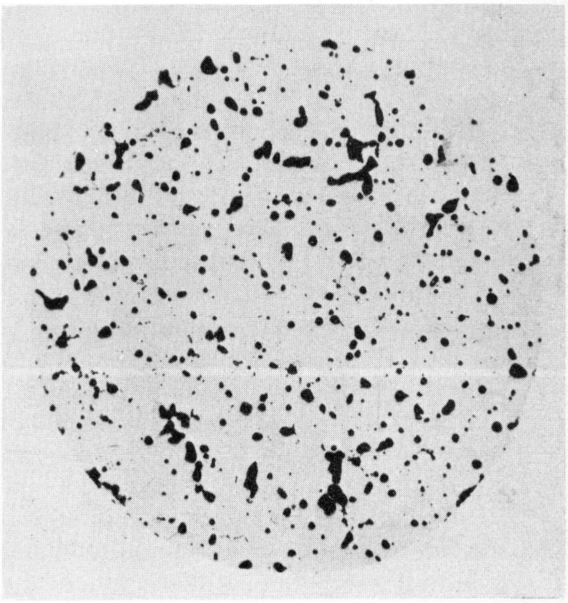

***Fig.* 14.7** Lead areas (dark) in 85% Cu, 5% Sn, 5% Pb, 5% Zn alloy. Unetched, ×100. (*From American Foundrymen's Society.*[6])

make machining soft, tough copper alloys to a fine finish easier by causing machining chips to form, break, and flow more easily from cutting tools.

Figure 14.6 shows that L_1, copper-rich liquid, begins to form as soon as the temperature drops below the liquidus temperature. Since L_1 has high density, it may separate and settle in melting pots or castings. As soon as the temperature drops low enough, below 953 C or 1747 F, L_2, which is over 90 per cent Pb, begins to form, and because of its high density it sinks rapidly if free to do so. Because of this behavior of lead in copper, the alloys must always be heated adequately to ensure solution in the melt and must not be allowed to segregate during the cooling in ladles. Stirring is frequently used to disperse the lead. In castings, the distribution of the lead islands is greatly determined by the lead content, rate of solidification of the casting, and the presence of other elements. Segregated lead, in grain boundaries, large blobs, or in the lower portion of castings, causes poor mechanical properties. The strength of brasses and bronzes is lowered below maximum by the presence of excess lead, and it therefore may be considered as an impurity in some of the high-strength alloys, even though it is beneficial in other alloys.

Copper-Aluminum Alloys

The aluminum-copper equilibrium diagram has been presented in Fig. 12.1. Solid solubility of Al in Cu exists up to about 7.4 per cent at the solidus, with solubility increasing to 9.4 per cent at 565 C (1049 F). A unique feature of this system is the existence of a eutectoid at about 11.8 per cent Al and 565 C (1049 F). This fact enables the high-aluminum-content alloy to be heat-treated in a manner similar to the steels. They may be quenched after holding at 1450 to 1600 F and then reheated to 650 to 1250 F to give optimum combinations of strength, hardness, and ductility. The as-cast and heat-treated microstructures of a commercial aluminum-bronze casting alloy are shown in Figs. 14.8 and 14.9, respectively.

The highest strength and hardness among copper-base alloys are found in heat-treated aluminum bronzes and also in heat-treated Cu-Be bronzes, as illustrated in Table 14.1, for example.

The narrow freezing-temperature range of copper-aluminum alloys is shown in Fig. 12.1. A range of 20 to 50 F in these alloys is seen to be very narrow compared with over 400 F in the tin bronzes. This condition results in a large apparent solidification shrinkage and requires heavy risering to produce sound castings. The narrow freezing range, however, makes it possible to produce castings of maximum soundness with less tendency for microshrinkage than in long-freezing-range alloys.

The aluminum bronzes are of two types. Low-aluminum-content ones are under 10% Al. They consist structurally of α solid solution and

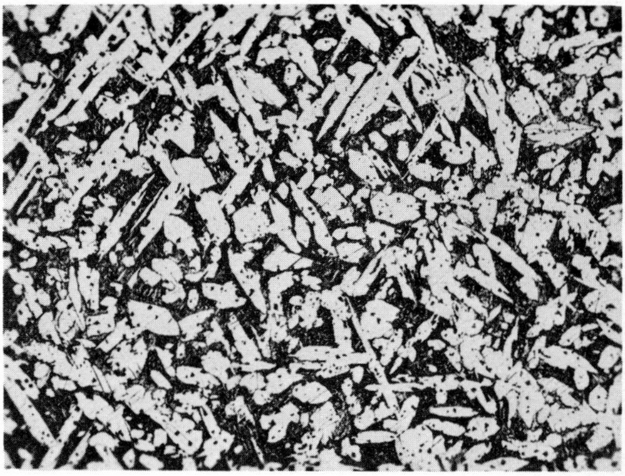

***Fig.* 14.8** As-cast microstructure of Cu, 10.5% Al, 3.5% Fe aluminum-bronze sand casting. White phase is the alpha constituent; dark matrix is eutectoid decomposition product. Etched with ferric chloride, ×100. (*Courtesy of Ampco Metal, Inc.*)

are softer, more ductile, and not heat-treatable to high strength like the higher-aluminum-content bronzes. The latter alloys, containing more aluminum, may make full use of the heat-treating possibilities of this system. Nominal compositions of some aluminum bronzes are given in Tables 14.1 and 14.2.

Effect of Iron

Both classes of alloys contain appreciable percentages of iron. This element is necessary to achieve grain-size control of the cast alloy. In its absence, very coarse grain size develops during solidification and cooling and poor mechanical properties result. The mechanism of the grain-refining effect is controversial but may be due to a change in freezing mechanism. When sufficient iron is present, more than about 0.75 per cent, the liquidus temperature is raised and freezing

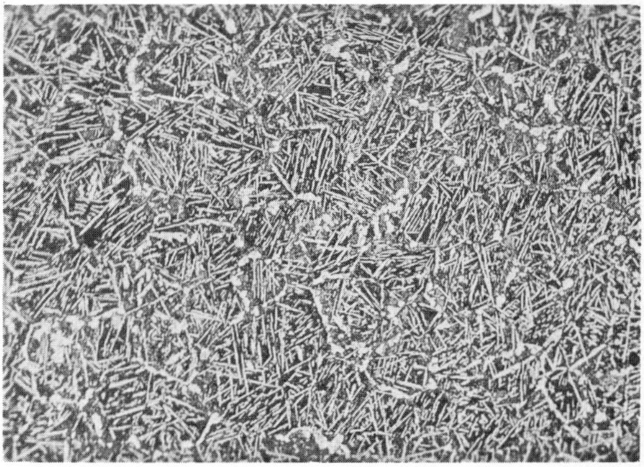

***Fig.* 14.9** Microstructure of alloy shown in Fig. 14.8 after heat-treatment. White phase is the alpha constituent; dark is the decomposition product. Heat-treatment consists in water quenching from 1450 to 1475 F, followed by reheating to 1200 to 1250 F and water quenching. Etched with ferric chloride, ×100. (*Courtesy of Ampco Metals, Inc.*)

begins with solidification of δ-iron, which serves to nucleate a fine grain size throughout the casting as freezing progresses and also prevents grain growth during cooling. Excessive iron content can cause iron segregation and hard spots in the casting.

Casting Properties

The narrow freezing range of the aluminum bronze has been pointed out earlier as requiring good risering practice. These alloys are also susceptible to gas defects because of their composition. Aluminum oxidizes readily, so that the oxygen content of the molten metal is always low. However, because of its ability to reduce water vapor, aluminum makes copper alloys readily susceptible to hydrogen pickup. It must be kept away from water-forming materials as much as possible in order to prevent it from absorbing hydrogen. A furnace atmosphere which is oxidizing to a red brass may be reducing to an aluminum bronze. Unfortunately, oxidizing melting causes severe drossing, especially if the metal is mechanically agitated as it is melted. The aluminum forms a low-surface-tension dross which can easily be entrained in the casting unless the gating introduces the metal very gently and with little agitation in the mold.

Aluminum bronzes also sometimes contain manganese and nickel as alloying elements. The alloys are used for applications requiring a combination of high strength, hardness, and corrosion resistance. Examples shown in Fig. 13.1 are worm gears, sliding plates, bearing sleeves, pickling baskets, bearings, and sleeves for paper mills, castings for marine use, and the like. Nonsparking tools such as those in Fig. 14.10 and nonmagnetic instrument elements are further uses of these casting alloys.

Copper-Beryllium Alloys

Copper and beryllium possess a solubility range which extends to 2.10% Be at 864 C (1587 F). Be-Cu casting alloys contain about 1.0% Be and sometimes cobalt and nickel (Table 14.1). The alloys can be solution heat-treated and precipitation-hardened to high hardness and strength.[1] Their combination of low alloy content and high strength obtainable by heat treatment qualifies them as high-strength–high-conductivity copper casting alloys (Table 14.1).

Nickel Brasses and Bronzes

Nickel brasses and bronzes are nickel-bearing alloys which have a silver or white color rather than the copper, brass, or bronze colors of the

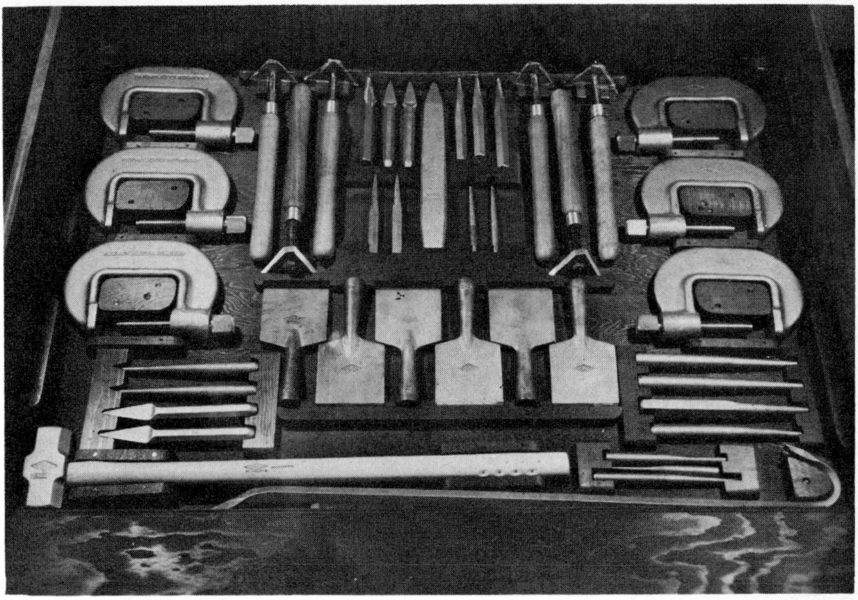

***Fig.* 14.10** Aluminum-bronze castings used as nonsparking safety tools. (*Courtesy of Ampco Metals, Inc.*)

other alloys. For this reason they may be called "nickel silver," or "german silver." The white or silver color presents a pleasing appearance, especially if the castings are required to blend with monel, stainless steels, aluminum, or other metals with a silvery luster. Two classes of nickel silvers are indicated in the ASTM classification. Nickel brasses have only enough of their zinc content substituted by nickel to give a white color. Nickel bronzes contain more nickel than zinc, over 10% nickel, and some tin. Nominal composition is given in Table 14.12. The leaded alloys contain 1.0 to 11.0% lead to improve casting, machinability, and pressuretightness. The uses of these alloys include hardware and ornamental fittings, valves, dairy and food-handling equipment castings, trim for ships and other marine use, soda fountains, valves, and the like: cases where a white color and moderate corrosion resistance are desired.

Cupronickel

Another group of white-colored copper-base alloys consists of the cupronickels. Their composition is given in Table 14.13. Their uses are similar to the nickel brasses and bronze, but they have somewhat better corrosion resistance.

Table 14.12a Chemical requirements for sand-cast leaded nickel brasses and bronzes*

Classification	Leaded nickel brass (leaded nickel silver)				Leaded nickel bronze (leaded nickel silver)			
Alloy Designation	10A		10B†		11A		11B	
	Min	Max	Min	Max	Min	Max	Min	Max
Copper, %	53.00	58.00	57.00	62.00	63.00	67.00	64.00	67.00
Tin, %	1.50	3.00	2.25	3.75	3.50	4.50	4.00	5.50
Lead %	8.00	11.00	4.25	5.75	3.00	5.00	1.00	2.50
Zinc, %	Remainder		Remainder		Remainder		Remainder	
Nickel, %	11.00	14.00	15.00	17.50	19.50	21.50	24.00	27.00
Iron, %	.....	1.50	.....	1.50	.....	1.50	.....	1.50
Manganese, %	.....	0.50	.....	0.50	.....	1.00	.....	1.00

* From American Foundrymen's Society[6] and ASTM Specification B149-52.

Analysis shall regularly be made only for copper, tin, lead, nickel, iron, and manganese. If the presence of excessive amounts of other elements is suspected, or indicated in the course of routine analysis, further analysis shall be made to determine that the total of these other elements is not in excess of 0.50%.

† The chemical requirements of SAE Specification 42 conform in general to the requirements for alloy 10B.

Table 14.12b Minimum physical properties for sand-cast leaded nickel brass and bronze alloys*

Classification	Leaded nickel brass (leaded nickel silver)		Leaded nickel bronze (leaded nickel silver)	
Alloy designation	10A	10B	11A	11B
Ultimate tensile strength, psi, min	30,000	35,000	30,000	45,000
Yield strength in tension,† psi, min	15,000	17,000	17,000	22,000
Elongation, % in 2 in., min	8	15	8	15

* From American Foundrymen's Society.[6]

† Yield strength shall be determined as the stress producing an elongation under load of 0.5%, i.e., 0.01 in. in a gauge length of 2 in.

Permanent-mold and Die-casting Alloys

Copper-base alloys have a low enough freezing range so that they may be cast in permanent molds or dies under pressure. Some of the factors in these casting processes are considered in Ref. 6. Alloys cast by the permanent-mold method are given in Table 14.14. These alloys have been found favorable in view of the requirement of resistance to tearing, pressuretightness, and good mechanical properties. Die-casting alloys

Table* 14.13 *Cupronickel composition*

Composition, %				Tensile strength, psi	Yield point 0.5% ext., psi	Elongation in 2 in., %	Charge melted, lb	Furnace type
Ni	Si	Mn	Fe					
30.19	0.50	1.11	1.03	63,200	31,500	39.0	250	Rocking electric
30.02	0.39	1.03	1.10	60,000	23,250	37.0	250	Rocking electric
30.23	0.50	1.10	1.29	66,500	35,000	35.0	150	Oil-fired crucible

* From "Nickel."[9]

are listed in Table 14.15. It may be noted that casting temperatures are lower in the latter group of alloys, a requirement for longer die life. Since die life is not so favorable as in the case of aluminum alloys, this field has not been so fully developed.

The influence of cooling rate on properties of copper-base alloys again is similar to the case of the aluminum alloys, though not so pronounced. Rapid cooling in metal molds favors better properties than slow cooling in sand molds. However, since solution heat-treatment and aging effects are not so common in copper alloys as in aluminum alloys, the influence of cooling rate on casting properties is not nearly so great.

Complex Alloys

The foregoing discussion has dealt with a number of the common copper-base alloys. The results of alloying have been considered from a simplified viewpoint. Obviously, with the number of elements involved, the complexity of microstructures possible is great. There is no intent in this textbook to consider the more profound metallurgical principles involved. Rather, it is expected that this material will provide the reader with a picture of some of the classes of copper-base casting alloys and their differences and similarity and their uses, in a broad way. Certainly, when alloys are extensively used for corrosion resistance and properties of that kind, only broad generalities are possible unless the subject is very comprehensively examined.

BIBLIOGRAPHY

1. American Society for Metals, "Metals Handbook," 1948.
2. O. W. Ellis, "Copper and Copper Alloys," American Society for Metals, 1948.
3. D. R. Hull, "Casting of Brass and Bronze," American Society for Metals, 1950.
4. R. A. Colton, How Copper-base Casting Alloys Are Used in Electrical Industry, *Materials and Methods,* June, 1950.

Table 14.14 ***Copper-base alloys in permanent-mold castings****

Alloy	Nominal composition, %								Temp, F		Average mechanical properties			
	Cu	Al	Fe	Ni	Mn	Si	Zn	Sn	Melting point	Casting range	Tensile strength, psi	Yield strength, 0.5%, elongation, psi	Elongation, % in 2 in.	Bhn
Aluminum bronze, A	88.0	9.0	3.0	....	†	...	......	...	1830	1850–2000	75,000	35,000	30.0	130
Aluminum bronze, B	89.0	10.0	1.0	....	†	...	......	...	1830	1850–2000	75,000	30,000	30.0	120
Aluminum bronze, C	85.0	11.0	4.0	....	†	...	......	...	1880	1900–2050	80,000	40,000	20.0	130
Aluminum bronze, D	80.0	11.0	4.5	4.5	†	...	......	...	1890	1900–2050	95,000	65,000	10.0	175
Aluminum bronze high nickel	76.0	12.0	5.0	7.0	†	...	......	...	1890	1925–2100	105,000	80,000	3.0	225
Silicon-aluminum bronze	91.0	7.0	...	....	...	2.0	......	...	1830	1850–1950	70,000	30,000	30.0	105
Yellow brass, 1	60.0	0.4	...	....	...	...	Rem.	1.0	1700	1750–1850	40,000	20,000	25.0	75
Yellow brass, 2	61.0	....	...	....	...	...	Rem.	...	1700	1750–1850	42,000	20,000	20.0	80
Nickel brass	55.0	0.4	...	5.0	...	...	Rem.	...	1750	1800–1875	50,000	30,000	20.0	95
Manganese bronze	57.0	2.0	1.5	....	1.0	...	Rem.	...	1750	1800–1875	75,000	55,000	15.0	100
Nickel silver	45.0	1.0	1.0	15.0	1.0	Pb 1.0	36.0	1.0	1700	1800–1900	90,000	50,000	8.0	170
Silicon brass	81.0	....	...	....	...	4.0	15.0	...	1700	1800–1900	85,000	55,000	15.0	140

* From American Foundrymen's Society.[6]

† May partially replace iron.

Table 14.15a Chemical requirements for copper-base alloy die castings*

Alloy designation†	Z30A‡		ZS331A‡		ZS144A‡	
	Min	Max	Min	Max	Min	Max
Copper, %	57.00	....	63.00	67.00	80.00	83.00
Tin, %	....	1.50	....	0.25	....	0.25
Lead, %	....	1.50	....	0.25	....	0.15
Zinc, %	30.00	....	Remainder		Remainder	
Iron, %	....	0.50	....	0.15	....	0.15
Manganese, %	....	0.25	....	0.15	....	0.15
Silicon, %	....	0.25	0.75	1.25	3.75	4.25

* From ASTM Specification B176-62.

† These alloy designations were established in accordance with ASTM Designation B275, Recommended Practice for Codification of Light Metals and Alloys, Cast and Wrought.

‡ Prior to 1952 these alloys were designated as A, B, and C, respectively.

Table 14.15b Minimum physical properties for copper-base alloy die castings*

Alloy designation	Z30A	ZS331A	ZS144A
Ultimate tensile strength, psi, min	45,000	58,000	90,000
Yield strength (offset = 0.2%), psi, min†	25,000	30,000	50,000
Elongation in 2 in., %, min	10	15	25

* From ASTM Specification B176-62.

† Yield strength as determined by the offset method.

5. A. B. Kinzel, High Conductivity Copper Castings, *Trans. AFS,* vol. 67, p. 779, 1949.
6. American Foundrymen's Society, "Copper-base Alloys Foundry Practice," 1952.
7. R. A. Colton, Copper-base Alloys Have Wide Range of Properties, *Am. Foundryman,* vol. 17, February, 1950.
8. H. E. Arblaster, Manganese Bronze, *Trans. AFS,* vol. 54, 1946.
9. The International Nickel Co., Inc., "Nickel," 1947.
10. American Society for Metals, "Metals Handbook," 8th ed., vol. 1, 1961.

15
Steel Castings

INTRODUCTION

Many of the advantages that make wrought steel such an outstanding material of construction can also be assigned to steel castings. In addition, the casting process confers special advantages not obtainable otherwise and, by the same token, is accountable for certain disadvantages.

Steel is strong, with tensile strengths ranging from 60,000 to about 280,000 psi. Steel is also ductile, and the combination of strength and ductility adds up to give steel great toughness and resistance to shock. The properties of steel can be controlled within rather wide limits by controlling its composition, specifically its carbon content. Steel is essentially an alloy of iron and carbon, and its remarkable properties and the ability to control its properties stem from the presence of carbon.* For example, when carbon is absent, iron is quite soft and weak. If carbon is added in as little as 0.2 to 0.3 per cent, the strength is raised appreciably and the ductility, although reduced, is still appreciable. The result is that steel exhibits a versatility found in no other metal. Figure 15.1*a* shows this effect of carbon on the tensile strength and percentage reduction of area of plain carbon cast steel. Curves for yield strength and percentage elongation showing similar trends are also available.[1]

Favored as it is with this means of controlling properties, steel is further favored by another control of its properties, namely, heat-treatment. This subject is discussed more fully in Chap. 17, but briefly, iron and steel undergo a change in their crystal-lattice structure (i.e., the arrangement of the atoms in the solid state) that makes it possible to control properties by controlling the cooling rate from an elevated temperature (1500 to 1650 F). Further control is also obtained by reheating (tempering or drawing) after rapid cooling (quenching). See Fig. 15.1*b*.

A special attribute of steel castings in comparison with wrought products is the fact that steel castings have a uniformity of properties regardless of the direction in which they are tested. This so-called "isotropic" behavior is absent in steel that has been worked down into

*See p. 467 for the amounts of other elements that are normally present in steel.

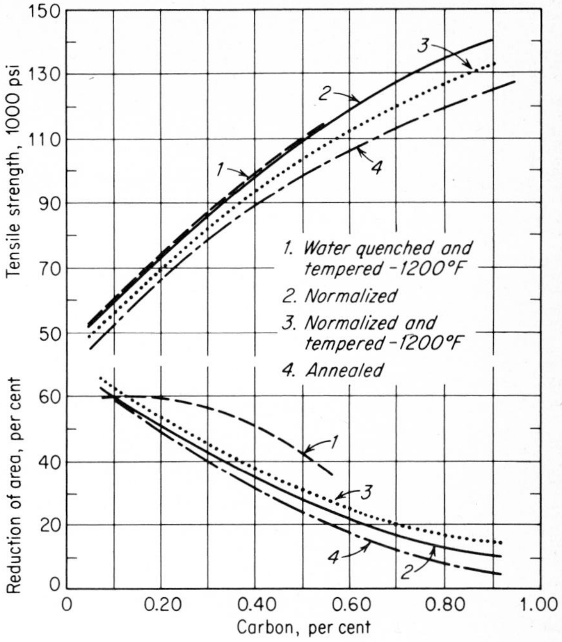

(*a*)

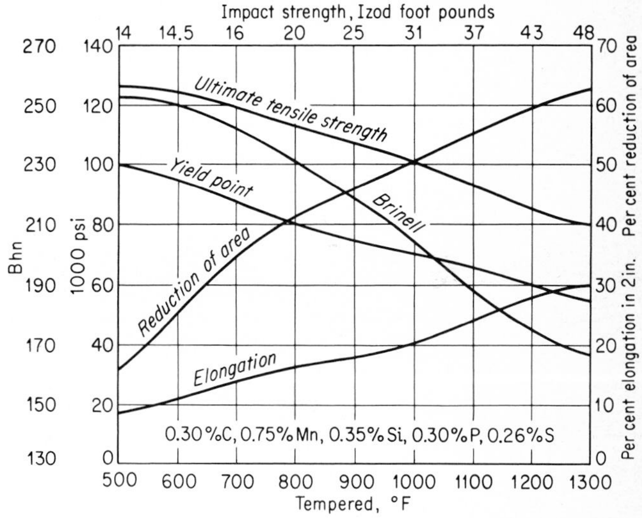

(*b*)

***Fig.* 15.1** (*a*) Tensile strength and reduction of area vs. carbon content for carbon cast steels after various heat-treatments, (*b*) the effect of tempering on the mechanical properties of a 0.30 per cent carbon cast steel. (*Courtesy of Steel Founders' Society of America.*)

structural shapes from ingots or billets because the working operation introduces a directionality in properties. Thus steel so worked is tough and strong when tested in the direction of greatest elongation but is weaker and more brittle if tested in a transverse direction. Cast steel does not possess this directionality and is therefore better suited to applications where this effect might prove harmful.

A distinct advantage of steel castings not readily realizable in other ferrous foundry products is ease of welding. The fact that steel can be readily welded with no serious loss of properties means that this valuable tool can be used in fabrication and in the repair and salvage of castings. Of perhaps greater potential importance is the opportunity to combine by welding steel castings with shapes fabricated by other means to produce a composite structure composed partly of castings and partly of wrought-steel parts.

Rather ironically, one of the major advantages of steel, namely, its strength and ductility, becomes a definite handicap in the foundry. As was discussed somewhat in Chap. 9 and is considered further here, steel castings require (as do certain other castings and alloys) extensive risering to compensate for a rather large shrinkage that occurs during freezing. After casting, removal of these sometimes quite massive gates and risers presents a definite problem since the ductility and strength of the metal preclude their being merely hammered off as in the case of brittle alloys like cast iron. Saws, abrasive cutoff wheels, torches, etc., are required for this purpose, leading to high finishing costs in many cases.

The excellent combination of properties found in steel has already been mentioned. From a foundry-practice standpoint, however, it taxes the ingenuity of the designer and metallurgist because of its casting properties and the close limits of its composition. The high pouring temperature of steel also demands that special attention be given to refractories, ladles, molding sands, metal transfer in the shop, filling the mold with no misruns, and related problems. The high solidification shrinkage of steel also introduces design and molding problems seldom exceeded in other alloys. In the melting of this alloy there are also special problems more or less unique to steel. The nature of the alloy and its reactivity with oxygen and other impurities require that a rather intricate procedure of melting and refining be established to ensure the production of good-quality metal.

It is the purpose of this chapter to discuss these problems, but because melting of steel is so specialized, it is considered separately in Chap. 16, and only a brief survey of melting methods is given here.

MOLDING PROCESSES AND SANDS

Molding for steel castings is no different from that for other casting alloys. However, because of certain characteristics of steel, certain methods cannot be used and others are not used to the extent that they are employed in other metals.

Steel can be cast into molds made by any of the sand-molding processes. Dry-sand molds, core-sand molds, skin-dried molds, and cement-bonded molds are used to a greater extent in steel foundries than for most of the other casting alloys. The reason for this is the severe conditions imposed by steel. The problems associated with various molding methods should become more apparent as these methods are discussed.

With reference to molding methods other than those using sand, the high pouring temperature required for steel prevents its being made by the permanent-mold process, except in certain special cases, or by die casting, or plaster molding. Steel can be poured in investment molds because the investment materials are sufficiently refractory. Graphite molds can be used for steel if precautions are taken to avoid carbon pickup. Ceramic molds can be and are being used.

Green-sand Molding

Many steel castings are made using green-sand molds. The general practice is no different from that for other alloys. However, steel-foundry sands differ from others chiefly in the following characteristics.

Refractoriness

Because sand in contact with steel may be heated to an excessively high temperature, the molding sand must be of sufficient purity so that it will not fuse together or deteriorate. Figure 15.6 illustrates that the sand at a metal-mold interface may reach high temperatures, but a short distance away the sand does not get so hot nor does it heat up so rapidly as at the interface.[2] As a consequence of the demand for high thermal stability, most green-sand molding for steel is done with compounded sand mixtures; the bond is usually bentonite. Associated with refractoriness of the sand is the problem of *durability*. The high-temperature exposure to which the sand is subjected alters the sand and its bond both physically and chemically, leading to a gradual change in its properties unless it is amply replenished with new sand. Unfortunately, there is no simple test to indicate the occurrence of these gradual changes. In one investigation[3] it was observed that the rate of deterioration of the sand could be linked with the development of relatively high hot strength and sensitivity to thermal shock, with progressive build-up of "cokey" coatings on the sand grains.

High Permeability and Low Moisture Content

These two requirements are linked together because they are interrelated. When sand is heated, part of the moisture in the sand is changed to steam. The air in the mold is heated and increases in volume, and organic additions may decompose to gaseous products. These gases must be vented away from the mold cavity. Steel heats the mold to higher temperatures than do other alloys; hence a greater gas volume may develop and more venting is needed. The necessary conditions can be achieved for steel by increasing the permeability above that required for other alloys and restricting the moisture content to a relatively low value (around 3 per cent). Much of the gas can escape through risers and other openings in the mold.

Organic and Other Additions

The use of synthetic sands with a relatively low binder content for steel is accompanied by a tendency toward certain casting defects such as scabs, buckling, and rattails that result from the expansion of the sand as it is heated. The addition of certain materials to the sand may reduce the tendency to form these defects. Principles related to the control of this defect are discussed in Chap. 5.

The net effect of these special conditions imposed by steel on green-sand properties results in establishing a range of properties that differ rather markedly from those for molding sand mixtures used for other alloys. These differences are demonstrated by the data in Table 5.9, which lists typical sand compositions and properties for various alloys, including steel.

Much green-sand work is done with a *facing sand* which is especially compounded to produce the desired properties, and a *backing sand* which, being essentially reused facing sand, is also controlled as to properties and grain size. This practice, although it adds to the complexity of molding since it involves delivery of both facing and backing sand to the molder, has the advantage of cutting down the quantity of sand that must be treated with additives and ensures sand properties at the metal-mold interface that are always under close control.

Green-sand-molding Casting Defects

In addition to such defects as rattails, buckles, scabs, hot tears, etc., which are discussed elsewhere in this book, and also treated thoroughly in reference material,[5] another defect that can develop is *pinhole porosity.*

It is characterized by small smooth-walled holes, elongated in a direction perpendicular to the mold wall and occurring immediately below the casting skin. The exact cause of this defect is still a matter of debate, but it is generally agreed that the formation of either CO or H_2O or both by a reaction at the metal surface or slightly below is responsible.[5-7] The fact that the defect occurs more frequently in green-sand molds suggests that it is at least aggravated by certain conditions existing at the metal-sand interface; and since the only major difference between green-sand and dry-sand molds would be in moisture content, the formation of H_2O by reaction between hydrogen and oxygen in the steel is strongly suspected as at least a contributing factor. Moisture in the sand could aggravate the condition by being dissociated to hydrogen, which could then diffuse into the steel and react with dissolved oxygen. This would explain why pinhole porosity can be prevented by deoxidizing the steel with aluminum before pouring, since the oxygen would react with the aluminum instead of the hydrogen.

Dry-sand Molds and Skin-dried Molds

Green-sand molding is preferable to other methods of molding because it is more economical and gives maximum production rates. There are times, however, when, because of the need to increase the strength of the mold or to avoid pinholes, or for other reasons, drying of the mold before pouring is desirable. Superficial drying can be accomplished by heating the surface with torches, infrared lamps, or hot air, or the molds can be dried in large car-type ovens at temperatures up to 500 F.

The moisture content of the green sand used for skin-dried or dry-sand molds may be somewhat higher than for ordinary green-sand work for greater moldability, and also because a higher moisture content leads to greater dry strength. These dry-sand properties have been illustrated in Chap. 5.

Other Types of Molds

A few foundries have used cement as a sand binder, but the practice has not been very popular in this country. Cement-bonded molds were discussed in Chap. 3.

Investment molding, also discussed in Chap. 3, has been used for specialty castings where close tolerances or intricacy of design dictated the use of this method. One field where investment molding has proved effective is in the castings of the special alloys and shapes used for gas-turbine blades and other parts subject to high-temperature service that cannot be readily formed by other methods.

Shell molds have been used with some success, but there is a tendency to form surface defects. These can be eliminated by use of chill-type shell molds.[8] Ceramic molds are also feasible.[9] These permit pouring thinner sections than with conventional sand molds. A special process combining graphite molds and air-pressure pouring has been used to produce steel car wheels and other shapes.[10]

Molding Methods

The usual methods of molding, such as hand ramming, jolt ramming, squeezing, and sand-slinger ramming, are used on steel sands; no difference exists in the ramming methods used for steel in comparison with other casting alloys.

CORES

Coremaking and core materials were discussed in Chaps. 6 and 7, respectively. Outside of the need to provide for higher operating temperatures, there is little basic distinction between cores for steel castings as compared with those used for other alloys, and the principles discussed in the aforementioned chapters are readily applicable to steel-foundry practice.

Because of the extreme conditions that develop from the high pouring temperature used for steel, certain special problems should be mentioned. One effect, for example, of the high pouring temperature is that cores are heated faster and to higher temperatures than cores for similar-sized casting pouring in lower-melting alloys. The result is that larger volumes of core gases are generated and must be removed from the mold. This necessitates cores of higher permeability for steel castings and more venting than may be required for most cast-iron or nonferrous castings. Data in Table 7.2 show the markedly greater permeability in sands recommended for steel cores. The use of hollow shell-molded cores has aided considerably in eliminating gas problems that originate from cores.

Other effects associated with cores in steel-casting work are discussed in the following paragraphs.

Hot-tear Formation

Steel is poured at a high temperature, but this temperature is low relative to the high-freezing-temperature range for steel. The result is that steel begins to freeze very soon after being poured, and in some instances before the cores have been heated to the point where they have lost their bond strength. The combination of a relatively rigid core and a weak contracting metal often results in the formation of cracks in the casting, referred to as *hot tears*. Steel is not the only metal subjected to hot tears—they are also formed in other metals—but the problem can be quite acute in certain steel castings, and for that reason the causes of hot tears have been the subject of considerable study. Nor can it be said that cores are the only cause of hot tears, since a *rigid* mold is also a potential cause of hot tears.[5,11] Since cores generally offer greater rigidity than molds, the hot-tear defect is discussed with relation to cores.

The defect, which is illustrated for malleable irons in Fig. 23.12, is associated with both metallurgical variables and sand variables. One opinion regarding the cause of this phenomenon is that hot tearing occurs during the last stages of freezing of steel when the solid metal grains are still surrounded by a thin liquid film.[12,13,16,17] The tearing occurs when the natural contraction of the steel is inhibited either by the geometry of the casting or by the mold. Others have submitted evidence indicating that tearing can occur after solidification.[18,19] In this case, the tears may be fine, hairline fractures, not readily visible without the use of special techniques such as magnafluxing or etching. Hot tearing is more likely to occur if the casting contains local areas that freeze at a later period than the balance of the surrounding metal. These so-called "hot spots" which remain fluid longer than the surrounding metal serve as a focal point for the concentration of contractual strains. Because hot tearing is associated with the freezing characteristics of metal, as well as variables introduced by the mold, there can be no established rule regarding the probability and intensity* of hot-tear formation. For example, a given core mix may prove perfectly acceptable in one application and completely unacceptable in another. Again, a specific composition of steel may not crack in one type of casting and yet show cracking in another case. The probability of attack may be even more critical than in the examples just given. A particular core-sand mix may cause cracking only if the metal is poured above a certain temperature, whereas another mix may or may not crack regardless of pouring temperature. If these interrelationships are kept in mind, it can be shown, however, that the probability and intensity of tearing are related to core composition and properties as follows:

1. Strong, hard cores and molds that collapse slowly under heat are more likely to cause hot tears than weak, easily collapsible cores or molds.
2. Increased core density increases the intensity (length) of hot tearing.[15]

As far as metallurgical variables are concerned, it appears that hot tearing is aggravated by elements such as sulfur and phosphorus.[14,19] In one investigation, aluminum deoxidation was found to give more re-

*Probability: whether or not a tear will appear; intensity: size or length of the crack.

sistance to hot tearing than silicon deoxidation.[16] By and large, however, metallurgical causes of hot tearing are believed to be of minor significance as compared with mold and core variables.[13,14]

Metal Penetration

Another characteristic which is more common in steel castings than in other casting metals is the tendency for steel to penetrate a finite distance into the mold or core. The result is either a steel-sand crust attached to the casting or fin-type attachments resulting from local or crevice penetration into the mold. Examples of the first type are shown in Fig. 15.2.

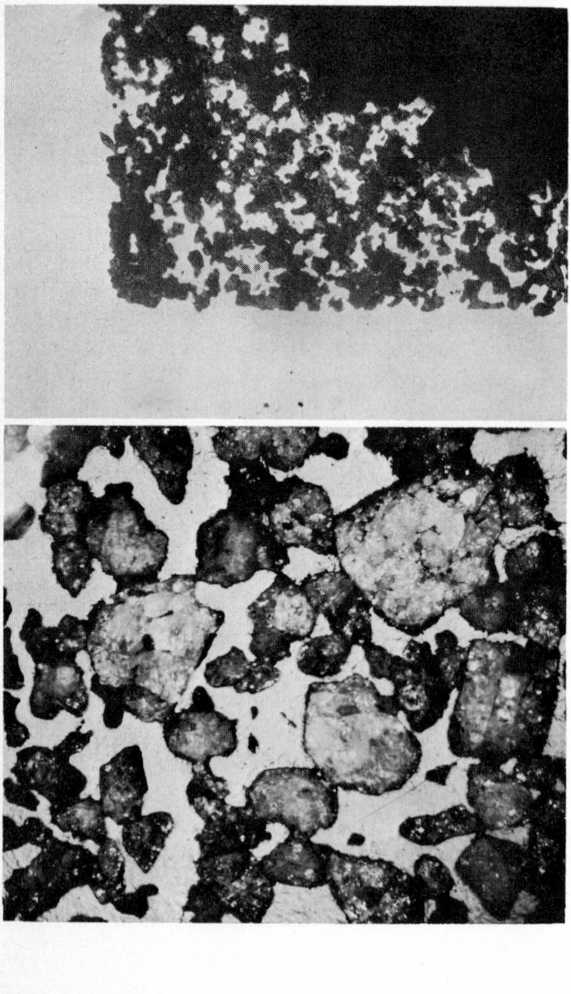

***Fig.* 15.2** Examples of metal penetration. Top, steel (light) penetrating sand at an inside corner, ×10. Bottom, enlarged view of penetration of steel between sand grains, ×50. (*From H. Pettersson.*[20])

Factors which have been found to affect metal penetration are:[20–25]

1. The *longer* molten steel is held in contact with sand, the greater the chance for metal penetration.
2. *Increased metal pressure* increases metal penetration. Since metal normally does not penetrate sand because of surface-tension effects, the effect of pressure is to overcome the normal resistance offered by surface tension. High metal pressures are, of course, directly related to the differential metal pressure head (height) that exists in the molten steel.
3. *High pouring temperatures* lead to penetration.
4. Increased penetration occurs with *increased grain size* or poor ramming of the sand.
5. *Mold washes* tend to prevent penetration.
6. Increased penetration occurs with *increased carbon content.*
7. *Large metal mass* compared with a small sand mass increases the penetration.
8. *Moisture or other gases* in the sand may react with the sand or metal to open channels for penetration.

Mold washes are probably effective in reducing metal penetration by closing the pores in the sand mold and also by reducing the amount of oxidation that occurs on the metal surface.

Besides the use of mold or core washes, areas that are troublesome from the standpoint of metal penetration can be improved by using zircon (zirconium silicate) sand mixtures as a facing material.[26,27] Zircon sands are highly refractory, have a high heat conductivity and a high density, and are not wet by metals. These factors are all instrumental in reducing metal penetration. Because of the cost, zircon sand is used only in severe cases where the cost is justified.

Burn-on

Burn-on is differentiated from metal penetration by the fact that it is related to oxidation of the casting surface. This results in penetration of the sand by the molten oxide which wets the sand grains. Progressive oxidation at the metal surface develops a pitted condition, with encrustations formed by the liquid-oxide penetration into the sand clinging to these areas because of the rough casting surface created by the oxidation.[5,28] Although burn-on may have the appearance of metal penetration, it is essentially oxide penetration into the casting surface (coupled with oxide penetration into the sand) rather than metal penetration.

Ceroxides

Closely related to burn-on is the accumulation of nonmetallic particles that normally occur on the cope surface of steel castings. These particles, low-melting mixtures of oxides of silicon, manganese, iron, and aluminum of variable composition, are called ceroxides. They solidify as a glassy material frequently intermingled with sand grains. They are attributable to the following factors:[29-36]

1. *Pouring practice.* Bottom pouring causes fewer ceroxides than lip pouring.
2. *Composition of ladle linings.* A high alumina lining results in less ceroxide on the casting surface than a silica ladle lining.
3. *Gating practice.* A streamlined gating practice produces less ceroxide than other methods tried, although a whirl gate is quite effective.
4. *Mold atmosphere.* If the mold atmosphere is made more reducing, ceroxide formation is reduced, but erosion of the mold may increase.
5. *Composition of the steel.* Increasing manganese in the steel increases the amount of ceroxide formed, and aluminum may react with fire-clay refractories to form a viscous product which may erode from the refractory lining surfaces and enter the mold cavity.

Core and Mold Washes

The greater difficulty in achieving good surface finish and avoiding metal penetration in steel castings suggests the use of mold or core washes to a greater degree than with other casting alloys. The functions of mold or core washes, as listed by Briggs,[18] are:

1. To prevent metal penetration
2. To eliminate cutting (sand erosion)
3. To prevent scabbing
4. To give smooth casting appearance
5. To obtain clean casting surfaces
6. To modify the mold atmosphere
7. To assist in cleaning the casting

Core coatings are discussed in Chap. 7, and typical coating materials for steel-casting molds are given in Table 7.8.

SOLIDIFICATION FACTORS

Principles of gating and feeding castings have been discussed in Chap. 9. However, it is evident from Chaps. 11 and 13, on aluminum and copper-base castings, that each alloy group has certain inherent characteristics which require special treatment for proper gating and feeding to exist. Steel, likewise, has certain properties which must be correctly handled in gating and risering of steel castings.

Fluidity*

The spiral-type fluidity test is used to describe the fluidity of molten cast steel. A spiral pattern is shown in Fig. 15.3.[37] Pouring temperature and composition are important factors influencing the inches of fluidity obtained with the spiral test. Accurate temperature determination is one of the most important factors in any spiral-fluidity test. Differences in fluidity at any particular temperature due to composition variables such as carbon, silicon, sulfur, chromium, manganese and to deoxidation treatment have been extensively studied.[18,37,38] The influence of some of these variables is indicated in Fig. 15.4. The type of melting practice appears to have little effect, whereas the composition, particularly the silicon content, has a more noticeable influence on fluidity. Chromium steels are regarded as having a very poor fluidity.

In pouring commercial steels limited to certain analysis ranges it appears that temperature rather than analysis may be viewed as the major factor which should be controlled to obtain the best conditions. This is not to imply that chemical-composition variables, mold conditions, melting practice, etc., can be ignored. Rather, from an engineering viewpoint, it should be emphasized that ladling, pouring, and handling of the steel should be done with a minimum of temperature drop in order to retain fluidity.

The relatively low fluidity of steel and its rapid loss of fluidity as it approaches the liquidus temperature must be compensated by gating design. There is an old rule, especially applicable to small or thin castings, "Never pour steel downhill." In the mold cavity, if streams of metal separate and run ahead of the main body of metal as the mold fills, freezing will occur. Because of the rapid temperature drop of the

*Discussion of fluidity in Chap. 8 should be reviewed.

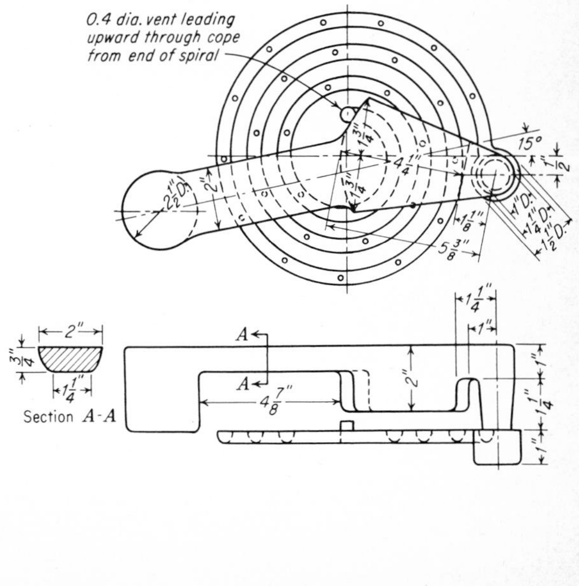

***Fig.* 15.3** Fluidity spiral used for steel. (*From H. Taylor, E. Rominski, and C. W. Briggs.*[37])

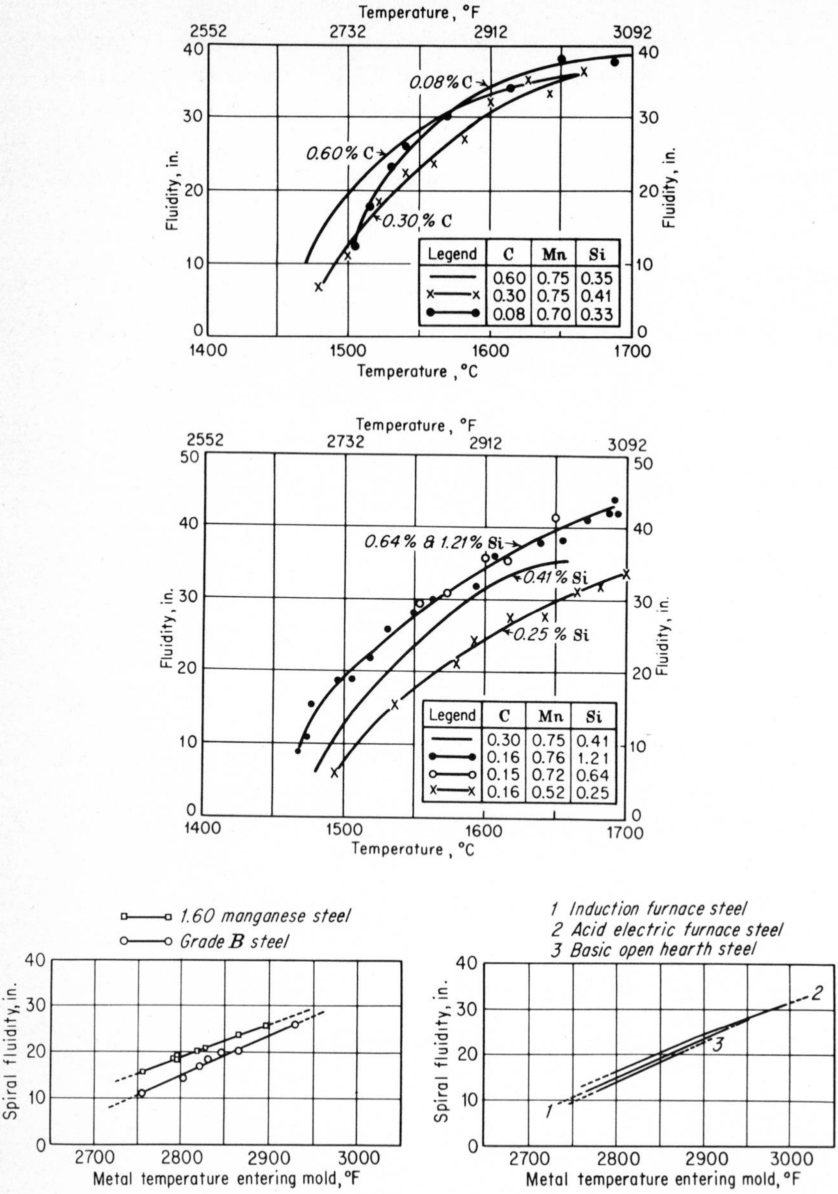

***Fig.* 15.4** Effect of melting variables and composition on the fluidity of steel. (*From H. Taylor, E. Rominski, and C. W. Briggs*[37] *and G. A. Lillieqvist.*[38])

small isolated metal streams, they do not readily remelt and fuse into the main body of the casting. Misruns consequently appear on the casting surface. Pouring hot, fast, and, of course, with gating that fills upward from the bottom with no cascading of metal over cores will minimize misruns from this source. Gating design for favorable metal flow is discussed later.

Solidification

Although solidification was discussed in Chap. 8, it seems appropriate to enumerate and discuss some of the variables that influence the solidification characteristics of steel:

1. Temperature level of solidification
2. Temperature range for solidification
3. Thermal conductivity of the mold
4. Thermal conductivity of steel
5. Gravity and convection effects
6. Solidification in a flowing stream
7. Solidification time
8. Shape factor

Temperature Level of Solidification

Because of its high solidification temperature, steel usually has a large temperature difference between the casting and the mold wall. This results in steep thermal gradients that favor progressive solidification. Of course, the characteristics of the mold are also a factor, as discussed later.

Temperature Range of Solidification

The temperature range of solidification is primarily influenced by the carbon content and secondarily by other alloying elements in low-alloy steels. In high-alloy steels, the effects of elements other than carbon may predominate. The effect of carbon was revealed in Fig. 8.11. This figure shows that solidification range increases with the carbon content. The net effect is that the differential distance from the casting surface to the start and end of the freezing interfaces becomes greater with carbon content, and hence the degree of progressive solidification becomes less.

Thermal Conductivity of the Mold

Figures 15.5 and 15.6 illustrate the effect of thermal conductivity of the mold material.[39,40] Figure 15.5 compares temperature gradients

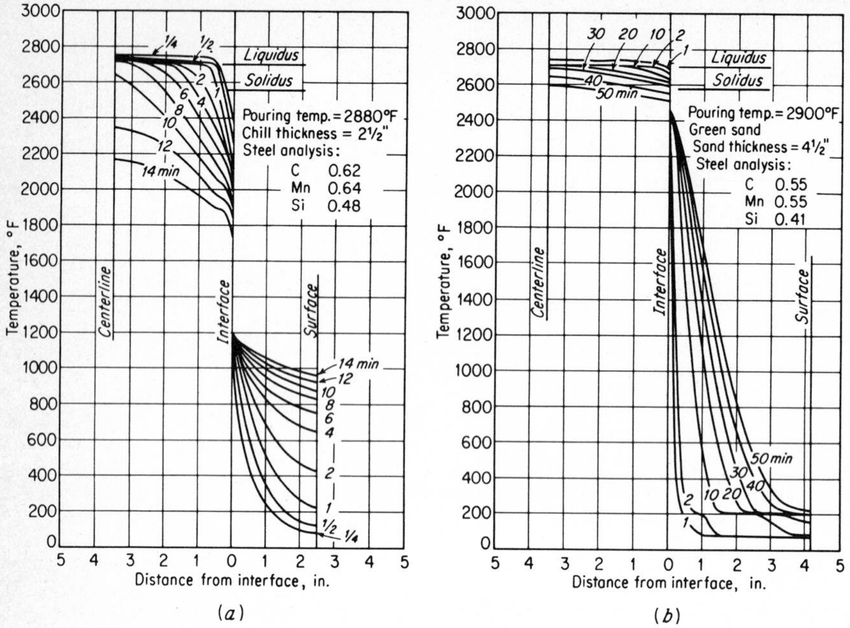

Fig. **15.5** Thermal gradients in the casting and in the mold when steel is cast (*a*) against a 2½-in. chill, and (*b*) in a green-sand mold. (*From H. F. Bishop and W. S. Pellini.*[39])

obtained by pouring steel into a 2½-in. steel chill with those obtained by pouring into a green-sand mold. Use of the chill contributes to a highly progressive freezing process.

The range of freezing that can be anticipated from a variety of mold materials, some of commercial significance and others not, is indicated in Fig. 15.6.

Thermal Conductivity of the Steel

Because of its relatively poor thermal conductivity, steel is inclined to develop sharp temperature gradients which favor progressive solidification unless the thermal conductivity of the mold is so low as to overshadow the effect of the metal. This latter condition usually arises in sand molds.

Nominal changes in carbon or alloy content would not be expected to change the thermal conductivity of the steel per se and therefore would not be expected to exert a noticeable influence on progressive solidification. (An effect from changing the temperature range of solidification could still occur.)

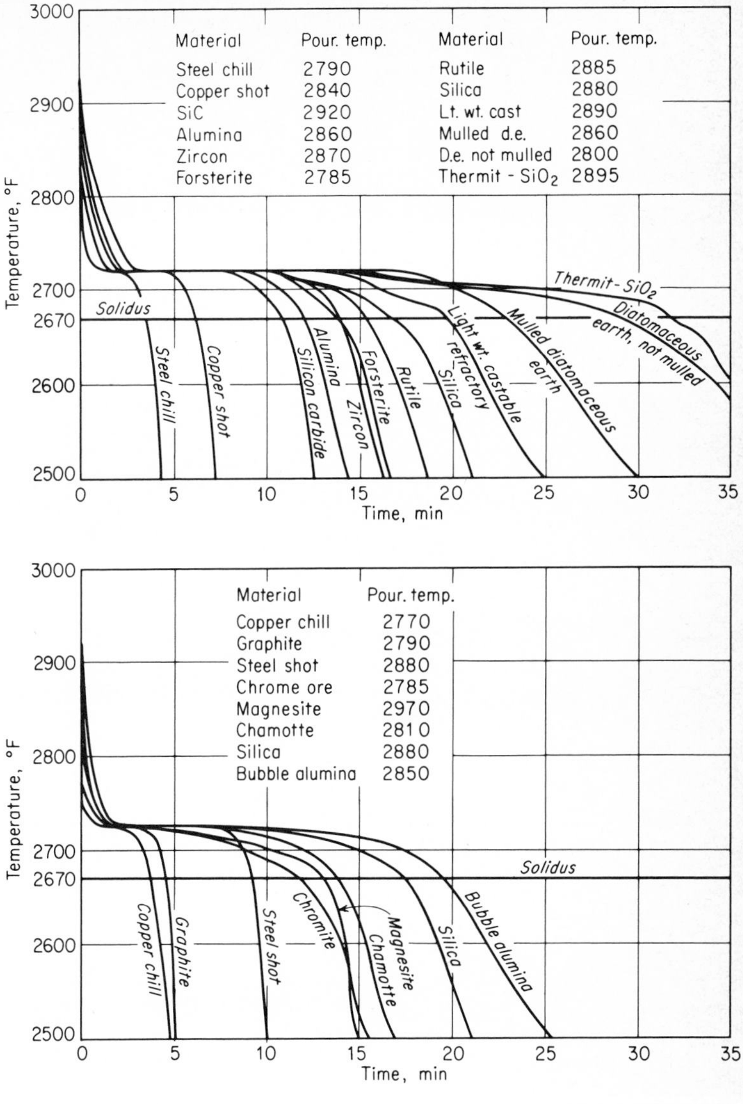

***Fig.* 15.6** Influence of mold material on cooling curves obtained at the center of 6-in. cast-steel spheres. (*From C. Locke, C. W. Briggs, and R. L. Ashbrook.*[40])

Gravity and Convection Effects

Some investigators believe that convection and gravity can affect the structure of the solidified casting.[41] They believe that, in addition to columnar grains and equi-axed grains formed during solidification, there are also "nuclear" crystal units that develop from a large number of nuclei. These units are not attached to the side walls and are free to move by convection and gravity. Maintenance of a large temperature gradient between the top and bottom of a casting causes a higher proportion of the metal to solidify about these nuclear crystallites, thereby producing a finer structure. Because the effect must be induced by chilling the top of the casting compared with the bottom, the procedures used to enhance nuclear crystallization are contrary to the principles of progressive solidification.

Solidification in a Flowing Stream

When liquid metal moves past a solidifying front, the columnar dendrites tend to point upstream. The effect is promoted by raising the pouring temperature; therefore, in pouring thin sections, the development of these dendrites tends to defeat the purpose of the higher pouring temperature by restricting the feed channels in the thin sections.[41]

Solidification Time

In Chap. 8, the formula $D = k\sqrt{t} - c$ was given to indicate the casting wall thickness as a function of time t, k and c being constants. A better fit for steel castings is obtained by using $D = K_1t^{0.4} + K_2t$, where K_1 and K_2 are constants, depending on the shape of the mold, etc.[41]

Modifications of Chvorinov's rule relating freezing time to surface area and volume of the casting provide the following equations for simple shapes:[43]

$$\frac{V}{A\sqrt{t}} = 0.25 \text{ in./min}^{1/2} \qquad \text{(steel plates or slabs)}$$

$$= 0.28 \text{ in./min}^{1/2} \qquad \text{(steel cylinders or bars)}$$

$$= 0.29 \text{ in./min}^{1/2} \qquad \text{(steel chunks, spheres, cubes)}$$

Figure 15.7 illustrates the influence of shape and size on freezing time.[41]

Shape Factor

External or internal corners pose special problems. A study of L- and T-shaped sections for a 0.25 per cent carbon steel is plotted in Fig. 15.8. The adverse effect of the low freezing rates at the internal corners can be compensated by using fillets at these points. For sections greater than 3 in., a fillet radius of $T/3$ is recommended.[41]

When calculating from surface-area–volume relations, the solidification times for flat-plate sections joined in L or T designs, the factors of $1\frac{1}{3}$ and $1\frac{1}{2}$, respectively, should be used to account for the lower freezing rates at the junctions, as compared with unjoined sections.[41]

Although core diameters would be expected to have an influence on heat extraction from a casting, studies of this effect should take into

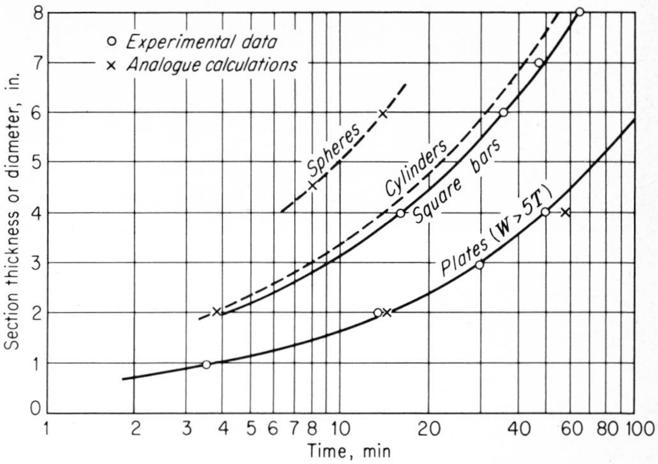

***Fig.* 15.7** Effect of casting shape and size on freezing time. (*From C. W. Briggs.*[41])

consideration whether the core is solid or hollow. Solid cores, however, do not begin to exert much influence on the freezing pattern until they reach a size of about 8 in., at which point a measurable amount of heat is extracted by the core. A 16-in. core produces essentially the same solidification time as a flat plate with a thickness equal to the wall thickness of the cylinder.[45] Comparable data for hollow cores are not available.

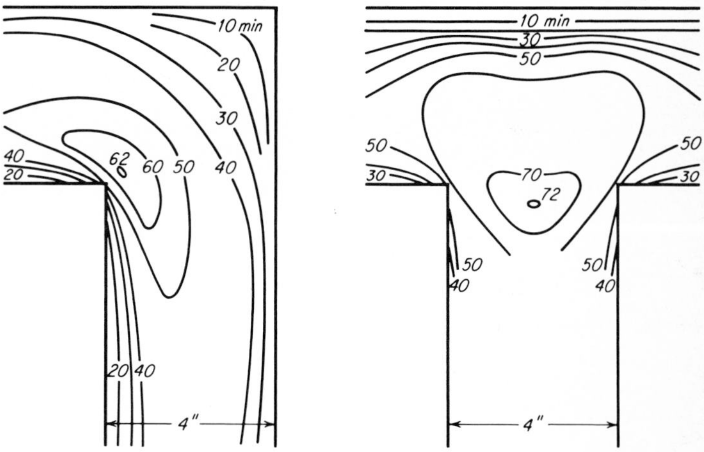

***Fig.* 15.8** Localization of the last stages of freezing as a result of joining sections. (*From F. A. Brandt, H. F. Bishop, and W. S. Pellini.*[45])

Porosity

Steel, of course, is subject to shrinkage during cooling from the casting temperature. The nature of this shrinkage was discussed in Chap. 8, and quantitative data were presented in Table 9.2.

Conditions giving steep temperature gradients in solidifying steel tend to decrease microporosity. Thus it has been found that samples tested from steel having an essentially columnar grain structure as induced by steep temperature gradients had lower microporosity and correspondingly higher ductility than samples taken from the equi-axed zone.[46] Tests of samples from high-strength-steel casting cylinders give the following variation in mechanical properties and porosity index:

Sample	Yield strength $\times 10^{-3}$ psi	Tensile strength $\times 10^{-3}$ psi	Elongation, %	Reduction of area, %	Porosity index
Columnar chill zone (transverse to grains)	218	270	10.7	27.0	0.38
Equi-axed zone	218	272.5	5	7.1	1.17

The soundness of commercial steel castings is largely determined by the effectiveness with which principles of risering are applied. At the outset it should be recognized that some castings, depending on their application, may be permitted to have various degrees of internal unsoundness or other defects. ASTM Specification E71-52, covering radiographic standards for steel castings and listing the types of castings and their service conditions, is set forth in Table 15.1. The degree of perfection required in each class for each of the defects listed at the bottom of this table is given in another table in this specification, each defect being classified on the basis of a set of standard radiographs published in the specification. Class 1 castings in Table 15.1 must be almost radiographically perfect for all the defects listed, whereas the other classes permit different degrees of unsoundness for each type of defect. The degree of soundness required may thus be specified by the ASTM class number upon mutual agreement between the supplier and purchaser of the casting.

GATING

Principles of gating were stated in Chap. 9, and this chapter should be referred to for the general aspects of gating. Specific gating problems arise in connection with steel castings because of high pouring tempera-

Table* 15.1 *Suggestions for the classification of castings to be used with radiographic standards*

Class	Service
1	High-pressure or high-temperature service castings, or both (wall thickness less than 1 in.). Machinery castings† subject to high fatigue or impact stresses (wall thickness less than ½ in.)
2	High-pressure or high-temperature service castings, or both (wall thickness 1 in. or greater). Low-pressure service castings (wall thickness less than 1 in.). Machinery castings subject to high fatigue or impact stresses (wall thickness of ½ in. and greater)
3	Low-pressure service castings (wall thickness of 1 in. and over). Machinery castings subject to normal fatigue or impact stresses
4	Structural castings‡ less than 3 in. in thickness and subject to high service stresses. Machinery castings subject to low impact stresses or vibration
5	Structural castings 3 in. or more in thickness and subject to high service stresses

* From ASTM Specification E71-52, ASTM Standards, Part 3, 1958.
† Machinery castings are dynamic parts or members in contact with working parts.
‡ Structural castings are construction parts for machinery castings.

Group	Defect
A	Gas and blowholes
B	Sand spots and inclusions
C	Internal shrinkage
D	Hot tears
E	Cracks
F	Unfused chaplets
G	Internal chills

ture and the need to fill the mold quickly. Defects attributable to poor gating practice include mold erosion, hot tears, dimensional instability, slag entrapment, cold shuts, oxidation, misruns, and wrinkles. The gating system must therefore be designed not only with respect to filling the mold, but also with the objective of avoiding these defects.

Mold Erosion

Mold erosion is reduced by utilizing one or more of the following procedures:[47,48]

1. Multiple ingates instead of a single-ingate system
2. Fairly large ingates
3. Low pouring temperatures consistent with adequate mold filling
4. Short sprue

5. Tile tubes for sections of the sprues or runners
6. Hard ramming of sand in the vicinity of the gates
7. Smooth gate surfaces
8. Elimination of loose sand from the system
9. Uphill pouring of the casting when possible
10. Selection of proper sprue-runner-gate ratio

Slag Entrapment

Despite the precautions used to prevent mold erosion by the foregoing methods, it still may be necessary to add other features to the gating system to avoid entrance of slag, sand, and dirt into the mold cavity. This can be done by the use of such devices as strainer cores, gate wells, whirl gates, and slag traps. Opinion is not unanimous regarding the advantages of the whirl or swirl gate.[47,48] One design for a whirl gate for steel castings which is advocated is found in Ref. 47. Although slag entrapment may be achieved with a given gate design, it is still possible to develop casting surface defects by excessive oxidation of the metal during pouring. This is a situation that can be remedied by designing the gate system to avoid aspiration of air and mold gases into the system. The discussion on ceroxide formation should be referred to again.

RISERS

Chapter 9 should be referred to for general principles of risering. The following riser design principles, introduced in that chapter, are given further attention here:

1. Riser size and feeding distance
2. Riser necks
3. Padding sections to gain directional solidification
4. Use of exothermic riser sleeves
5. Knock-off risers

Riser Size and Feeding Distance

As discussed in Chap. 9, Caine's curves can be used to determine riser size. When the riser is provided with some artificial means to prolong the liquid state, the riser need not be as large as when allowed to freeze normally. The effect of exothermic compounds or the use of an arc to

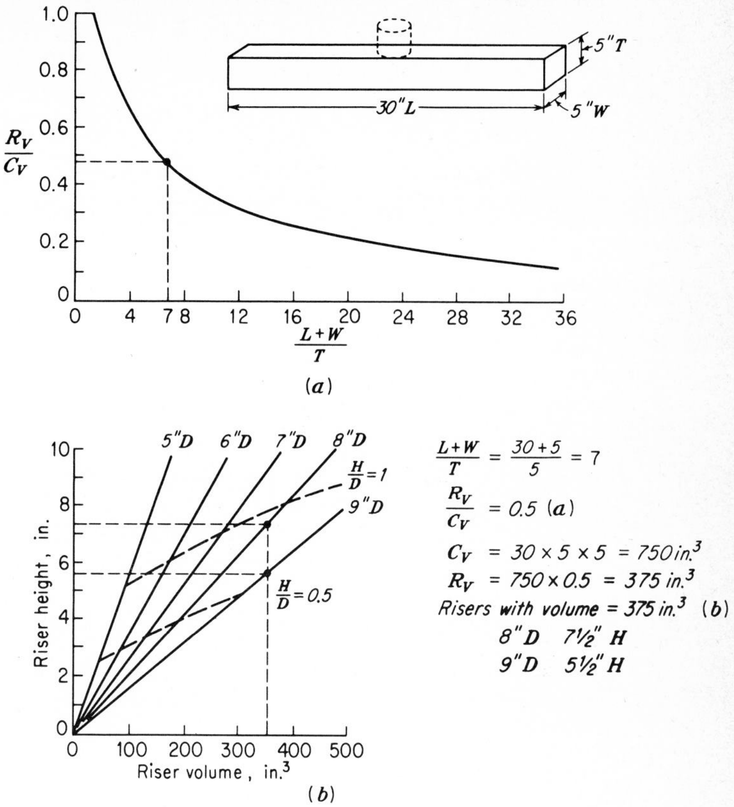

***Fig.* 15.9** Method of calculating riser size for a bar casting. The calculations show that either an 8-in.-diameter, 7½-in.-high or a 9-in.-diameter, 5½-in.-high riser can be used. *(From H. F. Bishop,[60] courtesy of Foundry.)*

prolong the liquid state was shown in Fig. 9.13. Figure 9.14 gave an example of one method of calculating riser size based on casting shape. An application of this method is presented in Fig. 15.9.

Considering the bar casting shown, the $(L + W)/T$ calculation at right gives a value of 7. From the curve at the left, the Rv/Cv ratio is found to be approximately 0.5. Knowing the casting volume, one can calculate the riser volume to be 375 cu in. This value is then applied to the set of curves in (*b*) to obtain two possible riser sizes, namely, either a 9-in.-diameter riser, 5½ in. high, or an 8-in. riser, 7½ in. high. Selection of one of these risers should theoretically provide for proper feeding of the casting. Additional examples are to be found in Refs. 59 to 61.

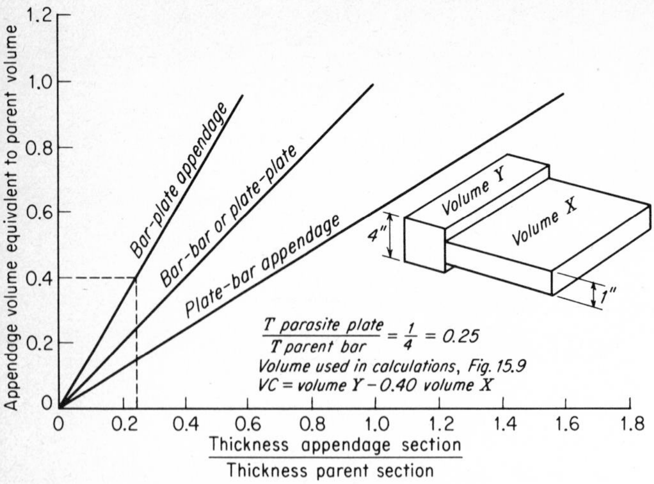

***Fig.* 15.10** **When an appendage is attached to a parent casting section, the equivalent volume of the appendage can be found in this plot and added to the volume of the parent casting to get the total casting volume.** (*From H. F. Bishop, E. T. Myskowski, and W. S. Pellini.*[62])

If the casting contains an appendage which would tend to lower the cooling rate, an additional increment must be added to the riser. The curves in Fig. 15.10 show how this adjustment is made.[62] For example, when the appendage on a bar-plus-plate type of casting is one-half the thickness of the casting, the additional volume to be added to the original volume is approximately 0.85 of the original volume. Thus, if the original volume were 200 cu in., the total casting volume for calculating riser size would be 200 + 170, or 370 cu in. This value would be used in conjunction with the curves in Fig. 15.9 to obtain the riser volume.

Often plate-type castings are reinforced with ribs. These ribs would have an adverse effect on the freezing pattern in the plate unless chilled. Calculating of the proper chill size can be made with the help of Fig. 15.11.[63]

For the rib shown, the ratio of rib to plate thickness is 3/4. The ratio of appendage depth to casting thickness is 8/4, or 2. From these data a chill-thickness ratio of 0.32 is determined. Therefore a chill of 4 × 0.32, or 1.28 in., is required. Note that all comparisons are made on the basis of the original plate thickness, T. Additional examples of adjustments by means of risers or chills for appendages added to castings can be found in Refs. 61 to 63.

The determination of riser size can also be made with the use of equations developed on the basis of surface-area–volume relations:[61]

$$D = 2.60t + \frac{M}{65t^2} \quad \text{(plates or slabs of length and width greater than four times thickness)} \qquad (1)$$

$$D = 1.16 + \frac{M}{13t^2} \quad \text{(cylinders or bars of length greater than four times thickness)} \qquad (2)$$

$$D = 0.93t + \frac{M}{6.7t^2} \quad \text{(chunks, spheres, cubes)} \qquad (3)$$

where D = riser diameter, in.
M = weight of section being fed, lb
t = section thickness or diameter, in.

To use these equations, a representative section size t must be calculated. Thus, for a rectangular long bar, of thickness a and width b, $1/t = 1/2\,(1/a \times 1/b)$. Other representative section thicknesses can be determined in a similar manner by the use of formulas.[61] Corrections must be applied in the use of these formulas if chills are used.

Alternative methods for calculating riser dimensions have been presented.[59,64–66] Included among these are charts to determine riser size based on the original riser-dimension equations.

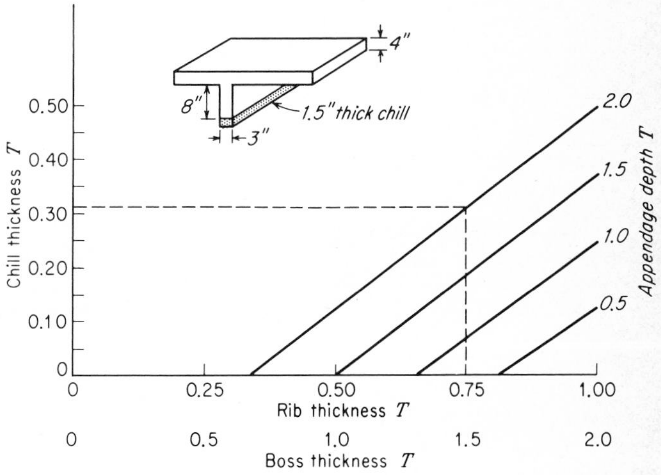

***Fig.* 15.11** Chart to be used to determine the correct chill thickness to counteract the effect of an appendage with dimensions given in terms of the original plate thickness, *T*. (*From E. T. Myskowski and H. F. Bishop.*[63])

The methods outlined in the foregoing paragraphs require the use of charts or formulas to determine riser dimensions based on casting weight or size. In the method outlined in Chap. 9, based on measuring the amount of feed required, knowledge of casting weight or dimensions is not necessary. The calculations were based entirely on a knowledge of the shrinkage which occurs in a riser of adequate size. Therefore complications arising from casting sizes or other intricacies are avoided, and the calculations are restricted purely to the riser dimensions, which are relatively simple.

The distance over which a riser can feed a casting effectively must be known or determined by experiment in order to ascertain the number of risers required for a given casting. Research on plates and bars has established the effective feeding distance of risers under a variety of conditions, as tabulated in Table 15.2. In this table the term "end effect" refers to the extra cooling effect obtained at the ends of a plate or bar; the feeding distance for "no end effect" means half the distance measured for that part of the casting between two risers. Note how the introduction of a chill midway between two risers greatly increases the feeding distance.

Table* 15.2 *Feeding distances of risers in terms of thickness* T

Condition	Without chill	With chill
Plate, no end effect	$D = 3.6\sqrt{T}$	$D = 11.6\sqrt{T} - 3.2$†
Bar, no end effect	$D = 3.6\sqrt{T}$	$D = 6\sqrt{T} + T$
Plate with end effect	$D = 11.6\sqrt{T} - 5.2$	$D = 11.6\sqrt{T} - 3.2$
Bar (horizontal) with end effect	$D = 6\sqrt{T}$	$D = 6\sqrt{T} + T$
Bar, vertical	$D = 7.15\sqrt{T}$	
Plate with parasite section	$D_H = 3(T_H - T_L) + 4.5$	
Plate with both light and heavy sections attached	$D_M = 3.5(T_H - T_L)$	
Plate with parent section	$D_L = 3.5T_H$	

* From J. F. Wallace.[61]

† Chill spaced uniformly between two risers. D = distance from one riser to chill. Therefore total feeding distance between two risers is $2D$.

When sections of different size adjoin, they have a mutual effect on the feeding distance of a riser for each section. Thus, when a light section is attached to the end of a heavier section, the so-called end effect is reduced and the presence of the light section tends to reduce the feeding distance of a riser for the heavy section in proportion to the section thickness of the light section, as shown by the equation for D_H in Table 15.2. If a heavy section is attached to a lighter section, it tends to increase the length of sound metal in the light section as compared with the case where the heavy section is absent. This is shown by the equation for D_L in Table 15.2.

Another situation is the case where both a light and a heavy section are attached to one of intermediate thickness. The formula covering this condition is given also in Table 15.2.

Riser Necks

Riser-neck dimensions were given in Table 9.4. Other types of riser necks for steel top risers have been studied.[61] These require the use of cores between the riser and casting to form the neck contours. The effectiveness of these necks is a function of core thickness. Large neck diameters can tolerate the use of thicker neck cores without shrinkage showing up in the casting. The greater effectiveness of round necks in comparison with rectangular necks is indicated in Ref. 61. This type of riser is known as the Washburn knock-off riser.

Padding Sections to Gain Directional Solidification

Previous discussion in this chapter and Chap. 9 has indicated what procedures can be used to obtain sound castings when casting regular plates, bars, or rounds. On occasion, it is expedient to obtain soundness in plates or bars by controlling directional solidification in the casting itself rather than by the judicious placement of risers or chills. This can be done by "padding" the casting, and Fig. 15.12 gives the necessary taper on plates of various lengths and thicknesses, to achieve directional solidification.

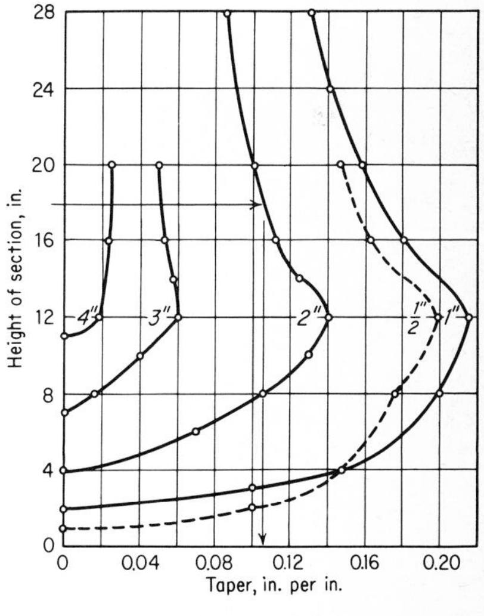

***Fig.* 15.12** Metal "padding" required to feed completely plate castings of various lengths and thicknesses. (*From S. W. Brinson and J. A. Duma.*[67])

Without this padding, progressive solidification would result in a zone of shrinkage along the center line of the plate. This padding causes the solidification to progress from the thin to the thicker sections, thereby eliminating *center-line shrinkage.*

Use of Exothermic Riser Sleeves

As discussed in Chap. 9, exothermic materials can be used to reduce the size of risers. For example, a 3½-in. riser with a 1½-in. sleeve of exothermic material is about as effective in feeding a casting as a 7-in. uninsulated riser. This is demonstrated in Fig. 15.13.

One precaution that should be emphasized is that, when using exothermic materials, the riser cavity should not be filled too high. A rule of thumb which has been given is that the riser should be no higher than its diameter.[71] Some authorities have advocated heights equal to one-third to one-half the diameter.[72] If the riser is filled too high, freezing occurs in the lower portion of the riser before the casting has frozen. Thus the molten metal at the top of the riser cannot feed the casting and *underriser shrinkage* occurs.

Knock-off Risers

Gates and risers must be removed from castings before shipment. Because steel is tough and ductile, this is not always so easy to do

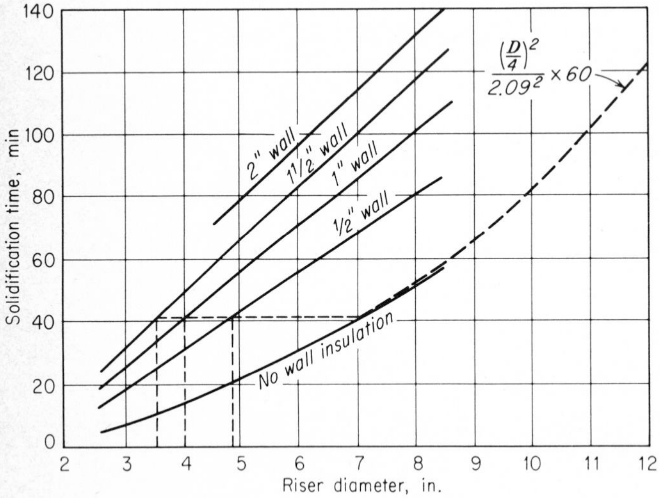

Fig. **15.13** Combinations of riser diameters and sleeve walls which match solidification times of uninsulated risers. (*From H. F. Bishop, H. F. Taylor, and R. G. Powell,*[71] *courtesy of Foundry.*)

merely by breaking them off, as in the case of more brittle alloys. The design of the connection between the gate or riser and the casting therefore becomes a matter of concern, and some examples of riser connections were provided in Chap. 9 as well as in this chapter. It should be obvious, also, that if exothermic materials are used to reduce the size of the riser, the riser connections can be reduced in size, thereby reducing the cleaning costs. A recent study of riser connections advocates that the knock-off core used to make the connection should provide a diameter of about 10 per cent of the riser diameter plus 0.2 in. A radius-tipped cross-shaped neck provides the best breakability.[73]

STEEL MELTING

Steel melting is discussed in more detail in the next chapter, but a brief survey is given here to complete the study of steel castings. Steel melting is substantially different from the melting of most other alloys in that a definite part of most steel-melting cycles is a refining action that is necessary to ensure good-quality steel. Refining operations are also employed in melting down other metals, but not to the extent and with the degree of control usually exercised with steel. Broadly speaking, the melting cycle consists of an oxidation period extending through and beyond the melting period in which certain impurities are removed by oxidation and collected in a *slag*. This is followed by a reducing period (deoxidation) in which the oxygen content of the molten metal is lowered (in one process, sulfur is also lowered). The steel is then adjusted in composition and poured.

The various steel-melting processes, classified according to furnace type, are:

1. Open-hearth (acid and basic)
2. Electric-arc (acid and basic)
3. Electric induction (acid or basic)

The choice of a particular melting method is governed by a large number of factors, some of which are enumerated in Chap. 16. The open-hearth furnaces are preferred for large tonnages, whereas the electric furnaces offer greater versatility in the type of metal to be melted and greater flexibility of operations.

Open-hearth Melting

Illustrations of open-hearth-furnace construction are given in Chap. 16. These furnaces are charged with scrap and pig iron (an impure iron produced in blast furnaces) and heated with oil, gas, or powdered coal.

The air used for combustion is heated in preheat chambers, called *checker chambers,* where it picks up heat from a brick checkerwork. The checker chambers are heated by the exhaust gases from the open hearth. Two chambers are required so that combustion air and waste gases can be alternately cycled between them. Preheating the air is necessary to obtain the high temperatures required.

The refractories in the melting zone of the furnace are either *acid* (SiO_2-base) or *basic* (MgO-base). The type of refractory controls the types of reaction that are possible during the refining period and the nature of the slag product.

During meltdown and after the steel is melted, silicon, manganese, iron, and carbon are oxidized. The oxidation products of the first three elements become a part of the slag, whereas the oxidized carbon leaves the furnace as CO or CO_2. Additional slag-making materials (lime in the case of the basic process, and sand in the case of the acid process) may be added to the furnace. The carbon content of the charge is adjusted so that after meltdown the carbon content of the molten metal is higher than desired in the final analysis. As the temperature of the metal rises, this carbon is gradually eliminated as CO, which bubbles up through the bath. This is known as the "carbon boil." The oxidation of carbon produces heat, and the bubbling action stirs the bath and aids in the removal of impurities. When the desired carbon content is reached or when it has reached a low value, additions are made to rid the steel of a large part of its dissolved oxygen and to adjust the manganese, silicon, and carbon contents. While the carbon boil is proceeding, the slag which floats on top of the steel is adjusted in composition to control the rate at which carbon is removed from the bath. This control is achieved through iron or manganese ore additions to the bath. Gaseous oxygen may also be used. When the bath has reached the desired pouring temperature, the slag has been adjusted by the melter to the proper viscosity for tapping. The refining period thus represents a proper balancing of metal composition, slag composition, time, and temperature so that metal of the desired quality and temperature is available for castings.

The acid practice is not capable of removing phosphorus from the steel; hence the charge must be low in phosphorus to meet the usual limit of 0.05 per cent phosphorus in the finished steel. Basic slags, on the other hand, are capable of dissolving the oxidized phosphorus, and phosphorus removal is therefore a part of the refining operation. As a consequence, there is not the restriction on phosphorus content of the charge as in the case of the acid practice. Some sulfur elimination is also obtained, but it is not very much, amounting to about 0.004 to 0.007 per cent.

Other Melting Methods

Essentially the same procedure outlined for the open-hearth furnaces is followed in arc-furnace melting, except, of course, that electrical power is used to melt the charge.

In the basic electric-arc furnace, it is possible to remove the initial oxidizing slag after the desired degree of oxidation has occurred and to add slag-making constituents that will create a reducing basic slag. This promotes the removal of sulfur. The basic electric furnace can therefore be used to remove both phosphorus and sulfur. The acid electric furnace removes neither element; consequently, the charge must be sufficiently low in both these impurities.

Reference should be made to Chap. 16 for discussions of melting in a converter and electric-induction furnace.

Deoxidation

The primary purpose of deoxidation is to lower the dissolved oxygen content of steel to improve its quality. This is accomplished by adding elements such as silicon and manganese shortly before the metal is tapped and adding aluminum to the ladle during tapping. The oxides of silicon and manganese tend to float out of the steel and become part of the slag. The aluminum oxide products may also float out, but regardless of whether silicon plus manganese alone or silicon plus manganese and aluminum additions are made, some of the deoxidation product invariably is visible upon microscopical examination of a solidified casting. Incomplete removal from the metal is one reason for this entrapment of these nonmetallic inclusions, but it is not the only one. Actually, the deoxidation reactions occur while the metal is cooling, and this effect would naturally not allow time for all the reaction product to leave the molten steel. In fact, the reactions are going on during the freezing process, making it impossible to rid the steel completely of these deoxidation products.

In addition to deoxidizing the steel, aluminum additions cause certain side reactions of extreme interest to steel foundrymen. These reactions are:

1. Prevention of pinhole porosity, described in an earlier section
2. Control of the sulfide distribution as described in Chap. 17
3. Control of austenitic grain size (of interest during heat-treatment)
4. Effect on fluidity

The effect of temperature and of various alloy elements on fluidity was discussed in an earlier section of this chapter. In addition to these factors, deoxidation has been found to affect fluidity, both insufficient deoxidation and overdeoxidation causing decreased fluidity. Overdeoxidation refers to the addition of so much deoxidizer, such as aluminum, to the steel that substantial residual quantities remain in solution.

Thus it is apparent that the physical metallurgy associated with cast-steel production is quite involved and complex. A complete discussion of this subject goes far beyond the scope of this book.

Tapping and Pouring

Temperature Measurement

The steel-furnace melter attempts to regulate conditions so that the steel is up to pouring temperature at the time of final deoxidation. Temperature control and determination are important in that a cold heat would lead to misruns or even the loss of an entire heat. At the elevated temperatures at which steel is tapped, temperature measurement becomes a real problem, and various devices have been used which give either a true reading or a relative measure of temperature.[11]

Tapping

The size of the taphole in the open-hearth furnace should be small enough so that no slag enters the ladle with the metal. This is necessary so that the ladle deoxidizers, such as aluminum, will not lose their effectiveness by being entrapped by the slag.

Tapping is usually made into a ladle large enough to hold the contents of an entire heat. From there the metal may be transferred to smaller ladles for pouring molds or taken directly to the molds to be poured. There is about a 50 to 200 F loss in each transfer of metal. Therefore a minimum number of metal transfers should be made. Ladles used in the steel foundry include bottom-pour, lip-pour, and teapot types. These are illustrated in Figs. 9.1 and 9.2.

CLEANING, CHIPPING, AND GRINDING

Once castings are solidified, the problem of sand removal, improvement of surface finish, removal of gates and risers, and repair of defective areas arises. This problem is much more difficult with steel castings than with other casting alloys because of greater sand adherence, tougher metal, and increased chance for casting defects to occur. The problems and methods associated with these finishing operations are adequately covered in Chap. 24, and the student should refer to that chapter for information on this subject.

WELDING

As mentioned in the introduction, welding can be used on cast steel either for repair or salvage work or to produce composite structures. The fact that certain steel castings are difficult to cast and high casting losses can occur makes welding particularly attractive to the foundryman. As long as he does not use this technique as a crutch to get out of difficulties created by poor foundry practice, it can prove a valuable part of the casting process, for it allows a versatility in design not possible with most of the other metals. Figure 15.14 is cited as an example where an improved product is obtained by weld joining.

In jobbing shops particularly, where only a few castings may be produced and where the foundry "bugs" have not been completely eliminated, welding can be used to salvage costly or intricate castings. For example, hot tears or blowholes may be removed and repaired by welding without affecting the quality of the casting.

Welding, as performed in cast steels, makes use of the same techniques

***Fig.* 15.14** Composite structure by welding. (*Courtesy of Steel Founders' Society of America.*)

used in wrought-steel products, and the same process controls must be adhered to. These involve:

1. Welding methods
2. Welding techniques
3. Selection of welding-rod size, type, and composition
4. Pre-heat-treatments
5. Post-heat-treatments
6. Control of composition, particularly carbon and alloy content
7. Testing methods
8. Grinding operations

To discuss all the factors involved in welding and welding metallurgy is a subject sufficiently large for another book, and the importance of it to the steel foundryman can only be indicated here.

INSPECTION AND TESTING

The tests most commonly used to evaluate the properties of cast steel are tensile, hardness, and impact tests. These are made on metal removed from the castings or on test bars machined from separately cast test coupons. The latter tests give the properties of the metal under the more or less ideal conditions prevailing in the test coupon. Two types of keel blocks are shown in Fig. 15.15. Each leg of the keel block provides one tensile specimen. Sometimes the keel block is molded along with the casting as a part of the total casting system.

Impact tests are often used when the steel is to be exposed to low temperatures. The impact resistance of steel drops off rather suddenly at certain subatmospheric temperatures. This "transition temperature" is quite sensitive to steel composition, steel quality, and heat-treatment, and for that reason tests over a range of temperatures are usually advocated.

Microscopical examination is often used to determine the effects of heat-treatment on the metal structure. Where production requirements are severe or where developmental work is being done on casting design, X-ray radiographic techniques are employed to show up the internal defects in the casting. Castings for aircraft applications, for example, may require 100 per cent inspection, and specially equipped laboratories may be required to accomplish this important phase of casting inspection. Since steel is quite resistant to X-ray penetration, high-voltage equipment may be necessary, and installations of as high as 1 million volts are not uncommon. Betatrons, which provide X rays at much higher energy than conventional X-ray machines, are also used for this purpose.

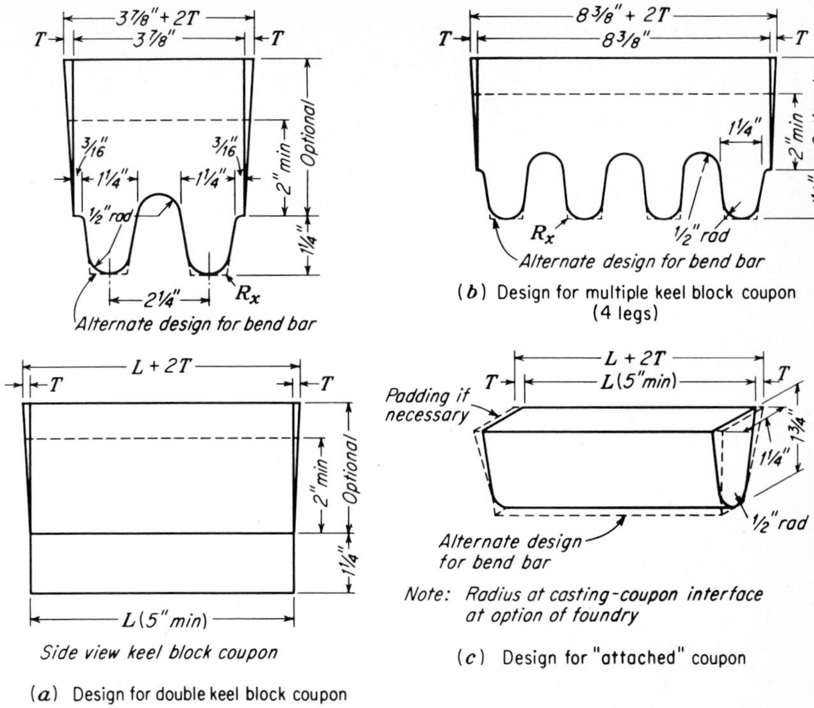

***Fig.* 15.15** Keel-block coupon (ASTM 370, Mechanical Testing of Steel Products.)

Sources of penetrating rays are radium, cobalt 60, and other radioactive isotopes. Radium or cobalt 60 as a source of gamma rays provides portability and the possibility of radiographing a number of castings at one time. The disadvantage of cobalt 60 is that it is too penetrating for thin sections, thereby reducing resolution of the defects.

Imperfections that are on or near the surface, such as cracks or sand inclusions, can be detected in magnetic materials by *magnaflux* testing. This test involves the use of fine iron powder applied either wet or dry to the casting while placed in a magnetic field. The powder lines up in a definite pattern, tending to outline the edges of the defect, as illustrated in Fig. 15.16.

PROPERTIES AND USES

Table 10.2 lists certain casting properties of cast steels, and Fig. 15.1 gives mechanical properties as affected by carbon content and heat-treatment. By a suitable selection of carbon content, alloy content, and

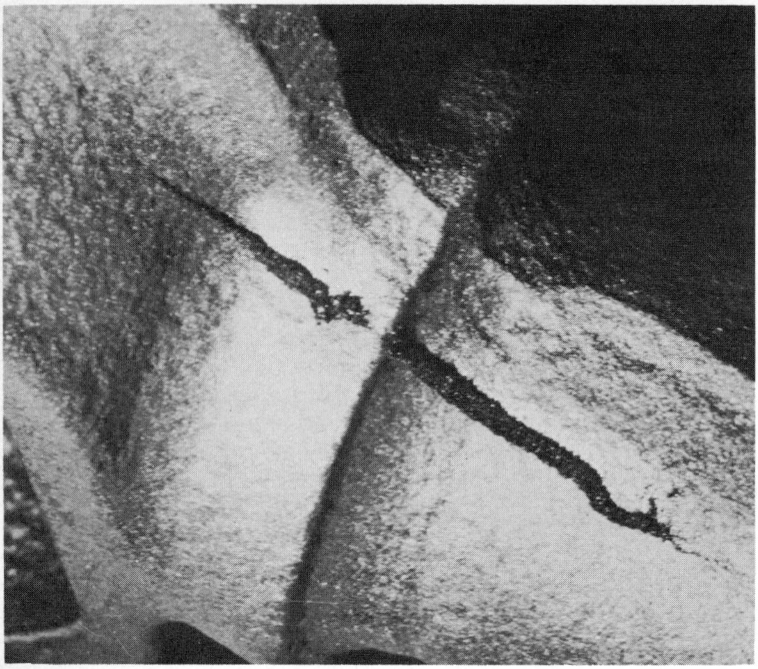

***Fig.* 15.16** Example of a crack in a casting exposed by magnaflux inspection. (*Courtesy of Magnaflux Corporation.*)

heat-treatment, cast steels can be produced having tensile strengths ranging from about 44,000 to over 200,000 psi. Similar broad variations in other mechanical properties, such as ductility and toughness, can likewise be realized. High strength and high ductility are not compatible, and one cannot be gained without a reduction in the other.

Table 15.3 lists the chemical and property specifications for a selected list of carbon and low-alloy cast steels.

Plain-carbon Steels

Low-carbon steel (<0.2% C) castings are used in considerable tonnages for railroad castings. Other uses include certain automotive castings, castings for the steel industry such as annealing boxes and ladles, castings for surface hardening by carburizing, and castings for electrical or magnetic applications. The low-carbon steels are the softest and most ductile of the various carbon grades available, and their properties are not influenced greatly by heat-treatment.

Medium-carbon steels (0.2 to 0.5% C) represent the bulk of the steel-foundry output and rarely are used in the as-cast condition because

Table 15.3 ***Chemical and property specifications for a selected list of carbon and low-alloy cast steels***

Specification and heat-treatment			Mechanical properties, minimum					Chemical composition, %, maximum								
Specification	Class	Heat-treatment*	Tensile strength, psi	Yield point, psi	Elong. in 2 in., %	Reduction of area, %	Other tests: bend, impact hardness†	C	Mn	P	S	Si	Ni	Cr	Mo	Other elements
ASTM A27-62	N-1	....	....	....	....	....	....	.25†	.75†	.05	.06	.80	.50	40	.20	Cu .30
	N-2	A, N, NT, or QT	....	....	....	....	....	.35†	.60†	.05	.06	.80	.50	.40	.20	Cu .30
	U-60-30	....	60,000	30,000	22	30	....	.25†	.75†	.05	.06	.80	.50	.40	.20	Cu .30
	60-30	A, N, NT, or QT	60,000	30,000	24	35	....	.30†	.60†	.05	.06	.80	.50	.40	.20	Cu .30
	65-35	A, N, NT, or QT	65,000	35,000	24	35	....	.30†	.70†	.05	.06	.80	.50	.40	.20	Cu .30
	70-36	A, N, NT, or QT	70,000	36,000	22	30	....	.35†	.70†	.05	.06	.80	.50	.40	.20	Cu .30
	70-40	A, N, NT, or QT	70,000	40,000	22	30	....	.25†	1.20†	.05	.06	.80	.50	.40	.20	Cu .30
ASTM A148-60	80-40	A, N, NT, or QT	80,000	40,000	18	30	....	‡	....	.05	.06					
	80-50	A, N, NT, or QT	80,000	50,000	22	35	....	‡	....	.05	.06					
	90-60	A, N, NT, or QT	90,000	60,000	20	40	....	‡	....	.05	.06					
	105-85	A, N, NT, or QT	105,000	85,000	17	35	....	‡	....	.05	.06					
	120-95	A, N, NT, or QT	120,000	95,000	14	30	....	‡	....	.05	.06					
	150-125	A, N, NT, or QT	150,000	125,000	9	22	....	‡	....	.05	.06					
	175-145	A, N, NT, or QT	175,000	145,000	6	12	....	‡	....	.05	.06					
SAE Automotive							Bhn									
	0022	A, N, or NT	....	....	....	....	187	.12-.22	.50-.90	.05	.06	.60				
	0025	A, N, or NT	60,000	30,000	22	30	187	.25	.75†	.05	.06	.80				
	0030	A, N, NT, or QT	65,000	35,000	24	35	187	.30†	.70†	.05	.06	.80	.50§	.25§	....	W .10+Cu .50§
	0050	N or NT	85,000	45,000	16	24	229	.40-.50	.50-.90	.05	.06	.80				
	0050	QT	100,000	70,000	10	15	255	.40-.50	.50-.90	.05	.06	.80				
	080	A, N, NT, or QT	80,000	50,000	22	35	207	....	....	.05	.06					
	090	NT or NQT	90,000	60,000	20	40	241	....	....	.05	.06					
	0105	NQT	105,000	85,000	17	35	248	....	....	.05	.06					
	0120	NQT	120,000	95,000	14	30	311	....	....	.05	.06					
	0150	NQT	150,000	125,000	9	22	363	....	....	.05	.06					
	0175	NQT	175,000	145,000	6	12	415	....	....	.05	.06					

* A, full anneal; N, normalize; NT, normalize and temper; QT, quench and temper; at the option of the manufacturer.

† For each reduction of .01% C below the maximum specified, an increase of .04% Mn above the maximum specified will be permitted to a maximum of 1.0% Mn. (1.40 maximum for grade 70-40, A27.)

‡ Alloying elements shall be selected by the manufacturer.

§ Total maximum content of undesirable elements is 1.0%. For each .10% below the specified maximum alloy content of 1.0%, an increase of .02% in the Cr plus Mo content and .06% in the Ni and Cu contents above the specified maximum will be permitted.

heat-treatment improves their ductility and impact resistance. About 60 per cent of all steel castings are of the medium-carbon grade, and their field of application is extensive and varied. Medium-carbon steels are used in the transportation industries, for machinery and tools, rolling-mill equipment, road and building machinery, and many other applications.

Because of their higher hardness and strength, *high-carbon cast steels* (0.5% C) are used for metalworking dies, rolls, and other tools where wear and abrasion resistance are necessary.

Low-alloy Steels

The low-alloy steels are limited to a total alloy content of 8 per cent, and differ from plain-carbon steels principally in their ability to be heat-treated to higher levels of hardness and strength in a given cross section. This ability is measured by the hardenability test (discussed in Chap. 17). As a result of having increased hardenability, the low-alloy cast steels can be made with better mechanical properties than plain carbon steels, or the same properties can be achieved without resorting to severe heat-treating operations that might normally distort or crack a casting.

The alloying elements commonly employed for the purpose of securing hardenability, given in the approximate order of their effectiveness, are:

Manganese
Chromium
Molybdenum
Nickel
Silicon
Copper
Vanadium

Various combinations of these elements are used, resulting in the numerous types of alloy steels listed under SAE (Society for Automotive Engineers), AISI (American Iron and Steel Institute), or other specifications. Outside of the effect of the alloys on hardenability, it may be generalized that the low-alloy steels are otherwise intrinsically no different from plain carbon steels. Of course, there are problems in connection with economy, ease of melting, availability of scrap, etc., that may dictate the selection of one alloy or alloy combination over another.

High-alloy Steels

In this category fall those alloys of iron and carbon that have over 8 per cent alloy content and have superior corrosion, heat, or wear resistance. The Alloy Casting Institute recognizes 16 standard grades of corrosion-resistant alloys and 12 standard grades of heat-resistant alloys. Included in these groups are alloys of:

1. Iron and chromium, with chromium varying from about 12 to 30 per cent
2. Iron, chromium, and nickel, with chromium varying from 18 to 32 per cent and nickel from 8 to 20 per cent
3. Iron, nickel, and chromium, with nickel varying from 33 to 41 per cent and chromium from 13 to 21 per cent
4. Nickel, iron, and chromium, with nickel varying from 58 to 68 per cent and chromium from 10 to 19 per cent

Other metals, such as silicon, molybdenum, and aluminum, may also be used in these alloys to confer special advantages.

A steel of outstanding wear resistance is an *austenitic manganese* steel, also referred to as Hadfield's manganese steel. It contains 10 to 14 per cent manganese, and is commercially unmachinable. It is used for mining equipment, railroad-track work such as crossing and frogs, pulverizers, quarrying equipment, and many other similar applications.

BIBLIOGRAPHY

1. Steel Founders' Society of America, "Steel Castings Handbook," 3d ed., 1960.
2. H. F. Bishop, F. A. Brandt, and W. S. Pellini, Solidification of Steel against Sand and Chill Walls, *Trans. AFS,* vol. 59, p. 455, 1951.
3. D. K. Fourshou, Durability of Foundry Sands and Properties of Deteriorated Foundry Sands, *J. Steel Castings Res.,* no. 5, p. 1, May, 1956.
4. L. DeBoer, Steel Wheels in Green Sand, *Modern Castings,* vol. 30, p. 34, October, 1956.
5. Steel Founders' Society of America, "Fundamentals of Steel Foundry Sands," 1959.
6. C. E. Sims and C. A. Zapffe, The Mechanism of Pin-hole Formation, *Trans. AFS,* vol. 59, pp. 255–281, 1941.
7. R. C. Savage and H. F. Taylor, A Thermodynamic Study of Pin-hole Formation in Steel Castings, *Trans. AFS,* vol. 58, pp. 393–399, 1950.
8. R. G. Powell and H. F. Taylor, Shell Molding for Steel Castings, *Trans. AFS,* vol. 66, p. 403, 1958.
9. D. C. Ekey and E. G. Vogel, Ceramic-mold Process for Steel Castings, *Trans. AFS,* vol. 64, p. 439, 1956.
10. H. H. Hursen, Graphite Molds plus Air Pressure Pouring Yields New Steel Car Wheels, *Modern Castings,* vol. 28, p. 26, September, 1955.
11. H. Chappie, Steps to Take in Eliminating Hot Tears, *Foundry,* vol. 86, p. 82, July, 1958.
12. H. F. Bishop, C. G. Ackerlind, and W. S. Pellini, Metallurgy and Mechanics of Hot Tearing, *Trans. AFS,* vol. 60, pp. 818–833, 1952.
13. J. B. Caine, Cracks and Hot Tears in Steel Castings, *Foundry,* vol. 81, p. 120, June, 1953.

14. W. S. Pellini, Strain Theory of Hot Cracking, *Foundry*, vol. 80, p. 125, November, 1952.
15. C. H. Wyman, C. A. Faist, and G. DiSylvestro, Hot-tear Investigation, *Trans. AFS*, vol. 60, p. 145, 1952.
16. V. K. Bhattacharya, C. M. Adams, Jr., and H. F. Taylor, Hot-tear Formations in Steel Castings, *Trans. AFS*, vol. 60, pp. 675–686, 1952.
17. C. F. Christopher, Hot-tearing Characteristics of Acid and Basic Steel Castings Determined by High Temperature Testing, vol. 64, p. 293, 1956.
18. C. W. Briggs, "The Metallurgy of Steel Castings," McGraw-Hill Book Company, New York, 1946.
19. V. K. Bhattacharya, C. M. Adams, Jr., and H. F. Taylor, Stress Required to Hot Tear Plain Carbon Cast Steel, *Trans. AFS*, vol. 62, pp. 557–567, 1954.
20. H. Pettersson, An Investigation of the Penetration of Steel into Molding Sand, *Trans. AFS*, vol. 59, pp. 35–55, 1951.
21. S. L. Gertsman and A. S. Murton, Metal Penetration, *Trans. AFS*, vol. 59, pp. 108–115, 1951.
22. G. J. Vingas (for Mold Surface Committee 8-H), Ramming Superheat and Alloys (Type of Metal Effects on Metal Penetration), *Modern Castings*, vol. 36, p. 671, November, 1959.
23. A. E. Murton and S. L. Gertsman, A Literature Review of Metal Penetration, *Modern Castings*, vol. 33, p. 37, January, 1958.
24. R. C. Emmons and J. Bach, Steel Penetration, *Foundry*, vol. 83, p. 108, April, 1955.
25. D. V. Atterton, Surface Finish of Steel Castings, *Foundry*, vol. 86, p. 79, January, 1958; p. 107, February, 1958; p. 92, March, 1958.
26. N. M. Peterson, Zircon and Its Foundry Application, *Foundry*, vol. 81, p. 93, April, 1953.
27. H. Chappie, Use of Zircon Sand in Producing Large Castings, *Foundry*, vol. 83, p. 126, October, 1955.
28. D. F. McVittie and T. P. Hoar, Sand Burn-on without Metal Penetration, *J. Steel Casting Res.*, no. 10, p. 8, January, 1958.
29. J. B. Caine, E. H. King, and J. S. Schumacher, A Microscope Study of Rammed Sand Surfaces, *J. Steel Castings Res.*, no. 21, April, 1961.
30. J. B. Caine, E. H. King, and J. S. Schumacher, A Study of the Influence of Mold Atmosphere on Ceroxide Defects in Steel Castings, *J. Steel Castings Res.*, no. 24, January, 1962.
31. An Investigation of Factors Producing the Ceroxide Defect on Steel Castings, SFSA Research Report 52, *J. Steel Castings Res.*, no. 27, October, 1962.
32. J. B. Caine, A Study of the Behavior of Molding Sand When in Contact with Liquid Steel, *Foundry*, vol. 75, p. 72, 1947.
33. G. A. Colligan, L. H. Van Vlack, and R. A. Flinn, Factors Affecting Metal-mold Reactions, *Trans. AFS*, vol. 69, p. 52, 1961.
34. J. B. Caine, E. H. King, and J. S. Schumacher, A Study of Some Foundry Variables Affecting the Occurrence of Visible Nonmetallic Surface Defects in Steel Castings, *J. Steel Castings Res.*, no. 23, October, 1961.
35. R. A. Flinn, W. B. Pierce, and L. H. Van Vlack, Cast Steel Nonmetallic Macroinclusions, Sources and Prevention, *Trans. AFS*, vol. 69, p. 193, 1961.
36. L. H. Van Vlack, J. P. Brokloff, and R. A. Flinn, Refractories as a Source of Macroinclusions, *Trans. AFS*, vol. 69, p. 178, 1961.
37. H. Taylor, E. Rominski, and C. W. Briggs, The Fluidity of Ingot Iron, and Carbon and Alloy Cast Steels, *Trans. AFS*, vol. 99, pp. 1–93, 1941.
38. G. A. Lillieqvist, Influence of Temperature on Fluidity and Surface Appearance of Steel Castings, *Trans. AFS*, vol. 58, p. 261, 1950.

39. H. F. Bishop and W. S. Pellini, Solidification of Metals, *Foundry*, vol. 80, p. 86, 1952.
40. C. Locke, C. W. Briggs, and R. L. Ashbrook, Heat Transfer of Various Molding Materials for Steel Castings, *Trans. AFS*, vol. 62, p. 589, 1954.
41. C. W. Briggs, Solidification of Steel Castings, *Trans. AFS*, vol. 68, p. 157, 1960.
42. C. A. Rowe, The Solidification of Steel in the Standard Fluidity Spiral, *MJI*, Research Report, February, 1959.
43. J. F. Wallace (ed.), "Fundamentals of Risering Steel Castings," Steel Founders' Society, 1960.
44. C. M. Adams, Jr., and H. F. Taylor, Flow of Heat from Sand Castings by Conduction, Radiation and Convection, *Trans. AFS*, vol. 65, p. 170, 1957.
45. F. A. Brandt, H. F. Bishop, and W. S. Pellini, Solidification of Corner and Core Positions, *Trans. AFS*, vol. 60, p. 451, 1953.
46. S. Z. Uram, M. C. Flemingo, and H. F. Taylor, High Strength Cast Steel Structure and Microporosity Effect on Mechanical Properties, *Trans. AFS*, vol. 68, p. 347, 1960.
47. C. W. Briggs, Gating Steel Castings, *Foundry*, vol. 88, p. 125, June, 1960; p. 86, July, 1960.
48. H. Chappie, Gating Affects Quality in Production of Steel Castings, *Foundry*, vol. 84, p. 90, April, 1956.
49. T. Finlay, Fin Gating: New Cost-cutting Steel Technique, *Modern Castings*, vol. 40, p. 53, September, 1961.
50. Armour Research Foundation, Fluid Flow Mechanics of Molten Steel, April, 1951.
51. M. J. Berger and C. Locke, A Theoretical Basis for the Design of Gates, *Foundry*, vol. 79, p. 112, February, 1951.
52. W. S. Pellini, W. H. Johnson, and H. F. Bishop, Velocities and Volume Rates of Metal Flow in Gating Systems, *Trans. AFS*, vol. 61, p. 439, 1953.
53. American Foundrymen's Society, "Symposium on Principles of Gating," 1953.
54. W. S. Pellini et al., Feeding Range of Joined Sections, *Trans. AFS*, 1953, p. 302.
55. E. T. Myskowski, H. F. Bishop, and W. S. Pellini, Feeding Range of Joined Sections, *Trans. AFS*, vol. 61, p. 302, 1953.
56. J. Caine, A Theoretical Approach to the Problem of Dimensioning Risers, *Trans. AFS*, vol. 56, pp. 492 and 501, 1948.
57. H. F. Bishop and W. S. Pellini, The Contribution of Riser and Chill-edge Effects to Soundness of Cast Steel Plates, *Trans. AFS*, vol. 58, p. 185.
58. W. S. Pellini, Relation of Riser Range and Feeder Adequacy, *Am. Foundryman*, November, 1953, p. 58; December, 1953.
59. H. F. Bishop and W. H. Johnson, Risering of Steel, *Foundry*, vol. 84, p. 71, February, 1956; p. 136, March, 1956.
60. H. F. Bishop, Risering of Steel Castings, *Foundry*, vol. 88, p. 75, August, 1960; p. 116, September, 1960.
61. J. F. Wallace (ed.), "Fundamentals of Risering Steel Castings," Steel Founders' Society, 1960.
62. H. F. Bishop, E. T. Myskowski, and W. S. Pellini, A Simplified Method for Determining Riser Dimensions, *Trans. AFS*, vol. 63, p. 271, 1955.
63. E. T. Myskowski and H. F. Bishop, Application of Chills for Neutralization of Rib and Boss Hot Spots on Plates, *Trans. AFS*, vol. 63, p. 295, 1955.
64. C. W. Briggs, Risering of Commercial Steel Castings, *Trans. AFS*, vol. 63, p. 287, 1955.
65. J. F. Wallace, Risering of Castings, *Foundry*, vol. 87, p. 74, November, 1959.

66. H. D. Merchant, Dimensioning of Sand Casting Risers, *Trans. AFS,* vol. 67, p. 93, 1959.
67. S. W. Brinson and J. A. Duma, Studies on Centerline Shrinkage in Steel Castings, *Trans. AFS,* vol. 50, p. 657, 1942.
68. E. J. Sullivan, Jr., C. M. Adams, and H. F. Taylor, Transport of Feed Metal during Solidification of Tapered Steel Bars, *Trans. AFS,* vol. 65, p. 394, 1957.
69. H. Present and H. Rosenthal, Feeding Distance of Bars in Investment Molds, *Trans. AFS,* vol. 67, p. 138, 1961.
70. M. C. Flemings, R. V. Barone, S. Z. Uram, and H. F. Taylor, Solidification of Steel Castings and Ingots, *Trans. AFS,* vol. 69, p. 422, 1961.
71. H. F. Bishop, H. F. Taylor, and R. G. Powell, Risering of Steel Castings with Exothermic Sleeves, *Foundry,* vol. 86, p. 54, June, 1958.
72. C. G. Lutts, J. P. Kickey, and Michael Bock II, Exothermic Materials, *Am. Foundryman,* vol. 13, p. 310, August, 1946.
73. P. K. Sandell, Breakability of Knock-off Risers, *Foundry,* vol. 88, p. 92, November, 1960.
74. "Steel Solidification Fundamentals and Their Importance to Steel Casting Design," The Pelton Steel Casting Company, Milwaukee, Wis., 1959.

16
Steel Melting in the Foundry

INTRODUCTION

Four types of furnaces are used to make cast steel:

Open-hearth (acid and basic)
Electric-arc (acid and basic)
Converter (acid side-blow)
Electric induction (acid and basic)

Of these the first two contribute most of the tonnage.

The distinction between acid and basic practice is in regard to the type of refractories used in the construction and maintenance of the furnace. Furnaces operated by the acid practice are lined with silica-base (SiO_2) refractories, and the slags employed in the refining process have a relatively high silica content. Basic furnaces, on the other hand, use a basic refractory such as *magnesite* or *dolomite* base* and have a high lime (CaO) content in the slag.

The acid process depends on having a good grade of scrap available, since neither phosphorus nor sulfur, both undesirable impurities, can be removed by this process. By employing one or another of the basic refining practices, however, either phosphorus or sulfur or both can be partially eliminated. The choice of furnace and melting practice depends on many variables, including:

1. The plant capacity or tonnage required
2. The size of the castings
3. The intricacy of the castings
4. The type of steel to be produced, i.e., whether plain or alloyed, high or low carbon, etc.
5. The raw materials available and the prices thereof

* Magnesite is $MgCO_3$, and dolomite is a calcium-magnesium carbonate. The magnesite is calcined to the oxide form before use or before making brick. Dolomite may be used raw or in the calcined form.

6. Fuel or power costs
7. The amount of capital to be invested
8. Previous experience

Generally, the open-hearth furnace is used for large tonnages and large castings, and the electric furnace for smaller heats or where steels of widely differing analyses must be produced. Special steels or high-alloy steels are often produced in an induction furnace. The converter is used where space is limited and almost continuous pouring is desired. Other advantages and disadvantages of the various methods will become more apparent after a specific process is discussed.

BASIC OPEN-HEARTH MELTING

Furnace Construction

A simplified sketch of a cross-sectional view of an open-hearth furnace is shown in Fig. 16.1. The air used for combustion purposes must be preheated to obtain the high temperatures required in an open hearth.* This is accomplished by passing the air over a brick checkerwork that has previously been preheated by outgoing gases. A companion checkerwork, in the meantime, is being heated by the outgoing gases. The cycle is reversed about every 15 min to prevent excessive cooling of the checkerwork bricks. This method of cyclically reversing the flow of air and gas is known as the *regenerative* method of preheating, and is used in all open-hearth furnaces. The regenerators (checkerwork) are located below the furnace hearth and off to one side as shown in Fig. 16.2.

* If producer gas is used as a fuel, it may also be preheated because of its low Btu content.

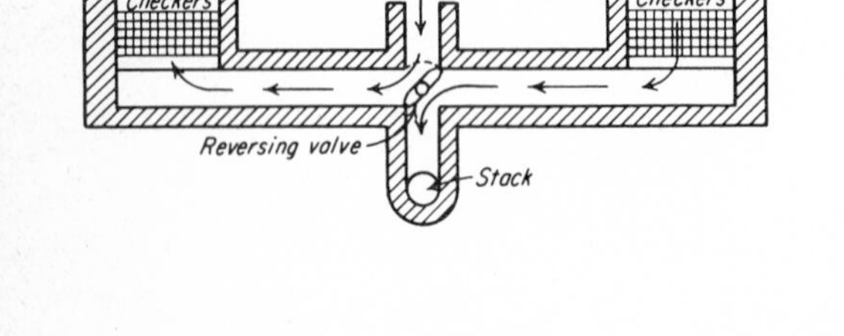

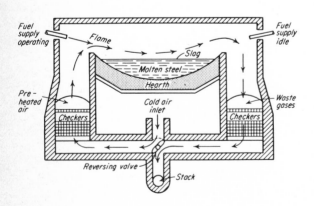

Fig. **16.1** Simplified sketch of a cross-sectional view of an open-hearth furnace. (*Courtesy of Steel Founders' Society of America.*)

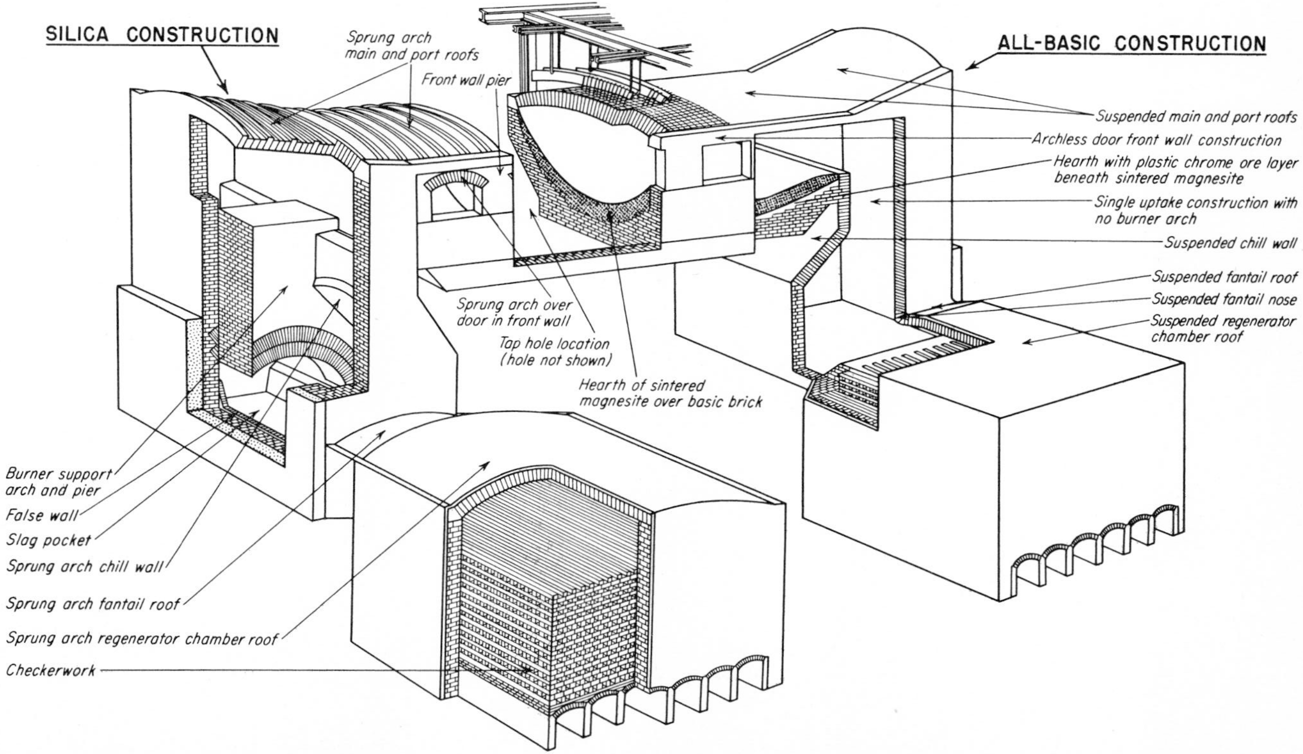

***Fig.* 16.2** Exploded view of an open-hearth furnace showing two types of roof construction. (*Courtesy of General Refractories Co.*)

The preheated air is mixed with the incoming oil or fuel gas at the burner ports. This creates a flame over the hearth which heats the charge and surrounding refractories. The slag pockets shown in Fig. 16.2 are provided to trap dust and slag carried over by the gases so that these particles do not clog the checkerwork system.

Roof Construction

As seen from Fig. 16.2, the open-hearth furnace construction is more complex than the sketch in Fig. 16.1. For example, the roof can be constructed in several different ways. This figure illustrates two methods of roof construction. Expansion allowances of about 1.25 per cent must be made to allow for the thermal expansion of the brick. Silica roofs are suspended by an arch construction supported by vertical stays at the side wall, and basic roofs are hung from an overhead-suspension system, as illustrated in Fig. 16.2.

Bottom Construction

The foundation of the hearth consists of fire-clay brick laid on the *pan* (concrete foundation). A *course* (layer) of chrome brick (30 to 40% Cr_2O_3, 12 to 30% Al_2O_3, 12 to 15% FeO, and about 17% MgO plus some impurities) is laid over this, usually followed by a course or two of basic brick. On top of the brick a monolithic lining is rammed into place, using granular dolomite or magnesite. The taphole is at the side of the furnace opposite the charging doors, and is prepared when the bottom is constructed.

Wall Construction

Walls at or below the metal line must be of basic refractories. Walls above the metal line are frequently of silica brick, 12 to 15 in. thick, but basic refractories, including metal-encased magnesite or chrome-magnesite brick, have been used.

The furnace is charged on one side through charging doors and is tapped from the opposite side. The floor elevation on the tapping side is lower than on the charging side so that the receiving ladle can be placed below the taphole. The tapping side of an open-hearth furnace is pictured in Fig. 16.3. The charging platform can be seen in the background at the extreme left. Capacities range from 25 to 75 tons, with 30 to 50 tons preferred in steel foundries.

Fig. **16.3** **A general view of the tapping side of an open-hearth furnace.** (*Courtesy of Steel Founders' Society of America.*)

Fuels and Charge Materials

Basic open-hearth furnaces are fired with either gas or oil. The oil may have to be preheated before it is burned. The sulfur content of the oil must be limited by selection in purchasing to avoid too much sulfur in the steel from this source. Consumption is about 28 to 35 gal per ton of metal charged. When producer gas (made from coal) is used as fuel, consumption is in terms of coal, about 550 to 600 lb of gas coal being required per net ton of steel melted. The gases resulting from the oil flame are more oxidizing than those from a gaseous fuel, and this controls the extent of the oxidation required from iron ore later in the heat.

The charge materials consist of pig iron, purchased scrap, foundry-scrap returns, lime, and ore. The pig iron has approximately the following composition:

3.50 to 4.40% carbon
1.50 to 2.00% manganese
1.25% maximum silicon
0.06% maximum sulfur
0.35% maximum phosphorus

The manganese is kept high to aid in desulfurization and in controlling the slag. Silicon is limited because it is an acid component in slag and hence tends to require excess lime in the charge and also may increase solution of the refractories. Only a slight sulfur removal, 0.01 to 0.02 per cent, occurs in the basic open-hearth process; therefore it must be restricted in the charge. The upper limit for phosphorus represents the maximum allowable phosphorus that can be handled practicably. A phosphorus content of 0.35 per cent in the pig iron would account for an over-all phosphorus content in the charge of about 0.10 per cent that would have to be reduced to less than 0.04 per cent during the refining stage.

The lime is of controlled composition and low in silica since increased amounts of lime would have to be used if the silica content were high in order to maintain desired composition of the slag. Lime is graded as to size. The ore is a high-grade lump ore. Some operators also use manganese ore as an addition. The scrap is composed of purchased scrap and foundry returns.

Charging and Melting

Several methods are used in placing the materials in the furnace, but the usual practice is to cover the bottom with scrap, followed by the lime spread as evenly as possible. This is followed by the pig iron. The lime addition will vary from 4 to 7 per cent of the weight of the metal charge.

The carbon content of the charge will vary from 1.0 to 1.75 per cent. This carbon content will give a value at meltdown that is about 0.3 to 0.5 per cent higher than the desired carbon content at tapping time. During the meltdown, considerable manganese and carbon are lost and almost all the silicon. The oxides so formed will float to the surface of the molten metal, where they mingle and dissolve with the lime that has also risen to the surface to form a slag. A bubbling action occurs on the bath during meltdown which results from the release of CO_2 gas from the calcination of the limestone. This is known as the "lime boil" (Fig. 16.4).

Oxidation and Refining

The principle underlying the melting and refining of steel in open-hearth and electric furnaces is to create an oxidizing condition that will oxidize such elements as carbon, manganese, silicon, and phosphorus. These oxides, with the exception of CO gas, dissolve in the slag. The bath is kept shallow to permit these reactions to proceed readily as well as to assure good heat transfer. The slag is conditioned to accept the oxides and is adjusted in viscosity to control reaction rates. Most of the manganese and silicon oxidation and part of the carbon oxidation occur during meltdown. The rest of the carbon is oxidized down to the

Fig. 16.4 **A steel bath during the "lime boil."** *(Courtesy of Loftus Engineering Co.)*

desired percentage by reacting with oxygen supplied by the furnace gases, by oxygen injection, or by the iron oxide added to the furnace after meltdown. The amount of the iron oxide addition is determined by the meltdown carbon content of the bath and the desired carbon content at tapping. The addition of iron oxide causes an evolution of CO from the reaction

$$FeO + C \rightarrow CO + Fe$$

The bubbles of CO originate in the melt at the hearth bottom and create a "carbon boil" as they percolate up to the surface. The carbon boil is an important part of refining since it aids in heat transfer by stirring the melt, cleanses the metal of retained oxides by bringing them to the slag, hastens reactions at the gas-metal interface, and aids in removing hydrogen and nitrogen. Hydrogen and nitrogen diffuse into the CO bubbles and are thereby flushed out of the liquid steel.

Although oxygen supplied by the atmosphere and the iron-ore (Fe_2O_3) addition is the original source of the oxygen which eliminates the carbon, the reaction actually is largely between oxygen dissolved in the steel and the carbon. At the temperatures used in steel refining (around 2900 F), the steel is capable of dissolving considerable oxygen as FeO.† This FeO is picked up from the slag or from a reaction between the added iron ore and the steel, such as

$$Fe_2O_3 + Fe \rightleftharpoons 3FeO$$

Figure 16.12 gives a schematic representation of the oxidation cycle in the open hearth.

In the early stages of the oxidation period after meltdown, the carbon content, being fairly high, largely controls the FeO content of the metal. At about 0.10 per cent carbon and below, the FeO content of the metal is controlled largely by the oxidizing character of the slag, which, in turn, is proportional to the FeO content of the slag. Therefore it is particularly important that the slag be adjusted in composition, or "shaped up," to create the proper conditions when the carbon has been reduced to the desired percentage.

Control of the oxidizing character of the slag can be achieved, in part, by the use of manganese. During the carbon boil there is virtually no change in the manganese content of the metal because the manganese dissolved in the metal is protected by the carbon. If manganese is added to the heat at a late stage of the oxidizing period, part will remain in the metal and part will be oxidized and dissolve in the slag. This, in effect, lowers the oxidizing power of the slag since the FeO content of the slag is lowered proportionately. The manganese is frequently added as *spiegel,* a pig iron containing about 15 to 30 per cent manganese.

Phosphorus removal is favored by having an oxidizing condition and a basic slag. Hence, if the manganese content of the steel is too high and thereby reduces the oxidizing character of the slag, phosphorus removal is not so effective.

In addition to the use of manganese for controlling the slag characteristics, *fluorspar* (CaF_2) may be used to increase the fluidity of the slag. This mineral acts essentially as a slag thinner. Further lime additions may also be used near the end of the refining period if the operator finds it necessary.

Since control of the slag is necessary in order to control the oxygen content of the melt and the degree of dephosphorization, attempts have been made to develop tests that will reflect the condition of the slag. Such tests include chemical analysis, viscosity tests, slag-color tests, and visual inspection of slag samples. The purpose of these tests is to make

† This dissolved FeO is frequently represented in chemical reactions by the symbol $\underline{O}$.

it possible to standardize operations so that good-quality steel is produced in each heat. Slag analyses just prior to stopping the boil (blocking) will usually fall in the following composition range:

CaO, 40 to 50%
SiO_2, 13 to 18%
MnO, 7 to 15%
FeO, 12 to 16%

Deoxidation and Tapping

When the heat is considered ready for tapping, deoxidizing agents are added. This step of adding a deoxidizing agent is referred to as "blocking the heat" because it prevents any further reaction between oxygen and carbon, the oxygen reacting with these additives to form nongaseous reaction products. The deoxidizers include spiegel, ferrosilicon, ferromanganese, and silicomanganese. Typical analyses of these ferroalloys are given in Table 16.1. About 10 min after adding deoxidizers, the heat is tapped. Temperatures are near 2900 to 3000 F.

Further deoxidation in the ladle may be done with ferrosilicon and ferromanganese, and occasionally with aluminum, if grain-size control is desired. If additional carbon is required, coal or petroleum coke may be added to the ladle.

Table* 16.1 *Typical analyses of ferroalloys used in steelmaking*

Name	C	Mn	Si	Cr	Ca	Al
Spiegeleisen (spiegel)	4.5–5.0	15–30	1.0–3.0 max			
Silicomanganese	1.5 max	65–70	17–20			
80% ferromanganese	6.0–8.0	78–82	1.0 max			
50% ferrosilicon	....	.....	46–52			
Ferrochromium	4–9	.....	2–3	65–70		
Calcium silicon	....	.....	60–65	.....	28–35	
Alsifer	....	.....	40	.....	.....	20

* From American Society for Metals, "Metals Handbook," 1948.

BASIC ELECTRIC MELTING

Furnace Construction

Basic electric furnaces are much smaller than open-hearth furnaces, ranging from ½ to 7½ tons capacity. A cross-sectional sketch of an electric furnace is shown in Fig. 16.5, and a photograph of a furnace ready for charging is shown in Fig. 16.6. The arc furnace is heated from the arc struck between the charge, or bath, and three large electrodes of carbon or graphite operating from a three-phase circuit. The height of the electrodes above the bath is controlled electrically. Voltages are fairly low, and current flow is high, necessitating large bus bars and heavy lead-in cables from the transformers. Charging is usually done by removing the furnace top. The roof of the furnace is silica brick, whereas the side walls are lined with magnesite brick or chrome-magnesite brick. Bottoms are rammed into place.

Melting and Refining

Although the general principles controlling the refining operation in the basic open-hearth furnace also apply to the basic electric, certain modifications in operation are possible which give the basic electric furnace greater flexibility.

Unlike the open-hearth charge, the charge for the electric furnace may not necessarily include pig iron, because not so much carbon is lost during melting as in the open-hearth. Since the atmosphere in the furnace is not appreciably oxidizing, most of the control of the oxidizing conditions comes from the charge itself. Lime is usually not added until a pool of metal is formed, and then it is added in small increments from time to time. Following meltdown, the heat may be handled in any of the following ways:

1. Iron ore is added and refining is accomplished by "complete oxidation," much in the same manner described for the open-hearth.
2. Iron ore is omitted, or very little used, and the carbon drop during refining is less than in the preceding case.
3. Melting without oxidation. This method, which is applicable to high-alloy and stainless steels, may be employed if the scrap is high in manganese and chromium. The scrap is selected to be as free of rust and scale as possible. Conditions are not oxidizing during refining, but rather are sufficiently reducing to return the small amount of manganese, chromium, and phosphorus that was oxidized during melting from the slag back to the melt.

In the heats made by methods 1 and 2, the slag is sufficiently basic and oxidizing to remove the phosphorus to about 0.02 per cent or lower. When the bath and slag have been adjusted to the proper temperature and composition, the slag is removed, or "slagged off." This practice is not followed in the basic open-hearth since the mechanical manipulation would be too difficult to carry out. Once this slag is removed, a *refining* slag composed of lime and fluorspar is added.* The purpose

* A variation is to deoxidize the metal after removing the first slag, then add slaked lime as a slag and add Ca-Mn-Si alloy to the steel bath.[5]

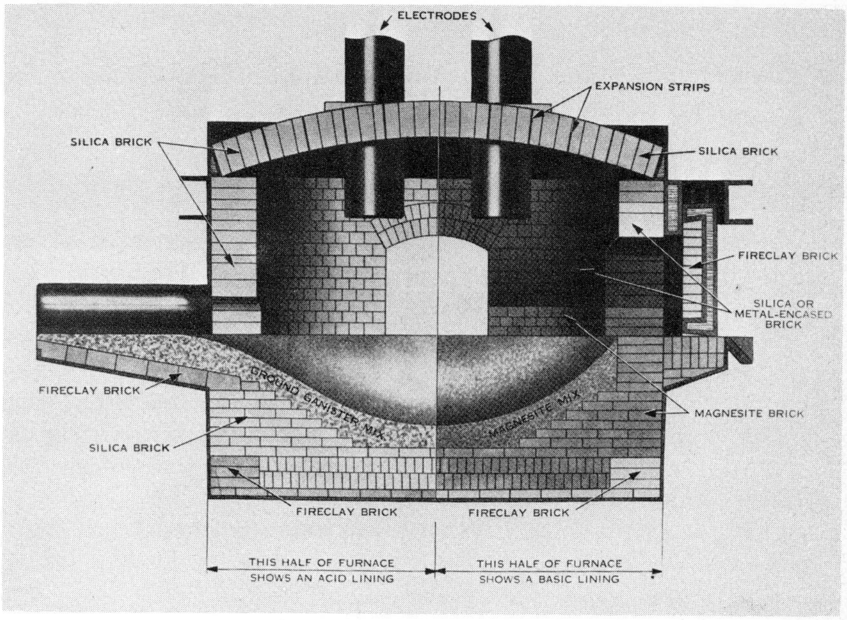

***Fig.* 16.5** Cross-sectional view of an electric arc furnace showing an acid lining (left) and a basic lining (right). (*Courtesy of American Bridge Division of U.S. Steel Corporation.*)

***Fig.* 16.6** Electric furnace being charged. (*Courtesy of Steel Founders' Society of America.*)

of this so-called refining slag is to remove sulfur, which can be accomplished only by establishing basic and reducing conditions. The necessary reducing agent in this case is carbon added to the top of the slag. The reaction is considered to be

$$\text{C (in steel)} + \text{CaO} + \text{FeS (in steel)} \rightarrow \text{CaS (in slag)} + \text{CO} + \text{Fe}$$

Refining proceeds for about 1 to 1½ hr, the completion of which is indicated by the appearance of a slag sample. The metal is usually tapped into bottom-pour ladles. Since the composition was adjusted before and during the refining period, no further additions are required at tapping.

If the phosphorus content is sufficiently low, the first, or oxidizing, slag can be eliminated, and a reducing slag established immediately at meltdown. The remainder of the process is similar to the refining procedure described in the preceding paragraphs.

In some cases, such as in the production of stainless steel, low carbon contents are required. Then carbon must be avoided in the refining slag, and aluminum is substituted.

One advantage of the two-slag process used in the basic electric furnace that cannot be realized in other melting practices for steel is the possibility of making alloy additions during the time the refining or reducing slag is on the bath. This is particularly important when additions of the readily oxidizable elements manganese and chromium are to be made. Alloys such as nickel and molybdenum can be charged with the scrap since they do not oxidize during meltdown.

As in the open-hearth practice, deoxidizers may be added 5 to 15 min before tapping. These deoxidizers may be ferrosilicon, ferromanganese, silicomanganese, ferrotitanium, and, in some instances, aluminum.

ACID OPEN-HEARTH MELTING

Furnace Construction

Outside of the different refractories used, the acid open-hearth furnace is similar to the basic open-hearth. The refining process is also the same, in that it is an oxidation process. However, sulfur and phosphorus cannot be removed and a given content of iron oxide in the slag is not so active as the same percentage in a basic slag. This is attributed to a combination of the FeO with the SiO_2 of the slag. This feature is probably the principal reason why the production of high-quality steel can be consistently carried out with a minimum of controls.

The bottom of the acid open-hearth furnace is built up in much the same manner as in the basic open-hearth, except that sand, instead of calcined magnesite, is laid over the base brick. The sand is fused in place at a temperature of about 2900 F. Some foundries mix some slag, fire clay, or ferrosilicon with the sand to obtain a better bond. Monolithic construction is used in some cases. The life of the furnace is dependent, among other things, on the grade of steel being produced. Low-carbon steels, because of the higher temperatures required for their melting and refining, cause rapid deterioration of the furnace bottoms.

Furnace Charge

As in the basic open-hearth, fuels are either gas or oil. The charge to the acid open-hearth will consist of pig iron, foundry scrap, and purchased scrap, with the average charge containing approximately 15 to 20 per cent pig iron. The percentage of pig iron is determined by the need for having sufficient carbon in the heat at meltdown to ensure a vigorous boil when iron ore is added. It is usually planned to have the total carbon content about 0.5 to 0.7 per cent above the finishing carbon value. The scrap must have a low sulfur and phosphorus content, preferably below 0.04 per cent each, since these elements cannot be eliminated in the acid process.

The silicon content of the charge will be between 0.6 and 1.0 per cent. This is higher than used in the basic open-hearth charge. Manganese may vary between the wide limits of about 0.4 to 1.75 per cent, with the average addition being between 0.75 and 1.0 per cent.

Melting and Refining

The carbon, silicon, and manganese are partly oxidized during meltdown. The carbon content at meltdown will be about 0.20 to 0.3 per cent above the finishing carbon. Silicon will not be over 0.2 per cent. If the silicon were much above this figure, a vigorous boil would not be secured immediately upon oxidation with ore or the oxygen lance.* If too low, the carbon drop during the boil would be faster and a higher meltdown carbon thereby indicated. Factors which determine the silicon and manganese content at meltdown include:

1. Amount charged
2. Working speed of the furnace (oxidation during meltdown)
3. Compactness of the charge
4. Content of the other element present, i.e., silicon or manganese, as the case may be

The manganese content of the charge will control the working of the heat to a certain extent. Thus a high manganese content in the charge

* See p. 443.

(1.25 to 1.75 per cent) will result in a slag of high MnO content. This produces a more fluid slag of lower FeO content. The slag is therefore less oxidizing toward the end of the refining period and thus assists in controlling the carbon drop.

Lime additions to the slag can also be used to control the heat. An addition of lime will aid in carbon removal since it serves to replace part of the FeO in the slag, and this FeO is then free to oxidize the carbon.

A heat is usually finished by "blocking" it with deoxidizers such as silicomanganese, spiegel, or ferrosilicon and ferromanganese. Final deoxidation is made about ½ hr later, using ferromanganese and ferrosilicon. Aluminum may be added to the ladle as a grain refiner and deoxidizer, but the amount used is critical, since this addition may result in low ductility, as explained in more detail later.

If the temperature is raised near the end of the heat to about 3100 F and the carbon is not too low, silicon can be picked up from the slag and furnace walls through the following reaction:

$$SiO_2 + 2C \rightarrow 2CO + 2Si$$

Such a reaction is generally considered undesirable, but it is practiced as a melting process in Europe and has been used in this country. The practice is said to lead to lower fluidity and greater opportunity for gas pickup.

As in the case of the basic-lined furnaces, slag control can be exercised by the use of such methods as viscosity measurements, slag-cake tests, or specific-gravity measurements. There is a close relationship between slag viscosity and acid content of the slag (SiO_2 plus Al_2O_3), as demonstrated by Fig. 16.7. Here, a high "viscosity" value actually means higher fluidity, since the longer the sample, the more fluid the slag. A drawing of the viscosity-test mold is given in Fig. 16.8. A relation between viscosity and FeO content of the slag can also be shown, the

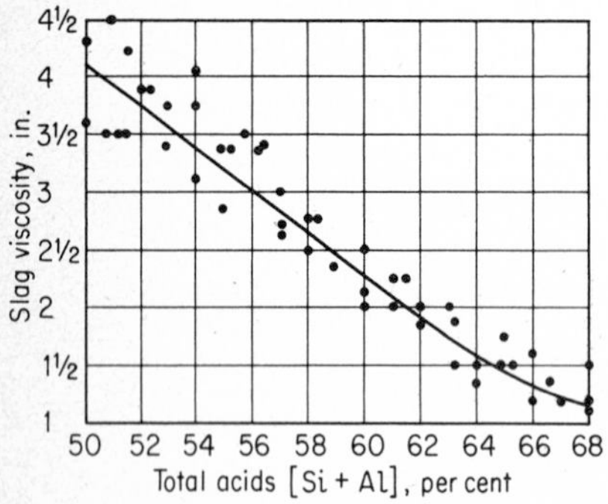

***Fig.* 16.7** Relationship between slag fluidity and acid content of the slag. (*From Briggs and Baldwin, Trans. AFS, vol.* 50, *pp.* 1104–1133, 1942.)

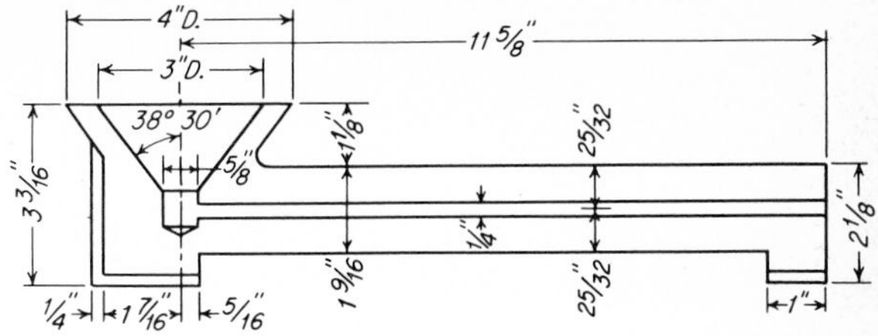

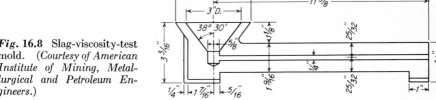

***Fig.* 16.8** Slag-viscosity-test mold. (*Courtesy of American Institute of Mining, Metallurgical and Petroleum Engineers.*)

viscosity decreasing with increasing FeO content, but a considerable scatter in the points indicates that other factors besides FeO content also contribute to the control of viscosity.

ACID-ELECTRIC MELTING

Melting in the acid-electric furnace is analogous to melting in the acid open-hearth, with the exception that it permits a greater latitude in the degree of oxidation because of the less oxidizing character of the furnace atmosphere as compared with the open-hearth.

The furnace construction is similar to that used for the basic electric steel, and is illustrated by Fig. 16.5. Three tons represents the average furnace rating, but the furnaces are generally charged beyond the rated capacity. There are a greater number of acid-electric furnaces in this country than of any other type of steel-melting furnace for producing steel castings.

The charge is usually foundry scrap and purchased scrap. The latter must be carefully selected to avoid high phosphorus or sulfur content.

Melting and Refining

Most foundries maintain a vigorous boil to ensure good-quality steel. This boil is secured from iron oxide supplied by rust on the steel and additions of iron ore or mill scale added to the bath or by use of the oxygen lance (see the section on oxygen injecting). The principle of operation of the heat is similar to that for an acid open-hearth. This method of melting is referred to as the *complete-oxidation* process. Slag-forming materials other than sand clinging to the charge are usually not added with the charge for acid heats.

When the *partial-oxidation* process is used, only a mild boil results, which is induced by the reaction of carbon with the small amount of FeO supplied by rust and oxide normally present on the charge. This method has the advantage of rapid production, but occasionally may lead to poor mechanical properties.

Slag control is effected by observation of the slag color or by using the viscosimeter test. The relation between viscosity and acid content is similar to that obtained with the acid open-hearth.

In some cases, the initial slag formed on the steel is removed at the time of recarburization, and a new neutral slag made from lime and sand is formed. The necessary manganese and silicon additions can then be made with a uniformly high recovery, and a better control of the heat can be achieved.

In addition to the usual deoxidizers added at the end of the heat, aluminum is frequently added to the ladle, particularly if the metal is cast in green-sand molds, where the danger of casting defects is great unless the metal is sufficiently deoxidized.

Silicon reduction from the slag or furnace walls is a more likely reaction in the acid-electric than in the acid open-hearth furnace because of the higher temperatures near the electrodes, and is practiced in a few foundries. The reduction is aided by a high manganese content in the charge.

ACID CONVERTER PROCESS

Some foundries produce steel in an acid-lined converter. This necessitates a source of liquid metal which is usually supplied by a cupola (Chap. 19). The converter used in the steel foundry is not the *bessemer* type, in which air is blown in from the bottom; it is a side-blown *Tropenas* converter, illustrated in Fig. 16.9.

Liquid metal having an analysis in the following range is charged into the converter:

2.75 to 3.5% carbon
1.30 to 2.00% silicon
0.50 to 0.60% manganese
0.04% max phosphorus
0.04% max sulfur

As obtained from the cupola, this metal is usually higher in sulfur and must be given a treatment to bring the sulfur down to the desired level. The treatment is with *soda ash* (sodium carbonate) or *caustic soda* (sodium hydroxide) or mixtures of the two placed in a forehearth in front of the cupola. These materials form fluid slags that react rapidly with the sulfur in the cupola metal, reducing it about 75 per cent.

As soon as the treated metal is poured into the converter, the air blast is turned on and oxidation of the silicon and manganese begins. The blow is completed by carbon oxidation, leaving a metal of about 0.05% C, 0.02 to 0.05% Si, and 0.01 to 0.03% Mn. The flame coming from the

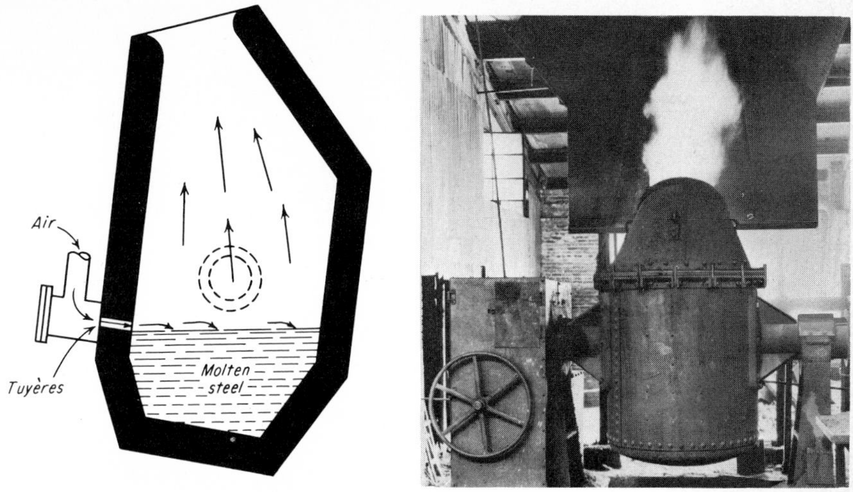

***Fig.* 16.9** Drawing and photograph of a Tropenas converter. (*Courtesy of Steel Founders' Society of America.*)

mouth of the converter varies in its characteristics, depending on the stage of the blow, and this variation can be measured through a photoelectric-cell apparatus, which enables good control of the process.

The steel is then prepared for pouring by deoxidizing and recarburizing to the desired specifications.

By employing an electric furnace as a holding furnace for the converter metal, greater flexibility can be obtained and further adjustments of composition and alloy content can be made. This is known as the *triplex method.*

INDUCTION FURNACE

The high-frequency induction furnace is essentially an air transformer in which the primary is a coil of water-cooled copper tubing and the secondary is the metal charge. Furnace capacity rarely exceeds 1 ton. A sketch of the furnace is shown in Fig. 16.10. The shell of the furnace consists of asbestos board, and is supported on trunnions on which the furnace pivots when pouring. Inside the shell is placed the circular winding of copper tubing. Firebrick is placed on the bottom portion of the shell, and the space between that and the coil is rammed with grain refractory. The furnace chamber may be a refractory crucible, or it may consist of a rammed and sintered lining. The general practice is to use ganister rammed around a steel shell which melts down with the

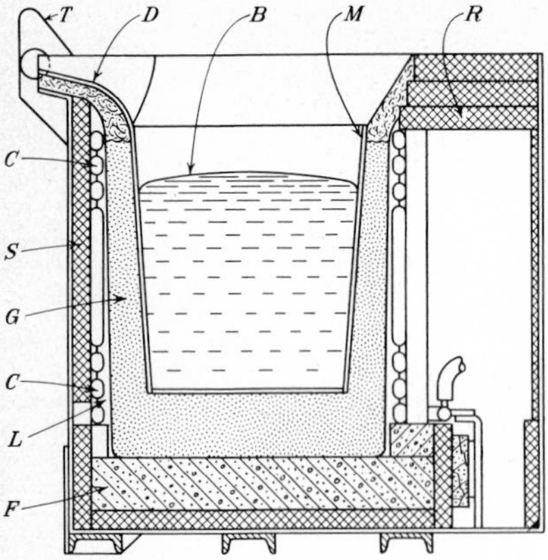

***Fig.* 16.10** Cross-sectional drawing of an induction furnace. *B*, metal bath; *C*, water-cooled copper coil; *D*, pouring spout; *F*, firebrick base; *G*, refractory packing; *S*, asbestos lumber; *T*, trunnions. (*Courtesy of American Society for Metals.*)

first heat, leaving a sintered lining. Basic linings are often preferred, and in this case either the lining may be rammed, using magnesia grain, or a clay-bonded magnesia crucible may be used.

The process consists in charging the furnace with steel scrap and then passing a high-frequency current through the primary coil, thus inducing a much heavier secondary current in the charge, which results in heating the metal charge by resistance. As soon as a pool of metal is formed, very pronounced stirring action in the molten metal takes place, which helps to accelerate melting. In this process, melting is quite rapid, so much so that there is only a slight loss of the easily oxidized elements. If a capacity melt is required, steel scrap is added continually during the melting-down period. As soon as melting is complete, the desired superheat temperature is obtained and the metal is deoxidized and tapped into ladles.

The time of melting depends upon the size of the furnace, the weight of the charge, and the power input. Since a period of only 10 or possibly 15 min elapses from the time the charge is melted down until the heat is tapped, there is not sufficient time for chemical analyses. Thus the charge is usually carefully selected from scrap and alloys of known composition so as to produce the desired analyses in the finished steel. A very close control of elements can be obtained in this manner.

In most cases, no attempt is made to melt under a slag cover, since the stirring action of the bath makes it difficult to maintain a slag blanket on the metal. However, a slag cover is not necessary since oxidation is slight.

The induction furnace is proving valuable to the steel foundry, particularly in the production of small lots of alloy castings, where the number of alloy types desired may be large. The fact that high-alloy-content metal can be remelted in these furnaces without loss of the alloy content through oxidation makes it a particularly valuable melting furnace.

VACUUM MELTING AND DEGASSING

Because of its compact size, the induction furnace is ideal to use for melting under a vacuum. This is a costly process because of the need for high-capacity vacuum equipment, but the cost may be justified in terms of improved properties or in the production of alloy steels.[7]

By melting in a vacuum, the normal deoxidation reaction between carbon and oxygen to form CO gas can be much more effective than in conventional melting, to the extent that carbon becomes a better deoxidizer than those elements that are normally used for this purpose. This reaction is favored by high temperatures. The result is a steel that is virtually free of oxide-containing nonmetallic inclusions. Harmful hydrogen and nitrogen gases should also be removed more effectively. Precaution must be taken that steel is poured carefully soon after melting to avoid gas pickup or reoxidation. Pouring in a vacuum eliminates this possibility. One disadvantage that might occur with vacuum melting is the loss by evaporation of those elements which have a relatively high vapor pressure.

Another use of vacuum is vacuum degassing. This is done after conventional melting by pouring the metal into a specially designed ladle or by enclosing the furnace in a chamber that can be evacuated rapidly to a low pressure. The metal might also be poured in a vacuum.

Vacuum degassing and pouring reduces the residual gas content of steel without markedly altering the composition. Improved toughness, better fatigue resistance, and better ductility are claimed for steels produced in this manner. High-quality, superstrength alloy steels are the most likely products[9] made by this process.

OXYGEN INJECTION IN OPEN-HEARTH AND ELECTRIC FURNACES

The advent of relatively cheap oxygen supplies in 1946 resulted in considerable investigation of the use of oxygen as an additional control in steel production. Although oxygen can and has been used to enrich the fuel mixture by injecting it into the open-hearth furnace below the burners, the principal use for oxygen has been in controlling the refining process.

Oxygen is injected into the metal bath through a steel pipe or a copper-tipped, water-cooled lance. The oxygen reacts vigorously with carbon, particularly when the latter is high, and increases the rate of carbon loss to two or three times as high as normal rates with ore. Since this reaction creates heat, ore may be added simultaneously to keep the temperature from becoming excessively high, the oxidation of carbon with ore being an endothermic reaction. Use of oxygen injection saves time in working the heat, and this can be extremely helpful when furnace capacity is limited.

In addition to its use to increase production, oxygen injection is also helpful in curing temporary difficulties such as low temperatures or incomplete lime solution of the lime in the slag. In stainless-steel production, carbon can be reduced without oxidizing much chromium by injecting the oxygen under a neutral slag at high temperature.

Besides giving increased production rates, oxygen injection gives better control, lower carbon contents without chilling the bath, and fuel savings. Disadvantages are increased fume, smoke, and splashing, the latter causing decreased refractory life because of the erosive effect of splashed slag and metal.

Briggs[10] has reproduced data from the British Steel Casting Research Association showing the amount of oxygen to inject as a function of initial carbon, final carbon, and injection temperature. These are provided in Table 16.2.

BASIC OXYGEN (LD) PROCESS

Steel is being produced in Europe and in the United States by using a converter similar to the one illustrated in Fig. 16.9, but using an oxygen lance inserted through the top of the converter rather than blowing air in through the tuyeres in the support trunnions. The lining is basic. Advantages of this process are an outstanding degree of dephosphorization; partial removal of sulfur; low residual contents of oxygen, hydrogen, and nitrogen; low capital outlay; flexibility; and low upkeep during shutdown.[11]

PHYSICAL CHEMISTRY OF STEELMAKING

The preceding descriptions of the various steelmaking processes indicate that, generally, steelmaking can be conveniently divided into three stages, although there is no clear-cut demarcation between the first two stages.

Table 16.2 Amount of oxygen required for producing steel for castings by oxygen injection*

Initial carbon, %									Final carbon, %
0.20	0.25	0.30	0.35	0.40	0.45	0.50	0.55	0.60	
For Use Where the Temperature prior to Injection Is 1550 C (2822 F)									
260	292	321	348	375	402	429	455	481	0.07
136	168	197	224	251	278	305	331	357	0.10
83	115	144	171	198	225	252	278	304	0.125
43	80	109	136	163	190	217	243	269	0.15
20	52	81	108	135	162	189	215	241	0.175
	32	61	88	115	142	169	195	221	0.20
		29	56	83	110	137	163	189	0.25
			27	54	81	108	134	160	0.30
				27	54	81	107	133	0.35
					27	54	80	106	0.40
						27	53	79	0.45
							26	52	0.50
For Use Where the Temperature prior to Injection Is 1600 C (2910 F)									
231	256	279	302	324	346	368	390	411	0.07
111	136	159	182	204	226	248	270	291	0.10
68	93	116	139	161	183	205	227	248	0.125
39	64	87	110	132	154	176	198	219	0.15
16	41	64	87	109	131	153	175	196	0.175
	25	48	71	93	115	137	159	180	0.20
		23	46	68	90	112	134	155	0.25
			23	45	67	89	111	132	0.30
				23	44	66	88	109	0.35
					22	44	66	87	0.40
						22	44	65	0.45
							22	43	0.50

* Courtesy of the British Steel Castings Research Association, Sheffield, England. From C. W. Briggs.[10]

These tables give the volume of oxygen in cubic feet per ton of steel that must be blown during *the period from the appearance of the carbon flame to the end of the blow* to give the stated final carbon contents from the given initial carbon contents.

These stages are melting, oxidation and refining, and deoxidation. Each of these stages will be considered from the standpoint of the major reaction involved and the relative differences between the several steelmaking methods; but before this is done, some facts regarding the thermochemical behavior of the important elements are briefly reviewed.

At steelmaking temperatures, carbon, silicon, and manganese are all readily oxidizable elements (so is phosphorus if a basic slag is maintained to dissolve the P_2O_5 which is formed). The relative amount of each of these elements, as well as of iron, which is oxidized, is dependent upon (1) its basic or fundamental oxidation tendencies; (2) the temperature, since the oxidation tendency varies with temperature; and (3) the relative amounts of these elements that are present, or concentration.

Standard Free Energy

The basic or fundamental oxidation tendency is given by the *standard free energy of formation of the oxide.* The greater the negative value of this thermodynamic function, the greater the tendency of the element to oxidize. Thus, at 1600 C, this value is about -126 kcal (kilogram-calories) for $Si + O_2 \rightleftharpoons SiO_2$ and about -117 kcal for $2Mn + O_2 \rightleftharpoons 2MnO$, which means that one gram-atomic weight of silicon is more readily oxidized by a given quantity of oxygen than are two gram-molecular weights of manganese.

The standard free energy change refers to the reactants in some specific, previously selected standard state, reacting to form products also in some specific, previously selected standard state. Thus, for the preceding reactions, the standard states which were arbitrarily selected were:

Si as a liquid
O_2 as a gas at 1 atm pressure
SiO_2 as a solid
Mn as a liquid
MnO as a solid

Had some other standard state been selected, for example, oxygen at some pressure other than 1 atm, or MnO as a liquid rather than a solid, the standard free energy values would be different. Therefore, implied for each of the equations is the following additional information:

$$\text{Si (as a liquid)} + O_2 \text{ (as a gas, 1 atm)} \rightarrow SiO_2 \text{ (as a solid)} \qquad \Delta G^\circ = -126 \text{ kcal/mole}$$

$$2\text{MnO (as a liquid)} + O_2 \text{ (as a gas, 1 atm)} \rightarrow 2\text{MnO (as a solid)} \qquad \Delta G^\circ = -117 \text{ kcal/mole}$$

where the ΔG° notation signifies a *standard* free energy change.

In reactions involving substances of variable composition or pressure, such as in the case of liquid or solid solutions or mixed gases of variable pressure, the standard free energy change can be related to the *equilibrium constant* K for the reaction

$$\Delta G^\circ = -RT \ln K$$

where ΔG° = standard free energy change
R = gas constant in cal/mole/deg
= 1.987 cal/mole/deg
T = degrees Kelvin
$\ln K$ = natural logarithm of K
= 2.3 logarithm of K to the base 10
= 2.3 log K

Thus, for the silicon reaction at 1600°C,

$$-126{,}000 = -1.987 \times 1873 \times 2.3 \log K$$

or

$$\log K = \frac{126{,}000}{4.575T} = 14.72$$

Now the equilibrium constant must be expressed in terms that define the *thermodynamical equilibrium* of the reaction. These terms are referred to as *activities.* Activity is a dimensionless quantity that is used to express *chemical potential,* or driving force, for a given substance involved in a reaction, or physical change, relative to some standard condition. Thus, if the standard state for a gas were 1 atm, an actual pressure of 2 atm would mean an activity of 2 for this gas. The activities of the products of a reaction are multiplied in the numerator of the constant, whereas the activities of the reactants are multiplied in the denominator. This is demonstrated as follows for the silicon reaction:

$$K_{Si} = \frac{a_{SiO_2}}{a_{Si} \times a_{O_2}}$$

and for the manganese reaction:

$$K_{Mn} = \frac{(a_{MnO})^2}{(a_{Mn})^2 \times a_{O_2}}$$

Note that the power of each term is determined by the number of moles in the reaction.

If pure solid or liquid substances are involved in a reaction, their reference states are identical with their actual states. Consequently, their activity values are unity. Then the preceding equations simplify to

$$K_{Si} = \frac{1}{1 \times a_{O_2}}$$

$$K_{Mn} = \frac{1}{1 \times a_{O_2}}$$

For gases, the standard states are so selected that the activities are equal to the numerical value of the pressure of the gas. Therefore

$$a_{O_2} \approx |P_{O_2}|\dagger$$

$$K_{Si} = \frac{1}{P_{O_2}} \quad \text{and} \quad K_{Mn} = \frac{1}{P_{O_2}}$$

Although a $1/P_{O_2}$ term occurs in each equation, one must note that these values are not the same, because in one case the oxygen is equilibrated with liquid silicon and solid silica and in the other case with liquid manganese and solid manganese oxide.

Returning now to the relation between $G°$ and K, we note that

$$\Delta G_{Si}° = -RT \ln K_{Si} = +RT \ln P_{O_2}$$

and

$$\Delta G_{Mn}° = -RT \ln K_{Mn} = +RT \ln P_{O_2}$$

Therefore the standard free energy change involved in the oxidation of *pure* elements to form *pure* oxides using one mole of oxygen gas is given by $+RT \ln P_{O_2}$. The value of P_{O_2} is either the total pressure of oxygen if it is the only gas present or the partial pressure of oxygen if other gases are present. Calculations will find that the pressure of gaseous oxygen in equilibrium with silicon or manganese at 1600 C is exceedingly low. This is shown in Fig. 16.11.

Temperature

Up to this point only one temperature has been considered. The standard free energy change for a given reaction will vary with temperature, and hence the equilibrium constant will also vary. Figure 16.11 plots the effect of temperature on the standard free energy of formation of oxide compounds formed from the elements and one mole of gaseous oxygen. From preceding relations it can be noted that the ordinate not only gives the numerical value for $RT \ln P_{O_2}$ but also for $\Delta G°$.

The effect of temperature would not have much significance in steelmaking if all the oxidation reactions were altered in the same direction to the same degree, but this is not the case. The negative value of the standard free energy change of formation decreases with an increase in temperature. This means that the oxides become less stable as the temperature increases. The one exception is the reaction between carbon

† Actually, of course, the activity is defined by $f/f°$, where f is the actual *fugacity*, and $f°$ is the *standard fugacity*. In most metallurgical problems, this ratio is equivalent to $p/p°$, where $p° = 1$. Therefore $a_{O_2} \approx |p_{O_2}|$.

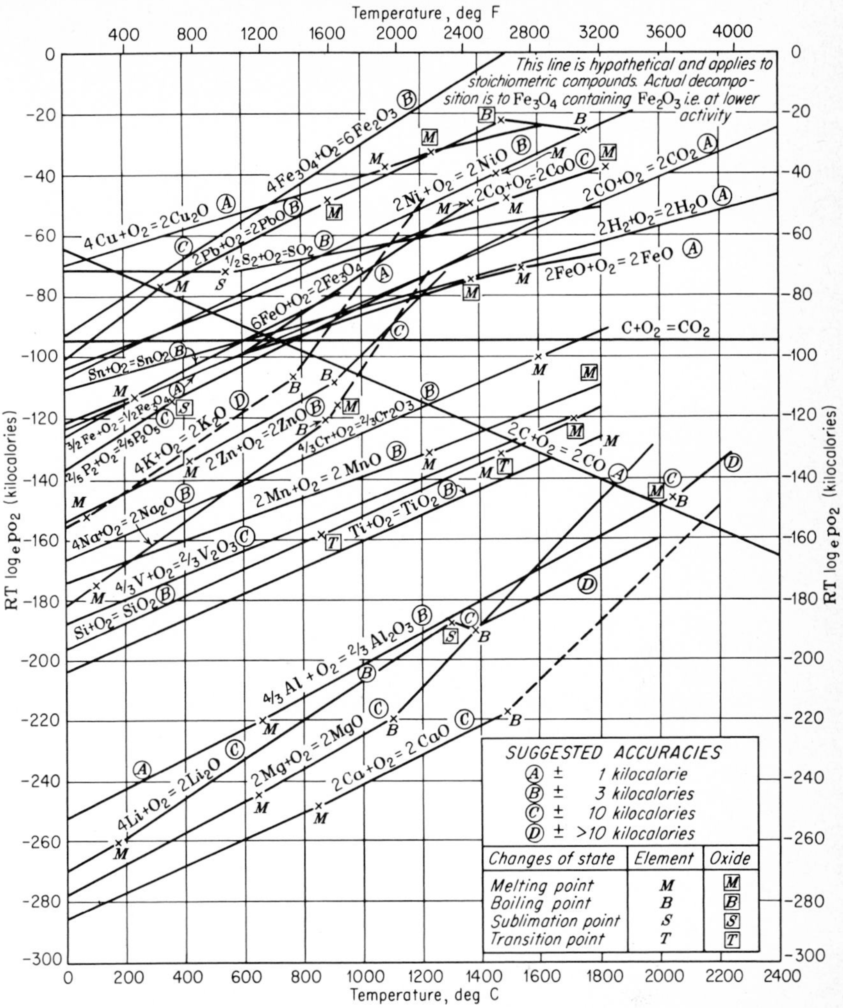

***Fig.* 16.11** Effects of temperature on the standard free energy of formation of a number of oxides. (*Courtesy of American Institute of Mining, Metallurgical and Petroleum Engineers.*)

and oxygen to form carbon monoxide. Carbon therefore becomes increasingly more effective as a deoxidizer as the temperature increases, whereas the effect of other deoxidizing elements decreases. Since carbon monoxide is a gaseous product, the effectiveness of carbon as a deoxidizer and reducing agent for other oxides not only increases with temperature, but also increases with a decrease in pressure. Vacuum deoxidation as previously described is therefore based on sound thermodynamic principles.

Effect of Concentration

According to the third factor listed, the relative concentration of each element must also be considered. This effect can be demonstrated only for oxygen if the data in Fig. 16.11 are used. Thus, if oxygen exceeds the equilibrium partial pressure given by Fig. 16.11, the metal will be oxidized. If the oxygen partial pressure is reduced below that of the equilibrium pressure, the oxide is reduced. Quantitatively, this effect is represented by

$$\Delta G = \Delta G^\circ + RT \ln Q$$

where ΔG = *actual* free energy change
ΔG° = *standard* free energy change
Q = quotient similar to that used to express K, but in which the actual activity values are used

For the oxidation of silicon, it was previously established that ΔG° at 1600 C is -126 kcal/mole. From Fig. 16.11 it can be determined that the *equilibrium* partial pressure of oxygen in contact with silicon and silica is about $10^{-14.72}$ atm. This value was also calculated on page 447. Then

$$\begin{aligned}\Delta G &= -126{,}000 + RT \ln \frac{1}{P_{O_2}} \\ &= -126{,}000 - 4.575T \log P_{O_2} \\ &= -126{,}000 - 4.575T \log 10^{-15} \\ &= -126{,}000 + 15 \times 4.575 \times T \approx 0\end{aligned}$$

This shows that the actual free energy change at equilibrium is zero. Now if the partial pressure of the oxygen in contact with silicon and silica were 10^{-10},

$$\begin{aligned}\Delta G &= -126{,}000 + 4.575(1873) \log \frac{1}{P_{O_2}} \\ &= -126{,}000 - 4.575(1873) \log P_{O_2} \\ &= -126{,}000 - 4.575(1873) \log 10^{-10} \\ &= -126{,}000 + 45.75(1873) = -40{,}310 \text{ cal/mole}\end{aligned}$$

A negative free energy change indicates a spontaneous reaction and demonstrates that a pressure of 10^{-10} atm will cause oxidation of silicon. Note that the ΔG value is less negative than the ΔG° value. This merely means that, for the specific condition selected, namely, 10^{-10} atm, the reaction would not be as spontaneous as it would be under standard conditions of 1 atm of oxygen.

The preceding example illustrates the influence of concentration (partial pressure) in the case of oxygen. In steelmaking reactions, the reactions actually occur between elements dissolved in steel and oxygen dissolved in steel to form a product that will dissolve in a slag. Such a reaction could be represented for silicon as follows:

$$\text{Si (in liquid iron)} + 2\text{O (in liquid iron)} \rightarrow \text{SiO}_2 \text{ (in liquid slag)}$$

Here it can be noted that the concentration of any one or all of the three components of the reaction can be varied rather than the partial pressure of oxygen only. The question naturally arises as to how this situation can be treated thermodynamically. This is done by selecting new standard states that more nearly represent the actual situation and then calculating or determining new standard free energy values representative of these new standard states. The procedure required is to calculate or determine the free energy change involved in going from the original standard state to the new one. It will be demonstrated for the oxidation of silicon, where the new standard states for silicon and oxygen dissolved in iron are a concentration of 1 per cent by weight and that for SiO_2 dissolved in slag is a mole fraction of 1, or $N_{Si} = 1$:

(*a*) $\text{Si}(s) \rightarrow \text{Si (in liquid iron, 1\% by wt)} \qquad \Delta G_a^\circ$

(*b*) $\text{O}_2 \text{ (1 atm)} \rightarrow 2\text{O (in liquid iron, 1\% by wt)} \qquad \Delta G_b^\circ$

(*c*) $\text{SiO}_2(s) \rightarrow \text{SiO}_2 \text{ (in liquid slag, } N_{\text{SiO}_2} = 1) \qquad \Delta G_c^\circ$

Note that ΔG_b° represents a situation that could not be realized in actuality inasmuch as the solubility limit for oxygen is about 0.22 per cent at 1600 C. However, this does not prevent making such calculations. There are methods available for calculating each of the foregoing standard free energy changes which depend upon having some knowledge of the thermodynamic behavior of each of these solution systems. The standard free energy changes for the SiO_2 would probably be small, relatively, because the change of state in going from pure solid silica to liquid silica does not entail much of a change in free energy.* Using Hess's law, the conversion from the original oxidation equation to the one involving the true steelmaking reaction is now made as follows:

$$\text{Si}(s) + \text{O}_2 \text{ (1 atm)} \rightarrow \text{SiO}_2(s) \qquad \Delta G_{\text{Si}}^\circ$$

(*a*) $-\ [\text{Si}(s) \rightarrow \text{Si (in liquid iron, 1\% by wt)} \qquad \Delta G_a] =$

$\text{Si (in liquid iron, 1\% by wt)} + \text{O}_2 \text{ (1 atm)} \rightarrow \text{SiO}_2(s) \qquad \Delta G_{\text{Si}}^\circ - \Delta G_a$

(*b*) $-\ [\text{O}_2 \text{ (1 atm)} \rightarrow 2\text{O (in liquid iron, 1\% by wt)} \qquad \Delta G_b] =$

$\text{Si (in liquid iron, 1\% by wt)} + 2\text{O (in liquid iron, 1\% by wt)} \rightarrow \text{SiO}_2(s)$

$\Delta G_{\text{Si}} - \Delta G_a - \Delta G_b$

(*c*) $+\ [\text{SiO}_2(s) \rightarrow \text{SiO}_2 \text{ (in liquid slag, } N_{\text{SiO}_2} = 1) \qquad \Delta G_c] =$

(*d*) $\text{Si (in liquid iron, 1\% by wt)} + 2\text{O (in liquid iron, 1\% by wt)} \rightarrow$

$\text{SiO}_2 \text{ (in liquid slag, } N_{\text{SiO}_2} = 1)$

$$\Delta G_d^\circ = \Delta G_{(\text{Si})} - \Delta G_a - \Delta G_b + \Delta G_c$$

* Both the enthalpy and entropy of solution should be small.

This new $\Delta G_d{}^\circ$ value can now be used to establish the effect of concentration through the relation

$$\Delta G^\circ = -RT \ln K = -RT \ln \frac{a_{SiO_2}}{a_{Si} \times (a_O)^2}$$

or the relation

$$\Delta G = \Delta G^\circ + RT \ln Q$$

In both K and Q, the activity values can be represented as given below, provided that the actual compositions do not deviate too far from the selected standard states. When such deviations do occur, their effect can be adjusted for if there is some prior knowledge of the system. Assuming that the deviations are moderate, the respective activity values are now numerically determined as follows:

$$a_{Si} \approx |\% \text{ Si}|$$

$$a_O \approx |\% \text{ O}|$$

$$a_{SiO_2} \approx |N_{SiO_2}|$$

The advantage of these choices of standard states is obvious from the above relations.

Standard free energy values for the oxidation of many of the elements that are in solution in iron during steelmaking have been established and are tabulated in several sources.[4,12,13]

There is also some knowledge of the effect of the addition of a third component in iron on the activity of the second component, e.g., the influence of manganese, chromium, or nickel on the activity of silicon in iron, but these data are incomplete.

Our knowledge of slag constitution is also incomplete, although progress is being made in this field. The theories of slag behavior are considered in the section on oxidation and refining.

With this brief consideration of the factors associated with the oxidation reactions, we can turn to their applications to steel melting.

Melting

During meltdown, oxidation of iron, manganese, silicon, and carbon occurs. Part of the oxygen comes from the atmosphere and part from the solid oxides such as rust or ore that may be charged with the metal. As soon as a slag forms, oxidation may be thought of as occurring between the metalloids dissolved in the metal and the FeO dissolved in the slag, although the original source of the oxygen in the slag could still be the atmosphere. Typical reactions would be

$$\underline{Si} + 2\underline{O} = [SiO_2]\dagger$$

$$\underline{Mn} + \underline{O} = [MnO]$$

FeO, SiO_2, and MnO become a part of the slag. In the case of the basic practices, the slag volume is further increased by the lime additions that have been made with the charge or during the meltdown.

The carbon content at meltdown is governed by the amount added with the charge and the amount lost during melting. The latter amount is determined to some extent by the furnace operation. In the open-hearth furnace, provision is made to have enough carbon at meltdown to provide for a carbon boil during the refining period. Such extra carbon may or may not be provided in the electric furnace, depending upon the particular practice employed. Because of the low temperature during meltdown, manganese and silicon oxidize more readily (for a given concentration) than carbon; so carbon is not removed so readily as these two elements. Therefore appreciable amounts of carbon remain after melting. The silicon content, on the other hand, is usually below 0.05 per cent in basic furnaces and below 0.20 per cent in acid furnaces at meltdown. The manganese losses are not so great as those of silicon, and the amount which remains at meltdown will range between 0.05 and 0.40 per cent, the low value coming from well-oxidized heats starting with a low manganese charge, and the latter from a fairly high manganese content in the original charge.

Oxidation and Refining

Carbon

The most important reaction during the oxidation period is the reaction between carbon and oxygen to form CO gas.

$$\underline{C} + \underline{O} \rightleftharpoons CO$$

This reaction stirs the melt, aids in removing dissolved hydrogen and nitrogen, and brings other deoxidation products to the slag-metal interface. The reaction actually is initiated on the furnace hearth or on the surfaces of any solid components such as scrap or iron ore that may be added to the bath. Surface irregularities at these interfaces provide the necessary

† The designation $\underline{Si}$ and $\underline{Mn}$ mean these elements are in *solution* in the metal. The bracket indicates solution in the slag.

nucleation of the CO bubble. The equation representing the pressure required to nucleate the bubble is

$$P_{CO} = P_h + \frac{2S}{r}$$

where P_h = pressure "head" due to metal slag and atmosphere
S = surface tension
r = diameter of bubble[13]

The surface irregularities make it possible to nucleate a bubble with a much larger radius than if it were to nucleate homogeneously. This reduces the CO pressure required for bubble formation. Figure 16.12 illustrates this effect.

Silicon

Silicon is brought down to fairly low levels during meltdown, as already mentioned. In acid heats at the end of the refining period when temperatures are high, silicon may be reduced from the slag or furnace lining through the following reaction:

$$2\underline{C} + [SiO_2] \rightleftharpoons \underline{Si} + 2CO$$

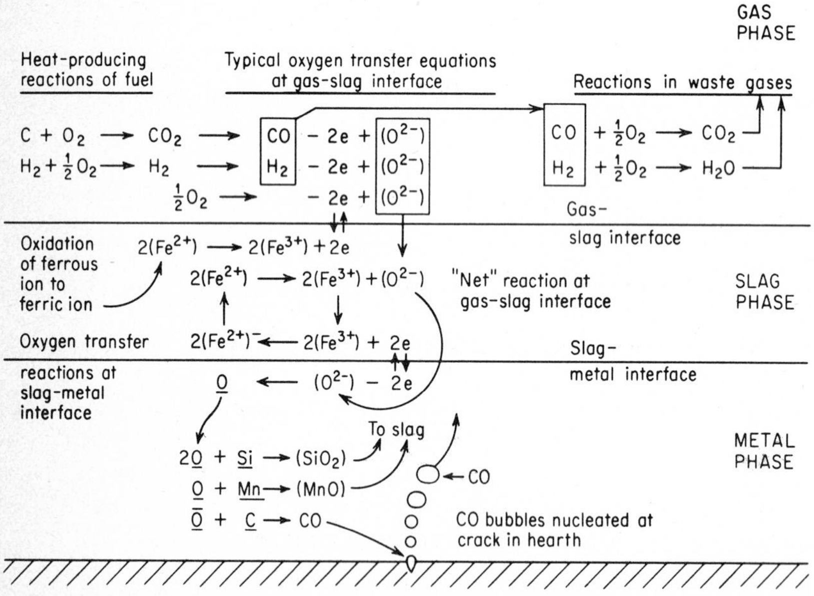

Fig. 16.12 Typical physicochemical cycle in an open-hearth furnace showing transfer of the Fe^{++}, Fe^{3+}, and $O^{=}$ ions in the slag and formation of CO bubbles at the hearth. Terms in parentheses are in the solution in the slag, and terms underlined are in solution in the metal. (*After R. G. Ward*[13] *and AIME "Basic Open-hearth Steelmaking."*[4])

This action is not unexpected in view of the fact that silicon becomes less readily oxidized and carbon more so as the temperature rises. There apparently is no simultaneous increase in the oxygen content of the bath, since the increased silicon content should prevent oxygen pickup. Silica reduction is also aided by having a high manganese content. This effect may result either from having a higher concentration of MnO in the slag, thereby lowering its FeO content, or from an actual reduction of SiO_2 by manganese as a result of mass action. At elevated temperatures there is little difference in the standard free energy of formation of SiO_2 and MnO; hence it is conceivable that a reduction of SiO_2 by manganese could take place if the manganese content were high enough.

Manganese

The manganese distribution between slag and metal depends on:

1. The amount of manganese in the charge
2. The amount of manganese in the ore that may have been added
3. The slag volume and slag composition
4. The carbon content of the metal
5. The oxidizing characteristics of the slag
6. Temperature

The manganese in the charge and that supplied by the ore determine the total amount of manganese that will be found in either the metal or slag. The distribution of manganese between slag and metal approaches very close to chemical equilibrium. Obviously, then, a greater slag volume will throw a larger proportion of manganese into the slag; and the extent of this distribution is affected by the slag composition. Both a high and a low base-acid ratio in the slag tend to decrease the residual manganese content of the metal. The carbon content is important because it will protect the manganese in the metal if it is high enough. If the FeO content of the slag is high, manganese is oxidized to MnO, until a new balance is struck between manganese in the metal and in the slag. Therefore a high MnO-FeO ratio in the slag results in a high residual manganese content in the metal. As with most of the other oxidizable elements in steel, an increase in temperature shifts the equilibrium toward a higher manganese residual in the metal. It is therefore possible that, during the refining period when carbon is dropping, the increased temperature occurring simultaneously may compensate for the lack of protection from the carbon, and manganese residuals may stay constant or even increase slightly.

Good manganese recovery obviously is a worthwhile objective, but sometimes this objective must be subordinated to other objectives that can be accomplished only by having a large percentage of the manganese appear in the slag. Because manganese reacts with FeO and can readily replace FeO in a slag without altering the properties of the slag, manganese is useful in controlling the state of oxidation. Manganese added to the bath during a refining period will react with FeO, reducing its concentration and thereby lowering the oxidizing character of the slag. In effect, part of the FeO in the slag is replaced with MnO, rendering the slag less oxidizing without changing its viscosity.

Typical reactions involving carbon, silicon, manganese, and iron with oxygen are shown schematically in Fig. 16.12. The equations involving iron transfer in the slag show the changes in the iron ions in the slag required to affect the transfer of oxygen to the metal bath from the atmosphere.

Phosphorus

In considering the removal of some elements from the melt it is essential to consider the state of the slag. Although this knowledge is helpful with reference to silicon or manganese distribution between slag and metal, it is particularly helpful in the case of the removal of phosphorus and sulfur. Our knowledge of slag constitution is incomplete, but two general theories have proved useful.

1. A molecular theory based on the concept that slags are composed of undissociated or partially dissociated complex molecules and free oxides.
2. An ionic theory which postulates the formation of certain simple and complex ions in slag melts. The interactions of these ions contribute to specific slag behavior. Typical positive ions would be Ca^{++}, Mn^{++}, Fe^{++}, etc., and typical simple and complex negative ions would be O^{-}, F^{-}, SiO_4^{4-}, PO_4^{3-}, FeO_3^{3-}, etc.[13]

Although the molecular theory of slags has been used to good advantage in steelmaking, the ionic theory has contributed to a better understanding of the constitution of slags and the nature and kinetics of reactions between slag and liquid-metal melts.

The use of the two theories will be demonstrated in connection with phosphorus removal. A commonly used equation representing the molecular theory is

$$2\underline{P} + 5[FeO] + 4[CaO] = [4CaO \cdot P_2O_5] + 5\underline{Fe}$$

This equation shows that phosphorus removal is favored by a *basic* and an *oxidizing* slag. A relation between phosphorus removal and FeO and CaO content of the slag is given in Fig. 16.13.

The equation representing the application of the ionic theory is[13]

$$\frac{N_{PO_4^{3-}}}{a/oP} = K^{1/2}\,(a/oO)^{5/2} \cdot (N_{O^=})^{3/2}$$

where $N_{PO_4^{3-}}$ = amount of PO_4^{3-} ion expressed as a fraction of all the anions (negative ions) present in the slag

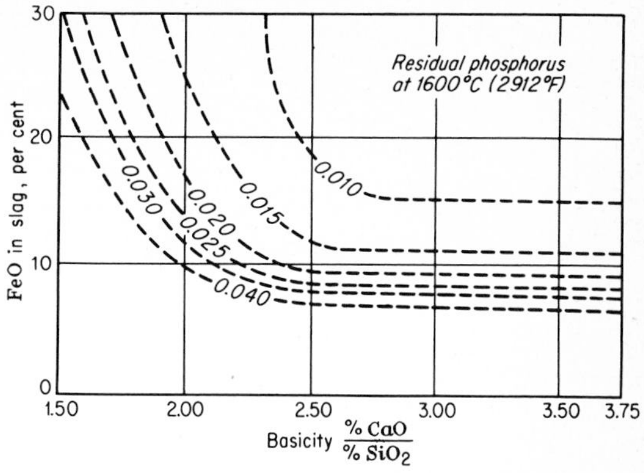

***Fig.* 16.13** Relation between phosphorus removal and FeO content and basicity of the slag. (*Courtesy of American Institute of Mining, Metallurgical and Petroleum Engineers.*)

$N_{O^=}$ = anionic fraction of $O^=$ in the slag calculated in the same way

a/oP, a/oO = atomic fractions of phosphorus and oxygen, respectively, in the iron melt

K = "equilibrium quotient" defined by

$$\log K = 21N'_{Ca^{++}} + 18N'_{Mg^{++}} + 13N'_{Mn^{++}} + 12N'_{Fe^{++}}$$

where each N' value is the electrically equivalent ionic fraction given by the general expression

$$N'_R = \frac{v \cdot n_{R^{v+}}}{n_{R^+} + 2n_{R^{++}} + 3n_{R^{3+}} + \cdots}$$

where n_{R^+} represents the moles of R^+ ion, etc., and v represents the ionic charge integer.

Although the ionic equation representing dephosphorization seems unnecessarily complex, its principal difference from the molecular equation is in its recognition of the contribution of the individual cations (Ca^{++}, Mg^{++}, Mn^{++}, Fe^{++}) toward dephosphorization. In this respect, it attempts to recognize the specific structure of slag and the interplay of forces between these ions and between the ions and the constituents in the metal bath.

In the case of either the molecular theory or the ionic theory, the factors that favor phosphorus removal from the metal are itemized in Table 16.3. Neither theory directly predicts the effect of temperature, but a low temperature favors dephosphorization. The curves in Fig. 16.13 are shifted upward and to the right by increased temperature. Other factors that influence dephosphorization which are not directly connected with the two slag theories are:

1. *Slag viscosity.* A viscous slag slows up reaction rates and hinders dephosphorization. This happens if the slag becomes too basic. In this instance the

Table 16.3 Factors favoring phosphorus removal from steel bath

Factor	Molecular theory	Ionic theory
Basic slag.	High CaO	High $N_{O^{=}}$
High lime content.	High CaO	Lime has the highest multiplying factor (21) of the various cations
Oxidizing conditions.	High FeO content in slag	High oxygen content in the metal —effected by high FeO content in slag—but note that log K tends to be lowered if $N'_{Fe^{++}}$ is too high, thereby lowering $N_{Ca^{++}}$

question is not one of thermodynamic equilibrium, but of reaction rates or kinetics.

2. *Active bath action.* A vigorous boil provides a stirring action which increases the contact area between metal and slag. Again, this is a question of kinetics rather than equilibrium.
3. *Time.*
4. MnO *content of the slag.* A high MnO content reduces the FeO content of the slag and the oxygen content of the metal. This is an indirect effect that basically would be predicted by either of the two theories.

For the detailed application of these theories to other solute elements, see Refs. 12 and 13.

Sulfur

Conditions in the average oxidizing basic slag are not particularly favorable for sulfur removal from the metal, and even less so in acid slags. The most effective way to reduce sulfur is to use a second refining slag in the basic electric furnace which is nonoxidizing in character. The basic reaction is

$$\underline{S} + [CaO] \rightarrow [CaS] + \underline{O}$$

The oxygen going into solution in the metal must, in turn, be kept low by using a reducing agent, such as carbon, in the slag.

The essential features of a desulfurizing slag are:

1. High basicity to keep the oxygen ion concentration high
2. High lime content
3. Low iron oxide content
4. Low temperature
5. High carbon, silicon, and phosphorus in the metal since these all increase the activity of sulfur in the iron

The rate of the reaction is increased by use of a fluid slag as promoted by fluorspar additions and by stirring of the bath to improve slag-metal contact.

Alloys

A chart showing the constituents of the charge and the products formed in a low-carbon basic open-hearth steel heat is given in Fig. 16.14. To this chart might be added such residual alloy elements as copper, nickel, chromium, and molybdenum. Copper and nickel will be found to be fully recoverable in all melts since these elements are not oxidized in the presence of the other more highly oxidizable elements such as iron, silicon, and manganese. Chromium and molybdenum are partially oxidized.

Oxygen

An understanding of the oxygen distribution during melting is of importance to the steel foundryman because high oxygen content at the time of pouring tends to reduce the quality of the steel. Furthermore, proper control of oxygen is necessary in order to achieve other desirable qualities in the metal and slag. Oxygen is distributed between the metal and slag. In open-hearth melts, oxygen is continually being supplied to the slag by the atmosphere. Therefore it is not possible to reach an equilibrium between the oxygen which is in the slag and that in the metal. In electric-

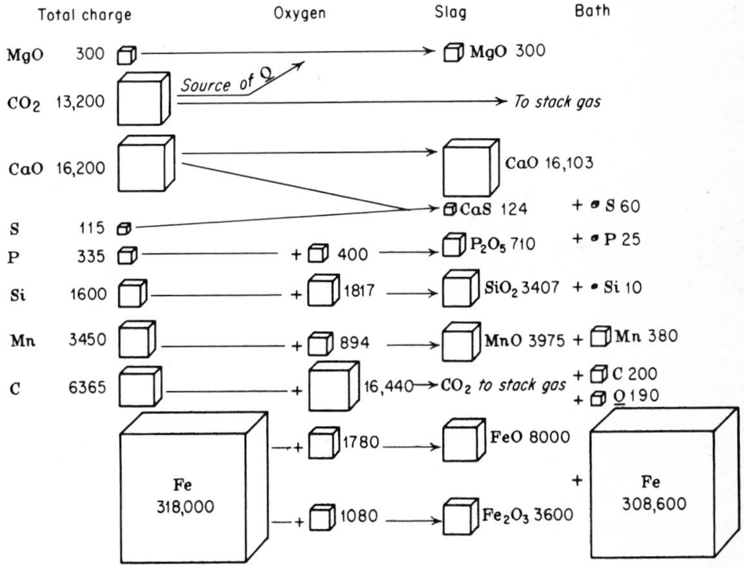

***Fig.* 16.14** Constituents and products of a basic open-hearth heat. *(Courtesy of American Institute of Mining, Metallurgical and Petroleum Engineers.)*

furnace heats, control of this distribution is better realized since the influx of oxygen to the melt is under control.

High oxygen content in the metal is caused by:

1. Low carbon or silicon contents
2. High FeO content in the slag
3. Basic slag composition and low slag viscosity
4. High temperature

The carbon boil occurs when the temperature and carbon content are sufficiently high and the silicon is sufficiently low. During this period of refining, the oxygen in the melt is controlled primarily by the carbon content and is fairly low.

When the carbon is low enough (about 0.20 per cent or less) carbon no longer is effective in controlling the oxygen content of the melt, and slag

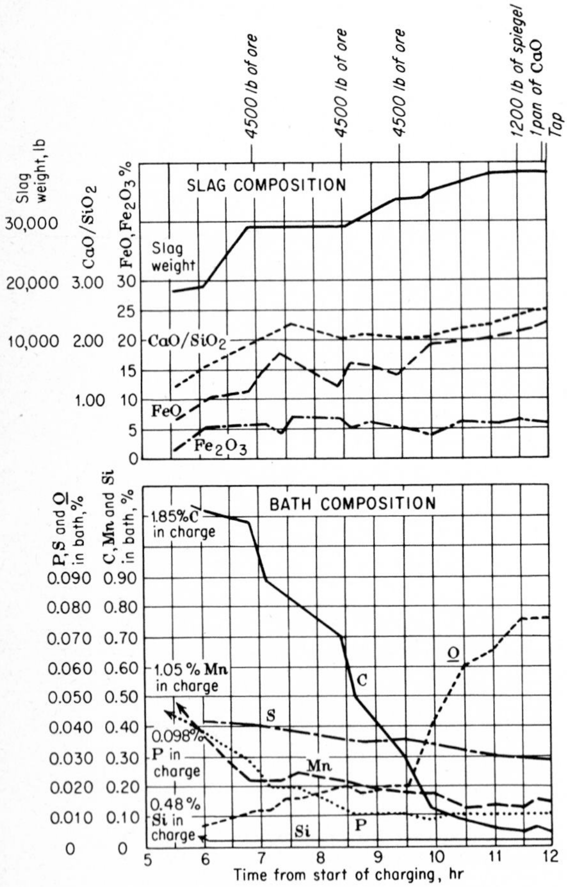

***Fig.* 16.15** Increase in FeO content of the steel occurs when the carbon content is lowered. (*Courtesy of American Institute of Mining, Metallurgical and Petroleum Engineers.*)

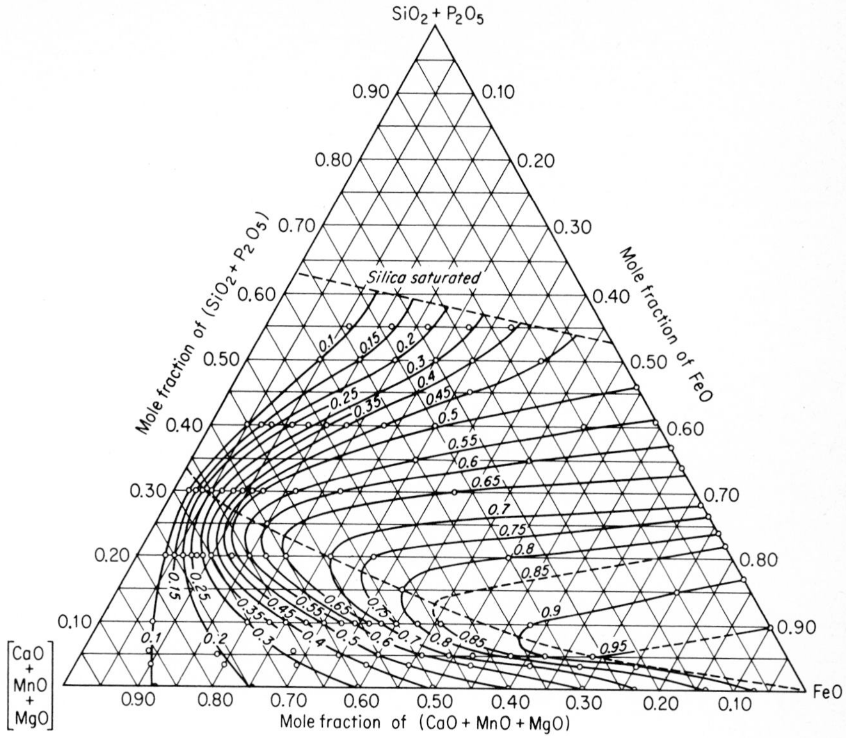

***Fig.* 16.16 Effect of composition on the oxygen activity in simple synthetic laboratory slags at steelmaking temperature. (*Courtesy of Journal of Iron and Steel Institute.*)**

composition then becomes an important factor. Thus a high FeO content of the slag at this time will not only tend to reduce the carbon further, but will also tend to raise the iron oxide content of the metal since at this stage more iron oxide can go into solution because of the lowered carbon. Figure 16.15 shows how rapidly FeO builds up in the steel when the carbon is lowered.

In the electric furnace, iron oxide content of the slag can be adjusted by the amount of oxide added to the heat. Therefore it should be possible to bring the FeO content to a fairly low value at the conclusion of the oxidation period. However, in open-hearth heats the control is largely through slag-composition adjustment because the atmosphere is continually furnishing more oxygen, and adjustment of slag is the only way that the oxygen can be controlled near the end of the refining period.

Not only a variation in FeO content of the slag per se, but a variation in other slag components affects the degree of oxidation obtained. This is demonstrated in Fig. 16.16. If attention is confined to slags of fixed

FeO content, it is seen that, for a given FeO content of the slag, the FeO content of the metal becomes increasingly less as the base-acid ratio approaches 0.7. With either acid or basic slags, control of the FeO content can be achieved, at least temporarily, through adjustment in slag composition. For instance, in an acid slag, lime may be added to achieve the transfer of oxygen to the bath because it replaces FeO in the slag, consequently making the FeO more available to oxidize the iron. In a basic heat, a lime addition would exert an opposite effect because it would thicken and chill the slag, thus tending to retain FeO and decrease its transfer to the metal.

If fluorspar is added to a basic heat, it will also affect the oxygen distribution by its effect on the fluidity of the slag. A thin or fluid slag obtained by adding fluorspar will transfer oxygen more rapidly than a viscous one. In other words, the addition of fluorspar tends to give a more rapid approach to equilibrium through its effect on the rates of reaction. If a slag is too viscous early in the refining period, it will build up in oxygen content. If it is subsequently made more fluid by an increase in temperature or increase in FeO content, the retained oxygen may then be transferred to the metal in excessive quantities. Because the question of slag composition and fluidity is so closely associated with steel refining, it is discussed further in the next section.

A high temperature of the metal increases the chance for a higher oxygen content in the bath because of the increased solubility of oxygen with increased temperature. Such increased solubility occurs despite the presence of deoxidizing elements in the bath (Fig. 16.19).

Slag Control

Aside from serving as a reservoir into which the various metallic oxides formed during melting and refining can dissolve, the slag serves as a measure of controlling the "condition" of the bath. This control can be exerted through an adjustment of the slag composition or of slag viscosity. For example, an increase in the FeO content of the slag will

Table* 16.4 *Approximate composition and weight of slags used in cast-steel refining

Furnace	Composition, %				Slag weight, % of metal charge
	CaO	SiO_2	MnO	FeO	
Basic open-hearth	40–50	13–18	7–15	12–16	5–10
Basic electric	35–50	12–16	3–13	12–25	5–7
Acid open-hearth	0–8	48–58	10–25	12–25	5±
Acid electric	0–10	57–66	15–25	12–20	5±

tend to make it more oxidizing, whereas the actual rate at which reactions take place will be dependent on the slag viscosity. Of course, slag viscosity is dependent indirectly on slag composition but can be varied somewhat independently of the oxidizing power of the slag.

In the acid practice the slags are fairly siliceous, as indicated in Table 16.4. At meltdown the iron oxide content is high, leading to a black color and good fluidity (low viscosity). After refining, the slag tends to be less fluid and have a lighter color. A slag low in FeO and MnO is usually dark green, but one low in FeO and high in MnO is light or pea green. The latter slag is desirable for retaining a higher manganese percentage in the steel. Although either slag appearance or slag viscosity serves as a measure of the FeO content of the slag, neither is an exact measure since changes in the lime or MnO content of the slag will also effect changes in color or viscosity that, however, will not reflect changes in the oxidizing power of the slag. The fluidity of acid slags is closely associated with the SiO_2 content, as was demonstrated by Fig. 16.7.

Adjustments in basic slags are made to aid in removing phosphorus and sulfur, as already described. Adjustments are also made to arrive at the desired degree of oxidation at the end of a refining period. This degree of oxidation is affected both by the carbon content of the melt and by the base-acid ratio of the slag. Figure 16.17, for example, shows that, for a given slag composition in an open-hearth furnace, the iron oxide content of the slag (and also of the metal) is higher, the lower the carbon content. It is also varied, however, by changing the base-acid ratio. An addition of lime to the slag should therefore result in a momentary stop in the transfer of FeO to the bath as already described, whereas a change in the other direction should momentarily increase oxidation rates.

Changes in slag fluidity due to temperature or composition changes

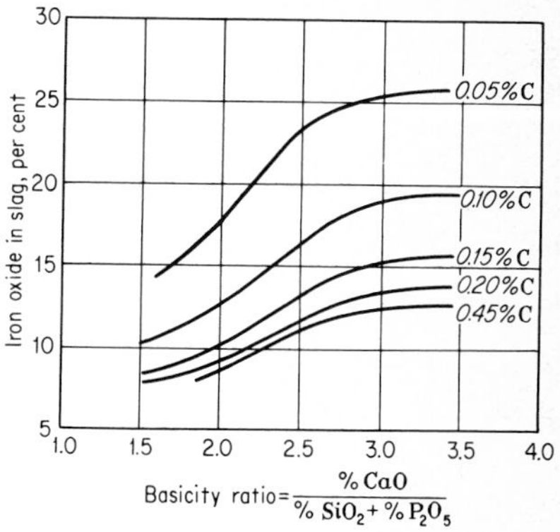

***Fig.* 16.17** For a given slag composition in an open-hearth furnace, the FeO content is higher, the lower the carbon content. Also, for a given carbon content, the FeO content of the slag is higher, the larger the basicity ratio. (*Courtesy of American Institute of Mining, Metallurgical and Petroleum Engineers.*)

affect the oxidation rate by affecting the reaction rate at the metal-slag interface. Such changes due to composition are obtained by changing the base-acid ratio or by adding fluorspar.

Deoxidation

At the end of the refining period in acid open-hearth and electric practices, and the basic open-hearth and single-slag electric practices, the metal is at the lowest carbon it will reach and at the highest dissolved oxygen content. The purpose of the deoxidation is, therefore, to restore the carbon to the proper level and to reduce the oxygen content to a low value. Although carbon would be the ideal deoxidizer if it could remove enough oxygen, it becomes relatively less effective compared with other elements as the temperature is lowered. Hence it cannot serve as a deoxidizer for steel melts. Instead, elements such as manganese, silicon, and aluminum are used. These elements, with the exception of aluminum, are added as ferroalloys.

The relative effectiveness of a deoxidizer is given by equilibrium data showing the concentration of oxygen that can remain in solution in steel in equilibrium with a given concentration of deoxidizer (also in solution). Examples of such equilibrium lines are given by solid lines in Fig. 16.18.

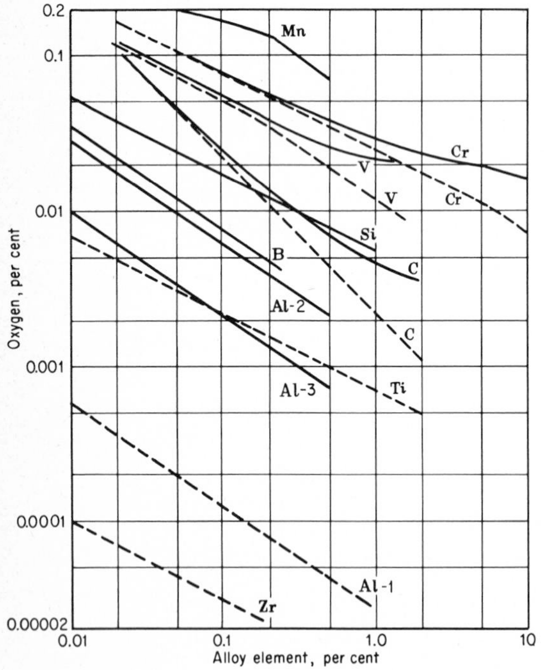

Fig. **16.18** Equilibrium between various deoxidizers and the oxygen content in steel. (*Courtesy of American Institute of Mining, Metallurgical and Petroleum Engineers.*)

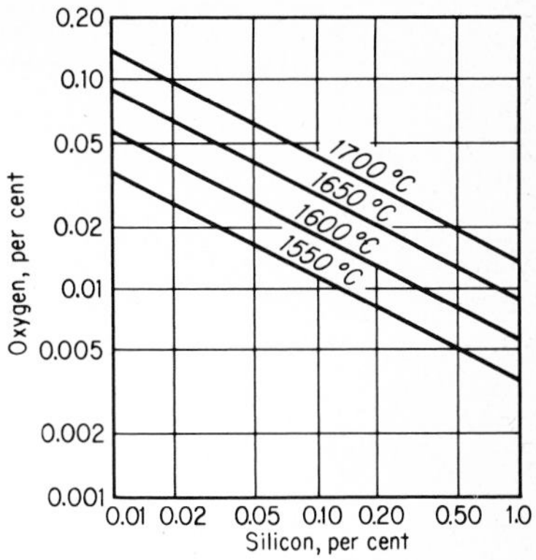

***Fig.* 16.19** Effect of temperature on the silicon-oxygen equilibrium in steel. (*Courtesy of American Institute of Mining, Metallurgical and Petroleum Engineers.*)

(The *dashed* lines in this figure are for calculated values based on thermodynamic data.) Actually, these lines represent the limits of solubility of oxygen in liquid steel in the presence of the added elements, and may be considered as lines on an isothermal section taken from ternary systems of iron, oxygen, and a deoxidizing element.

The lines in Fig. 16.18 are for a temperature of 1600 C (2912 F). If the temperature were lower, they would all shift to lower values, with the exception of that for carbon, which would be shifted upward. An example of the shift is given in Fig. 16.19 for the silicon-oxygen equilibrium.

The data presented so far are in regard to the formation of the pure oxides of the several deoxidizing elements. There is evidence, however, that some deoxidizers like manganese and silicon are more effective when they are added together rather than separately.[14] This has been attributed to the formation of complex deoxidation products such as manganese silicates. For that reason, some melters prefer to add ferromanganese and ferrosilicon together. Silicomanganese additions are preferred by some because in this ferroalloy the ratio of silicon to manganese is such that a relatively fluid deoxidation product is formed. Ferromanganese may be used after the silicomanganese to aid in coalescing these products. Not only is the oxygen content of the metal reduced to a low value by this procedure, but the deoxidation products are more fluid, and hence should coalesce and float out of the bath more readily.

The foregoing information reveals that deoxidation is not merely concerned with reducing the dissolved FeO to a low level, but also involves the problem of cleansing the steel of the reaction products. An understanding of the various binary and ternary equilibrium systems of oxides, such as FeO, SiO_2, MnO, and others, is therefore of considerable assistance in establishing a deoxidation practice that will ensure good-quality steel. An analysis of these systems will indicate which combination of oxides will have low melting points and hence be more likely to coalesce and float out of the bath.

The subject of steel deoxidation encompasses two practical phases of steel-castings production. Deoxidation with aluminum or other powerful deoxidizers is a useful tool, assisting in the making of sound steel castings, as discussed in Chap. 15. The metallurgical properties and microstructure of the steel are also influenced by deoxidation practice. The latter subject is considered in Chap. 17.

BIBLIOGRAPHY

1. Steel Founders' Society of America, "Steel Castings Handbook," 3d ed., 1960.
2. United States Steel Company, "The Making, Shaping and Treating of Steel," 7th ed., 1957.
3. C. W. Briggs, "The Metallurgy of Steel Casting," McGraw-Hill Book Company, New York, 1946.
4. American Institute of Mining and Metallurgical Engineers, Iron and Steel Division, Physical Chemistry of Steelmaking Committee, "Basic Open-hearth Steelmaking," 1951.
5. C. C. Wissmann, "Acid Electric Furnace Steelmaking Practice," American Society for Metals, 1947.
6. E. J. Dunn, Jr., Rapid Desulfurization to 0.002 Per Cent Sulfur, *Trans. AFS,* vol. 69, p. 276, 1961.
7. P. S. Schaffer, P. J. Ahearn, and M. C. Flemings, Vacuum Induction Melting High Strength Steels, *Trans. AFS,* vol. 68, p. 551, 1960.
8. T. F. Kaveny, Vacuum Induction Melting Alloy Quality Requirements, *Trans. AFS,* vol. 69, p. 680, 1961.
9. J. B. Dabney, M. C. Flemings, and H. F. Taylor, Vacuum Cast Steel Sulfur and Carbon Effect on Properties, *Trans. AFS,* vol. 69, p. 778, 1961.
10. C. W. Briggs, presentation at Electric Furnace Conference, Cincinnati, November, 1962.
11. R. Rinesch, H. Neudecker, and J. Eibl, Basic Oxygen LD Process for Foundries, *J. Steel Castings Res.,* April, 1963 (condensed and translated from *Giesserei*).
12. C. E. Sims, "Electric Furnace Steelmaking," vol. II, "Theory and Fundamentals," Interscience Publishers, Inc., New York, 1963.
13. R. G. Ward, "An Introduction to the Physical Chemistry of Iron and Steel Making," Edward Arnold (Publishers) Ltd., London, 1962.
14. E. J. Dunn, Jr., Cast Steel Deoxidation to Vacuum-melted Levels without Vacuum Processing, *Trans. AFS,* vol. 70, p. 743, 1962.
15. H. H. Fairfield and J. A. Ortiz, Some Factors Affecting the Toughness of Mild Steel Castings, *Modern Castings,* vol. 34, p. 70, July, 1958.
16. E. T. Turkdogan and J. Pearson, Activity of Constituents of Iron and Steelmaking Slags, Part I, *J. Iron Steel Inst.,* vol. 173, p. 217, 1953.

17

Metallurgy of Cast Steel

COMPOSITION

Cast steel was defined in Chap. 15 as basically an alloy of iron and carbon. In addition to carbon, which imparts basic properties to steel, the other elements that are normally present in wrought steel are also found in cast steels. These include manganese, silicon, phosphorus, and sulfur. These elements usually fall in the following ranges:

Manganese, %	0.5–1.0
Silicon, %	0.2–0.8
Phosphorus, max %	0.05
Sulfur, max %	0.06

Small precentages of other residual metals such as nickel and copper may also be present. For plain-carbon-steel castings, the carbon content determines one type of classification used for commercial steel.

1. Low-carbon steel (carbon less than 0.20%)
2. Medium-carbon steel (carbon between 0.20 and 0.50%)
3. High-carbon steel (carbon above 0.50%)

In addition to the three classes of plain carbon steels listed above, two other classes are also defined as:

1. Low-alloy steels (alloy content totaling less than 8%)
2. High-alloy steels (alloy content totaling more than 8%)

Classifications based on strength requirements are also provided for design purposes (Chap. 15).

If the important role of carbon in controlling the properties of cast steel is set aside for the moment, the significance of the other elements commonly present may be considered.

Manganese and Silicon

In carbon steels, both these elements are residuals resulting from the deoxidation practice. They occur in solution in the steel; i.e., they are dissolved in the iron and are not visible when a steel sample is examined under a microscope. Both elements confer strength and hardness through their influence on the transformation the steel undergoes when cooling from an elevated temperature. In other words, they increase the *hardenability* of the steel.

Sulfur

Manganese combines with the sulfur that is present in steel to form nonmetallic sulfide inclusions in the steel. The role of deoxidation with aluminum in controlling the shape and distribution of these sulfides is discussed later. Sulfides, of course, are readily identified in a sample prepared for microexamination since they are not soluble in solid steel. Since all the sulfur appears as sulfide inclusions, the sulfur content is limited to 0.06 per cent maximum to avoid the harmful effect on ductility and toughness that would result if excessive sulfur were present.

Phosphorus

Phosphorus is limited to 0.05 per cent because it tends to embrittle the steel at low temperatures, leading to "cold shortness." Like silicon and manganese, it is soluble in iron and *does not* appear in the microstructure. [It will be noted that in gray cast iron phosphorus occurs in a separate phase (steadite).]

STRUCTURE

Effect of Carbon

Carbon-free iron changes its crystallographic structure twice on cooling from the freezing point: once at 2538 F (1392 C) when it changes from a *body-centered cubic structure* (δ-*iron*) *to a face-centered cubic structure* (γ-*iron*), and again at 1670 F (910 C) when it changes back from face-centered cubic iron to body-centered cubic iron (α-*iron*). It is not necessary to discuss these crystallographic structures further here, except to point out that it is the allotropic transformation occurring at 1670 F, together with the effect of carbon on it, that makes it possible to control the properties of the steel by controlling (1) the carbon content and (2) the heat-treatment.

The iron-carbon equilibrium diagram shown in Fig. 17.1 depicts the changes effected by increasing the carbon content. It is seen that carbon dissolves in γ-iron to a maximum of about 2.0 per cent at about 2110 F. This solid solution is referred to hereafter as *austenite*. The solution of

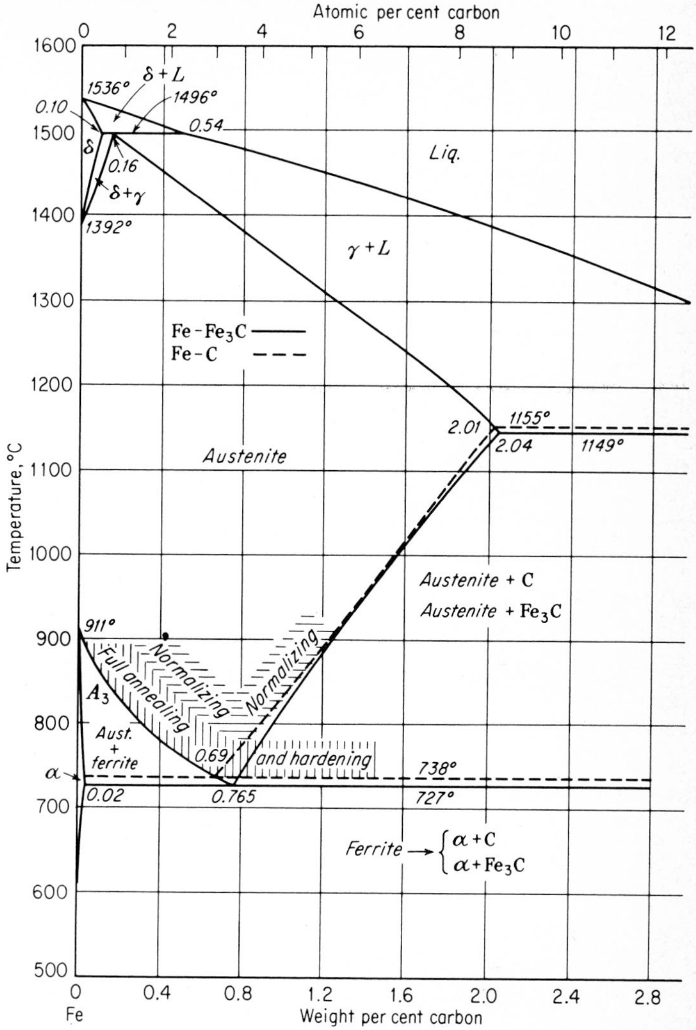

***Fig.* 17.1** A portion of the Fe-Fe_3C and Fe-C diagrams. (*After Kirkaldy and Purdy, courtesy of American Institute of Mining, Metallurgical and Petroleum Engineers.*)

carbon in γ-iron also extends the maximum and minimum temperatures at which austenite is stable, respectively, 2725 F at about 0.16 per cent carbon and 1340 F at 0.76 per cent carbon.

At room temperature, carbon is only slightly soluble in *ferrite,* which is the name given to the alpha solid solution. When carbon is present in excess of this slight solubility it appears as iron carbide, or *cementite.* In normally cooled steels, this cementite is associated with ferrite in a unique

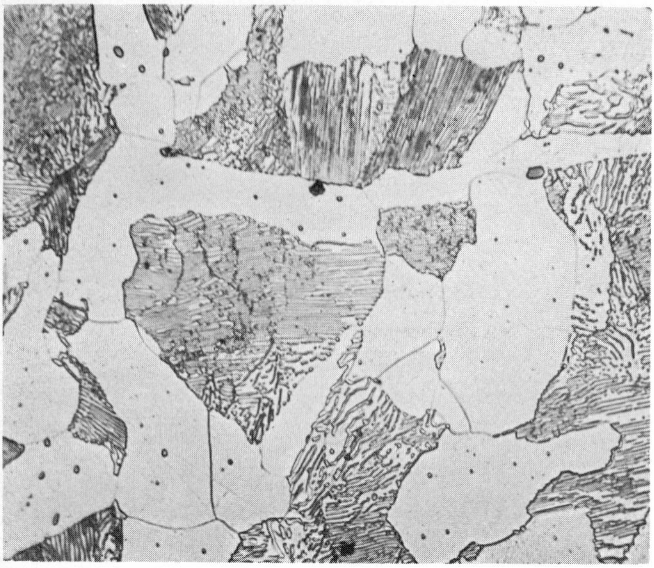

***Fig.* 17.2** Microstructure of ferrite and pearlite in a 0.50 per cent carbon steel, ×750.

lamellar structure referred to as *pearlite* (Fig. 17.2). At 0.76 per cent carbon this mixture of ferrite and carbide constitutes the entire microstructure of the steel, in other words, it is all pearlite. At carbon percentages less than this amount, ferrite and pearlite appear together in separate patches (Fig. 17.2), the relative proportions of these microconstituents being determined by the carbon content. Thus, with carbon changing from 0 to 0.76 per cent, the steel changes from an entirely ferritic material to an entirely pearlitic material. Ferrite is much softer and more ductile than pearlite, and it is the change from this material to a mixture of ferrite and pearlite, and finally to all pearlite at 0.76 per cent carbon, that accounts for the effect of carbon on the properties of cast steel.

Beyond 0.76 per cent carbon, cementite is present with the pearlite and becomes increasingly more prevalent as the carbon increases. Thus, in these higher-carbon steels, cementite is found not only in pearlite, but also in a more massive form as a network around the pearlite areas. Few steel castings are made, however, with carbon as high as this.

The contribution of carbon to the strength and hardening characteristics of cast steel is of the same degree and magnitude as in wrought steels. Cast steels, however, do not show the directional properties usually associated with wrought steels. The effect of carbon on the properties of cast steel was shown in Fig. 15.1.

Control of Properties

The relative proportions of ferrite and pearlite and the fineness of the pearlitic structure in steels of less than 0.76 per cent carbon are controlled by the rate of cooling from the austenite condition. Since this effect also makes it possible to control the properties of the cast steel, the result is that steel castings are heat-treated prior to use. The specific heat-treatments are discussed in succeeding sections. The preceding discussion of the structure of steel did not take cognizance of the effect of the casting process on the structure. However, if it is assumed that the effects of the casting process are superimposed on those microstructural conditions already established, it will be easier to place the effects of the solidification process in the proper perspective. These solidification effects will now be considered.

Solidification Process

Examination of the iron-carbon diagram in Fig. 17.1 will show that iron-carbon alloys freeze by a *peritectic* reaction in the carbon range of 0.10 to 0.54 per cent and as typical solid-solution alloys beyond these limits. At the peritectic temperature of 1496 C (2725 F), the first solid to freeze, δ-iron, combines with liquid metal to form austenite. The amount of austenite formed and the amount of either δ-iron or liquid iron remaining after this interaction are dependent on the carbon content, δ-iron being in excess below 0.16 per cent carbon and liquid in excess above this composition.

Austenite apparently forms from the δ-iron–liquid-iron combination by forming an encasement of austenite around each δ-dendrite. Subsequent diffusion during cooling should tend to promote chemical homogeneity. Just how much influence the peritectic reaction has on the microstructure and properties of cast steel is uncertain. Considering the high rate with which carbon can diffuse at the peritectic temperature, it would be expected that plain-iron-carbon alloys should approach an equilibrium structure quite readily. This is not so certain, however, if the casting contains elements such as phosphorus, nickel, chromium, and molybdenum, which segregate along with carbon and which are not nearly so ready to diffuse as carbon.

If one retains the mental reservation that the peritectic reaction may have some influence on the structure of alloy steels, it is probably safe to consider the freezing of cast steel as behaving essentially like that of a solid-solution alloy.

Solidification of a steel casting may be visualized as the gradual thickening of a skin of solid metal that forms first at the mold-metal interface and grows toward the center as heat is extracted. The principles of this solidification process were discussed in Chap. 8. The skin when first formed is an array of interlocking dendrites that extend into the liquid and grow laterally as well. Because of heat-flow effects, the inward growth is usually more rapid than the lateral growth, with the result that a "mushy zone" of part-solid–part-liquid metal separates the completely solidified skin from the interior liquid. The last liquid to freeze in this mushy zone is found (1) between the several branches of a dendrite (interbranchial areas) and (2) between separate dendrites or in interdendritic regions.

Segregation of carbon and of phosphorus and alloying elements follows the same pattern, with the last liquid to freeze highest in these elements and the first axes of the dendrites richest in iron.

The size and shape of the dendrites depend upon the rate of cooling (section size of the casting) and the direction of heat flow. Outside of these effects, there is as yet no practical way to control the size of these dendrites, although it is claimed that deoxidation with aluminum, vanadium, or titanium will cause some refinement.

The dendritic structure formed during the freezing process affects the macrostructure and the microstructure of the cast steel, and is related to the distribution of inclusions and pinhole porosity.

Macrostructure

The macrostructure of cast steel, as revealed by such evidence as hot tears, shrinkage areas, castings bled before completely solidified, and by etching of sections, is a typical dendritic structure (Fig. 8.13). The presence of numerous interlocking and interlacing dendrites is revealed. The fact that such structure is apparent after etching means that the chemical segregation which occurred during freezing was not eliminated by diffusion during the time the casting cooled to room temperature.

Microstructure

The microstructure of cast steel can be dealt with in the same way as that of wrought steel, provided one superimposes the effects accruing from the dendritic freezing process and the accompanying segregation. Thus the distribution and type of microconstituents present at room temperature are influenced primarily by the austenitic transformation characteristics of the steel as controlled by carbon content and cooling rate, and secondarily by the manner in which the steel froze and the segregation resulting therefrom. Since most cast steel is heat-treated in some way before use, it will greatly simplify matters if the microstructure is explained on this basis rather than attempting to rationalize all the possible as-cast structures that can be found. Such a procedure is justified by the fact that studies have indicated that as-cast structure and grain size have little influence on structure and grain size after the first reheating of cast steel.

If a wrought hypoeutectoid steel is subjected to increasingly higher rates of cooling from an austenitizing temperature, the effect is to change the microstructure from one of large masses of ferrite and pearlite to one of less and less ferrite and more but finer pearlite, the ferrite becoming more of a grain-boundary network as the cooling rate is increased. Ultimately, when the cooling rate is sufficiently high, these constituents can no longer form and the steel transforms to *bainite* or *martensite*. In cast hypoeutectoid steel, the changes in microstructure caused by changes in cooling rate in the molds are essentially the same except that the ferrite and pearlite in the more slowly cooled castings may not be distributed in the same manner as in wrought steels.

For example, slow cooling tends to cause the ferrite and pearlite to assume a dendritic pattern as that illustrated in Fig. 17.3 for an annealed 0.23 per cent carbon steel. This reflects the lack of chemical homogeneity induced by the freezing process. The ferrite shape in this photomicrograph is often referred to as *blocky* ferrite. More rapid cooling produces a more platelike or acicular arrangement of the ferrite, referred to as *Widmanstaetten* ferrite. This type of ferrite is shown in Fig. 17.4 for

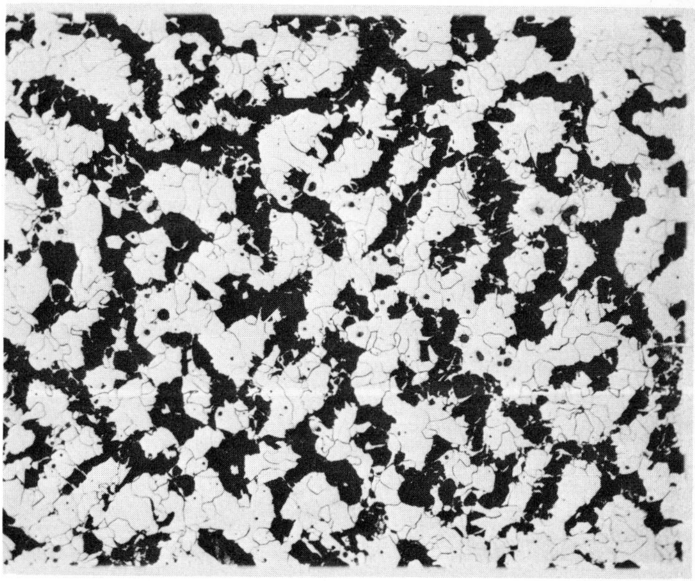

***Fig.* 17.3** Dendritic distribution of ferrite and pearlite resulting from annealing a 0.23 per cent carbon cast steel, ×100. (*Courtesy of R. A. Ragatz, Professor of Chemical Engineering, University of Wisconsin, Madison, Wis.*)

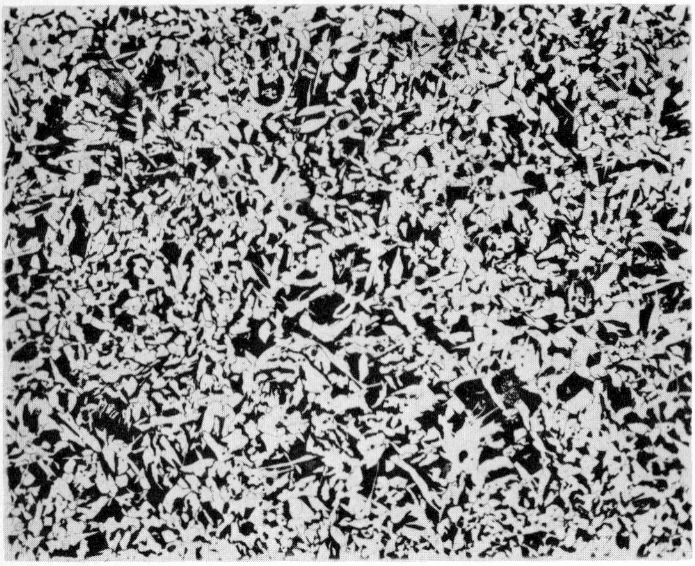

Fig. 17.4 Structure of an air-cooled (normalized) 0.23 per cent carbon cast steel, ×100. (*Courtesy of R. A. Ragatz, Professor of Chemical Engineering, University of Wisconsin, Madison, Wis.*)

an air-cooled specimen of the same steel illustrated in Fig. 17.3. The Widmanstaetten ferrite is even more marked in the as-cast structure of the same steel shown in Fig. 17.5. The network ferrite in this figure outlines the original dendrites developed during solidification of the casting. This network is eliminated by a heat-treatment, as exemplified by Figs. 17.3 and 17.4.

A schematic diagram showing the effect of cooling rate of the casting on the type of microstructure which develops is shown in Fig. 17.6 for a low-alloy 0.3 per cent carbon cast steel. Increasing the alloy content shifts the microstructural features to the right, with the result that a finer structure would tend to be developed for a given cooling rate.

Thus, depending on the cooling rate, segregation in the casting, and the alloy content in the steel, either the blocky or Widmanstaetten ferrite or a mixture of both can be obtained. In addition, a dendritic segregation of the pearlite and ferrite may be evident.

When blocky and Widmanstaetten ferrite coexist in a particular specimen, this effect can be attributed to segregation of alloying elements in the steel which cause the interdendritic areas to have a higher alloy content, and hence a slightly lower temperature of transformation as compared with adjacent lower-alloyed regions having the same cooling rate. Thus the core regions of the dendrites, being relatively deficient

***Fig.* 17.5** As-cast structure of a 0.23 per cent carbon steel, ×100. (*Courtesy of R. A. Ragatz, Professor of Chemical Engineering, University of Wisconsin, Madison, Wis.*)

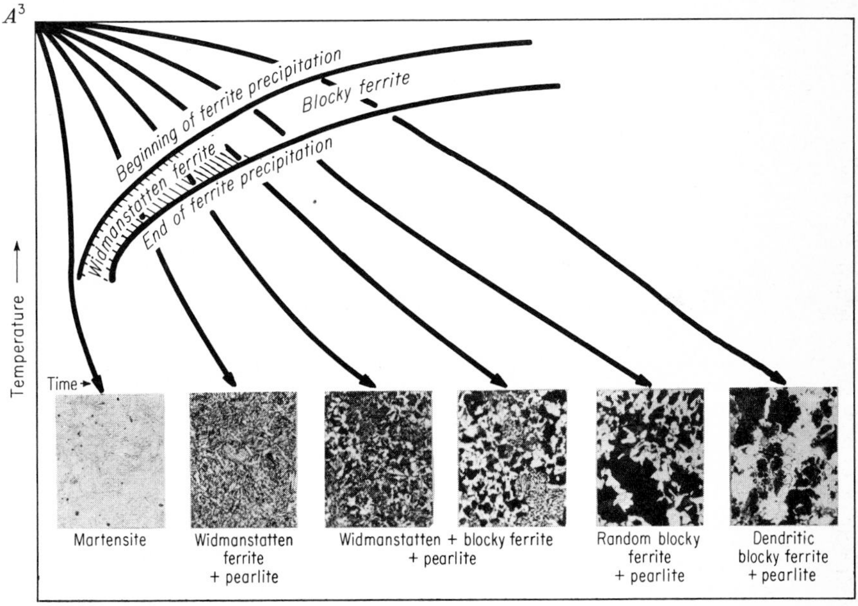

***Fig.* 17.6** Schematic diagram showing effect of cooling rate on microstructure for a hypothetical low-alloy 0.30 per cent carbon cast steel, ×100, reduced 25 per cent in reproduction. (*Courtesy of Steel Founders' Society of America.*[2])

in alloy and carbon content, transform first and at higher temperatures to blocky ferrite nucleated at austenite grain boundaries. On the other hand, the interdendritic regions transform later at lower temperatures which produce Widmanstaetten ferrite nucleated within the austenite grains as well as on the grain boundaries. The greater the degree of segregation in a cast steel, the greater the range of cooling velocities over which both blocky and Widmanstaetten ferrite are found together. Thus, in cast steels, not only the austenite transformation but also the composition of the austenite as determined by segregation control the final microstructure.

The interdendritic areas, being higher in alloy content, usually exhibit that structure, for example, less ferrite, and finer pearlite, or martensite, that is indicative of higher hardenability. Occasionally, however, and particularly in low-carbon material, the reverse effect is found and the interdendritic regions have more ferrite than the balance of the structure. In this case, another effect of the segregated alloy predominates. This effect is one of raising the A_3 line (Fig. 17.1) so that an alloy ferrite precipitates preferentially in the interdendritic areas. This leaves most of the carbon in lower-alloy material. Phosphorus, particularly, seems to exert this influence, accounting for the apparent tendency for carbon to diffuse out of phosphorus-rich areas.

Effect of Structure on Properties

A study of structure is important because there is a good correlation between structure and properties of the casting. Figure 17.7 illustrates schematically how the mechanical properties of cast steel are influenced by microstructure. Because of this variation, which may occur in a single casting before heat-treatment, it is usually beneficial to heat-treat to acquire greater uniformity of structure throughout a casting.

The effect of structure is also reflected in the so-called mass effect. The mass, or size, of the casting not only affects the microstructure of the metal through its influence on the cooling rate, but also through its influence on inclusion size and distribution and segregation. Increasing mass of the casting results in the following effects near the center of the section:[2]

1. A decrease in strength and ductility
2. A slight decrease in impact strength
3. A decrease in density

Inclusions

Inclusions usually result from nonmetallics that are rejected from solution during cooling of the liquid metal. Only occasionally are entrapped

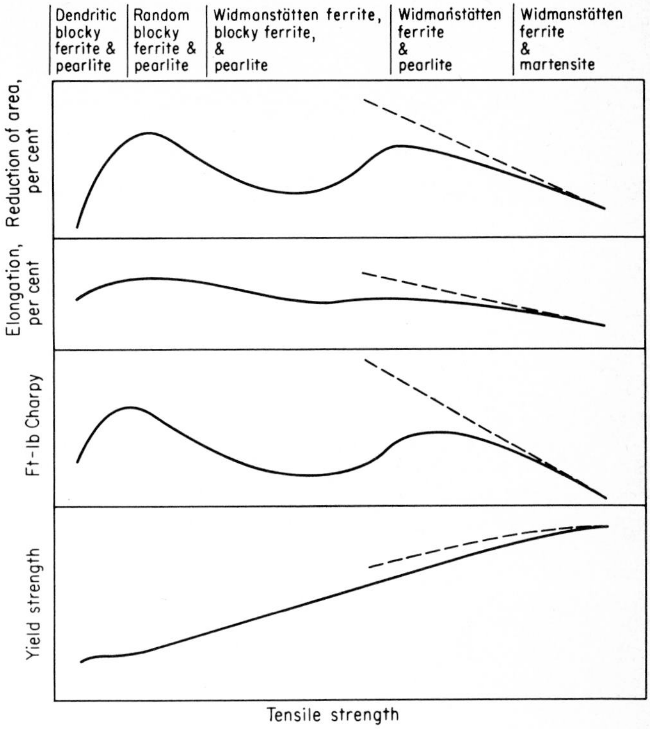

***Fig.* 17.7** Idealized diagram showing the effect of microstructure on mechanical properties of cast steel. Cooling rate decreases from left to right. (*Courtesy of Steel Founders' Society of America.*[2])

impurities the source of inclusions. The rejection of the inclusions may occur early in the thermal history of the cast metal, resulting in geometrically shaped particles more or less randomly distributed (Fig. 17.8 left), or the rejection may not take place until some metal has already solidified which will give rise to a segregation pattern for the inclusions.

Inclusions differ as to composition, with oxides, sulfides, silicates, and occasionally nitrides or carbonitrides being found. The form and type of these inclusions are strongly influenced by the deoxidation practice used. In Chap. 15, the effect of deoxidation in producing sound castings was discussed. Chapter 16 indicated that deoxidation was required to restore the dissolved oxygen content to the proper level in the steel. The tangible result of this deoxidation practice is the inclusions which are found in the solidified casting, and in cast steels this is a very important phase in the control of the properties of the steel. Therefore it is seen that not only is deoxidation of concern in producing castings free of

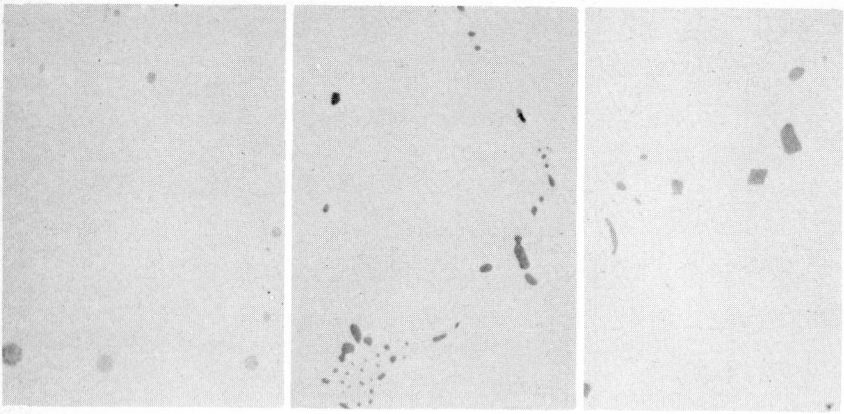

***Fig.* 17.8** Typical appearance of sulfide inclusions classified on the basis of shape, ×500. (*Courtesy of Steel Founders' Society of America.*)

pinholes and blowholes, but also it must be given serious consideration with respect to the microstructure and properties of the cast steel.

Steels deoxidized with manganese and silicon only will be found to contain two principal types of inclusions: (1) iron-manganese silicates and (2) sulfide inclusions.[4] The silicates are glassy and tend to be globular and translucent and vary in color, depending on their composition. They frequently are identifiable by showing a "maltese cross" type of reflection when examined under plane-polarized light (crossed nicols). The sulfides, on the other hand, are opaque and do not reflect polarized light. They are also globular in shape, but are dove or light gray in color under ordinary light and may be more irregularly shaped than the silicates. With a little experience, these two types of inclusions can be readily identified and distinguished. The actual quantity of these inclusions is controlled by the iron oxide of the molten-steel content prior to deoxidation. The size and distribution are controlled by the cooling rate, i.e., the size of the casting section.

The combination of globular silicates and sulfides characteristic of manganese and silicon deoxidation suggests relatively low solubility of these constituents in the liquid steel, so that they begin to precipitate at a rather early stage during the solidification process, giving rise to more or less randomly distributed particles. These are essentially spherical in shape because they have grown freely in liquid steel. The low solubility is attributed to the relatively high oxygen content of the steel. Sims and Dahle[4] designated these inclusions as type I inclusions, and as will be shown later, steels having these inclusions have a high degree of ductility. An example of type I inclusions is given in Fig. 17.8, left.

The addition of a small amount of aluminum (about 0.02 to 0.05 per cent) drastically changes the appearance of the inclusions. There is a definite decrease in the quantity of the silicate inclusions, or they may not appear at all. Also, the reduced oxygen content of the liquid steel results in a sulfide which is appreciably more soluble than in the case of straight manganese and silicon deoxidation. This increased solubility of the sulfides in the liquid steel causes them to precipitate at a late stage during the freezing of the steel. They are therefore restricted to the austenite grain boundaries, where they appear as fine and elongated particles, suggestive of a eutectic mode of solidification (Fig. 17.8, center). This type of sulfide distribution was designated type II by Sims and Dahle. Clusters of fine, angular, whitish alumina particles may also be present as inclusions in these steels. The concentration of sulfide inclusions as fine dots or elongated particles on the grain boundaries markedly reduces the ductility and toughness of the steel.

If the aluminum content exceeds this critical amount, more alumina is present as inclusions. The sulfides, although still persisting on the austenite grain boundaries, are larger, irregular in outline, and farther apart than the type II sulfides. These sulfides are designated type III, and their shape and distribution are attributed to the presence of aluminum in the sulfides, which lowers their solubility in the iron, causing them to precipitate earlier in freezing. The sulfides can also be duplex in structure, being mixtures of Al_2S_3 and MnS (Fig. 17.8, right). Because of the absence of a film-type distribution of the sulfides, the ductility and toughness of steels containing these sulfides are almost on a par with those of steels containing type I inclusions.

Other strong deoxidizers, such as titanium, boron, and zirconium, are also capable of producing the changes obtained from aluminum.[5] The percentages of these elements required for this will not, however, be the same as that for aluminum.

The effect of aluminum deoxidation results in property changes of the degree indicated in Fig. 17.9. These data indicate that, if aluminum additions are required to enhance casting characteristics (Chap. 15), a poor sulfide distribution can be avoided by using sufficient aluminum to exceed the critical concentration range. This usually means an addition of 2 to 2½ lb per ton (0.10 to 0.125 per cent). It should be noted that, if the sulfur content is low, the changes are not so drastic as with higher sulfur percentages. Thus steels produced in the basic open-hearth furnace may not suffer from the addition of a small quantity of aluminum because of the high oxygen and low sulfur content of the steel.

Other additions and combinations of deoxidizers have also been tried in an effort to improve the ductility of cast steel. Some foundrymen

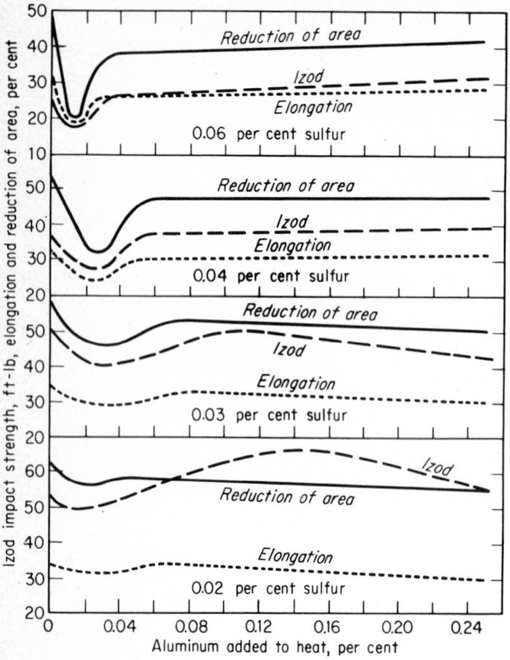

Fig. 17.9 Effect of aluminum on the properties of medium-carbon cast steels at various sulfur contents. (*From C. E. Sims and F. B. Dahle.*[4])

have had good success by using calcium alloys such as calcium-manganese-silicon, together with aluminum. Some of these deoxidizers are sold under proprietary trade names. A calcium-silicon addition preceding aluminum deoxidation has been found to give a ductility equivalent to that of a silicon-manganese deoxidized steel.[6] More recently, additions of rare-earth elements,* after the regular deoxidation with aluminum and followed by an addition of calcium-manganese-silicon, have been tried.[7] This treatment resulted in improved ductility, toughness, and resistance to hot tears. Inclusions were changed from type III to type I by the treatment, but this was not believed to account entirely for the improvement.

Another type of inclusion which can seriously affect the properties of cast steel is aluminum nitride. This inclusion precipitates on the original as-cast austenite grain boundaries in castings that cool relatively slowly. It causes the steel to fracture in a brittle manner along the as-cast grain boundaries. The type of fracture surface produced is sometimes referred to as "rock-candy" fracture.

* Combinations of lanthanum, cerium, praseodymium, neodymium, samarium, etc.

HEAT-TREATMENT

It has already been mentioned that steel castings are heat-treated in some manner. Heat-treatment can be given to accomplish any number of objectives, such as:

1. To diffuse carbon and alloying elements
2. To soften
3. To improve machinability
4. To harden
5. To toughen
6. To increase wear resistance
7. To stress-relieve
8. To remove hydrogen

So far as the heat-treatments designed to alter the mechanical properties are concerned, cast steel can be considered in the same light as wrought steel and is subject to the same principles. As a consequence, therefore, this subject will not be covered in detail, and standard texts on the subject of heat-treating steel can be consulted. There are, however, a number of additional features that should be mentioned.

Homogenization

A rather prolonged heating at an elevated temperature to achieve a better distribution of the segregated carbon and alloying elements is referred to as *homogenization.* For heavy sectional castings, segregation is such that a long time at higher than average temperatures may be necessary.

The efficacy of homogenization for alloy cast steels is not too certain since here we are concerned with diffusion of alloy segregation as well as that of carbon. Alloy diffusion is much slower than that of carbon, and calculations show that inordinately long times at temperatures in excess of 2000 F would be necessary to accomplish appreciable diffusion. The data available indicate that some benefit may be had in some instances from homogenization heat-treatments, particularly for certain compositions and where extremes in service requirements are encountered, but by and large, they do not appear to be justified on the basis of improved mechanical properties and the costs involved.

Annealing

The annealing treatment is essentially the same in principle as that employed on wrought steels and involves heating to the austenitic state and cooling in the furnace. Its purpose is:

1. To refine the austenitic grain structure
2. To soften for machinability
3. To relieve stresses
4. To improve toughness

Normalizing

Normalizing is similar to annealing, except that somewhat higher temperatures may be used and the castings are cooled in air. Normalizing gives a higher strength and hardness than annealing, and is used as the final heat-treatment where strength requirements do not exceed 100,000 psi.

The usual temperature range for annealing, normalizing, and quenching is shown in Fig. 17.1, and the effect of annealing, normalizing, and tempering on the properties of medium-carbon cast steels is illustrated in Fig. 17.10.

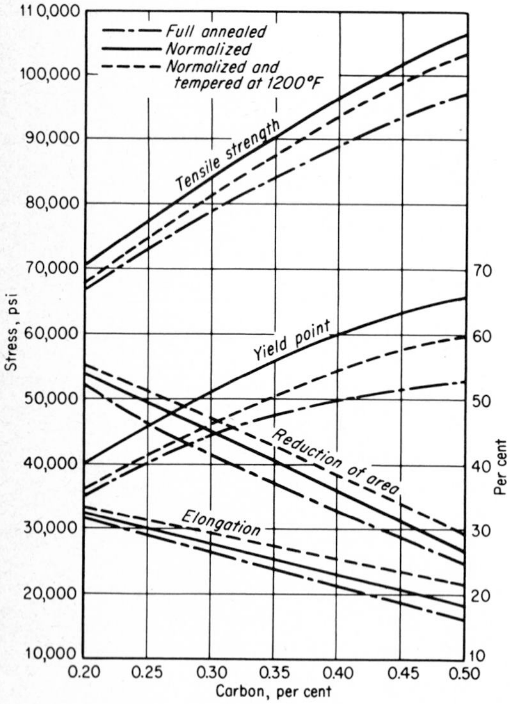

Fig. 17.10 Effect of various heat-treatments on properties of cast steel. (*Courtesy of Steel Founders' Society of America.*[2])

Stress-relief Anneal

Stress relief can be accomplished by a full anneal, as already described, or it may be done by using a subcritical temperature. Holding at 750 F will reduce stresses about 50 per cent, whereas a temperature of 1000 F will reduce stresses more than 90 per cent. Time at temperature is also a factor. If liquid quenching and tempering are employed, stress relief is accomplished by tempering.

Liquid Quench and Temper

As mentioned in a previous section, sufficiently rapid cooling will repress the transformation of steel to a ferrite-pearlite product and will produce martensite instead. Martensite is the hardest product obtainable for a given carbon content. Reheating martensite to a subcritical temperature (tempering) will produce a dispersion of fine carbide in ferrite and will lead to a gradual softening and toughening of the steel. Thus the quenching and tempering treatment provides a means of controlling the properties of a given steel within rather broad limits. Furthermore, this treatment gives the best combination of properties obtainable. In other words, a steel tempered to a given tensile strength (or hardness level) will have the highest ductility, toughness, or yield strength as compared with other methods of heat-treating leading to the same hardness. Figure 17.11 correlates the effect of carbon content and tempering temperatures on the properties of medium-carbon cast steel.

Quenching and tempering of cast steels follows the same principles and techniques used for wrought-steel products. Therefore the problems of quenching media, steel selection, quench cracking, tempering treatment, hardenability requirements, etc., are the same as those encountered with wrought steels.

Adequate discussion of these subjects, as well as of alloy steels considered in the next section, is much beyond the scope of this book; consequently, the student is referred to the many available books on this subject.[3,10,11]

ALLOY STEELS

If the distinction between low- and high-alloy steels already given is used as a basis, a very general summary of these two groups might be stated as follows:

The properties of low-alloy steels are controlled largely by the effects of the specific alloys on the allotropic transformation characteristics, especially under the influence of rapid cooling of the steel, and are not

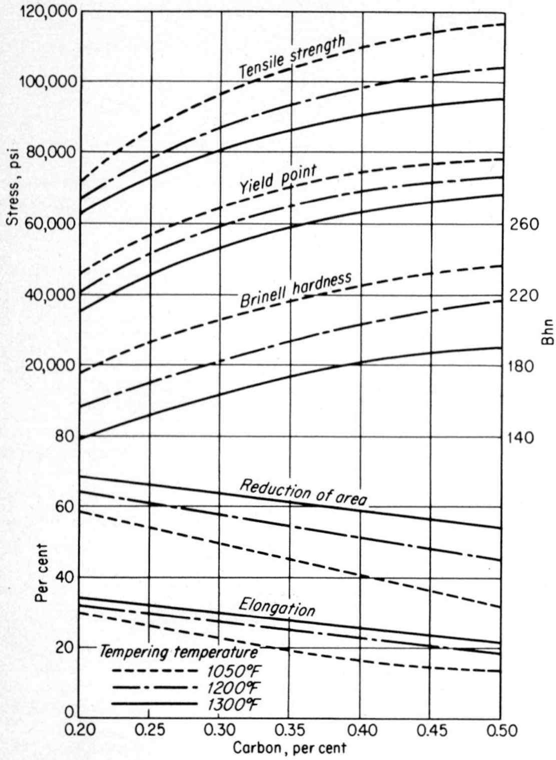

***Fig.* 17.11** Effects of carbon content and tempering temperature on the properties of medium-carbon cast steel. (*Courtesy of Steel Founders' Society of America.*[2])

dependent to any great degree on any intrinsic property that the particular alloy might confer. In other words, in this class of steels the alloying elements are used primarily to alter the response to heat-treatment, i.e., to increase the hardenability of the steel.

On the other hand, the high-alloy steels are designed primarily for some specific property conferred by the alloy, such as corrosion resistance or heat resistance or some other property, rather than for hardenability. In this group, for instance, would fall the austenitic manganese steels (14 per cent manganese), which have outstanding wear resistance, and the 18-8 stainless steels for their corrosion resistance. The metallurgy of these steels also differs considerably from that of plain carbon steels, and reference should be made to suitable texts or books on this subject.

The heat-treatment of the low-alloy steels is basically the same as that of the plain carbon steels. The fact that the alloy steels have higher hardenabilities means that less severe quenching practice (oil or air quench rather than water quench) can be employed to obtain the desirable martensitic structure prior to tempering, or that heavier sections can be heat-treated than would be the case for carbon steels.

Measurement of Hardenability and Its Significance

This difference in hardenability between alloy steels and plain carbon steels is best considered in terms of the Jominy end-quench test,[8] which is the most commonly used test to evaluate hardenability. In the Jominy end-quench test a 1-in.-diameter bar approximately 3½ in. long is heated to the desired austenitizing temperature in a protective container to prevent oxidation. After holding the desired time at temperature, the bar is removed from the furnace and placed in a vertical position in a fixture over a water jet which quenches only the bottom of the specimen. The water flow and height of the specimen above the stream are fixed to standardized conditions.[3] This manner of quenching produces a gradient in cooling rate along the length of the bar, with the highest rates at the quenched end. After quenching, the sides of the bar are carefully ground down about 0.015 in., and Rockwell C hardness measurements are made at frequent intervals along the length. Results are plotted in the form of a hardenability band, several of which are illustrated in Fig. 17.12.

It is apparent from Fig. 17.12 that the hardness is fairly constant for some distance along the bar and then drops off fairly rapidly, except for the HC steel. This distance of constant hardness is a measure of hardenability; the greater the distance, the higher the hardenability.

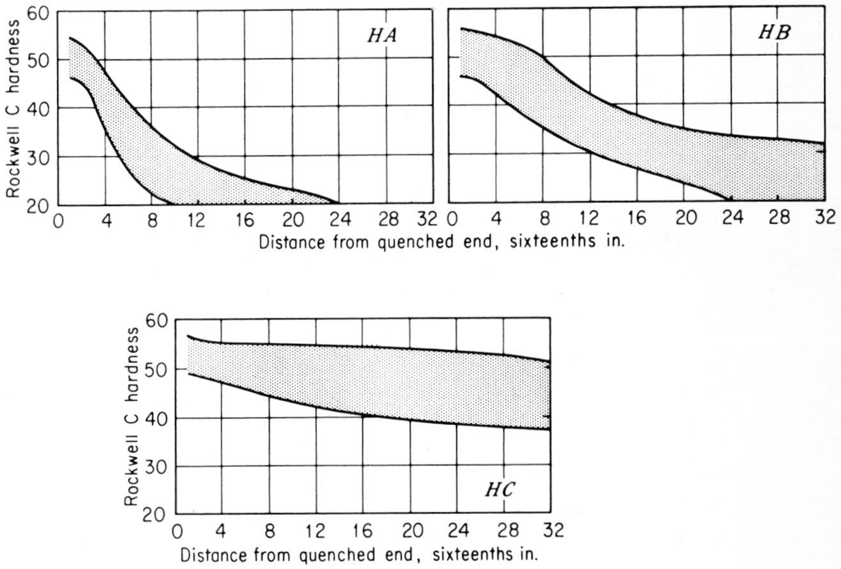

***Fig.* 17.12** End-quench hardenability bands for three cast steels of 0.3 per cent carbon content. (*Courtesy of American Society for Metals.*)

Note that the steels have essentially the same quenched hardness at the quenched end of the bar but that their hardenabilities as measured by the distance of constant hardness vary. (Actually, several methods have been used to measure hardenability quantitatively from the hardenability curve; further information on this topic can be obtained elsewhere.[3]) An alloy steel such as HC in Fig. 17.12 could be used in heavier sections than the HA steel and still produce martensite after quenching. Or alternatively, in a given section where a drastic quench might be required for the HA steel, an oil or even an air quench might suffice for the HC steel.

The common alloy elements used to confer increased hardenability include manganese, molybdenum, chromium, silicon, and nickel. They are listed in their approximate order of effectiveness. Other elements used are vanadium and boron. The latter element is used in percentages of less than 0.005 per cent and is frequently used to replace a portion of the more expensive elements.

Generally speaking, the low-alloy steels are used in the heat-treated

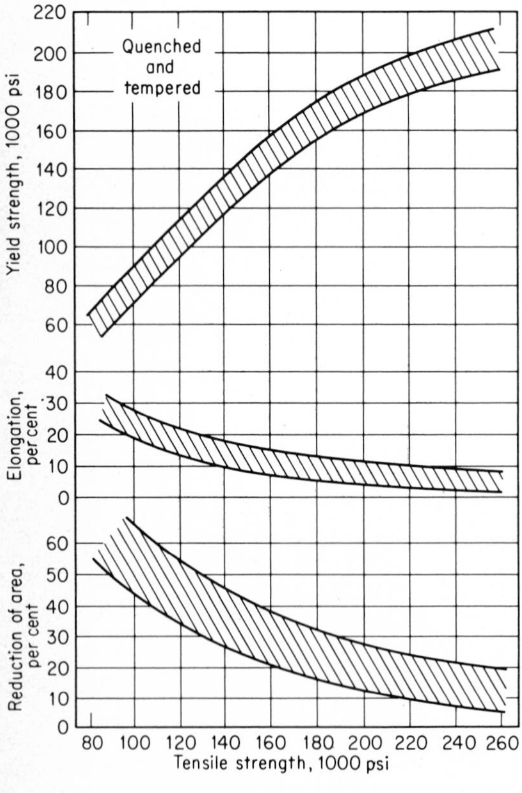

Fig. 17.13 Tensile properties of low-alloy cast steels in the quenched and tempered condition as a function of ultimate tensile strength. (*Courtesy of Steel Founders' Society of America.*[2])

conditions since this is the only way the beneficial effects of the alloying elements can be realized economically. Liquid quenching followed by tempering is common practice. In this connection one difference between low-alloy steels and plain carbon steels might be mentioned. The alloy steels when tempered or cooled through a tempering-temperature range of about 1075 to 825 F (580 to 440 C) exhibit a form of embrittlement referred to as *temper brittleness.* The exact cause of this embrittlement is not known, but it can be eliminated or reduced in severity by water quenching after tempering above the embrittlement range or by using upward of about 0.25 per cent molybdenum in the steel. The embrittlement is manifested by a reduction in notched-bar toughness values at room temperature or at subatmospheric temperatures.

Published hardenability data for a given steel are often presented as a single curve, but it is actually more realistic to plot a so-called "hardenability band" rather than a curve. The hardenability band would represent an allowable variation of several RC hardness numbers for a given steel. The use of a hardenability band recognizes the normal variations that may result from segregation in the casting. For this reason, hardenability data found in the "Steel Castings Handbook"[2] usually are presented as bands rather than lines.

Despite differences in hardenability when low-alloy steels are heat-treated, they have essentially identical properties when quenched and tempered to a given hardness or tensile-strength level. This is illustrated in Fig. 17.13.

PRODUCTION HEAT-TREATING

The heat-treating of a steel casting as carried out in most foundries is operated on a batch-lot basis in car-type or stationary batch-type furnaces. Where production is large, considerable mechanization of heat-treating operations can be achieved, and the entire process of heating, holding at temperature, quenching, and tempering can be placed on an automatic or semiautomatic basis.

The heating rate for the castings is limited primarily by the furnace capacity and the need to avoid cracking and warping during heating. Large uniform-sectioned castings do not exhibit a large differential in temperature between the surface and center of the casting during heating because of the greater heat conductivity of the steel as compared with the rate of heat transfer from the furnace to the steel surface. Representative heating curves for massive sections are shown in Fig. 17.14. Thus it is seen that the center and outside arrive at furnace temperature at about the same time. Even when the furnace is already at tempera-

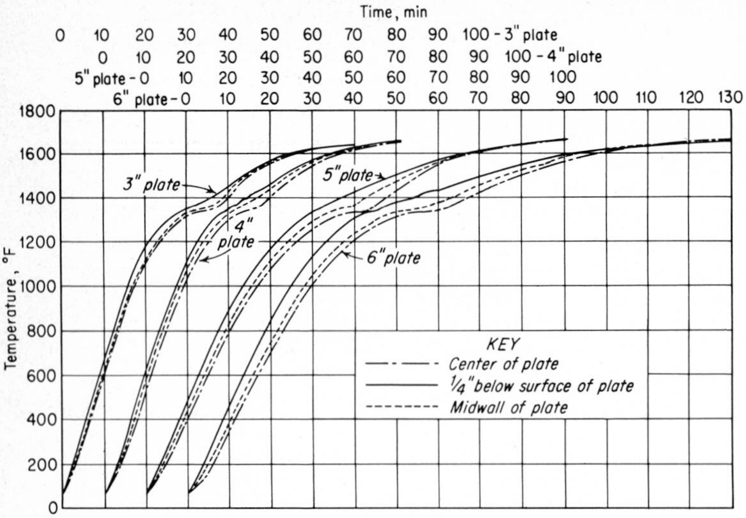

Fig. **17.14** **Heating curves for heavy-sectioned steel castings.** (*From P. C. Rosenthal and G. K. Manning.*[9])

ture before insertion of the steel, temperature gradients within a heavy section may not be over 200 F. For castings of nonuniform cross section, however, the thinner parts will heat up to furnace temperature much more rapidly than the heavier sections, and in so doing may develop sufficient stress to cause warping or cracking. In such cases lower rates of heating are required. Since most of the cracking or distortion takes place only after the steel has reached its critical temperature, heating in the early stages can be quite rapid. In this connection, some tempering furnaces are now started at a higher temperature than required for the castings, and are so regulated that this temperature drops while the castings heat. Thus more rapid heating rates are attainable than could be realized by simply placing the castings in a furnace maintained at the desired final temperature.

Effective use can also often be made of the various specialized heat-treating processes designed to avoid distorting or cracking during cooling. These processes, some of which are compared with the standard quench and temper (Fig. 17.15), include:

1. *Time quenching.* Quenched in oil or water until the thickest section is in the martensite transformation range, then returned to furnace for tempering.
2. *Martempering.* The initial quench must be in molten salt or metal.* The temperature of the casting is equalized before cooling to room temperature.

* Certain oils are also used.

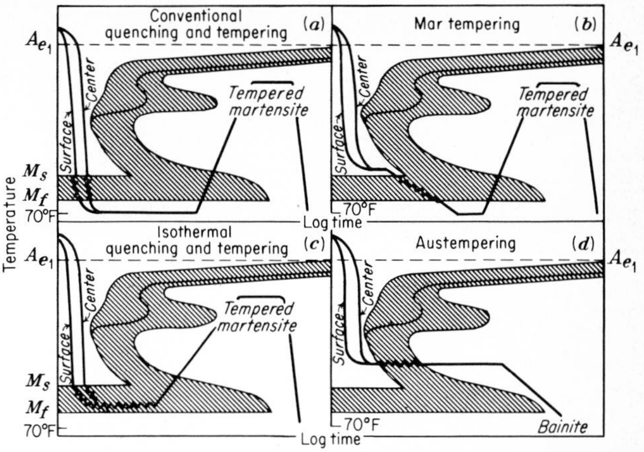

***Fig.* 17.15** Various types of quenching processes. (*Courtesy of Steel Founders' Society of America.*[2])

3. *Isothermal quench.* Again, a molten salt or metal bath must be employed, and temperatures are permitted to equalize before tempering. The isothermal temperature used here is lower than that used for martempering.
4. *Austempering.* This method is seldom used for castings because the castings must be small and thin.
5. *Differential hardening.* This is accomplished either by heating a part of the casting and quenching the whole or by heating the entire casting and quenching only a part of it.

More detailed information on production heat-treating can be obtained from Refs. 1, 2, 3, and 10.

BIBLIOGRAPHY

1. C. W. Briggs, "The Metallurgy of Steel Casting," McGraw-Hill Book Company, New York, 1946.
2. Steel Founders' Society of America, "Steel Castings Handbook," 1950 and 1960 editions.
3. American Society for Metals, "Metals Handbook," 8th ed., vol. 1, 1961.
4. C. E. Sims and F. B. Dahle, The Effect of Aluminum on the Properties of Medium Carbon Cast Steel, *Trans. AFS,* vol. 46, p. 65, 1938.
5. C. E. Sims, H. A. Shaller, and F. W. Boulger, Relative Deoxidizing Powers of Some Deoxidizers for Steel, *J. Metals,* vol. 1, p. 814, 1949.
6. K. E. Fenrich, Effects of Aluminum and Calcium-Aluminum Deoxidation of Cast Steel, Master's thesis, University of Wisconsin, Madison, Wis., 1946.
7. G. A. Lillieqvist and C. G. Mickelson, Properties of Cast Steel Improved with Rare Earth Element Additions, *J. Metals,* vol. 4, p. 1024, 1952.
8. W. E. Jominy, Commercial Aspects of Hardenability Tests, *Metal Progr.,* vol. 38, pp. 685–690, November, 1940.

9. P. C. Rosenthal and G. K. Manning, Heat Treatment of Heavy Cast Steel Sections, *Foundry,* vol. 74, August, 1946.
10. D. K. Bullens-Battelle, "Steel and Its Heat Treatment," 5th ed., vols. 1–3, John Wiley & Sons, Inc., New York, 1948.
11. W. Crafts and J. L. Lamont, "Hardenability and Steel Selection," Pitman Publishing Corporation, New York, 1949.
12. R. F. Harris and G. D. Chandley, High Strength Steel Castings Aluminum Nitride Embrittlement, *Trans. AFS,* vol. 70, p. 169, 1962.
13. C. H. Lorig and A. R. Elsea, Occurrence of Intergranular Fracture in Cast Steels, *Trans. AFS,* vol. 55, p. 160, 1947.
14. U. Kuhn and P. Detrez, Nitrogen in Cast Steel, *Trans. AFS,* vol. 70, p. 469, 1962.
15. J. Van Eeghem and A. DeSy, Side Effects of the Deoxidation of Steel, *J. Steel Castings Res.,* no. 33, p. 1, April, 1964.

18

The Family of Cast Irons

Cast irons are the tonnage product of the foundry industry. Cast-iron foundries produce over a million tons of castings monthly, and thus supply more than twice as much casting weight as all other foundries combined. Iron foundries are found everywhere that manufacturing occurs. Of the 5674 foundries in the United States and Canada, 2068 produce gray-iron, 350 nodular-iron, and 116 malleable-iron castings. These foundries send a steady stream of iron castings into every conceivable industry. The demand for iron castings is based on the nature of cast irons as engineering materials and their economic cost advantages. Cast irons offer a tremendous range of the metallic properties of strength, hardness, machinability, wear resistance, abrasion resistance, and corrosion resistance and other properties. Furthermore, the foundry properties of cast irons in terms of yield, fluidity, shrinkage, casting soundness, ease of production, and others make the material highly desirable for casting purposes. From all standpoints, the cast-iron family offers a variety of engineering properties which ensure its continued and widespread use. Since many cast irons of different properties are employed, it is desirable that a student engineer obtain an over-all picture of the entire field. This chapter offers such a picture and presents some of the simpler and more fundamental differences between members of the cast-iron family.

DEFINITIONS

The term *cast iron* is a generic one, referring to a family of materials differing widely in their properties. In general, a cast iron is an alloy of iron, carbon (up to about 4.0 per cent), and silicon (up to about 3.50 per cent) which ordinarily is not usefully malleable as cast. Definitions of specific types of cast irons are given below.

Gray cast iron. An iron having a chemical composition such that, after solidification, a large portion of its carbon is distributed throughout the casting as free or graphic carbon in "flake form." Gray cast iron always presents a gray sooty surface when fractured.

White cast iron. An iron having a composition such that, after solidification, its carbon is present in a chemically combined form as cementite (iron carbide). White iron presents a white crystalline surface when fractured. Figure 23.5 shows fractured surfaces of gray, white, and mottled irons.

Mottled iron. An iron of intermediate composition which freezes partly as a white iron and partly as a gray iron under prevailing cooling conditions (Fig. 23.5).

Chilled cast iron. An iron of such composition that it would normally freeze as a gray iron but which is caused to freeze white in some locations by rapid cooling during solidification, i.e., chilling. Fractured surfaces of chilled irons show areas of white iron where freezing was rapid and other areas of gray iron where the cooling rate was normal. The appearance of fractured surfaces of chilled iron is illustrated in Fig. 18.7.

Malleable iron. An iron with ductility, or malleability, produced by heat-treating (malleableizing) a white-iron casting of suitable chemical composition. The carbon in malleable iron is present as nodular-shaped aggregates of graphite (Fig. 23.3).

Nodular cast iron (also known as ductile cast iron, or spheroidal graphite cast iron). A specially prepared iron treated in the molten condition with a small percentage of magnesium, cerium, or other agent that will cause a large proportion of its carbon to occur as spheroids of graphite rather than as flakes. Ductility is obtained in the iron as a result of the spheroidal type of graphite formed. This type of cast iron presents a bright steely surface when fractured. The spheroidal type of graphite is illustrated in Fig. 22.1.

The definitions given above suggest certain factors of major importance controlling the nature of cast irons. These are chemical composition, solidification process, cooling rate, and microstructure. A number of other factors are involved, but the aforementioned ones are of prime importance. They are considered briefly in this chapter and are discussed in greater detail in Chaps. 21 to 23.

CHEMICAL COMPOSITION

The broad limits of chemical composition of some cast irons are given in Table 18.1. The over-all picture of the composition ranges in the table with respect to carbon and silicon in cast irons is illustrated in Fig. 18.1. The figure shows that even the terms "gray iron" and "white iron" are general ones in that they refer to a number of alloys falling within broad composition limits. Within the broad limits occur a number of irons with narrower composition limits and different properties. Typical chemical compositions, specifications, and uses of a few commercial

Table 18.1

Element	Gray iron, %	White iron* (malleable iron), %	High-strength gray iron, %	Nodular iron,† %
Carbon	2.5–4.0	1.8–3.6	2.8–3.3	3.0–4.0
Silicon	1.0–3.0	0.5–1.9	1.4–2.0	1.8–2.8
Manganese	0.40–1.0	0.25–0.80	0.5–0.8	0.15–0.90
Sulfur	0.05–0.25	0.06–0.20	0.12 max	0.03 max
Phosphorus	0.05–1.0	0.06–0.18	0.15 max	0.10 max

* Such compositions may be converted from white to malleable iron by heat-treatment.
† Necessary chemistry also includes 0.01 to 0.10% Mg.

cast irons are given in Table 18.2. A detailed list of chemical specifications of cast irons for a wide variety of applications may be found in the "Cast Metals Handbook."[1]

Composition and Graphitization

The influence of chemical composition on the properties and uses of cast irons is largely related to the two alloying elements carbon and silicon and their effects on the process of graphitization. Both elements promote the formation of graphite as their percentage increases in the iron. Carbon may occur in cast irons as iron carbide (cementite), and is then referred to as combined carbon. It may also occur in free form as graphite. Graphitization is the process whereby free carbon is precipitated in the iron or chemically combined carbon, Fe_3C, is changed

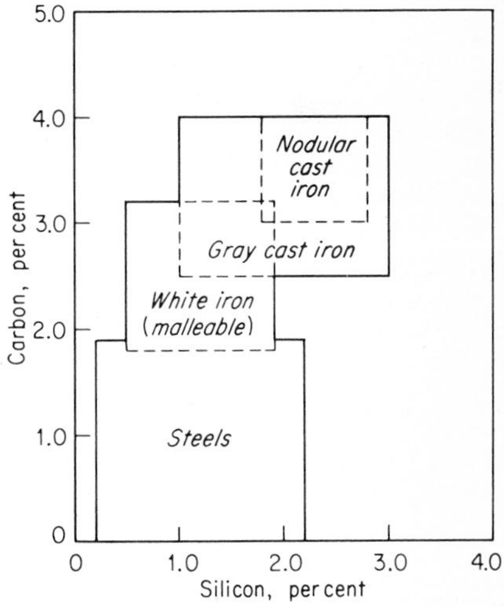

Fig. 18.1 The carbon and silicon percentage ranges present in cast irons. Note the overlapping compositions of the various grades.

Table 18.2 Typical chemical composition of a few commercial cast irons*

Iron	C, %	Combined carbon, %	Si, %	Mn, %	S, %	P, %	Other, %	Bhn	Tensile strength, min, psi	Use
Gray	3.30–3.60	....	2.30–2.60	0.50–0.80	0.20 max	0.30 max	....	192 max	....	General-purpose use
	3.10–3.50	0.40–0.70	1.90–2.30	0.60–0.90	0.125 max	0.12–0.18	....	163–228	30,000	Motor blocks
	3.50–3.90	....	2.20–3.10	0.40–0.80	0.10	0.30–0.80	....	222–267	....	Piston rings
	2.90–3.20	0.65–0.90	0.90–1.10	0.65–0.90	0.05–0.12	0.20 max	1.00–1.50 Ni 0.50 Cr	200–240	40,000	Heavy machine-tool bases, 2000–10,000 lb
	2.60–2.80	0.60–0.75	2.20–2.50	0.90–1.00	0.08 max	0.08 max	0.75–1.00 Ni 0.75–1.25 Mo 0.10–0.20 Cr	220–240	60,000	High-strength iron, large diesel-engine crankshafts
Chilled	3.25–3.60	....	0.50–0.65	0.40–0.60	0.15 max	0.30–0.45	....	45 RC as-cast	....	Chilled-iron freight-car wheels, rolls
White, malleable	2.20–2.40	†	0.90–1.10	0.35–0.50	0.12 max	0.14 max	0.03 Cr max	Over 320,‡ 135 max§	50,000	General-purpose malleable iron
cupola malleable	2.70–3.20	†	0.60–0.80	0.45–0.60	0.15 max	0.15 max	....	....	....	Malleable-iron pipe fittings
Nodular	3.60–4.20	0–0.20	1.25–2.00	0.35	....	0.08	0–1.0 Ni 0.05–0.08 Mg	140–200	60,000	Pressure castings, valve and pump bodies, shock-resisting parts
	3.20–3.80	0.70	2.25–2.75	0.60–0.80	....	0.10	1.5–3.5 Ni 0.05–0.08 Mg	200–270	80,000	Heavy-duty machinery, gears, dies, rolls, for wear resistance and strength

* Adapted from "Cast Metals Handbook."[1]

† Virtually all the carbon is present as carbide in the white iron, but is graphitized by heat-treatment.

‡ Before malleableizing heat-tretment.

§ After malleableizing heat-treatment.

to free carbon (or graphite). Increasing the percentage of carbon in an iron, especially above 2.00% C, increases the likelihood of graphitization. Furthermore, the presence of certain other elements in the iron, such as silicon, causes iron carbide to become less stable and thus promotes the formation of graphite; these are said to be graphitizing elements. Probably the simplest picture of the combined effects of carbon and silicon on graphitization is that presented by the diagrams in Fig. 18.2*a* and *b*. In Fig. 18.2 it can be seen that, if carbon and silicon are both below certain percentages, a white iron is formed during solidification. If either carbon or silicon is held at a constant percentage and the other is increased, the iron changes from white to mottled to gray. Carbon and silicon thus may be varied to produce a white or gray iron as

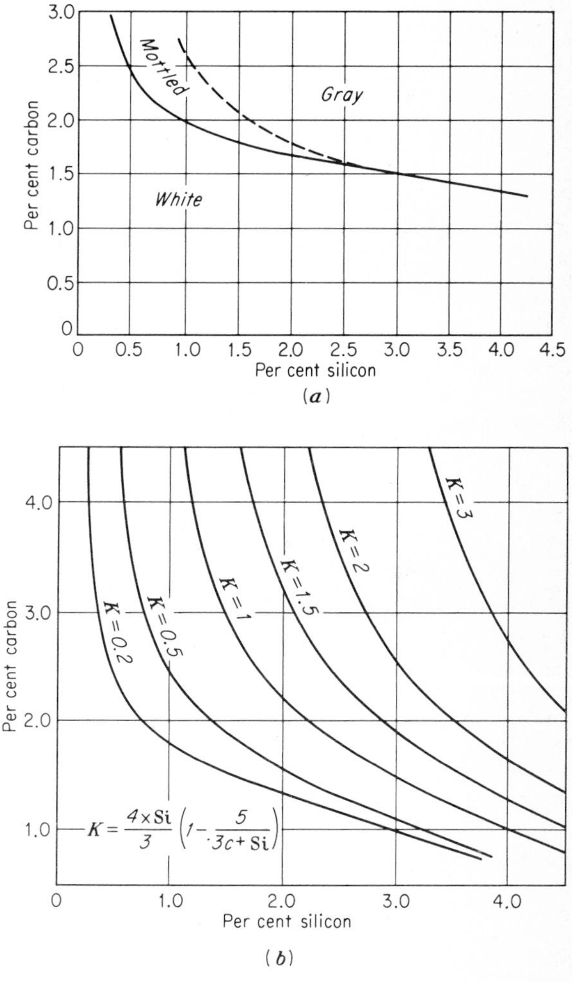

***Fig.* 18.2** (*a*) The effect of carbon and silicon percentages in the iron on the kind of cast iron obtained. This diagram is based on structure obtained for 4- by 4- by 8-in. castings produced under the conditions specified in Ref. 9. The diagram will be shifted when the effect of different cooling rates, section sizes, alloy additions, melting conditions, etc., is considered. Other diagrams are available for different section sizes. (*From C. R. Loper, Jr., and R. W. Heine.*[9]) (*b*) Laplanche's structural diagram for cast iron showing lines where equivalent structures will be obtained in different analyses of cast iron produced under similar conditions and compared in identical castings. For instance, each of these curves may be regarded as a boundary line between white and mottled fractures, pearlitic and pearlitic-ferritic structures, etc., depending on casting geometry and cooling rate. The diagram may be corrected at low carbon contents using Fig. 18.2*a*. (*From H. Laplanche.*[10])

desired. It must be recognized that the diagrams of Fig. 18.2 do not consider the variable of cooling rate or section size in castings. This is another variable affecting graphitization. Slower cooling rates (heavy casting sections) shift the lines on the diagram to the left, and rapid cooling (thin casting sections) shifts them to the right. Thus in practical situations, gray-iron piston rings are high in carbon and silicon percentages whereas heavy machine-tool-casting gray irons are low in carbon and silicon percentages. White irons for making malleable castings are even lower in carbon and silicon content, so that the carbon will be in combined form as cast. The carbides in this white cast iron, however, are still sufficiently unstable so that they can be graphitized slowly in the solid state by a malleableizing heat-treatment.

Carbon and silicon are not the only elements which influence graphitization and the structure of the iron. Consideration is given in Chap. 21 to the effects of other elements and a variety of other factors influencing the final properties of the iron. At this point, however, it is obvious that chemical composition is a prime factor in causing the differences in the various types of cast irons.

SOLIDIFICATION PROCESS

The differences between gray, mottled, and chilled irons are largely established during the freezing process. The fundamentals of the freezing process are related to the nature of the iron-carbide-silicon ternary equilibrium system (Fig. 21.2). However, a simplified schematic diagram presenting the essential ideas is given in Fig. 18.3. With reference to the diagram, the freezing and cooling of an iron, composition *A*, may be described by the following steps:

A. Liquid melt cools until freezing begins at point 1. At this point solid austenite dendrites begin to form and grow until the temperature at point 2 is reached. This step is omitted when the composition is eutectic, at *B*, on the diagram.

B. Eutectic (a liquid saturated with respect to two solids) freezing begins as the area at point 2 is entered with decreasing temperature. The eutectic solids which form may be a mixture of austenite and carbide or of austenite and graphite. If the former occurs, the iron is freezing as white iron. If the latter occurs, the iron is freezing as a gray or a nodular iron. Graphite will prevail if graphitizing factors, such as high silicon content and slow cooling rate, are operative. Low silicon content and rapid cooling will cause the eutectic to freeze as a mixture of carbide and austenite (white). When the temperature has dropped to point 3, freezing is completed. Thus an iron freezes, as white, gray, or nodular iron. Actually, the solidification of nodular cast iron is somewhat more complex than this.[11] If the iron freezes as gray or nodular, the nature of the graphite is established during freezing.

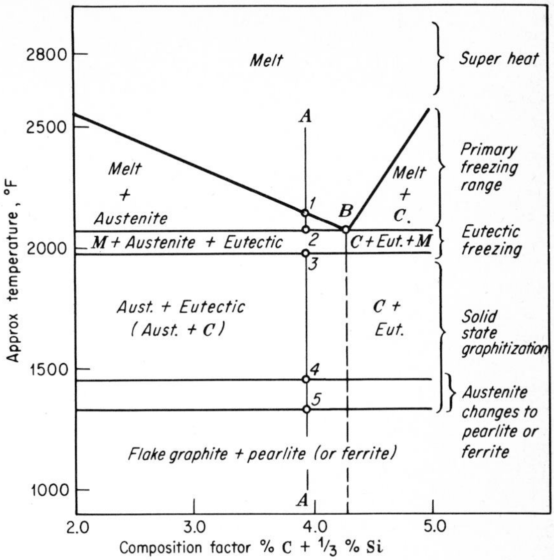

***Fig.* 18.3** **Schematic diagram showing approximate temperature range of solidification and graphitization in cast irons.**

Mottled irons are borderline cases where both graphite and carbide have formed.

C. At the end of freezing, the structure consists of the solids developed during steps *A* and *B*. In gray and nodular irons these are austenite and graphite, and in white irons, austenite and carbide.

D. Further cooling between points 3 and 4 results in the precipitation of carbon from the austenite present since the austenite may contain as much as 2.0% C at the end of freezing, but only about 0.60 to 0.80% as the temperature decreases to point 4. The excess of carbon in the austenite is precipitated as carbide in white irons and as graphite in gray and nodular irons.

E. Between points 4 and 5, the final change occurs in the solid state during cooling. Austenite transforms over the temperature range of points 4 to 5. Because this change is quite complex, only a few generalizations are offered. With the most favorable of graphitizing conditions, only ferrite is formed in gray and nodular irons. With less severe graphitizing conditions, ferrite and pearlite or only pearlite is formed. In nodular cast iron, mixed structures of ferrite and pearlite form as "bull's eyes" of ferrite around the graphite spheroid (Fig. 22.1). In white irons only pearlite is formed. The final microstructure of white iron such as is used to produce malleable castings is illustrated in Fig. 23.2.

F. Cooling below point 5 to room temperature produces little change in the iron.

From the foregoing it can be seen that the type of iron, whether white, mottled, chilled, or gray, is largely established during the freezing process. Furthermore, the room-temperature microstructure reflects the entire freezing and cooling process of the iron. Thus the properties of cast irons are greatly influenced by the thermal and chemical changes occurring during its entire history from liquid melt to cooled casting.

MICROSTRUCTURE

Cast irons provide examples of alloys which are structurally sensitive; i.e., the properties of the metal are greatly dependent on its metallographic structure and vary in a manner dependent on this structure. The structural components of cast irons differentiate the various types of irons, white, gray, malleable, and spheroidal carbon. The most important components are defined below.

Graphite

Carbon in cast irons may occur in the free, or elemental, condition as graphite. In gray irons, flakes of graphite develop as the iron freezes and, because of its low specific gravity, may amount to about 6 to 17 per cent of the total iron volume.

Several forms of graphite differing from the flake shape occur in cast irons. Temper-carbon or graphite aggregates are developed in malleable irons by heat-treatment of white irons (Figs. 23.2 and 23.3). Spheroidal graphite may develop when cast irons are treated with a small percentage of magnesium, cerium, or other special element (Fig. 22.1). Other special forms of graphite may also develop, and are discussed in later chapters.

The amount, size, shape, and distribution of the graphite in cast irons greatly influence their properties. The size and type characteristics of flake graphite in gray irons have been described in standards adopted by the AFS and ASTM (Fig. 18.4). In general, type *A* graphite, random or uniformly distributed, is desirable in gray cast irons. Flake graphite is responsible for the lack of ductility observed in tensile tests of gray irons. Graphite as temper carbon in malleable irons and as spheroidal carbon in "ductile" irons does not decrease ductility to the same degree as flake graphite.

Cementite

The carbon in cast irons may occur entirely or in part in the chemically combined form as Fe_3C, cementite. Free or massive cementite develops during the freezing of white or chilled cast irons (Fig. 23.2). Cementite is very hard and brittle and confers these properties on irons in which it is a major component. Carbon will form Fe_3C, to the extent of 15 times its weight percentage in the iron. Therefore a white iron with 2.50% C will contain about 37.50% iron carbide and will therefore be very hard and brittle. Cementite also occurs as a constituent of the pearlite.

Ferrite

Ferrite may be defined as a solution of the normal-temperature body-centered cubic crystalline form of iron and small amounts of carbon and as such is relatively soft, ductile, and of moderate strength. In cast irons, ferrite contains the silicon present in the iron. Silicon hardens and strengthens the ferrite, giving it a hardness of 100 to 140 Bhn, 20 to 30 per cent elongation, and 50,000 to 70,000 psi tensile strength, depending on the silicon percentage present.

Structurally, ferrite in cast irons may occur as free ferrite or as ferrite in pearlite. Free ferrite predominates in malleable irons (Fig. 23.3) and nodular irons of maximum ductility. In gray irons, ferrite occurs mainly as a constituent of pearlite unless a soft iron is especially desired. When incomplete graphitization is encouraged, the end structure of an iron consists of graphite and pearlite (or a mixture of pearlite and free ferrite or pearlite and free cementite). Figure 18.5 shows free ferrite, pearlite, and flake graphite in the microstructure of gray cast iron.

Pearlite

Pearlite consists of a mixture of ferrite and cementite arranged in alternate lamellae. Pearlite in cast irons is strong (about 120,000 psi tensile strength) and moderately hard (about 200 to 230 Bhn) and has some ductility. The amount of pearlite present in cast irons depends on the degree of graphitization of the iron. In gray and nodular irons, the combined carbon percentage reflects the presence of pearlite. A pearlitic gray iron will contain about 0.5 to 0.9 per cent combined carbon. Lower combined carbon percentages usually indicate the presence of free ferrite, the latter increasing as the percentage combined carbon decreases. Pearlite in the microstructure of a gray cast iron is shown in Fig. 18.5.

In white irons, pearlite and cementite are the chief structural components other than cementite (Fig. 23.2).

Steadite

The phosphorus present in cast irons, especially gray iron, often occurs as steadite, a eutectic of iron and iron phosphide of low melting point, about 1750 to 1800 F. Because phosphorus segregates into areas which solidify late in the freezing process, steadite areas in the microstructure often reveal a cellular pattern, as shown in Fig. 18.6. Iron phosphide, like iron carbide, is very hard. Excessive phosphorus content raises the hardness and brittleness of gray iron because of the steadite formed.[1]

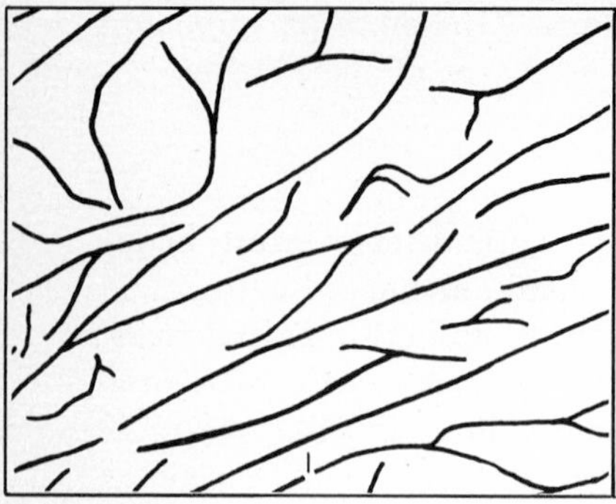

Longest flakes 4 in. or more in length

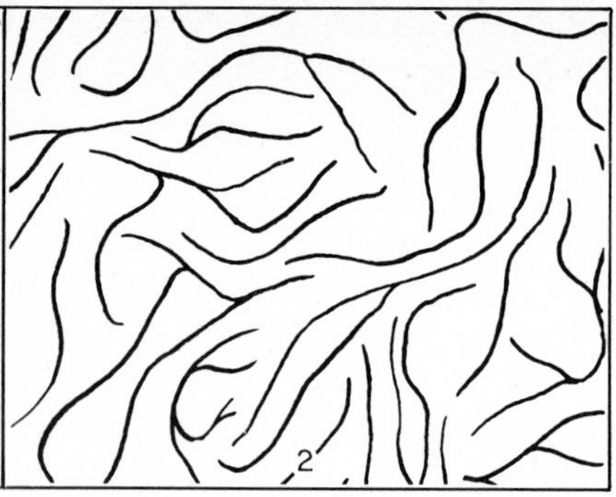

Longest flakes 2 to 4 in. in length

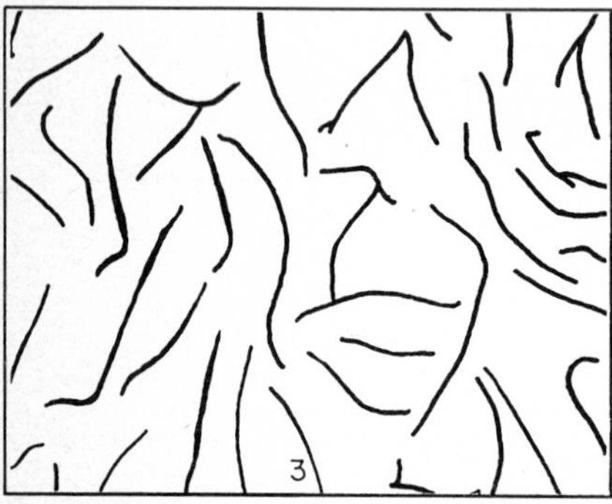

Longest flakes 1 to 2 in. in length

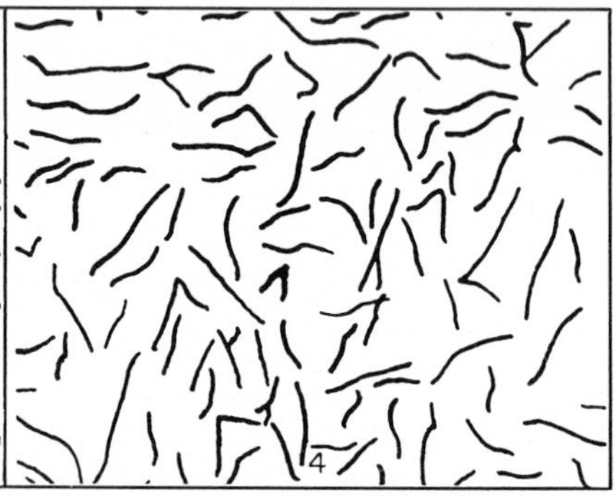

Longest flakes ½ to 1 in. in length

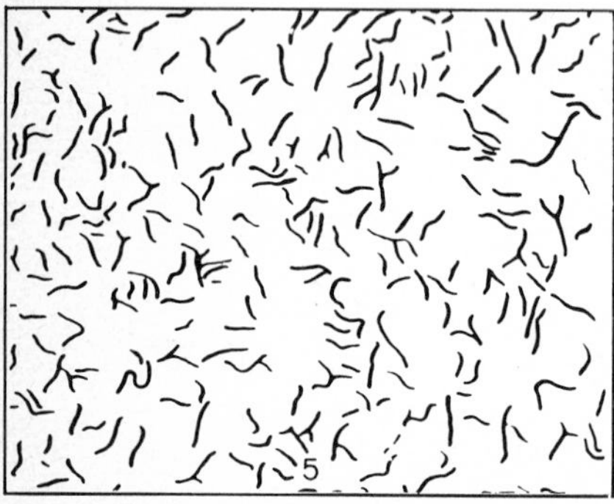

Longest flakes ¼ to ½ in. in length

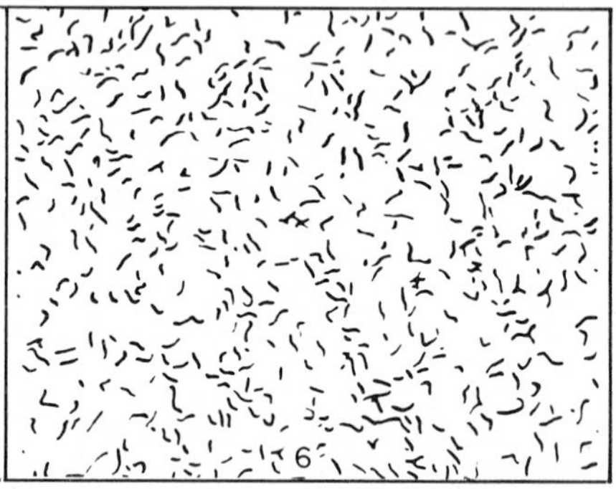

Longest flakes ⅛ to ¼ in. in length

***Fig.* 18.4** AFS and ASTM graphite-flake type and size rating charts, ×100. (*From American Foundrymen's Society.*[1])

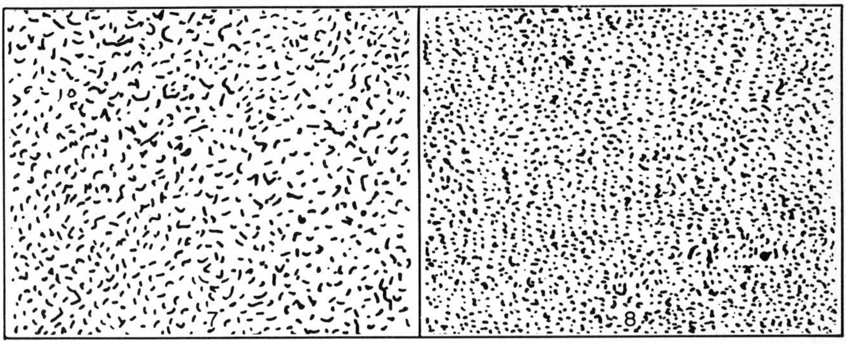

Longest flakes $\frac{1}{16}$ to $\frac{1}{8}$ in. in length

Longest flakes $\frac{1}{16}$ in. or less in length

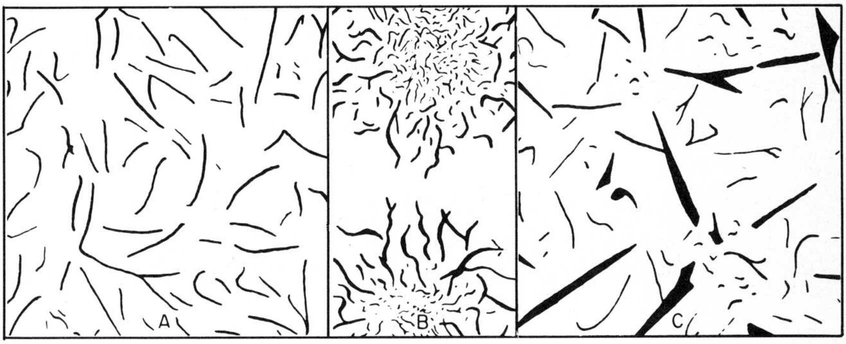

Uniform distribution, random orientation

Rosette groupings

Superimposed flake sizes, random orientation

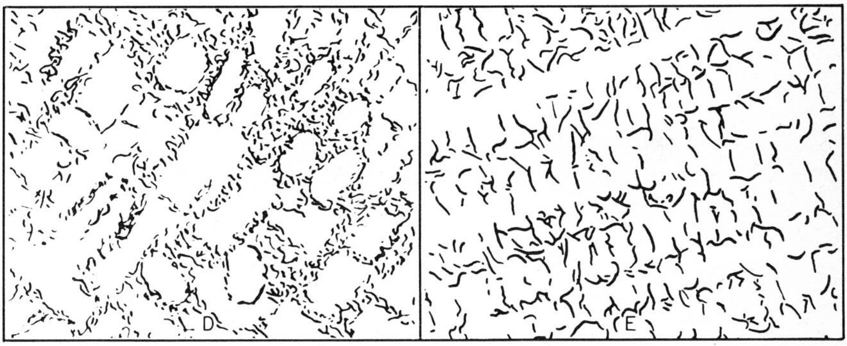

Interdendritic segregation, random orientation

Interdendritic segregation, preferred orientation

***Fig.* 18.4** *Continued.*

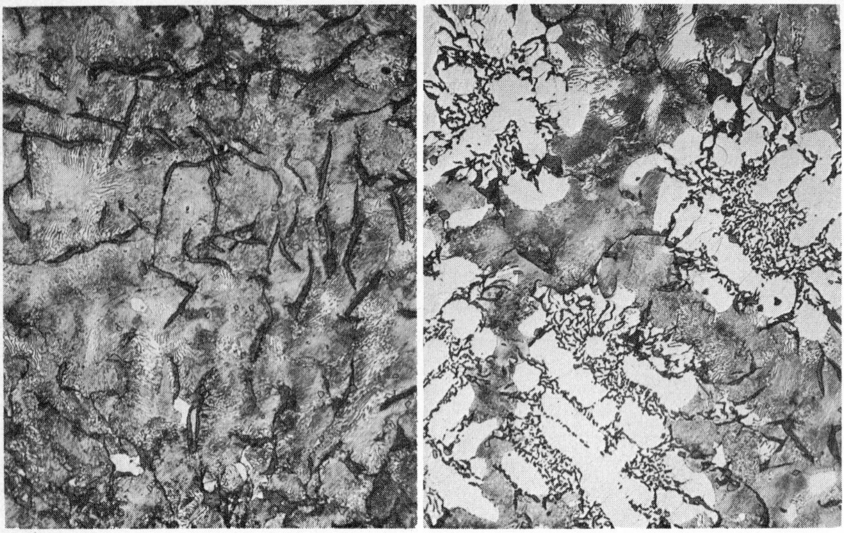

***Fig.* 18.5** Microstructure of two gray cast irons showing pearlite, flake, and some free ferrite. Etched, ×250.

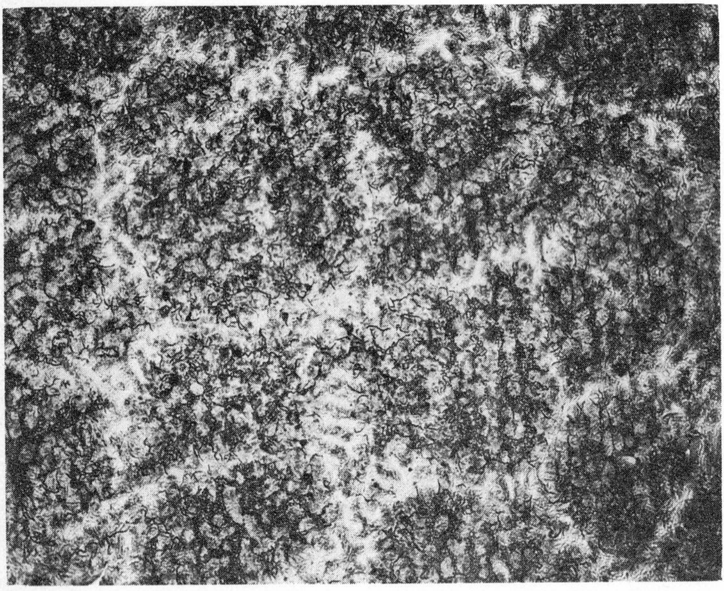

***Fig.* 18.6** Steadite in gray cast iron occurring in a cellular pattern because of its segregation during freezing.

Austenite

In cast irons, austenite may be defined as a solution of carbon and the high-temperature face-centered cubic crystalline form of iron which occurs during solidification and which, during slow cooling, changes to pearlite, ferrite, or a mixture of the two. Austenite, as a portion of the microstructure at room temperature, is encountered only in cast irons which are specially alloyed with nickel to make the austenite stable at room temperature.

In addition to the structural constituents defined above, cast irons may contain nonmetallic inclusions. These are mainly sulfides of manganese and iron due to the sulfur present and silicates of iron and manganese formed by reaction with oxygen.

For summary purposes, some properties of the microconstituents of cast iron are presented in Table 18.3. From this table it can be seen that structural components of widely varying properties may occur in them. In this connection, it should be noted that chemical composition is far from the only factor determining microstructure. Cooling rates, freezing mechanism, the evolution of certain gases from the metal, and a

Table* 18.3 *Properties of compounds and microconstituents of cast iron*

Constituent	Specific gravity	Tensile strength, psi	Elongation, %	Reduction of area, %	Bhn	Remarks
Ferrite[a]............	7.86[b]	39,500–42,000	61	30.9	75	
Silicoferrite[c].........	.....	45,150	50	91.6	...	Contains 0.82% Si
Silicoferrite[c].........	.....	63,500	50	85	...	Contains 2.28% Si
Silicoferrite[c].........	.....	77,400	21	28.7	...	Contains 3.4% Si
Cementite[b].........	7.66	....	..	....	550	
Pearlite[b]...........	7.846	120,000	15	....	240	
Pearlite[d]...........	.....	125,000	10	15	200	Pearlitic steel
Pearlite[e]...........	.....	105,000–125,000	..	....	...	0–0.80% manganese
Graphite[b]..........	2.55					
Ledeburite[f].........	.....	....	..	....	680–840	
Steadite[b]...........	7.32					
Manganese sulfide[b]...	4.00					
Iron sulfide[b]........	5.02					

* From American Foundrymen's Society.[1]

[a] G. P. Fuller, Some Properties of Electrolytic Iron, *Trans. Am. Electrochem. Soc.*, vol. 50, pp. 371–377, 1926.

[b] Symposium on Cast Iron, AFA-ASTM, *Proc.* ASTM, vol. 33, Part II, pp. 115–273, 1933.

[c] T. D. Yensen, Magnetic and Other Properties of Iron-silicon Alloys Melted in Vacuo, University of Illinois Engineering Experiment Station, 1915. Also E. S. Greiner, J. S. Marsh, and B. Stoughton, "Alloys of Iron and Silicon," McGraw-Hill Book Company, Inc., New York, 1933.

[d] A. L. Boegehold, "Physical Properties of 0.88 Carbon, 0.26 Manganese, 0.014 Phosphorus, 0.022 Sulphur Steel," personal file.

[e] R. P. Neville, and J. R. Cain, The Preparation and Mechanical Properties of Vacuum-fused Alloys of Electrolytic Iron with Carbon and Manganese, *Trans. Am. Electrochem. Soc.*, vol. 42, pp. 21–37, 1922.

[f] A. L. Boegehold, Influence of Composition and Section Size on the Strength-hardness Ratio in Cast Iron, *Trans. AFS*, vol. 45, pp. 599–625, 1937.

host of variables in the foundry practice may markedly alter microstructure, and consequently properties. The actual manipulations in the foundry may cause drastic changes in the microstructure and properties of the iron. For example, in gray irons, the type of graphite, whether A, B, D, or E, may be greatly altered by many variables in the melting practice. In nodular irons, the graphite shape, size, distribution, and nodule count may be varied by melting and metal-handling practice, resulting in property variation. In malleable irons, the melting practice and heat-treatment given the white iron are major factors affecting the properties. In all cast irons, the influence of section size and cooling rate is omnipresent. With all these factors involved, the family of cast irons can offer widely varying structures and properties for engineering use, each with its own advantages and limitations. It is a part of the foundryman's technology to produce the kind of iron desired for the casting.

PROPERTIES OF CAST IRONS

Because the cast irons are a family of iron-base alloys, their properties may be expected to vary over wide ranges. Furthermore, there are characteristic differences in properties of the various members of the family because of the inherent differences in their structure and composition. Each member of the family of cast irons should then be considered as a series of alloys, offering a range of properties. For this reason, it is not possible to consider merely the "properties of cast iron." Rather, a broad concept of the tremendous range of properties available in the individual members of the cast-iron family is necessary.

Engineering properties of the more widely used cast irons are discussed in Chap. 21 (gray iron), Chap. 22 (nodular iron), and Chap. 23 (malleable iron), to which the student should refer. Two other cast irons, however, are of importance and are considered below.

White Irons

The principal use of white iron is for the manufacture of malleable-iron castings. White irons for this use and the malleableizing process are discussed in Chap. 23. However, some white-iron castings are used as such because of the high hardness of the material. These properties are related to its microstructure, which consists of pearlite and a large percentage of iron carbide (Fig. 23.2). A hardness of 350 to 550 Bhn and over may occur in white irons. The abrasion resistance accompanying this hardness is used to advantage in tumbling-mill jack stars, pulverizing-mill plates, and similar applications. More common use of the abrasion-resistant type of white-iron microstructure is made in chilled-iron castings.

Chilled Iron

Where the abrasive wear resistance of white iron is desired on wearing surfaces, chilled-iron castings are often employed. Railroad freight-car wheels, grain-mill rolls, and rolls for crushing ores and rolling metals are examples of chilled-iron casting applications. Approximately 2 million freight-car wheels have been produced annually for a number of years.[1]

The fractured surface of a chilled-iron casting is shown in Fig. 18.7. The chemical composition of chilled-iron castings has the silicon and carbon content balanced so that the portions cast against a metal chill in the mold will freeze white whereas the more slowly cooled sections freeze gray. Between the white and gray areas shown in Fig. 18.7 is a zone of mottled iron.

Although the chilled zone has high hardness, it is also brittle. Brittleness of the chilled zone is often reduced with little loss of hardness by a heat-treatment. This may be accomplished by holding the chilled-iron castings at 1500 to 1600 F for 5 to 20 hr, the shorter time at the higher temperatures.

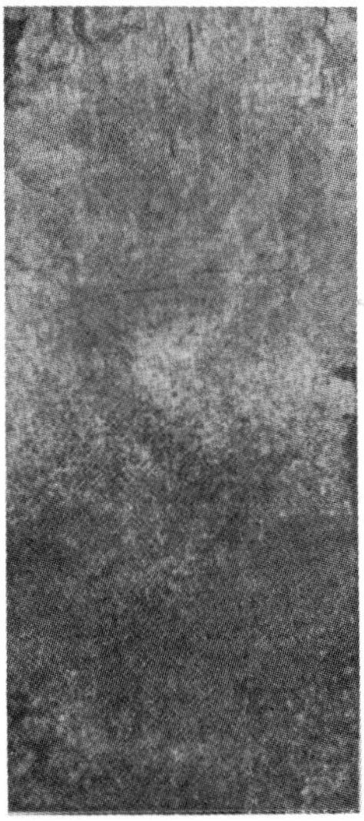

***Fig.* 18.7** Fractured surface of a chilled-iron casting. The upper surface on the figure was chilled by a metal block. (*From American Foundrymen's Society.*[1])

An alternative to heat-treatments where cooled castings are reheated consists in transferring hot castings to soaking pits or holding furnaces where cooling of the casting is delayed to provide an annealing effect. The combination of abrasion-resistant surfaces and the gray-iron core makes chilled-iron castings suitable for many applications such as sludge-pump liners, jaw-crusher plates, grinding-mill liners, camshafts, grinding balls, abrasive-materials-handling equipment, and others of this type.

Numerous other cast irons of specialized chemical composition, microstructure, and properties are also available, but have not been considered in this text. The student interested in more details is advised to study the "Cast Metals Handbook" and the "Alloy Cast Irons" handbook published by the AFS, as well as the numerous references cited in the following chapters on cast iron.

BIBLIOGRAPHY

1. American Foundrymen's Society, "Cast Metals Handbook," 4th ed., 1944.
2. American Foundrymen's Society, "The Cupola and Its Operation," 1954.
3. The Gray Iron Founders' Society, "Summary of Gray Iron Specifications," Cleveland, 1965.
4. T. E. Eagan and C. O. Burgess, Gray Iron: Its Mechanical and Engineering Characteristics and Details for Designing Cast Components, *Foundry,* vol. 76, August–September, 1948.
5. C. H. Lorig and T. E. Barlow, Gray Cast Iron, Tensile Strength, Brinell Hardness, and Composition Relationships, *Trans. AFS,* vol. 54, 1946.
6. A. P. Gagnebin, Ductile Iron, *Foundry,* vol. 80, June, 1952.
7. "Marketing Guide to the Metal Casting Industry," *Foundry,* Penton Publishing Co., Cleveland, 1964.
8. American Society for Testing Materials, Standards, Part I, Ferrous Metals, 1949, Specifications A48-48 and A159-49T.
9. C. R. Loper, Jr., and R. W. Heine, Heavy White Iron Sections Melt Additions Effects on Mottling Tendency, *Trans. AFS,* vol. 68, 1960.
10. H. Laplanche, A New Structual Diagram for Cast Iron, *Metal Progr.,* December, 1947.
11. C. R. Loper, Jr., and R. W. Heine, The Solidification of Cast Iron with Spheroidal Graphite, *Trans. ASM,* vol. 56, 1963.

19

Melting of Cast Irons

Historically, the development of the blast furnace for the reduction of iron ore gave birth to iron founding. At first, pig iron from the blast furnace was used directly for making iron castings. As time went on and the use of iron castings became more common, smaller shaft-type furnaces were introduced for remelting pig iron specifically for making gray-iron castings. Thus evolved the *cupola*. The first English patent on a cupola furnace was granted in 1794, and the first American cupola was erected in 1820. Since that time the cupola has gradually developed into a furnace especially adapted to the needs of cast-iron melting. Although other types of furnaces are used, by far the greatest tonnage of iron is produced by cupola melting. Statistics* on furnace capacity of all foundries in the United States and Canada for 1962–1963 are given in the following table.

Melting equipment	No. of units	Capacity	Average capacity
Cupolas....................	2,817	27,465 tons/hr	9.75 tons/hr
Open hearths..............	99	5,896 tons/charge	59.56 tons/charge
Air furnaces................	139	3,989 tons/charge	28.70 tons/charge
Electric arc furnaces.........	1,250	3,919 tons/charge	3.14 tons/charge
Electric induction furnaces....	2,159	1,215 tons/charge	0.56 ton/charge
Crucible furnaces............	14,402	3,802 tons/charge	0.26 ton/charge
Reverberatory furnaces.......	1,171	3,433 tons/charge	2.93 tons/charge
Noncrucible furnaces.........	837	529 tons/charge	0.63 ton/charge

THE CUPOLA

Widespread use of the cupola for gray-iron melting rests upon its unique advantages, which include:

1. Continuous melting. Foundry production is facilitated since a ladle of molten iron may be tapped from the furnace at regular intervals. The flow

* "Marketing Guide to the Metal Casting Industry," *Foundry*, Penton Publishing Company, Cleveland, 1964.

of molten metal and molds for pouring may be synchronized for quantity production as required by the automotive, agricultural equipment, and similar industries.

2. Low cost of melting. Raw materials and operating costs are lower than on any other type of melting furnace producing equivalent tonnage.
3. Chemical-composition control is possible by proper furnace operation with continuous melting.
4. Adequate temperature control for fluidity in pouring castings can be obtained.

Certain limitations also are characteristic of the cupola furnace. Low carbon percentages in the iron below about 2.80% C are difficult to attain because of direct contact of molten iron and the carbonaceous fuel. Some alloying elements such as chromium and molybdenum are in part lost by oxidation in the cupola. Higher temperatures are obtained with air-furnace and arc-furnace melting. The use of several furnaces by duplexing, i.e., transferring of the molten metal from one furnace to another, may be utilized to combine the advantages of each type of furnace. For example, white iron may be melted in the cupola and have its carbon percentage lowered from about 3.0 to 2.20 to 2.40 per cent by decarburization in the air furnace.

Mechanical Structure

The structural features of a conventional cupola are illustrated in Fig. 19.1. It consists of a vertical shaft or shell built of ¼- to ⅜-in. steel plate. The shell is lined with refractory brick. A wind box and tuyeres for delivering air into the shaft are shown in Fig. 19.1. About 20 or more feet above the bottom an opening in the side is provided for charging materials into the stack. The cupola bottom is hinged so that the furnace may be emptied by dropping the bottom doors. The cupola bottom itself is generally of molding sand rammed in place on top of the bottom doors. At the bottom in front is a taphole and spout for the molten iron. At the rear and above the taphole level is a slag hole. The stack is topped by a spark-arrester hood or dust suppressor. Finally, some type of blower and blast control is required to supply air for combustion.

Some of the dimensions of standard cupolas are given in Table 19.1. The figures in Table 19.1 define the characteristics of the various sizes of the common cupola and are worthy of some discussion, as follows:

1. *Cupola size.* Cupolas are rated by number from 0 to 12 and vary in capacity designated as melting rate in tons per hour from approximately 1 to 35 tons per hr.

2. *Shell diameter.* The outer shell diameter is the dimension which ultimately limits the capacity of the cupola. Shell diameters of common cupolas vary from 27 to 108 in., although they have been operated with much smaller and larger diameters.
3. *Thickness of lower lining.* This is the lining thickness in zones *A* and *B* (Fig. 19.1), where the maximum amount of refractory erosion occurs.
4. *Diameter, inside lining.* The inside diameter establishes the operating cross-sectional area of the cupola.
5. *Area, inside cross-sectional area in the melting zone.* This dimension determines the range of the melting rates of a particular cupola size. A cupola

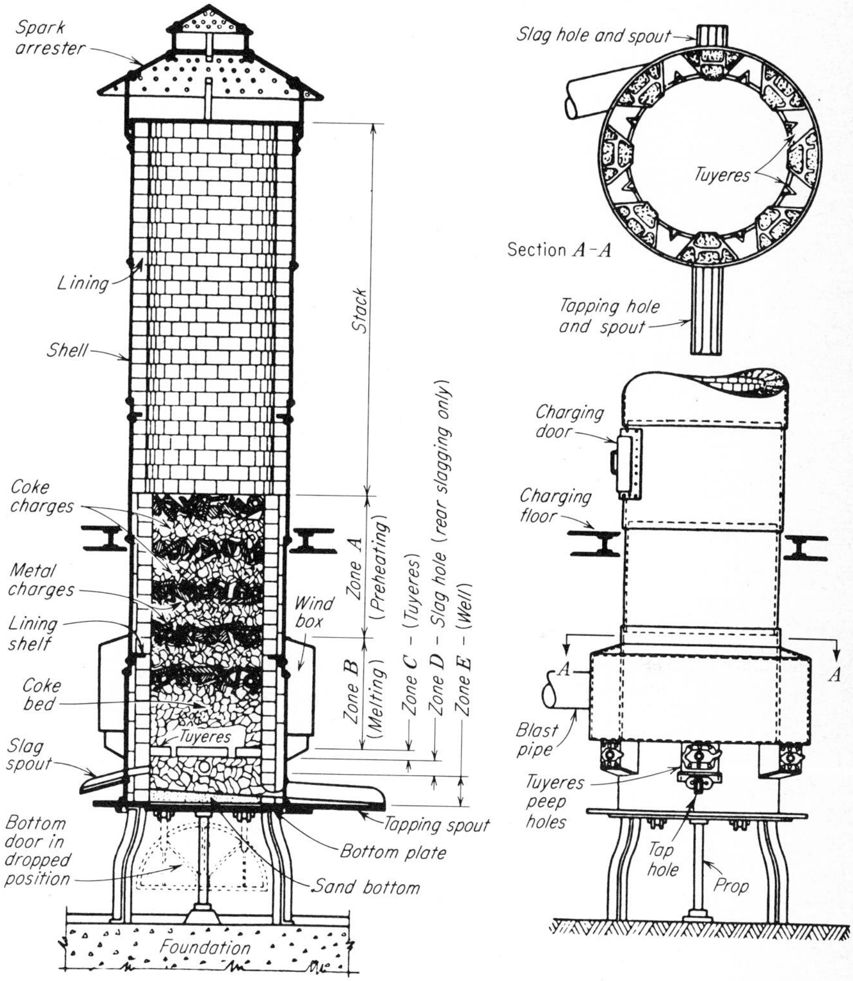

Fig. 19.1 Structure of the common cupola. (*From American Foundrymen's Society.*[4])

Table 19.1 ***General charging directions for cupolas****

Cupola size	Shell diam, in.	Thickness of lower lining, in.	Diam inside lining, in.	Area inside lining, sq in.	Melting rate, tons/hr with iron to coke (after bed) ratios of				Bed† coke height above tuyeres, in.	Coke and iron charges, lb					Flux lb	Cfm air through tuyeres	Normal wind-box pressure, oz.	Suggested blower selection		Total area of tuyeres, sq in.
											Iron									
					6	8	10	12		Coke	6:1	8:1	10:1	12:1				Cfm	Discharge pressure, oz.	
0	27	4½	18	254	¾	1	1¼	1½	28–34	20	120	160	200	240	4	570	7	640	8	32
1	32	4½	23	415	1	1½	2	2½	36–42	35	210	280	350	420	7	940	12	1,040	16	85
2	36	4½	27	572	1¾	2¼	2¾	3¼	36–42	45	270	360	450	540	9	1,290	12	1,430	16	118
2½*H*	41	7	27	572	1¾	2¼	2¾	3¼	36–42	45	270	360	450	540	9	1,290	12	1,430	16	121
2½*L*	41	4½	32	804	2½	3¼	4	4¾	40–46	65	390	520	650	780	13	1,810	14	2,000	16‡	121
3	46	7	32	804	2½	3¼	4	4¾	40–46	65	390	520	650	780	13	1,810	14	2,000	16‡	161
3½	51	7	37	1075	3¼	4¼	5¼	6½	40–46	85	510	680	850	1020	17	2,420	14	2,700	16‡	182
4	56	7	42	1385	4	5½	7	8¼	42–48	110	660	880	1110	1320	22	3,100	16	3,450	–24	263
5	63	9	45	1590	4½	6¼	8	9½	42–48	130	780	1040	1300	1560	26	3,600	16	4,000	–24	314
6	66	9	48	1809	5½	7¼	9	10¾	45–51	145	870	1160	1450	1740	29	4,100	18	4,500	–28	347
7	72	9	54	2290	7	9¼	11½	13¾	45–51	185	1110	1480	1850	2220	37	5,200	18	5,750	–32	466
8	78	9	60	2827	9	11¼	14	17	45–51	225	1350	1800	2250	2700	45	6,400	18	7,100	–32	546
9	84	9	66	3421	10½	13¾	17	20½	45–51	275	1650	2200	2750	3300	55	7,700	18	8,600	–32	640
9½	90	9	72	4071	12¼	16¼	20¼	24½	47–53	325	1950	2600	3250	3900	65	9,200	20	10,200	–36	802
10	96	9	78	4778	15	19	23¾	28¾	47–53	385	2310	3080	3850	4600	77	10,700	20	11,900	–36	919
11	102	12	78	4778	15	19	23¾	28¾	47–53	385	2310	3080	3850	4600	77	10,700	20	11,900	–40	919
12	108	12	84	5542	17	22¼	27¾	33¼	47–53	445	2670	3560	4450	5400	89	12,500	20	13,900	–40	860

* From American Foundrymen's Society.[4]

† Height of bed coke varies as square root of blast pressure.

‡ Recommend blowers with 20 oz discharge pressure when air-weight control is used.

The lining thickness for cupolas operated for 8- to 16-hr heats may be appreciably greater than shown in the table.

A practical guide for determining the height of the coke bed: Multiply the square root of the blast pressure by 10.5 and add 6. For example, suppose the blast pressure is 16 oz. The square root of 16 is 4; $4 \times 10.5 + 6 = 48$ in. So the bed coke (for 16-oz blast) should measure 48 in. above the tuyeres.

melts approximately 10 lb of iron per hr per sq in. of inside cross-sectional area in the melting zone when the weight of iron and coke charges is in the ratio of about 10:1. Thus the melting-rate figure in the column under iron-to-coke ratio of 10 in Table 19.1, expressed in pounds divided by 10, and the inside cross-sectional area are the same. A No. 0 cupola has 254 sq in. inside area and, at a 10:1 iron-to-coke ratio, will melt approximately 2540 lb per hr, or $1\frac{1}{4}$ tons per hr. Of course, within limits it may melt faster or more slowly than this figure, depending on the way in which it is operated.

6. *Total area of tuyeres, square inches.* The tuyere openings serve to introduce air for combustion of the coke. The combined area of the tuyeres in standard cupolas is usually on the order of one-fourth to one-eighth of the inside cupola cross-sectional area of the cupola at the tuyere level, although much smaller and larger ratios are sometimes used.

Other information in Table 19.1 will be considered relative to actual cupola-operating procedure.

Steps in Operation

A cupola heat includes not only the actual melting operation but all the operations which precede and follow the period during which iron is being melted. A certain cycle of events occurs each time a heat is made, including the following:

1. Preparation of the refractory lining, bottom, and taphole and slag hole
2. Lighting and burning in the coke bed
3. Charging
4. Melting
   a. Starting the air blast
   b. Charging
5. Tapping and slagging
6. Dropping the bottom

Each step above is an important one, and must be properly carried out for a successful heat.

Preparation of the Cupola

Preparation of the cupola usually begins with the cupola in the condition remaining after dropping the bottom at the conclusion of the previous heat. More or less slag, coke, and iron adhere to the side walls in the melting zone and well when the bottom is dropped. This extraneous material is chipped away and back to the original refractory. Normally, this work is confined to the high-temperature melting zone. In some cases, the brickwork is removed up to the first lining shelf. The taphole and slag hole are cleaned out and inspected. If they are too large or show iron penetration or cracking, the taphole area (breast) and slag hole are knocked out completely. In some foundries, the taphole and slag hole may be used for several heats before replacement is necessary.

Repair and maintenance of the lining require the use of several types of refractories. Cupola block is used for the original lining. Some standard sizes of brick for cupolas are listed in Ref. 4. Fire-clay-type refractories are most commonly employed for cupola-lining purposes. Cupola blocks have an analysis in the following range:[4]

Silica, %	52–62
Alumina, %	31–43
Titania, %	1.5–2.5
Fluxing oxides, %	3–6

Table* 19.2 *Refractory mixtures for patching* *Parts by volume*

	Fire clay	Ganister or silica	Ground fire-brick	Graphite	Crushed fire-stone	High-temp cement	Ground coke	Saw-dust	Cereal flour
Breast tapholes (rear slagging)	2	2	1						
	1		1	1					
	1	2							
					2	1			
Slag hole, taphole (front slagging)	1		1	1					
Botting	10	3					1	½	
	2			1					1
	1	1							
Patching	1	2							
Cupola linings					2	1			
Ladle linings	10				7				
Spouts	1		1					½–¾	
	2	2	1						
	1½		3						
	1	1	1						
	4		6						
Wash mixture for cupolas and ladles	17–18	80		2–3% bentonite (All materials 75–100 mesh)		Water to creamy consistency			

* From American Foundrymen's Society.[4]

NOTES: The cupola department should have its own muller for mixing plastic refractories, a crusher for crushing brick, and a set of screens for sizing. Fire clay should be plastic and refractory. The addition of goulac or molasses to the tempering water tends to reduce the amount required for bonding. All mixtures should be tempered with as little water as practicable, and mulled thoroughly. Ram material in place rather than use excessive water. Air ramming is preferable to hand ramming.

Basic slags (those rich in coke, MgO, and FeO) will slowly attack a silica lining; therefore points of excessive slag attack might well be lined with chemically neutral materials.

Patching a lining is sometimes performed with plastic mixtures of granular refractory, clay, and water of the kind listed in Table 19.2. It is more common, however, to use air placement of granular refractory. This is done with a pneumatic device which properly blends the refractory and water and hurls it into place by means of an air stream. An example of the equipment employed is shown in Fig. 19.2. The mixture blown is generally a combination of ganister, water, sand, and clay. Sizing of the components is important to obtain desired density, and quality is important to ensure effective application and refractoriness. Material selection to form a glaze is generally considered more important than refractoriness. In addition to proprietary mixtures, several homemade mixtures have been employed:

1. 50% ganister (¼ in. diameter), 30% silica sand (50 mesh), 20% clay
2. 75% amorphous silica (half coarse and half fine), 25% clay
3. 50% silica pebbles, 25% sand, 25% clay

The air gun may also be used for patching the melting zone and ramming of tapholes and slag holes. Since the air gun can be used to place the refractory where needed, it is a convenient method for obtaining a contoured patch. This type of patch is useful in those areas of the cupola where extreme lining erosion is experienced early in the heat, but dimin-

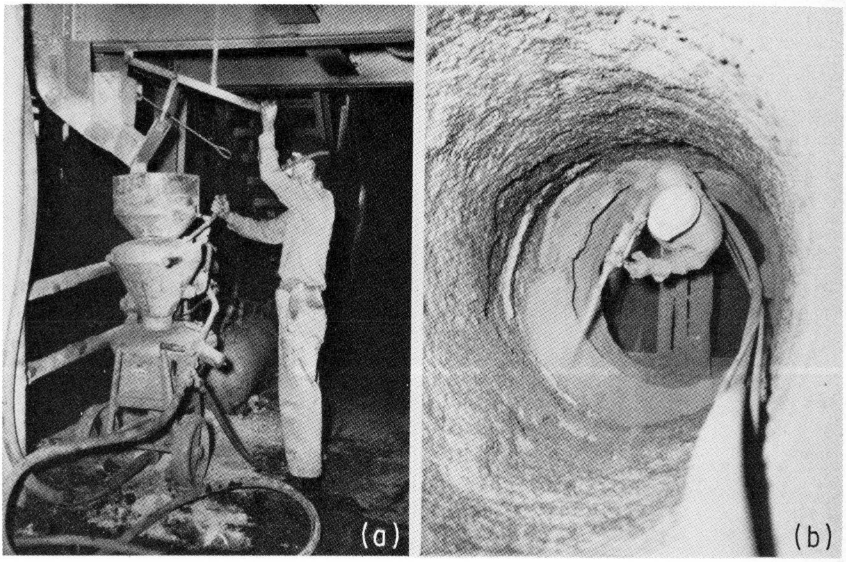

***Fig.* 19.2** (*a*) Discharging lining material from storage bin to pressure hopper in preparation for cupola lining with a pneumatic gun. (*b*) Operator installing monolithic lining with an air gun. (*From American Foundrymen's Society.*[4])

ishes at later stages. As a result, less refractory lining material is required in patching.

Taphole and Slag Hole

Tapholes and slag holes may be constructed in several ways. Plastic mixtures may be rammed in place by hand or with the air gun around a tapered plug. Tapholes and slag-hole bricks may be employed. A number of methods of putting in tapholes and slag holes are discussed in Ref. 4.

A dimension of importance is the vertical distance from the bottom of the taphole to the bottom of the slag hole. This distance determines the volume of metal which may be held in the cupola well when the slag hole is left open and the taphole is closed. Ordinarily, the dimension is such that one to two iron charges may be held in the well except when low-carbon-content irons are desired.

Bottom

Molding sand may be used for putting in the cupola bottom. The doors are closed and should fit snugly. Tempered sand, having green strength of about 6.0 psi or more, 60 or more permeability, and 3.0 to 6.0 per cent moisture, is rammed in place. The bottom is tapered toward the taphole, as illustrated in Fig. 19.3*a*. Uniform ramming of the bottom is important so that no iron leaks will develop.

Coke Bed

When the cupola lining is fully prepared, the heat begins with the building of the coke bed. Essentially, "putting in the bed" means starting a coke fire and building up a hot-burning coke pile within the cupola to a preselected height. Often kindling wood is put down, taking care not to damage the sand bottom. Then some coke is added and the kindling ignited. When the initial coke is burning well, more coke is added. As the coke becomes hot, more is added until the desired height is reached. Many foundries do not use kindling wood to start coke fires. Gas torches inserted through openings at the side near the bottom sometimes are used. The burner ports are later closed with bottom sand. Electric-spark ignitors are also used.

Coke-bed height. The coke bed is defined as the height of the coke above the tuyeres. Actually, then, the coke-bed height does not refer to the coke below the tuyeres in the well, but only to the height of coke above the tuyeres, because of its effect on proper combustion during melting. A correct bed height is necessary at the outset of the heat in order to cause combustion to occur so that metal will be melted and heated to the desired temperature. Hence the bed should be carefully put in and measured for correct height. The height measurement is ordinarily

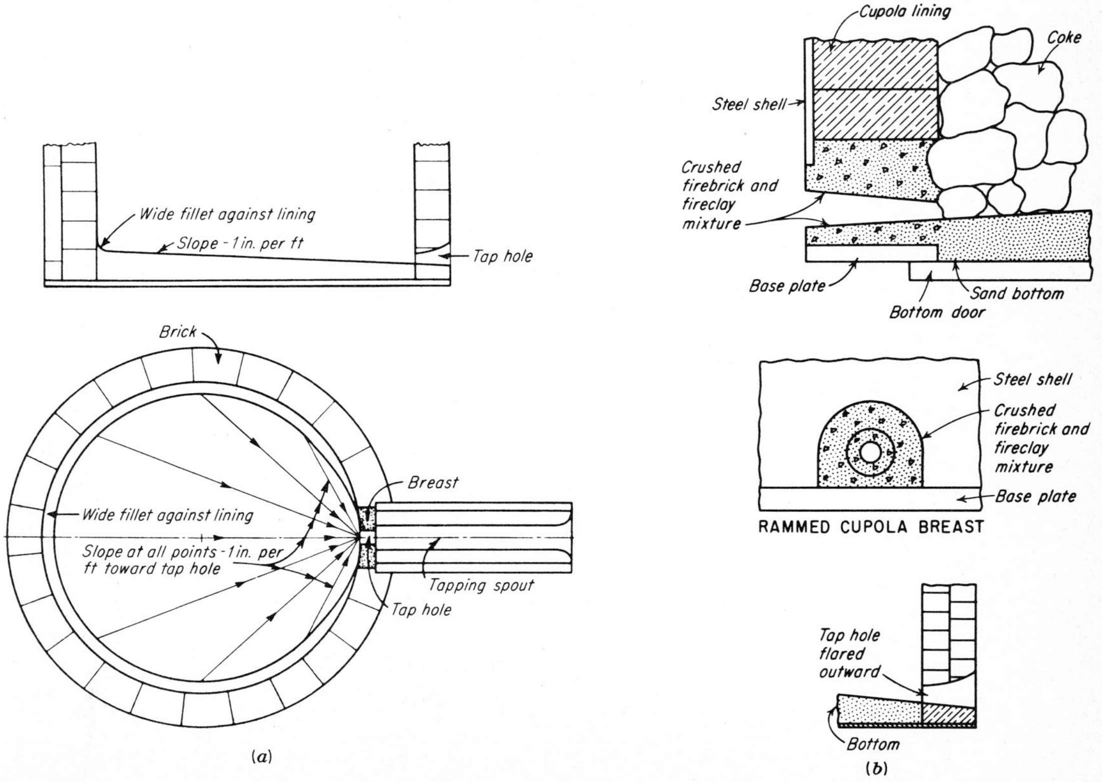

***Fig.* 19.3** (*a*) Sand-cupola bottom and taphole arrangement. (*b*) Construction of the cupola taphole, using either a monolithic breast or taphole blocks. (*From American Foundrymen's Society.*[8])

made from the charging-door sill down to the top of the bed with a chain or rod.

To complete building up the bed, a burning-in period is sometimes adopted. Air, at about half the normal blowing rate, is blown through the bed for 2 or 3 min to raise the coke temperature to a white heat and heat the refractory. After burning in, replenishing coke is added, and the bed is leveled at the desired height. The cupola is then ready for charging.

Charging

Charging the cupola consists in adding weighed batches of metal, coke, and flux. The weight of individual metal coke and flux charges recommended for various cupola sizes is given in Table 19.1. However, larger or smaller charges may be used. The weight of one coke charge, as listed in Table 19.1, corresponds approximately to the amount of coke required to produce a layer of coke 3 to 9 in. deep across the inside cupola area. The approximate weight of coke per cubic foot is given in the following table:

Approximate weight of coke per cubic foot

Size of coke*	Lb/cu ft
1 by 2½	33
3½ by 2½	30
3 by 4	28
4 by 7	27

* 3 by 4 means the coke pieces pass through a 4- by 4-in. screen opening but remain on a 3- by 3-in. screen opening.

The flux charge, usually limestone, as tabulated in Table 19.1, approximates 20 per cent of the weight of the coke charge, although as high as 50 per cent may be employed. The main purpose of the flux is to cause the slag formed from coke ash, refractory erosion, and metal oxidation to be fluid so that it may be readily tapped from the slag hole.

Melting

With the cupola fully charged, melting can be started. Often a soaking period of 20 min to 1 hr is used to permit the stack contents to preheat. The blowers are then started. After blowing for a few minutes the coke becomes hot enough to cause melting of the metal charge. Droplets of iron may be seen falling past the tuyere peepholes.

After 8 to 10 min from "wind-on," melting progresses sufficiently so that a trickle of iron appears at the taphole if it is open. The heat is usually started with the taphole closed so that first iron will not freeze in it. Since the first tap is often cold, it may be pigged rather than poured into molds.

The time for first iron at the taphole is an important measure of the correctness of the coke-bed height. A time of less than 8 min from wind-on suggests too low a bed and longer than 10 or 12 min suggests too high a bed for the air pressure and rate employed. Importance of the proper bed height is associated with temperature of the molten iron. It is usually desired to have the iron issue from the taphole consistently at 2750 to 2900 F. A low or high coke bed is one reason for iron colder than this temperature range. Of course, air at the proper rate in cubic feet or pounds per minute is necessary for combustion of the coke and melting to continue properly. Suggested wind-box air pressures and blower capacities are listed in Table 19.1. Several types of blowers are available with characteristics discussed in Ref. 4. As blowing continues, melting progresses, the cupola stack contents settle, and new charges must be added through the door as long as the heat continues. Metal and slag accumulate in the well, and may be handled by a sequence of tapping and slagging operations.

Tapping and Slagging

Intermittent tapping requires that the taphole be opened at intervals to deliver iron to pouring ladles. The taphole is then closed with a plastic clay bott. Refractory botting mixtures are given in Table 19.2. Opening the taphole is performed by picking out the clay plug with wedge-shaped tools. The intervals of tapping are usually predictable since the melting rate of a particular cupola and the capacity of the ladles are known. Hence ladles of iron may be withdrawn at regular intervals. If the well is allowed to overfill with iron, it will drip from the slag hole, where it can be quickly detected. Intermittent tapping is usually accompanied by intermittent slagging. As the melt level rises, slag will ultimately flow from the slag hole. Upon tapping, the drop in metal level results in cessation of slag flow. Ordinarily, a slag hole is first opened about 30 to 45 min after wind-on in order to allow time for sufficient slag to accumulate.

Continuous tapping of iron from the cupola is most commonly done by use of some type of dam on the spout. Such an arrangement is shown in Fig. 19.4. Critical dimensions in the system are the heights of the metal and slag dams above the top of the taphole. The former governs the height of the metal level in the cupola at a particular blast pressure whereas the latter controls the depth of slag layer floating on the iron. Similar principles apply to continuous tapping with rear slagging.

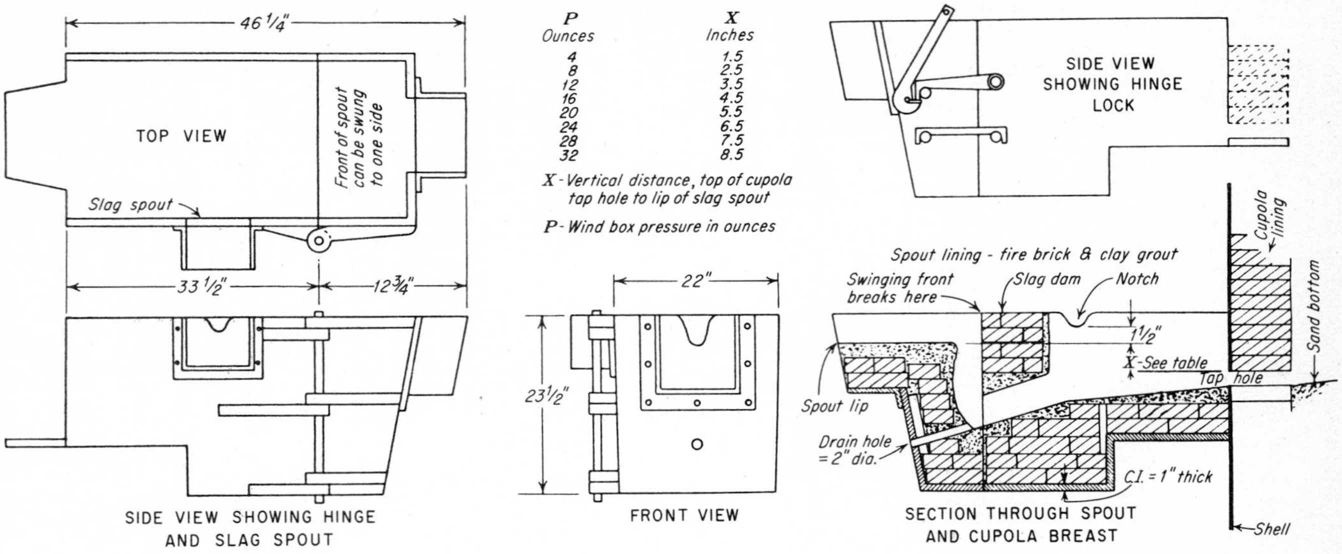

Fig. 19.4 Section drawing of a continuous-tapping front slagging spout for an 84-in. cupola lined to 66 in. (*From American Foundrymen's Society.*[4])

Dropping Bottom

The end of a cupola heat begins with cessation of charging. The stack contents are melted down until about one or two charges remain above the coke bed. During this period the air blast is often reduced. The bottom doors are then dropped, and the contents fall to the floor under the cupola. Water is sprayed over the white-hot drop to prevent it from damaging the cupola legs and bottom. In some cupola installations, the drop falls into a bucket or gondola and is removed from the foundry and quenched with water. Metal and coke from the drop may be recovered and worked into charges gradually in succeeding heats.

Although the details of cupola heats may vary greatly, the more common phases of the operation are those discussed in the preceding sections.

Water-cooled Cupolas

Current trends in cupola operations are to increase the production period of the cupola instead of using either larger cupolas and heavy refractory linings or more cupolas maintaining short runs. The latter imposes greater service requirements on the refractory and cupola shell in the combustion and tuyere zones. For these reasons, water-cooled cupolas are in general use in the industry.

Two types of water-cooled cupolas are in use, those with an external spray on the shell and those with water jackets. Water-spray cooling is shown in Fig. 19.5. This cupola makes use of a thin, continuous water film to maintain a cool shell. Additional water sprays may be incorporated at various places on the shell to ensure a continuous water film. In general, the cupola shell is sloped to a larger diameter just above tuyere so that the water film will adhere to the shell.

Water-jacket cooling is shown in Fig. 19.6. This type of cooling introduces cold water into the bottom of the water jacket while the warmer water is removed at the top. One advantage of water-jacket cooling is that cooling water is confined and not open to areas near molten metal. On the other hand, it is more difficult to convert an existing cupola to this type of cooling.

Many water-cooled cupolas, of either of the above types, are operated with little or no lining on the inside cupola shell in the melting zone. After a short period of operation a built-up layer of slag or slag plus refractory is formed on the shell which protects the shell from abrasion of the charge. If, in addition, the cupola well is lined with carbon block, the cupola may be used as either an acid or basic melting unit, depending on the charge material.

In order to confine combustion to a concentrated area and thereby minimize both the maximum-temperature zone (to prevent excess heat

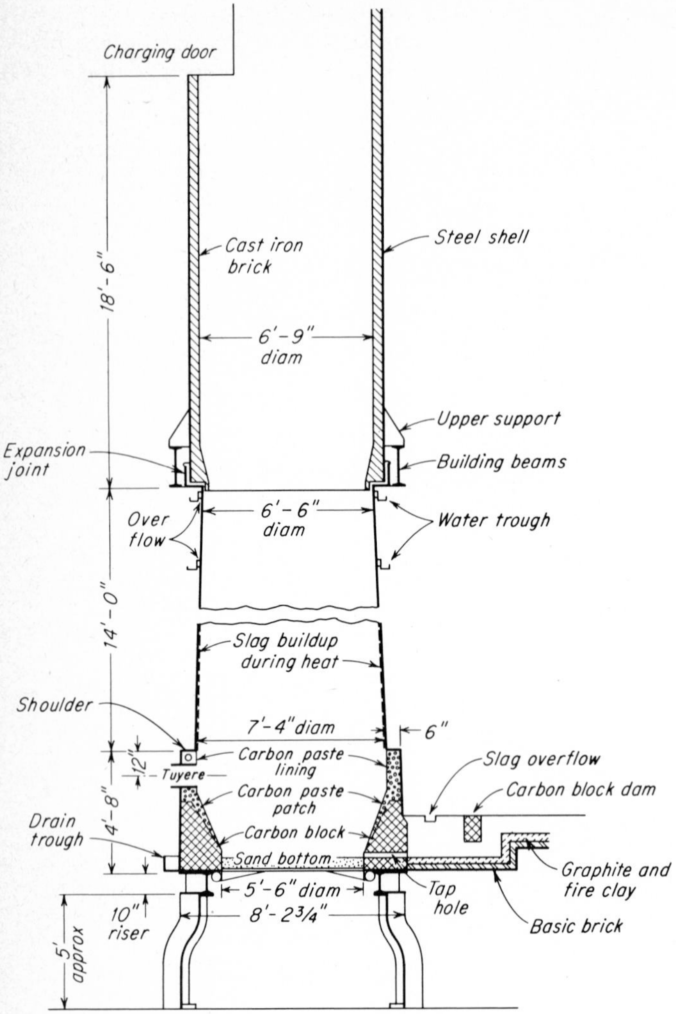

***Fig.* 19.5** Sectional view of a water-spray-cooled, open-top, drop-bottom-door, continuous-tapping, cold-blast cupola. (*From American Foundrymen's Society.*[4])

loss) and the zone of free oxygen, projecting tuyeres may be used.[4] Such tuyeres, which generally are made of copper, and therefore water-cooled, permit the introduction of air at predetermined distances from the shell. The result is a much more concentrated combustion zone and a smaller zone of free oxygen.

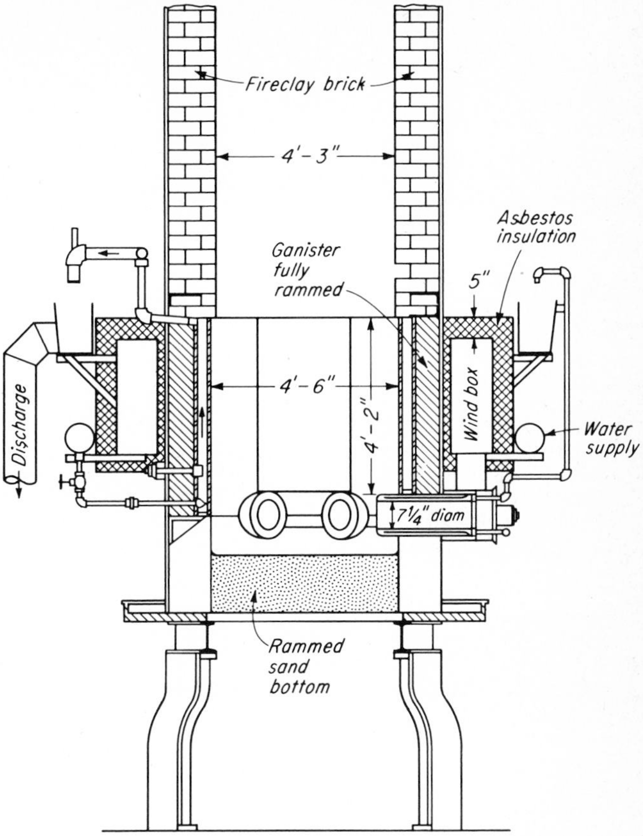

***Fig.* 19.6** Sectional view showing a water-jacket cupola utilizing water-cooled tuyeres. (*From American Foundrymen's Society.*[4])

CUPOLA MATERIALS

Cupola melting is a complex processing method occurring at high temperatures in which metallic raw materials, the combustion materials, the molten-iron product, and gas and the slag by-products are all intimately associated. The amount of material involved is large. To produce a ton of molten iron, materials to the extent listed in Table 19.3 are required.

The problem is one of selection and handling of materials as well as proper processing. Of course, a certain percentage of the iron, 15 to 40 per cent, is remelted from day to day in the form of foundry returns, sprues, runners, risers, and defective castings. The new material entering the cycle comes from pig iron, cast-iron scrap, and steel.

Table* 19.3 *Approximate amounts of materials per ton of iron in cupola melting

Cupola input*	Cupola output
1.0 ton pig, scrap iron, steel	0.98 ton molten iron
0.15 ton coke	0.05 ton molten slag
0.03 ton flux	1.35 tons stack gases
1.20 tons air	
2.38 tons total	2.38 tons total

* Assuming a 6.67:1 iron-to-coke ratio.

Pig Irons

Foundry pig iron is a blast-furnace product specifically produced for foundry use. Types of pig irons are classified in Table 19.4.

Since foundry pig irons are high in percentages of carbon, silicon, and manganese, the level of these elements in the cast iron may be kept high by the use of pig iron in the charge. Of course, pig irons also vary in content of other elements. So-called southern pig irons are higher in phosphorus content than northern pig iron. Malleable pig is a low-phosphorus pig iron especially used by malleable-iron foundries. A grade of pig having a very high silicon content, 5.0 to 17.0 per cent, is known as "silvery" pig and is used to enrich the silicon content of a cupola charge.

Scrap

Scrap may include gray iron, steel, and malleable iron. Cast-iron scrap originates in discarded machinery, automobiles, farming equipment, machine tools, etc. Gray iron, malleable iron, and steel scrap are separated to varying degrees by scrap dealers. Some typical grades of scrap are specified in Ref. 4.

Scrap may be the source of difficulties in gray-iron melting since it may contain small percentages of elements such as antimony, tin, lead, zinc, aluminum, and others that are harmful to the iron.[4] Furthermore, its average analysis is difficult to predict. Size of the scrap is an important factor in maintaining proper density in the stack. Bulky light steel and small bits of cast-iron scrap cause trouble in charging and in the smooth flow of material down the stack.

Proper proportioning of pig iron, gray iron, and steel scrap and remelt is performed by calculation and experience with the materials. Metal-composition control is discussed later in this chapter.

Table* 19.4 *Classification of pig irons*

A. Low phosphorus (LP):
- Phosphorus, 0.035% max—all grades
- Silicon, 0.50–3.00% in 25-point ranges
- Sulfur, 0.035% max—all grades
- Manganese, 0.15% max, 0.50–1.00 and 1.00–1.50

B. Intermediate low phosphorus (LPi):
- Phosphorus, 0.036–0.075%—all grades
- Silicon, 1.00–3.00%
- Sulfur, 0.05% max—all grades
- Manganese, 0.75% max and 0.76–1.25

C. Bessemer iron, used in making acid Bessemer steel (Bes):
- Phosphorus, 0.076–0.100%
- Silicon, 1.00–3.00%
- Sulfur, 0.05% max
- Manganese, 1.25% max—all grades

D. Malleable iron (M):
- Phosphorus, 0.101–0.300%—all grades†
- Silicon, 0.75–5.00%
- Sulfur, 0.05% max—all grades
- Manganese, 0.50–1.25%

E. Basic, northern, used in making basic open-hearth steel:
- Phosphorus, 0.40% max—all grades
- Silicon, 0.90% max, 0.91–1.15, 1.16–1.40
- Sulfur, 0.05% max—all grades
- Manganese, 1.25–1.75%—all grades

J. Basic, southern, used in making basic open-hearth steel:
- Phosphorus, 0.70–0.90%—all grades—manufactured in southern districts
- Silicon, 0.90% max, 0.91–1.15 and 1.16–1.40
- Sulfur, 0.05% max—all grades
- Manganese, 0.40–0.75%—all grades

F. Foundry, northern, low phosphorus (Fl):
- Phosphorus, 0.30–0.50%—all grades†
- Silicon, 1.50–5.00%
- Sulfur, 0.05% max—all grades
- Manganese, 0.50–1.25%

G. Foundry, northern, high phosphorus (Fh):
- Phosphorus, 0.501–0.70%—all grades
- Silicon, 1.50–5.00%
- Sulfur, 0.05% max—all grades
- Manganese, 0.50–1.25%

H. Foundry, southern (Fs):
- Phosphorus, 0.70–0.90%—all grades
- Silicon, 1.50–5.00%
- Sulfur, 0.05% max—all grades
- Manganese, 0.40–0.75%

S. Silvery (S):
- Phosphorus, 0.30% max—all grades
- Silicon, 5.00–17.00%
- Sulfur, 0.05% max—all grades
- Manganese, 0.50–1.25%

Carbon. The carbon content of pig iron is not closely controlled, and therefore it is not customary to specify limits. In conventional blast-furnace practice, low silicon generally accompanies high carbon, and vice versa.

* From American Foundrymen's Society.[4]

† Although the phosphorus ranges given correspond to those of the American Iron and Steel Institute, merchant blast furnaces supply and gray-iron foundries use pig iron with the following phosphorus ranges: malleable—phosphorus, 0.101–0.200%; foundry—northern, low phosphorus, 0.201% and up.

Composition Adjustment and Alloying

A number of alloying agents are utilized in the cupola charge and are employed as ladle additions to the molten iron. These materials are listed in Table 19.9. For increasing silicon and manganese content of the cupola charge, briquets of ferrosilicon, ferromanganese, or silicon carbide may be used. Such briquets are manufactured to contain 1 or 2 lb of the element desired. Silvery pig is also used for this purpose. When chromium, molybdenum, or nickel is to be increased, additions are commonly made in the ladle. If large percentages are added, alloying may be accomplished in an electric furnace.

Coke

Foundry coke is produced from bituminous coals in by-product or beehive ovens, the by-product type being in more general use. Some specifications on foundry coke are given in Table 19.5. A number of important properties of foundry coke influence its use in the cupola. Uniform cupola operation is favored by using coke of uniform combustibility, size, and good mechanical strength. Sulfur pickup by the iron comes from the coke.

A number of properties are listed in Table 19.5, and testing methods have been devised and their influence on cupola melting studied.[13,5] The most common specifications, however, include only the proximate analysis and sulfur-content values in the range given in Table 19.5 and rigid size requirements. A size of 4 to 6 in. is common. Fragile coke or rough handling may cause finer pieces to be formed even after it has been screened. This is undesirable since it interferes with gas and liquid-metal flow through the cupola.

Coke ash forms the principal constituent of the slag. About 6 to 12 lb of ash is formed from each 100 lb of coke. The chemical composition of the coke ash is ordinarily acid and in the range of 45 to 55% SiO_2, 25 to 35% Al_2O_3, about 7 to 10.0% iron oxide, and the balance oxides of

Table* 19.5 *Example of foundry-coke characteristics

Proximate analyses:	
Moisture, %	Less than 3.0
Volatile matter, %	Less than 2.0
Fixed carbon, %	More than 86.0
Ash, %	Less than 12.0
Sulfur, %	Less than 0.80
Physical properties:	
Size	4–6 in. common, about $\frac{1}{10}$ to $\frac{1}{12}$% cupola lined ID
Strength	See ASTM Standard Method D141
Hardness	See ASTM Standard Method D294
Bulk density	See ASTM Standard Method D292, or 24–27 lb/cu ft
Porosity and specific gravity	See ASTM Standard Method D167; for other properties, see Ref. 4

manganese, magnesium, and alkaline earths. Fusion of the coke ash occurs in the melting zone. The fused ash has high viscosity, however, and requires fluxes to make it fluid for ease in tapping it from the slag hole.

Fluxes

Fluxes are basic materials which will react with the coke ash and melted refractory to make a fluid slag. Fluxing agents used most often are limestone, fluorspar, and soda ash. Limestone is $CaCO_3$ of about 98 per cent purity, having a size of -2 in. and $+\frac{3}{4}$ in. The "stone" should have a low acid oxide content. Dolomitic limestones having 15 to 30% $MgCo_3$ replacing some of the $CaCO_3$ in straight limestone are also employed. The stone begins to decompose to CaO and CO_2 at a temperature of about 1470 F as it descends in the stack. The CaO freed from the $CaCO_3$ reacts with the acid constituents of the ash and refractory to produce the fluid slag, which may be tapped from the cupola. Additions of fluorspar and soda ash cause the slag to be more fluid than when only stone is employed. Chemical compositions of typical cupola slags and fluxes are given in Table 19.6.

Air

The materials necessary for cupola operation include air about equivalent in weight to each ton of iron produced. The air may vary in temperature, pressure, humidity, and uniformity of air delivery to the cupola. Air blowing and metering equipment has been devised to control the rate of flow. Humidity conditioning, or dehumidification, is practiced by some foundries. Preheated air, or hot blast, may also be employed. Because of the importance of the air blast, many attempts have been made to improve the quality of the blast by specially designed tuyeres, balanced blast with two or more rows of tuyeres, or other features. Such practices are outside the scope of the text but may be found extensively discussed in technical literature such as that included in the Bibliography.

PRINCIPLES OF CUPOLA OPERATION

Successful cupola operation hinges largely on combustion control. In order to have favorable melting conditions it is necessary to have a balanced combination of coke and air supplied at the proper rate. With proper combustion, the control of metal composition, temperature, and slagging can be accomplished.

Table 19.6 ***Typical slags and fluxes***

Chemical constituent	Limestone		Acid slags					Fluorspar	Soda ash	Coke ash		Basic slag	
	Regular	Dolomitic	A	B	C*	D†	E			B	A	A	B
Silica	0.35	0.40	48.60	40.60	45.54	37.64	52.42	...	...	46.40	46.23	26.0	25.8
Alumina	0.20	0.38	14.29	22.40	15.30	18.90	18.0	...	...	16.45	31.93	9.2	6.5
Lime	...	...	36.10	24.40	22.0	28.10	24.39	...	...	11.80	5.04	32.5	40.3
Magnesia	...	...	0.34	8.60	6.80	2.80	2.03	...	...	4.60	2.06	28.6	23.2
Calcium carbonate	98.40	53.72											
Magnesium carbonate	...	45.44											
Sodium carbonate	...	...	...	...	...	...	...	...	78–98%				
Iron oxide, as FeO	...	...	2.21	1.50	5.38	12.62	1.86	...	...	18.15	14.54	2.90	2.0
Manganese oxide, MnO	...	...	1.46	1.95	2.30	1.20	1.02	...	...	...	...	0.60	0.60
CaF_2	...	...	...	...	...	...	...	85% or more					
Sulfur	...	...	0.31	0.20	...	...	0.11	...	...	...	...	1.26	

* A dark-green slag.

† A black slag resulting from oxidizing melting conditions.

Combustion

The combustion principles applicable to cupola operation are not too different from those encountered in any combustion problem. Although the problem may be considered with the most intricate of thermochemical calculations, these are for the most part not within the scope of this book.

Coke and Air Supply

The rate at which coke is charged and air is delivered must be properly balanced. Assuming that a coke bed of proper height has been established, the balance of coke and air is probably best judged from the composition of the stack gases. Experience has shown that, under proper operating conditions, cupola stack gases should contain about 12 to 14% CO_2 and 11 to 15% CO (Ref. 4). The amount of air required for combustion of 1 lb of carbon to gases of the aforementioned composition may be easily calculated. For convenience, however, the quantities are tabulated in Table 19.7. From Table 19.7, it is evident that 1 lb of carbon will be burned to gases containing 12 to 14% CO_2 by 8.35 to 8.93 lb of air, or 109.1 to 116.8 cu ft of air, at 60 F and 29.92 in. Hg. A sample problem will be worked to show the application of the figures to cupola melting conditions.

Example. A No. 6 cupola with 48 in. inside diameter is found to be melting at a rate of 9 tons per hr at a coke ratio of 10:1. What are the air requirements of this cupola?

$$9 \text{ tons/hr} \times 2000 \text{ lb/ton} \times \frac{1 \text{ lb coke}}{10 \text{ lb iron}} \times \frac{0.90 \text{ lb carbon}}{1 \text{ lb coke}} \times \frac{1 \text{ hr}}{60 \text{ min}}$$

$$= 27.0 \text{ lb C burned/min}$$

$$27.0 \text{ lb C/min} \times 8.35 \text{ lb air/lb C} = 225.5 \text{ lb air/min}$$

or

$$27.0 \times 109.1 \text{ cu ft air} = 2945.7 \text{ cfm}$$

$$27.0 \text{ lb C/min} \times 8.93 \text{ lb air/lb C} = 241.1 \text{ lb air}$$

or

$$27.0 \times 116.8 \text{ cu ft air} = 3153.6 \text{ cfm}$$

Thus 2945.7 to 3153.6 cfm of air at standard conditions is required to burn the coke supplied in this cupola. A back check on the coke and air supply may be obtained by carefully determining the actual melting rate on several satisfactory heats. The melting rate helps to measure the actual rate at which coke is being burned once iron and coke are charged in a definite ratio. The air requirements may then be recalcu-

*Table 19.7 The air requirement for combustion**

Effluent gases			Fraction of 1 lb carbon burned to		Air requirements, lb/lb C			Gases produced, lb/lb C				Heat developed, Btu/lb C			Efficiency of combus-tion, %	Lb/lb C	Cu ft/lb C	Cu ft/ton iron 90% coke 10:1 ratio	54-in. cupola melting rate 12T/hr, cfm	
CO_2, %	CO, %	N_2, %	A CO_2	B CO	O_2	N_2	Air	CO_2	CO	N_2	Total	CO_2	CO	Total					Theo-retical	+ 5%
0	34.7	65.3	0.000	1.000	1.33	4.44	5.77	0.00	2.33	4.44	6.77	000	4350	4,350	29.9	5.77	75.4	13,600	2720	2860
1	33.0	66.0	0.029	0.971	1.37	4.57	5.94	0.11	2.26	4.57	6.94	422	4224	4,646	31.9	5.94	77.7	14,000	2810	2950
2	31.4	66.6	0.060	0.940	1.41	4.70	6.11	0.22	2.19	4.70	7.11	873	4089	4,962	34.1	6.11	79.9	14,400	2880	3030
3	29.7	67.3	0.092	0.908	1.45	4.85	6.30	0.34	2.11	4.85	7.30	1,338	3950	5,288	36.3	6.30	82.4	14,800	2960	3110
4	28.1	67.9	0.125	0.875	1.50	3.99	6.49	0.46	2.04	4.99	7.49	1,819	3806	5,625	38.6	6.49	84.8	15,300	3060	3220
5	26.4	68.6	0.159	0.841	1.54	5.14	6.68	0.58	1.96	5.14	7.68	2,314	3658	5,972	41.1	6.68	87.3	15,700	3140	3300
6	24.7	69.3	0.195	0.805	1.59	5.30	6.89	0.71	1.88	5.30	7.89	2,837	3502	6,339	43.5	6.89	90.0	16,200	3240	3400
7	23.1	69.9	0.232	0.768	1.64	5.47	7.11	0.85	1.79	5.47	8.11	3,376	3340	6,716	46.2	7.11	92.9	16,700	3340	3510
8	21.5	70.5	0.271	0.729	1.69	5.64	7.33	0.99	1.70	5.64	8.33	3,943	3171	7,114	48.8	7.33	95.8	17,200	3440	3620
9	19.8	71.2	0.312	0.688	1.75	5.82	7.57	1.15	1.60	5.82	8.57	4,540	2993	7,533	51.7	7.57	99.0	17,800	3560	3740
10	18.2	71.8	0.354	0.646	1.80	6.01	7.81	1.30	1.51	6.01	8.82	5,151	2810	7,961	54.7	7.81	102.1	18,400	3680	3870
11	16.5	72.5	0.400	0.600	1.87	6.21	8.08	1.47	1.40	6.21	9.08	5,320	2610	8,431	57.9	8.08	105.6	19,000	3800	4000
12	14.8	73.2	0.447	0.553	1.93	6.42	8.35	1.64	1.29	6.42	9.35	6,504	2406	8,910	61.2	8.35	109.1	19,700	3940	4140
13	13.2	73.8	0.496	0.504	1.99	6.64	8.63	1.82	1.17	6.64	9.63	7,217	2192	9,409	64.7	8.63	112.8	20,300	4060	4260
14	11.6	74.4	0.547	0.453	2.07	6.86	8.93	2.01	1.06	6.86	9.93	7,959	1971	9,930	68.3	8.93	116.8	21,000	4200	4410
15	9.9	75.1	0.602	0.398	2.13	7.11	9.24	2.21	0.92	7.11	10.24	8,759	1731	10,490	72.1	9.24	120.8	21,800	4360	4580
16	8.3	75.7	0.658	0.342	2.21	7.35	9.57	2.42	0.80	7.35	10.57	9,576	1488	11,064	76.0	9.57	125.1	22,600	4520	4750
17	6.6	76.4	0.720	0.280	2.29	7.63	9.92	2.64	0.65	7.63	10.92	10,476	1218	11,694	80.4	9.92	129.7	23,400	4680	4820
18	5.0	77.0	0.783	0.217	2.38	7.91	10.29	2.87	0.51	7.91	11.29	11,393	944	12,337	84.8	10.29	134.5	24,300	4860	5100
19	3.3	77.7	0.852	0.148	2.47	8.21	10.68	3.13	0.34	8.21	11.68	12,397	644	13,041	89.6	10.68	141.2	25,400	5080	5330
20	1.7	78.3	0.922	0.078	2.57	8.52	11.09	3.39	0.18	8.52	12.09	13,410	339	13,749	94.5	11.09	145.0	26,200	5240	5500
21	0.0	79.0	1.000	0.000	2.67	8.87	11.54	3.67	0.00	8.87	12.54	14,550	000	14,550	100.0	11.54	151.0	27,200	5480	5750

* From American Foundrymen's Society.[4]

lated as described above. In calculations of this type, corrections for air temperature, pressure, and humidity are sometimes employed,[4,14] especially when the cupola blast has been conditioned, i.e., by preheated air, moisture control, oxygen enrichment, etc. Those factors may also be controlled by air metering and blast dehumidification.

When the coke and air are in unbalanced supply, certain melting problems arise. An excess of coke results in wasted coke, a slow melting rate, high carbon percentage in the iron, lower iron temperature, excessive refractory erosion, and other operation difficulties. Oversupply of air causes the coke bed to be burned out and results in oxidation of iron, higher losses of silicon and manganese, low carbon percentages in the iron, and low metal temperatures. The required relationships of air and coke to combustion in the cupola are graphically illustrated in Fig. 19.7.

Coke Bed and Stack Gases

Coke-bed height was defined earlier as the height of the coke above the tuyeres before charging is begun. During melting the bed height fluctuates as coke descends into the melting zone from the stack above. Maintenance of an adequate bed height is reflected in metal temperature. If the bed is at its proper height, the molten iron will issue from the cupola at 2750 to 2900 F, the higher temperatures occurring under the most favorable conditions. Temperatures will drop if the bed burns away because of excess in the air supply. Concurrently, the carbon dioxide content of the stack gases increases and the carbon monoxide content decreases. Free oxygen may pass through the bed. Oxidation of the iron under these conditions results in a brown fume discharging from the cupola stack in place of a normal white fume. On the other hand, build-up of the coke bed due to insufficient air supply is accompanied by increasing CO content of the stack gases, and ultimately by decreasing

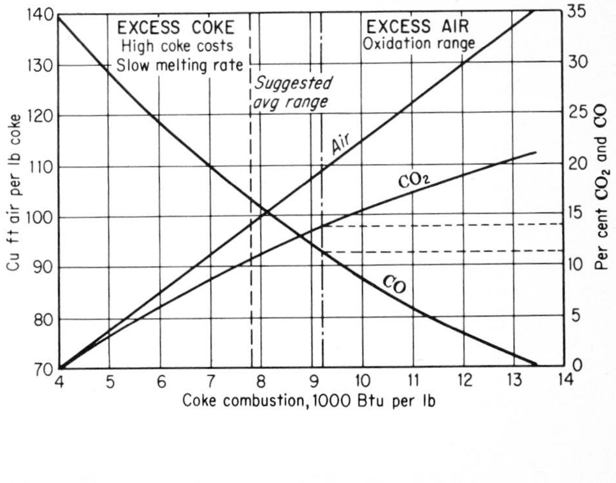

***Fig.* 19.7** Relation of air and coke to combustion in the cupola. (*From American Foundrymen's Society.*[4])

metal temperatures and melting rate. Thus it can be seen that the coke bed functions as a high-temperature reaction zone wherein combustion proceeds with the liberation of intense heat for melting and superheating under gaseous conditions favorable to the iron.

If air is to combine with carbon in this high-temperature reaction zone to form stack gases of the proper composition, it is necessary that the coke bed be of adequate height. However, bed height is also related to melting rate. Higher rates of melting in a given cupola can be obtained within limits by an increase in the rate of combustion. To blow air at a faster rate requires higher wind-box pressures and results in greater penetration of the blast in the coke bed. Generally, cupolas operated at the higher limits of their melting rate and at higher blast pressure are started with a high coke-bed height. An empirical relationship of starting bed height to wind-box pressure is given as a footnote in Table 19.1. The higher wind-box pressures are characteristic of cupolas being operated near the limit of their capacity.

Melting Rate, Combustion, and Temperature

The operating characteristics of cupolas are such that all the factors are interrelated. Coke bed, coke charge, air supply, melting rate, and melt temperature all influence the ultimate operation. Charts showing some of the relationships have been developed.[4] One of the operating charts is reproduced from Ref. 4 and illustrated in Fig. 19.8. The chart shows that higher melt temperatures result as the air blast is increased and iron-to-coke ratio is decreased. Of course, the chart assumes that coke and air are in balance and that a proper coke-bed height exists. Melting rate is increased with increased air blast and iron-to-coke ratio. The charts show that a given cupola may be operated over a wide range of melting rates and melt temperature by selection of the appropriate rate of air supply and iron-to-coke ratio. *In all cases, however, the air and coke supplies must be balanced in order to maintain consistent melting conditions.* Since the balance of coke and air is reflected in the stack gases, analysis of the gases may be utilized as a method of control,[4] or other means may be employed.[19]

Metal Composition and Properties

If proper combustion conditions prevail during melting, control of the analysis and properties of the iron is greatly facilitated. Basically, composition and property control depends on:

1. Charging metal charges of known analysis
2. Known and consistent composition changes during melting
3. Use of chill testing and inoculation

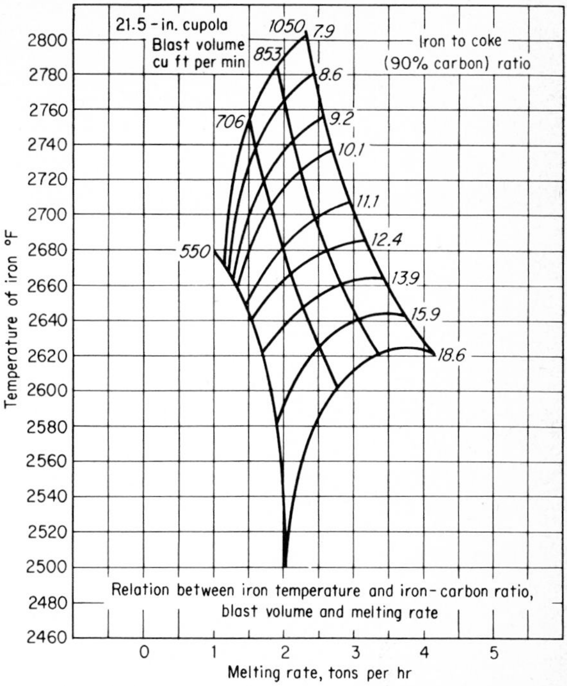

***Fig.* 19.8** Operating conditions for a 21.5-in. ID cupola. (*From American Foundrymen's Society.*[4])

The composition of metal produced during cupola melting may be estimated by means of computations usually called "mixture calculations." The usual methods of calculation are based on the following steps:

1. Empirically select a metal mixture which, on the basis of past experience, would be expected to melt down to approximately the desired composition.
2. Calculate the gross chemical composition on the basis of the analysis of the ingredients of the charge.
3. Determine the net chemical composition expected in the cupola melt by making corrections for the changes in analysis anticipated during melting.
4. Adjust the original mixture by trial-and-error calculations until the computed net chemical composition falls within the desired range.

It is essential that the composition changes during melting be known if calculations are to be made. Some typical melting losses or gains are given in Table 19.8. The method of calculation is most simply explained by an example.

Table* 19.8 *Composition changes during cupola melting*

Element	Adjustment for melting loss or gain	Remarks
Silicon........	Deduct 10% of the gross % silicon charged	Silicon loss enters slag
Carbon.......	Add 10–20% of the gross % carbon to the gross value to obtain the net % carbon	Carbon pickup depends on many factors; see Refs. 1, 25
Manganese....	Deduct 15% of the gross % manganese charged	Manganese loss enters the slag
Phosphorus...	No loss or gain, except below 0.06%	
Sulfur........	Add 0.03–0.05% to the gross calculated value	Sulfur absorbed from coke and varies with melting practice
Chromium....	No loss or gain	
Nickel........	No loss or gain	

* The changes listed are not intended to be generally applicable. The actual factors for a given operation must be determined by trial and error.

Example. Assume that an iron having an analysis similar to SAE 111 (Table 21.4) is desired. More specifically, 3.40% C, 2.10% Si, 0.75% Mn, and 0.12% S max is to be the estimated analysis at the cupola spout. Materials available are those having the analysis given below:

Materials analysis

Material	C, %	Si, %	Mn, %	P, %	S, %
Pig iron........................	4.0	3.05	0.92	0.25	0.030
Cast scrap.....................	3.0	1.90	0.71	0.25	0.12
Remelt..........................	3.40	2.15	0.70	0.18	0.12
Steel scrap.....................	0.30	0.15	0.30	0.05	0.050
Silicon briquets.................	1 or 2 lb per briquet				
Manganese briquets..............	1 or 2 lb per briquet				

A charge of 35% pig, 25% remelt, 15% steel, and 25% cast scrap, adjusted with briquets, has been used previously.

Following step 1 above for silicon, the calculations (slide-rule) for a 1000-lb charge are as follows:

Pig iron	350 lb	× 0.0305	=	12.25 lb Si per charge
Remelt	250	× 0.0215	=	5.37
Cast scrap	250	× 0.0190	=	4.75
Steel*	150	× 0.0015	=	0.22
				22.59 total lb Si in the charge

$$\frac{22.59}{1000} \times 100 = 2.26\% \text{ Si in charge}$$

To obtain metal containing 2.10% Si at the spout, the charge must contain silicon above this level to allow for oxidation losses. Assuming approximately a 10% loss, silicon in the charge = 2.10/0.90 = 2.34%.

The value obtained for the charge above, 2.26%, is insufficient to allow for oxidation; so additional silicon is required, and may be added as silicon briquets.

One silicon briquet containing 1 lb of silicon is added to the charge; then the calculation is completed as follows:

$$\begin{aligned} \text{Total silicon in 1000-lb charge} &= 22.59 \text{ lb} \\ \text{Plus one silicon briquet} &= 1.00 \text{ lb} \\ \text{Total silicon} &= 23.59 \text{ lb} \\ \text{Gross percentage of charge } \frac{23.59}{1000} \times 100 &= 2.36\% \\ \text{Minus 10\% loss, } 2.36 \times 0.10 &= 0.24 \\ 2.36 - 0.24 &= 2.12\% \end{aligned}$$

The value calculated is actually in the low end of the desired analysis range and could be left that way to allow for ladle inoculation. Similar calculations may be performed for manganese and other elements where a known analysis change occurs during melting. Carbon in the charge is calculated by many cupola operators.[1,25] A method of calculation of estimated percentage carbon at the cupola spout under certain melting conditions involves use of the following formula:[25]

$$\text{Total C (spout)} = K + \tfrac{1}{2}\,(\%\text{ C in charge} - 2.00\%)$$

where Total C (spout) = per cent carbon in the iron at the cupola spout

K = a constant, empirically determined, but assumed to be 2.85% for an iron of 2.0% Si, 0.20% P, at the spout under melting conditions described in Ref. 25

% C in charge = per cent carbon in the cupola charge

* Si in steel may be considered negligible.

Since the percentage carbon in the melt at the spout decreases with increasing percentage silicon, correction for this factor may be made. This can be done by adding as a correction to total C at the spout the following formula: (2.00% − % Si at spout)0.25. The formula which may then be used becomes

$$\text{Total C (spout)} + (2.00\% - \%\ \text{Si at spout})0.25 = 2.85\% + \tfrac{1}{2}\,(\%\ \text{C in charge} - 2.0\%)$$

HEAT SHEET

Cupola ____________ Date ____________
No. charges ____________ Day ____________
Coke charge ____________ Heat No. ____________
Stone charge ____________

CHARGE

Materials	Wt.	C		Si		Mn		Others*		Remarks
		%	Lbs	%	Lbs	%	Lbs	%	Lbs	
Pig iron	350	4.0	14.00	3.05	12.25	0.92	3.22	0.03	0.105	
Pig iron										
Remelt	250	3.40	8.50	2.15	5.37	0.70	1.75	0.12	0.30	
Scrap	250	3.0	7.50	1.90	4.75	0.71	1.77	0.12	0.30	
Steel	150	0.30	0.75	0.15	0.22	0.15	0.22	0.05	0.075	
Silvery										
Si briquet	1 Briq				1.0					
Mn briquet	2 Briq						2.0			
Total lbs charged	1000		30.75		23.59		8.96		0.780	
% gross of charge		3.07		2.36		0.90		0.078		
Melting loss or gain		+0.34		−0.24		−0.14		+0.04		
Calculated analysis		3.41		2.12		0.76		0.118		

*Sulfur

CHEMICAL LABORATORY

Time	No.	Base	Alloy	Chemistry					Physicals		Remarks
				Si	Mn	C	S		Chill	Bhn	
8:00am	1	Spout	—	2.08	0.69	3.42	0.11		9/32	205	

***Fig.* 19.9** **Mixture sheet and cupola-operation record.**

For the problem discussed above and tabulated in Fig. 19.9, the calculation is as follows:

$$\text{Total C} + (2.00 - 2.12)0.25 = 2.85 + \tfrac{1}{2}\,(3.07 - 2.0)$$

$$\text{Total C} = 3.41\%$$

Other methods of carbon calculation are employed.[4] It must be realized that the calculation used must be suited to the type of melting operation carried out in the particular foundry where it is used.

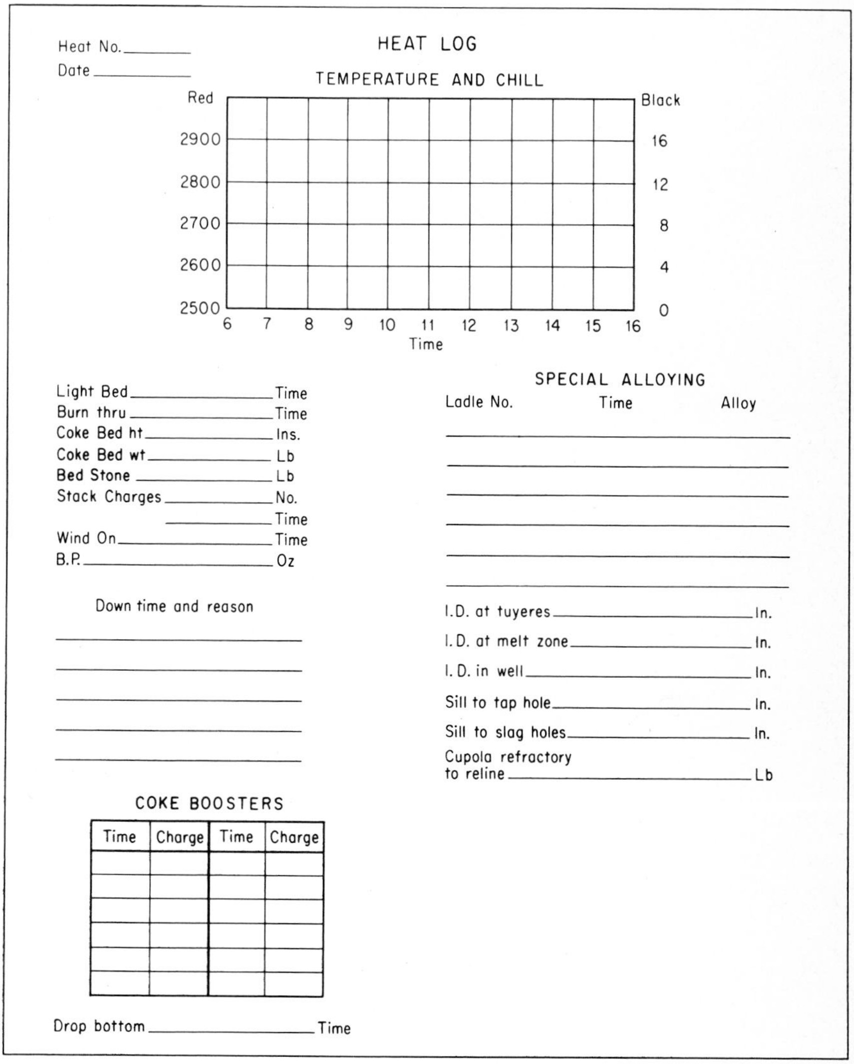

HEAT LOG

Heat No.________

Date________

TEMPERATURE AND CHILL

Light Bed________Time
Burn thru________Time
Coke Bed ht________Ins.
Coke Bed wt________Lb
Bed Stone________Lb
Stack Charges________No.
________Time
Wind On________Time
B.P.________Oz

Down time and reason

SPECIAL ALLOYING

Ladle No.	Time	Alloy

I.D. at tuyeres________In.
I.D. at melt zone________In.
I.D. in well________In.
Sill to tap hole________In.
Sill to slag holes________In.
Cupola refractory to reline________Lb

COKE BOOSTERS

Time	Charge	Time	Charge

Drop bottom________Time

***Fig.* 19.9** *Continued.*

Forms for mixture calculations are useful, and may serve as records of the entire cupola heat. The problem discussed above is completed on the mixture sheet shown in Fig. 19.9. The form shown in the figure provides a rather complete record of the entire cupola heat, as well as a form for making the mixture calculation.

Chill Control

Control of graphitizing tendency of the gray iron is an omnipresent problem in gray-iron melting. Chill testing is a procedure for evaluating to a degree the graphitizing tendency in the iron. A test sample of melt taken from the cupola spout or ladle is poured into a core-sand mold in which some sections are cooled more rapidly than others. Drawings of chill-test castings reproduced from Ref. 4 are illustrated in Fig. 19.10. A commonly used type of test is the flat bar (*a* in Fig. 19.10) with one edge cast against a chill plate. The depth of chill or white iron is measured in thirty-seconds of an inch. Of course, composition greatly influences chill depth, low carbon or silicon percentages in the iron causing

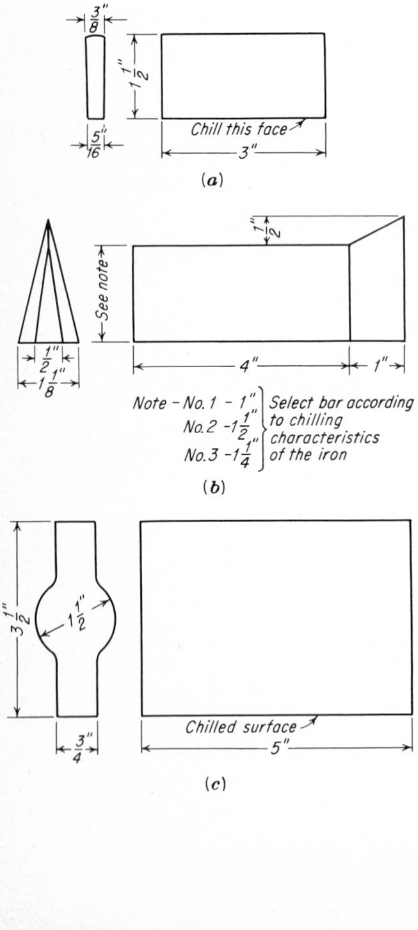

Fig. 19.10 Three types of chill castings.

a deep chill to develop. A relationship between chill depth and carbon equivalent is illustrated in Fig. 19.11. Fractured chill tests are shown in Fig. 19.12.

The chilling tendency of an iron may be greatly altered by the ladle additions of inoculants. An *inoculant* is defined as an addition to the ladle which produces major changes in graphite structure and chill depth

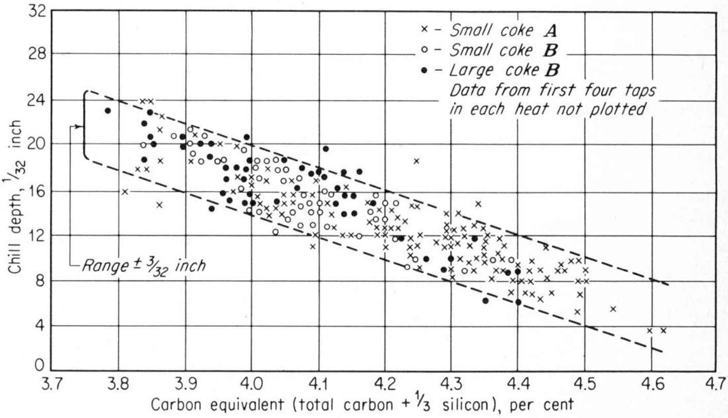

***Fig.* 19.11** Relationship of chill depth to carbon equivalent of iron melted with three cokes in a 10-in. cupola with coke ratios of 7.5:1 and blast rate of 12.5 lb air per min. (*From D. E. Krause.*[20])

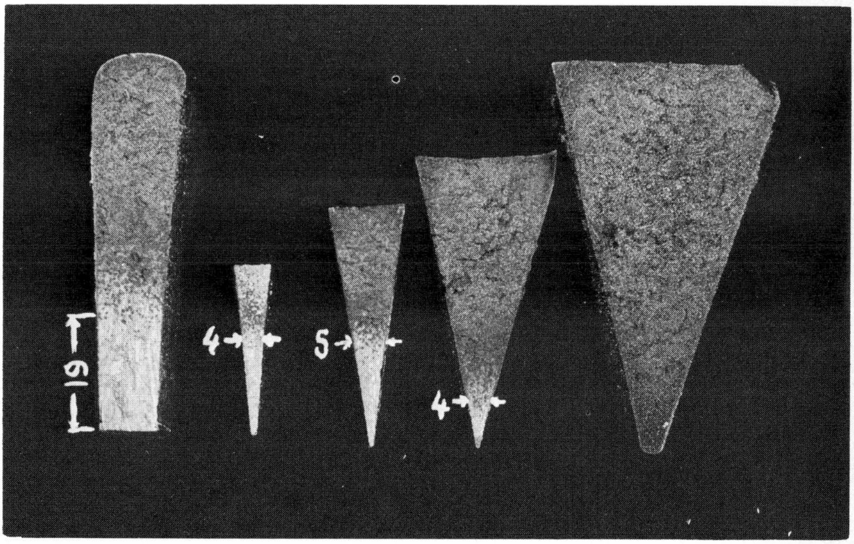

***Fig.* 19.12** Chill-test casting, showing appearance of fractured surface. (*From D. E. Krause.*)

not accountable by changes in normal chemical composition. Generally, it is desired to produce type A graphite and a controlled chill depth through ladle inoculation. In a particular foundry, it is possible to develop an inoculation schedule using ferrosilicon or some other inoculant as an addition to the ladle. The base-iron analysis of a particular operation will show a chill depth characteristic of its analysis. For example, base iron with an analysis corresponding to that of SAE 111 (Table 21.4) will have a chill depth of about $\frac{6}{32}$ to $\frac{9}{32}$ in. in the flat type of test bar A. A standard inoculation procedure to avoid chilled edges and hard spots in the iron might be adopted somewhat as follows:

Base-iron chill, thirty-seconds in.	Per cent inoculant*
6–8	0.10
8–10	0.15
10–12	0.25
12–16	0.33
Above 16	Melt should be pigged

* Weight percentage of ferrosilicon added to ladle. This inoculant schedule is intended to be illustrative only, and is not considered a standard practice.

The larger additions cause a significant change in iron analyses, and therefore the treatment should be called ladle addition rather than inoculation. The large additions compensate for analysis variations in the cupola metal, which should be avoided if possible. Melting of this type generally is aimed at producing iron at the spout which is slightly on the low side of the silicon specification range and adjusting the silicon and chill depth within the desired range by ladle additions. More uniform analyses and less fluctuation in chill depth *may* be obtained by the use of a mixing ladle or forehearth capable of holding several charges. A mixing ladle is especially convenient when continuous tapping is employed.

By chill testing, the graphitizing tendency and resultant properties of the iron may be made more consistent. A variety of inoculants and ladle additions can be used for these purposes. Table 19.9 lists a number of these materials. Some of the alloys in Table 19.9, such as those containing chromium, molybdenum, nickel, and vanadium, are mainly used for producing alloyed cast irons, whereas others are used specifically for inoculation. Inoculation of all the melt from each heat is a favored practice since there is the least danger from chilling, type D graphite, and undercooling during solidification of the gray iron. Furthermore,

Table 19.9 Nominal composition of alloying addition agents and inoculants

Name	C, %	Si, %	Mn, %	Zr, %	Ti, %	Al, %	Cr, %	Ni, %	Mo, %	Comments
75% ferrosilicon		73–78				1				3/8% by 12 mesh, inoculant
50% ferrosilicon		47–51				1.50–2				A low-aluminum grade may be obtained with 0.40% max
Silicon carbide										
SMZ		60–65	5–7	5–7						
Silicon briquet										1 or 2 lb of silicon per briquet
Manganese briquet										1 or 2 lb of manganese per briquet
Chromium briquet										2 lb Cr per briquet
Silicomanganese briquets										2 lb Si and 1/2 lb Mn per briquet
CMSZ-4	3–4.5	18–21	4–6	1.25–1.75			45–49			
Flake graphite	99%+									
Ca-Mn-Si		53–59	14–18							16–20% Ca
Ca-Si		60–65								30–33% Ca
Iron foundry ferrotitanium	0.03–0.10	20–23			20–23	0.5–1	0.1–0.8			
Foundry ferrochromium	4–6	6–9					62–66			6 mesh and finer
Ferromanganese			78–82							Less than 3/8-in. size if added to ladle
Ferromolybdenum									58–63	8- to 20-mesh size
Ferrovanadium	About 1	7–11								38–42% vanadium
Carbortam	4.5–7.5	2–4	0.3 max		15–21	1–2	0.3 max			1–2% boron
V-5		17–19	8–11				38–42			
Nisiloy		30						70		A low-melting-point eutectic alloy
Ni-shot								98		
Ferrophosphorus										20–25% phosphorus
Graphidox		48–32			9–11					5–7.0% Ca

certain low-carbon equivalent gray irons do not freeze completely gray unless they are heavily inoculated.[17]

Inoculation does not correct for all fluctuations in gray-iron properties because of the multitude of factors which influence chilling tendency.[4,20] However, it is a control measure which serves greatly to produce a more consistent quality. Furthermore, inoculated irons show generally improved mechanical properties over uninoculated irons.

Carbon-equivalent Meter

A recent and reliable means of rapidly evaluating the composition of gray iron is available in the carbon-equivalent meter.[28] This device is based on the change in thermal arrest temperature of the liquidus as a sample of molten cast iron freezes. This relationship is shown in Fig. 19.13. A simplified portion of the phase diagram for cast irons is shown in Fig. 19.13*a,* where composition is presented in terms of carbon equivalent (total carbon plus one-third silicon). The cooling curve of alloy S, Fig. 19.13*b*, shows the liquidus arrest at a temperature which can be correlated with the diagram of Fig. 19.13*a*. When cooling curves of this type are obtained in a reproducible manner, by using similar molds, thermocouples, thermocouple positioning, etc., the carbon-equivalent composition of the cast iron can be reliably determined. A relationship between liquidus arrest temperature and carbon equivalent is shown in Fig. 19.14. This relationship holds for most typical gray-iron analyses; however, similar curves can be obtained for other ranges of composition. It may also be noted that this method of obtaining a rapid evaluation of carbon equivalent appears to be more

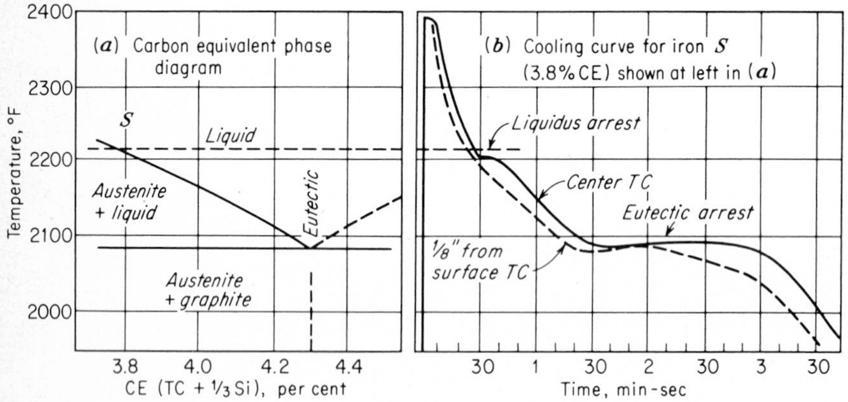

***Fig.* 19.13** **The relationship of the carbon-equivalent phase diagram in (*a*) to thermal arrests on the cooling curve in (*b*). (*From D. E. Krause.*[28])**

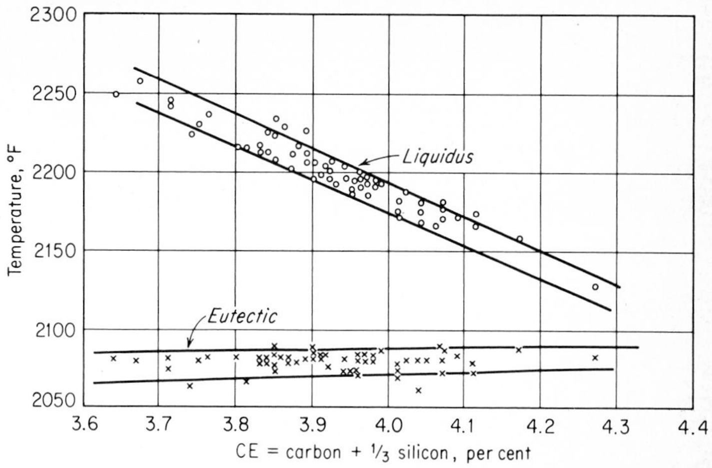

***Fig.* 19.14** **Correlation of liquidus and eutectic thermal arrest temperatures with carbon equivalent as determined by chemical analysis.** (*From D. E. Krause.*[28])

reliable than the chill-depth test discussed earlier (Fig. 19.11). A major reason for this is that many variables other than composition affect the chill depth.

In addition to chill tests and the use of the carbon-equivalent meter, other tests are often performed on the iron. Fluidity measurements may be taken at regular intervals. A fluidity test such as that discussed in Chaps. 20 and 23 may be employed. Fluidity tests, however, require accurate temperature measurements and are therefore difficult to obtain. Test bars for transverse and tensile properties are often poured at intervals throughout the heat. Brinell-hardness test blocks can be poured for rapid-hardness determinations. The aforementioned tests, however, are aimed more at determining the ability of the iron to meet mechanical specifications than as melting-control tests.

Slag Control

The cupola slag is often looked upon as a waste product of little significance and presenting only a materials-handling problem. In fact, the slag provides a measure of the results of the melting operation and, to a degree, a means of controlling metal composition. Slag effects include the following:

1. Controlled melting with normal oxidation is accompanied by the effluence of green or dark-green slags from the cupola.
2. Oxidizing melting conditions produce dark or black slags, and are accompanied by higher than normal melting losses.

3. Basic slags may be employed in basic-lined cupolas to produce low-sulfur- and high-carbon-content irons especially suited to nodular-iron production.

The principles relating to these effects of slags may be studied in Ref. 4 and other references given in the Bibliography.

Desulfurizing treatments are probably the best example of the influence of basic slags in lowering the sulfur content of the iron. Soda ash, sodium carbonate, and sodium oxide are added to the melt in a mixing ladle or forehearth. The soda ash may remove sulfur according to the following schedule:

	Sulfur, %			
Metal at spout	0.08	0.10	0.13	0.17
With 2 lb soda ash per ton	0.070	0.085	0.110	0.145
With 4 lb soda ash per ton	0.060	0.070	0.090	0.115
With 6 lb soda ash per ton	0.050	0.060	0.075	0.095

With sufficient contact time, the cupola spout metal will be reduced to the level shown above. If lower sulfur percentages are desired in the iron, basic cupola melting may be necessary.

Principles relating to basic melting and the effects of slags may be studied in Ref. 4 and other references given in the Bibliography.

Charging

Because of its influence on melting control, charging the cupola must itself be properly done. The pig iron, scrap, remelt, steel, etc., must be carefully segregrated in the foundry storage yard to maintain their identities. In some foundries the charge is made up and put into the cupola by hand. Mechanized foundries employ charging equipment which includes magnetic handling of the charge, weighing in buckets, and mechanical transfer into the cupola. A view of some charging equipment is illustrated in Fig. 19.15. A schematic layout of charging equipment is shown in Fig. 19.16. Distribution of material in the cupola by mechanical charging is important. A loose or open stack with channels through which the cupola gases may escape without proper reaction makes it difficult to keep melting in control. Channeling up the sides or through the stock permits the coke bed to burn out locally, causes melting outside the melting zone, and in general promotes poor melting conditions and nonuniform analysis. The type of charging bucket and emptying of the bucket are believed to influence profoundly the uniformity of melting. Several types of buckets are shown in Fig. 19.17. The cone bottom has been preferred by many operators

***Fig.* 19.15** Cupola yard crane and charging equipment. (*From R. J. Anderson, Trans. AFS, vol.* 61, 1953.)

because it is thought to give a charge more tightly packed around the outside of the cupola stack. A bucket having movable sides has been described in Ref. 3, and is said to have a similar charging effect. A uniformly packed stack, with limestone toward the center and density a little greater toward the outside of the stack so that the blast will penetrate to the center, is considered a desirable result from mechanical charging if it can be achieved. Skip-hoist chargers usually place the charge near one side and thus may promote channeling.

The cupola is usually operated with a full stack. However, as the contents settle below the charging-door sill, it is difficult to know when the next charge can be put in without actual observation. Since a low stack level changes the melting behavior of the cupola, constant observation is needed to keep the level up. Some magnetic and mechanical devices have been built which indicate the stack level to the charging crew, though these are not in general use.

Preheating Cupola Air

By preheating the cupola blast, the sensible-heat input into the cupola is increased, and less coke is required to produce a given quantity of molten metal at a given temperature. Data from actual foundry

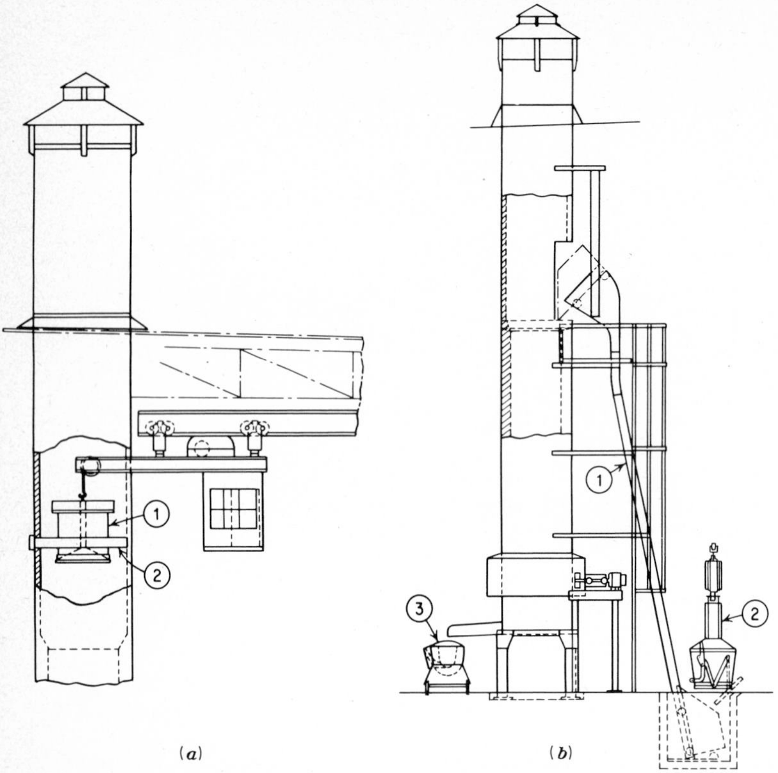

***Fig.* 19.16** (*a*) Diagram of charging equipment, with (1) bell-bottom charging bucket, and (2) device to hold bucket in discharge position; (*b*) charging equipment with (1) skip charger, (2) weigh lorry, and (3) holding U ladle. (*From H. W. Zimnawoda, Trans. AFS, vol.* 59, *p.* 56, 1951.)

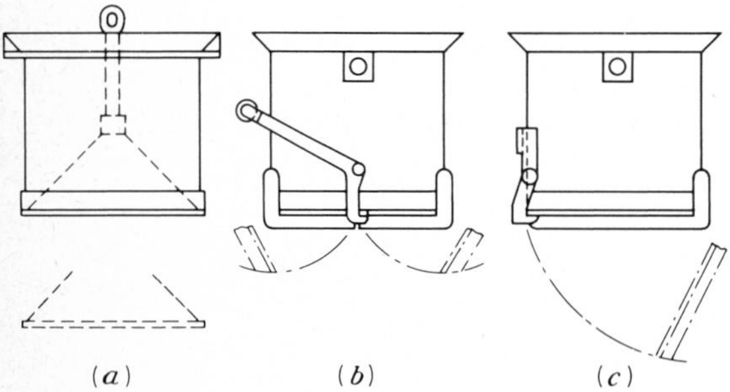

***Fig.* 19.17** Three types of charging buckets. (*a*) Cone-bottom, (*b*) double-door drop-bottom, (*c*) single-door drop-bottom.

operations have shown that when blast temperatures of moderate levels, 300 to 500 F, are used, resulting coke savings of 20 to 25 per cent may be obtained.[4] The hot-blast cupola may also be employed when the highest temperatures are necessary, as, for example, in iron piston rings. Air preheated to 400 to 1200 F serves to raise the metal temperature from the cupola 100 F or more over that obtained with a cold blast.

Other advantages include cupola operations due to the lack of bridging and tuyere plugging; lower sulfur pickup; decreased oxidation losses of silicon, manganese, iron, and other oxidation alloys; lower cupola refractory cost; and less use of fluxes.

The most widely used method for heating the cupola blast is the type shown in Fig. 19.18. This system makes use of both sensible and latent heat of the cupola gases. Separate air preheaters employing an external source of heat, gas, or oil fuel are also frequently used for this purpose. The principal advantage of externally fired units is that their operation is independent of cupola effluent-gas analyses and

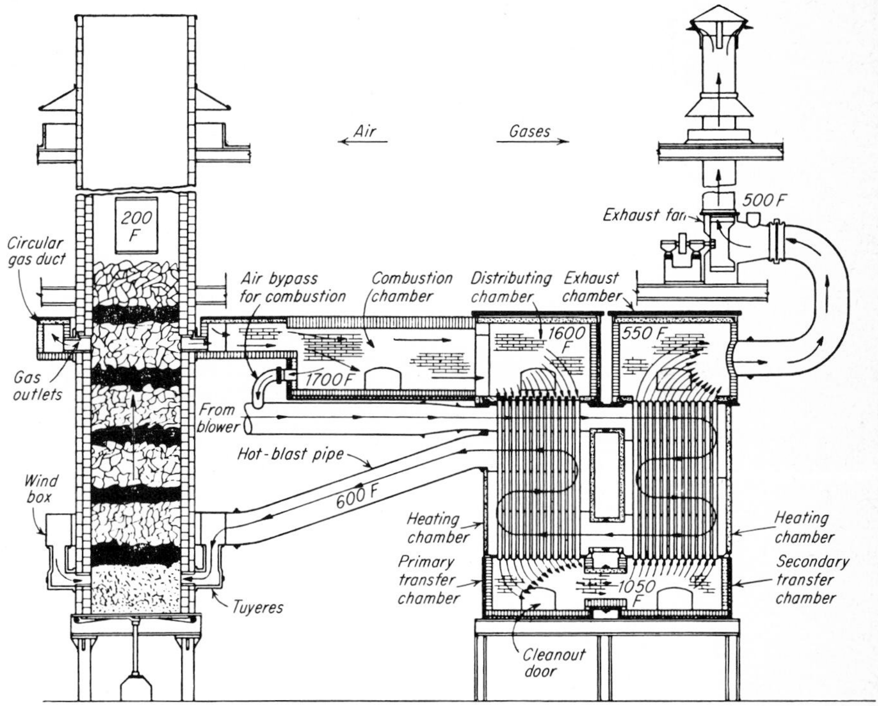

Fig. 19.18 Sectional view of hot-blast cupola of the Griffin type. (*From American Foundrymen's Society.*[4])

thus does not require control of cupola charges. At the same time the temperature of the preheated gas can be better controlled.

Pouring

Ladles should be clean and well preheated before use. New ladle linings or patching must be thoroughly dried at a red heat to avoid pickup of hydrogen by the iron and consequent defects. Typical ladle-lining mixtures are given in Ref. 4, and proprietary mixtures or ladle tiles are available in considerable variety.

Most gray-iron pouring is done with open or covered pot-type ladles. The capacities of various ladle sizes may be closely approximated by the use of the nomograph in Fig. 19.19. When alloy additions are required, they are made to the metal stream as the ladle is being filled. A maximum addition of 1.0 per cent by weight is recommended to avoid excessive cooling of the melt, although as much as 3 per cent can be added. "Over iron," that remaining in the ladle which is too cold or insufficient to pour a complete mold, should be pigged. Ladle heels, metal frozen in the ladle bottom and oxidized, injure the quality of the next melt poured into the ladle. Therefore ladles returning to the melting furnace for refilling should be completely empty. Uninterrupted pouring keeps the ladle hot and clean. However, slag accumulations do build up on ladle walls, and these should be frequently cleaned off and discarded.

Iron pourers may greatly influence casting quality. Interrupted pouring of a mold causes cold shuts and misruns. Pouring from excessive height may strain or crack the mold because of the pressures generated. Molds with thin sections often can be successfully run if the pourer fills the mold fast and with maximum pressure, whereas they may misrun if the pouring is done more slowly. This is particularly true if the gating is of questionable or borderline design. Some molds should not be poured below or above certain temperature ranges. Judicious pouring includes pouring the small castings first and heavier castings later as the metal cools in the ladle. Overfilling of molds may be harmful if it causes the molten iron to contact weights and freeze off risers and sprues needed for feeding.

CHEMICAL PRINCIPLES OF CAST-IRON MELTING

Many of the principles of chemical-composition changes during the melting of gray cast irons can be delineated. Although much of the high-temperature chemistry of molten metal, slags, and atmospheres is

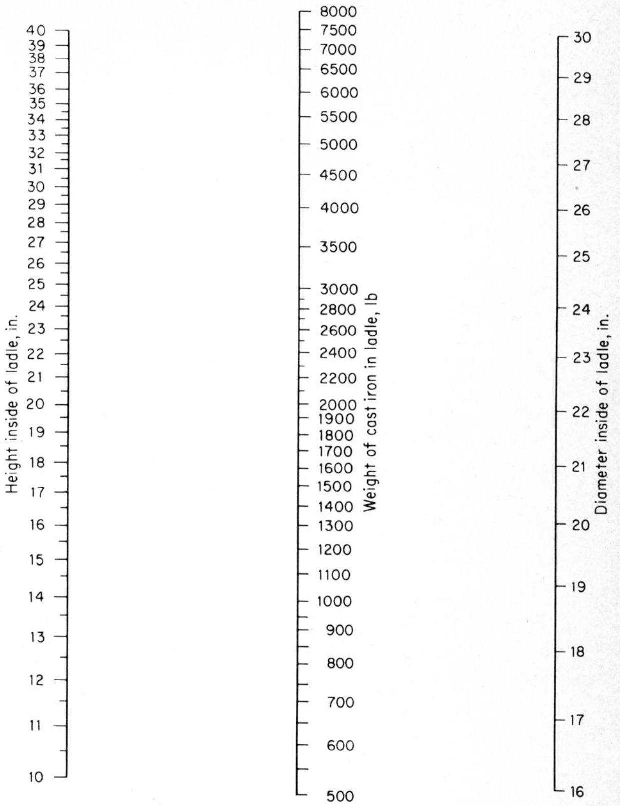

***Fig.* 19.19** Nomograph for determining the capacity of iron-foundry ladles. *Example:* Height inside ladle, 24 in.; diameter inside ladle, 18 in. Lay a straightedge from height (24 in.) to diameter (18 in.), and read iron capacity of ladle in pounds where straightedge intersects the weight scale, or weight, 1600 lb. (*From H. L. Campbell, Am. Foundryman, vol.* 15, *June,* 1949.)

known, the circumstances of cupola, air-furnace, arc-furnace, or induction melting require special interpretation of the principles.

Types of Chemical Reactions

Two principal types of chemical reactions, oxidizing and reducing, are encountered during the melting of cast irons. Some typical ones are as follows:

1. *Oxidizing reactions*
   a. $\underline{C} + O_2(g) = CO_2(g)$
   b. $\underline{2C} + O_2(g) = 2CO(g)$

c. $\underline{Si} + 2\underline{O} = SiO_2(s)$
d. $\underline{Si} + x$FeO (slag, solid) $= y$FeO · SiO_2 (slag) + 2Fe
e. $\underline{Mn}$ + FeO (slag, solid) = MnO(l) + Fe

2. *Reducing reactions*
a. SiO_2 (solid, refractory, slag) + $2\underline{C} = \underline{Si} + 2CO(g)$
b. MnO (liquid, slag) + $\underline{C} = \underline{Mn} + CO(g)$
c. Al_2O_3 (solid) + $3\underline{C} = 2\underline{Al} + 3CO(g)$

When the symbol is underlined in the above equations, it refers to the element dissolved in the molten iron.

All the aforementioned reactions are of course influenced by temperature and concentration.

Effects of Temperature

Temperatures encountered in gray-iron melting extend from room temperature to about 3500 F. Marked changes in chemical reactions occur over this temperature range. Oxidation reactions are usually considered to progress more readily with increasing temperature, although this concept is strictly true only for reactions involving carbon. If thermodynamic principles are employed, a clearer picture of the influence of temperature on the reactions may be obtained. Table 19.10 lists the free-energy equations for a number of the important reactions. Derivation of these equations will not be considered here (see Chap. 16 on Steel Melting). A few of the equations, however, are presented in graphical form in Fig. 19.20, on which is shown a plot of free energy of the reaction against temperature. Higher negative free-energy change implies greater spontaneity of reaction. On the graph, a line with negative slope indicates decreasing reaction tendency with increasing temperature. Thus the tendency of oxidation of silicon and manganese by oxygen decreases with temperature increase. Carbon, on the other hand, oxidizes more readily with increasing temperature. Furthermore, reduction of oxides of silicon and manganese by carbon occurs more readily as temperature increases.

As the result of these relationships, silicon and manganese are lost primarily at low temperatures during melting, under 2600 F, and carbon is lost at higher temperatures. A gain in silicon, silicon pickup, in the iron occurs at high temperature because of the ability of carbon to reduce silica. These composition trends may be most readily observed in induction-furnace melting of cast irons. Figure 19.21 illustrates composition changes in molten cast iron at various temperatures. The pronounced influence of temperature on carbon losses and silicon pickup is evident in Fig. 19.21. The influence of temperature on the formation of oxides may be readily observed by noting the melt surface

Table 19.10 ***Representative reactions in melting of ferrous alloys***

Reaction	$\Delta F°^{*} = \Delta H - T\,\Delta S$	Notes		K, 1600 C
Oxidation				
1. $\underline{C} + FeO(l) = Fe(l) + CO(g)$	$+20{,}390 - 21.03T$	For $FeO(l)$ and molten iron at 1600 C, $\Delta F° = -18520$ for 1, for 2 at 1600 C, $\Delta F° = -24{,}430$		
2. $\underline{C} + \underline{O} = CO(g)$	$-8510 - 7.52T$	Oxidation tendency increases with temp increase; $\underline{O}$ in iron		
3. $\underline{Si} + \underline{2O} = SiO_2(s)$	$-119{,}180 + 43.7T$	Oxidation tendency decreases with temp increase; $\Delta F° = -37{,}380$		$1/K = \frac{1}{5} \times 10^{-4}$
4. $\underline{Mn} + \underline{O} = MnO(l)$	$-59{,}100 + 26.97T$	Oxidation tendency decreases with temp increase; $\Delta F° = -9000$		
5. $\underline{2Al} + \underline{3O} = Al_2O_3(s)$	$-300{,}620 + 97.8T$	Oxidation tendency decreases with temp but high $-\Delta F$ at 1600C shows high affinity for oxygen		$1/K = 7 \times 10^{-13}$
6. $\underline{Si} + 4FeO(l) = 2FeO_1SiO_2(l) + 2Fe(l)$	$\Delta F° = -32{,}580$	Oxidation increases with temp decrease		
7. $Fe(l) + O = FeO(l)$	$-28{,}900 + 12.51T$	Oxidation increases with decreasing temp $\Delta F° = -5400$		
Reduction				
$\underline{C} + FeO(l) = Fe + CO(g)$	$+20{,}390 - 21.03T$	Reduction increases with temp increase	$T_e† = 1285$ F	
$\underline{C} + MnO(l) = Mn + CO(g)$	$+50{,}590 - 34.49T$	Reduction increases with temp increase	$T_e = 2178$ F	32.18
$\underline{2C} + SiO_2(s) = \underline{Si} + 2CO(g)$	$+102{,}160 - 58.70T$	Reduction increases with temp increase	$T_e = 2671$ F	8.29

* Cal/g-atom at 1% concentration at 1600 C.

† T_e = equilibrium temp.

Values of equilibrium constant K from R. W. Gurry, The Relative Deoxidizing Power of Boron in Liquid Steel and the Elimination of Boron in the Open Hearth Process, *Metals Technol. Tech. Pub.* 1641, December, 1943.

$K = 3.56 \times 10^{-16} = \%O \times \%Al^{2/3}$

$K = 2.67 \times 10^{-4} = \%O \times \%Ti^{1/2}$

$K = 2.52 \times 10^{-3} = \%O \times \%V^{2/3}$

$K = 1.62 \times 10^{-5} = \%O \times \%Zr^{1/2}$

$K = 0.006 = \%O \times \%Si^{1/2}$, Koerber and Oelsen; $0.0015 = \%O \times \%Si^{1/2}$, Darken (after Gurry)

$K = 1.07 \times 10^{-5} = \%O \times \%B^{2/3}$

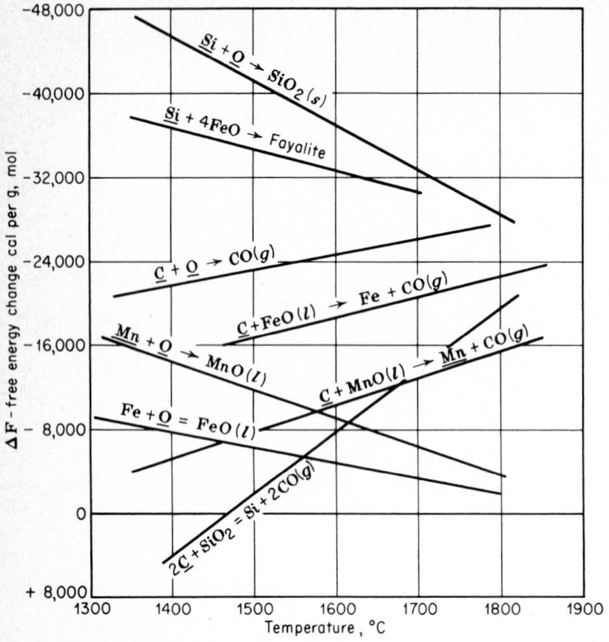

***Fig.* 19.20** Approximate free-energy changes of some iron-melting reactions as a function of temperature. Symbols underlined are elements dissolved in iron at standard concentrations of 1 per cent. Negative values indicate that spontaneous reaction is likely to occur.

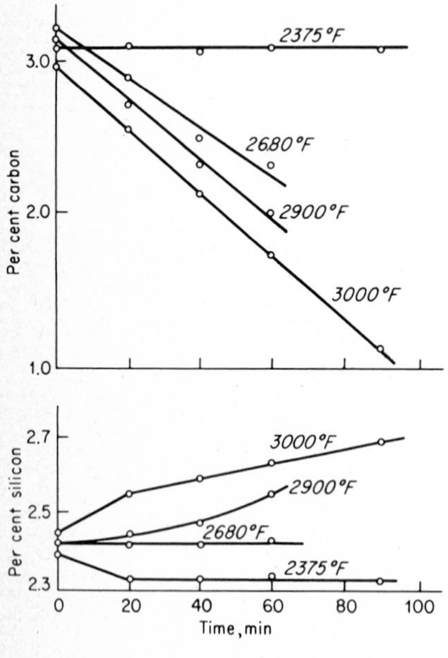

***Fig.* 19.21** Curves showing changes of carbon and silicon percentages in molten cast iron held at the temperatures indicated in a silica crucible in contact with air in an induction-melting furnace. (*From R. W. Heine.*[22])

during melting. At high temperatures where carbon is capable of reducing oxides, no slag scum forms and the melt surface is clear. As the iron cools, carbon loses its reducing power and a slag scum will form and cover the surface. Oxide formation proceeds readily, as evidenced by the appearance of the slag, which is an iron silicate. The aforementioned facts readily explain the nature of the curves in Fig. 19.21.

Effect of Concentration

The reactions under discussion are concentration-dependent as well as being influenced by temperature. Type of refractory, acid or base, slag composition, gas atmospheres, and melt composition become especially important when the composition factor is considered. In the usual case, irons are melted in furnaces having linings made of acid refractories and in contact with acid slags. At high temperatures, silica reduction becomes important. The concentration of silica and of silicon and carbon in the iron may be related by the chemical equilibrium constant as follows:

$$SiO_2(s) + \underline{2C} = \underline{Si} + 2CO(g)$$

$$K = \frac{\underline{Si} \times (CO)^2}{SiO_2(s) \times \underline{C}^2}$$

The K value may be calculated thermodynamically[22] for various temperatures with the results tabulated:

Temp		K value
C	F	
1400	2552	0.31
1466	2671	1.0
1500	2732	1.76
1600	2912	8.29

Using the equilibrium constant, equilibrium-concentration curves may be plotted for various temperatures, as has been done in Fig. 19.22. Certain limitations inherent in thermodynamic calculations apply to Fig. 19.22. However, the graph shows very nicely the directions of composition changes in molten irons at various temperatures. An iron of 3.50% C and 2.30% silicon at 2372 F lies to the right of the concentration curve for that temperature. It therefore contains an excess

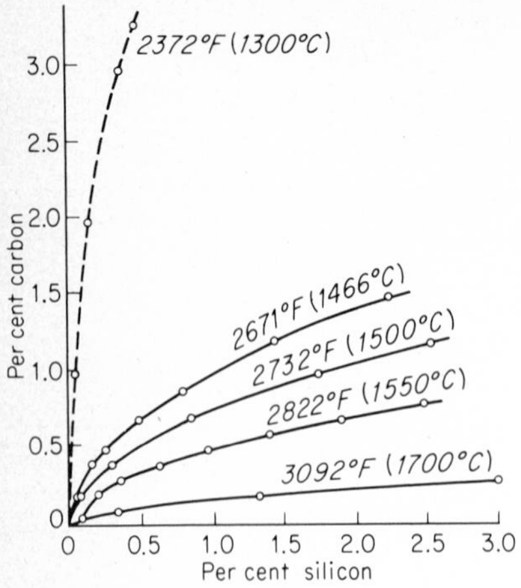

***Fig.* 19.22** Calculated equilibrium concentration of percentage carbon and silicon for $SiO_2(s) + 2\underline{C} = \underline{Si} + 2CO(g)$ in molten iron-carbon-silicon alloys contained in a silica crucible under 1 atm pressure of the CO. Solid curves indicate temperatures at which silica reduction will occur spontaneously if an excess of carbon is present. (*From R. W. Heine.*[22])

of silicon, and would not pick up silicon from a refractory or slag. With the iron at 2822 F, however, the composition lies to the left of the concentration curve and therefore contains an excess of carbon. Silica reduction will occur and the iron will gain silicon, if a sufficient supply of silica is available, from the refractory or slag. These facts were illustrated in Fig. 19.21.

The temperature at which the change from oxidation of silicon to reduction of silica occurs may be calculated for standard concentrations. Table 19.10 gives this temperature as 2671 F for silica and 2178 F for manganese oxide. Thus melting temperatures span the range of the two types of reactions. At high temperatures, above 2700 F, the iron will pick up both silicon and manganese if their oxides are available in sufficient concentration for reduction by carbon. With slags and refractories there usually is an adequate supply of silica but not of manganese oxide available for such reduction, and so only silicon pickup occurs. Concentration of carbon, silicon, manganese, silica, and manganese oxides and temperature of the melting environment are primary factors in weight-composition changes.

Effects of Iron Oxide

Oxidation may originate from several sources. Air or carbon dioxide may be oxidizing to a molten iron. Iron oxide is also oxidizing, and it occurs in slags or as rust in the charge, or it may form by reaction of iron with oxygen. The source of oxidation must be looked upon as a major factor in determining iron-composition changes. Oxidation of silicon by iron differs from other sources of oxidation in that it is relatively insensitive to temperature.[21] Silicon losses caused by reaction with iron oxide occur as readily at high temperature as they do at low. It has been proved that iron oxide in slags, as rust, or generated in any other way will cause silicon and manganese oxidation losses from cast irons even at high temperatures where these losses would not normally occur because of the protective action of carbon.[21]

Melting Down

In any type of furnace, the iron passes through a melting-down stage at temperatures up to about 2300 F. During this period furnace gases such as oxygen and carbon dioxide are important, whether in cupola, air furnace, or induction furnace, because they can form an iron oxide–rich skin on the iron. As the metal liquefies, silicon and manganese are oxidized by the aforementioned iron oxide. Rust initially present in the charge also contributes to this source of oxidation. Table 19.11 compares silicon losses from rusty and clean scrap during induction melting. The table also reveals that the oxidation loss during melt-down carries through the entire course of the heat.

Table* 19.11 *Effect of rust on analysis of melt*

Material	Clean scrap		Rusty scrap	
Sample during melting and heating	C, %	Si, %	C, %	Si, %
Melting stock	3.40	2.60	3.35	2.56
2375 F	3.28	2.42	3.20	2.38
2680 F, 0 min	3.27	2.42	3.16	2.36
2900 F, 0 min	3.21	2.47	2.94	2.30
2900 F, 60 min	Pickup in 60 min = 0.13 % Si		Pickup in 60 min = 0.13 % Si	

* Silica crucible, induction melting.

Considering the temperature effects, one may state that the losses of silicon and manganese, about 0.10 to 0.30 per cent, in induction and air-furnace melting occur during melting down. An added feature occurs in the cupola, since iron droplets must pass through an ascending gas stream and also a slag containing iron oxide. An oxidizing slag can cause silicon losses at high temperatures where silica reduction will occur simultaneously with the loss. The net change in analysis, a loss or gain, depends upon which reaction predominates. Oxidizing conditions during melting down thus favor increased silicon and manganese losses through an increased concentration of iron oxide in the melting environment.

During the meltdown, the molten cast iron is covered with a saturated, solid, flaky iron silicate slag.[21,22] At a certain temperature, the slag disappears because of the reducing power of carbon. For an iron containing about 2.40% Si and 3.40% C, this temperature of slag-scum disappearance is about 2550 F in a CO_2 or air atmosphere. However, the temperature of slag disappearance varies with carbon and silicon concentration, gas atmosphere, and refractory type. Appearance of the slag is a significant fact: It means silicon is likely to be oxidized from the iron. The same slag also forms when molten irons are cooled from high to low temperatures.

High-temperature Melting

Holding the molten iron at elevated temperatures, 2700 to 3200 F, is accompanied by well-defined composition changes. Molten cast irons decarburize rapidly at temperatures above about 2550 F during induction melting when CO_2 or air is the furnace atmosphere. Decarburization is illustrated graphically in Fig. 19.21. No silicon or manganese losses will occur at high temperatures, 2700 F and above, unless iron oxide is introduced from some source.[21] Carbon dioxide, even at 100 per cent concentration, will not cause silicon loss.[23] Nor will raw air, unless it is directed at the melt surface at a high enough rate. Raw air will then react with the molten iron to form FeO, and thus an iron silicate slag by reaction of silicon with the iron oxide. Silicon oxidation under these extreme conditions is accompanied by manganese loss in the ratio of about 10:4 points percentagewise and formation of a slag cover on the molten-iron surface.

Rate of decarburization at high temperatures is mainly affected by the rate of change of the atmosphere if CO_2 or air exists over the melt surface. Oxidation by CO_2 is an endothermic reaction and is thus much milder than air oxidation, which is exothermic.

Silica reduction and silicon pickup by the iron are additional features of high-temperature melting when silica is available, as in acid slags and refractories. This was illustrated in Fig. 19.21. The gross pickup of silicon is of course counterbalanced by some oxidation when iron oxide is present. A high-iron-oxide slag may cause a net loss of silicon, whereas low-iron-oxide slags may cause no loss or even permit a gain.[21] Highly reducing conditions, for example, the presence of coke and high temperatures, will cause a most rapid increase of silicon content of the iron.[21]

The application of these principles to malleable-iron-foundry melting in air furnaces has been well proved.[22] Pickup of silicon between preliminary and final chemical analyses for a number of air-furnace white-iron heats is shown in Fig. 19.23. The total pickup occurs over a period of 1 to 1½ hr as the temperature rises from about 2650 F, reaches

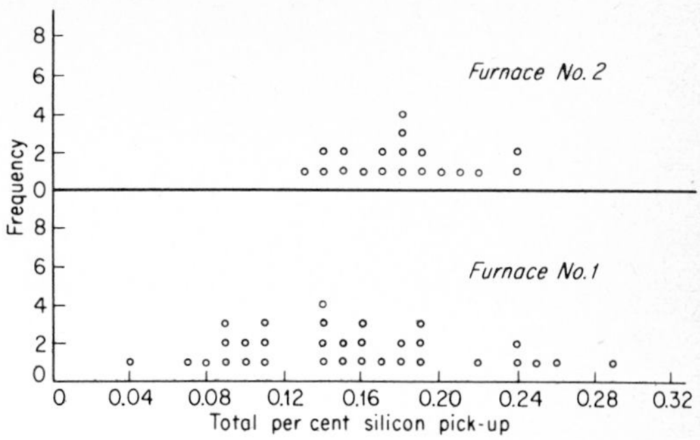

***Fig.* 19.23** Frequency of percentage silicon pickup in 51 heats made in air furnaces. Silicon pickup refers to net total increase from preliminary test to tail end of heat. (*From R. W. Heine.*[22])

2800 to 2900 F, and remains in this range. Silicon pickup no doubt also occurs in cupola melting, but is masked by the complexity of other factors involved.

Principles of changes in chemical composition during melting of cast irons with reference to cast irons have been described for C, Si, and Mn. Oxidation-reduction-type reactions also apply in the case of aluminum, titanium, and the other elements. These elements are readily oxidizable during most melting operations. It is known, however, that carbon in cast iron can reduce aluminum oxides at high temperatures and result in an aluminum residual in the iron. Both aluminum and titanium may carry through the melting process from scrap materials because of the protective action of carbon. The principles of reactions, temperature, and concentration effect are applicable to many of the elements, although much remains to be learned in the case of the less common elements.

AIR-FURNACE MELTING

Cast irons are melted in the air furnace as well as in the cupola. Since this furnace is most commonly used in malleable-iron foundries, air-furnace melting is discussed in Chap. 23, dealing with that type of iron.

BIBLIOGRAPHY

1. W. W. Levi, Operation of the Cupola, *Trans. AFS,* vol. 58, p. 1, 1950.
2. S. F. Carter, Basic Lined Cupola for Iron Melting, *Trans. AFS,* vol. 58, p. 376, 1950.
3. R. W. Heine, Cupola Charge Calculation, *Foundry,* vol. 76, February, 1948.
4. American Foundrymen's Society, "The Cupola and Its Operation," 1946, 1954.
5. B. P. Mulcahy, The Cupola: Its Raw Materials and Operation, *Foundry,* vol. 78, p. 77, February–March, 1950; first of a series of articles.

6. H. W. Lownie, Jr., Ladle Inoculation Improves Gray Iron Properties and Structure, *Foundry,* vol. 71, November–December, 1943.
7. W. R. Jaeschke, Development of Cupola Melting Equipment, *Trans. AFS,* vol. 62, pp. 339–353, 1954.
8. C. R. Loper, Jr., Design of a Gas Fired Cupola, *Trans. AFS,* vol. 70, pp. 531–536, 1962.
9. American Foundrymen's Society, "Cast Metals Handbook," 4th ed., 1944.
10. D. E. Krause and H. W. Lownie, Jr., Blast Humidity as a Factor in Cupola Operation, *Trans. AFS,* vol. 57, 1949.
11. E. Loebbecke, Hot Blast Cupola, *Trans. AFS,* vol. 64, pp. 171–196, 1956.
12. W. L. Heinrichs, Hot-blast Cupola Practice, *Trans. AFS,* vol. 64, pp. 532–542, 1956.
13. D. E. Krause and H. W. Lownie, Jr., A Survey of Foundry Coke Characteristics, *Trans. AFS,* vol. 55, 1947.
14. S. A. Herres and C. H. Lorig, Cupola Blast Control, *Am. Foundryman,* vol. 13, September, 1942.
15. "Symposium on Malleable Iron Melting," American Foundrymen's Society, reprint 43-47, 1943.
16. W. N. Witheridge, Cupola Dust Collection, *Foundry,* vol. 78, February–March, 1950.
17. A. Finlayson, Casting Diesel Engine Crankshafts in Gray Iron, *Foundry,* vol. 78, August–September, 1950.
18. D. E. Krause, C. T. Greenidge, and H. W. Lownie, How Iron and Steel Melt in a Cupola, *Trans. AFS,* vol. 60, 1952.
19. R. J. Taylor, How Thermocouples in the Stack Control Cupola Melting, *Am. Foundryman,* vol. 21, no. 6, p. 46, December, 1952.
20. D. E. Krause, Chill Tests and the Metallurgy of Gray Iron, *Trans. AFS,* vol. 59, p. 79, 1951.
21. E. A. Lange and R. W. Heine, Some Effects of Temperature and Melting Variables on Chemical Composition and Structure of Gray Irons, *Trans. AFS,* vol. 59, 1951.
22. R. W. Heine, Oxidation-Reduction Principles Controlling the Composition of Molten Cast Iron, *Trans. AFS,* vol. 59, 1951.
23. Whiting Corp., "Useful Information for Foundrymen," 1946.
24. D. Fleming, The Controlled-slag Hot-blast Cupola, *Trans. AFS,* vol. 66, pp. 113–124, 1958.
25. W. W. Levi, Carbon Control in the Cupola, *Am. Foundryman,* October, 1947.
26. H. E. Henderson, Acid Cupola Melting for Ductile Iron, *Trans. AFS,* vol. 67, pp. 661–668, 1959.
27. J. T. Williams, Basic Cupola Melting of Ductile Iron, *Trans. AFS,* vol. 67, pp. 669–670, 1959.
28. D. E. Krause, Rapid Control Test for Carbon Equivalent, *Foundry,* May, 1962.

20

Gray-iron Foundry Practice

Because of a fortunate combination of engineering properties, availability, excellent casting characteristics, and favorable cost, gray irons are produced in tonnages exceeding all other castings. The basic foundry operations of patternmaking, molding, coring, sand conditioning, melting, cleaning, etc., have been highly developed because of the tremendous amount of material and work involved in gray-iron-castings production. In fact, it is undoubtedly true that much of the engineering and mechanization which has developed in the foundry industry came through the needs for these improvements in order to meet the production demand of manufacturers for gray-iron castings. To a great extent, the automotive, truck, bus, and tractor industries were directly and indirectly responsible for these developments over the period of about 1915 to the present. Each of the millions of passenger cars presently in use has about 600 to 700 lb of gray-iron castings in its structure. Add the quantity in operating trucks, buses, and tractors, and it is evident that this industry alone accounts for a phenomenal consumption of gray-iron castings. Similar accounts might be cited in other manufacturing fields. The production of gray-iron castings is, in fact, such a large industry that twice as much gray iron is cast annually as all other cast metals combined. To supply this tremendous quantity of castings, all the casting processes discussed in Chap. 3 may be employed except die casting and plaster molding. Some of the specialized techniques of these processes as applied in gray-iron foundry practice are considered in this chapter.

MOLDING

Among the sand-casting processes, green-sand molding is the method most commonly practiced. The molding and other equipment discussed in Chap. 4 are employed, and to a large degree the foundries are modernized and mechanized.

The characteristics of molding sands have been discussed in Chap. 5. Of course, sand practice and related operations are carried out with due consideration for the unique properties of gray iron. Some examples of system sands for light and medium gray-iron castings are given in Table 20.1. These sands have been successfully used for producing many castings. The properties of green compression and shear strength, dry compression strength, permeability, moisture content, and others have not been given in Table 20.1 because they can be so greatly altered by variations in rebonding addition, moisture, the special additives, mixing, and molding methods. Almost any values can be obtained, depending on how the various factors are put together. It may be noted in Table 20.1 that in addition to features of thermal stability, reuse, and moldability, ease of cleaning and surface finish are considered highly important in molding sand mixtures.

When gray-iron castings are cooled sufficiently and shaken out, they may under proper sand conditions separate cleanly from the sand. Then the sand is said to "peel" from the casting. Little burned-on sand needs to be removed from the casting surface, and the work spent on cleaning is at a minimum. Light castings cool so quickly that there is insufficient temperature rise to permit the sand to burn onto the casting. When the sand is heated up to temperatures over 1500 F, however, the possibility of chemical reaction between metal and sand, fusion of the sand, and firm adherence of the fused-on material to the metal increases. The sand mixture may be modified to prevent or reduce the amount of fused-on sand-reaction products. Sea coal, gilsonite, coke, graphite, pitch, and other petroleum-base materials may be added to the sand for this purpose. Their effectiveness depends on producing reducing atmospheres in the mold or in preventing the oxidation reactions which occur when sand fuses to the iron.

Sea coal[3] is very commonly employed for improved casting finish and peel (see Chap. 5 for its characteristics). Amounts of 2 to 8 per cent by weight have been found beneficial. The appearance of the casting is the best criterion of the sea-coal percentage which should be maintained in the sand. Excessive sea coal can cause blow defects from the volatile constituents evolved on heating. The approach to this condition is often forecast by the appearance of a blue finish on castings when they are shaken out. The percentage of sea coal in the sand is kept up to the desired level by additions to the sand mixers during each cycle of reuse. The actual percentage in the sand may be estimated by running a proximate analysis on the dry sand to determine the percentage of volatile material and the percentage lost on ignition. Dead sea coal which has no volatile matter in it may be an undesirable ingredient in the sand since its ability to promote peel is low.

Gilsonite is another material used to improve casting finish. This asphalt-base mineral is almost completely volatile. Hence smaller percentages are used in the sand, 0.25 to 0.75 per cent, depending on casting size. The gilsonite is added during each cycle of reuse in amounts sufficient to keep the percentage at a level which gives a good casting finish, for example, 0.50 per cent. The amount in the sand

Table* 20.1 *Sands for gray-iron castings

Properties	General-purpose system sand*	General-purpose system sand†	General-purpose system sand‡
Sand base	Silica sand cores mainly	60% lake sand, AFS 52–58; 40% bank sand, AFS 90–100	Silica sand
Sieve analysis on 6 mesh			
12			
20	0.8	0.08	0.10
30	1.6	0.41	0.20
40	6.8	1.43	2.04
50	16.4	10.20	15.50
70	25.5	32.81	34.12
100	22.0	37.28	29.53
140	15.4	11.80	12.75
200	3.7	4.42	4.20
270	0.4	0.76	0.90
Pan	0.4	0.80	0.63
Total	93.0	99.99§	99.97§
Clay, %	7.0	6.0	7-8.0
AFS No.	62.0		
Rebonding clay	Western bentonite	Western or southern bentonite	Blend of western and southern bentonite
Special additives:			
a. Expansion control	Wood flour, cereal	Wood flour	Wood flour, 5–7.0% combustibles in sand
b. Finish	Sea coal	Carbonaceous facing	Gilsonite, 0.4–0.60% in sand
c. Strength in large molds	Pitch		
Rebonding, per 2000-lb batch	....	6 qt bentonite for heavy work, 1 qt for light work	3 qt southern, 4 qt western for medium work; 3 qt southern for light work but depends on core dilution

* From E. W. Fry.[1]
† From R. Clark.[2]
‡ Authors' experience.
§ Clay-free basis.

mixture may be determined by extraction since the material is soluble in a 50% carbon tetrachloride–50% benzol solution. Other materials such as soluble petroleum-base pitch dissolved in organic solvents, pulverized coke, and pitch may be employed to favor free shakeout of sand from castings. Recently, wood flours, treated with oils which volatilize, have been advocated as a means of combining the functions of expansion control and ease of cleaning.

Of course, the grain size basic to the sand mixture has a profound influence on the casting finish. Amounts of 6-, 12-, 20-, 30-, 40-, and 50-mesh sand grains in excess of about 15 per cent of the total promote a rough surface. Excessive fines, 270-mesh, pan, and finer sizes may reduce the ease of molding and permeability, and increase expansion difficulties, all of which can cause surface roughness or defects. These sand-grain effects are operative in spite of the use of sand additives to promote peel.

Mold coatings (Chap. 5) may also be employed to improve surface finish. Graphite coatings sprayed or swabbed onto the mold cavity and then dried are widely used.

GATING AND RISERING

Regardless of the most favorable sand conditions and good molding, casting quality may be improved or the castings ruined, depending on the gating system employed in the mold. The general principles of gating and feeding have been discussed in Chap. 9. Certain metallurgical characteristics make for specialized practices of gating peculiar to gray iron. These characteristics include:

1. Fluidity characteristics of the iron
   a. Relationships of superheat to pouring and liquidus temperatures
   b. Composition factors
2. Shrinkage characteristics
3. Relationship of gating design to:
   a. Time of pouring the casting
   b. Feeding of the casting
   c. Thermal-gradient effects
4. Mold effects as related to the iron

Fluidity of Gray Iron

Fluidity of molten gray irons is of principal interest in thin section castings having sufficient surface area so that it is difficult to avoid misruns. The gating system is then designed to introduce the melt into the mold cavity as rapidly and uniformly as possible at a number of locations in the mold cavity so that the metal will not freeze off until the mold cavity is completely filled. Cover castings, housings, and similar castings present a large surface for cooling the melt and can cause freeze-offs before the cavity is full. Where this problem is encountered in varying degree it is in part blamed on the gating and often, because it is less understood, on the fluidity of the melt.

Fluidity of molten gray irons, described in terms of the spiral-fluidity test (Fig. 21.7) as inches of spiral length for a given chemical composition and pouring temperature, has been established, and is presented in formula form in Chap. 21 and graphically in Fig. 8.19. These data show that decreasing carbon and silicon contents, low pouring temperature, and hypereutectic iron all result in a low fluidity. From a practical viewpoint, however, maximum fluidity can be obtained more readily by pouring at high temperature rather than overstressing the composition factor. In general, the composition of gray irons is limited to the kind in production by the foundry, for example, those in Table 21.1. A carbon increase of 0.15 to 0.20 per cent in the hypoeutectic range will increase fluidity only about 1 in. However, an increase of temperature of 20 F will increase fluidity 1 in. over most of the temperature range for pouring. The fluid life of the metal covers the temperature range of the maximum reached during the melting operation down to the liquidus. Iron tapped from a favorably operating cupola runs about 2800 to 2900 F. The liquidus is ordinarily reached about 2050 to 2100 F for most gray irons. It can be exactly defined as follows:[4]

$$\text{Liquidus temp, }^\circ\text{F} = 2981 - 218\ \text{F}$$

where $F = \%\ C + \frac{1}{2} \times \%\ P + \frac{1}{4} \times \%\ Si$, in the iron

It is evident, however, that actual pouring temperature in the range of 2800 down to about 2100 F is the most important single factor influencing the ability of the molten iron to run a casting. This is not to say that other factors such as composition variation, the effect of sulfur,[4,5] and mold conditions can be ignored. Rather, from an engineering viewpoint, the transport and pouring of the iron must be done with a minimum of temperature drop in order to retain maximum fluidity and reduce the difficulties of pouring thin castings.

Shrinkage Characteristics

Volumetric-shrinkage principles of casting alloys have been considered in Chaps. 8 and 9. Liquid volumetric shrinkage of gray irons has been found to be about 0.50 per cent per 100 F decrease in temperature down to the liquidus temperature. Liquid shrinkage can be compensated by transfer of molten iron from the gating system into the casting before the gates freeze off. Solidification shrinkage has been defined in Ref. 6 by the following equation:

$$\Delta V, \% = 2 \times (\% \text{ graphitic C} - 2.80\%)$$

where ΔV = percentage volume change, positive or negative.

Since the percentage of graphitic carbon enters the equation, it can be seen that readily graphitizable irons will have little or no solidification shrinkage whereas a white iron (0 per cent graphitic carbon) would have considerable shrinkage, about 5.6 per cent, according to this equation. A normal soft iron of 3.50% C, 2.20% Si, 0.4 to 0.60% combined carbon, 2.90 to 3.10% graphitic carbon will have virtually no shrinkage or may even expand on solidification. Hence, for ordinary gray irons little or no risering is needed for the purpose of feeding solidification shrinkage. The lower-carbon, lower-silicon, and less graphitizable irons, for example, SAE 121 and 122 in Table 21.4, do require risering, however. This discussion does not imply that no risers are needed on gray-iron castings. Rather, it is intended to point out that the metallurgical nature of gray iron is such that risers often need not be used unless some factors other than solidification shrinkage require their use. For example, risers may be useful in providing metal if mold-cavity enlargement occurs at some time after pouring has been completed. Also, pressure can be kept on the metal during solidification by suitably placed risers. Solidification under riser pressure favors casting soundness.

The solidification shrinkage of gray irons is not always quite as simple as indicated above. Some irons are susceptible to microshrinkage, which is difficult or sometimes impossible to eliminate by risering. Phosphorus, molybdenum, and other elements have been found to contribute to this effect. The reader is directed to Ref. 6 for a discussion of this phenomenon.

Gating Design

Gating design for iron castings can be expected to accomplish the following objectives:*

1. A casting without misruns or cold shuts, i.e., fully poured.
2. A clean casting. The gating must introduce only clean metal into the mold cavity.
3. A sound casting. The casting must be fed adequately to avoid shrinkage defects.

* Taken in part from Ref. 7.

4. A casting readily cleaned. Gate and riser removal must not unduly increase the cleaning costs.

These objectives are considered in separate categories in the following paragraphs.

Pouring Rate

Pouring rate, in pounds per second, determines the time required to fill the gating system and mold cavity. It has been observed by many foundrymen that an optimum pouring time exists. High-velocity pouring serves to entrain slag and drag it into the mold cavity and may cause mold erosion, entrained gases, and straining of the mold (enlargement) when it is abruptly filled. Low-velocity pouring, a long pouring time, may permit misruns to develop if the melt cools too much. An interesting point in this connection is the relation between pouring time and misruns. It appears that a casting which pours satisfactorily in a given time will require an increased time for filling when misruns occur. Apparently, the path of metal flow becomes longer because of freezing off in some spots and is reflected at first in increased pouring time. Of course, the time for pouring is influenced by casting size, pouring conditions, gating design, and other factors. If the gating system offers sufficient resistance to flow, it will be full of metal or nearly so during most of the pouring time. If no resistance, or choke, is offered by the gates, the gates will not remain full as the metal level rises in the mold cavity. The current practice in most foundries favors keeping a full sprue during pouring; i.e., during the pouring period the ladle operator is able to keep the sprue cup or pouring basin full of iron. This practice is encouraged by the belief that a full sprue provides opportunity for some of the entrained slag to float out and remain in the sprue cup. Strainer cores are often used in the sprue cup or at the base of the sprue for this purpose of regulating flow and maintaining a full sprue. A number of strainer cores are pictured in Fig. 20.1. The approximate delivery rate of these cores under a 2-in. metal head (typical if used in the pouring cup) is listed in Table 20.2. The delivery rate of strainer cores of the same total area but used at the base of the sprue or other locations in the gating as illustrated in Fig. 20.2 probably is somewhat different from that in Table 20.2 because of the differences in pressure head. However, one investigator[9] has reported that sprue height has little effect on pouring time of small molds (4- to 8-in. cope). The strainer cores in Table 20.2 do provide a wide range of pouring rates, and can be used to control the flow rate and hence pouring time. The height of the ladle lip above the mold may greatly affect the pouring time. Pouring high above the mold and directly into the sprue encourages

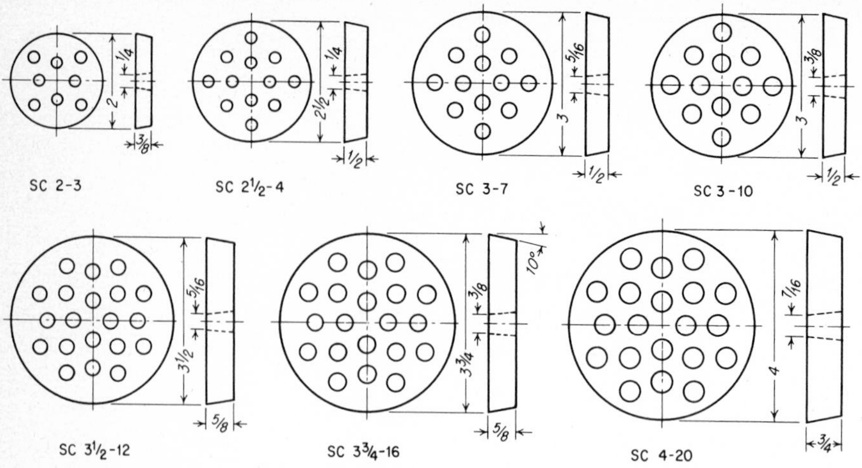

***Fig.* 20.1** Strainer core designs are shown having delivery rates which are listed in pounds per second in Table 20.2. (*From H. L. Campbell.*[8])

high-velocity pouring. Reference 9 cites the benefits to be obtained in production pouring of small castings by standardizing pouring height, gating design, pouring time, and other factors of filling the mold.

The selection of pouring time and gating to achieve this pouring time has been studied for a wide range of casting sizes by H. W. Dietert.[10] According to this author, optimum pouring times obtained by studying a large number of castings are those presented in the graph in Fig. 20.3. Pouring time may also be calculated by the following formula:

$$\text{Time, sec} = \left(A + \frac{T}{B}\right)\sqrt{W}$$

Table* 20.2** ***Strainer-core dimensions*

Designation	OD, in.	Thick-ness, in.	Diam single hole, in.	No. of holes	Total area of holes, sq in.	Delivery,† lb/sec
SC 2–3	2	⅜	¼	8	0.39	3
SC 2½–4	2½	½	¼	12	0.59	4
SC 3–7	3	½	5⁄16	12	0.92	7
SC 3–10	3	½	⅜	12	1.32	10
SC 3½–12	3½	⅝	5⁄16	20	1.53	12
SC 3¾–16	3¾	⅝	⅜	20	2.21	16
SC 4–20	4	¾	7⁄16	20	3.01	20

* From H. L. Campbell.[8]

† Delivery rate determined by trial with cast iron at 2700 F under a head of 2 in.

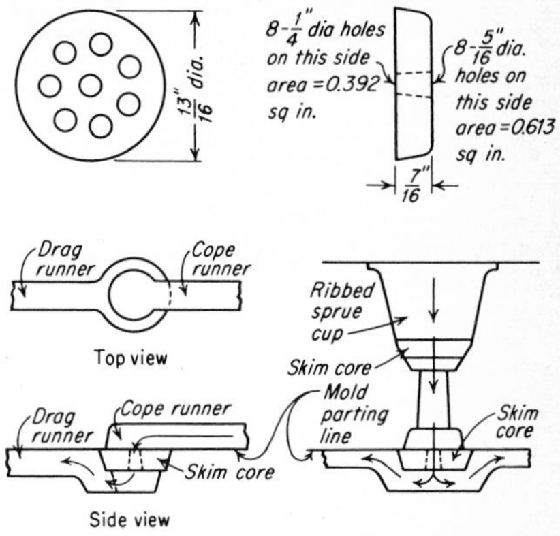

***Fig.* 20.2** Schematic diagram showing the use of strainer and skim cores at the base of the sprue and within a runner in the gating system. (*From F. J. McDonald.*[9])

where T = average metal thickness of the casting
A = 0.95 for gray iron
B = 0.853 for gray iron
W = casting weight, lb

Having selected a desired pouring time from Fig. 20.3, the gating necessary to approximate this pouring time is calculated as follows (quoted directly from Dietert[10]):

The first step is to determine the effective sprue height or the ferrostatic pressure on the gate. The effective sprue height can be calculated by formula ESH:

ESH, effective sprue height $= (2HC - Ca^2) \div 2C$

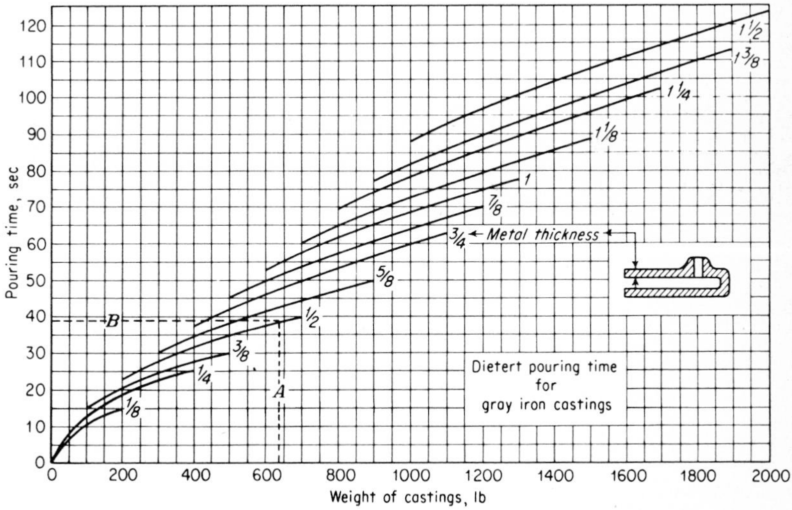

***Fig.* 20.3** Chart used for determining the optimum pouring time for castings of different weight and section thickness. (*From H. W. Dietert.*[10])

In this formula,

H = Distance of the gate from the top of the mold in inches.
C = Total height of the casting in inches.
Ca = Height of the casting above the gate in inches

The second step is to calculate the area of the gate by using

$$\text{Area of gate (sq. in.)} = X\sqrt{W} \div \sqrt{\text{ESH}}$$

In this formula,

W = Weight of casting in pounds
ESH = Effective sprue height obtained from formula ESH
$X = 0.23 \times T \div 2.22$ for gray iron, with T equal to the thickness of the casting.

As used here, the term "gate" refers to the ingate at the casting, unless the gating system contains a choke ahead of the ingate. If such a choke is used, effective sprue height must be calculated from the choke to the top of the mold, not from the ingate.

The calculated gate area can be used to select the dimensions of the ingate or ingates.

Modification of the calculated gating may be indicated after a few experiments to either increase or decrease the pouring time. In this type of gating it is assumed that the sprue is large enough so that it does not offer restriction to flow; i.e., the choke is at ingates or runners. The ratio of sprue to runner to total ingate cross-sectional area may be of the order 1:2:1, 1:2:0.5, 1:4:1, 2:7:1, etc. In this type of gating, small changes of ingate dimensions make for large changes in pouring time. Ratio gating as recommended for light metals (Chap. 11) does not follow this practice, and the choke is in the sprue itself. However, it should be recognized that many of these gating principles are as yet controversial, and no doubt revisions of practice will occur.

Dirt Prevention

Slag or dirt in the casting may develop from several sources. Slag, which should float out, forms as the metal cools and solidifies. Sulfides and silicates are the usual slag products. Silicate slags may also be formed by reaction between metal and sand. Sand molds may be eroded at critical points such as the sprue base or ingate locations and thus develop dirt. Various types of slag traps are used in an effort to prevent this slag and dirt from entering the mold cavity. Keeping the sprue full during pouring helps to prevent slag from the ladle entering the mold, provided that the metal is not poured directly down the sprue. Means of reducing the rate of metal flow in the runner are helpful. It has been suggested that, if the time the metal is in the runners can be increased about 1 sec by enlarging the runner over the sprue area by four to seven times, most slag will float out and become lodged on the cope-runner surface and will not enter the mold cavity. Reference 9 states that flow velocities in the runner of less than 0.75 fps will keep dirt from getting into small castings. Slag dams, whirl gates, and runner enlargements and chokes are other means of decreasing dirt by providing time for nonmetallics to float out. Some of these types of gates are illustrated in Chap. 9.

Feeding the Casting

Castings may be regarded as spread-out, platetype castings or as chunky, low surface-area-to-volume ratio shapes. The former freeze quickly and are generally not risered. The latter require varying degrees of risering, depending on the iron, pouring conditions, and mold factors. Since the actual total shrinkage of gray iron is low, it is often possible to use the runners for feeding purposes. An example is provided in Fig. 20.4 in match-plate molding.[11] Too small a runner freezes off and will not feed chunky castings, as shown in Fig. 20.4. A large runner remains molten, and the sprue keeps the liquid metal under pressure. If the runner is in the cope and casting in the drag, as in Fig. 4.6, then gravity helps the runner to feed the casting. The use of runners and risers in the runner as in Fig. 20.4 is good from the viewpoint of temperature gradients and pressure effects in compensating for possible mold-cavity enlargements. Edge gating is another means of feeding chunky castings from runners or runner enlargements (actually risers), as illustrated in Fig. 20.5.

Side risers, delivering feed metal through ingates to the casting, have in a number of cases been found more effective than top risers. Top risers require that the metal to fill the riser must flow through the mold cavity and up into the riser. Unfavorable thermal gradients then exist.[13] A difficult casting, a ball 8 in. in diameter, is shown side-risered through a small ingate in Fig. 20.6. Top risering was unsuccessful in this case because of shrinks under the riser. The gating in Fig. 20.6 is successful because of the thermal gradients set up by "hot" risering. Metal passing through the riser heats the sand and is itself cooled before entering the casting.

Top gating is another means of pouring some gray-iron castings which takes advantage of the fluid life of the melt, the pressure effect, and thermal gradients. A pouring cup and strainer core may be combined, as in Fig. 20.7, or the cup may be molded and a strainer core added or rammed up with the mold. The cup must be kept full during pouring. Feeding occurs because the ingates become very hot during pouring and the mass of the sprue is sufficient to cause it to remain molten longer than the casting. The same idea can be applied as a side-gate riser.

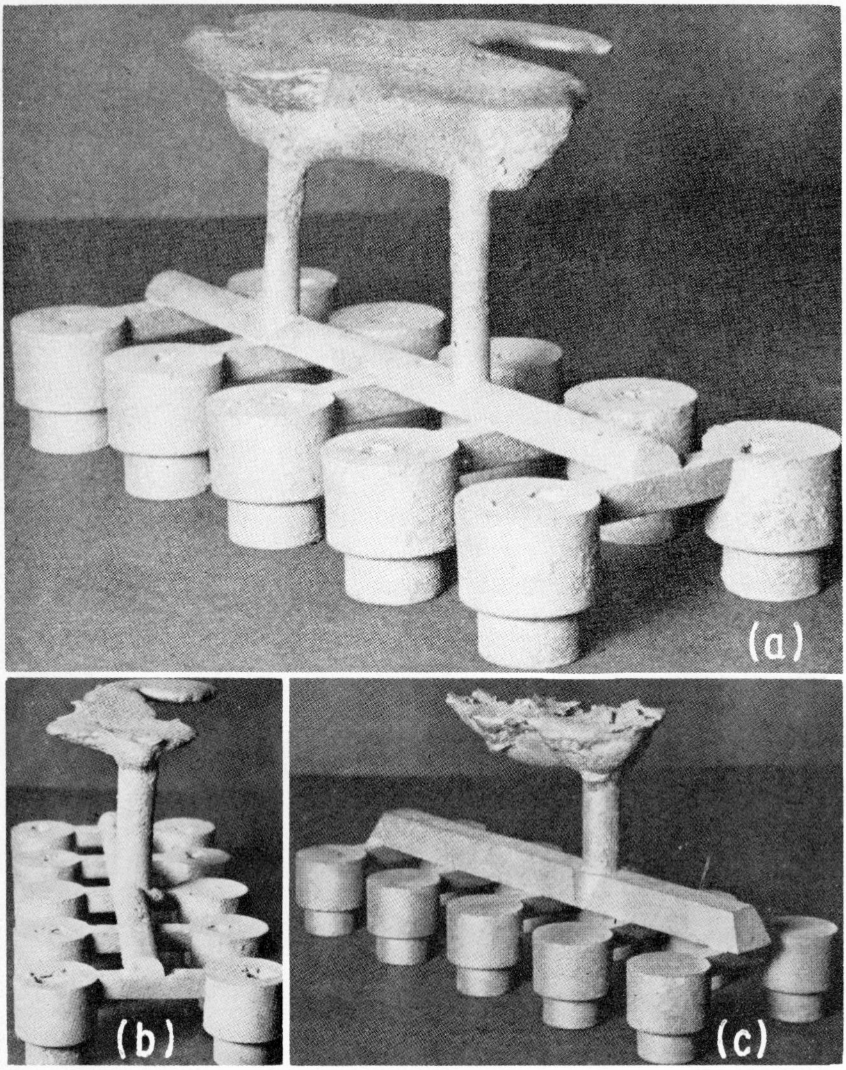

***Fig.* 20.4** Series of gating designs showing how an increase in runner and sprue size permits them to feed castings. (*a*) Improper gating of this match-plate group resulted in shrinkage defects; (*b*) the use of a large sprue did not eliminate shrinkage except in the two castings directly under the sprue, one of which shows an inclusion; (*c*) shrinkage was eliminated by use of a larger runner and sprue. (*From A. J. Howarth.*[11])

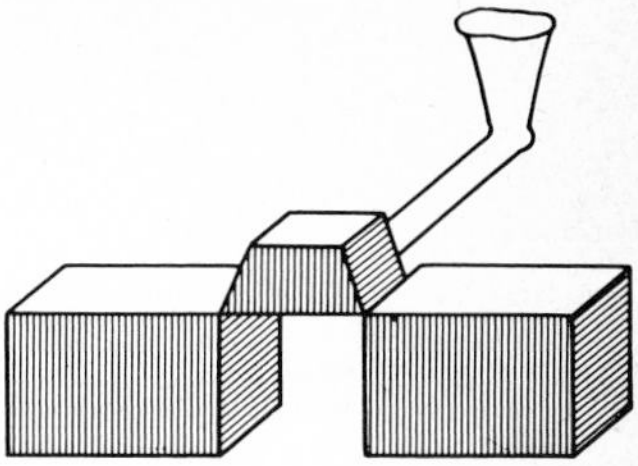

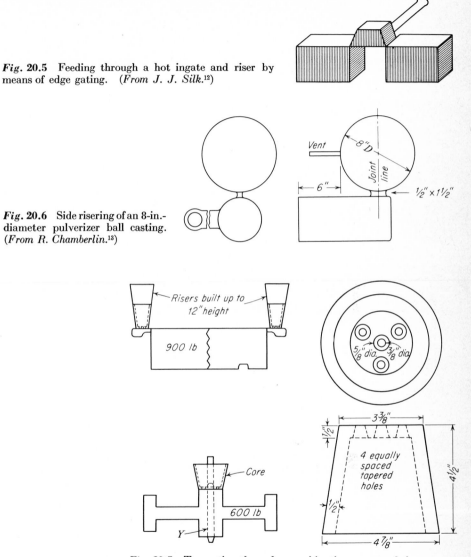

***Fig*. 20.5** Feeding through a hot ingate and riser by means of edge gating. (*From J. J. Silk.*[12])

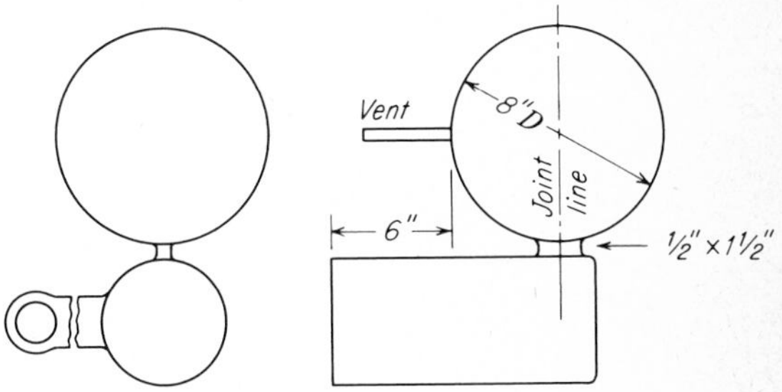

***Fig*. 20.6** Side risering of an 8-in.-diameter pulverizer ball casting. (*From R. Chamberlin.*[13])

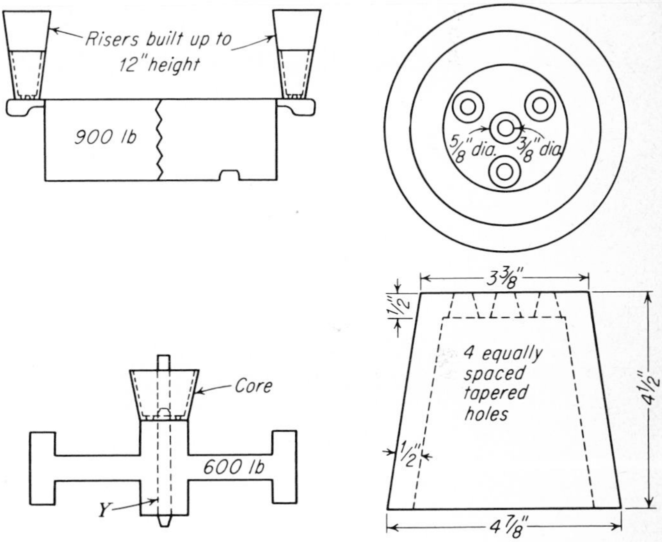

***Fig*. 20.7** Top gating through a combination sprue and riser. (*From B. F. Sweet.*[14])

The consideration of gray-iron gating and feeding has been quite limited since the nature of the textbook precludes further discussion. It should be noted, however, that the principles of gating and risering discussed in Chap. 9 are particularly adapted to gray iron.

SPECIAL CASTING PROCESSES

In addition to conventional casting employing green-sand molding, considerable amounts of gray iron are cast by specialized processes. Among these are:

1. Centrifugal casting of pipe
2. Permanent-mold casting
3. Casting in core-sand molds
4. Molding of heavy castings utilizing specialized techniques
5. Shell molding

Detailed considerations of these molding processes will not be taken up in this textbook. The interested student is referred to the bibliographies of Chaps. 3 and 4, as well as of this chapter, for further information.

METALLURGICAL OPERATIONS

Some of the principles and practices of gray-iron metallurgy, melting and preparing the iron for pouring, etc., are considered in Chaps. 18, 19, and 21. Other important foundry problems are affected by the composition of the iron and its suitability for the class of castings made in a particular foundry.

Selection of Iron Composition

Ordinarily, iron composition is established by specification agreed to by the user and the foundry and by circumstantial factors such as type and size of casting made in the foundry, casting process, melting materials, and availability of the alloy. Sometimes, however, the mechanical properties of the iron are the major concern of the user. Also, within many specification ranges, the iron properties may be quite different if either the low or high ends of the analysis range are adhered to. Thus the foundryman may in some cases have some degree of choice in the analysis of iron he chooses to produce.

Section Size, Cooling Rate, and Properties

The combined effects of composition and section size are summarized in Fig. 21.9 by two authors. The effect of section size for a given composition is of course related to the cooling rate of that section, slower cooling rates promoting softness and low strength. A relationship between factors which control cooling rate and mechanical properties of irons is pointed out in Ref. 15. It is based upon the cooling-rate factors of surface area of casting and volume of casting expressed as a ratio SA/V of the casting and is presented in Fig. 20.8. As an example of the use of this figure, consider a flat-plate casting ½ by 4 by 8 in. in which 40,000 psi tensile strength is desired.

$$SA = (4 \times 8) \times 2 + (0.5 \times 8) \times 2 + (0.5 \times 4) \times 2 = 76 \text{ sq in.}$$
$$V = 0.5 \times 4 \times 8 = 16 \text{ cu in.}$$
$$\frac{SA}{V} = \frac{76}{16} = 4.75$$

To obtain 40,000 psi tensile strength with an SA/V factor of 4.75, an ASTM No. 30 iron is required, according to the chart in Fig. 20.8. The composition of such an iron then might correspond to that of SAE 111 in Table 21.4. If the same casting-section thickness is checked in Fig. 21.9 for a Class 30 iron, it is seen that approximately the same strength may be expected. If the analysis for SAE 111 is used and checked against section size in Fig. 21.8, it again appears that the desired 40,000 psi tensile strength may be achieved by using this iron in the casting under consideration. Although the merit of these different methods of relating analysis, cooling rate, and properties has not been established, it appears that all the methods are useful in approximating

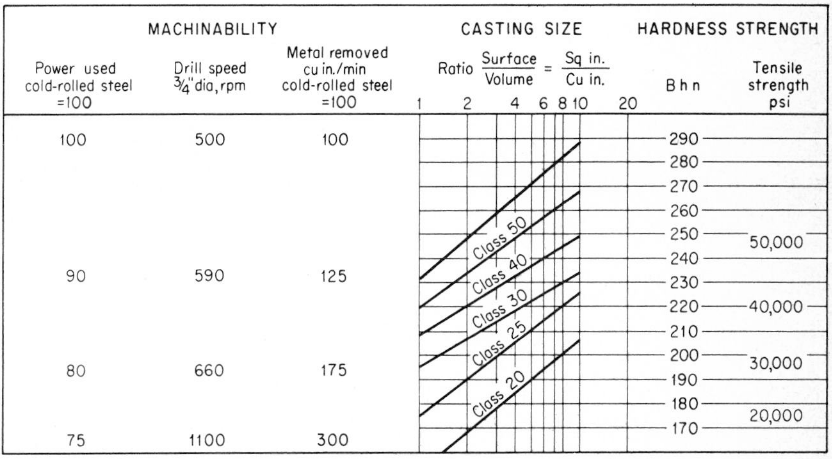

Fig. 20.8 Relationship of ASTM class number, tensile strength, hardness, and machinability of gray iron to ratio of casting surface area to volume. (*From H. H. Fairfield and F. W. Kellun.*[15])

the desired results without the hazard of a complete guess. Of course, the limitations of each method must be recognized, and are in the main recorded by their authors.

Other factors in the choice of gray iron may include:

1. Favoring fluidity by selecting high-carbon and high-silicon irons.
2. Favoring least shrinkage by selecting high-carbon and high-silicon irons.
3. Good machinability is effected by iron softness accompanying factors 1 and 2, but strength suffers.
4. Certain limiting minimum section sizes apply to each gray iron (Chaps. 18 and 21).

However, if casting specifications require higher strength and hardness, and especially in larger castings, the foundry has no recourse but to employ lower-silicon, lower-carbon irons, which are less favorable with respect to the above items.

CLEANING

Cleaning operations applied to rough castings include breaking off gates (flogging), blasting, chipping, grinding, or other of the conventional means of cleaning castings described in Chap. 24.

Surface-cleaning operations are thought to cease as far as the foundry is concerned when blasting, tumbling, or the other useful methods have been used. However, in a large number of cleaning and surface-treating processes, metallic, ceramic, and organic coatings can be applied which substantially extend the range of usefulness of gray-iron castings. A summary of the many useful surface-treating operations which can be applied to gray irons and their useful applications is presented in Ref. 16.

BIBLIOGRAPHY

1. E. W. Fry, Sand Control Should Include Mixer Operator Training, *Am. Foundryman,* vol. 22, November, 1950.
2. R. Clark, Silicon-Chromium Alloy in Complicated Castings, *Trans. AFS,* vol. 59, p. 401, 1951.
3. E. C. Zirzow, Factors Governing Sea Coal Selection and Control, *Am. Foundryman,* vol. 19, June, 1951.
4. L. F. Porter and P. C. Rosenthal, Factors Affecting Fluidity of Gray Cast Iron, *Trans. AFS,* vol. 60, 1952.
5. L. F. Porter and P. C. Rosenthal, What the Fluidity Test Reveals about Gray Cast Iron, *Foundry,* vol. 81, p. 94, August, 1953.
6. J. C. Hamaker, Jr., W. P. Wood, and F. B. Rote, Internal Porosity in Gray Iron Castings, *Trans. AFS,* vol. 60, p. 401, 1952.

7. N. A. Birch, Gating and Risering Principles, a talk given before Wisconsin Chapter AFS, 1952.
8. H. L. Campbell, Designing Strainer Cores, *Trans. AFS,* vol. 56, p. 574, 1948.
9. F. J. McDonald, Gating to Control Pouring Rate and Its Effect on the Casting, *Trans. AFS,* vol. 61, 1953.
10. H. W. Dietert, How Fast Should a Mold Be Poured? *Foundry,* vol. 81, p. 205, August, 1953.
11. A. J. Howarth, Gating Principles Applied to Gray Iron Castings Produced on Matchplates, *Am. Foundryman,* vol. 20, p. 28, July, 1951.
12. J. J. Silk, Gating Gray Iron for Production Foundries, *Am. Foundryman,* vol. 21, p. 41, February, 1952.
13. R. Chamberlin, Side Risers Cut Cleaning Room Costs on Alloy Iron Castings, *Am. Foundryman,* vol. 21, January, 1952.
14. B. F. Sweet, Core Serves as Gate and Riser, *Foundry,* vol. 80, September, 1952.
15. H. H. Fairfield and F. W. Kellun, Casting Surface: Volume Ratio Predicts Gray Iron Properties, *Am. Foundryman,* vol. 20, p. 30, August, 1951.
16. C. O. Burgess, Metallic and Non-metallic Coating for Gray Iron, *Foundry,* vols. 77 and 78, December, 1950, and January–February, 1951.
17. American Foundrymen's Society, "Cast Metals Handbook," 4th ed., p. 491, 1944.
18. American Foundrymen's Society, "The Cupola and Its Operation," 1954.
19. H. W. Zimnawoda, Mechanical Equipment for Medium-sized Gray Iron Foundry, *Trans. AFS,* vol. 59, p. 56, 1951.
20. C. O. Burgess, Gray Iron: Molding, Cutting and Brazing, *Am. Foundryman,* vol. 18, October–December, 1950.
21. H. L. Campbell, Convert Ladle Dimensions to Iron Weight, *Am. Foundryman,* vol. 15, June, 1949.
22. R. J. Anderson, Mechanics of Foundry Mechanization and Improved Methods, *Trans. AFS,* vol. 61, 1953.
23. A. W. Gregg, Mechanized Melting Methods for Foundries, *Iron Age,* May 8, 1947.
24. Modern Equipment Co., Bulletin on Cupola Charging, Port Washington, Wis.
25. G. Krumlauf, Cast Figure Process Reduces Machining Costs, *Am. Foundryman,* vol. 15, June, 1949.
26. W. F. Bohm, Mold Materials Are Factors in Gray Iron Shrinkage, *Am. Foundryman,* vol. 19, January, 1951.
27. C. C. Sigerfoos and C. A. Sanders, Gray Iron Shrinkage Related to Molding Sand Conditions, *Am. Foundryman,* vol. 19, February, 1951.
28. L. F. Porter and P. C. Rosenthal, Effect of Sulfur on Fluidity of Gray Cast Iron, *Trans. AFS,* vol. 60, 1952.
29. V. Pulsifer, Gray Iron Chilling Practice, *Foundry,* vol. 86, p. 67, September, 1958.
30. S. L. Gertsman, Desulfurization of Iron and Steel, *Foundry,* vol. 86, p. 46, August, 1958.
31. F. L. Arnold, Gray Iron Chemistry, *Foundry,* vol. 86, p. 86, December, 1958.
32. R. A. Clark, Inoculation of Gray Cast Iron, *Foundry,* vol. 87, p. 100, May, 1959.
33. H. H. Wilder, Inoculants for Production of High Strength Gray Iron, *Foundry,* vol. 88, p. 116, June, 1960.

34. W. C. Filkins, J. F. Wallace, and D. Matter, Chill Testing of Gray Iron, *Foundry,* vol. 89, p. 62, December, 1961.
35. J. V. Dawson, Pinhole Porosity in Gray Iron, *Foundry,* vol. 89, p. 116, September, 1961.
36. G. W. Form and J. F. Wallace, Gray Iron Structures and Properties, *Foundry,* vol. 90, p. 66, September, 1962; p. 58, October, 1962.
37. W. Hiller and R. Walking, Influence of Silicon:Carbon Ratio on Tensile Strength of Gray Iron, *Foundry,* vol. 90, p. 54, December, 1962.
38. A. Wittmoser and H. A. Krall, Shrinkage in Gray Iron, *Foundry,* vol. 90, p. 62, July, 1962.
39. F. G. Sefing, Alloyed Gray Irons, *Foundry,* vol. 91, p. 86, March, 1963.
40. J. F. Wallace, Effect of Carbon Equivalents and Section Size on Tensile Strength of Gray Irons, *Foundry,* vol. 91, p. 40, December, 1963.

21
Metallurgy of Gray Iron

Although "gray iron" denotes a certain type of cast iron, yet the chemical composition, structure, and properties of gray iron may vary over broad limits. The range of alloy compositions and properties produced as gray irons may be better understood by consideration of some of the principles of gray-iron metallurgy. Some of the more general principles and properties have been presented in Chap. 18, and it is assumed the student has studied that chapter before delving into this one.

The metallurgy of cast irons depends in large measure upon the nature of the iron-carbon equilibrium system. Superimposed on the solid-line phase diagram of the Fe-C system as demonstrated in Fig. 8.6 is a dashed-line diagram. The two diagrams show that iron-carbon alloys may exist in two different phase relationships. The solid lines apply to the system iron–iron carbide, and the dashed lines refer to the system iron-graphite.

THE METASTABLE IRON–IRON CARBIDE SYSTEM

In the phase system iron–iron carbide, carbon in the alloys occurs as the metastable compound iron carbide (Fe_3C). During solidification or melting and in thermal treatments in the solid state, the iron carbide functions according to normal principles of phase relationships as expected from the equilibrium diagram. For example, freezing of a hypoeutectic alloy, less than 4.30 per cent carbon, will begin with the formation of austenite dendrites and be completed by solidification of the eutectic austenite–iron carbide. After solidification, cooling in the solid state results in transformation of the austenite to pearlite. The room-temperature microstructure arising from the foregoing processes is given in Fig. 21.1*a*, which shows the primary austenite dendrites as pearlite areas and the austenite-carbide eutectic as a pearlite-carbide mixture. A eutectic Fe-C alloy containing 4.30% C should freeze without the formation of primary austenite dendrites and should consist only of the eutectic-type structure as illustrated in Fig. 21.1*b*. Heating and cooling of alloys with the microstructures shown in Fig. 21.1 are accompanied

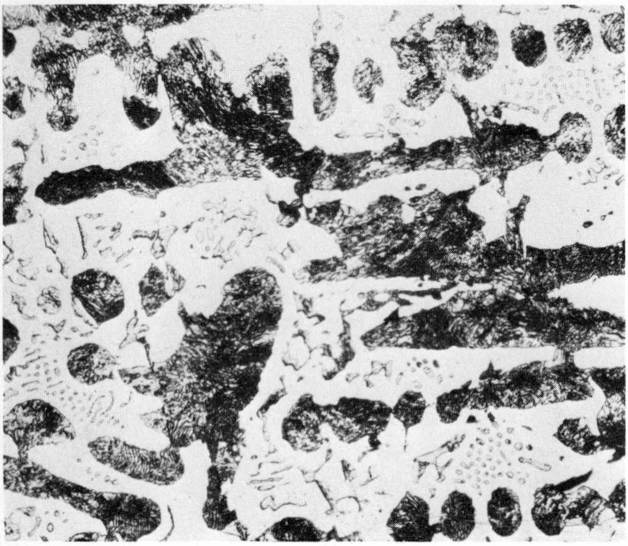

(a)

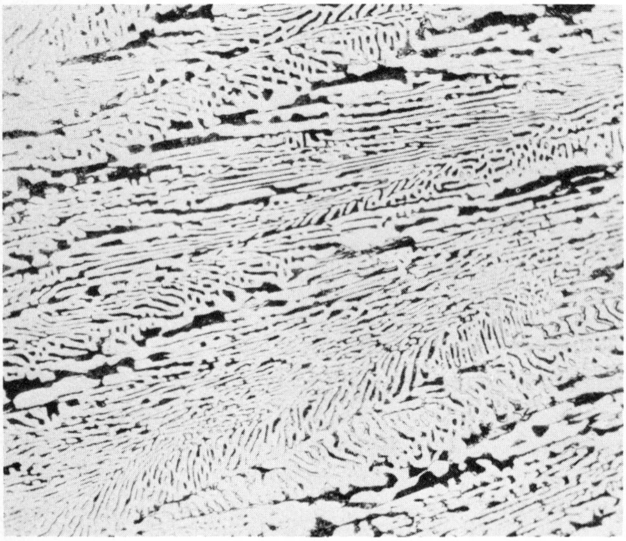

(b)

Fig. **21.1** (*a*) Typical structure of ungraphitized cast iron, (*b*) an ungraphitized eutectic Fe-C alloy. (*Courtesy of H. W. Weart.*)

by structural changes predictable from the iron–iron carbide phase diagram. Under such circumstances the iron carbide phase behaves as a stable phase although it is known to be metastable. A *metastable phase* is one which behaves as though it were stable but which actually is unstable. Iron carbide becomes unstable when it is in contact with graphite at elevated temperatures. Prolonged exposure to high temperatures or the presence of certain elements in the alloy may cause the formation of graphite nuclei and thus promote the change from the metastable iron carbide to the stable graphite phase. Conversely, rapid cooling and certain elements in the alloy tend to prevent nucleation of graphite and thus cause the metastable carbide phase to persist. In a particular case, the tendency to approach the complete equilibrium represented by the iron-graphite phase system results from the balance reached by the effects of all the factors that promote graphitization and those that oppose graphitization. A number of these factors have been briefly discussed in Chap. 18.

SOLIDIFICATION OF AN Fe-C-Si ALLOY

The presence of silicon in the alloy is the most important single composition factor promoting graphitization in gray cast irons. The effect of silicon may be visualized with the aid of vertical sections of the ternary alloy system Fe-C-Si as shown in Fig. 21.2. Consider the freezing processes for an Fe-C-Si alloy with 2% Si and about 3.50% C. Under equilibrium freezing conditions primary austenite dendrites are formed in the temperature range from the liquidus curve to the curve indicating the beginning of eutectic freezing, about 2300 to 2060 F. Simultaneous solidification of the eutectic austenite plus graphite completes the freezing process. The eutectic freezing occurs in a temperature range of about 2060 to about 2010 F. When solidification is complete in the alloy under consideration, the microstructure consists of about 20 per cent primary austenite dendrites and 80 per cent austenite-graphite eutectic. At the solidus temperature, austenite is saturated with carbon. Further decrease in temperature is accompanied by rejection of carbon from the austenite as graphite and its precipitation on the graphite flakes in the eutectic. Carbon precipitation continues until the eutectoid temperature range is reached (about 1475 to 1400 F with 2 per cent silicon). At the eutectoid temperature the 2.0% Si austenite contains about 0.60% carbon. *Equilibrium* cooling through the range results in the transformation of austenite to ferrite and precipitation of the remaining carbon on the graphite flakes. The final microstructure then consists of isolated areas of ferrite originating in the primary austenite dendrites and other

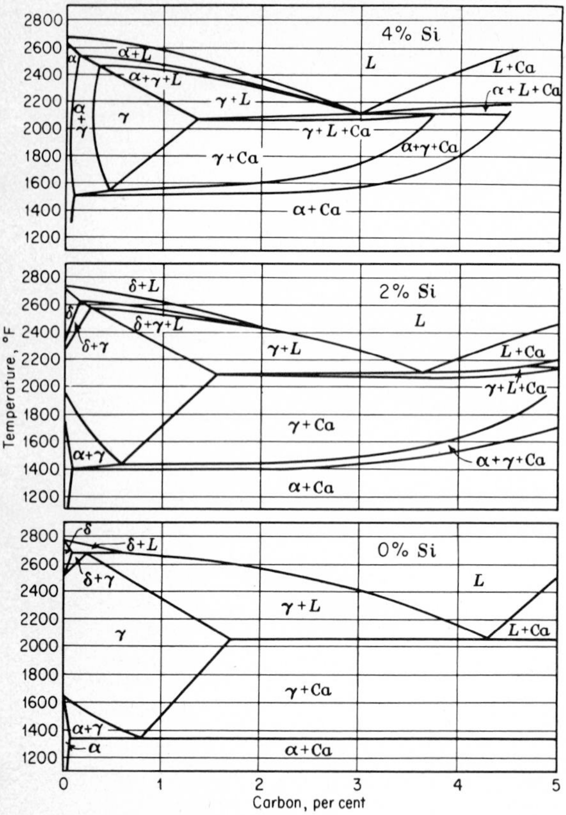

Fig. **21.2** Sections of the Fe-C-Si ternary equilibrium systems at 0, 2, and 4 per cent silicon. (*Courtesy of American Foundrymen's Society.*)

areas of mixed ferrite and flake graphite having their origin in the austenite-graphite eutectic. Figure 21.3 illustrates such a structure. Boyles[2] has demonstrated the freezing processes under consideration in Fe-C-Si alloys and commercial cast-iron alloys. The microstructural changes described above are those occurring in a ternary alloy of Fe-C-Si. Similar processes in commercial cast irons are much more complex since many other elements are present and a number of other factors are introduced. However, the simple alloy considered does point out the three important stages of graphitization:

1. Graphitization during solidification
2. Graphitization by carbon precipitation from austenite (solid state)
3. Graphitization during the eutectoid transformation (solid state)

Some graphitization also occurs below the transformation range down to about 1000 F, although this is of lesser importance unless the time spent at that temperature is very long.

These stages of graphitization and their effects on microstructure and properties will be referred to again.

CHEMICAL COMPOSITION EFFECTS

All the elements normally present in gray iron exert some influence on the microstructure of the iron. Carbon and silicon, of course, are fundamental in their effect on cast irons, and may be considered first.

Carbon

Carbon in gray iron is present from about **2.5 to 4.5** per cent by weight. Two phases occur, elemental carbon in the form of graphite and combined carbon as Fe_3C. The analysis reported ordinarily is the *total carbon* percentage in the iron. Since the two forms may be determined

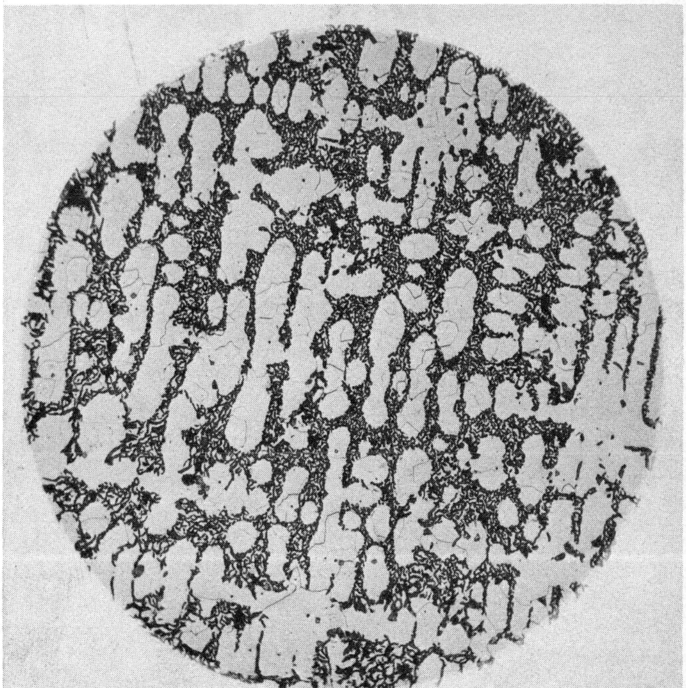

***Fig.* 21.3** Microstructure of a slowly cooled Fe-C-Si alloy, ×100. Note the ferrite areas formed from the original austenite dendrites and the austenite (now ferrite)-graphite eutectic. (*Courtesy of American Foundrymen's Society.*)

separately by chemical analysis, the degree of graphitization may be assessed by the following relationship:

$$\% \text{ total carbon} = \% \text{ graphitic carbon} + \% \text{ combined carbon}$$

If graphitization is complete, the percentage of total carbon and the percentage of graphitic carbon are equal. If no graphitization has occurred, the percentage of graphitic carbon is zero. If about 0.5 to 0.80 per cent combined carbon exists in a gray iron, it generally indicates that the microstructure is largely pearlitic since pearlite in gray iron having about 2 per cent silicon forms from the austenite eutectoid containing about 0.60 per cent carbon. Thus the relationship above offers a chemical criterion of the degree of graphitization in a gray iron. For sufficient graphitization to develop during solidification of a true gray iron, a certain minimum total carbon content is necessary, which is probably about 2.20 per cent, but this value depends on silicon percentage in the iron.

Silicon

Silicon is present in gray iron from about 1.0 to 3.50 per cent by weight. Of course, the important effect of silicon is its effect on graphitization. It may be noted from Fig. 21.2 that increasing silicon percentage shifts the eutectic point of the iron-carbon diagram to the left. The eutectic shift is often described by the following relationship:

$$\text{Eutectic carbon percentage (in Fe-C-Si alloy)} = 4.30 - \tfrac{1}{3} \times \% \text{ Si (in iron)}$$

Another term, the *carbon equivalent* (CE), is often used to describe the relationship of a particular iron to the eutectic point:

$$\text{CE} = \% \text{ C (in the iron)} + \tfrac{1}{3} \times \% \text{ Si}$$

If the carbon equivalent of a particular iron is calculated to be 4.3, then that iron corresponds approximately to a eutectic alloy (even though it is not a true eutectic in the sense of the ternary phase diagram). If the carbon equivalent of an iron is less than 4.30, the alloy is a hypoeutectic alloy. The carbon equivalent is a useful expression because many properties of gray iron have been found related to it. If the combination of carbon and silicon exceeds 4.30, according to the carbon-equivalent equation, the iron is a hypereutectic one. In this case, the freezing process begins with the formation of graphite. When graphite precipitates first during solidification, the melt is said to form *kish*. Because of its buoyancy, kish pops out of the melt into the air and can be observed as sparkly graphite flakes floating on the surface of the iron or in the air above the iron.

Not only is the eutectic point shifted by silicon in cast irons, but it also shifts the eutectoid point and the solubility limits of carbon in austenite to the left of equivalent points in the Fe-C system. For this reason pearlite in a 2.0% Si gray iron may contain only about 0.60% carbon rather than the 0.76% C value on the Fe-C diagram (Fig. 17.1).

Microstructurally, silicon occurs dissolved in the ferrite of gray iron. As such it hardens and strengthens the ferrite, as pointed out in Chap. 18. Ferrite in pure iron will measure 80 to 90 Bhn, whereas 2.0 per cent silicon in a ferritic iron raises the hardness to about 120 to 130 Bhn.

Silicon Content and Graphitization

Silicon promotes graphitization. Low percentages are not sufficient to cause graphitization during solidification, but will cause nucleation and graphitization in the solid state at high temperature, as, for example, during malleableizing heat-treatment. Certain silicon percentages will cause limited graphitization during solidification, and a mottled iron, partly white and partly gray, results.

A certain minimum silicon (and carbon) concentration is necessary for graphitization to proceed sufficiently during solidification to develop a satisfactory gray iron. These concentrations have been schematically illustrated in Fig. 18.2. The schematic diagrams of Fig. 18.2 do not take into account numerous effects, including cooling rate (section size of casting), and therefore have been modified by several authors.[5,6] More accurate diagrams have as their purpose a limiting description of the silicon and carbon percentages which will cause an iron to freeze gray in the section sizes of commercial castings poured into green sand molds. Although these diagrams are useful as a guide, successful metallurgical performance in the type of castings made in particular foundries remains the ultimate criterion for the carbon and silicon content. Hence foundries producing certain sizes of castings and types of gray irons will ultimately develop silicon and carbon combinations suitable to their work. Some silicon and carbon ranges which satisfy graphitization and other requirements for some automotive-type gray irons are given in Table 21.5.

Sulfur and Manganese

Sulfur, which may be present up to about 0.25 per cent, is one of the important modifying elements present in gray irons. A low-sulfur iron-silicon-carbon alloy, under 0.010% S, will graphitize most completely, as represented by Fig. 21.3. Boyles[2] has shown that higher sulfur percentages favor the retention of a completely pearlitic microstructure in

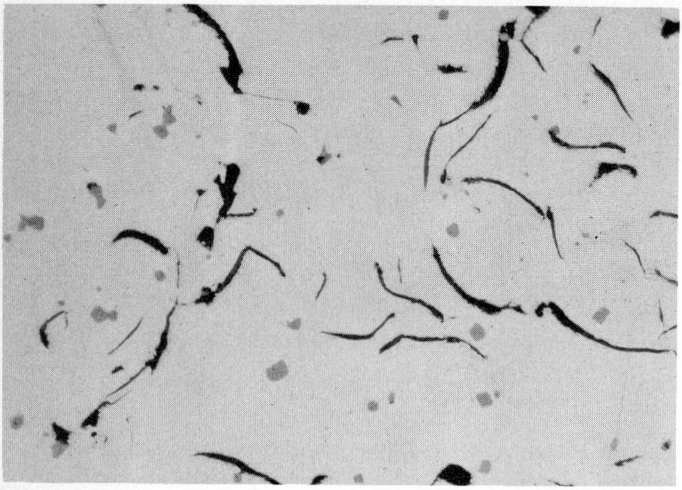

***Fig.* 21.4** Manganese sulfide inclusions (light gray) in gray iron. Unetched, ×250. (*Courtesy of L. F. Porter.*)

a gray iron. The latter effect causes sulfur to be known as an element restricting graphitization (carbide stabilizing). Above about 0.25 per cent, sulfur is considered to contribute undesirable hardness and decreased machinability because of its retardation of graphitization.

The influence of sulfur needs to be considered relative to its reaction with the manganese in the iron. Alone, sulfur will form FeS in cast irons. The latter compound segregates into grain boundaries during freezing and precipitates during the final stages of freezing.[2] When manganese is present, MnS, or complex manganese-iron sulfides, are found, depending on the manganese content. The manganese sulfides begin to precipitate early, and continue to do so during the entire freezing process, and are therefore usually randomly distributed. Manganese sulfides are illustrated in Fig. 21.4. As MnS, the effect of sulfur in causing a pearlitic microstructure to be retained is lost to a major extent. The effect of Mn alone as an alloying element is to promote resistance to graphitization. Therefore manganese above that necessary to react with the sulfur will assist in retaining the pearlitic microstructure. The following rules are advanced to express the relationship involved:

1. $\% \text{S} \times 1.7 = \% \text{Mn}$; chemically equivalent S and Mn percentages to form MnS.
2. $1.7 \times \% \text{S} + 0.15 = \% \text{Mn}$; the manganese percentage which will promote a maximum of ferrite and a minimum of pearlite.
3. $3 \times \% \text{S} + 0.35 = \% \text{Mn}$; the manganese percentage which will develop a pearlitic microstructure.[3]

For commercial gray irons in which a pearlitic microstructure is desired, rule 3 offers a favorable combination of manganese and sulfur percentage.

Phosphorus

The formation of steadite by phosphorus in gray iron has been mentioned in Chap. 18. Segregation of phosphorus may result in lowering of the temperature of final solidification to about 1800 F. The percentage of steadite present in the final structure may amount to ten times the percentage of phosphorus in the iron. Because of segregation, the steadite usually adopts a cellular pattern characteristic of the eutectic cell size developed during solidification.[7] This has been illustrated in Fig. 18.6. The microstructural appearance of steadite itself is illustrated in Fig. 21.5. In certain conditions of melting and chilling, iron carbide is associated with the phosphide in a ternary iron–iron phosphide–iron carbide eutectic. Then an amount of the latter constituent considerably in excess of ten times the per cent phosphorus may be formed. If the ternary eutectic is accompanied by graphitization of its carbide during solidification, expansion of the liquid occurs and beads of eutectic exude from the iron. These are often found at the surface of sprues and risers.

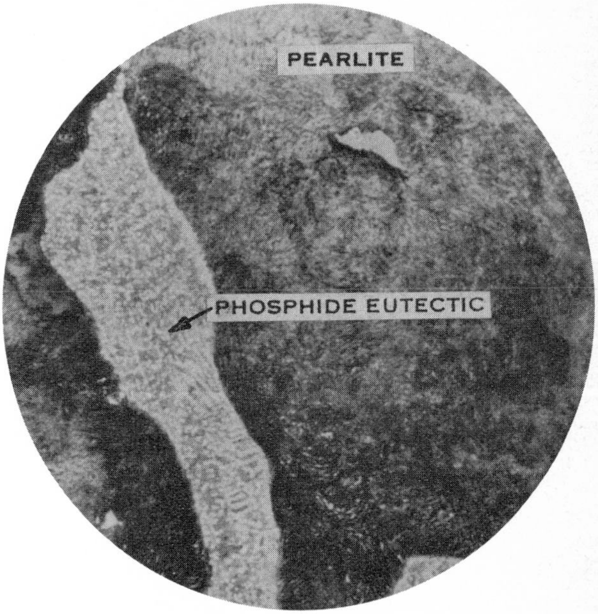

***Fig.* 21.5** Microstructure of steadite, the iron–iron phosphide eutectic, ×1000. (*From American Foundrymen's Society.*[4])

Because it forms a eutectic as it segregates, phosphorus is often looked upon as increasing the tendency for a particular iron composition to be a eutectic-type alloy. For this reason, the carbon-equivalent equation is sometimes modified to include a factor for phosphorus as follows:

$$CE = \% C + \tfrac{1}{3}(\% Si + \% P)$$

Another equation of this type for cast irons is given in Chap. 8, with respect to the effect of phosphorus on fluidity.

The phosphide of iron is hard and brittle, as is the carbide. Increasing phosphorus percentage in the iron causes a proportional increase of the hard constituent, and therefore increasing hardness and brittleness of the iron, especially above about 0.30% P. To a limited degree, improved fluidity of the molten iron is a desirable property contributed by phosphorus through its influence on carbon equivalent (Chap. 8).

GRAPHITIZATION DURING SOLIDIFICATION

The size, shape, and distribution of graphite flakes develop during solidification of the gray iron. Marked differences in graphite type and size are recognized. These are classified according to the standard type and size charts adopted by the ASTM and AFS (Fig. 18.4). A random distribution of flakes, type A, and small size, No. 5 or 6, is considered desirable. However, the dendritically segregated and cellular types are often encountered. Type E flakes, dendritically segregated with preferred orientation, are most often encountered in hypoeutectic irons, where the graphite flakes precipitate in the interstices of the primary austenite dendrites. It is more difficult to ascribe the type D flakes of the cellular pattern to a particular cause. Gray irons of identical composition may solidify with type A or D graphite. Much study has been given to this situation. Most researchers associate the type D graphite with an undercooling effect during solidification.[2,8,10,11,27] If the formation of the eutectic is suppressed from its normal temperature range of about 2100 to 2000 F down to below this range, the type of graphite formed changes from type A to types D and E. Suppression of eutectic freezing, as, for example, by chilling to still lower temperature, 1850 to 1900 F, results in formation of white iron (or chilled iron). The essential ideas of the effects of undercooling are summarized in Table 21.1.

Section Size and Graphite Type

The actual changes of graphite size, number of flakes, and their distribution are related to fundamental metallurgical nucleation and growth principles. Large flakes randomly distributed originate when the nucleation rate is low; there is ample time for diffusion; and graphitization

Table* 21.1 *Graphite type and related factors*

Temp of eutectic solidification	Type of structure	Other factors
2100–2040	Type A graphite, type B at lower temperatures	High carbon percentages, near eutectic carbon content, and ladle inoculation favors type A graphite
2040–1970	Increasing types E and D graphite as temperature decreases	Increased cooling rate, carbide stability favors type D, hypoeutectic carbon content favors type E. Superheating also favors types E and D graphite
1900–1950	Mottled and white iron, type D and/or E graphite present	Increased cooling rate (chilling) favors undercooling and white iron

* Adapted from H. W. Lownie.[8]

occurs readily. Small flakes are encouraged by rapid nucleation due to moderate undercooling under conditions where there is still time for diffusion and graphitization. Severe undercooling inhibits or prevents nucleation of graphite, and hence results in a chilled or white iron. The changes discussed above have been well demonstrated.[11,15] Figure 21.6 illustrates these changes in gray-iron castings made from the same melt but cast in various section thicknesses. Rapid cooling rates as illustrated by small-diameter test bars on the graph of Fig. 21.6 produce the effects of graphite modification. Slower cooling rates are accompanied by the formation of coarse types A and B graphite. It should be emphasized, however, that the entire range of graphite types and microstructures may occur in any gray iron, depending on its cooling rate during solidification and the treatments it receives.

Superheating

Superheating with respect to gray irons means heating the molten iron to temperature above about 2750 F. If the gray-iron melting cycle includes superheating, undercooling during solidification is most likely to occur.[10,16,24] The graphite flake size is reduced and types D and E graphite flakes are promoted by superheating. Chilling and mottled iron in thin sections are also more likely to occur in superheated irons unless they are properly inoculated.

Inoculation

An inoculant may be defined as an addition to the molten iron which produces effects far out of proportion to any resultant change in analysis. Marked change in graphite type may be obtained by inoculation of the molten iron. If ferrosilicon or some other graphitizing agent is added in small amount, 0.05 to 0.25 per cent, type A graphite formation is favored. It appears that undercooling is prevented by the inoculant. The effect is most pronounced when inoculants are added to superheated irons. By combining favorable melting and inoculation practices, type A graphite of the kind desired is most consistently produced in commercial gray irons.

GRAPHITIZATION IN THE SOLID STATE

At the end of the freezing process a gray iron of 3.60% C and 2.10% Si will contain about 2.0% graphitic carbon and 1.50% of carbon dissolved in austenite. Slow cooling permits the carbon to be rejected from the austenite as graphite as temperature drops to the eutectoid temperature of about 1450 F. This carbon rejection is a process of solid-state graphitization and proceeds until about 0.60 per cent remains in the austenite. The graphite precipitates on previously existing flakes. Very slow cooling through the eutectoid transformation range permits a large portion of the 0.60 per cent carbon that remains in the austenite to be rejected as graphite and is accompanied by austenite transformation to ferrite. The iron is then completely graphitized, as discussed earlier under Fe-C-Si alloys. Commercial practice, however, is generally aimed at retaining a pearlitic structure or some proportion of pearlite. The proper balance of manganese and sulfur assists in retaining pearlite even when castings are cooled in sand molds. The transformation of the eutectoidal austenite forms pearlite. The gray iron is not completely graphitized, and about 0.60 per cent combined carbon remains. Rapid solid-state cooling and the presence of carbide-forming elements can cause a substantially greater percentage of combined carbon to be retained.

Fine graphite flake size regardless of type promotes solid-state graphitization, with the flakes serving as precipitation centers for the carbon. Type D cellular graphite is often intermixed with ferrite because of the ease with which graphitization may occur. Figures 18.4 and 21.6 are examples.

SUMMARY—MICROSTRUCTURE OF GRAY IRON

Because of the many factors involved, the microstructure of the gray iron in a commercial casting may vary over the entire range discussed in the preceding sections. The essential points involved for each microconstituent are summarized as follows:

1. *Graphite.* Type and size of graphite are established during solidification of the iron. Chemical composition, undercooling, superheating, inoculation, and cooling rate are important factors.
2. *Ferrite.* Ferrite in the microstructure is promoted by strong graphitizing conditions. Slow cooling rate and a chemical composition causing effective graphitization during freezing and in the solid state are important factors.
3. *Pearlite.* Restriction of graphitization during the eutectoidal transformation, cooling rate, and proper balance of manganese and sulfur in the iron are important factors.

Although many of the factors which control the ultimate microstructure have been evaluated, there are still many unresolved problems. Anomalous behavior is encountered. Many items, such as the influence of gases in the metal and trace-element effects, and the like, have not been considered. The material presented here has attempted to picture in part the simpler phases of the present state of understanding of the metallurgy of gray iron.

FOUNDRY PROPERTIES OF GRAY IRONS

For several reasons, gray irons are among the most easily cast of all alloys. The practical difficulties of making castings require certain properties to a greater or lesser extent in casting alloys. Gray iron has many of these properties to an optimum degree.

Fluidity

Gray irons are the most fluid of ferrous alloys. Intricate and thin section castings may be produced. Bathtubs, piston rings, electrical-resistance grids, steam radiators, and motor blocks illustrate this point.

The fluidity of gray cast iron is expressed in terms of a standard-fluidity spiral casting as illustrated in Fig. 21.7. The metallurgical principles of fluidity were discussed in Chap. 8. A graph relating fluidity in inches of spiral length to iron composition and pouring temperature was presented in Fig. 8.20. The most fluid iron is one approximating a eutectic composition. To express the eutectic nature of a gray iron for fluidity purposes, the following composition-factor (CF) formula may be employed:

$$\text{CF} = \%\,\text{C} + \tfrac{1}{4} \times \%\,\text{Si} + \tfrac{1}{2} \times \%\,\text{P}$$

(CF of 4.55 for maximum fluidity)

Inches of fluidity in the spiral are related to composition and pouring temperature T by the formula

$$\text{Fluidity, in.} = 14.9 \times \text{CF} + 0.05T - 155 \qquad T = {}^\circ\text{F}$$

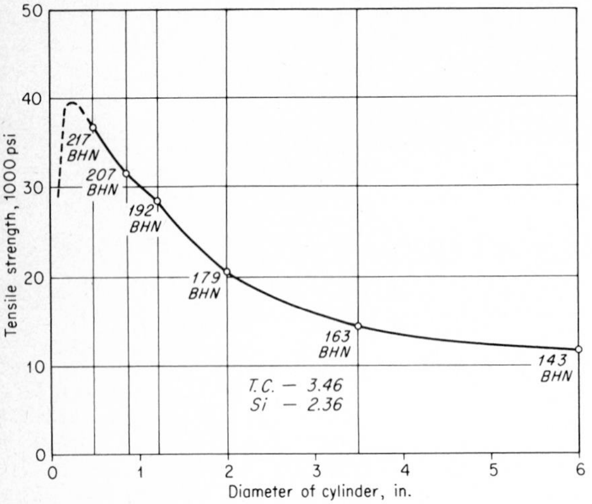

(*a*)

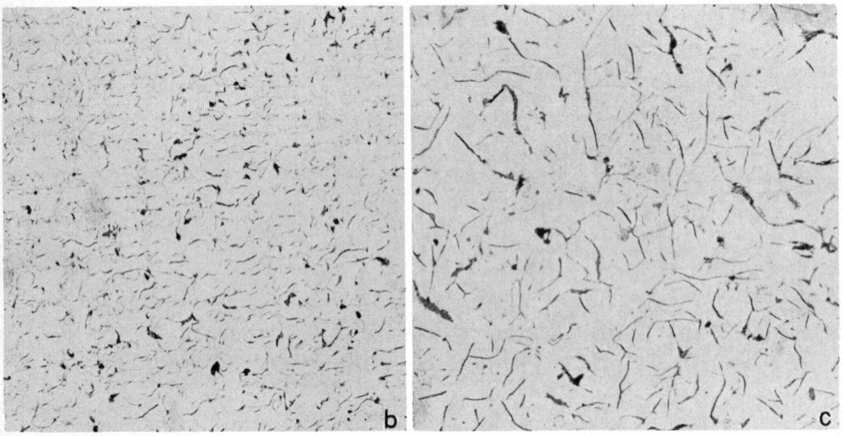

***Fig.* 21.6** (*a*) The effect of microstructure upon the tensile strength and hardness of a Class 20 cast iron. Test specimens were taken from sand-cast cylinders of the indicated diameters. (*b*) Graphite distribution of Class 20 cast iron from ½-in. cylinder. Fine interdendritic graphite of rating 6E, 7D. Unetched, ×100. (*c*) Graphite distribution of Class 20 cast iron from 1.2-in. cylinder. Small random graphite flakes of rating 5A. Unetched, ×100. (*d*) Graphite distribution of Class 20 cast iron from 2-in. cylinder. Moderately sized random graphite flakes of rating 4A. Unetched, ×100. (*e*) Graphite distribution of Class 20 cast iron from 6-in. cylinder. Very coarse random graphite flakes of rating 1A. Longest flakes are more than 4 in. in length at ×100. (*f*) Microstructure of Class 20 cast iron from ½-in. cylinder. Specimen contains moderately fine pearlite and interdendritic graphite. Picral-etched, ×1000. (*g*) Microstructure of Class 20 cast iron from 1.2-in. cylinder. Pearlite is slightly coarser than in (*f*), and a small amount of massive ferrite has formed. Picral-etched, ×1000. (*h*) Microstructure of Class 20 cast iron from 2-in. cylinder. Specimen contains coarse pearlite and massive ferrite. Picral-etched, ×1000. (*i*) Microstructure of Class 20 cast iron from 6-in. cylinder. The microstructure is composed of very coarse pearlite and a large amount of massive ferrite. Picral-etched, ×1000. (*From W. E. Mahin and H. W. Lownie.*[15])

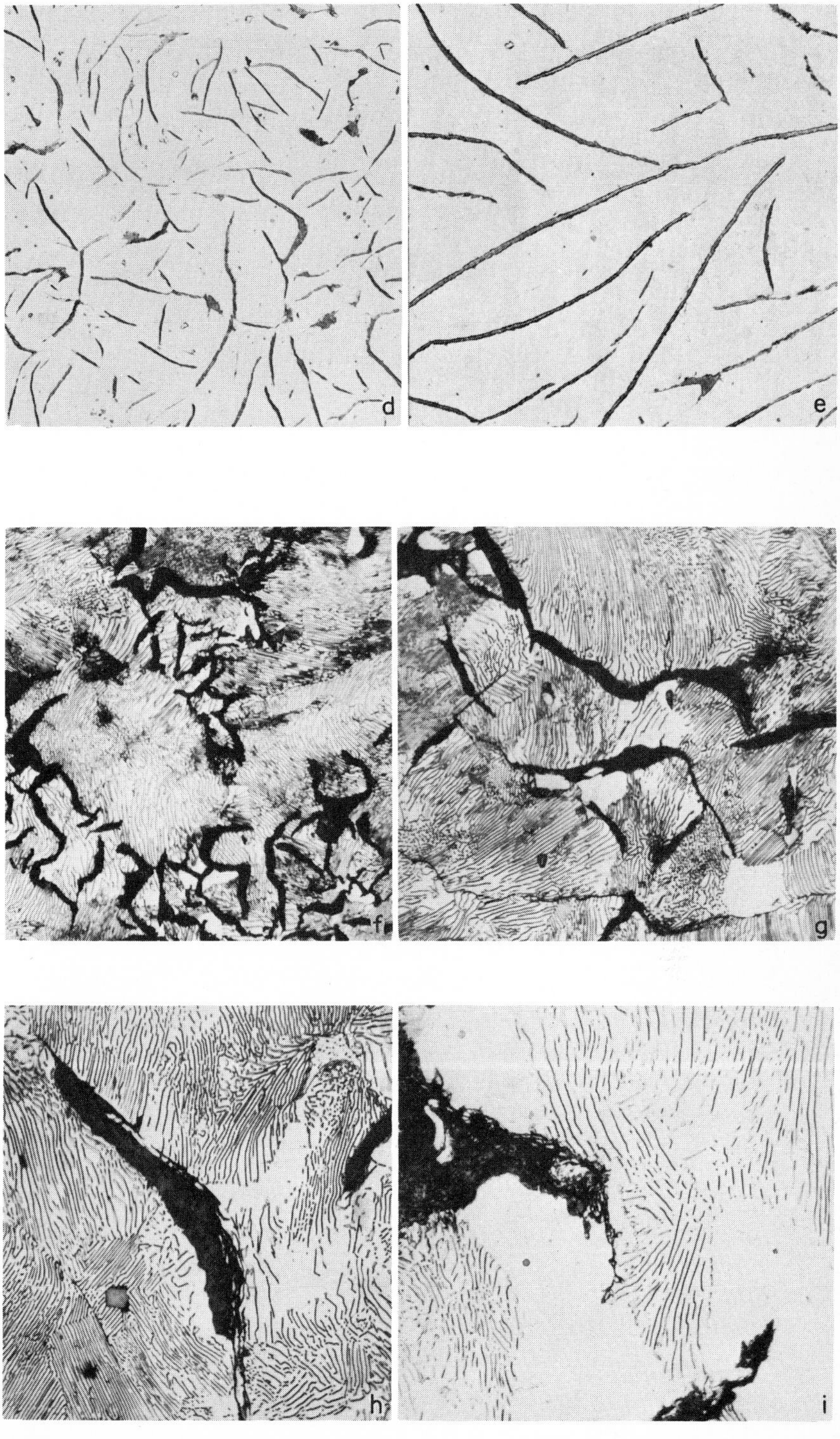
d
e
f
g
h
i

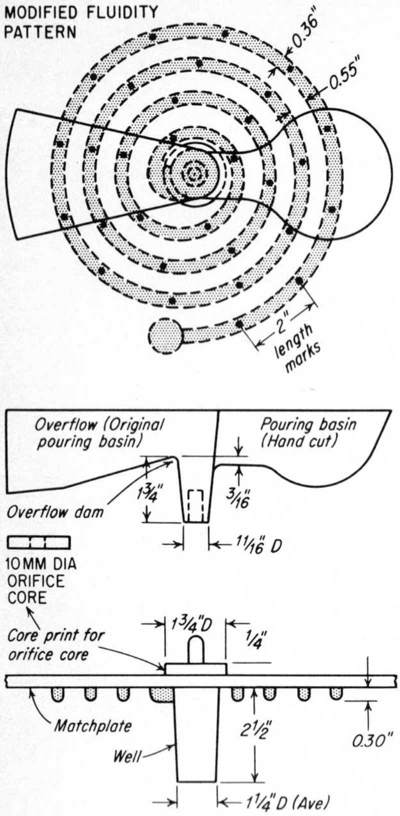

***Fig.* 21.7** **Fluidity-spiral pattern, a modification of the fluidity test of Saeger and Krynitsky.** (*From L. F. Porter and P. C. Rosenthal.*[29])

The entire relationship is expressed graphically in Fig. 8.20. Maximum fluidity exists when the pouring temperature is high and the composition is a eutectic one. In gray irons, however, hypereutectic compositions suffer an extreme loss of fluidity due to kishing, the precipitation of carbon flakes as the liquid metal cools. A hypereutectic iron which kishes may lose fluidity so greatly as not even to run through the ingates of the runner systems and into the simplest of castings. Composition factors other than those handled in the formulas listed above also influence fluidity—sulfur, for example.[7] Some of the additional factors are reported in the technical literature of this subject.

Pouring-temperature Interval

Augmenting the fluidity inherent in gray irons is the fact that the iron may be heated substantially above its melting point without damage. Gray iron may be heated to 2800 to 3100 F and handled in ladles until its temperature has dropped to 2200 F. The wide working-temperature range permits ease of manipulation in the foundry, reladling, and adequate time for pouring. Actual pouring temperatures range from about 2300 to 2800 F, depending on the casting requirements.

Shrinkage and Risering

Feeding of castings to compensate for solidification shrinkage has been discussed in Chap. 20.

Because of the favorable freezing mechanism and low shrinkage characteristics, the yield percentage is high compared with other ferrous metals. A yield of 60 to 75 per cent may be attained, and in some cases higher yields are possible. Although it is true that high-carbon-equivalent gray irons have the least shrinkage, it is not always true that they present the fewest problems in risering. Some casting designs are more easily cast in commercially acceptable soundness with lower-carbon-equivalent irons.

ENGINEERING PROPERTIES

From a metallurgical-engineering standpoint, gray iron may be viewed as a microstructurally sensitive alloy. Microstructure, chemical composition, and mechanical properties are intimately related. Of course, the many factors related to the processing of gray iron which influence microstructure, chemical-composition variations, and cooling rate also affect the properties.

Effect of Chemical Composition

Carbon and silicon are the most important composition factors influencing mechanical properties. The carbon equivalent has been related to a number of mechanical properties.[12,13,15] A graph of carbon equivalent and tensile strength is shown in Fig. 21.8. Decreasing carbon equivalent, brought about in part by a reduction of carbon percentage in the iron, results in increased tensile strength. The practical limit of strength by decreasing the carbon equivalent alone is probably about 45,000 psi tensile strength. Higher strengths require special alloying practices.

The relationship of hardness to tensile strength, the tensile-strength–Bhn ratio, is subject to substantial variations due to the influence of the various flake graphite types. Table 21.2 lists the relationships between tensile strength and Brinell hardness. The importance of graphite type and size is also emphasized in Table 21.2. It may be noted from the table that the highest tensile strength is obtained at a given hardness when small type A graphite flakes exist. On the other hand, a poor tensile strength is obtained at a given hardness when type D graphite prevails.

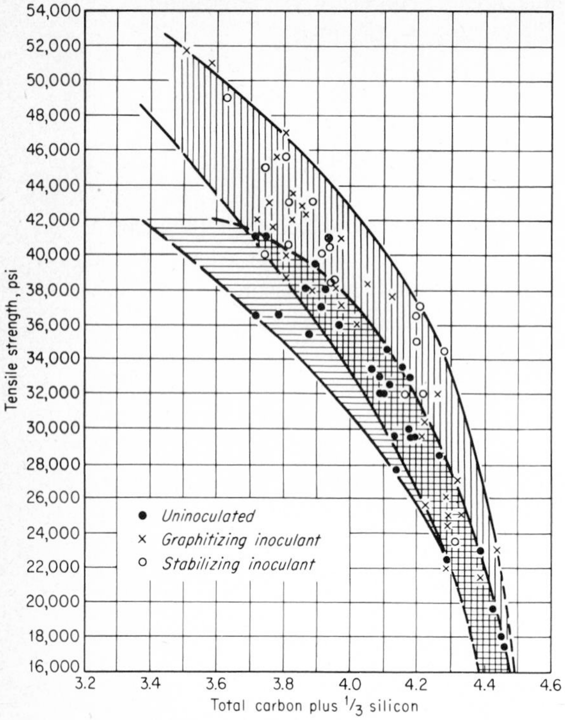

***Fig.* 21.8** Tensile strength of 1.20-in.-diameter gray-iron bars as affected by carbon equivalent. (*From T. E. Barlow and C. H. Lorig.*[12])

Manganese and sulfur seem to influence properties of commercial gray irons mainly through their effect on solid-state graphitization. Maximum strength obtains when a pearlitic matrix exists.

Mechanical properties above the range indicated in Fig. 21.8 require specially alloyed gray irons. However, the compositions of the gray irons of Class 40 or under in Table 21.4 fall within the limits of Fig. 21.8, and are the principal gray irons produced tonnagewise in commercial foundries.

Effect of Cooling Rate—Section Size

The influence of cooling rate on properties is profound because of its influence on microstructure. The principle has been illustrated in Fig. 21.6. Rapid cooling causes increased hardness and tensile strength. This is true, however, only so long as the rapid cooling does not cause white or chilled iron or an excessively bad type D graphite structure. Slow cooling in heavier sections results in progressive coarsening of the graphite flakes and lamellar pearlite, and finally the appearance of ferrite. The latter factors cause softening and weakening of the gray iron as illustrated in Fig. 21.6. Wear resistance is also lowered by type

Table 21.2 Relationship between structure and tensile strength and Brinell hardness ratio—listed by composition range*

Carbon equivalent, %	Tensile strength divided by Bhn	Structure
3.45–3.65	210 and over	Smallest cell, normal graphite
	190–210	Small cell, normal graphite
	180–190	Medium cell, some type D† graphite
	170–180	Large cell, some type D—medium cell, completely type D
	160–170	Large cell, partial type D
	160 and below	Large cell, complete type D
3.65–3.85	210 and over‡	Smallest cell, normal graphite
	190–210	Smallest cell, normal graphite
	180–190	Medium cell, normal graphite or small cell, partial type D
	170–180	Large to medium cell with partial type D graphite
	160–170	Large cell, type D graphite or free ferrite
3.85–4.20	190–210	Medium cell, normal graphite
	180–190	Medium cell, large normal graphite
	170–180	Medium or large cell, some type D
	160–170	Large cell, type D graphite
	160 or below	Free ferrite, type D graphite

* From T. E. Barlow and C. H. Lorig.[12]

† Type D graphite—AFA-ASTM graphite flake-size chart—also called modified, eutectiform, dendritic, pseudo-eutectic, etc. Undesirable for wear resistance; low deflection, low toughness values, and poor transverse properties.

‡ Very few irons in this range.

D flakes. Composition and foundry practice must be adjusted to produce the desired strength class of gray iron in the casting desired. Thus mechanical-property specifications are usually considered far more important than chemical specifications. However, certain combinations of carbon and silicon and other elements are used more commonly than others. Probably the most common gray irons are the Class 20 to 30 irons. The gray irons have minimum tensile strengths of 20 and 30 psi, respectively. They offer a desirable combination of good casting properties, strength adequate for many purposes, and excellent machinability.

The change of tensile strength and hardness with section size for gray irons of some of the various classes listed in Table 21.5 is illustrated in Fig. 21.9.

The properties of a Class 30 iron are seen to vary from 20,000 to 48,000 psi, depending on the diameter of the section from which the test bar is taken. Hardness changes in the same direction are evident in

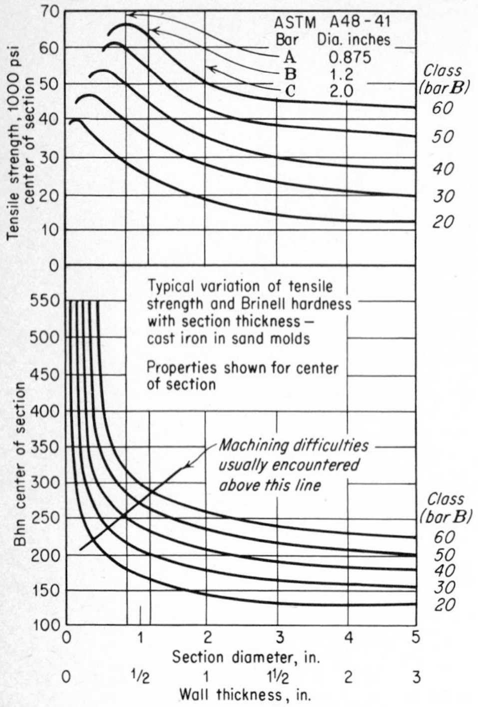

***Fig.* 21.9** Dependence of gray-iron properties on casting-section thickness. (*From T. E. Eagan and C. O. Burgess.*[35])

Fig. 21.9. Thus a gray iron which is a Class 30 iron in the B test-bar size may vary in hardness from Class 20 to almost Class 50 properties, depending on the section size of the casting.

Probably the most comprehensive summary of the relationships of carbon, silicon percentage, section size, and properties is that reproduced in Fig. 21.10.

Another section-size effect which may develop in the thinner sections of gray iron is the danger of misruns and chilled iron surfaces or internal hard spots. Certain minimum section thicknesses are therefore desirable to avoid this difficulty. Recommended minimum wall thickness desirable in gray iron castings is listed in Table 21.3. The information in the tables should not be interpreted as meaning that gray-iron castings with thinner sections than those listed cannot be produced satisfactorily, but rather that a minimum of foundry difficulties and cost will be possible if the suggested limiting thicknesses are followed.

Because composition, cooling rate, the graphitization process, and the structure and properties developed in the casting are so intimately related, these factors must all be considered when a certain end point is desired in the casting. Obviously, an automotive piston ring requires a different combination of the aforementioned factors than does a heavy

Table 21.3 ***Recommended minimum wall thickness****

ASTM class iron	Suggested min wall thickness, in.
20	1/8
25	1/4
30	3/8
35	3/8
40	5/8
50	1/2
60	3/4

* From "Metals Handbook." [1]

forging press frame. The selection of the proper combination of analysis, melting practice, and processing operations to produce the properties desired in castings of particular size and shape is a part of the foundryman's technology.

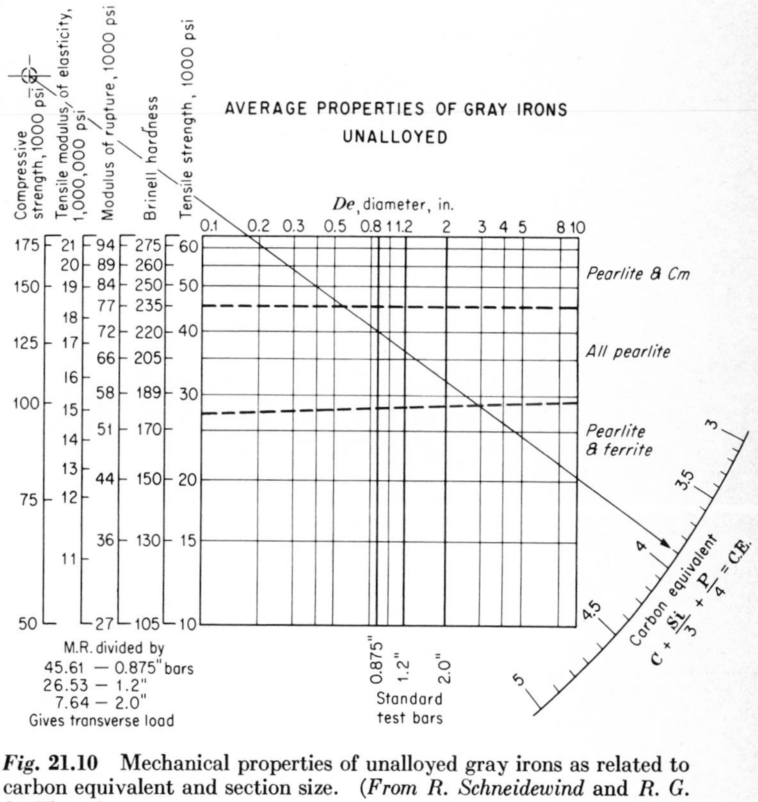

***Fig.* 21.10** Mechanical properties of unalloyed gray irons as related to carbon equivalent and section size. (*From R. Schneidewind* and *R. G. McElwee.*[6])

Other Properties

In addition to tensile and transverse properties, other properties of gray irons are significant. Specific data on these properties may be obtained from the "Cast Metals Handbook."[4] A few generalizations are offered in the following items:

Compressive Strength

This is an outstanding property of gray cast irons, being three to five times greater than its tensile strength.

Torsional Strength

Strength in torsion is about 1.20 to 1.40 times the strength in tension.

Modulus of Elasticity

The elastic modulus in tension varies from 12 to 22 million psi, depending on microstructure of the iron. A desirable microstructure of fine graphite and pearlite favors the higher values.

Shear Strength

The shear strength is about 1.0 to 1.60 times the tensile strength.[1]

Endurance Limit

The endurance limit of gray iron is about 35 to 50 per cent of its tensile strength. However, because it is less sensitive to notches, its endurance limit is as great in many applications as that of materials of substantially higher tensile strength.[4]

Hardness

The hardness of gray iron may vary in much the same way as its strength. This is illustrated in Fig. 21.9. Tensile strength and hardness are approximately related by the formula[16]

$$\text{TS} = \text{Bhn} \times K$$

where $K = 160$ to 210, depending on composition and microstructure.

The hardness, transverse, and tensile properties of automotive-type cast irons are given in Table 21.4. This table shows the general relationship of increasing hardness accompanying increasing strength. Pearlitic microstructures predominate in the higher hardnesses. Typical compositions for the irons are also given.

Wear Resistance

Gray iron is outstanding in its resistance to the sliding-friction type of wear, especially lubricated. This is exemplified in its use for piston rings, cylinder liners, crankshafts, clutch plates, brake drums, gears, and internal-combustion-engine blocks. Typical wear data are cited in the "Cast Metals Handbook"[4] and "Metals Handbook."[1]

Machinability

Gray iron is among the most machinable of ferrous materials. Best machinability in gray irons is encountered in the softer irons. A hardness range of 130 to 240 Bhn encompasses most gray irons. A combination of moderate strength and hardness, with emphasis on machinability, is listed in Table 21.4 as SAE G2000 (110) with a 187 maximum Bhn. Chilled-iron edges or hard spots in thin sections are very detrimental to machinability, although they should not occur with proper foundry practice.

Heat Resistance

Heat resistance in terms of resistance to scaling and retention of moderate strength at elevated temperatures is a desirable property of gray irons, advantageous in the use of gray iron for furnace and stoker parts, melting pots, gas burners, and similar applications. The property of heat resistance may be improved in alloyed gray irons.

Gray irons which are cycled through the critical range in service exhibit a gradual dimensional "growth" caused by oxidation. This growth can be reduced by alloying the gray iron with chromium or silicon or other alloying elements which will either increase carbide stability or raise the critical temperature range.

Damping Capacity

Damping capacity is the ability of a material to absorb energy due to vibrations and thus dampen the vibrations. The ability of gray iron to dampen vibrations as compared with steels is illustrated in Fig. 21.11 for a torsional vibratory impulse imparted to cast-iron and steel specimens.

The vibration damping capacity of gray iron assists markedly in producing smoothness of operation in internal-combustion engines or other structures where vibration is an operating characteristic.

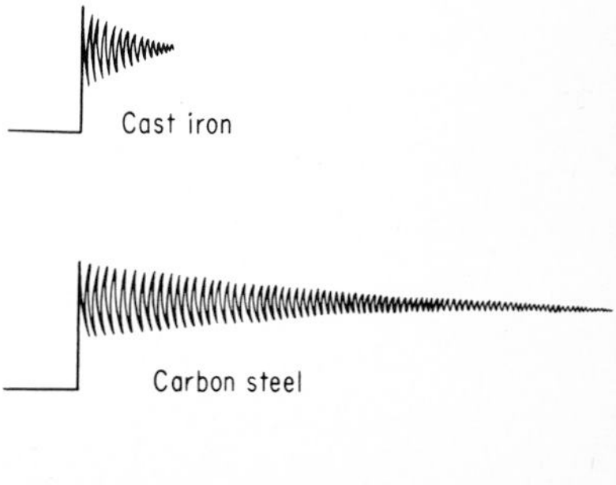

***Fig.* 21.11** Curves illustrating the damping of torsional vibrations in a carbon steel and a cast iron. (*From American Foundrymen's Society.*[4])

Table 21.4 ***Summary of gray-iron specifications***

Specifying body[a]	Specification No.[b]	Use	Class	Min tensile strength, psi	Brinell hardness
ASTM..... ASA....... AASHO.... CSA.......	A48-62 G25.1-1961 M105-62-I S61-1948	Castings intended for general engineering use where strength is a major consideration. Written exception to this specification takes precedence. These specifications are all basically the same	20[c] 25[c]	20,000[d] 25,000[d]	
			30[c] 35[c]	30,000[d] 30,000[d]	
			40[c] 45[c]	40,000[d] 45,000[d]	
			50[c] 55[c] 60[c]	50,000[d] 55,000[d] 60,000[d]	
ASTM..... SAE....... Federal.....	A159-62T[e] J431a[e] QQ-I-653	Gray iron for automotive castings	G2000[f] (110)	20,000[g]	187 max[h]
			G3000[f] (111)	30,000[g]	170–223[h]
			G3000a[f] (113)	30,000[l]	179–229[l]
			G4000b[f] (114)	40,000[l]	207–269[l]
			G3500c[f] (115)	35,000[l]	187–241[l]
			G3500[f] (120)	35,000[g]	187–241[h]
			G4000[f] (121)	40,000[g]	202–255[h]
			G4500[f] (122)	45,000[g]	217–269[h]
			G4000d[f] (123A) G4000e[f] (123B) G4000f[f] (123C)	40,000[g]	248–311[o]
Federal	QQ-I-652a[i]	Gray iron for general use. This specification may be referenced with special requirements for applications requiring special iron characteristics involving wear, corrosion, heat, or cold[q]	20	20,000[r]	....
			25	25,000[r]	....
			30	30,000[r]	....
			35	35,000[r]	....
			40	40,000[r]	....
			50[t]	50,000[r]	....
			60[t]	60,000[r]	....
			Special	[u]	....

Other requirements	Typical applications
1. At least two (2) test bars shall be cast and prepared for each casting lot, the lot size being designated	Lightweight and thin section castings requiring good appearance, high machinability, and close dimensions
2. Test bars shall be cast in dried sand molds made mainly of siliceous sand and binder. The average sand grain size shall approximate that in which the castings are poured. Test-bar mold should be approximately room temperature when poured	General machinery, municipal and water works, light compressors, automotive
3. Tension test specimens shall be tested under axial loading	Machine tools, medium gear blanks, heavy compressors, heavy motor blocks
4. Hardness, chemical composition, microstructure, pressuretightness, radiographic soundness, dimension, surface finish, etc., can be established as requirements upon written agreement between manufacturer and purchaser	Dies, crankshafts, high-pressure cylinders, heavy-duty machine-tool parts, large gears, press frames

Transverse test[i]		Chemistry				
1.2″ diam, 18″ span						
Strength, min, lb	Deflection, min, in.	Total carbon, %	Silicon, %	Alloys, %	Microstructure	Typical applications
1800	0.15	3.40–3.70[j]	2.30–2.80[j]	[k]		Miscellaneous soft-iron castings (as cast or annealed) in which strength is not of primary consideration
2200	0.20	3.20–3.50[j]	2.00–2.30[j]	[k]		Small cylinder blocks, cylinder heads, air-cooled cylinders, pistons, clutch plates, oil-pump bodies, transmission cases, gearboxes, clutch housings, and light-duty brake drums
2200[l]	0.20[l]	3.40 min mandatory	1.20–2.10 as required	As required	[m]	Brake drums and clutch plates or service requirements where high carbon is desired to eliminate heat checking
2600[l]	0.27[l]	3.40 min mandatory	1.10–1.80 as required	As required	[n]	Brake drums and clutch plates for heavy-duty service requiring both resistance to heat checking and higher strength
2400[l]	0.24[l]	3.50 min mandatory	1.10–1.80 as required	As required		Extra-heavy-duty service brake drums
2400	0.24	3.10–3.40[j]	1.90–2.20[j]	[k]		Automotive cylinder blocks, heads, liners, flywheels, pistons, medium-duty brake drums, and clutch plates
2600	0.27	3.00–3.30[j]	1.80–2.10[j]	[k]		Truck and tractor cylinder blocks and heads, heavy flywheels, tractor transmission cases, differential carrier castings, heavy gearboxes
2800	0.30	3.00–3.30[j]	1.80–2.10[j]	[k]		Diesel-engine castings, liners, cylinders, and pistons and heavy parts in general
2600	0.27	3.10–3.40	2.10–2.40	Cr 0.80–1.10 Mo 0.40–0.60	[p]	
		3.10–3.45	2.10–2.40	Cr 0.85–1.20 Mo 0.40–0.60 Ni 0.20–0.45		Automotive camshaft applications
		3.40–3.75	2.10–2.35	Cr 1.00–1.25 Mo 0.50–0.70 Cu 1.40–1.70		

Transverse strength, min pound load[s]			Other requirements	Typical applications
0.875″ bar; 12″ span	1.2″ bar; 18″ span	2.0″ bar; 24″ span		
900	1800	6,000	Unless otherwise specified, % S, 0.15 max % P, 0.25 max	General use in machinery, compressors, machine tools, motor blocks, valve bodies, chemical process equipment, etc.
1025	2000	6,800		
1150	2200	7,600		
1275	2400	8,300		
1400	2600	9,100		
1675	3000	10,300		
1925	3400	12,500		
[u]	[u]	[u]		

Table 21.4 ***Summary of gray-iron specifications*** **(continued)**

Specifying body[a]	Specification No.[b]	Use	Class	Min tensile strength, psi	Brinell hardness
ASTM ASME	A278-62T SA278	Pressure-containing parts for temperature up to 650°F	40[v]	40,000[r]	
			50	50,000[r]	
			60	60,000[r]	
			70	70,000[r]	
			80	80,000[r]	
ASTM	A319-53 Non-pressure-containing parts for elevated temperatures	For superior thermal shock resistance where strength requirements are unnecessary	I	Low strength[w]	Maximum hardness at casting locations to be machined shall be agreed on by manufacturer and purchaser
		For average thermal shock resistance and moderate strength	II	Above 30,000 may be expected[w]	
		For higher strength (at temperature)	III	As high as 40,000 may be expected	
U.S. Military	MIL-G-858A	High alloy for resistance to corrosion, scaling, warpage, and growth	1	25,000	120–180
			2	25,000	120–180
ASTM	A436-63	Austenitic-gray-iron[y] castings used primarily for their resistance to heat, corrosion, and wear. See full specification for prescribed heat-treatments covering stress relief, dimensional stabilization, or elimination of chilled edges or excessive carbides	1[z]	25,000[aa]	131–183
			1b[z]	30,000[aa]	149–212
			2[z]	25,000[aa]	118–174
			2b[z]	30,000[aa]	171–248
			3[z]	25,000[aa]	118–159
			4[z]	25,000[aa]	149–212
			5[z]	20,000[aa]	99–124
			6[z]	25,000[aa]	124–174

[a] Names and addresses are:
AASHO—American Association of State Highway Officials, 917 National Press Bldg., Washington 4, D.C
ASA—American Standards Association, Inc., 10 East 40th St., New York 16, N.Y.
ASME—American Society of Mechanical Engineers, 345 East 47th St., New York 17, N.Y.
ASTM—American Society for Testing and Materials, 1916 Race St., Philadelphia 3, Pa.
CSA—Canadian Standards Association, 235 Montreal Rd., Ottawa 7, Ontario, Canada
Federal—General Services Administration, 575 U.S. Court House, Chicago, Ill. (also eleven regional offices
SAE—Society of Automotive Engineers, Inc., 485 Lexington Ave., New York 17, N.Y.
U.S. Military—Bureau of Supplies and Accounts, Navy Department, Washington 25, D.C. (or neares Base or Military Installation for procurement of copies of specifications)

[b] The final number of most specifications indicates the year of latest revision.

[c] Each class number is followed by a letter, either A, B, C, or S, indicating the test-bar size required fo the class. All test bars must be separately cast and machined, and the tension-test result is required for castir qualification. At least two test bars required for each lot of castings intended to conform to this specificatio

[d] The test-bar size shall be determined by the controlling casting section if a test bar is not specified. Recom mended dimensions are as follows:

ASTM Tensile-bar Dimensions

Controlling section of castings, in.	Test bar	Cast-bar length, in.		Cast-bar average diam, in.	Machined-bar diam, in.
		Min	Max		
0.25–0.50	A	5.0	6.0	0.88	0.50
0.51–1.00	B	6.0	9.0	1.20	0.75
1.00–2.0	C	7.0	10.0	2.00	1.25
Under 0.25 Over 2.0	S	Intended for use when standard bars are not satisfactory. All dimensions shall be agreed upon by manufacturer and purchaser			

[e] Individual specification number given in "Class" column. This specification subordinates chemical compos tion to tensile strength and Brinell hardness except where specific application requires compositional contro

[f] New SAE numbering system adopted in 1963. Old numbers, i.e., "110," can be alternatively used for five-year period from 1963.

[g] Obtained from test bars separately cast but of same iron and thermal history as castings. Test-bar dimen

Other requirements	Typical applications
Carbon equivalent, 3.8% max CE = % C + 0.3(% Si + % P); % P, 0.25 max; % S, 0.12 max Castings and test bars must be stress-relieved by prescribed methods	Valve bodies, papermill drier rolls, chemical process equipment, pressure-vessel castings

Carbon equivalent	% C, min	% P, max	% S, max	Other requirements	Typical applications
3.81–4.40	3.50	0.60	0.12	When chromium is present as an alloying element, each class shall be subdivided as follows:[x]	Stoker and fire-box parts, grate bars, process furnace parts, ingot molds, glass molds, caustic pots, metal melting pots
3.51–4.10	3.20	0.60	0.12		
3.20–3.80	2.80	0.60	0.12		

Type	% Cr
A	0.20–0.40
B	0.41–0.65
C	0.66–0.95
D	0.96–1.20

	% total C	% Si	% Mn	% Ni	% Cr	% Cu	% S	% P	Typical applications
Min	2.60	1.25	1.0	13.5	1.8	5.5			For use at elevated temperatures, galley range tops; to resist acid, caustic, and salt solutions. (For galley range tops, maxima shall be 0.20% S, 0.70 %P)
Max	3.00	2.20	1.5	17.5	3.5	7.5	0.10	0.20	
Min	2.60	1.25	0.80	18.0	1.75				
Max	3.00	2.20	1.30	22.0	3.50	0.50	0.10	0.20	

	% total C	% Si	% Mn	% S	% Ni	% Cu	% Cr	% Mo	Typical applications
Min	....	1.00	1.00	......	13.50	5.50	1.75		Exhaust manifolds, valve guides, turbo supercharger housings, steam lines, grates, stove tops, furnace hoppers, pump casings, and impellers. Resistance to acid, caustic, and salt solutions. Resistance to heat and corrosion, as above
Max	3.00	2.80	1.50	0.12	17.50	7.50	2.50		
Min	....	1.00	1.00	......	13.50	5.50	2.50		
Max	3.00	2.80	1.50	0.12	17.50	7.50	3.50		
Min	....	1.00	0.80	......	18.00	....	1.75		
Max	3.00	2.80	1.50	0.12	22.00	0.50	2.50[bb]		
Min	....	1.00	0.80	......	18.00	....	3.00		
Max	3.00	2.80	1.50	0.12	22.00	0.50	6.00		
Min	....	1.00	0.40	......	28.00	....	2.50		
Max	2.60	2.00	0.80	0.12	32.00	0.50	3.50		
Min	....	5.00	0.40	......	29.00	....	4.50		
Max	2.60	6.00	0.80	0.12	32.00	0.50	5.50		
Min	....	1.00	0.40	......	34.00				
Max	2.40	2.00	0.80	0.12	36.00	0.50	0.10		
Min	....	1.50	0.80	......	18.00	3.50	1.00		
Max	3.00	2.50	1.50	0.12	22.00	5.50	2.00	1.00	

sions correspond to ASTM A48-62 (see footnote *d*) when transverse properties are not specified and to ASTM 438-62 when transverse properties are specified.

[h] Must be determined at the surface of the mid-length of the short bar or near fracture on broken halves of transverse bars. Hardness may be specified at definite casting location by mutual agreement.

[i] Unless otherwise specified, acceptance on mechanical properties will be based on tensile strength.

[j] Suggested. Not to be used as basis for material rejection.

[k] May be desirable to use alloying elements to obtain specific service requirements.

[l] Determined from 1.2-in. arbitration "B" bar as cast or stress-relieved at 1050 F maximum for 1 hr at heat.

[m] Graphite shall be type A, size 2–4 (see ASTM A247-47). Matrix of lamellar pearlite; ferrite not to exceed 15%.

[n] Graphite shall be type A, size 3–5 (see ASTM A247-47). Matrix of lamellar pearlite; ferrite, carbide, or both not to exceed 75%.

[o] Casting hardness shall conform to same range as specified for test bar and shall be taken on mutually located bearing surface.

[p] See full specification for specified microstructure.

[q] Temperatures above 450 F, only Classes 40, 50, or 60 should be used. Castings requiring dimensional stability or for use at elevated temperatures shall be stress-relief-annealed.

[r] Required test-bar size is similar to footnote *d* (except size A bar used for all sections under 0.50 in.).

[s] Transverse test shall be made in lieu of tensile test when specified, but shall not constitute basis for rejection.

[t] Must be relieved of stresses by prescribed methods for use below 450 F.

[u] Properties to be specified in contract.

[v] Classes 20, 25, 30, and 35 are also covered, but limited to use below 450 F.

[w] Low strength is desired for thermal shock resistance. Strength may be specified where essential (up to strength prescribed for Class 40, ASTM A48-62).

[x] Other alloys to increase strength and to improve and stabilize structure for elevated-temperature service may be used in all classes.

[y] Characterized by uniformly distributed graphite flakes, some carbides, and an austenitic matrix structure.

[z] See full specification for prescribed heat-treatments covering stress relief, dimensional stabilization, or elimination of chilled edges or excessive carbides.

[aa] Test bars machined from 1-in. keel block or a Y block in ½-in., 1-in., or 3-in. size by option of purchaser.

[bb] When some machining is required, the 3.00 to 4.00% Cr range is recommended.

Corrosion Resistance

The corrosion resistance of gray iron is important in some applications. Water mains and other pipe applications illustrate this property in use. Since gray irons may be porcelain-enameled, their usefulness may be extended to bathtubs, sinks, and other items of this type.

Electrical Resistance

The electrical resistance of gray iron is sufficiently high so that it is used extensively for resistance grids.[4]

Ability to Be Heat-treated

Gray iron may be hardened and tempered by heat-treatments similar to those applied to steel. For example, wear resistance in cylinder liners and sleeves is increased by hardening and tempering to the range of Rockwell 45 to 55 C.

Considering the range of properties available in gray irons, it is easy to understand the wide use of this material in all the basic industries. Although the property generalizations made above apply to the usual grades of gray irons, it should be recognized that certain of the properties may be enhanced by alloying or other metallurgical practices.

Gray-iron Specifications

Because gray iron is used in so many different engineering applications, numerous specifications covering its use in special fields have been developed. A most comprehensive summary of these specifications has been compiled.[22] It is presented in Table 21.4. Note that Table 21.4 gives the relationship between casting-section size and test-bar size in the table, in footnote *d*.

The specifications presented in Table 21.4 illustrate the idea of subdividing the wide range of properties of gray irons into smaller ranges. Thus these specifications recognize that this engineering material can be

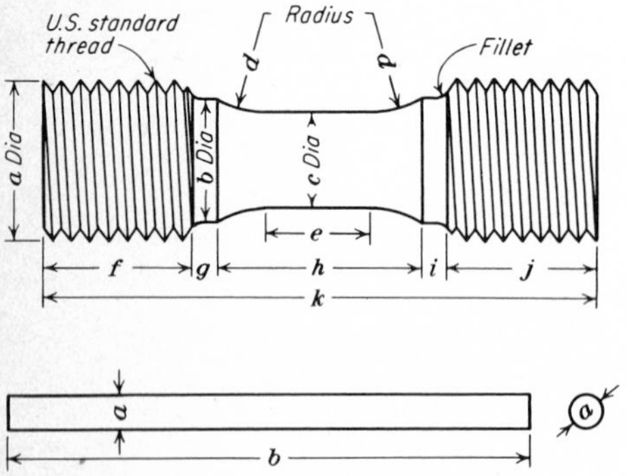

***Fig.* 21.12** Standard tensile and transverse test bars for gray iron with correction-factor table.

produced with a wide range of properties, and it is the foundryman's problem to produce an iron in the property range specified by the purchaser of the castings. Furthermore, it is the design engineer's problem to design the casting so that the foundryman can furnish the properties which are specified for the castings of a particular section, size, and shape.

Dimensions of the tension-test specimens and correction factors for transverse test bars are given in Fig. 21.12.

HEAT-TREATMENT OF GRAY IRON

Because gray irons may be heated into an austenitic temperature range, they are amenable to many heat-treatments applied to steels. Benefits which may be derived by a suitable heat-treatment are:

1. Improved machinability
2. Improved wear resistance
3. Improved strength
4. Dimensional stability and stress relief

Machinability

Annealing or normalizing may be utilized to soften and improve the machinability of gray irons. Subcritical annealing may be accomplished by heating to 1200 to 1250 F, holding 2 to 4 hr, followed by slow cooling. Spheroidization of pearlite and some graphitization occur during this treatment. More complete annealing may be accomplished by heating above the critical range to 1650 to 1700 F, holding, and slow cooling. The latter treatment can accomplish complete graphitization and softening of the iron to about 120 to 140 Bhn. Permanent-mold castings are often so treated. Normalizing by air cooling from the high temperature is accompanied by retention of pearlite and a higher strength and Bhn after treatment than result from annealing.

Wear Resistance

Hardening and tempering may be employed to obtain increased wear resistance in cast irons. Heating the iron to 1575 to 1700 F causes an austenitic structure with about 0.6 to 0.80 per cent dissolved carbon to be developed. Subsequent quenching in oil or water will produce a martensitic structure having the hardness characteristic of hardened steels. The quenched iron may then be tempered at various temperatures to reduce hardness to that desired. An example of these heat-treatments is provided in the case of hardened cylinder liners. Cylinder liners machined to the point of finishing may be given the following treatment:

1. Heat to 1660 to 1620 F in 30 min.
2. Hold at temperature for 20 to 30 min.
3. Quench on an arbor into oil at 160 to 180 F.
4. Drain and cool.
5. Temper at 400 to 420 F for 1 hr, cool.
6. Hardness after heat-treatment is Rockwell 45 to 55 C, usually about 48 to 50 C.

Cylinder liners treated according to this schedule are extensively used in diesel engines and heavy gas engines because of wear resistance superior to that of unhardened ones.

Added resistance to wear in cams, gears, rollers, and the like may be obtained by hardening. Flame or induction hardening of wearing surfaces may be more desirable than heat-treating the entire part, since many castings will crack when subjected to quenching from high temperature.

Strength

In rare cases, hardening and tempering heat-treatments are applied to produce a maximum tensile strength.[23] Hardening followed by tempering at 800 to 1000 F produces optimum tensile properties. However, because of the warpage or cracking difficulties of quench-hardening many castings, the treatment is not extensively used. Rather, alloying and combinations of alloying and heat-treatment are used to obtain greater strength.

Stress Relief

Stress relief is often desirable when castings are found to change dimensions to a harmful degree during machining or use. Such dimensional changes are due to residual stresses in the casting arising from the casting process. Annealing or normalizing heat-treatments may be applied to alleviate the stresses. A specific stress-relief anneal consists in heating slowly to about 900 to 1100 F, holding 1 hr or more, and cooling slowly, about 100 F per hr, to 400 to 600 F.[20,23] A subcritical stress-relief treatment causes less softening of the gray iron than the higher-temperature annealing treatment.

ALLOYING ELEMENTS

An "alloy" gray iron is one which has been alloyed with elements such as chromium, copper, nickel, or molybdenum to obtain some beneficial effect. Alloyed gray irons are produced in far less tonnage than regular gray iron, but their special properties make them more desirable for certain applications. Alloying effects in gray irons may be considered in two categories: (1) effect on microstructure, the metal matrix, and the graphitization process; (2) effect on the properties.

Effect on Microstructure

The microstructural effects of the alloying elements depend on their tendency to form carbides, dissolve in ferrite, alter the pearlite, or influence the graphite size and distribution. Some elements are capable of multiple effects. A summary of the alloying tendencies of the more important alloying elements is given in Table 21.5.

Elements such as Cr, Mn, and Mo, which form carbides and cause the transformation of austenite to pearlite to be sensitive to cooling-rate effects, are employed to develop completely pearlitic microstructures. Increasing percentages of these elements will cause the pearlite to contain more combined carbon and also produce pearlite of higher hardness and strength. Of course, these same elements also affect graphitization during solidification, and will increase chilling tendency if used in excess or with incorrect alloying practices. Ultimately, a white iron will prevail if large percentages of carbide-forming elements are added to gray irons.

Other elements, such as silicon, nickel, and copper, will dissolve in the ferrite phase of the microstructure. Such elements cause the ferrite to become harder and have higher tensile strength.[1] These same elements generally encourage graphitization. It is most common to use combinations of elements for their effects on the ferrite and carbide constituents.

Chromium [1,4]

Chromium in small amounts, about 0.15 to 0.75 per cent, is used to produce a fully pearlitic microstructure. A pearlitic structure of higher than 0.60% combined carbon content develops higher hardness and strength. An increase of combined carbon percentage from a value of 0.50 to one of 0.85% and hardness from 197 to 235 Bhn after adding 0.50% Cr to a 3.40% C–2.15% Si gray iron has been observed by the authors. However, the specific effects of adding an element such as chromium are greatly dependent on the initial condition and composition of the gray iron and nature of the addition agent.

Besides developing greater strength and hardness, chromium may be employed to obtain oxidation resistance. In applications calling for heating of the casting to temperatures where oxidation or scaling may occur, the use of 1.50 to 2.00% Cr has been found to improve the heat resistance of the iron. Furnace and stoker parts, grates, and pots are examples of this type of service.

Table 21.5 Summary of structural effects of some alloying elements in gray iron*

Graphitization effects	Effects on carbides	Effect on % combined carbon	Percentages used in pearlitic irons	Effect on metal matrix, pearlite, and ferrite	Effects on graphite structure
Decreased graphitization:					
Chromium	Strongly stabilizes	Increases	0.15–1.00	Refines and hardens pearlite and eliminates ferrite	Mildly refines
Vanadium	Strongly stabilizes	Increases	0.15–0.50	Refines and hardens pearlite and eliminates ferrite	Refines
Manganese	Stabilizes	Increases	0.30–1.25	Refines and hardens pearlite and eliminates ferrite	Mildly refines
Molybdenum	Stabilizes	Increases	0.30–1.00	Refines pearlite and in higher percentages produces an acicular or bainitic structure	Refines
Increased graphitization:					
Silicon	Strongly promotes instability	Decreases	....	Produces ferrite and softens	Coarsens
Nickel	Mildly decreases stability	....	0.1–3.0	Mildly refines pearlite and hardens	Mildly refines
Copper	Mildly decreases stability	....	0.25–2.0	Mildly refines pearlite and hardens	About neutral
Dual effects on graphitization:					
Aluminum	Above 8% Al, iron is white and carbides do not decompose by heat-treatment	Increases	....	Produces matrix of pearlite and stable carbides	Produces stable white iron
Aluminum	Small percentages, less than 0.50%, cause iron carbides to be unstable	Decreases	....	Produces ferrite and makes pearlite unstable	Complex, depends on many factors
Titanium	Forms very stable TiC which cannot be graphitized	Increases	....	....	Decreases, produces TiC particles in the matrix
Titanium	Small percentages, less than 0.25%, cause iron carbide to be unstable	Decreases	....	Produces ferrite and makes pearlite less stable	Refines graphite flakes

* Based in part on Table 12.1 and in part on research by authors.

Table* 21.6 *Suggested nickel-chromium-molybdenum combinations*

Cast-iron class	Composition range†		
	Ni	Mo	Cr
30	0.5–1.0	Optional	0.2–0.4
40	1.0–2.0	Optional	0.3–0.5
50	1.5–2.0	0.3–0.4	Optional
60	2.0–2.5	0.4–0.5	0.20 max
70	2.5–3.0	0.5–0.6	0.20 max
80	3.0–3.5	0.6–0.7	0.20 max

* From the International Nickel Co.
† Range for 1.2 to 2.0-in.-diameter arbitration bars.

Highly alloyed irons may contain as much as 30% Cr. However, these are white irons, and are used for very special conditions involving scaling or corrosion resistance.

Molybdenum, Molybdenum-Nickel[5,17,18]

Molybdenum is especially effective in strengthening and hardening irons because of its property of causing austenite to transform to fine pearlite or to bainite. The harder microstructures produce increased strength. Combinations of molybdenum and nickel have proved especially effective in this respect. Compositions and properties of some molybdenum- and nickel-bearing cast irons are given in Tables 21.6 and 21.7. The code designations of the irons in these tables are proprietary ones. The mechanical properties of the irons having 50,000 psi tensile strength or greater are obtained through a low carbon equivalent and modification of the pearlitic structure to the acicular bainite. This is illustrated in Fig. 21.13. Heat-treatments may be required to bring out optimum properties in these alloyed gray irons,[5,17,18] especially the higher tensile strengths listed in Table 21.7.

Nickel[1,4]

Nickel mildly promotes graphitization in gray iron. It dissolves in the ferrite and hardens this constituent. Used alone, nickel is somewhat effective in reducing the amount of silicon which must be present to develop a gray iron, and thus may cause refinement of the graphite and pearlitic structure. In combination with other elements, a wide range of properties may be developed, as was indicated in the previous section. More highly alloyed gray irons produce gray irons with austenitic or

Table* 21.7 *Properties of alloys listed in Table* 21.6

Cast-iron type†	30	40	50	60	70	80
Tensile strength, psi min	30,000	40,000	50,000	60,000	70,000	80,000
Modulus of elasticity, psi min	14×10^6	16×10^6	18×10^6	20×10^6	22×10^6	24×10^6
Compressive strength, psi min	110,000	130,000	145,000	165,000	180,000	200,000
Torsional strength, psi min	34,000	47,000	60,000	73,000	87,000	100,000
Modulus of rigidity, psi, typical	5×10^6	5.6×10^6	6.2×10^6	6.8×10^6	7.4×10^6	8.0×10^6
Impact strength, izod AB, ft-lb,‡ typical	26	35	43	52	61	70
Damping capacity	Excellent	Excellent	Good	Good	Fair	Fair
Endurance limit, psi, typical	15,000	19,000	23,000	27,000	31,000	35,000
Hardness, Bhn, typical	200	230	260	290	320	350
Specific gravity	7.10	7.20	7.30	7.40	7.40	7.40
Density, lb/cu in	0.257	0.260	0.264	0.268	0.268	0.268
Pattern shrinkage, in./ft	$\frac{1}{10}$–$\frac{1}{8}$	$\frac{1}{8}$	$\frac{1}{8}$	$\frac{1}{8}$–$\frac{3}{16}$	$\frac{1}{8}$–$\frac{3}{16}$	$\frac{1}{8}$–$\frac{3}{16}$

* From the International Nickel Co.

† The numbering system is similar to that used in ASTM Specification A48-48.

‡ A 120-ft blow struck 3 in. from the grips on a 1.2-in. cantilevered as-cast bar.

martensitic structure. Ni-resist* is an austenitic gray iron used for applications requiring corrosion resistance, for example, chemical equipment, pots, tanks, valves, etc. The microstructure of an austenitic gray iron is illustrated in Fig. 21.14.

Where exceptional wear resistance and hardness are required in service, a martensitic microstructure of the type illustrated in Fig. 21.15 may be

* Trade name.

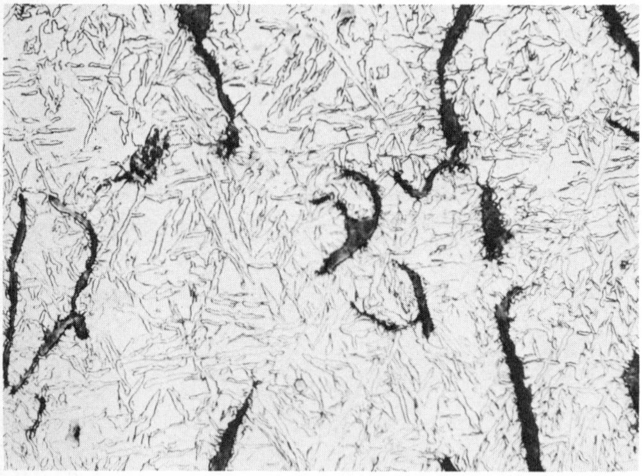

Fig. 21.13 Microstructure of an acicular cast iron. Chemical composition: 3.00% C, 1.50% Si, 0.70% Mn, 20% Ni, and 0.65% Mo. Mechanical properties: 300 Bhn, 60,000 psi ultimate tensile strength. Etched with 2% nital, ×500. (*Courtesy of International Nickel Co.*)

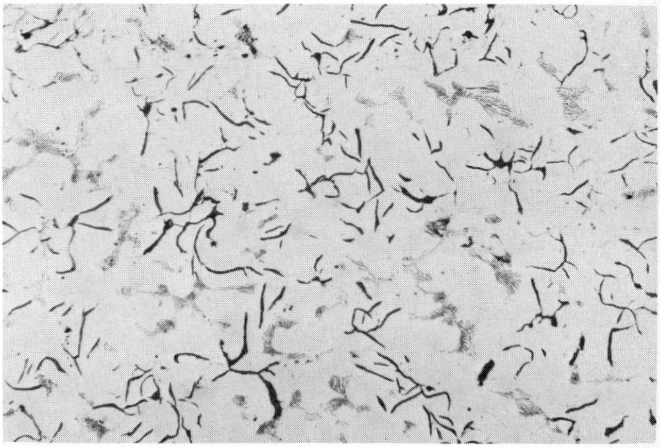

***Fig.* 21.14** Microstructure of an austenitic gray iron. Chemical composition: 2.70% C, 1.85% Si, 15.0% Ni, and 2.0% Cr. Mechanical properties: 130 Bhn, 30,000 psi ultimate tensile strength. Etched with 5% nital, ×500. (*Courtesy of International Nickel Company.*)

desired. Alloying gray irons with nickel, molybdenum, and chromium may be used to obtain this martensitic microstructure in the as-cast condition, usually in a white iron. Probably in excess of 12% chromium alone, or 4% nickel in combination with 1.50% chromium or more, is required to obtain martensitic structures in white irons.

Silicon

Silicon is also used as a special alloying element in cast irons. Cast irons containing 6 to 8% silicon have been found more resistant to scaling than ordinary irons. With 13 to 18% silicon (0.2 to 1.0% C), an alloy having corrosion resistance to sulfuric and other acids and corrosion media is obtained. These irons are useful for vessels, pump housing, pipe fittings, and other acid-handling equipment.

Copper[34]

Copper in gray irons functions as a mildly graphitizing element and dissolves in the ferrite phase. It is used in amounts up to 3.0 per cent to increase wear resistance in sliding friction, as in brake drums and cylinder sleeves, and to confer added corrosion resistance to mildly acid and to atmospheric conditions. Most gray iron contains some copper as a residual element from the raw materials.

***Fig.* 21.15** Microstructure of a martensitic white iron composed of needlelike martensite and massive white cementite. Chemical composition: 3.00% C, 0.50% Si, 0.50% Mn, 4.5% Ni, and 1.5% Cr. Mechanical properties: 600 to 650 Bhn. Picral-etched, ×500. (*Courtesy of International Nickel Company.*)

Aluminum and Titanium

Aluminum is at present little used as an alloying element in gray cast irons. However, since it is present in many ferroalloys used for adding other elements to gray irons, its effect may be mentioned. In small amounts, less than 0.25 per cent, it is known to be a powerful graphitizing element, both during solidification and afterward. An alloy containing over 8.0% aluminum and 3.0% C will freeze white and does not graphitize even if heat-treated. Aluminum thus functions as both a powerful graphitizer and carbide stabilizer, depending on the percentage employed. Some interest is being shown in irons alloyed with up to 12.0 per cent aluminum for oxidation- and scale-resistant purposes.

Titanium is another element behaving as does aluminum. The first small percentages of titanium, 0.05 to 0.25 per cent, promote graphitization, reduce chilling tendency, and refine the graphite flake size. Above this value, however, increasing titanium percentages result in the formation of TiC, a very stable carbide which cannot be decomposed by thermal treatments.

In the case of both these elements, the efficacy of the very small percentages is of great interest. The most common explanation offered is that these elements exert an indirect effect by their reaction with oxygen and nitrogen, which are always present in the iron. In this theory the latter two gases are held to be carbide-stabilizing, and their removal by aluminum or titanium results in a graphitizing effect.

Effect on Properties

The influence of alloying elements on properties of gray irons is complex. The objectives of alloying these irons, however, may be simply listed as follows:

1. Increased mechanical strength
2. Increased resistance to wear
3. Increased resistance to corrosion
4. Increased resistance to oxidation or scaling
5. Increased resistance to abrasion

The variety of specially alloyed irons developed to enhance these properties is great. Some typical compositions of alloyed gray irons and their uses are listed in Table 21.8. Detailed information of the specific quantitative effects on properties by each alloying element and their combination is beyond the scope of this book, and is in many cases lacking. Reference may be made to "Alloy Cast Irons" and "Cast Metals Handbook," AFS publications, *Transactions of AFS,* and the metallurgical literature for such information as exists.

BIBLIOGRAPHY

1. American Society for Metals, "Metals Handbook," 8th ed., vol. 1, 1961.
2. A. Boyles, The Microstructure of Cast Irons, American Society for Metals.
3. American Foundrymen's Society, "The Cupola and Its Operation," 1954.
4. American Foundrymen's Society, "Cast Metals Handbook," 4th ed., 1957.
5. R. A. Flinn, M. Cohen, and J. Chipman, The Acicular Structure in Nickel-Molybdenum Cast Irons, *Trans. ASM*, December, 1942, p. 1225.
6. R. Schneidewind and R. G. McElwee, Composition and Properties of Gray Iron, *Trans. AFS,* vol. 58, pp. 312–330, 1950; see bibliography also.
7. L. F. Porter and P. C. Rosenthal, Effect of Sulfur on the Fluidity of Gray Cast Iron, *Trans. AFS,* vol. 60, 1952.
8. H. W. Lownie, Jr., Theories of Gray Cast Iron Inoculation, *Trans. AFS,* vol. 54, 1946.
9. R. W. Lindsay, Graphite Phase in Gray Cast Iron, *Trans. AFS,* vol. 55, 1947.
10. H. LaPlanche, A New Structural Diagram for Cast Iron, *Metal Progr.,* December, 1947; New Structural Diagrams for Alloy Cast Irons, *ibid.,* June, 1949.
11. S. C. Massari and R. W. Lindsay, Some Factors Influencing Graphitizing Behavior of Cast Iron, *Trans. AFS,* vol. 49, p. 953, 1944.
12. T. E. Barlow and C. H. Lorig, Gray Cast Iron Tensile Strength, Brinell Hardness and Composition Relationships, *Trans. AFS,* vol. 54, 1946.

*Table 21.8 A few alloy-cast-iron compositions and properties**

Casting type	Si	Total C	Com-bined C	Mn	S max	P max	Ni	Mo	Cr	Others	Section size, in.	Weight, lb	Bhn	Transverse†		Tensile strength, psi
														Load, lb	Deflec-tion, in.	
Automotive cylinder block	2.15–2.35	3.10–3.40	0.50–0.80	0.50–0.80	0.12	0.20	0.10–0.20	...	0.15–0.25	...	¼–1.50	50	163–207	2200	0.20 min	37,000 min
Brake drums, coach and trucks	1.90–2.10	3.40–3.60	...	0.55–0.75	0.13	0.25	...	...	0.50–0.60	1.00–1.50 Cu	½–¾	50–150	207	2400–2700	0.25–0.30	34,000
Crankshaft, truck, diesel	2.20–2.50	2.60–2.80	0.60–0.75	0.90–1.00	0.08	0.08	0.75–1.00	0.75–1.00	0.10–0.20	...	1.25–3.00	200–1000	220–240	...	...	60,000–80,000
Cylinder sleeves	2.05–2.25	3.25–3.50	...	0.55–0.80	0.12	0.25	0.10–0.25	0.10–0.25	0.60–0.85	1.00–1.50 Cu	¼–½	Up to 25	192–241	3300	0.10	36,000
Ball-mill liners	0.40–0.60	3.50–3.70	...	0.60–0.80	0.13	0.25	4.25–4.75	4.25–4.75	1.40–1.60	...	3–5	200–500	700–750	Chill-cast		
Beds, heavy machine tools	0.90–1.10	2.90–3.20	...	0.65–0.90	0.12	0.20	1.00–1.50	1.00–1.50	0.50	...	¾–3	2000–10,000	200–240	4000–5000	0.10–0.175	40,000–50,000
Dies, metal forming	1.00–1.50	2.80–3.20	...	0.60–1.00	0.12	0.25	1.25–1.50	1.25–1.50	...	...	1½–6	500–10,000	...	3000–3200	0.26–0.30	48,000–55,000
Stoker links	1.50–2.00	2.85–3.75	...	0.50–0.80	0.12	0.35	...	...	12.00–17.00	...	½–1½	8–15	400–650			
Filter grids, brine solutions	2.00–2.20	2.80–3.00	...	1.00–1.10	0.10	0.20	14.00–16.00	...	2.00	5.50–6.50Cu	⅝–1½	25–200	160–180	...	...	25,000–30,000

* Adapted in part from American Foundrymen's Society.[4]
† Arbitration B bar.

13. J. T. MacKenzie, The Brinell Hardness of Gray Iron and Its Relation to Some Other Properties, *ASTM Proc.*, vol. 46, pp. 1025–1036, 1946.
14. J. T. Eash, Effect of Ladle Inoculation on the Solidification of Gray Cast Iron, *Trans. AFS,* vol. 49, pp. 831–849, 1941.
15. W. E. Mahin and H. W. Lownie, Microstructure Related to Properties of Cast Iron, *Trans. AFS,* vol. 54, 1946.
16. R. Schneidewind and D. A. D'Amico, The Influence of Undercooling on the Graphite Pattern in Gray Cast Iron, *Trans. AFS,* vol. 47, pp. 831–849, 1939.
17. R. A. Flinn, M. Cohen, and J. Chipman, The Acicular Structure in Nickel-Molybdenum Cast Irons, *Trans. ASM,* December, 1942, p. 1255.
18. R. A. Flinn and D. Reese, The Development and Control of Engineering Cast Irons, *Trans. AFS,* vol. 50, March, 1942.
19. A. Finlayson, Diesel Engine Crankshafts Cast in Gray Iron, *Foundry,* vol. 78, August–September, 1950.
20. J. H. Schaum, Stress Relief of Gray Cast Iron, *Trans. AFS,* vol. 56, 1948.
21. V. T. Malcolm and S. Low, Some Tests on Relaxation of Cast Iron, *Trans. AFS,* vol. 58, 1950.
22. The Gray Iron Founders' Society, Summary of Gray Iron Specifications, Rev., January, 1964.
23. J. S. Vanick, Engineering Properties of Heat Treated Cast Irons, *Trans. AFS,* vol. 52, 1944.
24. A. W. Silvester, Graphitization of Gray Cast Iron by Heat Treatment, *Trans. AFS,* vol. 57, 1949.
25. A. Boyles, Some Principles Involved in the Heat Treatment of Gray Cast Iron, *Trans. AFS,* vol. 56, 1948.
26. G. M. Lahr, Conventional vs. Salt Bath Hardening of Cast Iron Cylinder Liners, *Trans. AFS,* vol. 56, 1948.
27. C. K. Donoho, Mechanical Testing and Properties of Gray Iron, *Foundry,* vol. 68, p. 96, June, 1940.
28. A. W. Schneble and J. Chipman, Factors Involved in the Superheating of Gray Cast Iron and Their Effects on Its Structure and Properties, *Trans. AFS,* vol. 52, pp. 113–158, 1944.
29. L. F. Porter and P. C. Rosenthal, Fluidity Testing of Gray Cast Iron, *Trans. AFS,* vol. 60, 1952.
30. A. Boyles and C. H. Lorig, Notes on the Undercooling of Gray Cast Iron, *Trans. AFS,* vol. 49, p. 769, 1941.
31. H. Morrough and W. J. Williams, Graphite Formation in the Cast Irons and in Nickel-Carbon and Cobalt-Carbon Alloys, *J. Iron Steel Inst. (London),* vol. 155, p. 321, January–April, 1947.
32. H. W. Uhlitzsch and A. Keller, Beitrag zur Kenntnis der Aluminum legierten Gusseisen, *Neue Giesserei,* vol. 36, pp. 227–232, August, 1949.
33. C. H. Lorig and R. R. Adams, Copper as an Alloying Element in Steel and Cast Iron, McGraw-Hill Book Company, New York, 1948.
34. J. C. Hamaker, Jr., W. R. Wood, and R. B. Rote, Internal Porosity in Gray Iron Castings, *Trans. AFS,* vol. 60, p. 401, 1952.
35. T. E. Eagan and C. O. Burgess, Gray Iron: Its Mechanical and Engineering Characteristics and Details for Designing Cast Components, *Foundry,* vol. 76, August–September, 1948.
36. A. DeSy, Alloyed Gray Cast Iron for Machine Components, *Trans. AFS,* vol. 70, p. 390, 1962.

22
Ductile Iron

Ductile cast iron was first announced to the foundry industry as a new engineering material at the 1948 annual meeting of the American Foundrymen's Society. This revolutionary material, discovered independently by the British Cast Iron Research Association (BCIRA) and the International Nickel Company (INCO), is also referred to as nodular, or spheroidal, graphite cast iron. The BCIRA process consists of an addition of cerium to molten, hypereutectic cast irons of essentially the same analysis as gray cast iron. Cerium removes the sulfur and, with about 0.02 per cent residual cerium, produces graphite spheroids instead of flakes. The INCO process, on the other hand, similarly employs magnesium additions to either hypo- or hypereutectic cast irons. After initial exposure to these processes, the industry soon realized the greater potential and economy of the magnesium process, which is now almost universally practiced.

Essentially, ductile cast iron consists of graphite spheroids dispersed in a matrix similar to that of steel (Fig. 22.1). The only significant difference between gray cast iron and ductile cast iron is in the shape of the graphite phase; the matrices can be similar.

The ease with which ductile iron can be processed and cast into complex shapes is very dependent on a high carbon (or carbon-equivalent) content. During solidification most of the carbon forms as graphite spheroids which exert only a minor influence on the mechanical properties in contrast to the effect of flake graphite in gray cast iron. The matrix structure then has the greatest effect on the properties of the iron. Ductile cast irons are therefore a family of alloys which combine the principal advantages of gray iron (low melting point, good fluidity and castability, excellent machinability, and good wear resistance) with the engineering advantages of steel (high strength, toughness, ductility, hot workability, and hardenability). The matrix of ductile iron can be controlled by the base composition, by foundry practice, and/or by heat-treatment to produce 60,000 psi minimum tensile strength, with over 25 per cent elongation, up to 150,000 psi minimum tensile strength, yet having 1 to 4 per cent elongation. A summary of the principal types of ductile iron is shown in Table 22.1. A few examples of ductile-iron

Table 22.1 Principal types of ductile iron*

Type No.†	Brinell hardness no.	Characteristics	Applications
80-60-03	200-270	Essentially pearlitic matrix, high-strength as-cast. Responds readily to flame or induction hardening	Heavy-duty machinery, gears, dies, rolls for wear resistance, and strength
60-45-10	140-200	Essentially ferritic matrix, excellent machinability and good ductility	Pressure castings, valve and pump bodies, shock-resisting parts
60-40-15	140-190	Fully ferritic matrix, maximum ductility and low transition temperature (has analysis limitations)	Navy shipboard and other uses requiring shock resistance
100-70-03	240-300	Uniformly fine pearlitic matrix, normalized and tempered or alloyed. Excellent combination of strength, wear resistance, and ductility	Pinions, gears, crankshafts, cams, guides, track rollers
120-90-02	270-350	Matrix of tempered martensite. May be alloyed to provide hardenability. Maximum strength and wear resistance	

*Courtesy Gray and Ductile Iron Founder's Society.

† The type numbers indicate the minimum tensile strength, yield strength, and per cent of elongation. The 80-60-03 type has a minimum of 80,000 psi tensile, 60,000 psi yield, and 3 per cent elongation in 2 in.

applications which reflect the unique combination of properties available in these alloys are presented in Fig. 22.2.

Ductile iron is currently being produced by 209 companies in the United States and 16 in Canada. The phenomenal growth of the use of this material is illustrated by the statistics on castings shipped presented in Table 22.2. A considerable percentage increase in total shipments for recent years may be noted.

Table 22.3 shows the industries which are the principal users of ductile-iron castings. Projected estimates for 1966 and 1971 are also included in these data. The percentages listed do not include the tonnage of ductile iron cast into pipe, an application which accounts for a substantial amount of the total ductile iron produced.

Ductile iron requires foundry operations which are similar to those for other cast metals. Process control is critical, however, and the

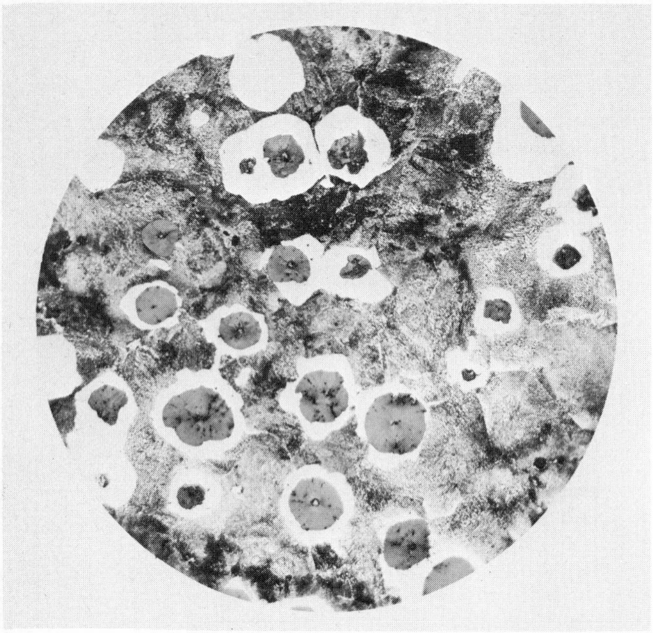

Fig. **22.1** Typical as-cast microstructure of ductile iron showing graphite spheroids surrounded by ferrite. The darker, lamellar structure in the matrix is pearlite. Etched, ×250. *(Courtesy of International Nickel Co., Inc.)*

Table **22.2** ***Total shipments of ductile-iron castings in the United States****

Year	Tonnage
1949–1953	Minor
1954	18,000
1955	33,600
1956	52,800
1957	140,300
1958	126,500
1959	193,400
1960	191,200
1961	215,000
1962	300,000
1963	442,400
1966 (est.)	856,000
1971 (est.)	1,315,000

* Courtesy of International Nickel Co., Inc.

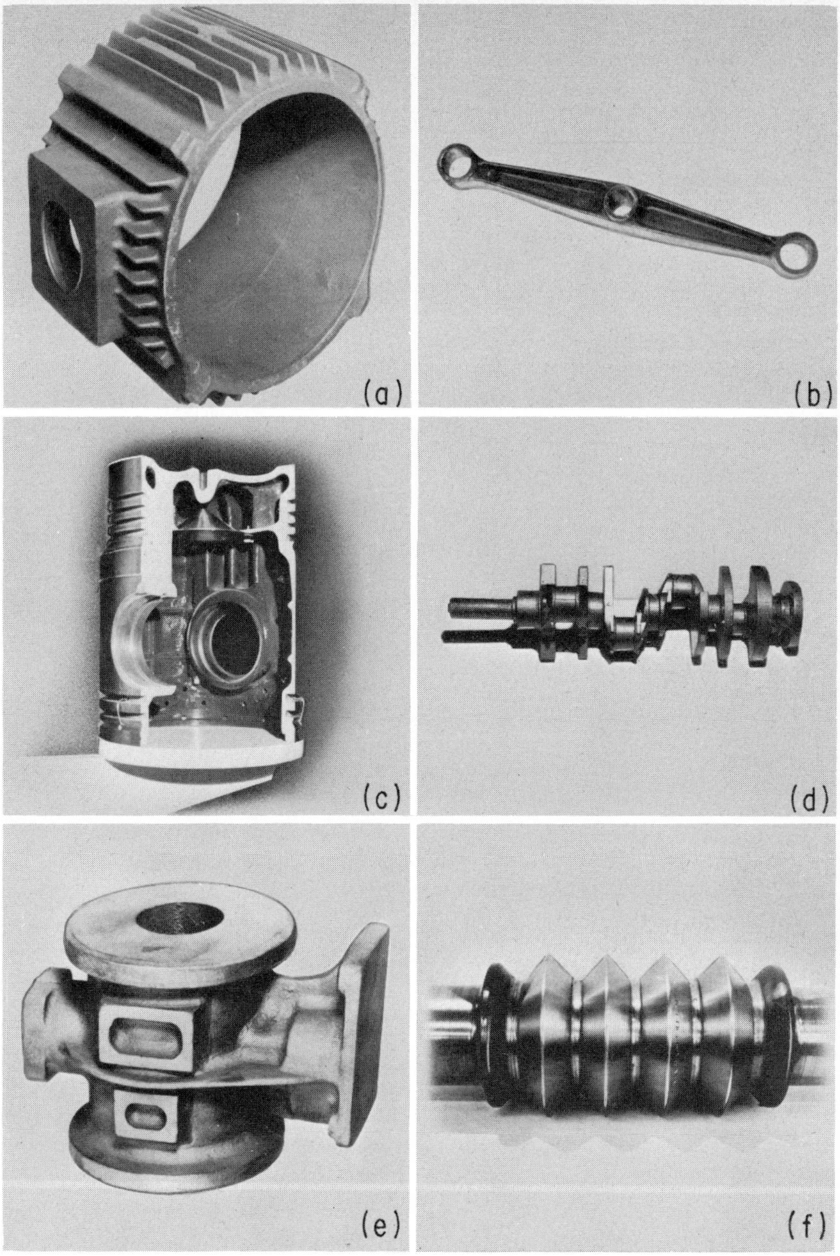

***Fig.* 22.2** Examples of the application of ductile-iron castings. (*a*) Motor frame for U.S. Navy made of 60-40-15 ductile iron because of its high resistance to explosion impact. (*b*) Axle equalizer beam for heavy-duty truck produced in normalized ductile iron selected to replace a steel forging. (*c*) Sectioned diesel-engine piston produced of ductile iron. (*d*) Shell-molded ductile-iron automotive crankshaft. (*e*) Rough casting of hot-air valve for the Caravelle plane. Ductile-iron alloy containing Ni, Cr, and Mo, selected for necessary hot strength. (*f*) Alloyed ductile iron used for 2½- by 2½-in. angle-finishing roll. (*a to d, courtesy of International Nickel Co., Inc.; e and f, courtesy of Climax Molybdenum Company.*)

Table 22.3 Principal users of ductile-iron castings*

Industrial markets	1961		1966 (est.)		1971 (est.)	
	Tons	%	Tons	%	Tons	%
Motors, vehicles, and parts	82,433	42.2	317,000	48.3	428,000	44.4
Farm machinery and equipment	27,848	14.2	93,000	14.2	157,400	16.3
Fabricated platework (boilershops)	14,981	7.7	56,200	8.6	83,300	8.6
Paper-industries machinery	7,917	4.1	17,600	2.7	26,600	2.8
Internal-combustion engines	7,560	3.8	20,000	3.0	30,100	3.1
Metalworking machinery (except machine tools)	7,391	3.8	18,400	2.8	27,700	2.9
Pumps and compressors	6,403	3.3	23,100	3.5	34,600	3.6
Construction machinery	4,280	2.2	12,500	1.9	19,100	2.0
Motors and generators	3,660	1.9	9,400	1.4	14,500	1.5
Power-transmission equipment (except ball and roller bearings)	3,497	1.8	11,000	1.7	16,700	1.7
Other	29,491	15.0	77,800	11.9	127,000	13.1
Subtotal	195,461	100.0	656,000	100.0	965,000	100.0
Ductile-iron pipe†	20,000	......	200,000	......	350,000	
Total	215,461	......	856,000	......	1,315,000	

* Courtesy of International Nickel Co., Inc.

† In 1961 ductile-iron pipe accounted for 9.3 per cent of the total, 23.4 per cent estimated in 1966, and 26.6 per cent estimated in 1971.

conventional foundry operation must be adapted to the requirements of ductile iron. Since the development of graphite as spheroids is of principal concern in this material, factors affecting this part of the structure are considered first.

SOLIDIFICATION OF DUCTILE IRON

Although the base chemistry of gray and ductile iron is essentially the same (with the exception of sulfur and magnesium), these alloys solidify according to quite different modes. These dissimilarities are especially pronounced in the solidification of the eutectic, and are responsible for many of the processing variations experienced in gray- and ductile-iron production.

Development of Graphite Spheroids

In Chap. 21, the solidification of gray cast iron was shown to involve the formation of a flake-graphite–austenite eutectic. This eutectic solidifies in a more or less conventional manner with both the austenite and the graphite in contact with the eutectic liquid. Solidification proceeds by the growth of cells of austenite and flake graphite at the expense of the liquid. Since gray iron is essentially an Fe-C-Si alloy, the eutectic solidifies over a temperature range, usually about 60 F. Further cooling of the completely solidified alloy results in the rejection of carbon from the solid austenite and the precipitation of graphite on the preexisting graphite flakes. This process continues until the eutectoid temperature range is attained. Cooling through the eutectoid range will result in a variety of matrix structures, from all ferrite to all pearlite, depending on the rate of cooling and/or the influence of alloying elements.

In comparison, solidification of the spheroidal graphite eutectic in ductile iron starts at temperatures above those of the flake-graphite eutectic for similar carbon equivalents. In this case the graphite spheroid is enveloped by a shell of austenite so that only one phase, austenite, is in contact with the eutectic liquid. Solidification of this type has been termed neoeutectic. Each unit of a graphite spheroid and austenite shell may be considered a cell where carbon must diffuse through the shell of austenite in order for the spheroid to grow. The result is that this process is slower than that of gray-iron eutectic solidification, and the neoeutectic freezing range is extended to about 120 F. Liquid metal is then present over a wider temperature range and to lower temperatures for ductile iron than for gray iron.

No nucleation of spheroidal graphite occurs once growth of the neoeutectic starts. The number of graphite spheroids is therefore determined at an early stage of solidification. Subsequent cooling of the solidified ductile iron is accompanied by graphite precipitation on the existing spheroids at temperatures down to the eutectoid range. As with gray cast iron, the cooling rate through the eutectoid range and/or alloying treatment determines the matrix structure. Bull's-eye patterns like those shown in Fig. 22.1 are typical of the ferrite-plus-pearlite matrix of as-cast ductile iron.

The importance of an adequate number of spheroids in obtaining fully spheroidal graphite structures must be stressed. When the number of spheroids is low, there are an inadequate number of sites to which the carbon of the liquid may diffuse. Depending on the composition and processing variables, either flake graphite or iron carbide will form from the liquid during further cooling. Both alternatives result in properties inferior to fully spheroidal graphite structure.

Role of Magnesium

As mentioned earlier, a magnesium addition is the most commonly accepted method of obtaining spheroidal graphite in either hypo- or hypereutectic analyses. Other elements have been suggested, but all these have proved inadequate. Among them are cerium, calcium, and yttrium. The mechanism by which magnesium causes graphite spheroids to occur is unknown; however, the function of magnesium additions is well known. First, magnesium serves as a deoxidizer and desulfurizer of the molten metal. If the oxygen and/or sulfur content of the melt is too high, a substantial amount of magnesium will be consumed in the formation of magnesium oxides and sulfides. Second, magnesium promotes the development of graphite as spheroids by a mechanism not yet defined. Finally, magnesium prevents the nucleation of flake graphite during the solidification process and thereby promotes the growth of graphite spheroids. Generally, only 0.05 per cent residual magnesium is necessary to achieve spheroid formation in most ductile irons. Methods of magnesium addition are discussed in a later section.

Control of the Common Elements

Carbon

The carbon content for commercial ductile iron is from 3.0 to 4.0 per cent, although much narrower limits are usually desired. Nodule counts are directly affected by the carbon content—greater numbers of spheroids formed at the higher carbon contents. Increasing the carbon content also increases castability by improving fluidity and feeding. The carbon-content level should be correlated with the carbon-equivalent formula:

$$CE = \% C + \tfrac{1}{3} \% S + \cdots$$

Carbon equivalents greatly in excess of 4.3 promote the development and growth of graphite spheroids. Since graphite is far less dense than molten iron, these spheroids may become buoyant and float toward the cope surface of a casting, resulting in gross carbon segregation. Flotation, as this phenomenon is called, is prevalent in analyses having carbon equivalents greater than 4.60 and in section sizes greater than 1 in.

Silicon

The normal range for silicon in ductile irons is 1.80 to 2.80 per cent. Since silicon affects the carbon-equivalent value, it also affects the number of spheroids and the occurrence of flotation. Silicon increases the amount of ferrite formed during the eutectoid transformation and also strengthens the iron by strengthening the ferrite. Additions of silicon are more influential in spheroidal-graphite control when the additions are made late (inoculation). This operation is described in a later section.

Sulfur

The most important effect of sulfur in ductile iron is to increase the amount of magnesium required to achieve spheroidal graphite. The level of sulfur in the iron prior to magnesium treatment is a function of the melting practice used. Sulfur content after treatment is usually 0.015 per cent.

Phosphorus

Phosphorus forms the very brittle structure known as steadite in ductile iron as well as in gray cast iron. Since phosphorus adversely affects toughness and ductility, a maximum of 0.05 per cent is usually specified.

Other Elements

In addition to the elements carbon, silicon, sulfur, and phosphorus discussed above, a number of other elements may be present in ductile iron. Most alloying of ductile iron makes use of manganese, nickel, molybdenum, and copper. Alloys involving these elements may be designed for higher strengths, greater toughness, or increased high-temperature- or corrosion-resistant properties. Other elements, however, even in trace amounts, may be avoided because of their deleterious effect on the development of the ductile-iron structure. Lead, titanium, aluminum, antimony, and zirconium, for instance, have been cited as promoting the development of flake graphite. On the other hand, arsenic, boron, chromium, tin, and vanadium are known to promote the formation of pearlite and/or iron carbide. Accordingly, close control over the quantities of these elements is usually exercised.

MELTING PRACTICES

The relationship of melting practice to the type and amount of spheroidizing alloy used is important to casting quality and physical properties. Considerable reduction of the amount of spheroidizing alloy and the percentage of defective or inferior castings can be realized by paying close attention to charge materials, melting methods and control, and iron composition. Ductile-iron producers have therefore found it necessary to improve normal melting practices and to exercise a greater degree of control than that used for gray iron.

Cupola melting is the most common method of melting for ductile iron; however, electric induction furnaces are in use in a number of foundries. About 75 per cent of the ductile-iron producers employ the acid cupola. In nearly all these instances, the cupola is used for both gray- and ductile-iron production. Among those foundries which have provided separate melting facilities for ductile iron, the basic cupola is preferred. Approximately 70 to 85 per cent of the tonnage of ductile iron produced is melted in basic cupolas.

Acid Cupola Melting

Since many ductile-iron producers also produce gray iron, and are generally limited to using a common cupola for melting both materials, the acid cupola has been adopted. Acid melting is much less costly than basic melting. Estimates of the cost differential in lining and maintenance of refractories for the basic cupola have been as high as four to five times as much as for acid refractories. Using acid cupolas necessitates close control over charge materials and coke since the acid slags produced are not capable of reducing the sulfur content of the iron. This results in sulfur content of 0.06 to 0.12 per cent, which, if not lowered, necessitates the use of increased amounts of spheroidizing alloy. Acid cupola melting, however, is capable of controlling the more readily oxidizable elements in the charge, such as chromium and manganese, since it is a more oxidizing process than basic cupola operation. Because of the moderate carbon pickup in acid cupola melting and the desired base-iron chemistry, the use of pig iron in the charge is required and the use of returns is somewhat limited. Close composition control and high metal temperatures, however, can be produced without the need of a hot blast.

Desulfurization

If the high sulfur content of acid-cupola iron is not reduced prior to treatment with the spheroidizing agent, an appreciable amount of the high-cost magnesium alloy will be consumed before graphite spheroidization can occur. A reduction of 0.01 per cent sulfur requires approximately 0.01 per cent magnesium by this technique. It is therefore desirable to desulfurize the iron by one of a number of commonly used methods.

Desulfurization from 0.12 to 0.02 per cent has been reported from the injection of calcium carbide into the melt. These injections are commonly made either in the forehearth or in the ladle and have an efficiency of approximately 15 per cent. The fine calcium carbide is injected through a refractory tube, using dry nitrogen gas as the carrying agent. The calcium sulfide formed floats to the surface of the melt as a readily removable dross.

Soda ash additions are also used to reduce the sulfur level of the melt, and can cause desulfurization from 0.14 to about 0.06 per cent. A second treatment with soda ash may lower the sulfur to between 0.030

and 0.025 per cent. Desulfurization with lime is also used by some producers, either alone or in conjunction with other materials.

A recent innovation of desulfurization has been the development of the "shaking ladle." In this process, desulfurization occurs by the reaction of lime with the sulfur of the melt. Shaking the ladle increases the contact of the iron with the lime, resulting in sulfur levels as low as 0.02 per cent at a 70 to 75 per cent efficiency.

Basic Cupola Melting

Basic cupola melting is characterized by the definite advantage of sulfur control. Average sulfur content of the basic melt before spheroidizing ranges from 0.025 to 0.035 per cent. This decreased sulfur level in the melt is obtained at the expense of higher operating costs, higher silicon losses during melting, less effective temperature and composition control, and a greater carbon pickup during melting. Attempts to reduce the refractory cost and to provide greater operating control have resulted in the widespread use of water-cooled cupolas and the incorporation of hot-blast equipment. When operated on a steady and continuous basis, however, basic cupolas are capable of producing a high-carbon-, low-sulfur-content melt at a lower cost than acid cupola melting.

Induction-furnace Melting

The most widely used induction furnaces for ductile-iron production are the low-frequency, 60-cycle type of unit. These furnaces can be operated either for cold melting or for duplexing, i.e., using the induction furnace to superheat an existing melt. Very close control must be exercised over raw materials in these furnaces since the rust on scrap and other slag-forming ingredients rapidly attacks furnace linings. Extremely close control of composition and of metal temperature is possible in these furnaces, so that quality ductile iron can be produced. Future trends in the ductile-iron industry indicate that an increased use of low-frequency induction furnaces is to be expected.

The use of melting units other than those mentioned for ductile-iron production is not widespread because of either their cost of operation, lack of versatility, or the degree of control which can be exercised over metal composition and temperature.

MAGNESIUM TREATMENT

Although a number of elements can be used to promote at least partial spheroidization of graphite in cast irons, magnesium is by far the most effective and economical method. The amount of magnesium required to produce spheroidal graphite is dependent largely on the sulfur and oxygen content of the base iron. In general, a minimum retained magnesium content of 0.015 to 0.050 is considered adequate.

The base-iron temperature at treatment is usually 2800 to 2850 F for both acid- and basic-melting practice, considerably above the boiling point of magnesium. As a result, the magnesium vaporizes on contact with the iron, and the reaction may be quite violent if it is not carried out properly. Magnesium recovery is dependent on the depth of liquid iron through which the vapor rises before entering the air. The time required to cover the alloy and the depth to which it is covered are therefore important in magnesium recovery. Lower magnesium recovery is also experienced at higher metal temperatures.

To reduce the volatility of the reaction, magnesium is usually alloyed with other elements. A number of alloys have been developed for this purpose. The main alloy types are:

1. Magnesium-nickel alloys
   a. 15% Mg, 85% Ni
   b. 15% Mg, 55% Ni, 30% Si
2. Magnesium-ferrosilicon alloys
   a. 9% Mg, 45% Si, 1.5% Ca, balance Fe
   b. 9% Mg, 45% Si, 1.5% Ca, 0.5% Ce, balance Fe
3. Magnesium-silicon alloys
   a. 18% Mg, 65% Si, 2.0% Ca, 0.6%

Magnesium recovery is usually higher when the lower-magnesium-content alloys are used.

Recovery is also dependent on the method by which the magnesium alloy is added to the melt. The most common methods of adding magnesium are (1) the open-ladle method, (2) the plunging method, and (3) the mechanical feeder.

The *open-ladle method* consists in first placing the magnesium alloy in the bottom of a treatment ladle and then tapping the melt onto the alloy. Treatment ladles are designed to be deep and narrow, having a height-to-diameter ratio of 2:1. The violent reaction of magnesium vapor with the liquid iron is therefore confined to the ladle. Magnesium vapor can then permeate a greater depth of molten iron than is possible with other ladle designs. The reaction with magnesium produces a dross containing magnesium sulfide and oxide which floats to the surface and is then removed. The open-ladle treatment offers a flexible method of treatment at a low equipment cost and a minimum loss in melt temperatures.

Since the open-ladle magnesium-treatment method is not efficient, several improvements on it have been suggested. The most commonly used modification is known as the "sandwich" method. Here the magnesium alloy is placed into a recession in the refractory bottom of the ladle. The alloy is then covered by a steel plate, iron chips, steel punchings, ferrosilicon, or an inert material such as sand before tapping the iron onto the alloy. In this manner the reaction time is delayed until the ladle is at least partially filled with metal, thus increasing the magnesium recovery to a level comparable with plunging.

Plunging techniques of magnesium treatment involve placing the magnesium alloy into a container positioned within a vented graphite or refractory bell fastened to a refractory-covered plunging rod. The bell is then plunged into a ladle filled with iron. Plunging offers a greater degree of control over the residual magnesium level and a higher magnesium recovery than does the open-ladle method.

The third method by which spheroidization is commonly accomplished makes use of a *mechanical feeder* whereby the magnesium alloy is continuously added to the melt stream emitting from the cupola or forehearth. This technique permits continuous and uniform treatment of the melt at generally greater magnesium recoveries than other methods.

Techniques have also been developed permitting the use of metallic magnesium; however, they are not popular in the United States and Canada. In these methods, magnesium metal is added either by a plunging technique in a covered ladle under several atmospheres of pressure or by injection through a refractory tube into the melt, using an inert gas as a carrier.

It is apparent, then, that the total magnesium recovery is dependent on a number of factors. Table 22.4 lists approximate magnesium recoveries based only on the alloy type used and the method of addition. These figures can be applied only after corrections have been made for magnesium consumption in desulfurizing the melt.

INOCULATION

Although the magnesium treatment is responsible for the development of spheroidal graphite, quality ductile iron also requires the use of an inoculant. Inoculation, or postinoculation, refers to the practice of making an addition to the melt which will increase the number of spheroids formed during solidification. A greater number of graphite spheroids provides an increased number of sites for graphitization, thereby increasing the graphitizing tendency of the solidifying melt or reducing the chilling tendency. Since eutectic carbides result in greater hardness and generally inferior mechanical properties, ensuring their elimination by inoculation has become a standard practice.

The most effective inoculants used for ductile iron are the ferrosilicon alloys. These alloys are produced in a variety of grades; the most common, however, are the 50, 65, 75, 85, and 90 per cent silicon grades. All these grades can also be obtained with or without calcium additions. The most widely used grade for inoculation is 85 per cent silicon.

Table 22.4 Per cent recovery of magnesium as related to alloy type and method of addition

Type of alloy	Method of addition		
	Open ladle	Plunging	Pressure ladle or injection
Mg-Ni	50	60	
Mg-Ni-Si	40		
Mg-Fe-Si	35	45	
Mg-Si	....	35	
Mg chips	....	....	20
Mg ingot	....	....	50

Silicon additions to the iron as postinoculants are much more effective in increasing the number of spheroids than an equivalent increase in the base silicon content. Approximately 0.5 to 1.5 per cent silicon, as ferrosilicon, is added during inoculation. These additions are made by reladling the treated iron onto ferrosilicon placed in the bottom of the ladle or added to the metal stream. Since the effect of this treatment fades with time, the addition of a small amount of ferrosilicon to the iron has been suggested each time the iron is transferred. Recent studies have also demonstrated the utility of adding a very small amount of ferrosilicon to the sprue or runner system during the pouring of the mold when it is necessary to ensure that no eutectic carbide will be formed. The increased number of spheroids also promotes an increase in the amount of ferrite formed during the eutectoid transformation because of the increased number of sites available for spheroidal-graphite growth.

METALLURGICAL PROCESS CONTROL

Production of ductile iron is a process highly sensitive to process variations. As a result, it is necessary to exercise a greater degree of control than normally used in gray-cast-iron production. Methods of control are designed to provide and maintain reliability of the cast product and to ensure the effectiveness of the magnesium treatment and inoculation.

Base-iron Analysis

Although the final carbon-equivalent content of ductile iron is usually hypereutectic, the base analysis, before magnesium treatment and inoculation, is hypoeutectic. Accordingly, control over base-iron chemistry is similar to that described in an earlier chapter for gray-cast iron.

After the magnesium treatment and inoculation it is desirable to obtain samples to determine the final chemical analysis of the iron. Methods described for gray iron are also applicable to ductile iron, except that special consideration is given to the analysis of the magnesium residual. In this case, spectrographic analysis of a chilled, graphite-free sample is preferred.

Test Coupons

The keel block, or Y block, shown in Fig. 22.3 is used to produce tensile-bar specimen for routine control or customer-acceptance tests. These castings are produced in dry-sand molds and allowed to cool to a black heat in the mold. Tests are made in the as-cast condition or, if so specified, after annealing, from standard 0.505-in. test coupons machined from the leg of the bar. Specifications for ductile iron referred to in Table 22.1 are for bars cast in this manner.

Special test coupons designed to indicate rapidly the effectiveness of the magnesium treatment are widely used. One such test coupon, referred to as a "micro lug," is approximately ¾ by ¾ by ½ in., and is

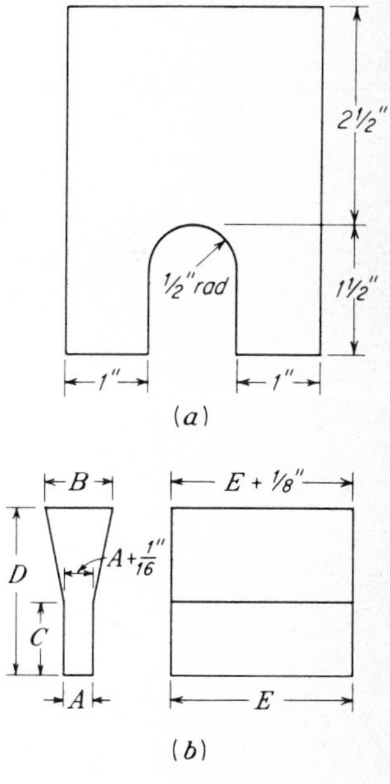

Fig. 22.3 (*a*) Keel block for ductile-iron test coupons. The length of the keel block is 6 in. It is recommended that the keel block be cast in a core sand mold with a minimum of 1½ in. of sand surrounding the casting. (*b*) Y block for ductile-iron test coupons.

cast adjacent to a heavier section of the casting in a one-piece core sand mold. The sample is allowed to cool to a black heat, is water-quenched, broken off from the heavy section, and then ground and polished. It is not necessary to remove the scratches to determine the acceptability of the iron under the metallurgical microscope at $\times 100$. The entire procedure can be completed in 3 min. This procedure is a control tool, and tells the foundryman that if the iron does not contain spheroidal graphite in the micro lug, the chances are that spheroidal graphite will not be present in the casting.

A number of factors must be controlled in ductile-iron production to avoid the occurrence of structural imperfections. Several of these factors are considered in the following paragraphs.

Graphite Shape

Quality ductile iron is produced so that the graphite is developed as spheroids. A number of other types of graphite may develop, however, if the process is not carried out properly. Charts classifying these graphite shapes have been proposed, and are presented in Figs. 22.4 and 22.5. This classification is similar to that established for gray cast iron, presented in Chap. 18. Type I graphite is the accepted graphite form in ductile iron, although the presence of type II graphite will have little effect on properties. Up to 10 per cent of type III, with the remaining graphite as type I or II, has been reported to have no noticeable effect on properties. Increased amounts of type III graphite are not desirable. Types IV and V graphite are undesirable and have significantly lower mechanical properties. Six sizes of graphite spheroids have also been proposed in Fig. 22.5.

The graphite shape developed in ductile iron has been shown to be dependent on pouring temperature, casting section size, amount of effective magnesium added, postinoculation, and base analysis of the iron. In general, the poorer graphite shapes are developed with low pouring temperature, heavy section sizes, insufficient magnesium addition, lack of inoculation, and low carbon equivalent.

An exception may be noted in high-carbon-equivalent ductile irons, over 4.6 per cent carbon equivalent, which are subject to graphite flotation and the development of exploded graphite, type V. This problem is magnified by heavy section sizes. Flotation occurs because the graphite developed early in the solidification process rapidly grows to a large size in these analyses, and thus becomes buoyant and floats to the cope surface. A considerable amount of graphite may accumulate if sufficiently heavy sections are cast. This of course results in a portion of the casting containing excessive graphite (up to 15 per cent carbon) and deteriorated properties.

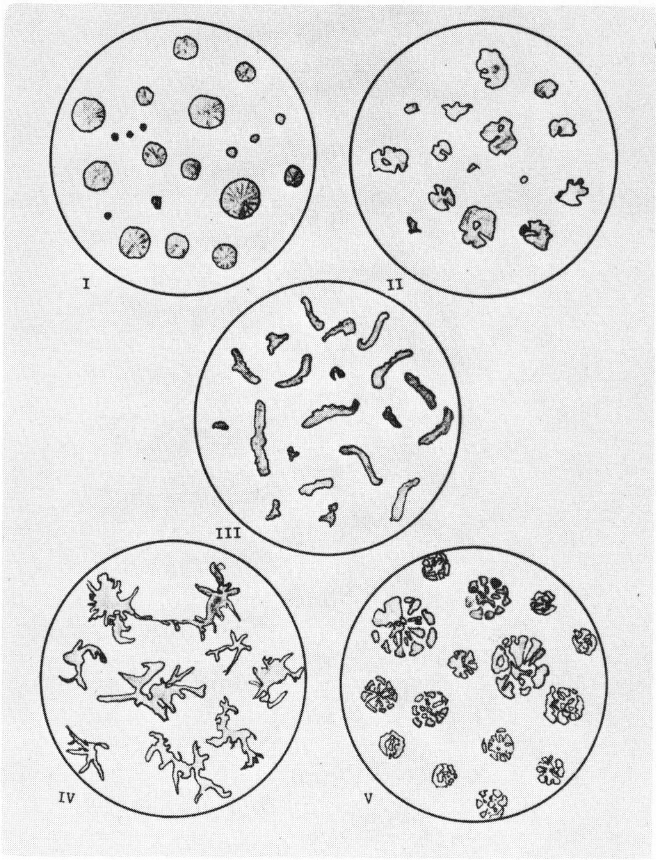

Fig. 22.4 **Proposed classification of graphite shapes in ductile cast iron, ×100.** (*From C. K. Donoho.*[30])

Carbide Formation

Just as in gray cast iron, ductile iron is subject to the occurrence of eutectic carbides during solidification. Prevention of these primary carbides is dependent on a sufficiently high base-carbon equivalent and the development of an adequate number of graphite spheroids. This number is processing-cycle-dependent; however, an estimate of the nodule counts required can be obtained from Table 22.5.

Dross

Since magnesium functions first as a desulfurizer and deoxidizer of the base iron, magnesium sulfide and magnesium oxide or silicate are formed. The dross defect appears on cope surfaces of ductile-iron

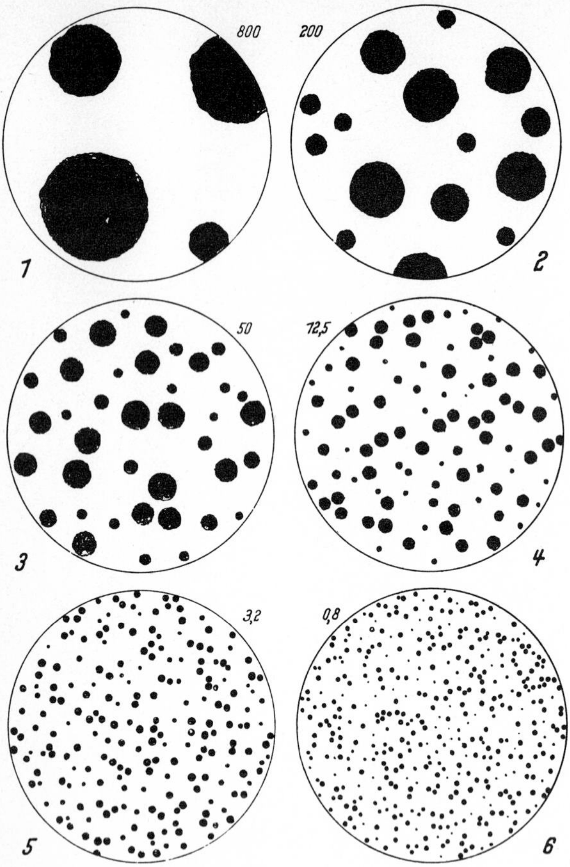

***Fig.* 22.5** Proposed classification of spheroidal graphite sizes based on size of spheroid at ×100. (*From C. K. Donoho.*[30])

castings, and is believed to be due to the retention of these magnesium compounds in the melt. The defect is aggravated by high magnesium additions, high pouring temperatures, and turbulence in the gating system and mold cavity.

FOUNDRY PROCESS CONTROL

Most ductile-iron castings are made in green- or dry-sand molds. Molding media for ductile-iron castings are similar to those used in gray-cast-iron foundries, with the possible exception that the moisture content of the sand must be more carefully controlled. This is considered a necessary measure because the ductile-iron melt, having been treated with magnesium, oxidizes easily. Total combustible material in the sand is usually limited to 6 to 7 per cent. Use of the sand mixture and manufacture of the molds reflect the type of castings produced and follow the principles set forth in Chap. 5.

Pouring and Gating Practices

When a sufficient amount of magnesium has been added to ductile iron, the iron is readily oxidized. The pouring and gating practices adopted by the ductile-iron foundrymen are based on this property. For instance, it has been reported that when the pouring temperature falls below 2550 F, oxidation products occur more readily. A pouring temperature of 2600 F or higher is therefore preferred, to avoid dross formation.

Table* 22.5 *Minimum nodule count obtained in carbide-free and vermicular (type III)-free structure

Bar diameter, in.	Nodules per sq in. in structure	
	Carbide-free	Vermicular-free
0.5	465	88
1.0	80	88
1.5	59	59

Magnesium additions increase the surface tension of the iron compared with gray cast iron. The sand mold then is not as easily wetted by the iron, and burn-in and penetration problems are not experienced as commonly as in other ferrous metals.

Design of Gating System

The ductile-iron gating system should be designed to fulfill the following requirements:

1. Retain the slag and dirt in the gating system ahead of the mold cavity
2. Introduce the metal into the mold with as little turbulence as possible
3. Control the rate of entry of the metal into the mold cavity
4. Establish the best possible metal distribution

It is therefore necessary to use a gating system which will minimize turbulence in the mold cavity. It should also introduce metal at the bottom of the mold cavity through a sufficient number of ingates so that a minimum amount of metal flows from each ingate. Positive-pressure systems of the 4:8:3 type are suggested. It is also desirable to provide runners with a height equal to twice the width. The total ingate area is a function of the pouring weight and the pouring time. It has been established that the best average time to pour ductile iron is given by

$$\text{Pouring time} = 0.65\sqrt{\text{pouring weight}}$$

These optimum pouring times and corresponding choke areas are presented in Fig. 22.6. This information, together with the gating-design rules discussed in Chap. 9, can then be incorporated into a gating system meeting the established requirements. An example of the type of gating required for quality ductile-iron production is shown in Fig. 22.7.

Riser Design

Since ductile iron solidifies according to a mechanism quite different from gray cast iron, the risering of these irons can be expected to be substantially different. Ductile iron solidifies by the growth of a large number of "cells" consisting of graphite spheroids surrounded by a shell of austenite. Accordingly, ductile iron does not freeze in layers from the surface inward as gray cast iron and steel do. Instead, solidification takes place with liquid and solid metal throughout the casting and with a very wide liquid-plus-solid temperature range.

The extent to which dispersed shrinkage will occur is largely dependent on the metal analysis, with hypoeutectic alloys showing greater shrinkage than hypereutectic alloys. This type of solidification also emphasizes the need for stable molds not subject to mold-wall movement (discussed

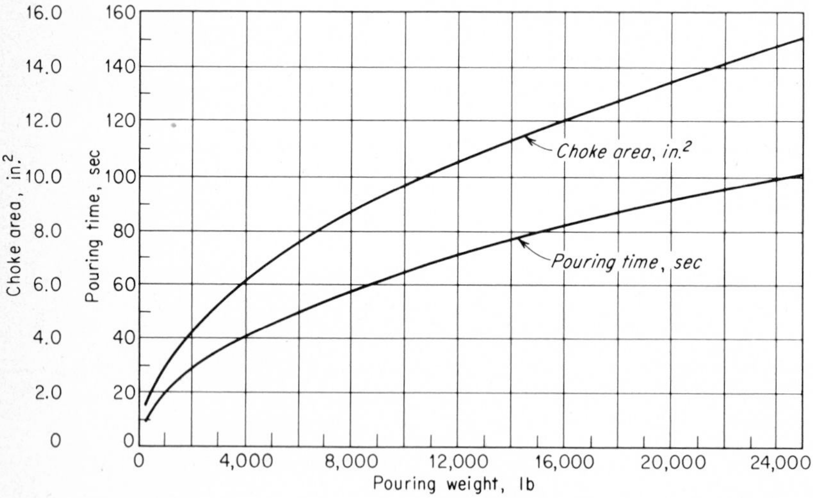

Fig. 22.6 **Chart used for determining optimum pouring times and respective choke areas for ductile iron.** (*From R. W. White.*[31])

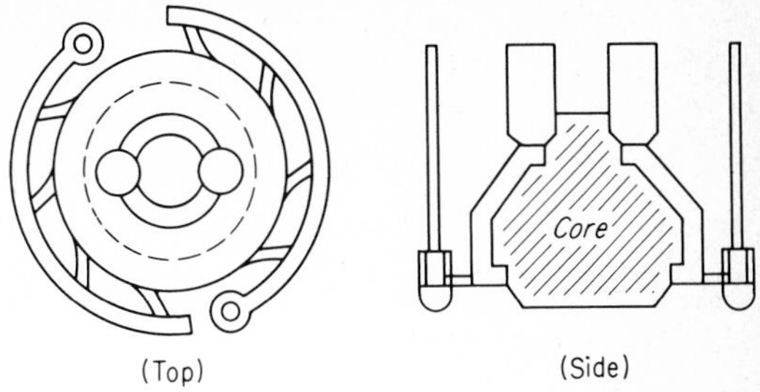

***Fig.* 22.7** Example of bottom gating as suggested for ductile iron. The metal enters the ingates at a number of points, and is directed to flow in a circular motion, eliminating direct impingement on the center core. (*From R. W. White.*[31])

in Chap. 5). Soft rammed molds will yield to the metal weight and solidification pressures resulting in the bulging of the casting, thereby increasing the section size and resulting in shrinkage.

These factors have not permitted riser dimensions for ductile iron to be well established. Suggested top- and side-riser dimensions for green-sand molds are shown in Fig. 22.8. This type of riser will effectively feed a distance of 4.5 times the diameter for plates up to 3 in. thick. Less risering is required in hypereutectic irons cast in dry-sand molds; however, even these castings are subject to shrinkage in isolated heavy sections. Location of the risers should follow the rules set forth in Chap. 9.

The effectiveness of the magnesium treatment and inoculation must also be considered in ductile-iron riser design. The development of eutectic carbide or vermicular graphite (type III, Fig. 22.4) in the structure alters the solidification behavior of the alloy and increases the risering requirements. Proper treatment of the iron is therefore an important factor in controlling solidification shrinkage.

HEAT-TREATMENT OF DUCTILE IRON

Because of its excellent response to heat-treatment, ductile-iron castings can be produced with a wide range of properties. The carbon content of the matrix can be adjusted from almost zero to over 0.80 per cent by metal analysis, alloying elements, foundry-process control, and/or

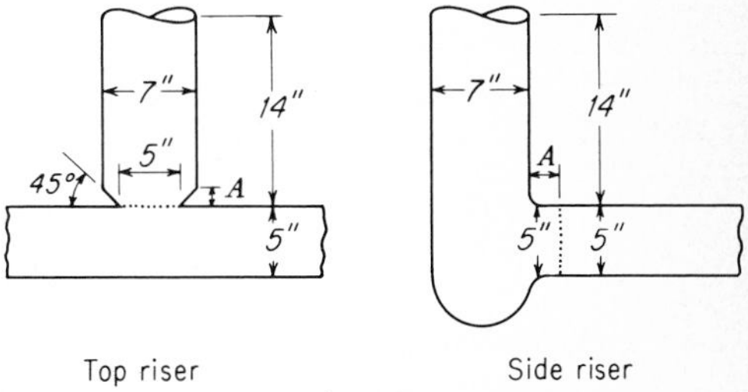

***Fig.* 22.8** Typical top- and side-riser configurations suggested for ductile iron. (*From R. W. White.*[32])

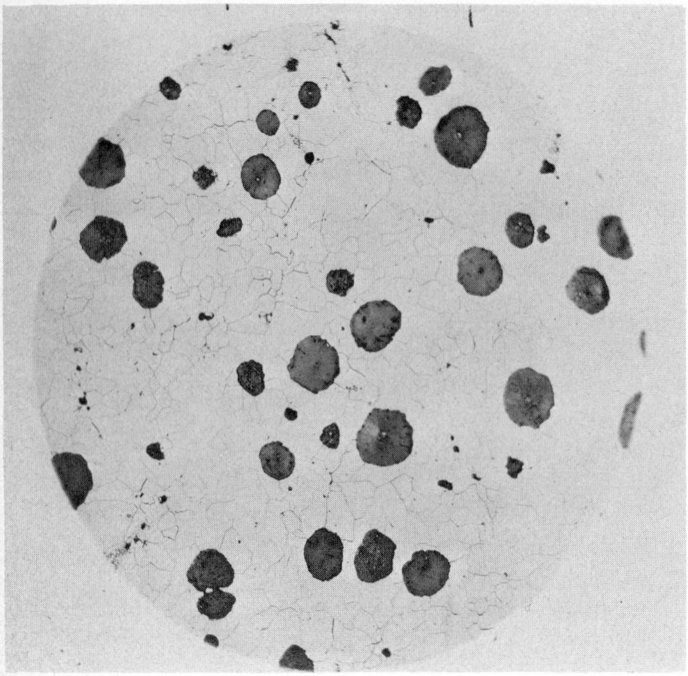

Fig. 22.9 **Ductile iron annealed to produce a fully ferritic matrix.** Etched, ×250. (*Courtesy of International Nickel Co., Inc.*)

heat-treatment. Accordingly, matrix structures may be all ferrite (Fig. 22.9), ferrite and pearlite (Fig. 22.1), all pearlite, martensite (Fig. 22.10), tempered martensite, or banite and may, in special alloys, contain carbides or an austenite matrix.

Control of the processing cycle can be used to produce ductile-iron castings to specifications without heat-treatment. It is common, however, to heat-treat most ductile iron either for stress relieving or to develop desired properties. Alloying elements in ductile iron behave in ductile iron as they do in steel and/or gray iron. The principal types of heat-treatments are also similar:

1. Stress relief. Used to remove internal stresses in castings by holding at 1000 to 1250 F for 1 hr, plus 1 hr per in. of thickness.
2. Annealing. Used to develop maximum ductility and the best machinability. Several methods may be used:

   a. Heat to 1650 F for 1 hr, plus 1 hr per in. of thickness. Cool to 1275 F and hold for 5 hr, plus 1 hr per in. of thickness, and then uniformly cool to room temperature.

b. Heat to 1650 F and hold as above, but furnace-cool from 1450 to 1200 F at a rate less than 35° per hr.

c. Subcritically anneal by heating to 1300 F and holding for 5 hr, plus 1 hr per in. of thickness. Furnace-cool to at least 1100 F.

3. Normalizing and tempering. Used to develop properties in the 100-70-03 and 120-90-02 types of ductile iron. Normalizing is generally section-size-sensitive, and alloying elements such as Ni and Mo may be used to counteract this partially. Normalizing is usually carried out at 1600 to 1700 F, followed by an air cool. Temperatures of 950 to 1150 F for 1 hr following normalizing.
4. Other heat-treatments which can be given ductile iron include quenching

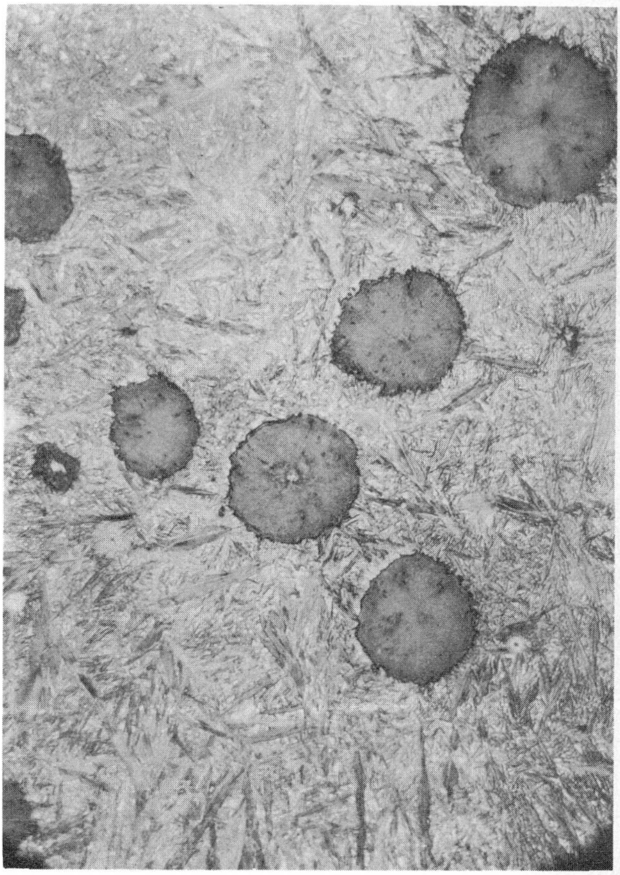

***Fig.* 22.10** Ductile iron quenched from 1650 F into an oil bath resulting in this acicular mixture of martensite and bainite. Etched, ×500. (*Courtesy of International Nickel Co., Inc.*)

and tempering, austempering, and martempering, all of which are similar to steel heat-treatment. Ductile irons are commonly surface-hardened by flame or induction methods. In this instance pearlite matrices are preferred prior to hardening since they are more readily austenitized.

ENGINEERING PROPERTIES

The principal types of ductile iron have been presented in Table 22.1, along with characteristics of the types and typical applications. Other properties of ductile iron are presented in Table 22.6.

Effect of Section Size

The section-size effect on properties in ductile iron, although present, is not as outstanding as has been discussed for gray cast iron. Because of their influence on the cooling rate during solidification and the resulting structures formed, thin sections are prone to carbide formation and heavy sections may contain deteriorated graphite shapes. The influence of these structures on properties has previously been discussed.

Nodule number and size affect properties through their ability to influence the remaining structure of the iron. Low nodule counts are generally accompanied by a carbidic matrix and/or deteriorated graphite shapes. As the number of nodules is increased, the amount of ferrite in the as-cast structure increases. The effect of section size on nodule size and number is shown in Figs. 22.11 and 22.12.

Effects of Other Engineering Properties

The unique position among engineering materials which ductile iron has attained is probably due to the fact that no other ferrous material can

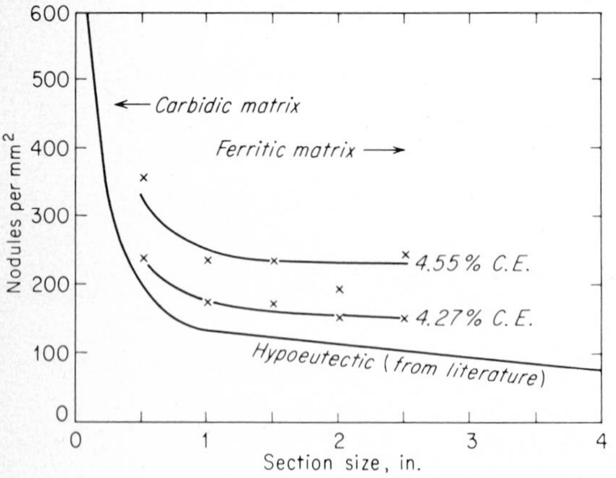

Fig. 22.11 Effect of section size of castings on the number of nodules produced from a standardized treatment procedure.

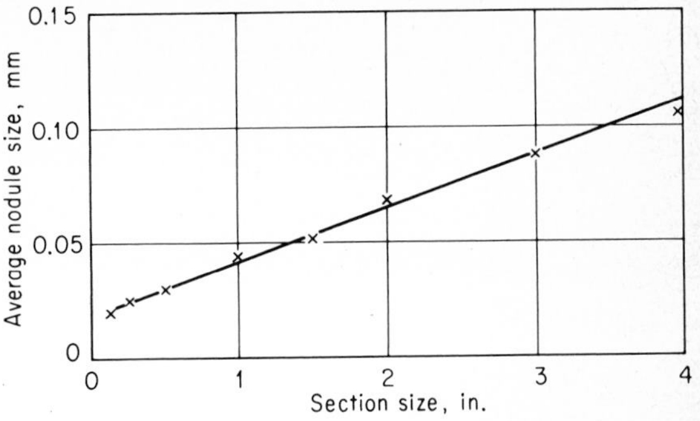

***Fig.* 22.12** Effect of section size on the average nodule size of the same castings as in Fig. 22.11.

equal the unusual combination of castability and mechanical properties of ductile iron. A few of the engineering advantages not cited elsewhere in this chapter include:

1. *Machinability.* The machinability of ductile iron is superior to that of gray iron at equivalent hardnesses and better than that of steel at equivalent strength levels.
2. *Corrosion resistance.* The resistance of ductile iron to corrosive media has been shown to be equivalent to that of gray iron and generally superior to steel.
3. *Wear resistance.* The spheroidal graphite in ductile iron acts as a reservoir to store lubricant for starting-up periods and to prevent galling and scuffing during periods of positive lubrication failure. Service-performance data and cylinder liners, crankshafts, metalworking rolls, dies, and gears have demonstrated that the wear resistance is equal to that of the best grades of gray iron and superior to that of carbon steel.
4. *Thermal shock resistance.* Ferritic ductile iron can be heated to temperatures above 1300 F and drastically quenched in cold water without cracking.

In general, it may be considered that ductile iron combines the processing advantages of gray cast iron with the engineering advantages of steel. Detailed information on the properties of ductile iron can be obtained from the "Gray Iron Castings Handbook," *Transactions of AFS,* and publications from the International Nickel Co.

BIBLIOGRAPHY

1. H. Morrogh, Production of Nodular Graphite Structures in Gray Cast Irons, *Trans. AFS,* vol. 56, pp. 72–90, 1948.
2. H. Morrogh and J. W. Grant, Nodular Cast Irons, *Foundry,* November, 1948.
3. D. J. Reese, Symposium on Nodular Graphite Cast Iron, *Trans. AFS,* vol. 57, pp. 576–587, 1949.

*Table 22.6 Other properties of ductile iron**

<table>
<tr><th></th><th>Types 80-60-03 and 100-70-03</th><th>Type 60-45-15</th><th>Austenitic† ductile iron</th></tr>
<tr><td>Compression strength, ratio of compression yield strength to tensile yield strength (approx)</td><td colspan="2">1.2</td><td></td></tr>
<tr><td>Endurance ratio (EL/TS):</td><td></td><td></td><td></td></tr>
<tr><td>Unnotched</td><td>0.35–0.45</td><td>0.45–0.55</td><td></td></tr>
<tr><td>Notched</td><td>0.20–0.30</td><td>0.25–0.35</td><td></td></tr>
<tr><td>High-temperature mechanical properties:</td><td></td><td></td><td></td></tr>
<tr><td>Creep strength (1% in 10,000 hr), psi:</td><td></td><td></td><td></td></tr>
<tr><td>At 800 F</td><td>11,000/25,000</td><td>14,000/26,000</td><td></td></tr>
<tr><td>At 1000 F</td><td>2,500/4,000</td><td>3,000/6,000</td><td></td></tr>
<tr><td>Creep strength (1% in 10,000 hr) of 0.5–1.0% Mo alloyed ferritic ductile iron, psi:</td><td></td><td></td><td></td></tr>
<tr><td>At 800 F</td><td>...</td><td>22,000/30,000</td><td></td></tr>
<tr><td>At 1200 F</td><td>...</td><td>5,000/10,000</td><td>8,000/11,000</td></tr>
<tr><td>Stress rupture, psi:</td><td></td><td></td><td></td></tr>
<tr><td>100 hr at 800 F</td><td>40,000/54,000</td><td>30,000/35,000</td><td></td></tr>
<tr><td>1000 hr at 800 F</td><td>34,000/42,000</td><td>25,000/27,000</td><td></td></tr>
<tr><td>100 hr at 1200 F</td><td>4,100/5,000</td><td>3,400/4,000</td><td></td></tr>
<tr><td>1000 hr at 1200 F</td><td>2,600/3,000</td><td>2,200/2,400</td><td></td></tr>
<tr><td>Stress rupture of 0.5–1.0% Mo alloyed ferritic ductile iron, psi:</td><td></td><td></td><td></td></tr>
<tr><td>1000 hr at 1100 F</td><td>...</td><td>6,500/8,000</td><td></td></tr>
<tr><td>Stress rupture of 1.4% Mo–5.4% Si alloyed ferritic ductile iron, psi:</td><td></td><td></td><td></td></tr>
<tr><td>1000 hr at 1100 F</td><td>...</td><td>11,000/15,000</td><td></td></tr>
<tr><td>Modulus of elasticity in tension, million psi</td><td colspan="2">23–26</td><td>13–19</td></tr>
<tr><td>Modulus of elasticity in torsion, million psi</td><td colspan="2">9.2–9.5</td><td></td></tr>
<tr><td>Shear strength, ratio of shear strength (in torsion) to tensile strength (approx)</td><td colspan="2">0.90</td><td></td></tr>
<tr><td>Proportional limit, psi</td><td>41,900</td><td>31,000</td><td></td></tr>
<tr><td>Poisson's ratio</td><td colspan="2">0.28–0.29</td><td></td></tr>
<tr><td>Electrical resistivity, μohms/(cm/sq cm) at 23.0 C:</td><td></td><td></td><td></td></tr>
<tr><td>2.5% Si</td><td>...</td><td>57.8</td><td></td></tr>
</table>

For peak induction B of 10,000 gauss:			
Peak H, oersteds	25.5	8.9	
Residual Br, gauss	6,100	6,400	
Coercive force Hc, oersteds	5.8	2.3	
Hysteresis loss W, (sec/cycle) lb	0.1093	0.0396	
For peak induction B of 15,000 gauss:			
Peak H, oersteds	225	150	
Residual Br, gauss	7,150	7,200	
Coercive force Hc, oersteds	7.8	2.6	
Hysteresis loss W, (sec/cycle) lb	0.187	0.075	
Maximum permeability at induction B:			
Of 5700 gauss	570		
Of 5600 gauss	....	1,580	
Magnetic permeability at room temperature	....	....	1–500
Melting range, °F	2050–2150		
Thermal conductivity, cal/(sq cm/cm)/°C/sec:			
At 100 C	0.074–0.076	0.084–0.105‡	
At 400 C	0.075–0.077	0.078–0.086	
Thermal expansion, mean value in./in./°F $\times 10^{-6}$ over the temperature range:			
68–212 F	5.9	6.2	
68–392 F	6.5	6.8	2.2–10.5
68–572 F	6.9	7.1	
68–752 F	7.3	7.3	
68–932 F	7.4	7.5	
68–1112 F	7.5	7.6	
Damping capacity (intermediate between cast iron and steel)	Approx 1.8–2.0 times that of steel		
Density:			
Lb/cu in	0.245–0.26		0.268–0.272
Lb/cu ft	423–449		
Specific gravity	7.2	7.1	

* Courtesy of International Nickel Co., Inc.

† Alloy content 18 to 35% Ni, up to 5% Cr.

‡ Higher values can be obtained with ductile irons with low silicon contents.

4. C. K. Donoho, Producing Nodular Graphite with Magnesium, *Am. Foundryman,* February, 1949.
5. G. E. Holdeman and J. C. H. Stearns, Variables in Producing Nodular Graphite Cast Iron, *Am. Foundryman,* August, 1949.
6. A. P. Gagnebin, K. D. Millis, and N. B. Pilling, Ductile Cast Iron: A New Engineering Material, *Iron Age,* Feb. 17, 1949.
7. E. T. Myskowski and R. P. Dunphy, Improved Nodulizing Alloy, *Steel,* Sept. 5, 1949.
8. J. E. Rehder, An Introduction to the Annealing of Nodular Iron, *Trans. AFS,* vol. 58, pp. 298–311, 1950.
9. J. L. Yarne and W. B. Sobers, Magnesium Determinations in Nodular Cast Iron: Sampling and Analysis Methods, *Am. Foundryman,* June, 1950.
10. J. E. Rehder, Effect of Phosphorus Content on Mechanical Properties of Nodular Cast Iron, *Trans. AFS,* vol. 59, pp. 501–508, 1951.
11. H. Morrogh, Influence of Some Residual Elements and Their Neutralization in Magnesium Treated Nodular Irons, *Trans. AFS,* vol. 60, pp. 439–452, 1952.
12. J. Keverian, C. M. Adams, and H. F. Taylor, Time of Formation of Spherulites in Hypo- and Hypereutectic Irons, *Trans. AFS,* vol. 60, pp. 849–853, 1952.
13. R. P. Dunphy and W. S. Pellini, Solidification of Nodular Iron in Sand Molds, *Trans. AFS,* vol. 60, pp. 775–782, 1952.
14. C. F. Reynolds and H. F. Taylor, Mechanical Properties of Spherulitic Graphite Cast Iron, *Trans. AFS,* vol. 60, pp. 687–713, 1952.
15. D. J. Reese, F. B. Rote, and C. A. Conger, Chemistry and Section Size on Properties of Ductile Iron, *Trans. Quart. SAE,* July, 1952.
16. S. F. Carter, American Experiences with Basic Cupola Melting, *Trans. AFS,* vol. 61, pp. 52–60, 1953.
17. C. C. Reynolds, C. M. Adams, and H. F. Taylor, Prediction of Mechanical Properties from Chemical Composition for Fully Annealed Ductile Cast Iron, *Trans. AFS,* vol. 61, pp. 510–515, 1953.
18. R. C. Shnay and S. L. Gertsman, Risering of Nodular Iron, *Trans. AFS,* vol. 62, p. 632, 1954.
19. R. A. Flinn, D. J. Reese, and W. A. Spindler, Risering of Ductile Cast Iron, *Trans. AFS,* vol. 63, pp. 720–725, 1955.
20. F. G. Sefing, Nickel Austenitic Ductile Irons, *Trans. AFS,* vol. 63, pp. 638–641, 1955.
21. W. S. Pellini, G. Sandoz, and H. F. Bishop, Notch Ductability of Nodular Iron, *Trans. ASM,* vol. 46, pp. 418–445, 1954.
22. C. Reynolds, J. Maitre, and H. F. Taylor, Feed Metal Requirements for Ductile Iron Castings, *Trans. AFS,* vol. 65, p. 386, 1957.
23. J. F. Ellis and C. K. Donoho, Magnesium Content and Graphite Forms in Cast Iron, *Trans. AFS,* vol. 66, pp. 203–209, 1958.
24. J. T. Williams, Basic Cupola Melting, *Trans. AFS,* vol. 67, p. 669, 1959.
25. A. H. Rauch, J. B. Peck, and G. F. Thomas, Carbon Flotation in Ductile Iron, *Trans. AFS,* vol. 67, p. 263, 1959.
26. A. H. Rauch, J. B. Peck, and E. M. McCullough, Ductile Iron As-cast and Annealed Tensile Properties, *Trans. AFS,* vol. 67, p. 187, 1959.
27. H. E. Henderson, Acid Cupola Melting for Ductile Iron, *Trans. AFS,* vol. 67, p. 661, 1959.
28. W. D. McMillan, Heat Treatment of Ductile Iron, *Trans. AFS,* vol. 67, p. 215, 1959.

29. J. A. Davis, J. C. McCarthy, D. M. Marsh, and H. O. Meriwether, Gating and Risering of Ductile Iron, *Trans. AFS,* vol. 68, p. 509, 1960.
30. C. K. Donoho, Ductile Iron Graphite Form Classification, *Trans. AFS,* vol. 69, p. 297, 1961.
31. R. W. White, Gating of Ductile Iron, *Foundry,* vol. 88, p. 101, February, 1960.
32. R. W. White, Risering of Ductile Iron Castings, *Foundry,* vol. 88, p. 96, March, 1960.
33. S. Tunder and L. Hohle, Shaking Ladle for the Economic Production of High Grade Cast Iron, *Foundry Trade J.,* Jan. 11, 1962.
34. J. V. Dawson, Effect of Carbon Equivalent on the Soundness of Nodular Iron Castings, *BCIRA J.,* vol. 10, no. 1, January, 1962.
35. C. R. Loper, Jr., Ductile Iron Solidification Study Using the Electron Microscope, *Trans. AFS,* vol. 70, p. 963, 1962.
36. W. Heinrichs, Magnesium Treatment of Gray Iron Melts to Produce Ductile Iron, *Trans. AFS,* vol. 70, p. 1121, 1962.
37. T. E. Rieger, Production of Ductile Iron, *Foundry,* vol. 90, p. 96, February, 1962.
38. R. S. Thompson, How Do We Know It's Ductile? *Foundry,* vol. 90, p. 76, June, 1962.
39. T. H. Burke, Melting Ductile Iron in an Acid Cupola, *Foundry,* vol. 90, p. 46, July, 1962.
40. Gray Iron Founders' Society, "Gray Iron Castings Handbook," Cleveland, 1958.
41. R. J. Christ and M. J. O'Brien, Inverse Chill in Ductile Iron, *Trans. AFS,* vol. 71, pp. 75–80, 1963.
42. J. Pelleg, Influence of Silicon on Ductile Cast Iron, *Trans. AFS,* vol. 71, pp. 108–116, 1963.
43. C. Vishevsky and J. F. Wallace, Effect of Heat Treatment on Impact Properties of Ductile Iron, *Trans. AFS,* vol. 71, pp. 290–295, 1963.
44. W. C. Wick, Metallurgical Properties of Continuous Cast Ductile, Gray, and High Alloy Iron Bar Stock, *Trans. AFS,* vol. 71, pp. 544–555, 1963.
45. D. Matter, H. H. Wilder, R. A. Clark, and R. W. White, Factors Affecting Application and Behavior of Magnesium Additives for Ductile Iron, *Trans. AFS,* vol. 71, pp. 625–627, 1963.
46. R. W. White, Application of Sandwich Method to Produce Ductile Iron, *Trans. AFS,* vol. 71, pp. 628–631, 1963.
47. W. H. Dawson, Injection of Magnesium Metal, *Trans. AFS,* vol. 71, pp. 632–637, 1963.
48. R. Carlson, Experiences with Plunging, Open Ladle, and Sandwich Methods, *Trans. AFS,* vol. 71, pp. 638–640, 1963.
49. C. R. Loper, Jr., and R. W. Heine, The Solidification of Cast Iron with Spheroidal Graphite, *Trans. ASM,* vol. 56, pp. 135–152, 1963.
50. C. R. Loper, Jr., and R. W. Heine, Variables Influencing Graphitization and Carbon Flotation, *Gray Iron News,* pp. 4–16, May, 1963; pp. 4–9, June, 1963.
51. C. R. Loper, Jr., P. Banarjee, and R. W. Heine, Risering Requirements for Ductile Iron Castings, *Gray Iron News,* May, 1964, pp. 5–16.
52. C. R. Loper, Jr., P. S. Nagarsheth, and R. W. Heine, Nodule Counts and Ductile Iron Quality, *Gray Iron News,* June, 1964, pp. 5–17.
53. W. J. Dell and R. J. Christ, Chill Elimination in Ductile Iron by Mold Inoculation, *Trans. AFS,* vol. 71, pp. 408–416, 1964.
54. C. R. Loper, Jr., and R. W. Heine, Graphitization and the Processing Cycle in Producing Ductile Iron, *Trans. AFS,* vol. 71, pp. 495–507, 1964.

23
Malleable Iron

American malleable iron occupies the unusual position of being truly a product born of the American foundryman's inventiveness. The first "blackheart" malleable-iron castings were developed by Seth Boyden at Newark, N.J., starting in 1826. Boyden's work eventually resulted in the growth of the American, or blackheart, malleable-iron industry, until it has become the third largest tonnage producer in the castings field.

Malleable iron is an important engineering material, largely because its properties offer certain special advantages among the family of cast irons. Desirable properties include ease of machinability, toughness and ductility, corrosion resistance in certain applications, strength adequate for wide usage, magnetic properties, and uniformity resulting from 100 per cent heat-treatment of all castings produced. Applications of malleable castings usually reflect a need for one or more of the foregoing properties. Principal users of the castings are the automotive and truck industries, construction-machinery producers, and agricultural-equipment makers.

Examples of truck malleable-iron castings are shown in Fig. 23.1.

The properties of malleable iron are mainly related to its metallographic structure. Malleable iron may be defined microstructurally as a ferrous alloy composed of temper carbon in a matrix of ferrite containing dissolved silicon. The structure is the result of heat-treatment applied to white-iron castings. The chemical composition of the common grades of white iron which may be heat-treated to malleable iron is given in Table 23.1.

Table 23.1 ***Typical chemical composition of white irons heat-treatable to malleable iron***

	ASTM No. 32510	ASTM No. 35018	Cupola-malleable
% C	2.30–2.65	2.00–2.45	2.80–3.30
% Si	0.9–1.40	0.90–1.30	0.60–1.10
% Mn	0.25–0.55	0.21–0.55	Less than 0.65
% P	0.18	Less than 0.18	Less than 0.20
% S	0.05–0.18	0.05–0.18	Less than 0.25

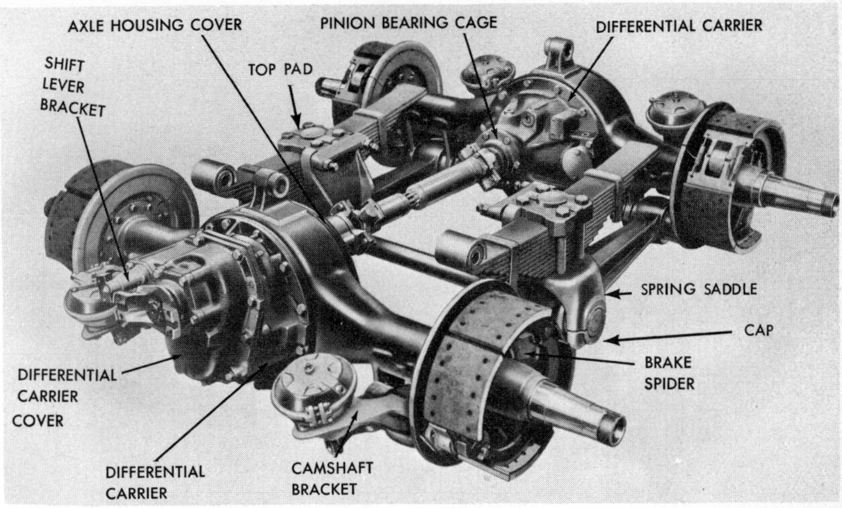

***Fig.* 23.1** Truck tandem axle assembly showing malleable- and pearlitic-malleable-iron parts. (*Courtesy of the Malleable Founders' Society.*)

The structure of the white iron as cast is shown in Fig. 23.2. After heat-treatment, the structure appears as in Fig. 23.3. Heat-treatment converts the massive carbides and pearlite of the white iron to ferrite and temper carbon. Chemically, heat-treatment causes a change from combined carbon to graphite or temper carbon, the combined carbon generally being less than 0.15 per cent by weight after heat-treatment.

Table* 23.2 *Tensile properties of malleable and pearlitic malleable irons *After ASTM Specification A220*

Type	Minimum tensile strength, psi	Minimum yield strength, psi	Minimum elongation, % in 2.0 in.	Brinell-hardness range, typical
Standard ferritic malleable:				
35018	53,000	35,000	18.0	110–145
32510	50,000	32,500	10	110–145
Pearlitic malleable:				
45010	65,000	45,000	10	163–207
45007	68,000	45,000	7	163–217
48004	70,000	48,000	4	163–228
50007	75,000	50,000	7	179–228
53004	80,000	53,000	4	197–241
60003	80,000	60,000	3	197–255
80002	100,000	80,000	2	241–269

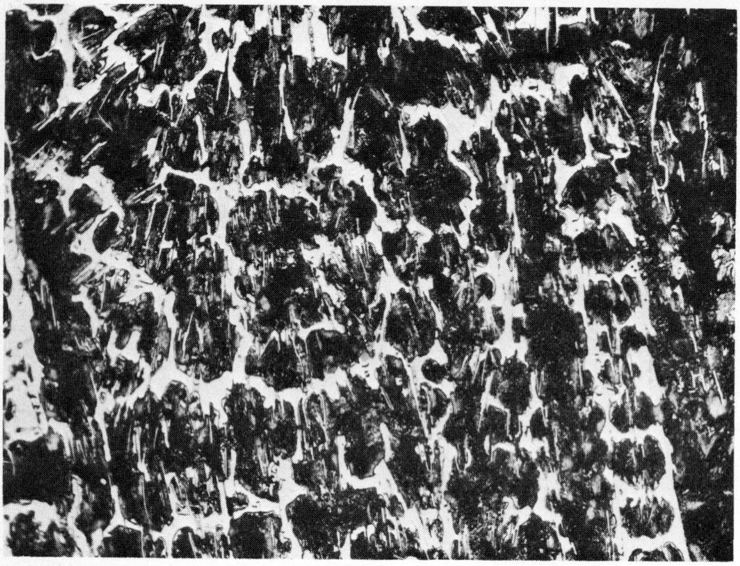

Fig. **23.2** Microstructure of white cast iron: white, massive carbide areas; dark, pearlite areas. RC 31. Nital-etched, ×150.

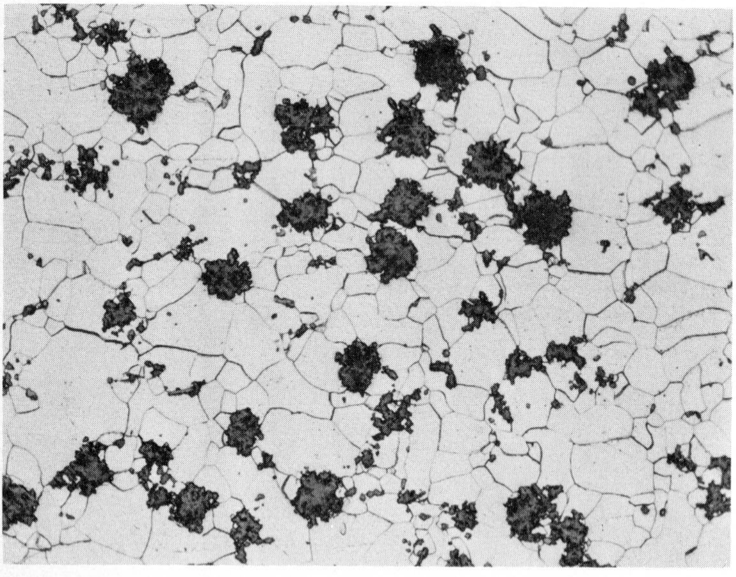

Fig. **23.3** Microstructure of standard malleable iron: ferrite and graphite, 125 Bhn. Nital-etched, ×150.

The ferrite structure with interspersed graphite gives malleable-iron mechanical properties in the range of those specified in Table 23.2, under standard malleable iron. The tensile properties and Bhn are characteristic of ferrite alloyed with 1 per cent silicon.[18]

Except for annealing or malleableizing, the manufacture of malleable-iron castings involves the same basic foundry processes used with other alloys. Molding, coremaking, cleaning, melting, pouring, etc., are adapted to the special casting properties of malleable iron, which are primarily related to its metallurgical nature. This area will therefore be considered first.

MELTING

Melting iron for malleable castings is generally performed in the air furnace, the cupola, induction, or direct arc electric furnaces, or a combination of these furnaces when duplexing is employed.

Batch-melting Process

The cold-melt air furnace shown in Fig. 23.4 is used for batch melting. The air furnace is a reverberatory-type furnace fired with pulverized coal or oil. Common furnace capacities range from 15 to 40 tons. The furnace hearth is rectangular and provides a molten-bath depth of generally less than 12.0 in. Tapholes are provided on the side of the furnace. The side walls are made of firebrick supported by steel, and the bottom is either silica sand or firebrick. The furnace top consists of a series of removable firebrick arches known as "bungs." By removing some of the bungs, the furnace may be charged with cold metal through the top. A typical furnace charge[1] is given below:

Material	Batch melting (air-furnace charge)	Duplexing (cupola charge)
Pig iron (malleable), %	25–35	12
Sprue, %	45–55	50
Malleable scrap, %	5–20	10
Steel scrap, %	0–10	38
Fuel:		
Coke, lb/ton melt	0	160–220
Coal, lb/ton melt	700–1000	180–220
Electricity, kw/ton melt	0	480 (duplex, arc furnace)
Flux, lb/ton melt	0	60–80 (cupola)

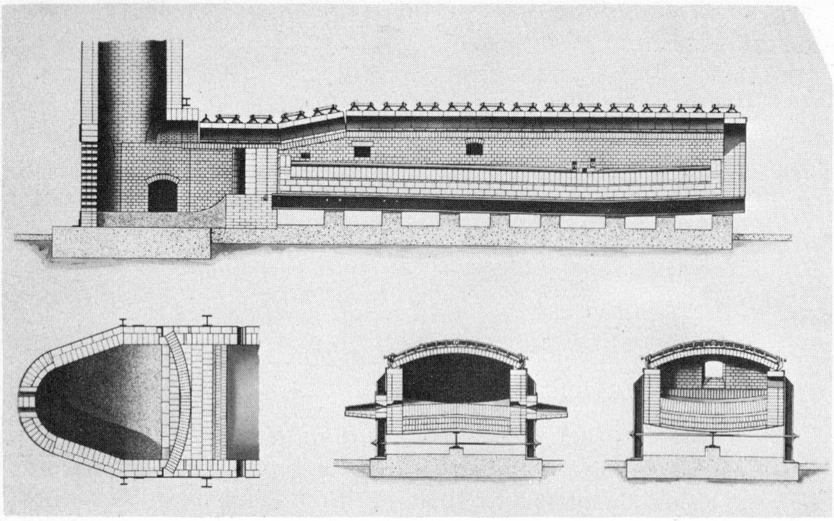

Fig. **23.4** View of ventilated bottom-arch furnace. Cross-sectional views of stack, tapholes, and firing end. (*Courtesy of Whiting Corporation.*)

Smaller-size charge materials are usually placed on the bottom of the furnace. Both charges listed above contain about 50 per cent sprue because this is the usual percentage of remelt in a malleable foundry. The balance of the air-furnace charge is selected so that the iron will melt down at about 2.65 to 2.85 C, phosphorus and sulfur percentages below the maximum permitted, and silicon and manganese within or slightly below the desired analysis range. Less than 0.07 per cent, and preferably less than 0.03 per cent, chromium should be in the charge, since this element interferes with annealing. Melting down is performed with a fuel-air mixture which will produce flame temperatures of about 3080 to 3150 F and hold oxidation of the metal to a minimum. A slag forms during melting down from metal-oxidation products and refractory attrition. During melting down and as the bath reaches a temperature of about 2600 F, the slag is skimmed. The bath temperature is then raised to the desired pouring temperature, usually 2800 to 2900 F. Chemical-composition changes during the process follow principles discussed in Chap. 20. Losses of silicon and manganese occur during melting down and until the metal has reached a temperature of about 2700 F. At higher temperatures, carbon losses can occur rapidly under oxidizing atmospheres, but there may be a silicon pickup from the refractories and slag. The iron gains about 0.05 to 0.15 per cent silicon per hour at 2800 to 2900 F from reduction of silica by carbon in the iron.[23] Typical composition changes during a heat are given in Table 23.3.

Table* 23.3 *Typical chemical-composition changes of air-furnace heat

Period of heat	% C	% Si	% Mn	% P	% S
Charge	2.80–3.20	1.10–1.25	0.45–0.55	0.14 max	0.09
After meltdown	2.70–2.90	0.90–1.10	0.30–0.40	0.14 max	0.09
Preliminary analysis 40-60 min before tapping	2.50–2.60	0.96	0.37	0.14 max	0.10
Final analysis	2.30	1.05	0.35	0.14 max	0.10

Carbon losses are counteracted by melting with a higher fuel-to-air ratio (reducing), by adding graphite, petroleum coke, or proprietary recarburizer, or by dropping powdered coal on the metal surface from the burners.

The analysis changes occurring in the course of an air-furnace heat are accompanied by structural changes in the solidified iron. A sprue fracture test of the type shown in Fig. 23.5 is often used to observe the condition of the iron. Early in the heat, iron cast into a bar about 1¾ to 2 in. in diameter and 8 to 10 in. long will freeze gray or mottled. Mottling results from the formation of flake graphite during freezing, the iron then not being a completely white iron. As the temperature increases above 2600 F and the carbon percentage in the iron drops, mottling gradually disappears. Finally, before tapping, the test bar will cast white and will have a completely white fracture as illustrated in Fig. 23.5. Generally, the objective of quality malleable-iron melting is to produce a completely white iron with no free flake graphite in the castings since flake graphite lowers the properties of malleable iron. Melting may be conducted to favor white iron by using high temperatures, oxidizing conditions, low carbon and silicon percentages in the

***Fig.* 23.5** Sprue test. The sprue at left shows a gray fracture characteristic of a high-carbon iron at the beginning of the heat. Decarburization of the iron causes a change from gray to mottled to white fracture-test sprues as carbon content of the iron decreases. (*Courtesy of the Malleable Founders' Society.*)

iron, additional steel in the charge, moisture in the air, and a number of other practices.[2,4] When the iron has reached the necessary composition limits and is known to freeze white, it is tapped from the furnace. Furnace addition of ferrosilicon and ferromanganese may be employed if it is necessary to adjust the analysis of the iron. Tapping is usually done at 2800 to 2900 F, and pouring occurs at 2600 to 2800 F, depending on casting-section thickness. Tapping in air-furnace heat may require from 30 min to over an hour, depending on the furnace size and pouring facilities.

Duplexing

The cold-melt air-furnace process is supplanted by duplexing when continuous melting and tapping is desired. In duplexing, the iron is melted in the cupola and transferred to an air or electric furnace for refining and temperature control. Equipment for duplexing is shown in Fig. 23.6. Duplexing installations may employ cupola–air furnace or cupola–electric arc furnace melting. In either case, melting down is done in the cupola. A typical cupola charge was given earlier. More steel and less pig are used than in the cold-melt process in order to compensate for carbon pickup in the cupola. Chemical-composition changes during duplex melting are illustrated in Table 23.4.

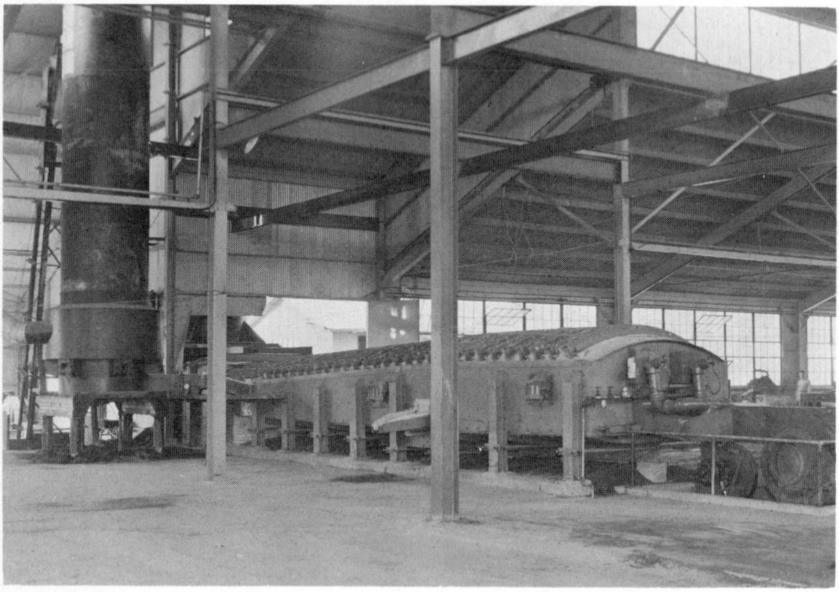

***Fig.* 23.6** View of duplexing installation. Metal is transferred from the cupola to the air furnace. (*Courtesy of the Whiting Corporation.*)

Table 23.4 Typical composition changes during duplex melting

Period of melting	% C	% Si	% Mn	% P	% S
Cupola charge.	1.40–2.20	1.50–1.65	0.55–0.60	0.05	0.12
Cupola gains or losses.	Gain	10–25 (loss)	15–20 (loss)	No change	Gain
Cupola tap.	2.60–3.0	1.20–1.40	0.45–0.50	0.05	0.12–0.17
Air-furnace tap (2 hr in the furnace). . . .	2.35–2.65	1.25–1.50	0.45–0.50	0.05	0.12–0.17

The cupola is continuously tapped into the air furnace. The air furnace is tapped intermittently into transfer ladles for pouring into the molds. Thus it can be seen that the air furnace mainly accomplishes carbon removal and serves to decrease analysis variations of metal coming from the cupola. If an electric furnace is used, steel may be added to the metal to lower carbon and silicon from the cupola metal. A 4 per cent steel addition will lower carbon and silicon about 0.05 per cent in the electric furnace and markedly decrease mottling tendency. Superheating for pouring can, of course, readily be accomplished.

MOTTLING

In all the processes discussed, the production of a white iron without primary graphite or mottling in the structure is essential to quality malleable-iron castings. The sprue test reveals the progress of the melt in each heat toward a fully white iron. The melting process exerts considerable influence on the mottling tendency of the iron. Flake or primary graphite is promoted by high carbon and silicon percentages in the iron. Cooling rate as influenced by various section sizes of a casting is another extremely important factor. Slow cooling promotes mottling. The relationship of these three factors is illustrated in Fig. 23.7. The figure does not, however, show that mottling tendency may be greatly shifted by melting conditions.[2,3,6,27] Graphite-bearing materials in the charge, such as pig iron and malleable scrap, promote mottling at lower silicon and carbon contents. Steel has the effect of decreasing mottling tendency. Oxidizing melting conditions raise the carbon and silicon limit for mottling.[3,4] Experimental work[27] has proved that melting-furnace atmospheres exert a profound effect on mottling tendency. Hydrogen, water vapor, nitrogen, and oxygen all promote resistance to mottling. The effects of the gases become more pronounced at higher temperatures. Minor additions of certain elements to the iron, such as 0.001 to 0.01% Bi or Te, decrease mottling tendency

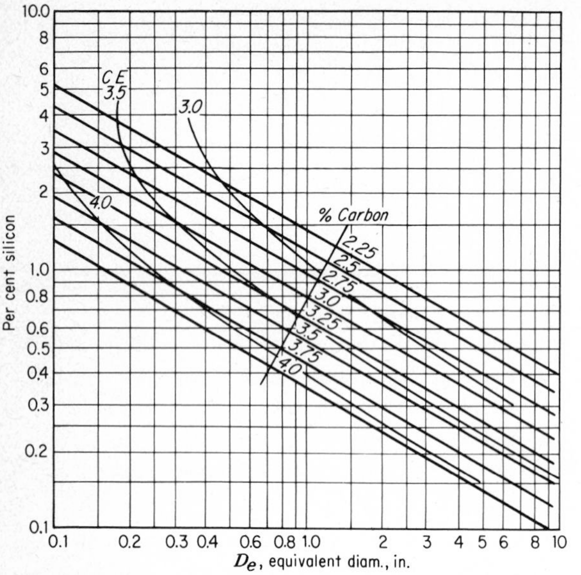

Fig. **23.7** Graph showing relationship of percentage carbon, silicon, and section size for mottling in sand molds. (*From R. Schneidewind and R. G. McElwee.*[20])

even in very heavy sections.[26] Because of the manifold factors involved, standardization of melting practices is adopted as a control measure in the production of white-iron castings free of mottling and with satisfactory annealing characteristics.

CASTING PROPERTIES

Foundry characteristics which require special consideration in making white-iron castings are fluidity, shrinkage, hot-tearing tendency, and temperature.

Shrinkage and Feeding

Because it freezes white, the iron has a solidification shrinkage of about 3 to 6.0 per cent. This is reflected in a foundry yield of about 50 per cent. Feeding the solidification shrinkage of white iron is aggravated by its two-step solidification process. Freezing begins with formation of primary austenite dendrites as temperature decreases below 2450 F. It is completed by eutectic freezing in the range of 2060 to 2020 F. Figure 23.8 shows the network of interlocking dendrites which develop early in freezing and which make it difficult for metal to pass from a feeder into the casting. Unfed shrinkage usually results in cavities with a dendritic pattern because of the freezing mechanism.

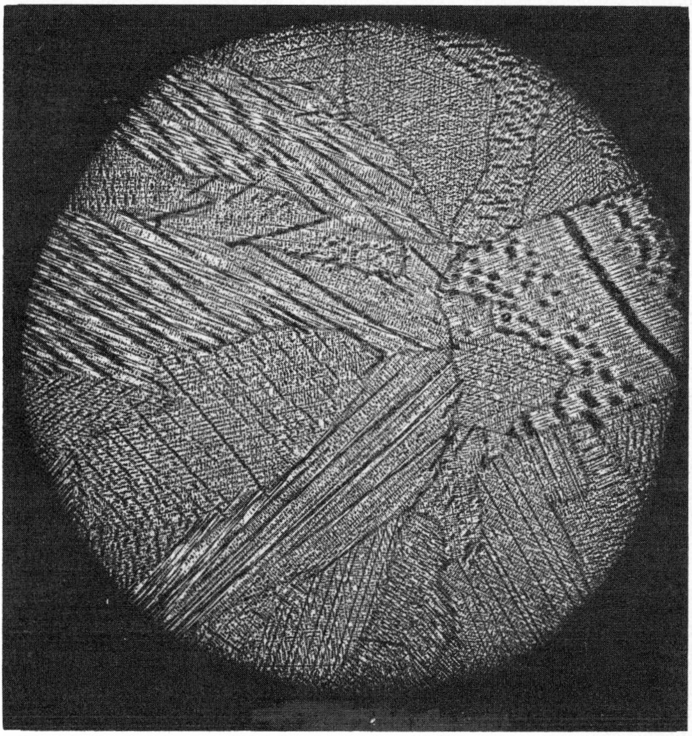

Fig. 23.8 **Dendritic freezing pattern across section of a ½-in.-diameter by 9-in. bar cast in sand. Dark streaks reveal original austenite dendrites freezing first, and light areas contain the eutectic carbides freezing last, during solidification. Nital-etched.**

Feeding distances from risers into the casting will be short. To improve feeding, chills are frequently employed to cause sharp temperature gradients. An illustration of the problem in a slab is given in the casting shown in Fig. 23.9. Chills serve to cause rapid solidification in locations which would not be reached from a riser if normal temperature gradients existed. To be effective, a chill must lower temperature in the area of shrinkage below the freezing-temperature range ahead of the time when feeding from the riser to the casting is prevented by dendrites in sections close to the riser. The freezing and feeding problem is especially emphasized where any heavier section is isolated by thinner sections. An example of this is shown in Fig. 23.10. In the original design, metal would be required to feed from a side riser through the thin section and into the enlarged section. The redesign overcame this problem.

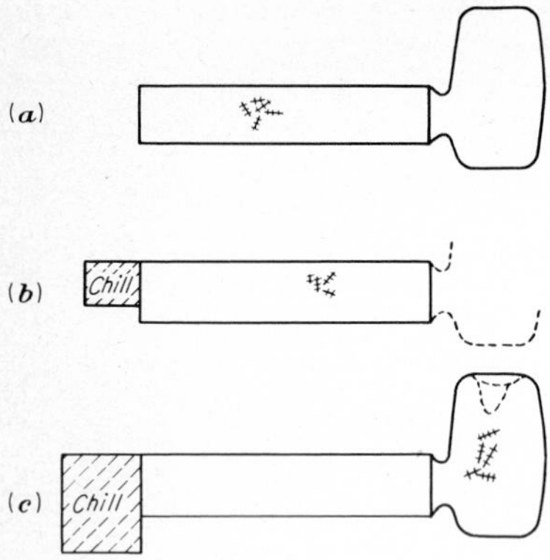

***Fig.* 23.9** Feeding problem caused by dendritic freezing of white iron in slab casting. (*a*) The metal is not able to flow from the riser into the casting because of the dendrite obstacle; (*b*) the shrinkage area has been moved closer to the riser by a chill not close enough for complete feeding; (*c*) sufficient chill has been employed to solidify rapidly the area which would not feed, whereas areas close to the riser are satisfactorily fed.

Fluidity

The fluidity of white iron is regulated largely by temperature and composition. The normal limits of fluidity measured with a fluidity spiral follow the general limits for cast irons described in Chap. 22. These limits for malleable iron are summarized in Fig. 23.11. Some changes in fluidity are caused by melting practice and other variables, but these are usually secondary to the major effects of temperature and composition. Reference 27 contains further information on these points. With high temperature and silicon or carbon on the high side, small castings down to $\frac{1}{16}$ in. section thickness or less may be cast.

Hot Tearing

Hot tearing of white-iron castings may occur under certain conditions. In white irons, a hot tear is a rupture which occurs during the latter

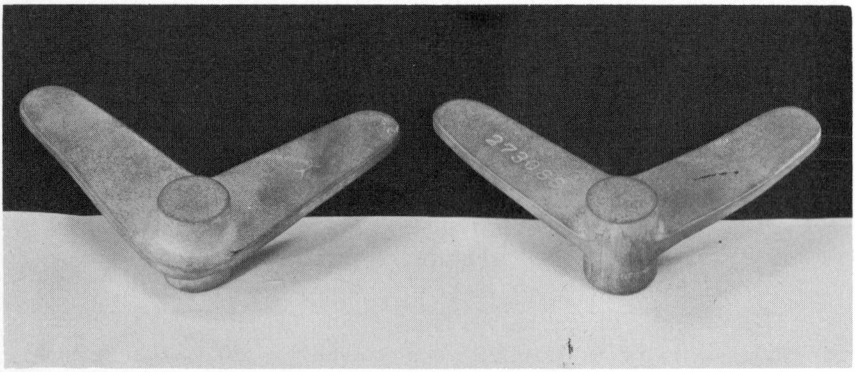

***Fig.* 23.10** Feeding problem caused by isolation of heavy section from riser by thin section and redesign to correct the condition. (*Courtesy of the Malleable Founders' Society.*[1])

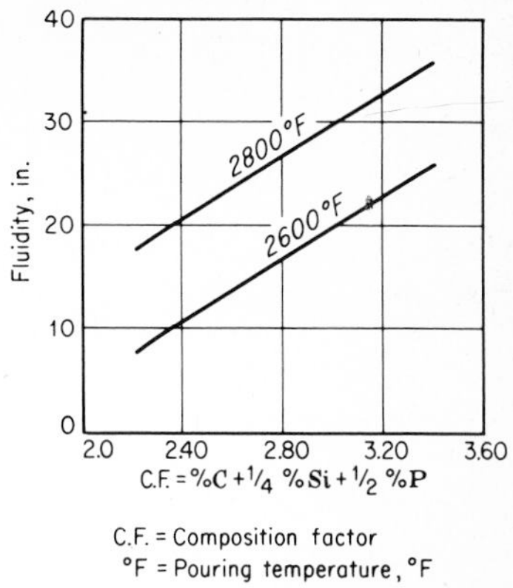

***Fig.* 23.11** Fluidity range, inches spiral length, as related to composition and temperature of white iron. The fluidity values are those obtained with the test casting shown in Fig. 22.7.

stages of freezing, i.e., eutectic freezing. The characteristic appearance of a hot tear is shown in Fig. 23.12. Tears are usually the result of restraint of contraction in combination with temperature gradients. Stresses develop in the metal if the casting is prevented from contracting, and eventually rupture occurs where the metal is weakest, which is at

***Fig.* 23.12** Degrees of hot tearing of white iron when cast around a noncollapsible steel bar. The variations in appearance of the tear are due to the effect of iron composition on the resistance to tearing. (*From E. A. Lange and R. W. Heine.*)

the location of the highest temperature (i.e., hot spot). Because tearing of white iron is usually associated with casting design, gating, or other foundry practices, a number of tricks are used to cope with it. Soft, collapsible cores permit castings to contract more freely. Chills and cracking strips are helpful. Use of a cracking strip in the case of a housing casting is shown in Fig. 23.13. The strip is a thin metal fin attached to the pattern and, consequently, the casting over the area where tearing has been troublesome. The fin freezes quickly, extracts heat, and helps to hold together the iron where it might rupture. The iron can vary in its strength to resist hot tearing, depending on its composition, pouring temperature, and melting practice.[27] Under many conditions, however, the casting and gating and the mold are the principal factors to be considered.

Pouring Temperature

The temperature of the iron for pouring is generally between 2800 and 2600 F at the molds, with an optimum of 2680 to 2700 F. This is substantially higher than for gray cast irons, which may be poured down to 2300 F. This means that molding and core sands must be more heat-resistant. Synthetic molding sands are most generally used, although some natural sands are employed.

FOUNDRY OPERATIONS

Most malleable-iron castings are light in weight, generally under 50 lb, although some castings are made with weights of several hundred pounds. Section thicknesses are correspondingly thin, generally under 2 in., with a majority in the range of $\frac{3}{16}$ to $1\frac{1}{2}$ in.

Molding and core sands reflect the type of work and the nature of the metal. Some typical mixtures are given for molding sands in Table 5.10 and for core sands in Chap. 7.

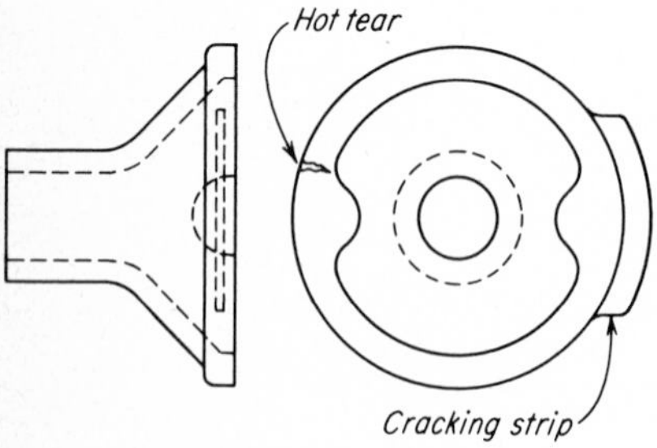

***Fig.* 23.13** Use of cracking strip to prevent hot tears. Stresses cause the tear to develop. The fin on the casting freezes quickly and strengthens the spot where the tear would occur.

Since white iron is susceptible to hot cracking, internal cores may be required to be especially collapsible. This may be achieved with core sands containing only organic binders and a minimum amount of core oil. Otherwise coremaking follows conventional means.

Sprues on white-iron castings are knocked off. Core and parting-line fins are readily broken off because of the brittleness of the iron as cast. Further cleaning and grinding is commonly delayed until after annealing. Grinding of gates and parting lines is usually less costly after annealing because of decreased metal hardness. For the same reason, finishing cleaning operations are delayed until after annealing.

ANNEALING

The annealing heat-treatment is often called malleableization since it converts the hard, brittle, white cast iron to a malleable iron. The initial structure at the beginning of the treatment consists of pearlite, massive carbides, and usually some eutectic areas (Fig. 23.2). The temperature-time cycle of the heat-treatment is illustrated schematically in Fig. 23.14. The treatment involves three important steps. The first step involves nucleation of graphite. This occurs mainly during heating to the high holding temperature and very early during the holding period. The second step, holding at temperature of 1600 to 1750 F, involves first-stage graphitization (FSG). The objective of the second step is to eliminate massive carbides from the iron structure. The last step in the treatment involves slow cooling through the allotropic transformation range of the iron, and is referred to as second-stage graphitization (SSG). The objective of the last step is the formation of a completely ferritic matrix free of pearlite and carbides, as illustrated in Fig. 23.3. The fundamentals of the annealing or graphitizing treatment are related to the metastability of iron carbide in the iron-carbon-silicon equilibrium system discussed in Chaps. 19 and 22, especially the latter. The carbide is sufficiently stable during freezing so that the iron freezes white, i.e., without flake graphite, provided the time required for freezing is not unduly long. The carbide is sufficiently unstable, however, so that graphitization will begin, and may be completed in the solid state by a suitable annealing heat-treatment.

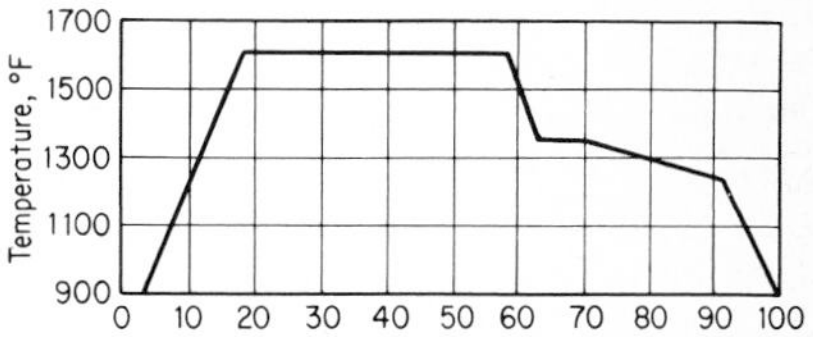

***Fig.* 23.14** Cycle of temperature and time for malleableizing white iron. Actual duration of the cycle may be much less or more than indicated. (*Courtesy of the Malleable Founders' Society.*[1])

Nucleation

The success of the later phases of the heat-treatment is greatly dependent on the first step, nucleation of graphite. If sufficient graphite nuclei develop, the balance of the treatment will usually proceed satisfactorily. During heating, pearlite changes completely to austenite when the allotropic-transformation temperature range is exceeded. When the high temperature of holding has been reached, the structure consists of carbon-saturated austenite, undissolved massive carbides, and graphite nuclei. The nuclei first appear within prior pearlite, at the interfaces of the iron carbide and austenite or at nonmetallic inclusion locations. Among factors known to influence nucleation of the graphite are the following:

1. Heating rate.[8,6] Rapid heating decreases the number of nuclei developed.
2. Section size.[19,12] Thin casting sections develop more nuclei.
3. Chemical analysis.[10–12] High silicon percentage and the proper balance of manganese and sulfur ($2 \times \%\ S + 0.15 = \%\ Mn$) favor nucleation.
4. Pretreatment.[14] A preliminary heat-treatment of holding the iron at 600 to 1200 F for a period up to 20 hr increases nucleation upon subsequent malleableization.
5. Prequenching.[7] Heating into the austenitic temperature range followed by quenching causes the most marked increase of all effects on nucleation when the iron is subsequently malleableized.
6. Slags high in FeO, over 25 per cent, drastically decrease nucleation during malleableization.[13]
7. Ladle additions. Nucleation during malleableization is increased by the addition of 0.001 to 0.003 per cent boron or a few hundredths per cent aluminum or titanium to the molten iron.[2]
8. Graphite bearing materials in the melting-furnace charge promote nucleation during heat-treatment.[6,3,7]
9. Steel in the charge decreases nucleation.
10. Oxidizing melting conditions in cupola or electric furnace decrease nucleation.[27,3]
11. Nucleation is decreased by excessive additions of Bi and Te.[26]

Other factors influence nucleation of graphite during malleableization, but these remain to be studied. In any event, graphite nuclei develop during the FSG holding period.

Nodule Counts

Because the number of graphite nodules developed during heat-treatment is so important, methods of measuring this variable have been employed.

Nodule counts are usually made on the completely annealed iron rather than at some intermediate stage. One of the simplest procedures is to count the number of nodules observed with a microscope in the field of view at a given magnification, ×100, for example. This number may be used as such or converted to number of nodules per square millimeter by dividing it by the area (actual sample) observed with the particular microscope. An average value obtained by counting 5 to 10 areas is used. The number may vary from just a few to over 150 nodules per square millimeter. The number of nodules per square millimeter may then be converted to nodules per cubic millimeter, using the graph in Fig. 23.15. Schwartz[17,18] has discussed the principles of nodule counting, and offers the graph in Fig. 23.15 as a simple approximate method of determining the number of nodules per cubic millimeter. With the procedure, values in the range of 2000 to 4200 nodules per cubic millimeter may be considered characteristic of readily annealable irons. When less than 3000 nodules per cubic millimeter are developed, the iron will anneal at less than its maximum rate, especially in the second stage.

The size and distribution and shape of graphite nodules may vary as well as the number. In quality malleable iron, temper carbon nodules are usually compact clumps, as shown in Fig. 23.3.

First-stage Graphitization

Graphitization proceeds at the FSG temperature by a process of solution and precipitation. The carbide dissolves in the austenite, and then carbon diffuses to the nuclei and precipitates as graphite. Growth of a

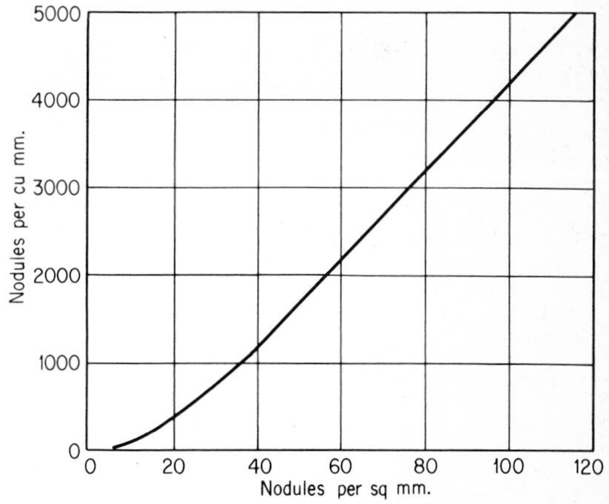

Fig. 23.15 Relationship of graphite nodules per cubic millimeter to number of nodules per square millimeter according to the method of Schwartz. (*From H. A. Schwartz.*[17,18])

temper carbon nodule during FSG occurs at the expense of the carbide, and the process is complete when the carbide has disappeared from the austenite. The time required for first-stage graphitization is largely a function of the number of nuclei, solution of the carbide, and the diffusion rate of carbon at the temperature. The time required for FSG has been directly related to silicon content and temperature, as shown in Fig. 23.16. Additional composition factors may alter the FSG rate and its degree of completion. Carbide-stabilizing elements such as chromium, excessive manganese, and molybdenum delay or prevent complete FSG. Over 0.03 per cent chromium is undesirable;[3] manganese should be in the proper balance with sulfur, namely, $\%\ \text{Mn} = 2 \times \%\ \text{S} + 0.15$; excess manganese functions as a carbide stabilizer, whereas too little permits sulfur to function as a stabilizer.[11,24] It is probably true that FSG is most directly influenced by nucleation of graphite, for if sufficient nodules develop, graphitization usually proceeds with ease, although there are some exceptions.

Second-stage Graphitization

The second stage of graphitization requires slow cooling through the transformation range of the iron, usually from about 1450 down to about 1300 F. The cooling rate must allow time for austenite to change to ferrite and precipitate carbon as graphite. Too rapid a rate will cause pearlite to be formed as in steels, whereas a quench will develop martensite. Cooling rates employed may vary from about 3 to 30 F per hr; the higher rates are successful when sufficient temper carbon nodules are present and with high silicon percentage in the iron. The slow cooling process may be carried to temperatures as low as 1200 F as a safety precaution since pearlite developed during the cooling process will graphitize below the transformation range. Many of the factors discussed as influencing FSG will also influence SSG, but less is known about this step. It is again true that SSG will proceed most readily if a sufficient number of graphite nodules are present.

Annealing Operations

The practical operations of annealing are carried out by batch or continuous processes.

Batch annealing is often done by packing the castings in metal boxes, stacking the boxes in the furnace, and then firing the furnace according to the temperature-time annealing cycle. Powdered coal is often used as a fuel in ovens of this type. Since the furnace and casting mass is large, heating and cooling are slow, and the cycle is a long one. The

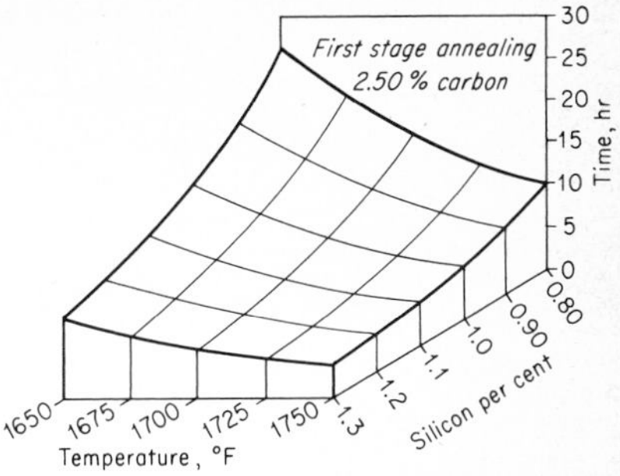

Fig. **23.16** Relationship of temperature to silicon percentage in white iron and time required for FSG; schematic. (*From J. E. Rehder.*[9])

tunnel kiln may be employed to make the process continuous. More rapid annealing is carried out in the electric furnaces or in continuous, conveyor-type, gas-fired, radiant-tube furnaces. In the latter furnaces, the casting is annealed in its own atmosphere or in a specially generated atmosphere. Typical cycles of temperature and time are given in Table 23.5.

Table* 23.5 *Annealing cycles

Type	Heating	Holding at first-stage temperature	Cooling and second stage of graphitization	Total
Periodic oven, pot-annealing, packed	To 1650 F in 40 hr	40 hr at 1650 F	1650–1100 F in 75 hr	155 hr
	To 1600 F in 45 hr	45 hr at 1600 F	1600–1100 F in 60 hr	150 hr
Continuous furnace	To 1700–1750 F in 3–5 hr	5–13 hr at 1700–1750 F	Cooling to 1300 F in 8–36 hr	14–60 hr

Faster cycles are used by foundries having a suitable combination of furnace equipment, casting size, and metal analysis. Considering these factors, the total time of the annealing cycle may vary from 15 hr to 8 days. After annealing, the castings are cleaned. Sometimes shearing or milling may be used to remove metal. Shot or grit blasting and tumbling are commonly used for removing sand or scale. Straightening or coining may be applied to castings which warp during annealing. After cleaning, the castings are subjected to dimensional, surface, and quality inspection by the usual methods (Chap. 24).

ENGINEERING PROPERTIES

The tensile properties of malleable iron were presented in Table 23.2. Other mechanical properties[1] are tabulated below:

Bhn	110–145 (115–135 usual range)
Endurance ratio	0.40–0.575
Notch endurance ratio	0.35
Modulus of elasticity in tension	25×10^6 psi
Shear strength	0.80 UTS
Compressive strength	Greater than UTS
Impact resistance	6.5–16.5 ft-lb, depending on test conditions
Machinability rating	120%*

* The Malleable Founders' Society; compared with cold-rolled or cold-drawn B1112 Bessemer screw stock with a rating of 100 per cent.

The strength of malleable iron combined with its ductility makes it suitable for many applications. Probably its greatest engineering value rests in the combination of its mechanical properties, service life, cost, and suitability to many fabricating and processing operations. Among these advantages are:

1. Machinability. Malleable iron is among the most machinable of ferrous alloys. Especially desirable is the fact that a high degree of uniformity of machinability in large numbers of castings can be maintained because every casting has been heat-treated.
2. Ductility in processing. Many processing operations such as coining, crimping, press fits, punching, and straightening can utilize or require ductility.
3. Ductility or toughness in service. Many applications are best served when the casting is capable of deforming rather than fracturing when overstressed. Clamps, pipe-fitting threads, chain links, tractor bolster posts, and many other cases may be cited.
4. Surface coatings.[1,2] Corrosion resistance of malleable iron may be greatly increased by coatings of zinc, cadmium, aluminum, and lead. Hot-dip galvanizing may be applied to clean malleable castings to provide good corrosion resistance to exposure in a wide variety of outdoor conditions which may be encountered by electrical conduct boxes and fittings, fence fixtures, playground-equipment castings, and numerous other applications.
5. Wear resistance. Malleable iron with a ferritic structure does not have inherent wear resistance other than that normal to soft-ferrous alloys. It may be hardened, however. If the metal is heated to the austenitic temperature range, carbon goes back into solution and permits a hard martensitic structure to be obtained by quenching. Caster wheels, cams, rollers, and other items may be flame- or induction-hardened to give wear resistance.
6. Magnetic properties.[2]

PEARLITIC MALLEABLE IRONS

Another type of malleable iron finding increasing use is pearlitic malleable iron.[2] Increased strength and wear resistance combined with reasonable toughness are obtained in these irons. As the name implies, the structure of this iron consists of a matrix of pearlite (or spheroidized pearlite or tempered martensite) and temper carbon, as shown in Fig. 23.17. Pearlitic malleable iron is produced by the following methods:

1. By preventing complete SSG by adding alloying elements such as manganese, molybdenum, or chromium
2. By arresting the anneal during second-stage graphitization
3. By heat-treatment of standard malleable iron

Type 1 pearlitic malleable iron often utilizes manganese between 0.5 and 0.90 per cent to retain pearlite during the regular annealing cycle. The annealing cycle may then be modified as shown in Fig. 23.18, and a spheroidized rather than pearlitic matrix is produced. Type 2 pearlitic irons depend for their production on the fact that rapid cooling through the transformation-temperature range produces pearlite rather than

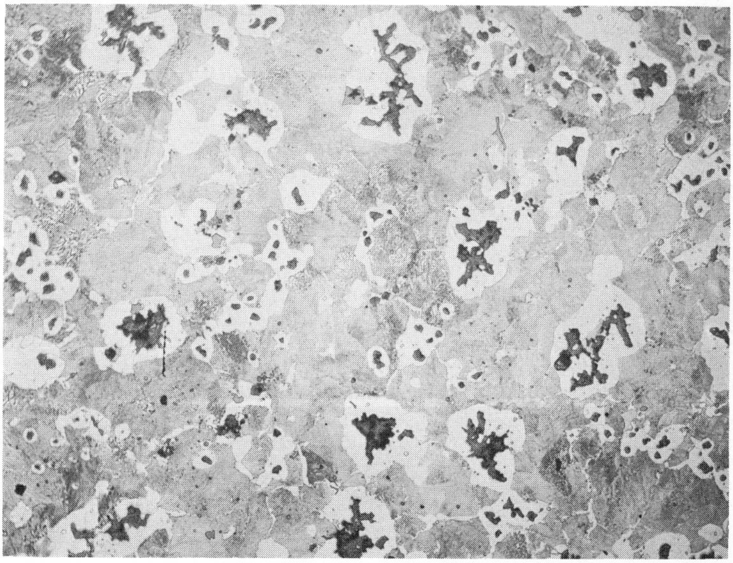

Fig. **23.17** Microstructure of one type of pearlitic malleable iron. Bull's-eye pattern, temper carbon, ferrite, and pearlite. The pearlitic irons can be made without free ferrite showing in the structure, and may be spheroidized. Nital-etched, ×100.

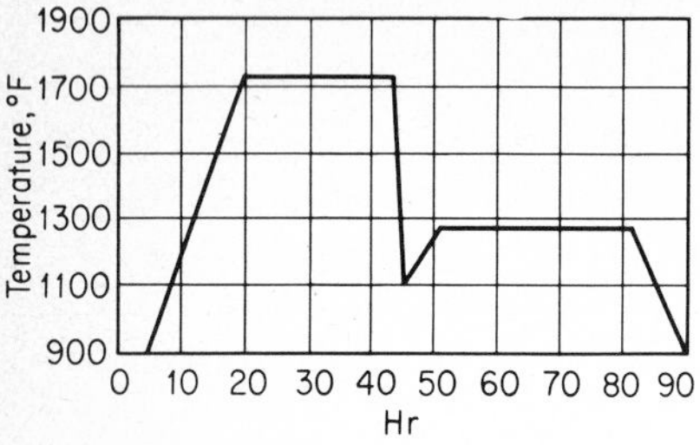

***Fig.* 23.18** Annealing cycle for spheroidized malleable iron. (*Courtesy of the Malleable Founders' Society.*[1])

ferrite. Type **3** pearlitic irons are made by reheating a ferritic iron to a temperature just above the critical range, followed by air or liquid quenching. The quenched iron is then tempered to produce the desired Bhn and tensile properties. Since the amount of pearlite, combined carbon percentage, degree of spheroidization, or hardness of tempered martensite may be greatly varied in pearlitic irons, the properties can be correspondingly varied by the manufacturer. The tensile requirements of pearlitic malleable irons are listed in Table 23.2. The pearlitic or tempered-martensite matrix can be hardened by heating and quenching to about 55 to 62 RC for wear resistance. Surface hardening by flame or induction heating is another advantage of pearlitic irons.[2] These properties are reflected in the use of pearlitic irons for gears and gear blanks, crankshafts, camshafts, rocker arms, chain links, tractor treads, and like applications.

OTHER MALLEABLE IRONS

Malleable irons are sometimes alloyed with 0.25 to 1.25% copper and up to 0.25% molybdenum for increased strength and corrosion resistance. These special irons are employed where additional strength and corrosion resistance are desired in the fully annealed material. The Malleable Iron Castings handbook[1] furnishes information on these irons and other details of the malleable-iron-casting field.

BIBLIOGRAPHY

1. "American Malleable Iron: A Handbook," The Malleable Founders' Society, 1944.
2. "Malleable Iron Castings: A Handbook," The Malleable Founders' Society, Cleveland, 1963.
3. American Foundrymen's Society, Malleable Iron Melting Symposium reprint 43-37.

4. G. Joly, Influence of Chromium on Graphitization of White Cast Iron, *Trans. AFS,* vol. 56, p. 66, 1948.
5. J. E. Rehder, Silicon Pick-up in Malleable Iron Melting, *Am. Foundryman,* vol. 10, no. 4, p. 50, 1946.
6. A. L. Boeghold, Some Unusual Aspects of Malleable Iron Melting, Campbell Memorial Lecture, *Trans. ASM,* vol. 26, 1938.
7. Symposium on Graphitization of White Cast Iron, *Trans. AFS,* vol. 50, no. 1, p. 1, July, 1942.
8. R. Schneidewinde and D. J. Reese, Influence of Rate of Heating on First Stage Graphitization of White Cast Iron, *Trans. AFS,* vol. 57, p. 497, 1949.
9. J. E. Rehder, Effect of Temperature and Silicon Content on First Stage Annealing of Black-heart Malleable Iron, *Trans. AFS,* vol. 57, p. 173, 1949.
10. J. E. Rehder, Influence of Silicon Content on Critical Temperature Range during Slow Cooling of Black-heart Malleable Iron, *Trans. AFS,* vol. 57, p. 549, 1949.
11. J. E. Rehder, Effect of Mn-S Ratio on the Rate of Anneal of Black-heart Malleable Iron, *Trans. AFS,* vol. 56, p. 138, 1948.
12. R. Schneidewinde, A Summary of the Quantitative Effects of Some Factors on the Annealing of White Cast Iron, *Trans. AFS,* vol. 58, p. 202, 1950.
13. H. N. Bogart and G. Vennerholm, Effects of Slag Types and Heat Treatment of Malleable Iron, *Trans. AFS,* vol. 57, p. 222, 1949.
14. C. H. Lorig and M. L. Samuels, Some Effects of Hydrogen on the Time of Malleablization, *Trans. AFS,* vol. 50, p. 107, July, 1942.
15. H. A. Schwartz and W. K. Bock, Effect of the Common Alloying Elements on the Tensile Properties of Malleable Iron, *Trans. AFS,* vol. 56, p. 458, 1948.
16. R. Schneidewinde, D. L. Reese, and A. Tang, Graphitization of White Cast Iron: Effect of Section Size and Annealing Temperature, *Trans. AFS,* vol. 55, p. 252, 1947.
17. H. A. Schwartz, The Metallographic Determination of the Size Distribution of Temper Carbon Nodules, *Metals and Alloys,* vol. 5, no. 8, p. 139, June, 1934.
18. H. A. Schwartz, A Simple Approximate Method for Determining Nodule Number, *Metals and Alloys,* vol. 7, no. 11, p. 278, November, 1936.
19. R. W. Heine, Oxidation Reduction Principles Controlling the Composition of Molten Cast Irons, *Trans. AFS,* vol. 59, p. 121, 1951.
20. R. Schneidewinde and R. G. McElwee, Composition and Properties of Gray Iron, *Trans. AFS,* vol. 58, p. 312, 1950.
21. R. W. Heine, Hardenability of Pearlitic Malleable Iron, *Trans. AFS,* vol. 66, p. 12, 1958.
22. R. W. Heine, Observations on Pinhole Defects in White Iron Castings, *Trans. AFS,* p. 31, 1958.
23. American Foundrymen's Society, Malleable Iron Microstructures: Effect and Cause, *Trans. AFS,* vol. 66, p. 166, 1958.
24. F. B. Rote et al., Malleable Base Spheroidal Irons, *Trans. AFS,* vol. 64, p. 197, 1956.
25. R. W. Heine and C. R. Loper, Jr., Formation of Flake, Spheroidal, Lacy, Film, and Compact Graphite during Solidification of Cast Iron, *Trans. AFS,* vol. 69, 1961.
26. R. W. Heine and C. R. Loper, Jr., Heavy White Iron Sections Melt Additions Effects on Mottling Tendency, *Trans. AFS,* vol. 68, p. 312, 1960.
27. R. W. Heine, Melting Variable Effects on Malleable Iron Properties, AFS bulletin, 1959.

24

Cleaning and Inspection

The *cleaning* of castings generally refers to all the operations involved in the removal of adhering sand, the gating system, and fins, wires, chaplets, or other metal not a part of the casting. Cleaning operations may also include a certain amount of metal finishing or machining to obtain the required casting dimensions, the salvage of castings having minor defects, and the inspection of the finished castings.

CLEANING OPERATIONS AND EQUIPMENT

The series of operations performed in the cleaning department may be classified as follows:

1. Removal of gates and risers, rough cleaning
2. Surface cleaning, exterior and interior of casting
3. Trimming, the removal of fins, wires, and protuberances at gate and riser locations
4. Finishing, final surface cleaning, giving the casting its outward appearance
5. Inspection

Sometimes heat-treatments are involved which necessitate cleaning the castings after the heat-treatment. This might be done between steps 3 and 4 above. Often steps 1 to 5 are carried on simultaneously. Some of these, such as gate removal, may occur during shakeout operations.

Removal of Gates and Risers

The sprue, runners, and risers are firmly attached to the solidified casting. If the casting alloy is brittle, the gating system may be broken off by impact when the castings are dumped and vibrated in shakeout and knockout devices.

Flogging

Flogging with a hammer or sledge is a positive means of gate removal by impact. A man may be stationed at the shakeout to flog the sprue and risers as the sand falls away from the casting. When the molds are set out on floors and dumped by hand, men with hammers knock off the gates and toss the castings and gates into separate boxes for transfer to the cleaning room. To *sprue* the castings is to remove gates in this way. Gray- and white-iron castings are especially amenable to gate removal by this method. An inherent danger of breaking off the gates is that the break may extend into the casting proper. This condition may be remedied by notching the ingate ahead of the casting. The protuberance remaining on the casting can then be ground flush with the casting wall.

Flogging may be applied advantageously to steel castings as long as the gates are of a size that can be knocked off by a man using about a 12-lb maul. One author[1] estimates that the maximum size of gate which may be flogged from carbon-steel castings is one with 4.4 sq in. cross-sectional area connection to the casting ($2\frac{5}{8}$-in.-diameter round

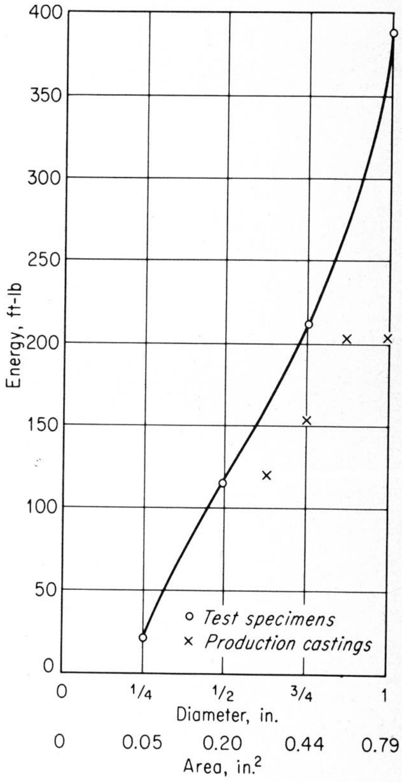

***Fig.* 24.1** Impact load necessary to rupture necked-down steel risers. (*From S. W. Brinson and J. A. Duma.*[1])

riser). The same author studied the impact in foot-pounds necessary to break steel knock-off risers and developed the graph shown in Fig. 24.1. It is important to note that the diameter referred to in Fig. 24.1 is the necked-down diameter of a Washburn riser, and not the enlarged diameter. Notching, or necking down, is a common means of making flogging easier. Even certain brasses and bronzes, relatively ductile as cast, may have risers flogged off if Washburn risers are used.

Mechanical Cutoff

Gates may be removed by band sawing, power sawing, abrasive cutoff wheels, or with sprue cutter. A rapid method of removing a number of small castings from a central runner is provided by the sprue cutter. This machine, illustrated in Fig. 24.2, shears off the casting at the ingate. Ductile metal castings such as steel, brass, copper, and aluminum are conveniently handled by the sprue cutter, provided the gate and casting size is not too large to shear. Gates of $\frac{1}{8}$ to $\frac{1}{2}$ in. in thickness may be readily sheared on the sprue cutter. In some cases, fins may be removed and gates cut off simultaneously by using a punch press fitted with a die for performing these operations. Die castings are often treated in this way.[2]

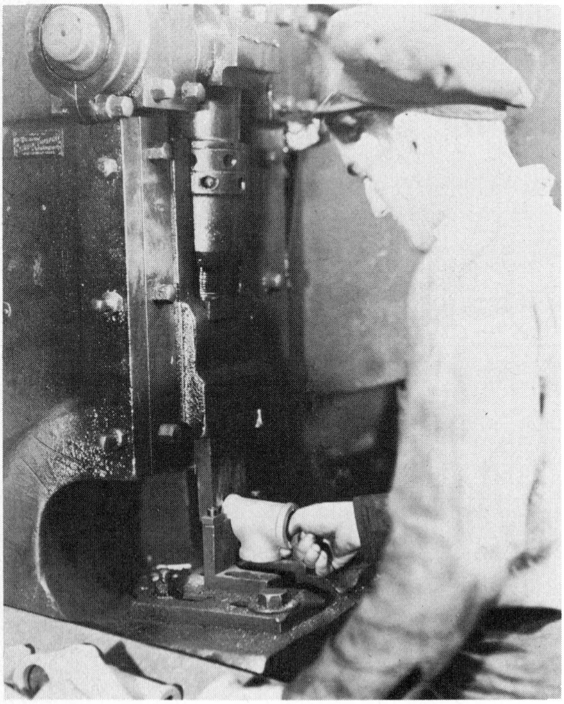

***Fig.* 24.2** Sprue cutter machine for shearing off ingates. (*From D. E. Sawtelle.*[10])

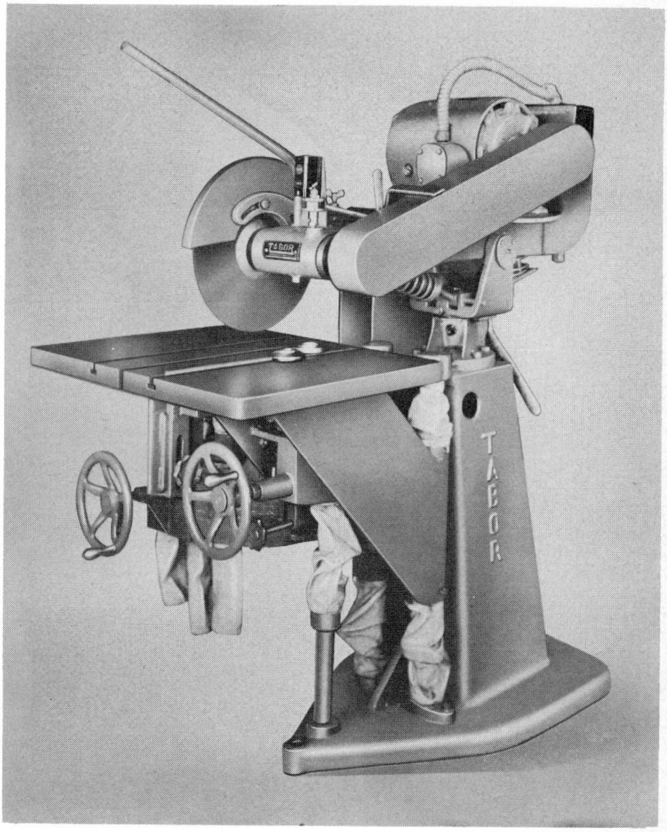

***Fig.* 24.3** Abrasive cutoff wheel used for cutting gates and risers. (*Courtesy of the Tabor Manufacturing Co.*)

Abrasive cutoff wheels may be used for gate removal. The machine illustrated in Fig. 24.3 will cut hard or difficult-to-saw alloys, as well as the more common foundry alloys.

Band sawing can be used for removing gates from many castings, both ferrous and nonferrous. Its most extensive use is on nonferrous castings and involves equipment such as that shown in Fig. 24.4. Band sawing may be done by cutting or friction sawing. Actual sawing involves cutting, chip formation, and removal at speeds up to about 3500 fpm.

Friction sawing requires cutting speeds up to 15,000 fpm which will heat the metal to temperatures approaching its melting point. Friction sawing is used almost entirely on ferrous materials. Gate removal by sawing under the proper conditions requires a consideration of cutting speed, cutting pressure, section thickness, lubricant, saw-blade type, alloy type, and other conditions. Numerical data for a few of these

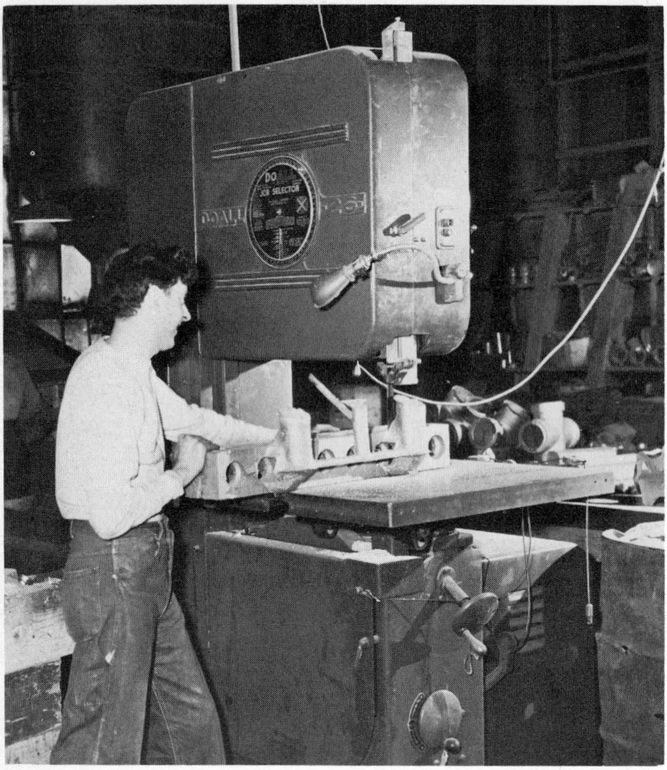

Fig. 24.4 Band-sawing machine. The operator is cutting off gates on a brass casting. (*From G. H. Shippard.*[3])

Table* 24.1 *Band-sawing conditions for gate removal*

Alloy	Speed, fpm		Feeding pressure	Lubricant	General information
	Low speed	High speed			
Copper-base alloy...	400 or less	2000 or less, buttress type	25 lb to 1 in. thickness	Used if chips weld to saw blade	Sawing speed decreases as hardness increases
Aluminum and magnesium	Up to 500 buttress blade	Up to 3500 on ½-in. section	Low	Ordinarily dry	4-pitch, 0.50-in. buttress blade; sawing speed decreases with section thickness
Ferrous (band sawing)	40–500	1500 or less	Moderate	May be used if chips weld to saw blade	
Ferrous (friction sawing)	....	3000–15,000	20–40 lb	No	¼- to 1-in.-width saw blade with 10–18 teeth per in.

* Adapted from Refs. 3 and 4.

factors are listed in Table 24.1. Low-speed sawing, ordinarily at less than 500 fpm of saw-blade velocity, is conventional band sawing. Sawing at higher speeds, however, is used whenever possible for gate removal. Band sawing makes it possible to a degree to follow the contour of the casting when removing gates and risers, something which cannot be done so easily with a sprue cutter or abrasive cutoff wheel.

Torch Cutting

Large risers and gates on steel castings are most conveniently removed by cutting torches. The sprue cutter is limited in metal thicknesses, whereas the cutting torch and oxygen lance may cut risers of practically any size. The principle of the oxyacetylene cutting torch, illustrated in Fig. 24.5, requires that the slot, or kerf, be controlled by the operator or cutting machine so that the temperature and oxidation rate of the metal can be maintained. Metal-section thickness determines the proper torch-nozzle size and oxygen pressure necessary to keep the cutting reaction and kerf moving along. Table 24.2 lists some of the combinations required for effective cutting.

If castings of a given size and type are lined up on work benches as in Fig. 24.6, the speed and ease of gate removal are increased. The same type of setup is occasionally conveyorized. Hand cutting, as illustrated in Fig. 24.6, is most commonly employed in jobbing foundries

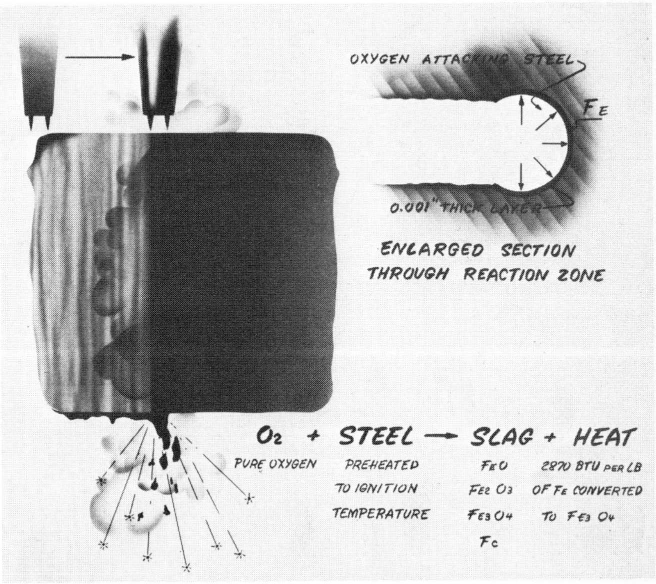

***Fig.* 24.5** Principle of the oxygen-cutting reaction. (*From R. S. Babcock.*[5])

Table 24.2 Data for hand-cutting carbon steel*

Section thickness, in.	Diam cutting orifice, in.	Oxygen pressure, psi	Cutting speed, in./min	Oxygen, cu ft/hr	Acetylene, cu ft/hr
1.0	0.0465–0.0595	28–40	9–18	130–160	13–16
2.0	0.0670–0.0810	22–50	6–13	185–231	16–20
3.0	0.0670–0.0810	33–55	4–10	207–290	16–23
4.0	0.810 –0.0860	42–60	4–8	235–388	20–26
6.0	0.098 –0.0995	36–80	3–5.4	400–567	25–32
10.0	0.0995–0.110	66–96	1.9–3.20	610–750	36–46
12.00	0.110 –0.120	58–86	1.4–2.60	720–905	42–55
24.00	0.221 –0.332	22–48	....	1600–3000	
36.00	0.290 –0.500	12–38	....	3000–4600	

* Adapted from American Welding Society.[6]

on a variety of castings. Sometimes mechanized cutting may be used, employing a motorized cutting carriage, with a form template to guide the cutting torch around the casting surface. Extremely large risers require an oxygen lance as well as cutting torch to complete the cut. This is illustrated in Fig. 24.7. The torch maintains the cutting reaction zone on the near side of the riser, and the lance carries it through to the far side. Thus cutting by hand or machine is seen to be an exceedingly versatile means of gate removal.

Some ferrous alloys, cast irons, and high-alloy steel are oxidation-resistant and do not cut well with the oxygen torch alone. *Powder*

Fig. 24.6 Steel castings lined up on a cutting bench. (*From R. S. Babcock.*[5])

Fig. 24.7 Removing riser from a large casting by means of the gas torch and oxygen lance. The casting has not been removed from the mold. (*From R. S. Babcock.*[5])

cutting has been developed to handle these materials. Iron powder is introduced at the oxygen stream after being preheated in the flame. The iron powder is picked up by an air stream and discharged through the preheat flame into the oxygen stream. The combination of the oxygen stream and burning iron attacks the metal by fluxing and oxidation. By this means, 18-8 stainless steel, high-chromium irons, high-temperature alloys, cast irons, and other oxidation-resistant alloys can be cut to remove gates rapidly.

Gouging and powder washing are processes allied to torch and powder cutting which assist in cleaning up castings. Gouging is used to clean out or remove surface defects on steel castings. Gouging is performed with the cutting torch, and involves preheating the defective area and cutting it or washing it out with a low-velocity, large-bore oxygen stream.[9] Slag inclusions, blowholes, cracks, fins, and wires may be cleaned out by gouging. A steel casting with surface defects removed by gouging and ready for repair by welding is illustrated in Fig. 24.8. Powder washing is a similar process but is used on the more oxidation-resistant alloys and in removing sand-metal encrustation due to metal penetration of molds or cores. Powder washing differs from gouging in that iron powder is required as in powder cutting. Much of the trimming of riser pads, heavy fins, chills, and other metal protuberances on medium and large steel castings may be done in this way.

Surface Cleaning

Surface-cleaning operations ordinarily follow the removal of gates and risers. However, surface cleaning may facilitate gate removal. For instance, elimination of sand from the casting favors sawing and torch cutting, so that surface cleaning may then be done before gate removal in the case of nonferrous alloys and sometimes steel. When flogging is used on steel or cast iron, it is easier to perform the surface cleaning after gate removal.

Tumbling

Sand, scale, and some fins and wires may be removed by tumbling in a tumbling mill. The mill is filled with castings and some jack stars.

***Fig.* 24.8** View of casting having surface defects removed by flame gouging. (*From R. S. Babcock.*[5])

Table 24.3 Typical cleaning shot and grit sizes*

SAE Shot Numbers and Screening Tolerances

Shot size No.	None on screen opening, in.	Min on screen		Max through screen	
		%	Opening, in.	%	Opening, in.
S1320	0.187	85	0.132	5	0.111
S1110	0.157	85	0.111	5	0.0937
S930	0.132	85	0.0937	5	0.0787
S780	0.111	80	0.0787	10	0.0661
S660	0.0937	80	0.0661	10	0.0555
S550	0.0787	80	0.0555	10	0.0469
S460	0.0661	75	0.0469	15	0.0394
S390	0.0555	75	0.0394	15	0.0331
S330	0.0469	75	0.0331	15	0.0232
S230	0.0394	70	0.0232	20	0.0165
S170	0.0331	70	0.0165	20	0.0117
S110	0.0232	65	0.0117	25	0.0070
S70	0.0165	65	0.0070	25	0.0049

SAE Grit Numbers and Screening Tolerances

Grit size No.	None on screen opening, in.	Min on screen		Max through screen	
		%	Opening, in.	%	Opening, in.
G10	0.111	80	0.0787	10	0.0661
G12	0.0937	80	0.0661	10	0.0555
G14	0.0787	80	0.0555	10	0.0469
G16	0.0661	75	0.0469	15	0.0394
G18	0.0555	75	0.0394	15	0.0280
G25	0.0469	70	0.0280	20	0.0165
G40	0.0394	70	0.0165	20	0.0117
G50	0.0280	65	0.0117	25	0.0070
G80	0.0165	65	0.0070	25	0.0049
G120	0.0117	60	0.0049	30	0.0029
G200	0.0070	55	0.0029	35	0.0017
G325	0.0049	20	0.0017		

* From American Wheelabrator and Equipment Corp.[7]

Rotation of the mill causes the castings and stars to tumble and abrade each other. Twenty minutes to an hour of tumbling is used on gray- and malleable-iron castings. Tumbling has a burnishing action on the casting surfaces and causes the corners to be rounded. Excessive tumbling can cause overabrasion and deformation of the casting corners.

The tumbling action can be combined with sand, grit, or shot blasting in blast mills. Wet tumbling using water treated with caustic is employed for dust suppression. Continuous tumbling mills in which the castings and stars are charged at one end and discharged at the other are usually operated wet.

Tumbling for deburring and brightening of copper-base castings is also practiced. The castings may be cleaned and deburred by using water and detergents in combination with sand or pumice stone in the tumbling barrels. Ball burnishing provides a means of imparting high luster to copper-base castings by tumbling. Steel balls and the castings in a ratio of 2:1 are charged into the barrel along with dilute soap solution. After tumbling, the castings are dried in another mill by tumbling them in sawdust or wood shavings.

Blasting

Blasting the surface of castings is the most rapid means of removing sand and scale. Abrasives employed are sand, metal grit, and metal shot. Sand blasting may be performed using coarse sand, 6- to 30-mesh size, as the abrasive and air as the carrying medium. When air blasting is employed the blasting must be done in cabinets or rooms provided with a means of handling the dust arising from the disintegrating sand. Water blasting eliminates the dust problem.

Grit or shot blasting can be done by the airless-blast method. The metallic particles are thrown by centrifugal force from a rapidly rotating wheel such as that illustrated in Fig. 24.9. The blasting wheel is incorporated in a variety of devices which tumble castings or rotate them under the shot or grit stream so that all casting surfaces are exposed to its abrasive action. The combination of tumbling and mechanical blasting is shown schematically in Fig. 24.10*a* and *b*. Another machine has a series of rotating tables that pass under the shot or grit stream.

Table* 24.4 *Recommended sizes of abrasive*

Castings	SAE size No.
Average gray or annealed malleable, with pockets, burned-in sand, etc	S390 shot
Light gray iron or annealed malleable	S330 shot
Hard malleable	S330 shot
Brass (all types)	G50 or G120 grit
Die castings	G50 grit
Aluminum	G50 grit
Steel	S390 shot

* From American Wheelabrator Equipment Corp.[7]

Rebound of the shot assists in cleaning surfaces not in direct line of the shot stream. On table-type models, the castings must be turned over for cleaning all surfaces. The mechanical-impact cleaning method may also be applied to conveyorized cleaning. Castings, suspended from conveyor hooks, enter a room where they are subjected to a shot or grit stream. The castings are rotated in the stream to expose all the surfaces to cleaning.

Metallic abrasives. Shot or grit may be made of white iron, malleableized iron, or steel. Shot is produced by allowing a stream of molten iron or steel to pass through a steam jet. The jet breaks up the stream into fine particles which fall into a water quenching tank. Grit may

***Fig.* 24.9** Phantom view of airless shot- or grit-blasting machine head (wheelabrator). (*Courtesy of the American Wheelabrator and Equipment Co.*)

be produced from brittle shot by crushing. Malleableized iron or steel shot has less tendency to break down into smaller particles than does white-iron shot. Typical shot and grit sizes are listed in Table 24.3, and recommendations for use on various casting types in Table 24.4. Shot blasting has a battering effect on the metal surface and causes surface-metal flow as it is continued. Grit appears to have more of a gouging action and seems to be removing small particles of metal from the casting surface as blasting continues. Shot blasting therefore produces a rather shiny surface, whereas grit dulls the surface. Only very light shot blast-

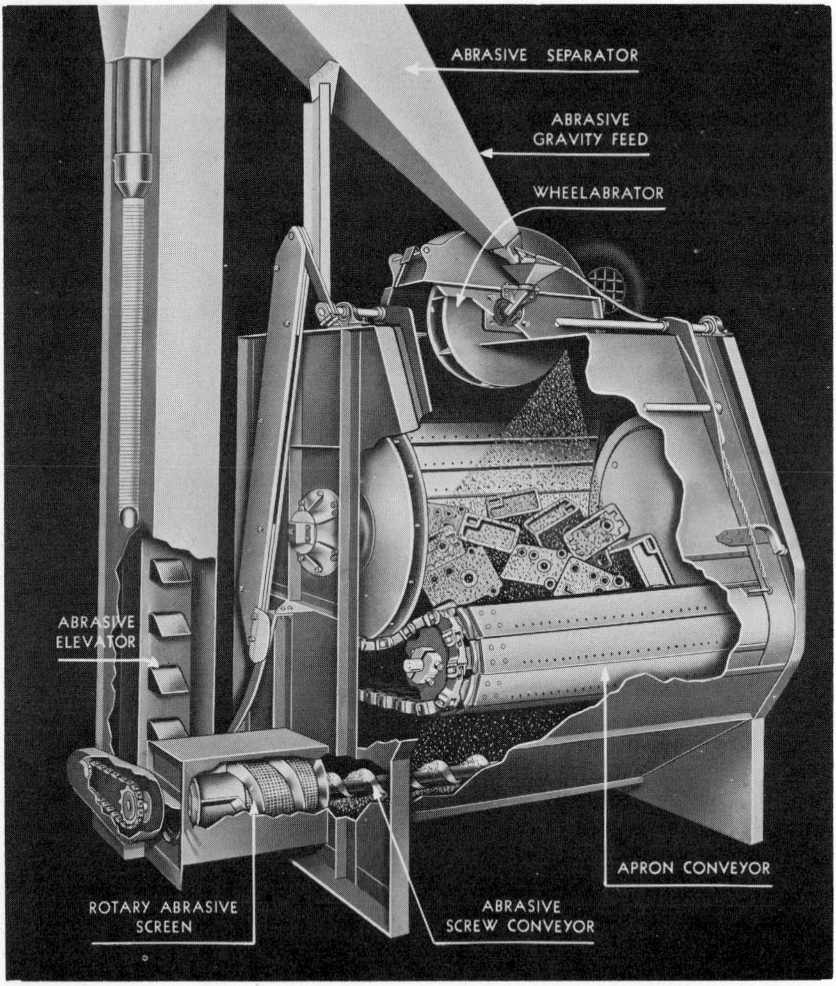

***Fig.* 24.10a** Phantom view of machine combining airless blasting with tumbling for cleaning castings. (*Courtesy of the American Wheelabrator and Equipment Co.*)

Table 24.5 Specifications for chipping hammers*

Piston stroke, in.	Piston diam, in.	Length, in.	Weight, lb	Hose, in.	Work adapted for
1	5/8	8	3	1/2	Very light chipping
1 3/8	3/4	10	5 1/2	1/2	Light chipping and scaling
1	1 1/8	11 1/4	10	1/2	Aluminum casting and light cast-iron calking
2	1 1/8	13 1/2	13 1/4	1/2	Heavy cast iron; light-steel casting; flue beading
3	1 1/8	14 1/2	14 1/2	1/2	Heavy-steel casting; billet chipping
4	1 1/8	15 3/4	15 1/4	1/2	Extra-heavy chipping

* From A. G. Ringer.[8] A composite table of all manufacturers' most popular sizes.

ing can be applied to nonferrous castings or the surface will be severely battered. Grit is not desirable because it will become embedded in the surface of copper or aluminum castings. Malleable iron, soft steel, copper, or bronze shot seems best for that application. In either shot or grit blasting, effectiveness is greatly reduced if the abrasive is contaminated with excessive amounts of sand or fine metal particles. Hence

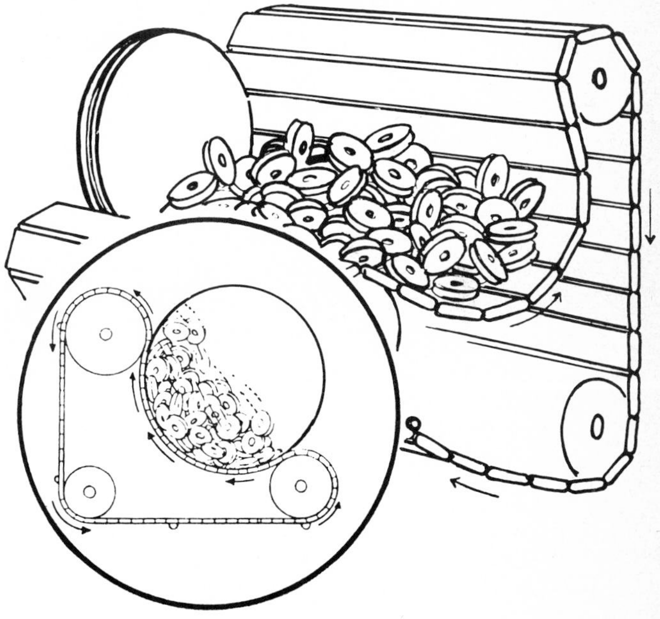

Fig. 24.10b Schematic diagram showing the tumbling action of the machine in (*a*). (*Courtesy of the American Wheelabrator and Equipment Co.*)

the cleaning units are equipped with a means of removing the fines as well as recycling the shot.

Other Types of Surface Cleaning

A number of methods of casting-surface cleaning other than those mentioned above are in use. Wire brushing, buffing, pickling, and various polishing procedures may be applied. Simple wire brushing can be an adequate means of taking off surface sand of nonferrous castings. Most of the other means of cleaning mentioned are used to impart a specially desirable surface finish for final cleaning of the casting.

Trimming

Either after, before, or during the initial surface cleaning, the castings are trimmed to remove fins, gate and riser pads protruding beyond the casting surface, chaplets, wires, parting-line flash, or other appendages to the casting which are not a part of its final dimensions.

Chipping

Pneumatic chipping hammers may be used to remove fins, gate and riser pads, wires, etc., and to remove cores. A variety of hammer and chisel sizes are used for various casting alloys. A No. 2 hammer, with 2-in. piston stroke, will handle most iron and steel foundry work. Specifications for chipping on different types of casting are given in Table 24.5. Chisel types and the relationship of air operating pressure to air-hose setup are illustrated in Fig. 24.11. An air-hose arrangement that causes more than about 10 per cent pressure drop from the source to the pneumatic tool seriously lowers the efficiency of the tool. Air-hose combinations of length and diameter which are favorable and unfavorable at various flow rates are listed in Table 24.7. Pneumatic grinders or other tools are subject to the same conditions. Chipping operations may be speeded up by having chipping stations at conveyors used to transport castings in the cleaning room. Much chipping may be done most conveniently by hand with a hammer. Light-gray- and white-iron castings are especially adaptable to hand chipping. Pneumatic chipping is then done on the areas that are heavier and more difficult to trim.

Grinding

Grinding, or "snagging," of castings is practiced to remove excess metal. Three principal types of grinders are employed for this purpose: floor or bench-stand grinders, portable grinders, and swing-frame grinders. In addition, specialized machines such as disk grinders, belts, and cutoffs may be used.

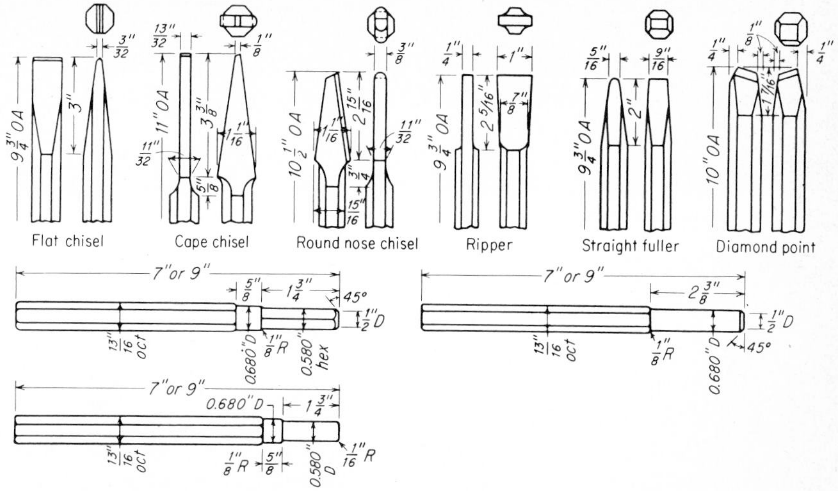

***Fig.* 24.11** Chisel types for chipping castings. Air-hose arrangements for maintaining the efficiency of pneumatic tools are given in Table 24.7. (*From A. G. Ringer.*[8])

Stand Grinding

Stand grinders are usually of the double-end type and may be of constant- or adjustable-speed type, the latter compensating for wheel wear. Low-speed machines operate at speeds up to 6500 surface feet per minute (sfpm), high-speed machines at 9500 sfpm. Castings which can be handled manually are ground on machines of this type. The operator presents the areas to be ground to the wheel face under suitable pressure. Traversing of the wheel face is desirable to prevent rounding or grooving of the wheel and the need for frequent dressing of the wheel.

Stand grinding is ordinarily hand work, depending upon the judgment of the operator for the selection of areas to be ground and amount of grinding. When many castings of one type are ground, special guide fixtures or mechanized feeding and positioning fixtures may be used to speed up grinding.

Abrasive wheels. Grinding wheels used for cleaning castings are made of either the aluminum oxide or silicon carbide types of abrasives. The aluminum oxide abrasives are bonded with vitrified clay or with a resinoid bond. The vitrified-clay-bonded wheels are limited to 6500 sfpm. The silicon carbide abrasives are resinoid-bonded and may operate up to 9500 sfpm. Application of various abrasives and bonds is given in Table 24.6. In general, the silicon carbide abrasives are used for casting materials of lower tensile strength. Coarser abrasive sizes are used for fast cutting whereas fine grits produce a smoother finish. Grits may be graded by sieve number similar to foundry sands. High grain-size numbers in Table 24.6 indicate finer abrasives. Grain spacing and structure determine the number of cutting edges per unit area of wheel face. Snagging usually requires wide grain spacing to get rapid metal removal unless the loading pressure is high.

Table 24.6 ***Abrasive wheels used for grinding castings****

Casting	Grain size	Wheel type	Bond	Speed and equipment
Gray iron..	16–24	Silicon carbide	Vitreous	5000–6000 sfpm, floor stand and swing frame
		Silicon carbide	Resinous	7000–9500 sfpm, floor stand and swing frame
Brass......	24–30	Silicon carbide	Vitreous	5000–6000 sfpm, floor stand
		Silicon carbide	Resinous	7000–9500 sfpm, floor stand
Steel.......	14–20	Aluminum oxide	Vitreous	5000–6000 sfpm, swing frame, floor stand, and portable
		Aluminum oxide	Resinous	7000–9500 sfpm, swing frame, floor stand, and portable
Aluminum.	24–30	Silicon carbide	Vitreous	5000–6000 sfpm, floor stand
		Aluminum oxide	Resinous or shellac	7100–9500 sfpm, floor stand
Malleable..	20	Aluminum oxide or silicon carbide		

* Adapted from Refs. 10, 11, 13, and 15.

A wheel diameter of 14 to 36 in. is common in foundries. The wheel velocity in sfpm varies as the wheel is worn. Of course, the maximum wheel diameter is limited by the safe upper limit of sfpm for the particular wheel and rpm of the grinding machines at hand. Worn wheels and stubs from heavy grinders may be transferred to smaller grinders for light work. Specific wheel applications are best determined by experience and testing.

Swing grinders. Swing grinders are employed when the castings are too heavy to be carried to the work. In this case, the grinder is mounted on a swing frame, the casting positioned under the grinder, and the grinder is then worked over the casting surface as illustrated in Fig. 24.12. Wheel sizes run from 12 to 24 in. in diameter. When the wheel is worn to the point where an excessive loss in sfpm occurs, the rpm on the wheel may be increased by changing the position of belts on the motor and wheel pulleys. The work piece must be firmly positioned under the grinder. This may require supports or fixtures to hold pieces that do not have large stable flat surfaces.

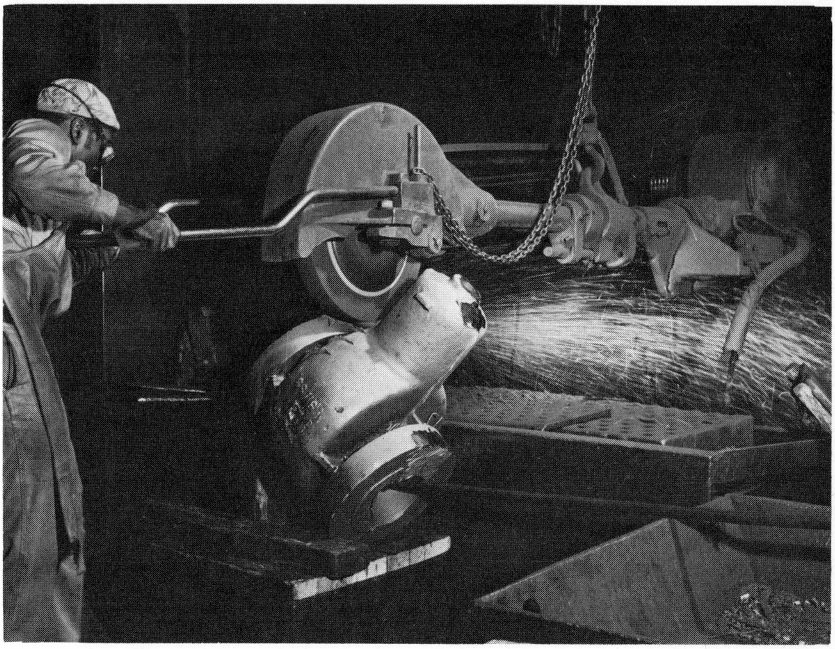

***Fig.* 24.12** Swing-frame grinding. (*From Steel Founders' Society of America.*)

Portable grinders. Electric or air-operated portable grinders are employed for working over surfaces of castings that cannot be handled by swing or stand grinding. Cone, cup, disk, special shapes, and straight grinding wheels up to about 14 in. in diameter may be mounted on portable machines. Generally, only light grinding is intended. Disk grinding is sometimes practiced in this way. Specially shaped wheels have safe operating speeds which are lower than those of regular wheels, and these must be observed to avoid the hazards of wheel disintegration.

Rotary Tools

Cleaning of softer nonferrous alloys such as aluminum or magnesium alloys may be done by rotary filing tools or cutters. These may be electrically or air operated, and are usually of the portable type. The tool operator may then file off excess metal on any casting surface accessible to the tool.

Trimming and Sizing

Shearing, punching, coining, and straightening are mechanical operations which may be employed to complete trimming and sizing castings. Coining or straightening is done with dies in presses under hydraulic pressures up to about 1000 tons, as described in Refs. 17, 22, and 33. In mild-steel and malleable-iron castings, holes may be punched out to eliminate drilling operations. Some castings may have surfaces which are milled, broached, or ground to a specified accuracy as required by the customer.

Finishing

The latter stages of cleaning are often referred to as finishing. Many castings have received their final cleaning operations when grinding is completed. Others are given additional surface finishing such as machining, chemical treatment, polishing, buffing, blasting, and painting to put them into a suitable appearance for sale. Heat-treatments may come at various stages of cleaning. Since scaling, oxidation, or discoloration occurs during heat-treatment, steel and malleable-iron castings receive their final surface cleaning after heat-treatment. In nonferrous castings, chemical, electrolytic, and mechanical means of making the casting surface attractive may be utilized.

A special salt-bath cleaning operation may be used on ferrous castings to obtain maximum freedom from scale, sand, dirt, and grit. For example, gray-iron castings may be immersed into a molten salt bath of caustic, 95% sodium hydroxide, 5% sodium nitrates and nitrites, at 800 F for cleaning. The castings are then rinsed, dipped in acidified water, 15% hydrochloric acid, hot-water-rinsed, and treated with a soluble oil. The oil coating provides rust protection. Treatments of this type are utilized only when the additional cost is justified in a particular application or processing sequence.[16]

INSPECTION

Inspection comprises those operations which check the quality of the castings and result in their acceptance or rejection. Inspection procedures may be classed as follows:

1. Visual, surface inspection for foundry defects
2. Dimensional, requiring gauges for measurements
3. Metallurgical, requiring chemical, physical, and other tests for metal quality

Complete inspection usually embraces all these types of procedures.

Visual Inspection

Certain types of casting defects are immediately obvious upon visual examination of the casting. Cracked castings, tears, dirt, blowholes, scabs, metal penetration, severe shifts, runouts, poured short, swells or strains, cracked mold or cores, and numerous other defects can be identified by the inspector. Casting defects of this type are usually associated with defective molds, cores, their materials of construction, flask equipment, the operations of molding and coremaking, and the rest of the factors in making and pouring the mold. Many of the causes of these defects have been discussed in previous chapters. Evidently, if excess amounts of these defects occur, faulty practices are being employed in the foundry. Their correction is a necessity and can be facilitated if the cause of the defect can be located. Inspectors identify the casting defects and assign their cause to some foundry operation or material so that corrective measures can be taken.

Visual inspection is the simplest method of inspection, and carried to its ultimate it will ensure a casting that "looks" good. This degree of inspection is satisfactory for some castings such as sash weight, manhole covers, drains, and counterbalance weights. However, countless numbers of castings for manufacturing require more exacting inspection for dimensional accuracy and metallurgical standards.

Dimensional Inspection

Dimensional inspection of castings involves the principles of gauging as it is applied to any machine elements. Surface plates, height and depth gauges, layout tables, dividing heads, go and no-go gauges, snap and plug gauges, templates, dies, contour gauges, etc., as used in standard layout and inspection procedures may be applied to castings. Agreement between the machine shop and foundry, or purchaser and vendor, is necessary so that gauging and dimensional checking may be carried out in a mutually acceptable way. Locating points used as starting points for machining and dimensional inspection should be selected by common consent. Castings must be sectioned to check metal-wall thickness. The area of dimensional inspection and accuracy involves the entire field of castings utilization by the machine shop. There is no intent in this textbook to discuss this mechanical-engineering field. It needs to be pointed out, however, that the closest cooperation between the foundry, pattern shop, and machine shop utilizing the casting will result in the most efficient use of good gauging and machining practice.[34,35]

Metallurgical Inspection

Metallurgical inspection includes chemical analysis, mechanical-property tests, evaluation of casting soundness, and product testing of special properties such as electrical conductivity, resistivity, magnetic effects, corrosion resistance, response to heat-treatment, strength in assemblies, surface conditions, coatings and surface treatments, and others.

Chemical Analysis

The methods of chemical analysis for many casting alloys, ferrous and nonferrous, have been developed and adopted as standard through the work of the ASTM. The ASTM "Methods of Chemical Analysis of Metals" sets forth the standard and tentative standard procedures adopted for ferrous and nonferrous metals by American industry. Many short-cut methods of analysis have been developed for specific casting alloys. Since this textbook does not deal with chemical analytical methods, there will be no further discussion of this subject.

Casting Soundness

Shrinkage cavities, blowholes, gas holes, porosity, hot tears, cracks, entrained slag, lapped or cold-shut surfaces, etc., are all considered as contributing to lack of casting soundness when they are present. These defects are of greater or lesser importance, depending on the casting application. Many castings with internal shrinkage, porosity, or other defects that do not interfere with the functioning of the castings are quite acceptable to the user. Where the requirements are high and factors of safety low, however, the very highest degree of metallurgical quality is required. In castings for aircraft, ordnance, and other highly precision-engineered applications, absolute soundness and optimum properties are needed. These objectives will be met only when the casting inspection includes methods which check the casting for soundness defects not visibly detectable. Diverse methods of discovering soundness defects have been devised, and are exhaustively treated by various authors.[24–27,32–34,36,37]

Pressure testing. Pressure testing is used to locate leaks in a casting or to check the over-all strength of a casting in resistance to bursting under hydraulic pressure. Equipment for sealing off castings and finding the leaks is discussed in Ref. 23. Proof loading by hydraulic pressure involves introducing a fluid, oil or water, into the casting. The casting is then subjected to a pressure which is in excess of the maximum stress that the casting is supposed to encounter in service. Case pipe or tubes are often proof-tested in this way.

Sectioning. Castings may be sawed up, and the sections examined for soundness. This procedure is desirable since the interior of the casting, section thickness, as well as its soundness, may be studied. Macroetching may be used to locate suspected shrinkage, porosity, or cracks.

Radiographic inspection. Nondestructive testing of casting soundness may be determined by X-ray radiographic means. The source of short-wavelength rays which can penetrate metals may be either an X-ray tube (radiographic machine), a radium capsule, a cobalt-60 capsule, betatron, or other radioactive source. Whatever the source, X or gamma rays are passed through the test piece, and the intensity of transmitted rays is recorded on a photographic film. Film is positioned behind the casting sections being radiographed. The distance from X-ray source to casting, section thickness, exposure, time, and many other details must be properly selected to give satisfactory results. Since most defects transmit the short-wavelength light better than the sound metal does, the film is darkened more where the defects are in the line of the X-ray beam. The darkening of defective areas is shown in Fig. 24.13, where an internal hot tear is revealed by radiographic examination. Figure 24.13 is a positive print of the normal X-ray negative film. Other internal defects can be located in this way. The penetrating power of the short-wavelength source limits the section thickness that can be examined in this way.[37]

Magnetic-particle inspection. This method of inspection is used on magnetic ferrous castings for detecting invisible surface or slightly subsurface defects. The object is magnetized, and magnetic particles applied to the casting surface. When a current or magnetizing force is passed through the metal, fields are set up as illustrated in Fig. 24.14. Polar effects exist at the defects, which cause magnetic particles to be aligned around the defect. The magnaflux indication is obtained when magnetic particles align themselves preferentially in the flux field. Magnaflux equipment may be of the portable type which has electrodes that can be positioned anywhere desired on the casting. Larger units are stationary and have fixed electrodes which are clamped to the casting and provide low-voltage high-current magnetization. The magnetic particles are applied dry, by an air stream, with the portable machine, or wet on the larger machines. Magnetic indications are not obtained from defects alone. Certain shapes, sharp corners, fillets, and welds

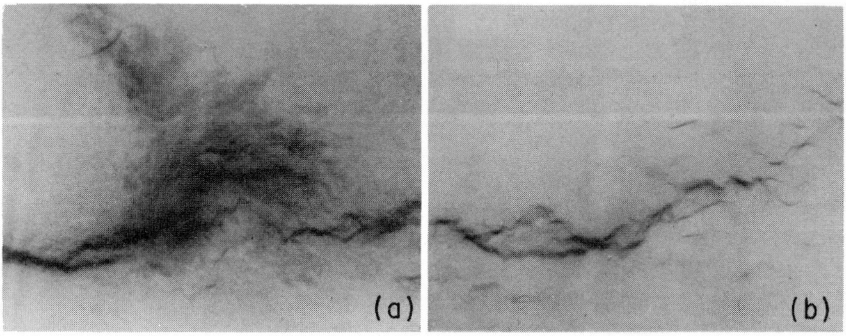

***Fig.* 24.13** Internal hot-tear defect revealed by radiographic inspection. (*a*) Dispersed spongy shrinkage with severe hot tear; (*b*) hot tear with shrinkage at a minimum. (*From W. H. Baer.*[25])

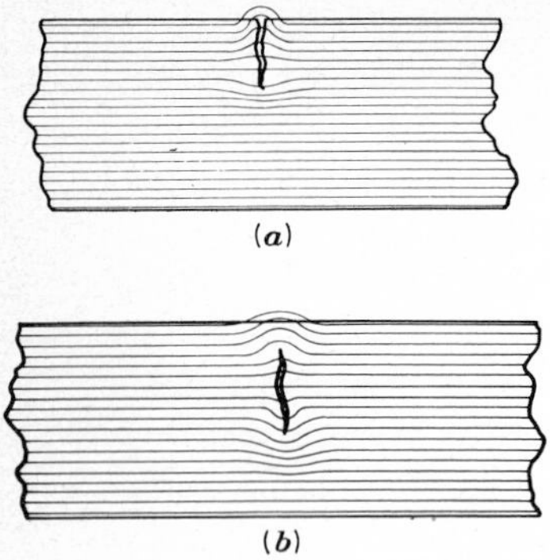

(a)

(b)

Fig. **24.14** Magnetic flux field in a magnetized bar containing (*a*) surface and (*b*) subsurface defects. (*From W. E. Thomas.*[27])

give indications that might look like defects. Hence experienced inspection is required to use this tool effectively. After magnafluxing, the parts must be demagnetized. Reference **36** is suggested for review of the principle of this inspection method.

Fluorescent penetrant. Invisible surface defects of nonmagnetic alloys cannot be located by magnaflux inspection. However, a similar inspection tool is available. A penetrating oil, mixed with whiting powder, may be applied to the casting surface. After the casting has been wiped dry, the oil will creep out of cracks or other defects and become visible at those places. Recent developments of this technique have employed fluorescent liquids. When these are wiped or cleaned off the casting, the defects filled with the fluorescent oil may be readily observed under black light. These tests are limited to surface defects.

Supersonic testing. Sound waves above the audible frequency (16,000 cycles per sec) may be used to locate defects. If supersonic vibrations are initiated at one casting surface, they will be reflected from the opposite surface after a suitable time interval. Defects will also reflect the sound waves, but the time required for reflection will be less than that of the opposite casting surface. The sound vibrations and reflection measurements are made with equipment known as the "supersonic reflectoscope." A vibrating quartz crystal applies the waves, and an oscilloscope can be used to detect the reflections from casting surfaces and defects. Of course, the problem of locating the defects is great since the entire casting must be laboriously surveyed by hand with the equipment. Reference **32** may be studied for further details on this inspection tool.

Mechanical-property Testing

Castings and test bars must be tested to see that mechanical-property specifications are met. Tensile, hardness, transverse, impact, fatigue, and other properties are tested in accordance with standard procedures

Table 24.7 Recommended hose arrangements* *A chart for use in determining hose arrangements for any pneumatic tool*

Air flow, cfm	10 ft of 1/4-in. hose	8 ft of 5/16-in. hose	10 ft of 3/8-in. hose	12½ ft of 1/2-in. hose	25 ft of 1/2-in. hose	50 ft of 1/2-in. hose	12½ ft of 3/4-in. hose	25 ft of 3/4-in. hose	50 ft of 3/4-in. hose	50 ft of 1/2-in. hose + 10 ft of 1/4-in. hose	50 ft of 1/2-in. hose + 10 ft of 3/8-in. hose	50 ft of 1/2-in. hose + 8 ft of 5/16-in. hose	50 ft of 1/2-in. hose + 12½ ft of 1/2-in. hose	50 ft of 3/4-in. hose + 25 ft of 1/2-in. hose	50 ft of 3/4-in. hose + 12½ ft of 3/4-in. hose
	Pressure drop, psi, based on 100 psi line pressure														
10–11	5.0	0.9								5.3	0.7	1.4			
11–12	5.9	1.0								6.2	0.8	1.6			
12–13	6.8	1.2	0.4							7.2	0.9	1.9			
13–14	8.0	1.4	0.5							8.4	1.1	2.2			
14–15	9.3	1.6	0.6							9.8	1.3	2.5			
15–16	11.0	1.9	0.7							11.6	1.5	2.9			
16–18	14.0	2.4	0.8							15.0	1.9	3.5	1.7		
18–20	19.6	3.0	1.0							21.4	2.4	4.5	2.0		
20–25		4.3	1.4	0.7	1.0	1.3					3.5	6.4	2.6	1.3	
25–30		6.6	2.1	1.0	1.5	2.3					5.2	9.8	3.8	1.9	
30–35		9.5	3.1	1.3	2.1	3.6					7.3	13.7	5.3	2.6	
35–40		12.8	4.2	1.7	2.8	5.2					9.6	18.4	7.1	3.5	
40–50		19.3	6.3	2.4	4.1	8.0					14.0		10.4	5.2	1.8
50–60			9.6	3.7	6.3	12.2					21.8		16.0	7.8	2.3
60–70			13.5	5.3	9.0	17.4	0.9	1.4	1.9				22.8	11.1	3.0
70–80			18.7	7.1	12.4		1.1	1.7	2.5					15.0	3.7
80–90			25.0	9.0	16.1		1.4	2.2	3.2					19.8	4.6
90–100				11.1			1.7	2.7	4.0						5.8
100–120							2.3	3.5	5.6						7.9
120–140							3.2	4.8	8.0						11.2
140–160							4.3	6.6	11.0						15.5
160–180							5.6	8.7	15.2						20.4
180–200							7.2	11.0							
200–220							9.0								

* A. G. Ringer.[8] Combinations of hose size, air flow, and pressure drop below the black line are undesirable.

adopted by ASTM and other specifying groups. Since these tests may be studied in the ASTM standards books and other technical works, they will not be considered in this book.. Some special test bars peculiar to certain casting alloys have been considered in earlier chapters. Special proof tests are used on certain types of castings. Pipe, for example, may be subjected to a pressure test to prove its reliability. Assemblies of cast chain links are often subjected to a maximum tensile proof load to ensure quality. Thus mechanical tests may be used to qualify castings for their service requirements, as well as for determining the normal strength properties.

SALVAGE

Castings which have been rejected because of failure to meet inspection requirements are not necessarily scrapped. If the defects are not too serious, salvage is possible in many cases by welding or other treatment and refinishing. Whether salvage is permissible or economical depends greatly on factors such as the casting alloy, casting size and shape, relative cost of new castings vs. repairing the defects, difficulty of salvage, availability of repair equipment and methods, quality requirements, and any agreements between the foundry and castings user relative to salvage castings. The salvaging process ordinarily consists in welding the defective areas. Castings that are defective because they are leakers under pressure tests may be reclaimed by sealing processes (Chap. 12).

Welding

Castings reclaimed by welding defects are ordinarily treated as follows:

1. The defective areas are prepared for welding by chipping, grinding, gouging, or powder washing in the case of ferrous alloys. Nonferrous alloys require defect removal by mechanical means such as filing, grinding, or other tooling. Cracks should be completely removed before welding.
2. By welding, the actual repair process. The welding of castings is discussed in references in the bibliography of this chapter.
3. By cleaning. The welded areas may be cleaned by the methods described earlier, and then the castings must be reinspected to pass the required standards.

BIBLIOGRAPHY

1. S. W. Brinson and J. A. Duma, Observations on Knock-off Risers as Applied to Steel Castings, *Trans. AFS,* vol. 56, p. 586, 1948.
2. D. Hannah, Die Casting Trim Die Procedure, *Trans. AFS*, vol. 69, p. 784, 1961.
3. G. H. Shippard, Band Sawing in Foundries, *Trans. AFS,* vol. 58, p. 621, 1950.
4. H. J. Chamberland, Band Sawing Nonferrous Castings, *Foundry,* vol. 60, September, 1952.

5. R. S. Babcock, Oxygen Cutting Processes in Steel Foundries, *Trans. AFS,* vol. 58, 1950.
6. American Welding Society, "Welding Handbook," vol. 1, 1962.
7. American Wheelabrator and Equipment Corp., "Wheelabrator Operators Manual," 1965.
8. A. G. Ringer, Use of Portable Air Tools in Foundry Cleaning Rooms, *Trans. AFS,* vol. 58, p. 510, 1950.
9. Carborundum Co., "Safe Speeds for Grinding Wheels," 1965.
10. D. E. Sawtelle, Mechanized Malleable Foundry Finishing and Inspection, *Trans. AFS,* vol. 55, p. 388, 1947.
11. L. N. Schuman, Equipment and Methods of Straightening and Dimensional Inspection of Malleable Iron Castings, *Trans. AFS,* vol. 59, p. 418, 1951.
12. C. Schneider and L. Ulsenheimer, Production Hardness Testing in a Malleable Shop, *Trans. AFS,* vol. 56, p. 473, 1948.
13. B. H. Work, Foundry Cleaning Room Abrasive Operations, *Trans. AFS,* vol. 58, p. 685, 1950.
14. D. Van Order, Grinding Standards Help Eliminate Cleaning Room Bottlenecks, *Trans. AFS,* vol. 56, p. 473, 1948.
15. H. W. Wagner, Snagging Operations, *Foundry,* vol. 81, p. 112, January, 1953.
16. R. H. Herrman, Salt Bath Cleaning of Gray Iron Castings, *Foundry,* vol. 78, August, 1950.
17. American Foundrymen's Society, Malleable Straightening Dies, *Trans. AFS,* vol. 68, p. 801, 1960.
18. P. E. Kufer, Finding the Most Profitable Snagging Wheel, *Am. Foundryman,* vol. 24, p. 32, July, 1953.
19. S. Kreszewski, Selection and Application of Cleaning Room Equipment, *Trans. AFS,* vol. 58, 1950.
20. M. G. Diett, The Nonferrous Cleaning Room, *Am. Foundryman,* vol. 22, p. 44, September, 1952.
21. N. L. Smith and R. J. Wolf, Material Transport in the Cleaning Room, *Trans. AFS,* vol. 58, p. 550, 1950.
22. D. T. Martin, Outline of Inspection for Pearlitic Malleable Castings, *Trans. AFS,* vol. 58, p. 692, 1950.
23. K. M. Smith, Dimensional Checking and Pressure Testing of Gray Iron Castings, *Trans. AFS,* vol. 59, p. 304, 1951.
24. C. H. Hastings, Choosing Equipment for Nondestructive Testing, *Trans. AFS,* vol. 59, p. 309, 1951.
25. W. H. Baer, Radiography of Gun Metal Castings, *Trans. AFS,* vol. 55, p. 153, 1947.
26. E. L. La Grelius, Importance of Radiography to Inspection, *Trans. AFS,* vol. 55, p. 375, 1947.
27. W. E. Thomas, Castings Industry Application of Magnetic Particle Inspection, *Trans. AFS,* vol. 55, p. 482, 1947.
28. A. V. Lorch, Repair Welding Light Metal Castings, *Foundry,* vol. 77, January, 1949.
29. T. E. Kihlgren and L. C. Minard, Arc Welding of Cast Iron with Nickel Electrodes, *Trans. AFS,* vol. 55, p. 357, 1947.
30. J. H. Hall, Steel Castings in Welded Assemblies, *Trans. AFS,* vol. 57, p. 1, 1949.
31. G. E. Bellew, Salvage of Castings by Welding of Defects, *Trans. AFS,* vol. 58, p. 669, 1950.

32. G. L. Kehl, "Principles of Metallographic Laboratory Practice," 3d ed., McGraw-Hill Book Company, New York, 1949.
33. American Foundrymen's Society, "Cast Metals Handbook," 1957.
34. E. Suring, Dimensional Control of Production Castings, *Trans. AFS,* vol. 70, p. 364, 1962.
35. AFS Committee 8 H, Surface Finish of Castings, *Trans. AFS,* vol. 70, p. 584, 1962.
36. AFS Committee 6 G, Magnetic Particle Testing of Malleable Castings, *Trans. AFS,* vol. 70, p. 1235, 1962.
37. L. J. Venne, Betatron Radiography of Heavy Section Castings, *Trans. AFS,* vol. 69, p. 743, 1961.
38. F. Newberry, Pad Washing with Carbon Arc Process, *Trans. AFS,* vol. 64, p. 430, 1956.

25
Casting-design Considerations

Castings are born on a designer's drawing board, but the final shape is often altered during the course of its development. As machine elements, tools, or other objects, their functional purpose is given, first and foremost, attention by the designer. Ultimately, after testing, the design, or possible modification, is found to work. The next step is manufacturing. If metal casting is selected as the primary metal-shaping process, certain features of the design may be modified to favor the casting process. This, of course, is also true if the part is to be made primarily by welding, forging, stamping, or any other process.

For casting purposes, designing may include the following areas of planning:

1. Functional design
2. Simplification of foundry practices
3. Metallurgical design; selection and optimum use of casting alloy
4. Economic considerations

FUNCTIONAL DESIGN

Sometimes there is only one design which will perform the service intended by the designer. In this case, the foundryman may be required to use all the technical abilities available to produce the casting as it is, whether the design is a favorable or an unfavorable one for foundry practices. It is of course a unique advantage of the casting process that any intricate shape may be cast. Often, however, several designs are possible, and one of these may be especially suited to the casting process. In many cases it is possible for the designer to alter the structural characteristics of the part so that a better or more economical casting may be produced without interfering with functioning of the part. The latter situation is one which is most advantageous to all, the designer, user, and the foundryman. This textbook, of course, offers no discussion of the elements of machine design as such. Considerations of the functioning of machine elements, stresses, stress distribution, stress measurements, proportioning of member size and shape, etc., are the proper field of design engineers and the technical literature pertaining thereto. References 14, 15, and 17 to 23 describe some of these design procedures as applied to castings. Of special import in arriving at a suitable design for a casting are the characteristics of the casting process. The mechanical strength of cast metals must be known for stress calculation. Characteristics of minimum section thickness, dimensional accuracy, various allowances needed, proper webbing, limiting shapes for soundness, and many other factors of the various casting processes need to be known to the designer. Then he can design the casting so that it will perform its functional requirements and still be a part that can be economically and favorably cast.

Mechanical Strength

On a drawing board, the sections of a casting are assumed to be of metal uniformly sound, homogeneous, and having a certain mechanical strength. Stress calculations and most experimentally determined stresses in castings are made with the same assumption. The factual relation between these assumptions and practical castings depends greatly on the casting design, foundry practices, and the nature of the alloy.

Accuracy of Mechanical-property Information

Assuming the metal is sound, accurate knowledge of its mechanical properties is needed before the casting can be designed for strength. A general knowledge or at least sources of information about the properties of casting alloys should be available to the designer. Mechanical properties such as tensile, yield, compressive, torsional, shear, and impact strengths; endurance limit; notch sensitivity; creep characteristics; hardness; elevated-temperature strength; and modulus of elasticity or rigidity all need to have quantitative values for the casting alloys if designers are to employ calculations and empirical design formulas. Unfortunately, many handbooks provide only very limited information about the properties of cast metals. For example, the whole family of gray cast irons may be simply classed as "cast iron" and given one set of properties. Actually, there are many gray irons of widely differing mechanical properties, as pointed out in Chaps. 18 and 21. Similar conditions exist in the case of cast steels and nonferrous casting alloys. It is extremely important, then, that accurate sources of information be consulted so that the designer may intelligently use the properties available. Recognized sources are such publications as the ASTM Standards, AFS "Cast Metals Handbook," handbooks of the various foundry societies, Refs. 1, 4 to 8, 24, and 25, the SAE handbook, Federal Specifications, U.S. Navy Specifications, and so on. These specifications give minimum and typical properties which can be expected of the casting alloys in the as-cast conditions and for different conditions of heat-treatment. Generally, the minimum and typical property data from the references cited are adequate. However, when the most accurate values are required, as, for example, in aircraft-casting design and design of cast crankshafts or other highly stressed critical parts, special testing procedures are necessary. Then test samples cut from the casting itself give the most accurate data.

Metal Soundness and Strength

Lack of metal soundness in a casting is one reason for lower than optimum mechanical properties. The foundryman, by using a sufficient number of foundry techniques such as gating, risering, chills, padding, and thermal gradients, can generally produce soundness even in exceedingly difficult cases of poorly designed castings. If certain design principles are observed, however, the job of producing soundness and uniformly good properties can be made much easier and less costly.

Directional solidification. Castings solidify toward areas of large mass or low SA/V ratio (Chap. 9). If the last sections to freeze solidify slowly and fully feed those which freeze earlier, then soundness can be obtained by risering. Castings may be intentionally designed to favor directional solidification. Figure 25.1 shows two designs of a valve body, one of which promotes directional solidification toward risers. The initial design (Fig. 25.1, right section) permits freezing off below the risers, and will most likely have porosity in the unfed lower portion of the casting. A circle may be inscribed in the bottom section below the point x to show the presence of a heat mass. By changing the bottom section to a wedge shape, feeding is improved. Further improvement

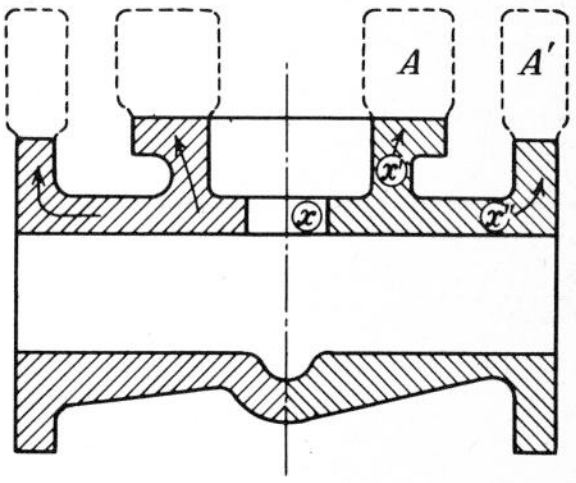

***Fig.* 25.1** Progressive solidification as applied to a cast-steel valve body. The right half represents an original valve design. The left half represents a design modified to permit progressive solidification. Risers are indicated by dashed lines. Since solidification will begin at thinner sections, points x, x', and x'' will solidify first, and solidification will proceed from these points. It is evident that the cross-hatched area included within x, x', and x'' will not be fed adequately by risers A and A'. In the design at the left, the section has been modified to permit controlled progressive solidification as indicated by the arrows. Solidification proceeds from the thinner sections, through the heavier sections, to the riser. (*From American Foundrymen's Society.*[1])

in Fig. 25.1 would accentuate wedge-shaped sections from the bottom toward the top risers and in the sectional between the two flanges. The use of the principle of directional solidification by a designer requires either that he be versed in risering practice in the foundry or that he obtain the advice of foundrymen with respect to improving the casting design. The latter is usually the better course since more phases of foundry practice than risering may be involved.

Columnar solidification. The solidification mechanisms of casting alloys have been discussed in Chap. 8. Because of the columnar growth of dendrites, planes of weakness can be developed during freezing. Figure 25.2 illustrates how columnar freezing develops directional weakness at sharp corners, in rectangular sections, and at perpendicular surface junctions. The use of generous fillets as illustrated in Fig. 25.2 can eliminate this factor as a source of lower than optimum mechanical properties.

Center-line shrinkage in plate sections, shown in Fig. 25.3, is also the result of columnar solidification or progressive solidification, depending on the alloy in question. This defect is an actual shrinkage defect, whereas planes of weakness may occur in sound metal.

The aforementioned defects can interfere with soundness and uniformity of strength in any casting alloys. However, they are much

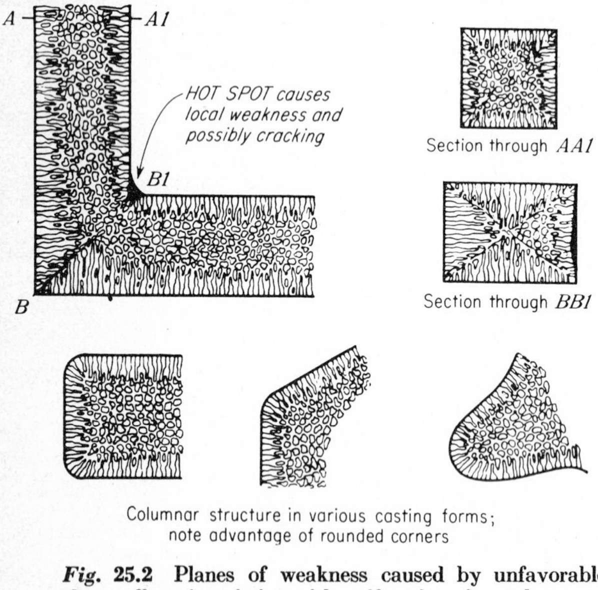

***Fig.* 25.2 Planes of weakness caused by unfavorable shape effects interfering with uniformity of metal properties. Adequate filleting corrects for these shape effects. (*From Meehanite Metal Corp.*[9])**

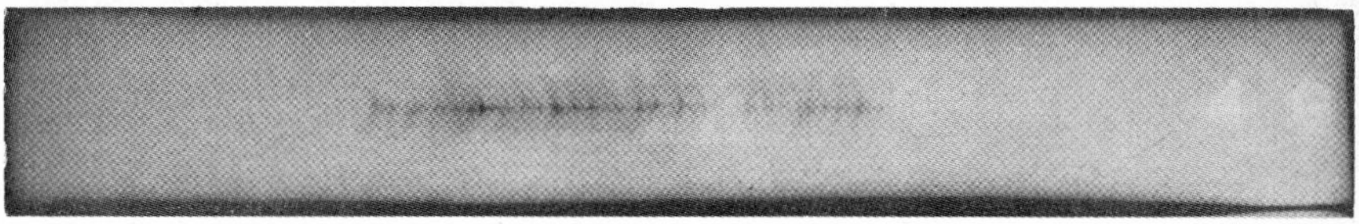

***Fig.* 25.3** Reproduction of radiograph showing center-line shrinkage due to columnar solidification in a section of cast steel. (*From W. S. Pellini.*[21])

more likely to cause trouble in some alloys than in others because of differences in the solidification mechanism. A relative rating of major casting alloys with respect to this problem follows:

Steel	Severely troublesome
White irons	Severely troublesome
Tin bronzes	Severely troublesome
Other copper alloys	Moderately troublesome
Aluminum-base alloys	Moderately troublesome
Low-carbon-equivalent gray irons	Slightly troublesome
High-carbon-equivalent gray irons	Not troublesome

Percentage of volumetric shrinkage during freezing and mode of solidification are principal reasons for differences of the alloys listed above. Fortunately, center-line shrinkage in even the more troublesome alloys can be eliminated by applying the principle of directional solidification.

The extent of center-line shrinkage is governed greatly by size and shape factors of the casting sections. In steels, it occurs most frequently in sections under 4 in. thickness. In sections 4 in. thick, center-line shrinkage occurs most commonly in casting walls having a length (horizontal position in mold) or height (vertical position in mold) exceeding 16 in. The size-and-shape effect is related to the distance that may be fed from risers into the casting whether located as top or as side risers. Figure 25.4 shows how increasing section thickness of steel from 0.25 to 4.0 in. in a wall 12.0 in. high gradually decreases the amount of metal containing center-line shrinkage. When the larger sections are reached in Fig. 25.4, risering could feed the damaged topmost metal. However, if much additional height, above 12 in., were added to the 4-in. section, then a top riser might no longer feed down sufficiently far to prevent center-line shrinkage. Padding or taper, the wedge-shape effect, may be used to combat this problem. If the section is tapered to become larger toward the riser, temperature gradients will exist, so that the heavier portion of the casting will feed the thinner portions and the former can be fed by risers. Figure 25.5 illustrates how taper decreases the amount of metal damaged in a 1- by 12-in. steel section. According to Fig. 25.5, tapering from 1 in. at the bottom

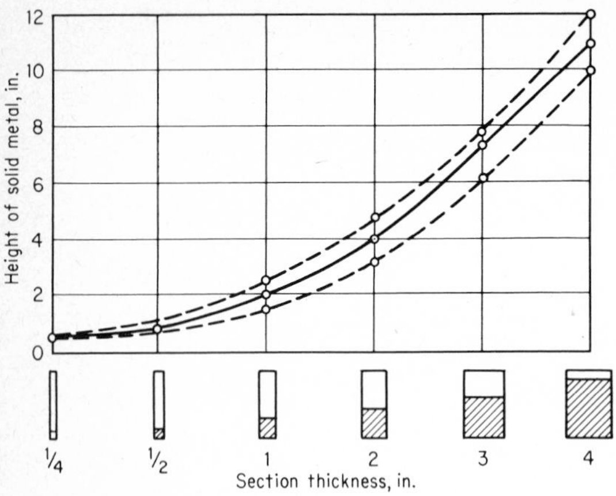

Fig. 25.4 Effect of cast-steel section thickness on center-line shrinkage, showing the height of solid metal in vertical sections 12 in. high. (*From American Foundrymen's Society.*[1])

to 4 in. at the top of a 12-in.-high section completely eliminates damaged metal. The combinations of vertical taper, section thickness, and height of section for steel castings are given in Fig. 25.6. It may be noted in Fig. 25.6 that the sections under 4 in. require much more taper to obtain soundness than do the heavier sections. This does not mean that center-line shrinkage does not occur in heavy sections. Ordinarily, the heavier sections are sufficiently compact so that the shrinkage can be fed by risers. If they are spread out enough, they will also show center-line shrinkage, and then tapering would be helpful.

The foregoing discussion has been concerned largely with cast steel. In many alloys center-line type of shrinkage does not occur to the point of developing gross shrinkage cavities but does cause dispersed shrinkage, especially toward the center of the section. This is but a lesser degree of the same problem, i.e., feeding uniform plate-type sections

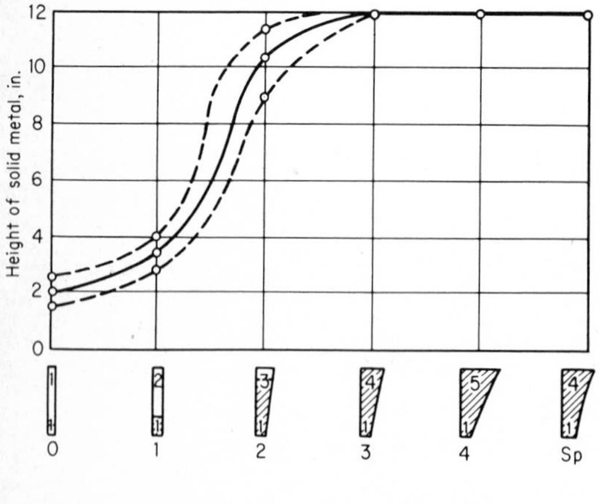

Fig. 25.5 Effect of taper on center-line shrinkage in cast-steel sections 1 in. thick at bottom, varying thickness (taper) at the top, and 12 in. high. (*From American Foundrymen's Society.*[1])

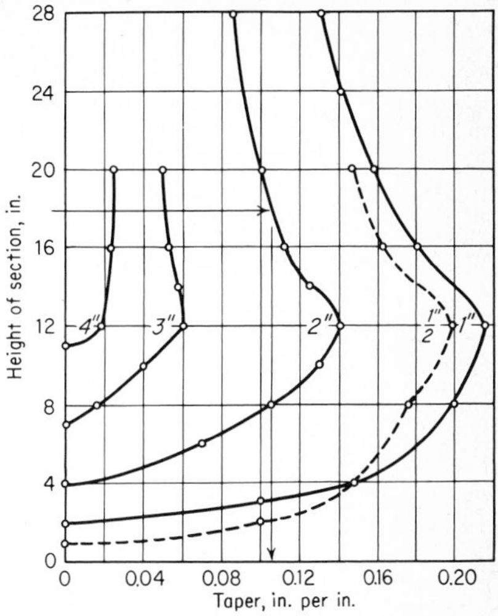

***Fig.* 25.6** Taper of section in inches per inch required to obtain solid metal in cast-steel sections of various heights and thickness. (*From American Foundrymen's Society.*[1])

through some substantial distance from risers. The alloy rating on susceptibility to center-line shrinkage given earlier was intended to mean that steel is more likely to give gross mid-wall cavities whereas the copper- and aluminum-base alloys are more likely to have dispersed shrinkage. By comparison, gray irons are unlikely to display this defect.

Padding applied to patterns is one of the foundryman's means of combating center-line shrinkage and of promoting directional solidification. Padding is excess metal added to the casting to develop temperature gradients for directional solidification. Padding on a pattern is illustrated in Fig. 25.7. In this case the foundry has added the padding and may be required to remove it by machining before the casting is accepted.

Mass shape and size effects (*hot spots*). Shrinkage cavities of any kind are of course harmful to metal properties. Certain shapes, because of their influence on heat extraction during solidification, are likely to cause shrinkage cavities. Whenever solidification is delayed at a particular location, that section will show a shrinkage cavity unless adequate feeding from risers occurs. An enlargement for a rib or corner is a typical case illustrated in Fig. 25.8. The cavity in the rib, on the right-hand side in Fig. 25.8, results because the riser cannot feed through the thin section to reach the rib. Freezing is delayed in the junction of the rib and the main section because this is a location of greater mass, or SA/V relationship, also called a "hot spot" by foundrymen. The location of hot spots at L, T, X, and Y junctions can be proved by the inscribed-circle method, as illustrated in Fig. 25.9. The locations

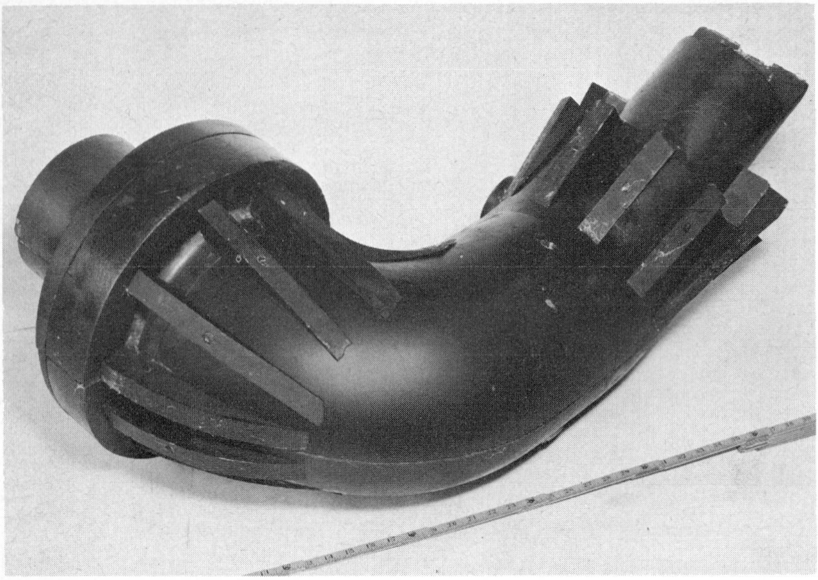

***Fig.* 25.7** Padding on a steel-flanged branch casting, showing the rib method of adding padding. The ribbing shown serves as a guide to molders for applying the full padding needed to promote soundness. Current pattern practice would include putting the full padding on the pattern to eliminate hand work by molders. (*From American Foundrymen's Society.*[1])

of joining members in Fig. 25.9 are sections wherein shrinkage cavities are likely to develop. The L section may be redesigned as in Fig. 25.10 to improve its heat-dissipating characteristics. The ultimate design, case *c* in Fig. 25.10, is one in which the section thickness at *R* is less than that at *d*. Details of L, V, Y, T, and X junctions are given in Fig. 25.12. Similar designs of various junctions are given in Refs. 1, 4, 5, 9, 12, 22, and 23 for different casting alloys. The application of the principle of minimizing hot spots in joining members of a casting is illustrated in Fig. 25.11. A variety of methods of treating joining

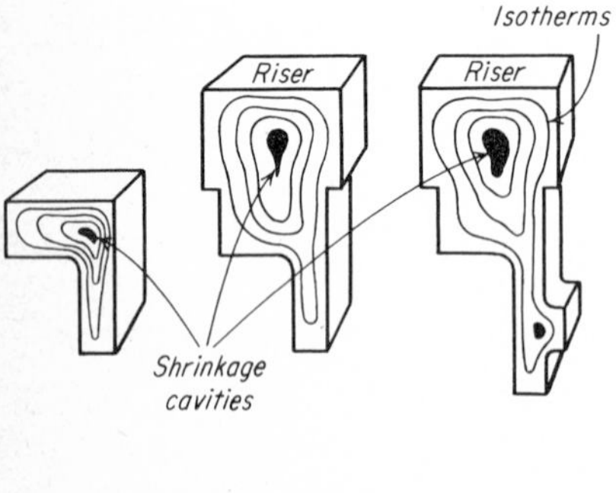

***Fig.* 25.8** Formation of shrinkage cavities in corners and ribs. (*Courtesy of Steel Founders' Society of America.*)

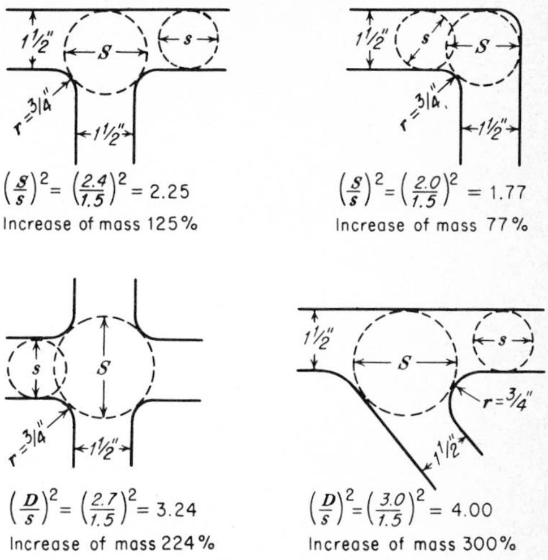

Fig. 25.9 **Use of inscribed circles to determine the increase in mass at joining members of T, L, X, and Y junctions.** *(Courtesy of Steel Founders' Society of America.)*

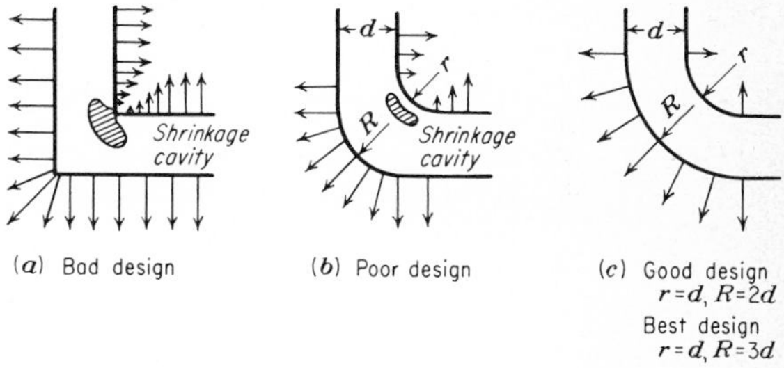

Fig. 25.10 Evolution of an L junction to eliminate a hot spot and thus promote soundness. *(Courtesy of Steel Founders' Society of America.)*

members of castings are illustrated in Fig. 25.12. It may be noted in Fig. 25.12 that the problem may be solved in two ways, one by the foundry when poor designs exist, the other by the designer, making the foundry correction unnecessary. The latter solution is preferred, of course.

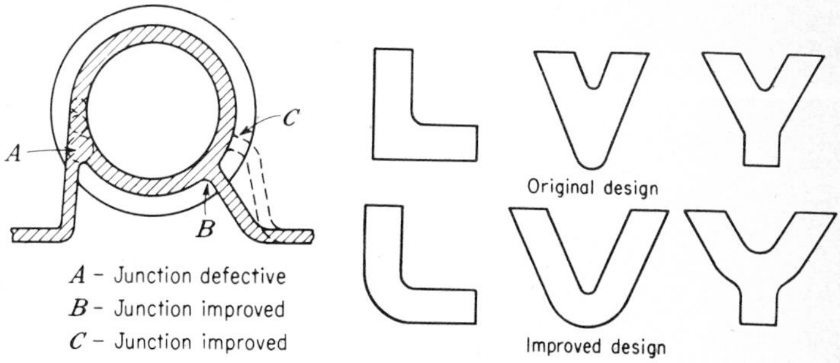

Fig. 25.11 **Minimizing hot spots on joining members of a casting.** *(Courtesy of Steel Founders' Society of America.)*

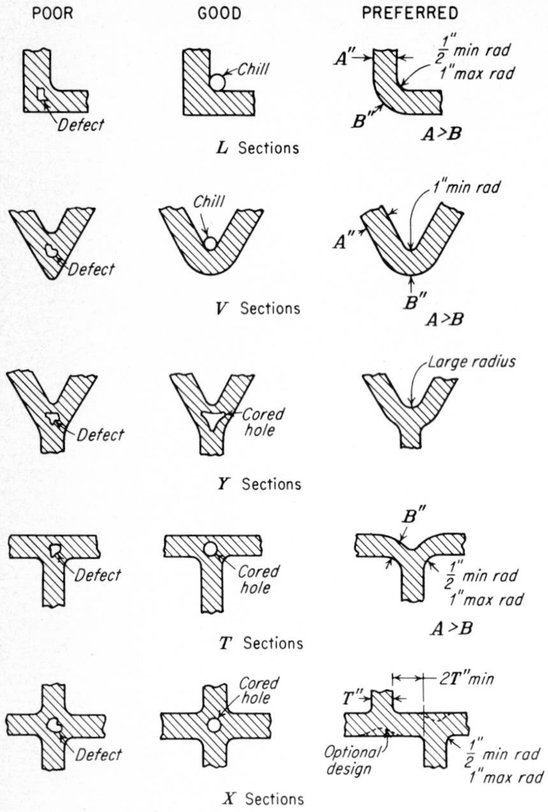

Fig. **25.12** Methods of treating joining members of castings to avoid hot-spot troubles. (*From R. W. Bolz.*[13])

Freezing delay from hot spots can occur in many different places. Bosses, pads, and flanges are examples illustrated in Fig. 25.13. When a thick section pad is joined to a thinner casting member, as in the upper right of Fig. 25.13, unsound metal results. These problems can be corrected by methods similar to those discussed. Flanges in which a perpendicular or other angled corner is needed are examples of designs where the use of filleting is not a suitable solution. A recommended design is offered in Fig. 25.14. In the latter figure, prevention of gross shrinkage is accomplished by feeding through section *D*, usually with a top riser.

Often the effect of a hot spot at the junction of members is obtained from the sand rather than the actual metal section. Thin sand projections, reentrant angles, for instance, are to be avoided for this reason. Figure 25.15 illustrates this condition. Since thin sand projections are heated rapidly, they do not extract so much as surrounding areas. These sand projections then have the effect of delaying freezing, are therefore a hot spot, and can cause shrinkage cavities.

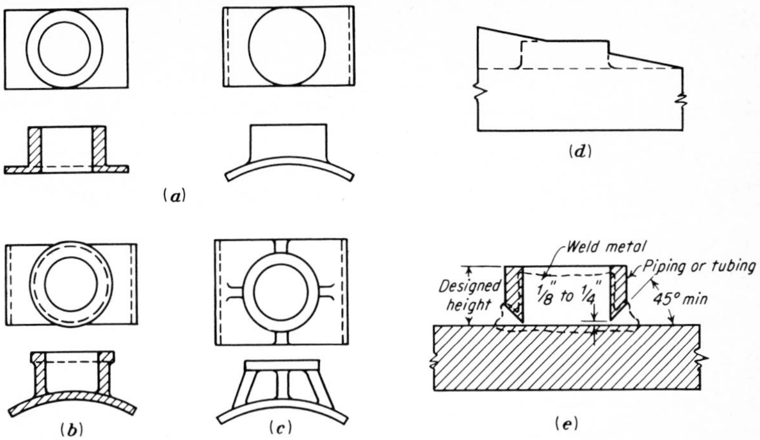

Fig. **25.13** Improved designs for various types of projections, bosses, lugs, and pads. (*a*) Common but improper designs showing thick sections conjoined to a thin main-casting section through which the heavy sections are fed; (*b*) design of projection on cylinder cored for equalization of section; (*c*) design of bolting pad on cylinder, either cored or welded construction; (*d*) pad method for making sound bosses, padded in the direction of nearest riser; (*e*) weld method for attaching bosses. (*From American Foundrymen's Society.*[1])

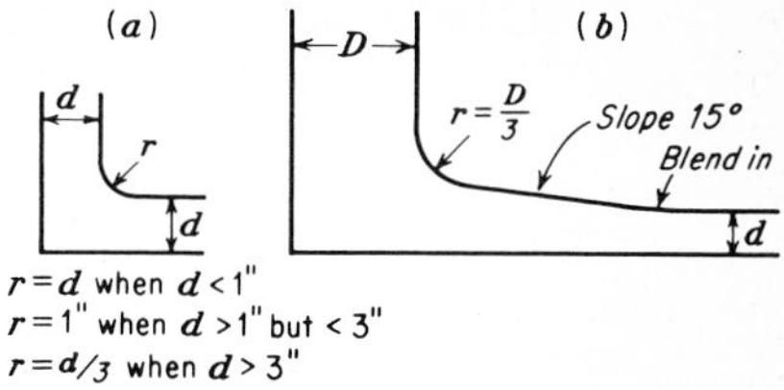

Fig. **25.14** Recommended flange design for cast-steel L junction with exterior corners. In this design, feeding is expected to occur through section *D*. (*Courtesy of Steel Founders' Society of America.*)

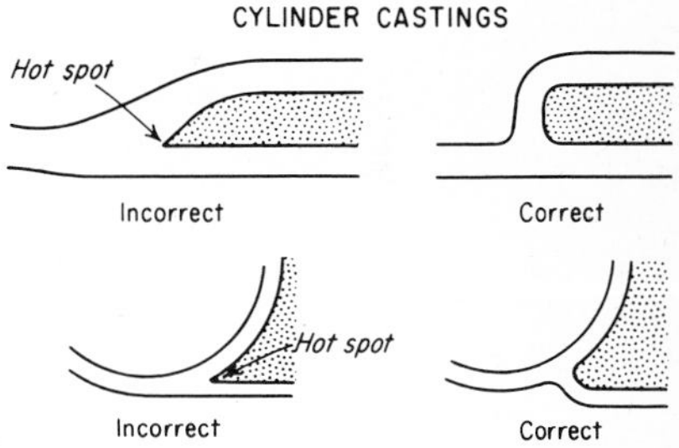

Fig. **25.15** Hot spot caused by thin sand pockets which heat rapidly and therefore do not extract heat from the casting. (*From Meehanite Metal Corp.*[9])

In general, because of hot-spot problems, it is considered desirable to blend and proportion the sections of castings. Abrupt changes in section, thin to thick, are considered harmful. Figure 25.16 illustrates section blending and recommends straight uniform sections rather than any change. By using tapered sections, however, it may be possible to achieve soundness more readily than with the perfectly uniform sections.

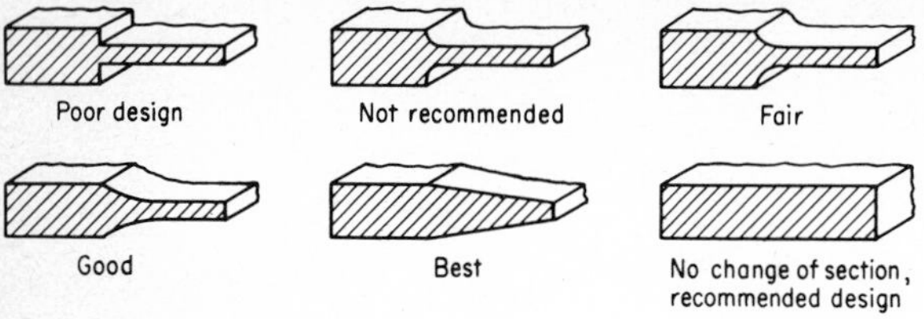

***Fig.* 25.16** Recommended section changes. (*Courtesy of Steel Founders' Society of America.*)

Hot tears. Hot tears are another form of metal unsoundness developed during or at the end of freezing in the casting. Some casting alloys have little tendency to hot-tear, whereas others hot-tear easily. Contraction stresses produced by resistance of the mold or other portions of the casting may become large enough to cause rupture (tearing) of the casting as illustrated in Fig. 25.17. If the reduced section shown in Fig. 25.17 were made the same size as the balance of the casting, the tear might not occur. The incidence of tearing is reduced by having a minimum of areas where sand is completely or partially surrounded by metal and by uniform distribution of metal thickness.

Dimensional-design Factors

Functional design of castings must take into account the ability of the various casting processes to produce the desired dimensions. Certain dimensional characteristics result from the nature of the casting processes.

Minimum Section Thickness

Minimum section thickness which may be cast in sand is given in Table 25.1. The values in Table 25.1 are useful only as guides since several factors are involved. For instance, gray irons may chill to white iron if any extended sections of ⅛ in. are employed. Sections of low-carbon-equivalent irons under ½ in. may cast too hard for machining (Chaps. 18 and 21). Furthermore, the thin section can be run only a certain limiting distance without having misruns appear on the casting. Thinner sections than those listed in Table 25.1 may be cast if they are short and are located so they can be run with hot metal from the ingates. Casting processes differ in this dimension of minimum section, as is evident in Table 25.1. If large areas of a casting are designed with section thicknesses approaching the limiting ones in

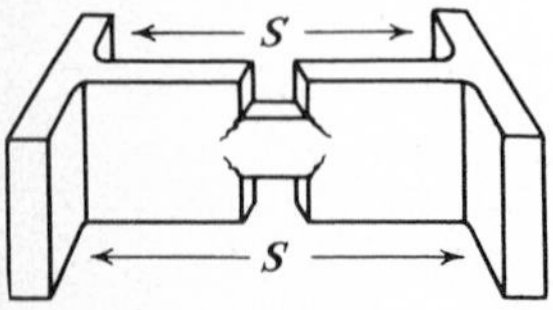

***Fig.* 25.17** Formation of hot tears because of stresses in a casting. (*Courtesy of Steel Founders' Society of America.*)

Table 25.1 Suggested minimum sections for castings

Metal	Sand castings, in.*	Die castings†		Permanent-mold castings, in.*	Plaster-mold castings, in.*
		Over large areas, in.	Over small areas, in.		
Aluminum alloys	1/8–3/16	0.075	0.045	1/8 over small areas	0.040 over small areas 0.093 over small areas
Copper alloys	3/32	0.100	0.060	1/8 over small areas	0.060 over small areas
Gray irons‡	1/8	.....	.....	3/16 over small areas	
Lead alloys	......	0.075	0.040		
Magnesium alloys	5/32	0.080	0.050	5/32–3/16	
Malleable iron	1/8				
Steel	3/16				
Tin alloys	......	0.060	0.030		
White iron	1/8				
Zinc alloys	......	0.045	0.015		

* From R. W. Bolz.[13]
† From H. K. Barton.[11]
‡ See Table 21.3 for the influence of gray-iron ASTM class number on minimum wall thickness of sand castings.

Table 25.1, the danger of misrun castings is increased. The percentage of foundry scrap from this source is then increased, and consequently over-all casting cost.

Cored-hole Sizes

The minimum size of cored holes which can be cast depends greatly on the accuracy of core location and tolerance required. In general, the figures listed in Table 25.2 may be used as a guide. If a cored hole

Table 25.2 Minimum size of cored holes*

Sand casting	$D = \frac{1}{2}t$; D = diam core in in., usually not less than 1/4 in., t = section thickness in in.
Permanent molds	$D = \frac{1}{2}t$, usually greater than 0.25 in. diam
Die castings:	
Copper-base	3/16 in. diam
Aluminum-base	3/32 in. diam
Zinc-base	1/32 in. diam
Magnesium-base	3/32 in. diam
Plaster molds	Cores under 1/2 in. diam normally drilled

* From R. W. Bolz.[13]

must be located with extreme accuracy with respect to other surfaces, it is often desirable to drill it rather than core it. However, dimples may be put on the casting surface to locate the drill holes. In the case of die castings, metal cores may be quite accurately located. Reference 11 gives more exact information regarding limiting dimensions of cores in die-casting dies.

Dimensional Tolerances

The question of dimensional accuracy is always involved in the design of any casting. Certain surfaces may of necessity be machined. These require a machining allowance as well as allowances for shrinkage and perhaps drafts as they finally appear on the pattern. In green-sand molding, dimensions ultimately obtained on the casting are the result of the faithfulness with which shrinkage, changes in dimensions of mold cavity, hardness of mold, stability of molding sand, mechanical alignment of flasks, temperature effects, and so on, are reproduced in the casting process. Of course, many of the variables related to sand molding are not encountered in die or permanent-mold casting. Thus the dimensional variations found in die castings may be considered as a degree of accuracy which may be aimed for in sand castings and, in certain cases, reached. Table 25.3 lists the dimensional variations which may be expected from die castings in the various alloy groups: tin, lead, zinc, aluminum, magnesium, and copper-base die-casting alloys. Ferrous alloys are not included in Table 25.3. This table indicates some principles for die castings which in many cases are true for sand castings as well. The following items may be noted from the table:

1. Dimensions which are on the same side of the parting vary less than those on opposite sides of the parting. Compare *A* and *B, C* and *D* in Table 25.3.
2. Dimensions tend to vary more on cored surfaces which are located (in core prints or in dies) separately from each other, whether located on the same side of the parting or on opposite sides; see cases *H, J, K* in Table 25.3.
3. Because of items 1 and 2, all critical dimensions which must be accurate should be formed in the same die half, mold as well as core.

Items 1 to 3 are emphasized to an even greater degree in sand casting because the mold segments for sand castings are not usually so accurately located by flasks as are the mold segments in a die-casting machine or in permanent molds. Some dimensional tolerances used for small- and medium-sized sand castings of various alloys are given in Table 25.4. The values given in Table 25.4 would not be sufficient for large castings, dimensional tolerances for castings weighing over 1000 lb being given in Table 2.3.

While the tolerances given in Table 25.4 are general ones, it should be recognized that the principles delineated in items 1 to 3 above have a great bearing on the actual tolerance limits which may be achieved in the foundry using a given casting design. Furthermore, the foundry itself may greatly influence limiting tolerances which can be achieved, depending on the effort it expends in striving for dimensional accuracy. By concentrating on flask equipment, flask pins, and bushings, cope and drag shifts which cause variation in dimension B in Table 25.3 can be held from 0.025 in. down to less than 0.010 in. This approaches die-casting accuracy, but is obtained only when strict attention is paid to flask pins and bushings, their initial alignment, wear, and fit. Permanent flasks are usually better than removable flasks for this purpose. In sand castings, dimensions such as C in Table 25.3, completely in cope or drag, can be much more closely held than dimension B. Dimension A can vary greatly because of foundry practices. Soft-mold ramming, lack of weights, pattern off size, shrinkage effects, etc., are more likely to affect a vertical dimension such as A. On the other hand, good foundry practices can hold this dimension considerably below the tolerances given in Table 25.4, especially in small castings. In recent years, the dimensional accuracy of uncored, small sand castings has been improved to the point where dimensions equivalent to those indicated for die casting have been obtained in certain cases. The full potential of the green-sand molding process with respect to dimensional accuracy has not yet, however, been fully exploited.

Surface Finish

The as-cast finish of the various casting processes is compared in Table 25.5. Roughness of sand casting varies more than those made by other processes.

Surface smoothness of mold cavities made with sand depends on sand fineness number, hardness or denseness of mold, materials in sand, molding pressure, and other foundry variables not present in the other processes listed in Table 25.5 and discussed previously in Chap. 5.

Flanges, Ribs, and Junctions

The influence of junctions and ribs on metal soundness was considered earlier. Principles of designing to avoid hot spots and unsoundness have been advanced. Often it is necessary, however, to join light and heavy sections in the interests of functional design even though it may not be most suited to best casting practice. Some recommended junctions for light and heavy sections of magnesium alloys are shown in Fig. 25.18. Note that L junctions of light and heavy sections in Fig.

*Table 25.3a Commercial tolerances for die castings**

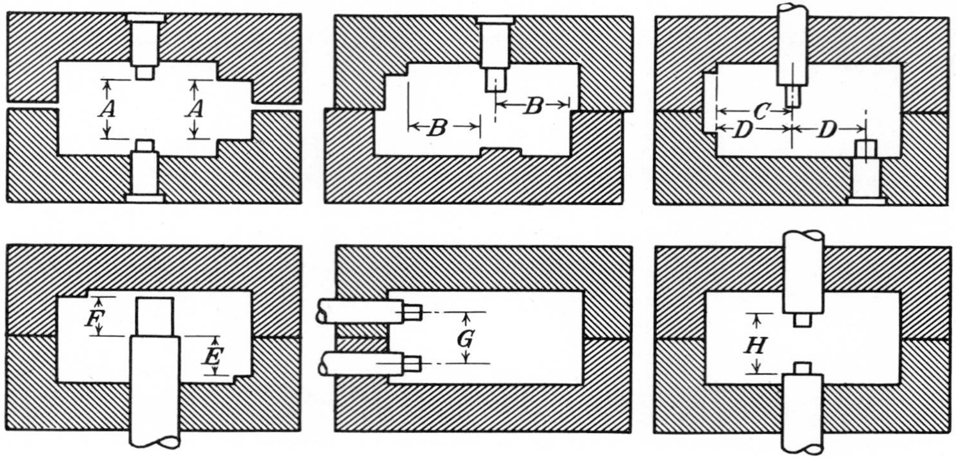

Alloy group		Tin	Lead	Zinc	Aluminum	Magnesium	Copper
A. Dimensions between fixed points in opposite die members, taken across the die parting	Basic variation	+0.003 −0.000	+0.003 −0.000	+0.004 −0.000	+0.006 −0.000	+0.006 −0.000	+0.009 −0.000
	Add for each inch of the dimension	±0.0003	±0.0003	±0.0005	±0.0008	±0.0008	±0.0015
B. Dimensions between fixed points in opposite die members parallel to die parting	Basic variation	±0.002	±0.002	±0.003	±0.004	±0.004	±0.006
	Add for each inch of dimension	±0.0003	±0.0003	±0.0005	±0.0008	±0.0008	±0.0015
C and *D*. Dimensions between a moving core and a fixed location in the same (*C*) or opposite (*D*) member at right angles to the core axis and parallel to the die parting.	Basic variation *C*	±0.001	±0.001	±0.0015	±0.002	±0.002	±0.004
	Basic variation *D*	±0.001	±0.004	±0.006	±0.008	±0.008	±0.10
	Add for each inch of dimension	±0.0003	±0.0003	±0.0005	±0.0008	±0.0008	±0.0015
E and *F*. Dimensions between a moving core and a fixed location in the same (*E*) or opposite (*F*) member parallel to the axis of die parting and core withdrawal	Basic variation *E*	±0.001	±0.001	±0.0015	±0.002	±0.002	±0.004
	Basic variation *F*	+0.004 −0.001	+0.004 −0.001	+0.0055 −0.0015	+0.008 −0.002	+0.008 −0.002	+0.012 −0.004
	Add for each inch of dimension	±0.0003	±0.0003	±0.0005	±0.0008	±0.0008	±0.0015
G. Dimensions between centers of moving cores housed in opposite die members, taken at right angles to the die parting	Basic variation	+0.003 −0.001	+0.003 −0.001	+0.004 −0.002	+0.006 −0.003	+0.006 −0.002	+0.008 −0.003
	Add for each inch of dimension	±0.0003	±0.0003	±0.0005	±0.0008	±0.0008	±0.0015
H. Dimensions between locations on moving cores housed in opposite blocks, taken across the die parting	Basic variation	±0.004	±0.004	±0.006	±0.008	±0.008	±0.010
	Add for each inch of the dimension	±0.0003	±0.0003	±0.0005	±0.0008	±0.0008	±0.0015

* From H. K. Barton.[11]

Table 25.3b Commercial tolerances for die castings*

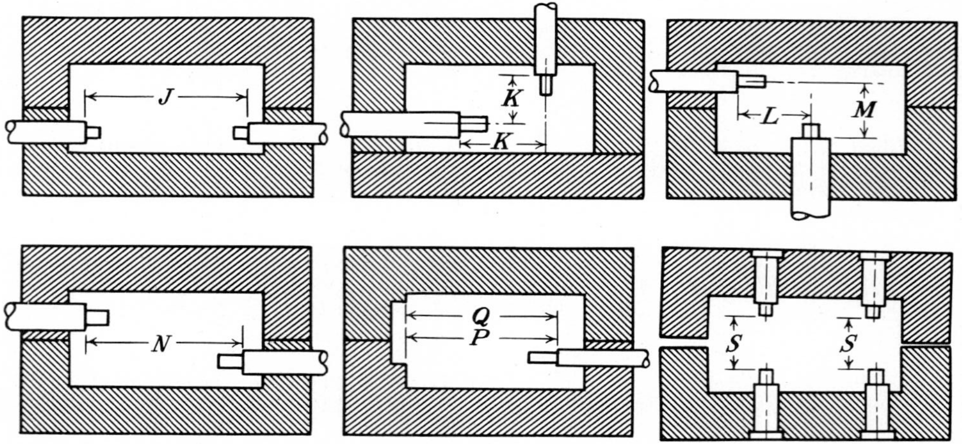

Alloy group		Tin	Lead	Zinc	Aluminum	Magnesium	Copper
J. Dimensions between locations on opposed moving cores in the same die member	Basic variation	+0.006 −0.000	+0.006 −0.000	+0.008 −0.000	+0.010 −0.002	+0.010 −0.002	+0.014 −0.004
	Add for each inch of dimension	±0.0003	±0.0003	±0.0005	±0.0008	±0.0008	±0.0015
K. Dimensions between moving cores housed at right angles in the same die member	Basic variation	+0.004 −0.002	+0.004 −0.002	+0.006 −0.002	+0.008 −0.004	+0.008 −0.004	+0.010 −0.005
	Add for each inch of dimension	±0.0003	±0.0003	±0.0005	±0.0008	±0.0008	±0.0015
L and *M*. Dimensions between moving cores housed in opposite die members taken at right angles to (*M*) and parallel to (*L*) the plane of die parting	Basic variation *L*	±0.004	±0.004	±0.006	±0.006	±0.006	±0.010
	Basic variation *M*	+0.005 −0.002	+0.005 −0.002	+0.008 −0.002	+0.010 −0.003	+0.010 −0.003	+0.017 −0.005
	Add for each inch of dimension	±0.0003	±0.0003	±0.0005	±0.0008	±0.0008	±0.0015
N. Dimensions parallel to the plane of die parting between opposed moving cores in opposite die members	Basic variation	±0.005	±0.005	±0.007	±0.007	±0.007	±0.010
	Add for each inch of dimension	±0.0003	±0.0003	±0.0005	±0.0008	±0.0008	±0.0015
P and *Q*. Dimensions between a moving core and a fixed location in the same (*P*) or opposite (*Q*) die member, taken parallel to the plane of die parting and the axis of core withdrawal	Basic variation *P*	+0.003 −0.001	+0.003 −0.001	+0.004 −0.001	+0.006 −0.002	+0.008 −0.002	+0.009 −0.003
	Basic variation *Q*	±0.004	±0.004	±0.006	±0.008	±0.008	±0.010
	Add for each inch of dimension	±0.0003	±0.0003	±0.0005	±0.0008	±0.0008	±0.0015
S. Possible variation due to warpage and other factors between two identical dimensions (see *A*) taken between different pairs of locations across the plane of die parting	Variations for each inch between the pairs of locations *S*	0.0003	0.0003	0.0005	0.0008	0.0008	0.0015

* From H. K. Barton.[11]

Table* 25.4 *Tolerances for sand castings*
Inches per foot, plus or minus

Metal	Tolerance, in.
Aluminum alloys	1/32
Be-Cu	1/16
Cast irons	3/64
Copper-base alloys	3/32
Cast steels	1/16
Magnesium alloys	1/32
Malleable iron	1/32

*From R. W. Bolz.[13] Tolerance indicated generally for all dimensions, including wall thickness, core shift, etc. For dimensions under 12 in. tolerance indicated is minimum.

Table* 25.5 *Surface smoothness of castings*

	Finish, microinches, rms
Green-sand casting	250–1000
Special sand-casting processes	250 and down
Die casting	40–100
Precision casting	30–100
Plaster molding	30

* From R. W. Bolz.[13]

25.18 are treated for magnesium alloys similarly to those for steel in Fig. 25.14. Junctions of light and heavy sections of malleable iron are shown in Fig. 25.19. The fillet R in Fig. 25.19 may be selected by using the graph in Fig. 25.20.

Ribbing is used to stiffen castings, especially large areas of uniform section. Some typical ribbing designs are shown in Fig. 25.21 for light-metal sand castings. The rib with beading on the edge, shown in Fig. 25.22 for malleable iron, is useful for strengthening. However, beaded ribs such as those in Figs. 25.21 and 25.22 increase molding difficulties since they cannot be pulled from molding sand unless they are located on the parting line. Such ribs in the cope or drag mold cavity must be molded with cores. Although ribs are useful for obtaining stiffness, in some designs stiffening may cause fatigue failure. Reference 19 may be studied for examples.

In the light metals, bosses are needed to strengthen holes for bolting castings. A typical flange bolthole is shown in Fig. 25.23 and in a thin straight section in Fig. 25.24. These designs may also be used for other alloys, but the need is not so great as in light metals, where the added strength is needed.

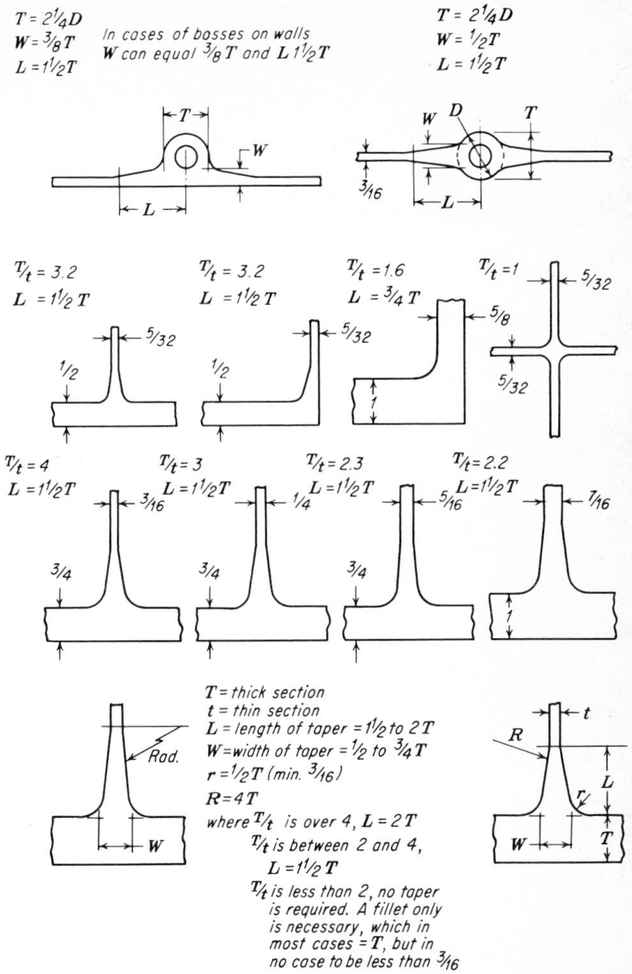

***Fig.* 25.18** Design recommendations for sections in magnesium-alloy sand castings. (*From R. W. Bolz.*[13])

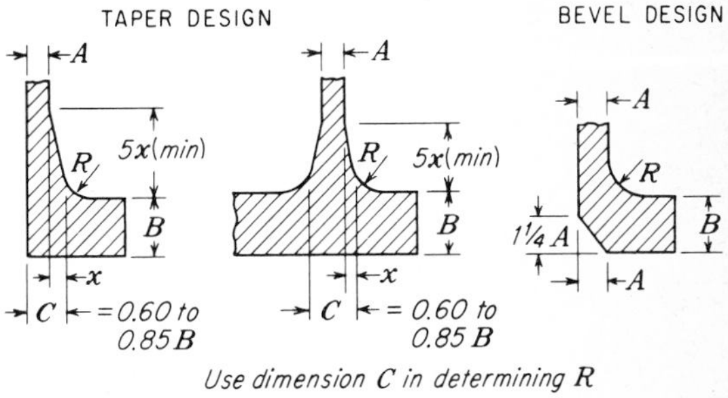

***Fig.* 25.19** Recommended design procedure for malleable iron when a light section joins a section more than 1.66 times its thickness. (*Courtesy of the Malleable Founders' Society.*)

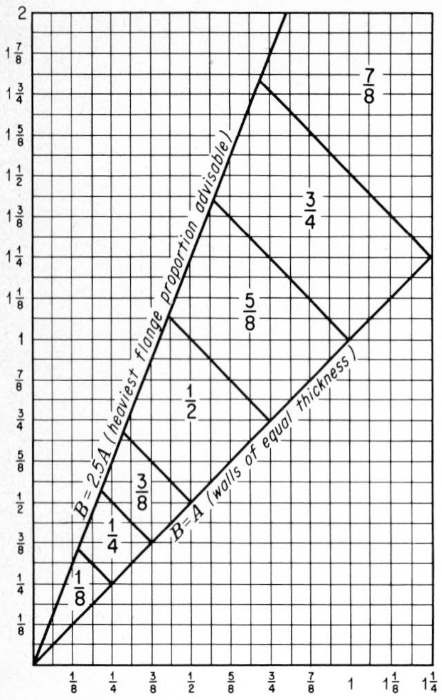

***Fig.* 25.20** Recommended fillet radius to be used in casting design for all joints with walls at right angles to each other and for walls of usual thicknesses and combinations of thicknesses. (*Courtesy of the Malleable Founders' Society.*)

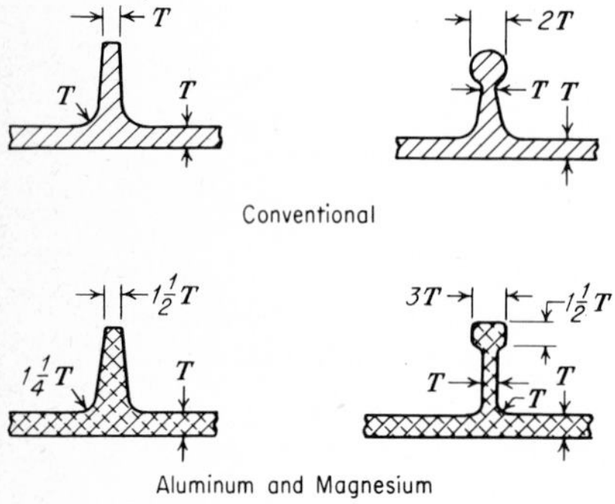

***Fig.* 25.21** Ribbing design for light-metal sand castings. (*From R. W. Bolz.*[13])

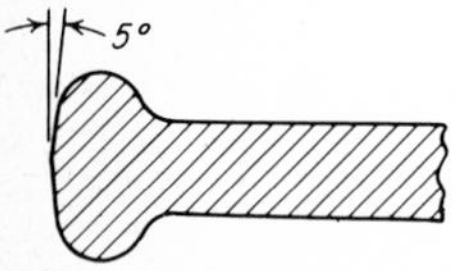

***Fig.* 25.22** Bead-edged rib or plate design recommended for malleable-iron castings. (*Courtesy of the Malleable Founders' Society.*)

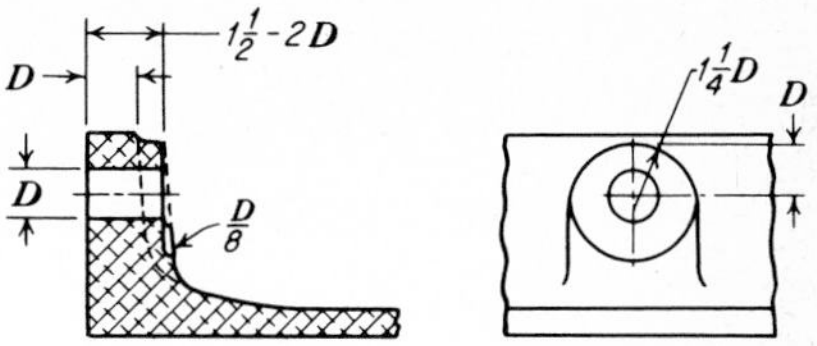

***Fig.* 25.23** Flange-bolthole design for light-metal castings. (*From R. W. Bolz.*[13])

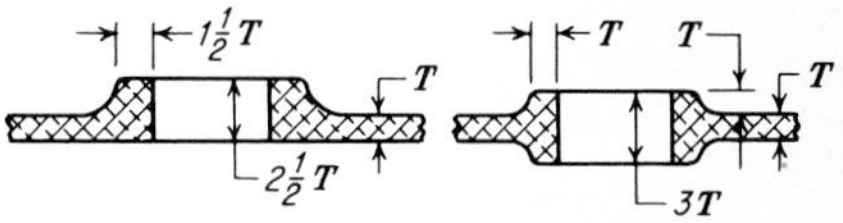

***Fig.* 25.24** Stiffening bolthole in straight-section light-metal castings. (*From R. W. Bolz.*[13])

SIMPLIFICATION OF FOUNDRY PRACTICE

The steps of molding, coring, and cleaning may be greatly simplified if the casting is designed with a view to the needs of these operations.

Molding and Coring

Any changes in the casting design which make molding easier or less costly or result in improved molds help to make a better foundry practice. Some of the likely factors which are involved may be considered.

Pattern Drawing

Any casting shape that makes patterns more difficult to draw or molds more complex is to be avoided if possible. Undercuts or protruding bosses, flanges, etc., which are above or below the parting line require the use of cores or loose pieces which might be eliminated with a better design. An example is given in Fig. 25.25. Deep pockets, especially if they are thin in section, are difficult to draw in green sand. Generally, they must be molded in the drag so that the sand does not hang down as it would if it were in the cope, green sand being more easily broken in tension. An example of such improvement in pattern drawing is shown in Fig. 25.26.

Of course, the use of maximum draft on patterns improves drawing. On many castings it is completely unnecessary to have vertical inner or outer surfaces and generous use of draft is possible. Especially where the casting must have some deep pockets, they can be more easily molded

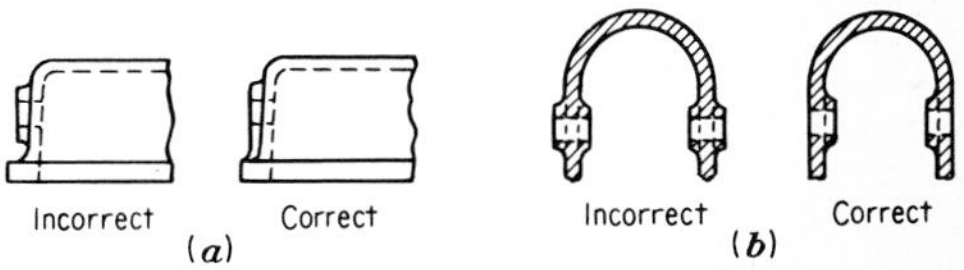

***Fig.* 25.25** Elimination of undercut by extending bosses down to parting line. (*a*) Undercuts should be eliminated wherever possible; (*b*) omit outside bosses to obtain straight draft. (*From Meehanite Metal Corp.*[9])

if the pockets have generous draft as in Fig. 25.26. Inner portions of the casting which can be molded in green sand should have plenty of draft. Ordinarily, draft is an allowance on the pattern. However, if the casting is designed with a minimum of vertical surfaces and good taper on side walls and ribs, then draft is not needed as an allowance on the pattern but is actually built into the casting.

Although draft has been emphasized in this discussion, it should be noted that straight outside surfaces are not impossible. A number of patterns can be drawn without draft up to depths exceeding 4 in. This is a necessity on some castings where these vertical surfaces may be required for locating machining operations or by the nature of the casting itself. Whenever possible, however, adequate draft is to be preferred.

Any consideration of pattern-drawing difficulties must involve establishing the parting line on the castings, an important aspect of the pattern-drawing problems. Figure 25.27 illustrates this point by presenting seven different parting lines possible on a simple casting. A flat parting surface, as shown in *a* and *e,* is convenient and least liable to drops, but may not always be the most desirable. In those cases where draft cannot be tolerated in the hole or on the sides of the casting, parting surfaces *f* and *g* may be employed. This necessitates that the faces be tapered in order to provide draft. Concentricity between the hole and side of the casting is ensured in *a*. Parallel sides and normal draft in the hole are provided in *b*; however, it is more difficult to maintain concentricity between the hole and sides. A minimum of stock removal is necessary if the hole is to be machined in *c* and *e*, but again misalignment of the hole and sides may occur. These examples serve to illustrate the adaptability of parting-line location to casting-design requirements. In addition, some offset parting planes are necessary and may be desirable since they often permit bottom gating on some castings.

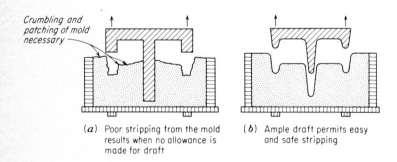

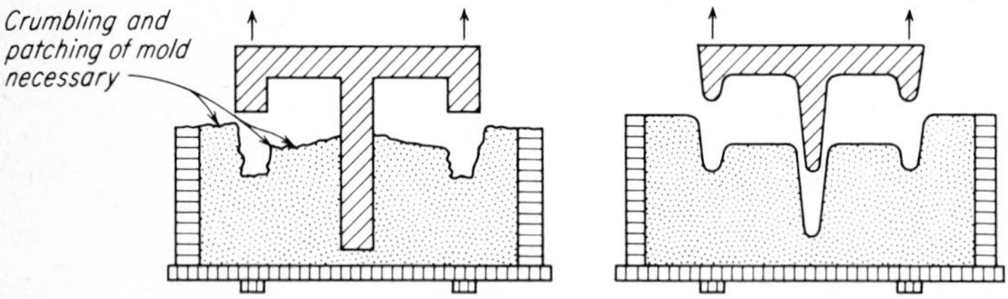

(*a*) Poor stripping from the mold results when no allowance is made for draft

(*b*) Ample draft permits easy and safe stripping

***Fig.* 25.26 Illustrating redesign with deep pockets to minimize tearing of mold during pattern drawing.** (*From Meehanite Metal Corp.*[9])

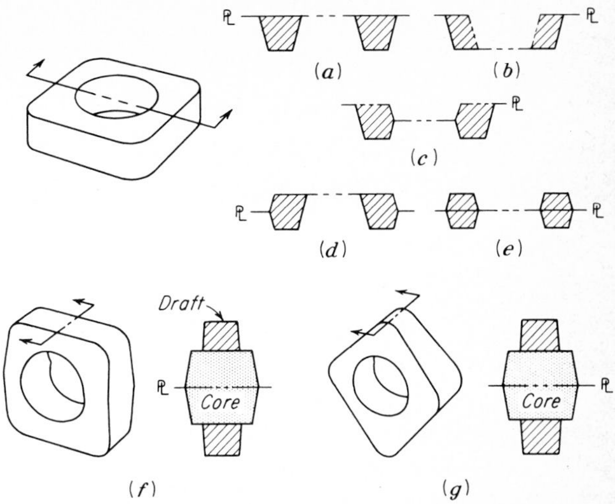

Fig. 25.27 Seven different parting lines are possible in producing this simple casting. Each parting line may have a different influence on the casting. (*Courtesy of American Society for Metals.*[23])

The parting surface, however, should be one that does not produce isolated, thin, or weak sand surfaces that may drop or be damaged during pattern drawing or mold handling. The foundryman is accustomed to searching for the best parting line on casting blueprints. However, the designer does not frequently enough consider the parting-line problem. If the design cannot be simply parted in two halves that can be drawn from the mold, it is necessary to use cores to help establish the parting. The latter is always a more costly process.

Elimination of Coring

Costs of mold construction with cores are generally greater than with green sand alone. Castings are not often originally designed with the elimination of coring in mind. However, redesign for greater economy may involve the elimination or reduction in coring in the mold. Figure 25.28 illustrates redesign to eliminate coring and incidentally retains a flat parting surface. Another example is given in Fig. 25.29. In the original design undercuts were needed to provide clearance for other components in the assembly. These undercuts were eliminated, along with the need for cores in the redesign (Fig. 25.29*b*). Greatly reduced coring is also illustrated in Fig. 25.30. In the latter case, the reduction of coring reduces the labor of making the mold for this casting.

Cleaning problems are also generally reduced with a decrease in coring. Internal cores, small, long passages, and thin cores relative to the

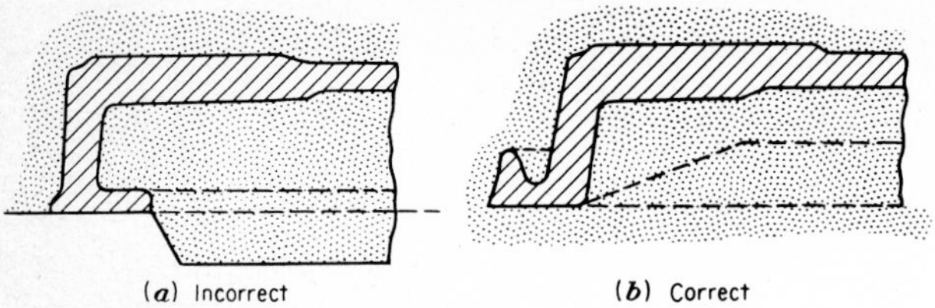

***Fig.* 25.28** Casting design to eliminate coring. (*a*) Complicated molding involving the use of cores; (*b*) redesign avoids unnecessary use of cores and simplifies molding and reduces cost of manufacture. (*From Meehanite Metal Corp.*[9])

sections surrounding them often pose difficulties in cleaning. Sand burned into core holes, and fins or veins, are very difficult to remove when they are hard to get at. Access holes or cleanout holes may be helpful in several ways. They provide additional core prints for support. They may also serve to vent core gases as well as permit the core sand to be removed. Figure 25.31 illustrates vent holes in a casting to permit escape of gases and core-sand removal.

Over-all dimensional accuracy of a mold assembly may be improved by decreasing the number of cores required since the errors in core assemblies are additive. Furthermore, cores may shift relative to the

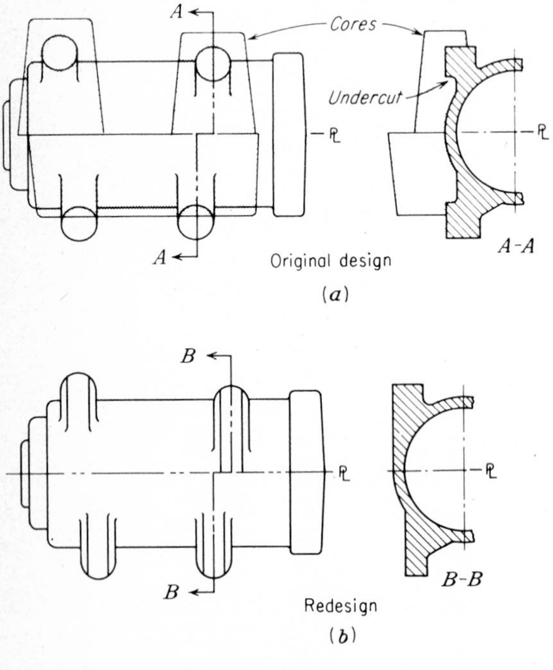

***Fig.* 25.29** (*a*) Undercuts require cores, as shown, to permit withdrawal of the pattern from the sand mold; (*b*) redesign eliminates the undercuts and the need for cores. (*Courtesy of American Society for Metals.*[23])

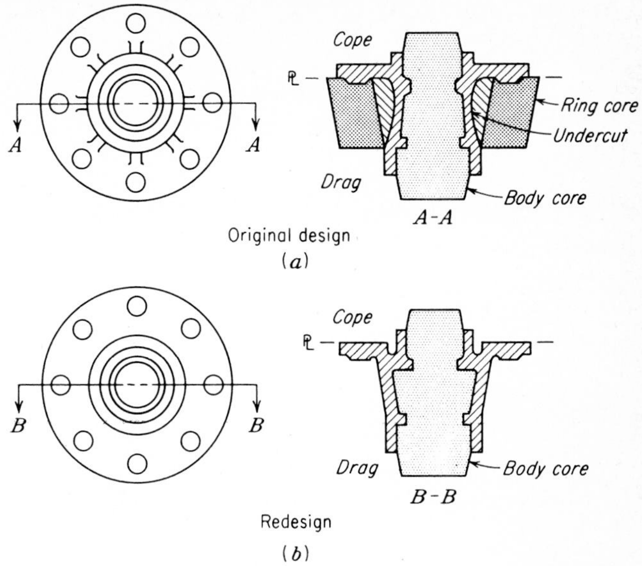

***Fig.* 25.30** (*a*) A reduced diameter adjacent to the flange of this sand-cast wheel hub necessitated a core. In addition, eight ribs were required to provide the desired strength. (*b*) Redesign as shown eliminated the ring core and the ribs, and a stronger casting was produced. (*Courtesy of American Society for Metals.*[23])

mold. For instance, in the cored cavity in Fig. 25.28 a shift in the core would result in a nonuniform wall thickness. As redesigned in Fig. 25.28, however, the core is green sand, formed and positively located by the pattern and flask pins.

Anchoring cores. Cores must always be securely anchored with prints and chaplets to prevent shifting or raising and consequent casting inaccuracy. The principles of securing cores with core prints and chaplets were discussed in Chap. 6. The use of chaplets is to be avoided if possible, especially in castings which must be leakproof. Setting chaplets is additional molding labor. Hence, if cored castings are designed to permit adequate anchoring at core prints without the need for chaplets, molding has been simplified. Decreasing the length of cores or increas-

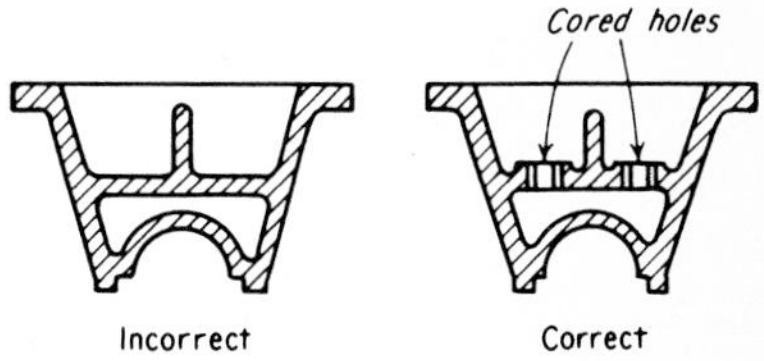

***Fig.* 25.31** Cored holes for venting and removal of sand. (*Courtesy of Meehanite Metal Corp.*[9])

ing the number of prints helps in this connection. The casting redesign shown in Fig. 25.33 is a substantial improvement in shortening a core and reducing the need for chaplets, although this particular illustration was used as an example of more efficient use of flask and molding sand (see following paragraphs).

Castings Simplification

Actually, one of the important means available to the designer for facilitating molding and coring operations is simplification of the casting itself. In some cases, a casting made in one piece might be made in two or more pieces. The pieces might then be assembled by welding or bolting them together. Figure 25.32, for example, shows the steel castings being positioned for welding together. In this case, each casting is intricate, but if the assembly were cast as one piece, the molding problems would be greatly multiplied.

Shape and size. Compactness in design favors more economical molding practices. A casting which is unnecessarily long or has portions which stick out considerably from the main body of the casting requires

Fig. 25.32 Cast-weld construction of cylinder and valve chest to produce final structure. Upper section of casting is shown in position for welding. (*Courtesy of Steel Founders' Society of America.*)

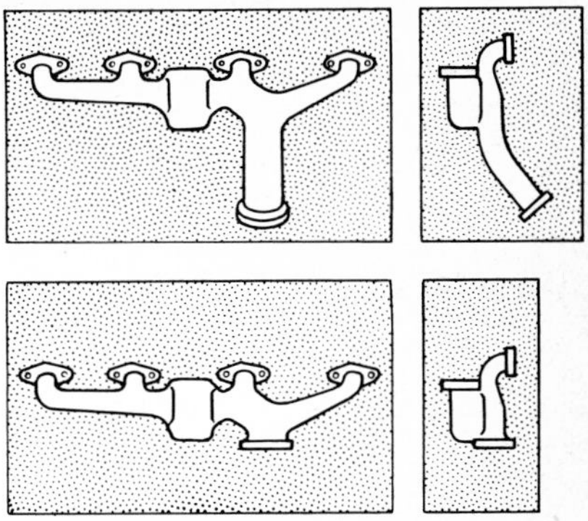

Fig. **25.33** Two designs of an exhaust manifold. The compact design may be molded with less sand or more pieces per mold. (*From American Foundrymen's Society.*)

large flasks, or they may be unduly limited in number of castings per mold. Figure 25.33 shows two designs of an exhaust manifold. The compact design permits more castings per mold and requires less molding sand per casting. Compactness of design does not imply a large concentrated mass, but simply the elimination of unnecessary extensions attached to the main body of the casting. As pointed out earlier, compactness also may decrease the need for chaplets in coring and make castings rejected for misruns less likely.

METALLURGICAL DESIGN

Not commonly recognized as a facet of design procedure is the intentional and purposeful application of metallurgical principles for developing optimum properties of alloys in castings. The designing engineer is concerned primarily with functional design; secondarily, with design for economical manufacturing. His concern with metallurgical design is usually limited to a selection of one of the more obvious alloys which will more or less satisfy his primary concerns. Usually, his knowledge of metallurgical principles is such that this area is not considered. In fact, because of the complexity of factors involved, these considerations are best handled by engineers who are thoroughly versed in metallurgical principles and foundry practices. Cooperation with those concerned with making castings is thus indicated.

Areas of metallurgical design may include:

1. Selection of the most suitable alloy
2. Effects of the casting process

    a. Importance of thermal effects, heat dissipation, mass, etc.
    b. Relationship to metal properties

3. Importance of heat-treatment in producing the desired properties
4. Special metallurgical processing, techniques of foundry practice, which assist in obtaining the desired properties
5. Alternatives of alloy selection, some of which may be more advantageous economically or otherwise at one time whereas others may be more suitable at another time (during a war, for example, when the availability of materials is greatly affected)

Detailed consideration of the multitude of factors which can be involved in items 1 to 5 is of course outside the scope of this textbook. Needless to say, much of the information upon which decisions in these areas are based is found only in the accumulated experience of engineers and in some cases widely scattered in the technical literature. Much of the information needed to use a scientifically sound technical approach is lacking in several areas. A few examples will be given to illustrate some of the items in metallurgical design listed above.

Example 1. A flywheel is designed to have the dimensions shown:*

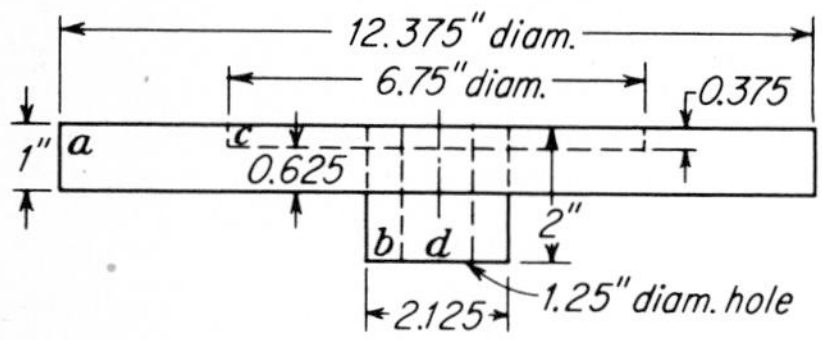

The designer has decided that a green-sand gray-iron casting will be used because of cost and machinability considerations and has specified a minimum of 40,000 psi tensile strength. The actual strength of each wheel will be proof-tested by requiring that it be spun 5500 rpm, the latter exceeding any service condition. Someone, in considering this problem, will need to answer the following questions:

1. What gray-iron composition should be used?
2. What test-bar size and shape should be submitted as representative of the iron in the flywheel?
3. What foundry practices should be followed to see that strength requirements are met, the dimensional tolerances are held so that a minimum of dynamic balancing is required, and machinability is good?

A simple answer to question 1, perhaps by the designer, would be to specify an ASTM Class 40 iron on the blueprint of the part or perhaps a hardness of 202 to 255 Bhn. As pointed out in Chaps. 18, 20, and 21, however, there is no guarantee that a Class 40 iron will produce a 40,000-psi minimum tensile strength in this casting because of the influ-

* Filleting, rib proportioning, blending of sections, etc., not shown in this sketch to simplify calculations.

ence of cooling rate on gray-iron properties. As a solution to this problem, the foundryman might study the blueprint and then conclude, because of his past experiences with similar castings, that an ASTM Class 40 iron, such as that in Table 21.4, would produce the desired properties. Another approach would be to consider the maximum section thickness, 1 in. in this case, as determining the minimum tensile strength of the casting and then use Fig. 21.9 or 21.10 as a means of determining the nominal iron composition and ASTM type. The latter graph indicates that a Class 40 iron would produce the desired strength in this casting if the aforementioned assumptions are true. A third method of attack which has been used involves calculations of the SA/V ratio and the procedure described briefly in Chap. 20 and in Ref. 15 of that chapter. The calculations in this problem are given below (see Chap. 20 for review of principles):

Total-volume calculation:

$$V = V^a + V^b - V^c - V^d$$

$$V^a = 120.30 \text{ cu in.}$$

$$V^b = 3.545 \text{ cu in.}$$

$$V^c = 12.10 \text{ cu in.}$$

$$V^d = 2.458 \text{ cu in.}$$

$$V = 120.30 + 3.55 - 12.10 - 2.46$$

$$= 109.29 \text{ cu in.}$$

Total-surface-area calculation:

$$SA = \text{wheel} + \text{hub}$$

$$\frac{\pi \times 12.375^2}{4} \times 2 = 240.50 \text{ sq in.}$$

$$2\pi \times \frac{12.375}{2} \times 1 = 38.90$$

$$2\pi \times \frac{6.75}{2} \times 0.375 = 7.95$$

$$2\pi \times \frac{2.125}{2} \times 0.375 = 2.50$$

$$2\pi \times \frac{2.125}{2} \times 1.0 = 6.66$$

$$2\pi \times \frac{1.25}{2} \times 2.0 = 7.85$$

$$\text{Total } SA, \text{ sq in.} = 304.36$$

Ratio SA/V calculation:

$$SA/V = 304.36 \div 109.29 = 2.78$$

According to the calculated SA/V ratio of 2.78 and the information in Fig. 21.10, a Class 40 unalloyed gray iron should easily produce the specified minimum tensile strength desired. On the basis of considerations of the type coming under item 4, it might be decided that it would provide a greater margin of safety to carry some alloying elements in the iron, and a Class 40 alloy iron such as that listed in Table 21.5 might be selected rather than the unalloyed iron composition listed in Table 21.4. The alloys might be added as ladle treatments rather than being melted in the cupola, a decision involved in item 4. Other ladle additions not involving a specific alloy composition such as the Class 40 iron in Table 21.5 might be used by the foundry as a safety factor in promoting minimum Class 40 properties in this casting.

The surface-area–volume method might also be used as a means of selecting the representative gray-iron transverse-test-bar size for this casting. The ratio is calculated below:

Bar A, 0.875 in. diam × 15 in. length:

$$SA = 42.61 \text{ sq in.}$$
$$V = 9.06 \text{ cu in.}$$
$$SA/V = 4.70$$

Bar B, 1.20 in. diam × 21 in. length:

$$SA = 81.36 \text{ sq in.}$$
$$V = 23.70 \text{ cu in.}$$
$$SA/V = 3.43$$

Bar C, 2.0 in. diam × 27 in. length:

$$SA = 175.27 \text{ sq in.}$$
$$V = 84.90 \text{ cu in.}$$
$$SA/V = 2.07$$

From a heat-dissipation standpoint, using the SA/V ratio as a criterion, it would appear that the properties of the casting would be better than those obtained in C arbitration bars but not so good as those in a B bar. However, according to the arbitrary relationship of these test-bar sizes to casting-section size either the B or C bar would be used. The latter bar would reflect unfavorably on the properties actually obtainable in the casting from a Class 40 iron if these calculations are true. This point is also indicated in Fig. 21.10. Actual experience with this casting definitely proved that the *B* bar was more representative of the casting than was the *C* bar.

A final approach to solution of the problem described above would be to make test castings of the several gray irons selected as possibilities and subject them to mechanical-property studies. Samples for mechanical-property tests could be cut directly from the casting, and their properties correlated with separately cast test bars.

Example 2. Suppose that the casting considered in Example 1 were to be made as a steel gear-blank casting and the designer required 85,000 psi yield strength, 105,000 psi tensile strength, 17 per cent elongation, and 217 Bhn as minimum mechanical properties with flame- or induction-hardened gear teeth. What steel is required to obtain these properties in the light of over-all costs? These properties are not obtained in the as-cast condition, but must be produced by heat-treatment. Assuming the foundry problems are satisfactorily answered, the selection of the proper steel requires a knowledge of the hardenability characteristics of cast steels. An arbitrary selection might involve specification of cast steel ASTM grade 105-85 (Chap. 17). There is no guarantee, however, that selection of this steel will produce the desired properties in this casting after heat-treatment. To establish this, a knowledge of hardenability (response to heat-treatment) of the steel available is required. Certain tests and calculations can be performed that will narrow down the choice to a relatively few steels. These principles belong to the realm of advanced ferrous metallurgy, however, and are not considered in this textbook. At any rate, it is evident at this point that the steel may be intentionally and purposefully selected and designed to fill the requirements of the casting.

In conclusion, it is evident that a well-engineered casting can be the result of much cooperation and exchange of knowledge. Engineers versed in mechanical design, production, foundry practices, metallurgical principles, etc., may all be involved in establishing the most favorable designs for castings. This fact has become so well recognized by some forward-looking manufacturing organizations that standard practices for designing castings have been set up involving the consultation and cooperation of all concerned.[14,15,17–19]

BIBLIOGRAPHY

1. American Foundrymen's Society, "Cast Metals Handbook," 4th ed., 1944.
2. C. T. Marek, "Fundamentals in the Design and Production of Castings," John Wiley & Sons, Inc., New York, 1950.

3. J. S. Campbell, Jr., "Casting and Forming Processes in Manufacturing," McGraw-Hill Book Company, New York, 1950.
4. Steel Founders' Society of America, "Steel Castings Handbook," 1950.
5. The Malleable Founders' Society, "American Malleable Iron: A Handbook," 1944.
6. American Foundrymen's Society, "Copper-base Alloys Foundry Practice," 1952.
7. American Foundrymen's Society, "Patternmakers' Manual," 1953.
8. American Society for Testing Materials, Standards, Parts 1 and 2, Ferrous and Nonferrous Metals, 1949.
9. O. W. Smalley, "Fundamentals of Casting Design as Influenced by Foundry Practice," Meehanite Metal Corp., White Plains, N.Y., 1950.
10. H. K. Barton, Commercial Tolerances for Die Castings, *Product Eng.*, vol. 22, p. 169, April, 1951.
11. H. K. Barton, Establishing Tolerances for Die Castings, *Product Eng.*, vol. 22, p. 119, April, 1951.
12. Aluminum Co. of America, "Design Details for Aluminum," 1944.
13. R. W. Bolz, Production Processes: Their Influence on Design, *Machine Design,* January–December, 1949; Sand Casting, August, 1949; Centrifugal Casting, September, 1949; Permanent Mold Casting, October, 1949; Die Casting, November, 1949; Plaster Mold Casting, December, 1949.
14. R. J. Franck, How to Develop Cast Products, *Foundry,* vol. 80, p. 120, October, 1952.
15. T. E. Eagan, Design of Gray Iron Castings, *Foundry,* vol. 81, p. 108, April, 1953.
16. C. O. Burgess, Metallic and Nonmetallic Coatings for Gray Iron, *Foundry,* vol. 79, December, 1950–January, 1951.
17. A. S. Grot and L. H. Carr, Standardizing Casting Practice, *Am. Foundryman,* vol. 21, p. 42, June, 1952.
18. G. H. Found, Design Light Metal Castings, *Trans. AFS,* vol. 57, p. 409, 1949.
19. W. T. Bean, Jr., Simplification of Light Metal Casting Design and Its Effect upon Serviceability, *Trans. AFS,* vol. 55, p. 430, 1947.
20. W. F. Wilson, Centrifugal Casting in Permanent Molds, *Product Eng.*, vol. 21, p. 112, November, 1950.
21. W. S. Pellini, Factors Influencing Riser Range and Feeding Adequacy, *Am. Foundryman,* vol. 24, no. 6, November–December, 1953.
22. J. B. Caine, "Design of Ferrous Castings," American Foundrymen's Society, 1963.
23. American Society for Metals, "Casting Design Handbook," 1962.
24. Gray Iron Founders' Society, "Gray Iron Castings Handbook," 1958.
25. Malleable Research and Development Foundation, "Modern Pearlitic Malleable Castings Handbook," 1958.
26. J. B. Caine, What Foundrymen Should Know about Casting Design, *Foundry,* vol. 87, p. 94, January, 1959.
27. J. B. Caine, Dynamic Loading: Its Effect on Casting Design, *Foundry,* vol. 87, p. 92, May, 1959.
28. G. L. Werley, Die Design Improves Zinc Diecastings, *Foundry,* vol. 88, p. 109, June, 1960.

Index

Index

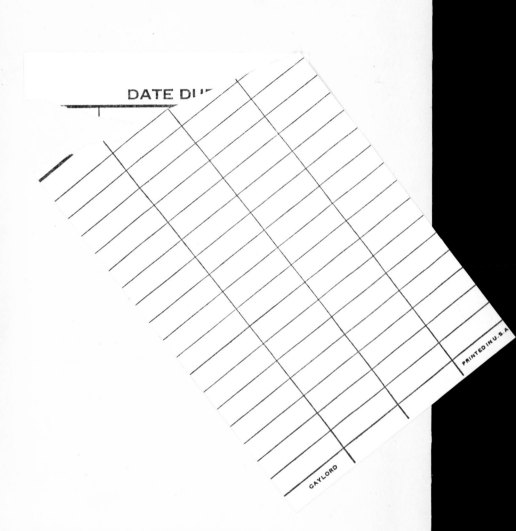